TimeOut
Barcelona Guide

Penguin Books

PENGUIN BOOKS

Published by the Penguin Group
Penguin Books Ltd, 27 Wrights Lane, London W8 5TZ, England
Penguin Putnam Inc., 375 Hudson Street, New York, New York 10014, USA
Penguin Books Australia Ltd, Ringwood, Victoria, Australia
Penguin Books Canada Ltd, 10 Alcorn Avenue, Toronto, Ontario, Canada M4V 3B2
Penguin Books (NZ) Ltd, 182–190 Wairau Road, Auckland 10, New Zealand

Penguin Books Ltd, Registered Offices: Harmondsworth, Middlesex, England

First published 1996
Second edition 1998
10 9 8 7 6 5 4 3 2 1

Copyright © Time Out Group Ltd, 1996, 1998
All rights reserved

Colour reprographics by Precise Litho, 34–35 Great Sutton Street, London EC1
Printed and bound by William Clowes Ltd, Beccles, Suffolk NR34 9QE

Edited and designed by
Time Out Magazine Limited
Universal House
251 Tottenham Court Road
London W1P 0AB
Tel + 44 (0)171 813 3000
Fax + 44 (0)171 813 6001
Email guides@timeout.co.uk
http://www.timeout.co.uk

Editorial
Managing Editor Peter Fiennes
Editor Nick Rider
Copy editor Angela Jameson
Researcher Laia Oliver
Indexer Douglas Matthews
Proof reader Tamsin Shelton

Design
Art Director John Oakey
Art Editor Mandy Martin
Designers Benjamin de Lotz, Scott Moore
Scanner operator Chris Quinn
Picture Editor Kerri Miles
Picture Researcher Emma Tremlett

Advertising
Group Advertisement Director Lesley Gill
Sales Director Mark Phillips
Advertisement Sales (Barcelona) Barcelona Metropolitan

Administration
Publisher Tony Elliott
Managing Director Mike Hardwick
Financial Director Kevin Ellis
Marketing Director Gillian Auld
Production Manager Mark Lamond

Features in this guide were written and researched by:
Introduction Nick Rider. **Barcelona by Season** EM Butterfield, Nick Rider. **History** Marcy Rudo, Nick Rider. **Architecture** Jane Opher, David Howel Evans. **Barcelona Today** Richard Schweid. **Wishful Thinking** Matthew Tree. **Sightseeing** EM Butterfield, Nick Rider. **Museums** Jeffrey Swartz. **Art Galleries** Jeffrey Swartz. **Accommodation** Anne Heverin. **Restaurants** William Truini. **Cafés & Bars** William Truini. **Nightlife** William Truini. **Shopping** Anne Heverin; *Fashion & Fashion accessories* Glòria Sallent. **Services** Anne Heverin. **Children** Esther Jones. **Dance** Richard Schweid. **Film** Richard Schweid. **Gay & Lesbian Barcelona** Martin Montoya. **Media** Richard Schweid, Nick Rider. **Music: Classical & Opera** Marcy Rudo. **Music: Rock, Roots & Jazz** Suzanne Wales. **Sport & Fitness** Jon Rolfe. **Theatre** Jeffrey Swartz. **Trips Out of Town** William Truini; *Festa!, Walking the hills* Jesús Rodríguez Rubio, Nicholas Law. **Directory** Nick Rider, Laia Oliver.

The editors, writers and publisher wish to thank the following: Maria Lluïsa Albacar, Consol Vancells, Mònica Colomer and the rest of the staff of Turisme de Barcelona; Transports Municipals de Barcelona; Col.lecció Thyssen-Bornemisza; Inés del Maschio, Museu Nacional d'Art de Catalunya; Laura Velades, TV3; Adrian, Luci and Bhã; Sonia Casas; Farrell Cleary; Daniel Gómez; Eva Guarch; Steven Guest; Jeff King; Carmen Martínez; Alfonso Martínez Aguado; Jacqueline Minett; Roger Perales; Salvador Rigol; Helen Rowson; Caroline Taverne; Matthew Tree; Esther Zarrillo.

Maps by Mapworld, 71 Blandy Road, Henley-on-Thames, Oxon RG9 1QB, except for p289, courtesy of Tubsal S.A.; p290, courtesy of Transports Municipals de Barcelona.

Photography by Jordi Oliver except for pages iii, 141, 157 Arnhel de Serra; 15, 82, MNAC; 20, 22, 25, 26, 28 Arxiu Històric de la Ciutat, Barcelona; 67 Angela Jameson; 80 Col.lecció Thyssen-Bornemisza; 95 Martí Llorens; 192 Lanònima Imperial Cia de Dansa; 194 Cinemes Renoir; 201 TV3; 216 FC Barcelona; 219 Marius Alexander; 230 Carlos de Andres/Cover; 232, 237, 238, 243 Quim Llenas/Cover. Pictures on pages 99 and 228 (right) supplied by featured establishments.

Contents

About the Guide

This is the second edition of the *Time Out Barcelona Guide*, one in a series of city guides that includes London, Paris, New York, Rome, Prague, Brussels, Las Vegas, Madrid and several other cities around the world. For the new edition our team of resident writers has checked out and revisited museums and cafés, back-street shops and harbourside clubs, to give as complete a picture as possible of this fast-changing city as it is today.

We cover every aspect of Barcelona – from its history and traditions to current politics, fashions and the alternative arts scene. The *Barcelona Guide* is also more than a book solely for tourists and casual visitors. We point you towards obscure venues and hidden-away shops, and, if you're thinking of staying for a while, give tips on handling local bureaucracy and other aspects of living.

CHECKED & CORRECT

We've tried to make this guide as useful as possible. All addresses, telephone numbers, transport details, opening times, admission prices and credit card details were correct at the time of going to press. In any city, though, places can close, arts programmes can be unpredictable and things can change at any time. In addition, in Barcelona small shops and cafés do not keep strictly to their stated hours. Before going anywhere out of your way it's as well to phone ahead to check on current times, dates and so on.

LANGUAGE

Barcelona is a bilingual city; however, the majority language is Catalan, and this is now the sole language used on street signs, and on most maps. We have followed Catalan usage in all addresses and in most other parts of the guide. In many areas, though, Catalan and Spanish are frequently mixed, and you may hear Spanish equivalents that can be very different. Where both versions of a word or phrase can be useful we give both, always with the Catalan first, as in *demà/mañana* (tomorrow). *See also pages 41 and 248.*

TELEPHONE NUMBERS

In 1998 the Spanish national phone company Telefónica made it necessary to dial provincial area codes with all numbers, even for local calls. Hence all Barcelona numbers have to begin with 93, whether you are calling from outside the city or within it. From abroad, you must dial 34 (Spain) + 93. This change was introduced with little warning, and the 93 is not shown on the stationery of many hotels, restaurants and so on.

PRICES

The prices listed should be regarded as guidelines, not gospel. Fluctuating exchange rates and inflation can cause prices to change unpredictably. However, if prices anywhere vary wildly from those we've quoted, ask if there's a reason. If there's not, go elsewhere, and then please let us know. We aim to give the best and most up-to-date advice, and always want to hear if you've been overcharged or badly treated.

CREDIT CARDS

The following abbreviations have been used for credit cards in this guide: **AmEx** – American Express; **DC** – Diners' Club; **EC** – Eurocheque card; **JCB** – Japanese credit bank card; **MC** – Mastercard; **TC** – travellers' cheques in any currency; **$TC**, **£TC** – travellers' cheques in US dollars or pounds sterling; **V** – Visa.

RIGHT TO REPLY

It should be stressed that the information we give is impartial. No organisation, venue or business has been included in this guide because its owner or manager has advertised in our publications. Their impartiality is one reason why *Time Out* guides are successful and well-respected. We hope you will enjoy the *Time Out Barcelona Guide*, but we'd also like to know if you don't. We welcome tips for places that could be included in future editions, and take notice of your criticisms of any of our choices. You'll find a reader's reply card at the back of this book.

> There is an online version of this guide, plus weekly events listings for Barcelona and other international cities, at
> http://www.timeout.co.uk

Introduction

You're walking down a street in the old city of Barcelona, the sky far above you at the top of a ravine of ancient houses. Everything is in shade, the walls seem ready to collapse in on you, their centuries-old stones stained black. Then you turn a corner, look up, and a brilliant shaft of misty sunlight hits the top floors, catching iron railings and bringing out the slatted wooden shades and potted geraniums in near-luminous reds and greens. This clash of dark and light is very characteristic of Barcelona. The same applies to space: one minute you're struggling up a gloomy, cramped old staircase, all deep shadow and like something drawn by Piranesi, then a flat door opens and you're in a huge, white, airy space with lofty ceilings.

These contrasts form part of the city's particular theatricality. It's ideally compact in size, but contains an enormous variety of settings, laid out for dramatic effect. All to fit different performances. There are medieval alleyways, and long, long avenues of apartment blocks, their endless rows of windows often picked out with superbly elaborated details. There are intransigently modern stages of glass and steel. Barcelona's most famous arena of all, the Rambla – however accidentally it came together in history – is a giant boulevard given over to the purpose of allowing people just to walk up and down, observing each other.

Sometimes it gets too much, all this anonymous scrutiny and eye contact. You have a bad Rambla day, when you can't face the crowd and so exit left through quiet back streets. I once met a New Zealander in Barcelona on his first trip abroad. He couldn't understand how anyone could live here. 'Everyone on top of each other', he said, 'back home, everyone has a quarter-acre'. Well no, Barcelona is not a city where everybody has their own little space to cultivate. Rather, they occupy and personalise a space in the surrounding warren.

Contrasts also apply in the city's people. There is a certain classic model of Catalan shopkeeper, who no matter what you look like, no matter how stupid you seem or how weird the request you make will still look at you over his half-moon glasses and reply in lugubriously deep vowels without cracking a trace of a smile. This is the *Català sec* (dry Catalan), or even *esquerp* (untranslatable, but meaning self-contained, stubborn, a bit brusque), who has raised not giving anything away into a performance in itself. At other times you can find the friendliest, most helpful, most welcoming people you could ever want.

Barcelona's public face has lately been taken over by bright young people in sharply-sculpted suits, who spend their time expounding how modern the city is. This is another piece of Barcelona theatre: paradigm of modernity, dream city of the new millenium. All well and good, really, if it keeps the money rolling, but it is to be hoped that Barcelona will not lose its essence – which is not one, but many things.

Barcelona has always been a great city for eccentrics, which has indulged and even promoted them. Barcelona's most famous citizen, Antoni Gaudí, was mad as a hatter, an austere modern mystic with dark religious visions. Until quite recently, Gaudí's buildings were widely regarded as vulgar, silly, kitschy and possible candidates for the wrecking ball. It was the 1960s that rediscovered Gaudí. Some hippies wandered down to Barcelona, saw the Sagrada Família and said, wow, that's amazing. Had Gaudí been able to meet the hippies he would probably have given them a clip round the ear and recommended abstinence, spiritual exercises and maybe a tasty bowl of gruel. But then, contradiction is the spice of life. *Nick Rider*.

In Context

Barcelona by Season

Folkloric fire-runners and pre-Christian saints make the Catalan calendar pretty special.

Thanks to Barcelona's friendly climate and Mediterranean character, at any time of the year there is certain to be some kind of festival – *festa* in Catalan, *fiesta* in Spanish – coming up. They give an opportunity for Catalans to bely their reputation for constant *seny*, earnestness, stolidity and common sense, by displaying their *arrauxament*, craziness and capacity for going wild. Most city *festes* follow the Catholic calendar of Saints' days and holy days, but only a few are still solidly religious. Some have pre-Christian roots, such as **Sant Joan**, others are modern urban inventions. *Festes* and events rise and fall in popularity, so that some, such as **Santa Eulàlia**, have gained in importance in recent years, while others, like **May Day**, have lost prominence.

Most celebrations are marked by concerts, parades, processions, exhibitions, street parties, children's competitions, and music and dancing outdoors into the small hours. There's also a unique body of Catalan folklore to go with them: the *correfoc* (fire-running), *gegants i capgrossos* (giants and big heads) *castells* (human towers) and *sardanes*, traditional dancing. Except maybe on Sant Joan or New Year, most Catalans don't drink huge amounts at *festes* (so non-Catalans tend to stand out), but there's no objection to alcohol.

In addition to city-wide events, every district has its own annual festival or *festa major*, when streets are decked out in bunting and garlands, and street parties go on into the night. An essential part of any district *festa* is the participation of children, dressing up, going in for shows and competitions and just staying up late. Most are purely local events, but a few – above all the one in Gràcia in August – are highly organised and bring in people from all over the city.

Barcelona also hosts nearly 60 trade shows each year, some of which attract major crowds. Practically all take place in the **Fira de Barcelona** buildings, off Plaça d'Espanya or in

*A friendly fathead from **El Ingenio** carnival shop. See page 10 and chapter **Shopping**.*

Don't forget your mother tongue

From time to time it's good to be spoken to in your own language. With TV3 it's possible. Because with Sistema Dual you can listen to programmes from all around the world in their original language.
So you too can feel at home.

Sistema Dual de TV3

(Also, by using Dual with our Teletext Subtitles you can learn or improve your Catalan!)

T V
3

D = Sistema Dual
(◊) = Subtitles

the Montjuïc 2 area near the airport (*see page 266*). Some important trade shows are listed below.

The best sources of information on what's on are tourist offices, the **Centre d'Informació de la Virreina** on the Rambla and the **010** line (*see page 251*). Programmes are also listed in the local press. In the listings below public holidays are marked *. For more on children's involvement in *festes*, *see chapter* **Children**, and for music festivals, *see chapters* **Music: Classical & Opera** *and* **Music: Rock, Roots & Jazz**. For festivals outside the city, *see chapter* **Trips Out of Town**.

Spring

Festes de Sant Medir de Gràcia
Gràcia to Sant Cugat and back, usually via Plaça Lesseps, Avda República Argentina & Carretera de l'Arrabassada. Metro Fontana/bus 22, 24, 28. **Information** City information line (010). **Date** 3 March. **Map D1-2/E1-2**
A popular celebration held since 1830, in which a procession of riders on horses and carriages leaves Gràcia in the morning after parading around Plaça Rius i Taulet with special banners, one for each of the *colles* or groups who organise the event. They head over Collserola by the winding Arrabassada road from the Hermitage of Sant Medir ('saint of the broad beans') near Sant Cugat, where they have a beany lunch. In the afternoon, as they return, they parade down Gran de Gràcia, throwing thousands of sweets into the crowd – a local version of the *Cavalcada dels Reis*.

Setmana Santa
Information City information line (010).
Dates Easter, Mar-April.
Holy Week, the most important festival of the year in southern Spain, is of relatively little importance here, although there is a small procession in C/Carme in the Raval. However, three different groups run by Andalusian migrants organise southern-style processions: most interesting is the lay procession, celebrated since 1978, known as the *Procesión del Santo Cristo de la Expiración*, which sets off from the Parc de les Bòbiles in Hospitalet de Llobregat (Metro Can Vidalet) at 9pm on Good Friday. In addition, *L'Ou com Balla* (*see below*) is repeated in the Cathedral cloister, which is decorated with flowers and herbs. For most people, though, Holy Week is simply a holiday when the city closes down – with the notable exception of the pastry shops. Having produced the sweet cakes called *bunyols* every Wednesday and Friday through Lent, they sell their *mones* (chocolate sculptures) for Easter. A run-of-the-mill *mona* will be a rabbit or a figure of whichever cartoon character is the rage that year, but many *pastisseries* also make elaborate set-pieces, including reproductions of famous buildings, people and events. The most spectacular are usually in **Escribà** (*see chapter* **Shopping**).

Sant Jordi
La Rambla, and all over Barcelona. **Date** 23 April.
Saint George, patron saint of Catalonia and a true romantic, slew the dragon and saved the lady, and so his day has been celebrated here by men giving roses to their ladies – a kind of alternative to St Valentine's Day. In 1923 a local bookseller noticed that the date also coincided with the birthdays of Shakespeare and Cervantes, and declared it the *Dia del Llibre*, the Day of the Book, obliging women to reply in kind for their flowers by giving men a book. In these enlightened times, everybody can give everybody else a book and/or a rose at their discretion. Bookshops set up stalls on pavements, and it's an important day for authors to make contact with readers through book signings. Half of total book sales in Catalonia take place on this day – and the rose industry does-

The *Sardana*

The sedate Catalan dance the *sardana* is not limited to seasonal celebrations, since it can be seen throughout the year, but it is also a part of every local *festa*. Its origins are believed to go back to ancient Greece; the name comes from the *ballo sardo* of Sardinia, an island occupied by Catalans for centuries, and the first written reference to it is from 1587. It consists of a moving circle, whose members hold hands and mark a set pattern of paces that shift from left to right and back again. The description of 'dancing in the streets' doesn't quite give the right idea: it's more like a folk dance invented by mathematicians, as serious dancers have to concentrate to follow the step sequences. The *sardana* was already popular as a folk dance in the Empordà, the coastal area near the French border, before 1800, but was given its modern form in the middle of the last century by a self-taught musician, Pep Ventura. He established the line-up of the traditional *sardana* band, the *cobla*, combining traditional and brass instruments, and gave the dance a definitive musical form, writing 400 scores for it himself. After his death in 1875 other musicians took up the baton, and the *sardana* quickly spread across the country. Charged with symbolic references to unity and equality, it was adopted as Catalonia's national dance, and has become one of its best-known symbols.

In Barcelona, as well as during *festes*, *sardanes* are danced every Sunday in front of the Cathedral from about noon to 2pm, and in the Plaça Sant Jaume from 7pm to 9pm. You don't have to be an expert to join in, and anyone wanting to try just has to enter a circle.

n't do badly either. The best way to see this colourful and civilised festival is to make your way down the Rambla: it's lined with book stands, surrounded by packed crowds, and the flower stalls have truly spectacular displays of roses. This is also the only day of the year that the **Generalitat** is fully open to the public, with its own rose display, but the queues to enter are, again, huge (*see chapter* **Sightseeing**).

Feria de Abril
Can Zam, Santa Coloma de Gramenet. Metro Santa Coloma, then special buses from the Metro. **Information** Federación de Entidades Culturales Andaluces en Cataluña (93 453 60 00). **Date** end April-early May.
The Feria, inspired by the famous month-long fair in Seville, has been the main event of the year for Catalonia's Andalusian community since 1971, with hundreds of different groups saving up all year to provide food and drink

Rio or the Rambla, you can still shake your stuff. The **Carnestoltes** *parade. See page 11.*

stalls. Non-members can also watch dozens of live events, including very authentic flamenco. Continuing for over a week, the fair is enormously popular with Catalans and Andalusians alike, attracting a million visitors.

Dia del Treball* (May Day)

Date 1 May.
Celebrated by the different labour unions: the largest demonstration is run by the mainstream trade unions and goes from Passeig de Gràcia to Plaça Sant Jaume. The anarcho-syndicalists of the CNT hold a meeting at the Cotxeres de Sants on C/Sants before their march. Attendance, massive in the first days of democracy, has fallen in recent years and for most people it has become simply a day off work.

Sant Ponç

C/Hospital. Metro Liceu/bus 14, 18, 38, 59, 64, 91.
Date 11 May. **Map C5**
Sant Ponç is patron saint of beekeepers and herbalists, and on his day C/Hospital is packed from end to end with stalls – some of whose owners travel from the other end of Spain to take part – selling honey, herbs, *fruta confitada* (very sweet candied fruit), perfumes, sweet wine and other natural products. It's a charming, crowded and very colourful event, and the scents of the bunches of fresh herbs are exhilarating.

Saló de l'Automòbil

Fira de Barcelona, Avda Reina Maria Cristina (93 233 20 00). Metro Espanya/bus all routes to Plaça d'Espanya.
Dates usually May, every two years (1999). **Map A4**
A very popular car show, with all the latest models and prototypes. Another crowd favourite is the section given over to an exhibition of vintage cars.

Marató de l'Espectacle

Mercat de les Flors, C/Lleida 59, & Teatre Grec. Metro Espanya/bus 9, 13, 38, 61, 65, 91. **Information** 93 268 18 68. **Dates** late May/early June. **Map B5**
And perhaps the main event for Barcelona's alternative arts-performance-club-and-much else scene. Over a weekend the **Mercat de les Flors** and **Teatre Grec** (*see chapter* **Theatre**) are taken over by comedians, theatre groups, musicians and other creator/performers, including art installations and performance art, who start up and keep going, in a real 'cultural marathon'. With tremendous participation by performers and audience, it's a real showcase for new talents. Things usually start around 8pm, and go on from there.

Festival Internacional de Poesia de Barcelona

Palau de la Música Catalana. Metro Jaume I/bus 17, 19, 40, 45. **Information** Centre d'Informació de la Virreina and 010. **Date** late May. **Map D4**
A free evening of poetry readings by around a dozen international and Catalan poets, in Barcelona's most *Modernista* venue, the Palau de la Música. A booklet of the poetry is sold, with Catalan translations only.

Festa de la Bicicleta

Information Servei d'Informació Esportiva (93 402 30 00). **Date** one Sunday in May.
Celebrated as the 'Day of the Pedal' before the Civil War in 1936, this event was revived by former Mayor Pasqual Maragall in 1982 in an effort to encourage local residents to use their cars less, though in the same period the number of cars here has risen by 50 per cent. On the day, though, some 30,000 cyclists ride around the city, and anyone with a bike can join in. For cycle hire shops, *see page 260*.

Summer

L'Ou com Balla

Venues *Ateneu Barcelonès, C/Canuda 6; Casa de l'Ardiaca, C/Santa Llúcia 1; Cathedral Cloister; Museu Frederic Marès, Plaça Sant Iu 5. Metro Jaume I/bus 17, 19, 40, 45.* **Dates** Corpus Christi (May or early June) and the following Sunday. **Map D5**
L'Ou com Balla (roughly, 'The Egg that Dances') is a curious custom that traditionally took place only during Corpus Christi, which until the last century was the most important festival in Barcelona. A previously emptied eggshell is left to bob on top of the jet of a fountain in the Cathedral cloister, on the patio of the Casa de l'Ardiaca in front of the Cathedral, and in other patios of the Barri Gòtic. This is a very old tradition, reported in the sixteenth century. The fountains, wonderfully garlanded with fragrant-scented broom and carnations, may represent the model of the cathedral that was carried in the Corpus procession, with the 'canopies' formed by the eggshells over the fountain-tops representing the monstrance that was held over the model cathedral. *L'Ou com Balla* can also be seen in the Cathedral cloister during Easter week (*see above* **Setmana Santa**).

Trobada Castellera
(Meeting of human-tower builders)

Plaça Catalunya. Metro Catalunya/bus all routes to Plaça Catalunya. **Information** 010. **Date** June. **Map D4**
A non-competitive display of human-tower building involving all the existing *casteller* groups in Catalonia (for an explanation of *castells, see page 10*).

Sant Joan*

All over Barcelona. **Date** night of 23 June.
The night of 23 June, Midsummer's Night and, less importantly, the eve of the feast of Saint John the Baptist, is *la Nit del Foc*, the Night of Fire, throughout Catalonia and the Balearics. As the summer solstice, its origins are obviously pagan, and it's the wildest night of the year, mad and magical. Days before the event kids start letting off bangers all over town, with the noise culminating on the night itself, when the city sounds like a war zone. Bonfires are lit at street junctions, despite Ajuntament attempts to prohibit them, and cava is drunk through the night, accompanied by a sweet cake, rather like a pizza base with candied fruit, called a *coca de Sant Joan*. If you don't want to celebrate at a club – expensive and closed-in – join in the more reasonably priced mass parties organised in the Monumental bull ring, the Tibidabo funfair or the Velòdrom in Horta. Alternatively, walk along the Rambla, lined with cava vendors, and watch the small *correfoc* at Plaça Barceloneta; or head for Montjuïc, where there's music for free. At midnight, fireworks erupt into the air at many points around the city, with two huge displays mirroring each other on Montjuïc and Tibidabo. A favourite way to end the night of Sant Joan is to watch the sunrise over the sea or to head for one of the beaches for the first swim of the year. Traditionally it has often occasioned a first of a different nature: as one student memorably remarked 'I went out a girl and came back a woman!' The holiday is the day after, 24 June, so there's plenty of time to sleep it off.

Festival del Grec

Information & tickets Centre d'Informació de la Virreina. **Dates** late June-July. **Map** (Grec theatre) **B5**
The Grec is the Barcelona Ajuntament's annual summer arts festival, mainly of theatre, contemporary dance and music, with a strong representation of world music. Many shows, particularly theatre, take place at the Greek-style amphitheatre on Montjuïc from which the festival gets its name, but performances go on in several other venues, mostly open-air: the Poble Espanyol, the Mercat de les Flors, Plaça del Rei – a superb setting for concerts, with the Gothic walls floodlit – the Palau de la Música, in parks, or on the streets.

Festa Major de Gràcia

All over Gràcia. Metro Fontana/bus 22, 24, 28. **Information** 93 291 66 00. **Date** late Aug. **Map D1-2/E1-2**
Held every year since the 1820s, Gràcia's *festa major* has now almost outgrown the *barri* itself, and attracts thousands from all over the city – to an extent that can irritate local residents. A unique feature is the competition between streets for the best decoration: they are decked out to represent elaborate fantasy scenarios, from desert-island themes to satires or comments on current events. Each street also has its own programme of events, entertainment and dancing, plus an open-air meal in the street for all the neighbours. District-wide events are centred on the Plaça Rius i Taulet, and there's also music nightly in the Plaça de la Revolució, Plaça del Sol and Plaça de la Virreina. The *festa* opens with *gegants* and *castells* in the Plaça Rius i Taulet, and reaches its climax on the last night with the *correfoc* and fireworks display.

Festa Major de Sants

All over district of Sants. Metro Plaça de Sants, Sants Estació, Plaça del Centre/bus 44, 54, 56, 57, 109. **Date** around 24 Aug. **Map A3**
Sants' *festa major*, once one of the most important in Barcelona, has not had the benefit of the same historical con-

tinuity as the Gràcia festival, and had to be revived after the dictatorship. Major events such as the *correfoc*, are held in the futuristic Parc de l'Espanya Industrial. Other events are centred on the Plaça del Centre, C/Sant Antoni, Plaça de la Farga and Plaça Joan Peiro, behind Sants Station.

Diada Nacional de Catalunya*
(Catalan National Day)

All over Barcelona. **Date** 11 Sept.
After being left in the lurch by perfidious Albion, on 11 September 1714 Barcelona fell to the Castilian/French army in the War of the Spanish Succession, a national disaster that led to the loss of all Catalan institutions for 200 years (*see pages 19-20*). This heroic defeat is commemorated as Catalan National Day. In 1977, the first time it could be celebrated openly in Barcelona after the dictatorship, over a million people took to the streets. It's now lost its force somewhat, but is still a day for national reaffirmation and demonstrations, with Catalan flags displayed on balconies. At night, separatist groups have confrontations with the police.

La Diadeta de la Barceloneta

All over Barceloneta. Metro Barceloneta/bus 17, 39, 45, 57, 59, 64. **Date** weekend in mid-Sept. **Map D/E6**
Held shortly before the Barceloneta's full *festa major* (*see below*), the Diadeta (little day) is an unusual, very local celebration organised by dozens of *penyes* (local associations), each of which is connected to a different bar or restaurant. The men of these groups, wearing an assortment of traditional regalia, disappear for a day, then come back – usually drunk – and laden with rabbits and other animals they have supposedly hunted for food, while the rest of the area celebrates their return with a procession of symbols of all the different guilds linked to the fishing industry in this old fishermen's district. Little-known among the city's popular festivals, this is one that's well worth a visit.

Mostra dels Vins i Caves de Catalunya

Information INCAVI (93 487 67 38).
Dates two weeks mid-Sept. **Map D6**
The official showcase for Catalan wines and *caves*, coinciding with the Mercè. It is held in stands outside Maremàgnum. Virtually every wine producer in the country sets up their wares, and there is plenty of opportunity for tastings. The association also organises an exhibition of *vi novell* (new wine) on 11 November in the Generalitat, invitation-only alas, and a *fira d'oli* (oil fair) in Maremàgnum in December.

Festes de la Mercè*

All over Barcelona. **Information** Centre d'Informació de la Virreina and 010. **Date** one week around 24 Sept.
Our Lady of Mercy – *Nostra Senyora de la Mercè* – housed in the church of the same name close to the port, joined Santa Eulàlia as one of the city's patrons in 1637, when she saved the city from a plague of locusts; in 1871, her name was given to the whole city's *festa major*, Barcelona's biggest celebration of itself. Official ceremonies include a mass and the reading of a speech of dedication by an invited cultural figure – in 1997, Yehudi Menuhin. In the same year 3,000 people held up *bengales* (sparklers) for a *piromusical* (firework mega-spectacular) in Plaça d'Espanya, and human jigsaw puzzles, exhibitions, conferences, fly-pasts and acrobatic parachuting, and parades have been just some of the events of recent years. There's a big music programme, including jazz, flamenco, Catalan folk and dance music, and other shows, some of them free. Concerts are held in many squares in and around the old city: usually Plaça Catalunya, Plaça Sant Jaume, Plaça del Rei and Plaça Reial, and the Poble Espanyol out on Montjuïc. Another fixture of the modern Mercè are large-scale rock concerts, held at waterside venues such as the Moll de la Fusta. The many associated sports events include the *Cursa de la Mercè* (24 Sept), a fun run with 20,000 participants from Plaça Catalunya to Montjuïc, and swimming competitions across the harbour. As well as this, there's the folklore of the *festa*,

with *gegants* and *castellers* on the mornings of the first and last days, and Barcelona's biggest *correfoc*, usually (but not always) on the evening of 23 September, for a grand climax.

Autumn

Festa Major de la Barceloneta
All over Barceloneta. Metro Barceloneta/bus 17, 39, 45, 57, 59, 64. **Date** end-Sept-early Oct. **Map D/E6**
One of the liveliest of the smaller district *festes*. Activities are centred around Plaça de la Barceloneta and Plaça de la Font, and a grotesque – supposedly French – general,

General Bum Bum (Boom Boom, possibly named after Prosper Verboom, the French army engineer who designed the *barri*), leads a procession of kids round the district firing off a cannon – a tradition dating from 1881. There's dancing on the beach every night, and some people take to boats to eat, drink and watch the fireworks display from the sea.

Tots Sants (All Saints' Day)*
All over Barcelona. **Date** 1 Nov.
All Saints' Day is the day for remembering the dead, and traditional Barcelonans visit the city's cemeteries to pay their respects. Around this time, roast *moniatos* (sweet potatoes) and chestnuts – deemed the favourite food of the dead – are

Giants, dragons, human towers...

Festivals in Barcelona are very varied, but have in common some very special popular traditions. Some hark back to pagan revels of ancient epochs, and all are at least four centuries old. Today, scarcely a town in Catalonia is without its dragon association and resident devils, not to mention its giant clubs, tower-builders and *sardana* groups, and all expanding by the year.

Gegants & capgrossos
The *Gegants* or giants – five-metre-high figures of wood and papier-mâché, each supported by a person peeping out through a mesh in the skirts – were originally part of the festival of Corpus Christi, instituted by the Church in 1264, partly in order to incorporate popular pre-Christian figures into conventional ritual. There are many theories regarding their origin, one being that they are based in David and Goliath, but they represent many folkloric characers. In Barcelona two of the most historic giants are the *Gegants del Pi*, kept in the church of Santa Maria del Pi. Equally popular are the *capgrossos* ('fatheads') who accompany the parade of giants, wearing huge papier-mâché and wood heads, usually with bizarre fixed smiles. Archetypal leprechaun-like figures, they once represented the biblical tribes of Sem, Cam and Japhet, but these theatrical set-pieces have long been dropped, and the heads can now resemble celebrities or all sorts of popular figures. Like the *Correfoc* (*see below*), and other events in the *festa*, these parades are accompanied by special music played on traditional instruments. One of the most skilled makers of them is **El Ingenio** (*see chapter* **Shopping**). The festival of Corpus went into decline, but in the meantime the giants and heads had been incorporated into the *festa major* developed in the nineteenth century. Like other *festa* traditions *gegants* and *capgrossos* have enjoyed a boom in popularity since the 1980s, their numbers increasing tenfold (today, there are 197 in Barcelona alone). *Gegants* and all their friends can be seen in every district *festa* as well as at the city-wide **Mercè**.

Dracs, dimonis & the Correfoc
If you see the giants and fatheads during the day, you can be near-certain that at sunset you will see the *dracs* (dragons) and *dimonis* (devils) come out to play, waving fireworks and scuttling after crowds of screaming spectators. The dragon is a recurrent feature in Catalan folklore, in contrast to the bull-obsession of much of Iberia. The *festa* dragons are big, wood-and-canvas monsters, carried by teams, with fireworks in their snouts; their attendant devils are men and women in demon suits carrying pow-

erful fireworks that spin round on sticks. Their procession is the *Correfoc* (literally 'fire-running', *above*), the wild climax of the *festa*, when the dragons spin and swirl through a surging crowd amid a manic atmosphere and clouds of smoke. If you intend to be at the front of the crowd, it's advisable to cover as much of your body as possible, with hoods and handkerchiefs over the mouth, which is how you'll see dedicated fire-runners dressed, even in August. Once the dragons are worn out, the party continues with yet more fireworks, and dancing.

Castells
The formation of *castells*, or human towers, has become a major spectator sport in Catalonia. *Castells* possibly have their origins in medieval prowess games, and in a popular dance of the seventeenth-century, the *moixiganga*. At the end of this dance, men would form a human tower up to six people high. Later, the tower-building began to take precedence over the dancing, and by the last century, tower-building clubs, known as *colles*, began to form. In each *castell*, a large group links arms at the bottom to form the base, the *pinya* (pine-cone), with the crowd joining in around them for extra support. Then successive layers climb on top of them, the upper levels getting smaller until it comes down to a single small boy or girl who tops the tower off with a wave. There are several distinctive formations of towers: the most difficult are combinations like a *5 de 8* (five people in each level, eight levels) or anything with nine levels. The completion of each level is accompanied by its own music, and there's a tremendous sense of suspense and excitement in the final, most precarious stages. Interest in *castells* waned over the last century, until the early 1980s, when a major revival began. And, as with the dragons and other *colles*, *castells* are now entirely women and girls. There are now 38 *colles castelleres* around Catalonia, including places that have never before had a tower-building tradition.

sold at street stalls, and *panellets* (ground almond cakes coated in pine-nuts) at pastry shops. This event has also become increasingly festive, with people holding All Saints' Eve parties at which these traditional foods are washed down with sweet wines such as *moscatell* or *malvasia*.

Fira del Disc de Col.leccionista (Record Collectors' Fair)

Fira de Barcelona, Avda Reina Maria Cristina (93 233 20 00). Metro Espanya/bus 9, 13, 38, 51, 53, 61, 65, 91, 109. **Dates** usually first or second weekend Nov. **Map A4**
Organised by rock enthusiast Jordi Tardà, this is the largest fair of its kind in Europe. With a different musical theme each year, it offers a vast selection of second-hand LPs, 45s, tapes and CDs, and ends with an auction of rock memorabilia that attracts buyers from around the world.

Winter

Fira de Santa Llúcia

Pla de la Seu & Avda de la Catedral. Metro Jaume I/bus 17, 19, 40, 45. **Dates** usually 8-24 Dec. **Map D5**
Christmas in Barcelona begins with the Christmas fair in front of the Cathedral, at which hand-made pieces are sold for the nativity scenes that Catalan and Spanish families build up year by year. They include not only the usual Josephs and Marys but also the exclusively Catalan figure of the *caganer*: a man, sometimes a woman, having a realistically sculpted crap within spitting distance of the King of Kings. It's by far the most popular figure in the Catalan crib, and local artesans compete each year to create new *caganer* designs. As for the origins of Catalans' scatological obsession (especially visible in Christmas traditions), it awaits full anthropological explanation. At the fair you can also find Christmas trees – a foreign import, but well established – and a range of craftwork.

Nadal* & Sant Esteve* (Christmas Day & Boxing Day)

All over Barcelona. **Dates** 25, 26 Dec.
The centrepiece of Barcelona's Christmas decorations is an extravagant life-size crib in Plaça Sant Jaume, surrounded by real palms. Some people have their main Christmas dinner late on Christmas Eve, as is the custom throughout the rest of Spain, but many Catalans have two big lunches, one on Christmas Day with the family of one parent and another on Boxing Day with the family of the other. Around Christmas children get to expend their energies in a ritual known as the *Caga Tió*, when the kids 'beat the crap' – more incorrigible scatology – out of a wooden log with sticks, and then run into an adjoining room. When they return, they find the log has crapped them out small presents. A skeleton transport service is provided during Christmas Day.

Cap d'Any (New Year's Eve)

All over Barcelona. **Date** 31 Dec.
As on Sant Joan (*see above*), discos and bars charge outrageous entrance fees for New Year parties: cheaper are the mass celebrations around the city, the best of them at the Monumental bullring. Wherever you are, at midnight – well announced on TV – you'll be expected to start stuffing 12 grapes into your mouth, one for every chime of the bell, without stopping until the New Year has been fully rung in. Otherwise, it's bad luck. Many taxi drivers take the night off and transport stops at 1am, so it isn't a good night to travel unless you have access to a car.

Cavalcada dels Reis* (Three Kings' Parade)

Route *Kings normally arrive at Moll de la Fusta, then parade up the Rambla to Plaça Sant Jaume, and continue to Passeig de Gràcia; detailed route changes each year.* **Information** City information line (010) or 93 301 41 98. **Date** 5 Jan. **Map D4-6**

Attracting crowds a politician can only dream of, this festival should not be missed by anyone with children. Epiphany, the Day of the Three Wise Men (Three Kings), on 6 January is celebrated in many Latin countries, and until the recent advent of Father Christmas was the time when children, and often adults, received their main presents. On 5 January the 'Kings' arrive by sea (from across the harbour) and are formally welcomed by the mayor. They then parade around the city, with accompanying floats, and throw sweets to children in the crowd along the route. Some hold umbrellas inside out to catch as many as they can. A toy fair is held on Gran Via (usually 2-6 Jan), which stays open through the night for late present-buyers. And, in case you'd forgotten the scatology, they also sell sugary coal and turd-lookalikes made from fig-paste, for kids who have been naughty in the preceding year.

Festa dels Tres Tombs

All over district of Sant Antoni. Metro Sant Antoni/bus 24, 41, 55, 64. **Date** 17 Jan. **Map C4**
Sant Antoni Abat (Saint Anthony the Abbot) is the patron saint of domestic animals and muleteers. There may no longer be any members of this trade left, but a small procession of horsemen, dressed in tailcoats and top hats, still commemorates his day by riding three times (the *Tres Tombs* or Three Turns) around a route that goes from the Ronda Sant Antoni, through Plaça Universitat, Pelai and Plaça Catalunya, down the Rambla and back along Nou de la Rambla. This parade coincides with the *festa major* of the nearby *barri* of Sant Antoni, which continues for a week, complete with *sardanes*, *castellers* and neighbourhood giants. There are smaller parades in other districts of the city.

Festes de Santa Eulàlia

All over Barcelona. **Date** around 12 Feb.
With La Mercè, Santa Eulàlia, whose remains repose in the Cathedral, is the co-patron saint of the city. Through February the Ajuntament organises a series of activities for adults and children – concerts, dances, games, *correfocs*, *diables*, walking tours, exhibitions – many related to traditional culture and the city's history. The Ajuntament building also opens its doors to the public. The climax is a parade of *mulasses* (dragons) and *mules guites* (mules with a kick) in Plaça Reial, *gegants* and *capgrosses* on the Rambla and *castellers* in Plaça Sant Jaume. It overlaps with Carnival.

Carnestoltes (Carnival)

All over Barcelona. **Date** usually late Feb.
The opening event is a procession of figures in outrageous outfits, from scantily clad Brazilian dancers to the usual Catalan monsters, making its way through the city centre led by *el Rei Carnestoltes* and *Don Carnal*, amid a confusion of confetti, blunderbuss salvos and fireworks. The origins of Carnival are in a once-traditional outburst of eating, drinking and fornicating prior to the limitations of Lent. King Carnestoltes – the masked personification of the Carnival spirit – also used to criticise the authorities and reveal scandals, a tradition which has unfortunately died out. Other events in Barcelona's modern carnival include a *Gran Botifarrada Popular* on the Rambla, when sausage is handed out to the public, dancing in Plaça Catalunya and concerts in different venues. During the ten-day celebration, children's fancy-dress carnivals are organised, so it's common to see kids in the street dressed up as bees or Marie Antoinettes. Carnival is also a big show in the city's markets, where traders get dressed up too, and parties are put on in clubs and bars. The end of Carnival on Ash Wednesday is marked by the *Enterrament de la Sardina*, the Burial of the Sardine, on Montjuïc or in Barceloneta, when the fish – symbol perhaps of the penis – is buried to emphasise that not even such frugal fare will be consumed for 40 days. More spectacular than Barcelona's Carnival are those in Vilanova i la Geltrú and Sitges, which both benefit from an unbroken tradition. A gay parade is now part of Sitges Carnival (*see chapters* **Gay & Lesbian Barcelona** *and* **Trips Out of Town**).

Key Events

Origins

c15 BC *Barcino* founded by Roman soldiers.
Fourth century AD Roman stone city walls built.
415 Barcelona briefly capital of Visigoths under Ataülf.
719 Moslems attack and seize Barcelona.
801 Barcelona taken by Franks, under Louis the Pious.
878 Guifré *el Pilós* becomes Count of Barcelona.
985 Moslems under Al-Mansur sack Barcelona; Count Borrell II renounces Frankish sovereignty.

A medieval Golden Age

1035-76 Count Ramon Berenguer I of Barcelona extends his possessions into southern France.
1064-8 First Catalan *Usatges* or legal code written.
1137 Count Ramon Berenguer IV marries Petronella of Aragon, uniting two states in the 'Crown of Aragon'.
1148-9 Lleida and Tortosa taken from the Moslems.
c1160 *Homilies d'Organyà*, first Catalan texts, written.
1213 Battle of Muret: Pere I is killed and virtually all his lands north of the Pyrenees are seized by France.
1229 Jaume I conquers Mallorca, then Ibiza (1235) and Valencia (1238); second city wall built in Barcelona.
1265 *Consell de Cent* (Council of 100), municipal government of Barcelona, established; Ramon Llull devotes himself to thought and writing.
1282 Pere II conquers Sicily.
1298 Gothic Cathedral begun. Population of city c40,000.
1323-4 Conquest of Corsica and Sardinia.
1347-8 Black Death cuts population by half.
1391 Thousands of Jews massacred in Barcelona *Call*.
1401 *Taula de Canvi*, first deposit bank, founded.
1412 Crown of Aragon given to Fernando de Antequera.
1462-72 Catalan civil war.
1474 First book printed in Catalan, in Valencia.
1479 Ferran II (Ferdinand) inherits Crown of Aragon, and with his wife Isabella unites the Spanish Kingdoms.

The fall of Barcelona

1492 Final expulsion of Jews, and discovery of America.
1516 Charles of Habsburg (Charles V), King of Spain.
1522 Catalans refused permission to trade in America.
1640 Catalan national revolt, the *Guerra dels Segadors*.
1652 Barcelona falls to Spanish army.
1659 Catalan territory of Roussillon is given to France.
1702 War of Spanish Succession begins.
1714 Barcelona falls to Franco-Spanish army after siege.
1715 *Nova Planta* decree abolishes Catalan institutions; new ramparts and citadel built around Barcelona. Population of the city c33,000.
1775 Paving of the Barcelona Rambla begun.
1808-13 French occupation.

Factories, barricades & poets

1814 Restoration of Ferdinand VII after French defeat.
1824 Building of Carrer Ferran begun on former church land; in 1827, route of the Passeig de Gràcia is laid.
1832 First steam-driven factory in Spain, in Barcelona.
1833 Aribau publishes *Oda a la Pàtria*, beginning of Catalan cultural renaissance. Carlist wars begin.

1836-7 Dissolution of most monasteries in Barcelona.
1839 First workers' associations formed in Barcelona.
1842-4 Barcelona bombarded for the last time from Montjuïc, to suppress a liberal revolt, the *Jamancia*.
1848 First railway line in Spain, between Barcelona and Mataró; Liceu opera house inaugurated.
1850 Population of Barcelona 175,331.
1854 Demolition of Barcelona city walls begins.
1855 First general strike is violently suppressed.
1859 Cerdà plan for the Barcelona *Eixample* approved.
1868 September: revolution overthrows Isabel II.
November: first anarchist meetings held in Barcelona.
1873 First Spanish Republic.
1874 Bourbon monarchy restored under Alfonso XIII.
1882 Work begins on the Sagrada Familia.
1888 Barcelona Universal Exhibition.

The city of the new century

1892 *Bases de Manresa*, demands for Catalan autonomy.
1897 Gràcia and Sants incorporated into Barcelona.
1898 Spain loses Cuba and Philippines in war with USA.
1899 FC Barcelona founded; first electric trams.
1900 Population of Barcelona 537,354.
1907 Via Laietana cut through old city of Barcelona.
1909 *Setmana Tràgica*, anti-church and anti-army riots.
1910 CNT anarchist workers' union founded.
1919 CNT general strike paralyses Barcelona.
1920 Spiral of violence in labour conflicts in Catalonia.
1921 First Barcelona Metro line opened.
1923 Primo de Rivera establishes Dictatorship in Spain.
1929 Barcelona International Exhibition on Montjuïc.
1930 Population 1,005, 565. Fall of Primo de Rivera.
1931 14 April: Second Spanish Republic. Francesc Macià declares Catalan independence, then accepts autonomy.
1934 October: Generalitat attempts revolt against new right-wing government in Madrid, and is then suspended.
1936 February: Popular Front wins Spanish elections; Catalan Generalitat restored. 19 July: military uprising against left-wing government is defeated in Barcelona.
1937 May: fighting within the republican camp in Barcelona, mainly between anarchists and Communists.
1939 26 January: Barcelona taken by Franco's army.

Grey years

1951 Barcelona tram strike.
1953 Co-operation treaty between Spain and the USA.
1959 Stabilisation Plan opens up Spanish economy.
1975 20 November: death of Franco.

The new era

1977 First democratic general elections in Spain since 1936; provisional Catalan Generalitat re-established.
1979 First local elections in Barcelona won by Socialists.
1980 Generalitat fully re-established under Jordi Pujol.
1982 Pasqual Maragall becomes Mayor; urban spaces programme gains momentum.
1986 Barcelona awarded 1992 Olympic Games.
1992 Barcelona Olympics.
1996 *Partido Popular* wins Spanish national elections.
1997 Joan Clos replaces Pasqual Maragall as Mayor.

History

Roman fortress, capital of an empire, bourgeois ideal, city of the Revolution and design mecca: Barcelona has been reinvented many times.

Origins

It was in the first thousand years of Barcelona's history that the foundations were laid of Catalan identity and language. Multiple invasions between periods of growth and decay left the isolated, self-reliant people of the city and surrounding countryside with traditions and character quite distinct from those of others in the Iberian peninsula.

The Romans founded Barcelona, in about 15 BC, on the *Mons Taber*, a small hill between two streams with a good view of the Mediterranean, today crowned by the Cathedral. The plain around it was sparsely inhabited by the *Laetani*, an agrarian Celtic-Iberian people known for producing grain and honey and gathering oysters. Named *Barcino*, the town was much smaller than the capital of the Roman province of *Hispania Citerior*, *Tarraco* (Tarragona), but had the only harbour, albeit a poor one, between there and Narbonne.

Like virtually every other Roman new town in Europe it was a fortified rectangle with a crossroads at its centre, where the Plaça Sant Jaume is today. It was a decidedly unimportant, provincial town, but nonetheless the rich plain provided it with a produce garden, and the sea gave it an incipient maritime trade. It very early acquired a Jewish community, and was associated with some Christian martyrs, notably Barcelona's first patron saint Santa Eulàlia. She was supposedly executed at the end of the third century via a series of revolting tortures, including being rolled naked in a sealed barrel full of glass shards down the alley now called Baixada (descent) de Santa Eulàlia.

Nevertheless, Barcelona accepted Christianity shortly afterwards, in 312 AD, together with the rest of the Roman Empire, by then under growing threat of invasion. In the fourth century *Barcino*'s rough defences were replaced with massive stone walls, many sections of which can still be seen today. It was these ramparts that ensured Barcelona's continuity, making it a stronghold much desired by later warlords (for more on relics of Roman Barcelona, *see chapter* **Sightseeing**).

These and other defences did not prevent the empire's disintegration. In 415, Barcelona briefly became capital of the kingdom of the Visigoths, under their chieftain Ataülf. He brought with him as a prisoner Gala Placidia, the 20-year-old daugh-

The blood of Hairy Wilfred

The Catalan flag, the *Quatre Barres* (Four Bars), also called *La Senyera*, is the oldest national flag in Europe. Its creation is one of many feats attributed to the founder of Catalonia, Wilfred the Hairy, Count Guifré *el Pilós*, and the legends surrounding its design of four red stripes on a gold background have all served to justify its special status.

In the ninth century, when from his base in the Pyrenees Wilfred was carving out the first possessions of the House of Barcelona and so the Catalan nation, he was nevertheless still a vassal of the Frankish Emperor. The story goes that he was called to serve his lord (appropriately, in some versions, Charles the Bald), and was mortally wounded in battle against the Saracens. In recognition of his heroism, the Emperor dipped his fingers into Wilfred's bloody wounds as he lay dying and traced his fingers down the Count's golden shield, creating the four red stripes on yellow, the *Quatre Barres*. Whatever their mythical origin, the four bars first appeared on the Romanesque tomb of Count Ramon Berenguer II in 1082, thus predating the flag of Denmark, its nearest competitor, by a hundred years.

As well as providing the flag and the genesis of the country, Wilfred became a figure of legend in many other ways, credited with wrestling down dragons (in a cave at Sant Llorenç del Munt) and all manner of enemies. What is not known is just why, and in what way, Catalonia's founding patriarch was so hairy, but he can perhaps be seen as the prototype of every deep-voiced, barrel-chested Catalan man with a beard.

ter of a Roman emperor, who he forced to marry him. She is famous, though, as a woman of strong character, and is credited with converting the barbarian king to Christianity. She was also perhaps fortunate in that Ataülf died shortly afterwards, whereupon Gala Placidia left, married her relative the Emperor Constantius I, and for a time became the most powerful figure in the court of Byzantium. Back in Barcelona, meanwhile, the Visigoths soon moved on southwards to extend their control over the whole of the Iberian peninsula, and for the next 400 years the town was a neglected backwater.

It was in this state when the Moslems swept across the peninsula after 711, easily crushing Goth resistance. They made little attempt to settle Catalonia, but much of the Christian population retreated into the Pyrenees, the first Catalan heartland. Then, at the end of the eighth century, the Franks began to drive southwards against the Moslems from across the mountains. In 801 Charlemagne's son Louis the Pious took Barcelona and made it a bastion of the *Marca Hispanica* or 'Spanish March', the southern buffer of his father's empire. This gave Catalonia a trans-Pyrenean origin entirely different from that of the other Christian states in Spain; equally, it is for this reason that the closest relative of the Catalan language is Provençal, not Castilian.

Loyal counts were given sections of the Catalan territories to rule, charged in exchange with defending the frontier against the Saracens. At the end of the ninth century, Count Guifré *el Pilós*, 'Wilfred the Hairy' (approx 860-98), succeeded in gaining title to several Catalan counties. He united the area, founded the dynasty of the Counts of Barcelona and created the basis for a future Catalan state, making Barcelona his capital and so setting the seal on the city's future (*see also* **The blood of Hairy Wilfred**).

In 985 the great minister of the Caliph of Córdoba, Al-Mansur, attacked and sacked Barcelona. Wilfred's great-grandson Count Borrell II requested aid from his theoretical feudal lord, the Frankish king. He received no reply, and so repudiated all Frankish sovereignty over Catalonia. From then on – although the name was not yet in use – Catalonia was effectively independent, and the Counts of Barcelona free to forge its destiny.

A medieval Golden Age

In the year 1000 Barcelona had a growing population of nearly 6,000, and was witnessing the first glimmerings of mercantile and artisan activity. During the first century of the new millennium

Exorcism before the Tomb of St Vincent *(1455-60), by Jaume Huguet, now in the* **MNAC** *(see page 82-3).*

Catalonia was consolidated as a political entity, and entered an era of great cultural richness.

The Catalan Counties retained from their Frankish origins a French system of aristocratic feudalism – another difference from the rest of Iberia – but also had a peasantry who were notably independent and resistant to noble demands. In the 1060s the *Usatges* ('Usages') were established, the first legal code in Europe to grant commoners equal rights in law against the nobility. The Counts of Barcelona and lesser nobles also endowed monasteries throughout Catalonia, consecrating the influence of a powerful clergy.

This provided the background to the years of glory of Romanesque art, with the building of the great monasteries and churches of northern Catalonia, such as **Sant Pere de Rodes** near Figueres, and the painting of the superb murals now in the **Museu Nacional** on Montjuïc. There was also a flowering of scholarship, reflecting the confluence of Islamic and Carolingian cultures. In Barcelona, shipbuilding and trading in grain and wine all expanded, and a new trade developed in textiles. The city grew both inside its old Roman walls and outside of them, where *vilanoves* or new towns appeared at Sant Pere and La Ribera.

Catalonia – a name that gained currency, in Latin, in the eleventh century – was also gaining more territory from the Moslems to the south, beyond the Penedès. For a long time, though, the realm of the Counts of Barcelona continued to look just as much to the north, across the Pyrenees, where the Provençal-speaking Languedoc was then the most sophisticated society in western Europe. After 1035, during the reigns of the four Counts Ramon Berenguer, large areas of what is now southern France were acquired through marriage or with Arab booty. In 1112 the union of Ramon Berenguer III 'the Great' (1093-1131) with Princess Dolça of Provence extended his authority as far as the Rhone.

A more significant marriage occurred in 1137, when Ramon Berenguer IV (1131-62) wed Petronella, heir to the throne of Aragon. This would, in the long term, bind Catalonia into Iberia. The uniting of the two dynasties created a powerful entity known as the 'Crown of Aragon', each element retaining its separate institutions, and ruled by monarchs known as the 'Count-Kings'. Since Aragon was already a kingdom, it was given precedence and its name was often used to refer to the state, but the court language was Catalan and the centre of government remained in Barcelona.

Ramon Berenguer IV also extended Catalan territory to its current frontiers in the Ebro valley. At the beginning of the next century, however, the dynasty lost virtually all of its lands north of the Pyrenees to France, when Count-King Pere I 'the Catholic' was killed at the battle of Muret in 1213. This was a blessing in disguise. In future, the Catalan-Aragonese state would be oriented decisively towards the Mediterranean and the south, and was able to embark on two centuries of imperialism equalled in vigour only by Barcelona's burgeoning commercial enterprise.

MEDITERRANEAN EMPIRE

Pere I's successor was the most expansionist of the Count-Kings. Jaume I 'the Conqueror' (1213-76) abandoned any idea of further adventures in Provence and joined decisively in the campaign against the Moslems to the south, taking Mallorca in 1229, Ibiza in 1235 and then, at much greater cost, Valencia in 1238. He made it another separate kingdom, the third part of the 'Crown of Aragon'.

Barcelona became the centre of an empire extending across the Mediterranean. The city grew tremendously under Jaume I, and in mid-century he ordered the building of a new, second wall, along the line of the Rambla and roughly encircling the area between there and the modern Parc de la Ciutadella, thus bringing La Ribera and the other *vilanoves* within the city. In 1274 he also gave Barcelona a form of representative self-government, the *Consell de Cent,* or council of 100 chosen citizens, an institution that would last for over 400 years. In Catalonia as a whole royal powers were limited by a parliament, the *Corts*, with a permanent standing committee, known as the *Generalitat*.

Catalan imperialism advanced by conquest and marriage well beyond the Balearic Islands. The Count-Kings commanded a sail-powered fleet, more flexible than oar-driven galleys, and a mercenary army, the 'Catalan Companies' (*Almogàvers*). For decades they were led by two great commanders, the fleet by Roger de Llúria and the army by Roger de Flor. The *Almogàvers*, in particular, with their sword-raised battle cry *'Desperta ferro!'* ('Awaken, iron!'), made themselves feared equally by Christians and Moslems, as they travelled the Mediterranean conquering, plundering and enslaving in the name of God and the Crown of Aragon.

In 1282 Pere II 'the Great' annexed Sicily, of vital strategic importance and a major source of grain. Catalan domination over the island would last for nearly 150 years. Shortly afterwards an episode occurred that has been depicted as a great military feat (by Catalan romantic historians) or as utterly discreditable (by many others). In 1302 Roger de Flor and his *Almogàvers* were sent to Greece to assist the Byzantine Emperor against the Turks. Finding he could not pay them adequately, they turned against the Emperor and carved out an independent dukedom for themselves in Athens that would last for 80 years.

The Catalan empire reached its greatest strength under Jaume II 'the Just' (1291-1327). Corsica (1323) and Sardinia (1324) were added to the possessions of the Crown of Aragon, although the latter would never submit to Catalan rule and would be a constant focus of revolt.

BARCELONA IN THE GOLDEN AGE

The Crown of Aragon was often at war with Arab rulers, but its capital flourished through commerce with every part of the Mediterranean, Christian and Moslem. Catalan ships also sailed into the Atlantic, to England and Flanders. Their ventures were actively supported by the Count-Kings and burghers of Barcelona, and regulated by the first-ever code of maritime law, the *Llibre del Consolat de Mar* (written 1258-72), an early example of the Catalans' tendency to legalism, the influence of which extended far beyond their own territories. Barcelona had a lighthouse in place as early as 1094, and by the late thirteenth century nearly 130 consulates ringed the Mediterranean, engaged in a complex system of commerce involving spices, coral, grain, slaves, metals, textiles, olive oil, salt fish and leather goods.

Not surprisingly, this age of power and prestige was also the great era of building in medieval Barcelona. The Catalan Gothic style reached its peak between the reigns of Jaume the Just and Pere III 'the Ceremonious' (1336-87). The Count-Kings' imperial conquests may have been ephemeral, but their talent for permanence in building can still be admired today. Between 1290 and 1340 the construction of most of Barcelona's major Gothic buildings was initiated. Religious edifices such as the **Cathedral**, **Santa Maria del Mar** and **Santa Maria del Pi** were matched by civil buildings such as the **Saló de Tinell** and the **Llotja**, the old market and stock exchange. As a result, Barcelona today contains the most important nucleus of Gothic civil architecture in Europe.

The ships of the Catalan navy were built in the monumental **Drassanes** (shipyards), begun by Pere II and completed under Pere III, in 1378. In 1359 Pere III also built the third, final city wall, along the line of the modern Paral.lel, Ronda Sant Pau and Ronda Sant Antoni. This gave the 'old city' of Barcelona its definitive shape, although large areas of the Raval, between the second and third walls, would not be built up for centuries.

La Ribera, 'the waterfront', was the centre of trade and industry in fourteenth-century Barcelona. Once unloaded at the beach, wares were taken to the Llotja (the Lodge), the porticoed market place and exchange. Just inland, the Carrer Montcada, built around this time, was the street *par excellence* where newly enriched merchants could display their wealth in opulent Gothic palaces. All around were the workers of the various craft guilds, grouped in their own streets: Agullers (needle-makers), Espaseria (swordsmiths), Mirallers (mirror-makers) and so on, names that still survive today.

Women's domains in this Barcelona were initially limited to home, market, convent or brothel, although in 1249 they gained the right to inherit property, a necessary measure for the perpetuation of Catalan land rights. As well as working as midwives and wet nurses – respected professions

Jewish Barcelona

The Jewish quarter, or *Call*, founded in Barcelona in the second century AD within the city's original Roman walls was home to one of the most important Jewish populations in medieval Spain. Under the Visigoths, in 694, all Jews were decreed slaves. Later, the Count-Kings improved their status to that of serfs. Heavily taxed with no civil rights, Jews were required to wear special dress in order to be identifiable at all times by a law of Jaume I of 1243.

The Barcelona *Call* was nevertheless highly reputed as a very learned, religious community. Rabbi Benjamin of Tudela, a famous twelfth-century chronicler, wrote of the 'wise and learned men among the Jewish community in Barcelona'. Jewish women too were unusually well educated. Though the inhabitants of the *Call* were mostly artisans and farmers, they were also known for their excellence as fiscal agents and money changers, and as doctors, Arabic translators, scholars and booksellers. Many worked for the Catalan nobility and as advisors to the Crown of Aragon. It was here that the famous 'Disputation of Barcelona' took place in 1263 between the Girona Jewish mystic Moshe ben Nahman (Nachmanides, known locally as Bonastruc da Porta) and Dominican monks, under the watchful eye of Jaume I. They debated the divinity of Christ and other great questions of faith for three whole days, and though the monks naturally did not accept defeat, the King was said to be so impressed by the Rabbi's eloquence that he gave him a large reward.

By this time the community was enclosed from dusk to dawn behind the arches that once lined the Carrer del Call, the quarter's eastern boundary, and between the present Generalitat to the north and Banys Nous to the south. Eventually their enemies had their way: the *Call* was sacked in a pogrom of 6-8 August 1391, which spread to every Jewish quarter in Catalonia, Valencia and the Balearics. A Christian mob, incited by monks, massacred hundreds of its inhabitants. The *Call* never recovered, and no Jews were left in Barcelona when they were officially banned from the city in 1424, a prelude to the expulsion of all Jews from Spain in 1492.

Today, a walk around these silent, winding streets can still turn up fragments from this centuries-old past. Recent studies have identified the north-west corner of the intersection of C/Marlet and C/Sant Domenec del Call as the site of the *Sinagoga Major*; the dank half-basement seen through the windows at knee-level corresponds to the model of synagogue permitted under the Crown of Aragon, while the odd angle on C/Marlet suggests a wall oriented towards Jerusalem. A private project is under way to convert the site into a museum and information point. A separate water fountain for the Jewish quarter was once located in the middle of C/Sant Honorat at the junction with C/Fruita, and a smaller synagogue (the *Sinagoga Poca*) stood on the site of the Sant Jordi chapel in the Generalitat, where a continuation of Fruita once ran. Arc de Sant Roman del Call housed the Jewish women's school, and at Carrer Marlet 1 we can still read a twelfth-century Hebrew inscription, placed here in the last century.

After the 1391 pogrom, the Jewish cemetery was desecrated and tombstones were used as building materials. Hebrew inscriptions can be seen on stones on the eastern wall of Plaça Sant Iu, across from the Cathedral, and at ankle-level in the Plaça del Rei, near the north entry to the Museu d'Història de la Ciutat. Jewish archaeological remains can also be seen in the **Museu Militar** on Montjuïc and in the Gothic section of the **MNAC** (*see chapter* **Museums**). Neither the Museu d'Història de la Ciutat nor the Museu d'Història de Catalunya, though, deal with Jewish history in Barcelona with the respect and attention the subject requires.

– women were at one time the principal textile workers, involved in all phases of production, even though officially the guilds still barred them from many trades. At the very top of society some women became very powerful, as it was unusually common – for that era – for Catalan Count-Kings to delegate their authority to their queens while they were away on imperial campaigns, as happened with Eleanor of Sicily, wife of Pere III.

The Catalan 'Golden Age' was an era not only of economic expansion, but also of cultural greatness. Catalonia was one of the first areas in Europe to use its vernacular language, as well as Latin, in written form and as a language of culture. The oldest written texts in Catalan are the *Homilies d'Organyà*, translations from the Bible dating from the twelfth century. Not just monks, but also the court and the aristocracy seem very early to have attained an unusual level of literacy, and Jaume I wrote his own autobiography, the *Llibre dels Feits* or 'Book of Deeds', dramatically recounting his achievements and conquests.

The adventures of Friar Anselm

For a people with such a strong collective identity Catalans also have a marked strain of quirky individuality, and there's no better example than poet-philosopher Anselm Turmeda, one of the great mavericks of the Middle Ages. He was born in Mallorca in about 1352. He stood out for his intellectual ability at an early age, studying logic, theology and physics in Palma and Lleida and becoming a Franciscan Friar at the age of 20. He then spent ten years as a wandering scholar around Europe, mainly in Bologna but also in Paris. He was particularly known for his knowledge of the Greeks and the Islamic Andaluz scholar Averröes.

On his return to Catalonia in the 1380s he was in great demand from Church and state for his knowledge of many fields and languages, as well as being known for his sophisticated, worldly wit, which perhaps already put other churchmen on their guard. He kept moving, however, and next turned up in Sicily. Then, in about 1388, Anselm appeared in Tunis, and announced he had become a Moslem.

In that era, there was no greater heresy. Much about Turmeda's life and motives is clouded in mystery. He immediately became the target of a sustained attempt at character assassination, especially by some of his former Franciscan brothers, who put around the story that he had fled together with another errant monk and several 'fallen women', driven only by 'a desire for adventure and lustful passions'. Just how highly regarded he was by others, though, is shown by the fact that both King Marti I and Pope Benedict XIII sent letters pleading with him to reconsider, and many years later Alfons IV offered the ageing Anselm safe conduct if he wished to make a visit home. In his new life, however, he soon won just as much prestige, serving the Bey of Tunis as diplomat and interpreter, marrying a sultan's daughter and being appointed head of the Tunis customs house.

His verse dialogues were all written in Tunis, but in Catalan: corrosive, clever satires of the life of the Catalan-Aragonese kingdom and the corruption of the Church, and no more orthodox in Islam than they were to Christians. In the *Disputa de l'Ase* ('Dispute with the Ass', 1418), the animals choose a donkey as their king, declaring their moral superiority over humans. Turmeda himself supposedly comes forward to defend humanity, but in the 'debate' he puts into the mouth of the ass a comprehensive, sarcastic demolition job of late-medieval society and its pervasive hypocrisy, until Anselm has to concede the beast has a point.

Despite its 'Islamic' origin the 'Dispute' was quite widely distributed for a book of its time, until it was banned absolutely by the Inquisition in 1583. Near the end of his life Anselm wrote his own book in Arabic, an anti-Christian polemic called *Refutation of the Followers of the Cross*, which apparently is still in print in some Arab countries. He died in 1432 in Tunis, where (as Abdullah Al-taryuman) he still has a street named after him.

Incipient Catalan literature was given a vital thrust by the unique figure of Ramon Llull (1235-1316). After a debauched youth, he turned to more serious pursuits after a series of religious visions, and became the first man in post-Roman Europe to write philosophy in a vernacular language. Steeped in Arabic and Hebrew writings, he brought together Christian, Islamic, Jewish and Classical ideas, and also wrote a vast amount on other subjects – from theories of chivalry to poetry and visionary tales. In doing so he effectively created Catalan as a literary language. Catalan translations from Greek and Latin were also undertaken at this time; troubadours brought legends and tales of courtly love to Barcelona, while chroniclers such as Ramon Muntaner recorded the exploits of Count-Kings and *Almogàvers*. In the very twilight of the Golden Age, in 1490, the Valencian Joanot Martorell published *Tirant Lo Blanc*, the bawdy story considered the first true European novel.

PLAGUE & DECLINE

Barcelona was not, though, a peaceful and harmonious place during its Golden Age, especially as the fourteenth century wore on. Social unrest and violence in the streets were common: grain riots, popular uprisings, attacks on Jews and gang warfare. An ongoing struggle took place between two political factions, the *Biga* (roughly representing the most established merchants) and the *Busca* (roughly composed of smaller tradesmen).

The extraordinary prosperity of the medieval period was not to last. The Count-Kings had over extended Barcelona's resources, and over-invested in far-off ports. By 1400 the effort to maintain their conquests by force, especially Sardinia, had exhausted the spirit and the coffers of the Catalan imperialist drive. The Black Death had arrived in the 1340s, and had had a devastating impact on Catalonia. This only intensified the bitterness of social conflicts, between the aristocracy, merchants, peasants and the urban poor.

In 1410 Marti I 'the Humane' died without an heir, bringing to an end the line of Counts of Barcelona unbroken since Guifré *el Pilós*. After much deliberation the Crown of Aragon was passed to a member of a Castilian noble family, the Trastámaras, Fernando de Antequera (1410-16).

His son, Alfons IV 'the Magnanimous' (1416-58), undertook one more conquest, of Naples, but the empire was under ever-greater pressure, and Barcelona merchants were unable to compete with the Genoese and Venetians. At home, in the 1460s, the effects of war and catastrophic famine led to a collapse into civil war and peasant revolt. The population was depleted to such an extent that Barcelona would not regain the numbers it had had in 1400, 40,000, until the eighteenth century.

The fall of Barcelona

In 1469 an important union for Spain initiated a woeful period in Barcelona's history, dubbed by some Catalan historians *la Decadència*, which would lead to the end of Catalonia as a separate entity. In that year Ferdinand of Aragon (reigned 1479-1516) married Isabella of Castile (1476-1506), and so united the different Spanish kingdoms, even though they would retain their separate institutions for another two centuries. It was theoretically a union of equals, but it soon became clear that the new monarchy would be dominated by Castile.

As Catalonia's fortunes had declined, those of Castile had risen. While Catalonia was impoverished and in chaos, Castile was larger, richer, had a bigger population and was on the crest of a wave of expansion. In 1492 Granada, last Moslem foothold in Spain, was conquered, Isabella decreed the expulsion of all Jews from Castile and Aragon, and Columbus discovered America.

It was Castile's seafaring orientation toward the Atlantic, rather than the Mediterranean, that confirmed Catalonia's decline. The discovery of the New World was a disaster for Catalan commerce: trade shifted decisively away from the Mediterranean, while Catalans were officially barred from participating in the exploitation of the new empire until the 1770s. The weight of Castile in the monarchy was increased, and it became the clear seat of government.

In 1516 the Spanish crown passed to the House of Habsburg, in the shape of Ferdinand and Isabella's grandson the Emperor Charles V. His son Philip II of Spain established Madrid as the capital of all his dominions in 1561. Catalonia was managed by appointed Viceroys, the power of its institutions increasingly restricted, with a down-at-heel aristocracy and meagre cultural life. Instead of the kings and merchant-magnates of former years, the main patrons of new building in Barcelona were the Church and state governors, who built baroque churches and a few official buildings, many of them since demolished.

THE GREAT DEFEATS

While Castilian Spain went through its 'Golden Century', Catalonia was left more and more on the margins. Worse was to come, however, in the following century, with the two national revolts, both heroic defeats, that have since acquired a central role in Catalan nationalist mythology.

The problem for the Spanish monarchy was that, whereas Castile was an absolute monarchy and so could be taxed at will, in the former Aragonese territories, and especially Catalonia, royal authority kept coming up against a mass of local rights and privileges. As the empire became bogged down in endless wars – against the English, the Dutch, the French – and expenses that not even American gold could meet, the Count-Duke of Olivares, the great minister of King Philip IV (1621-65), resolved to extract more money and troops from the non-Castilian dominions of the crown. The Catalans, however, felt they were taxed quite enough already.

In 1640 a mass of peasants, the 'Reapers', gathered on the Rambla in Barcelona, outside the Porta Ferrisa or 'Iron Gate' in the second wall. They rioted against royal authority, surged into the city and murdered the Viceroy, the Marqués de Santa Coloma. This began the general uprising known as the *Guerra dels Segadors*, the 'Reapers' War'. The authorities of the Generalitat, led by Pau Claris, were fearful of the violence of the poor and, lacking the confidence to declare Catalonia independent, appealed for protection from Louis XIII of France. French rule, however, created another, new set of problems, and French armies were in any case unable to defend Catalonia adequately. In 1652 a destitute Barcelona capitulated to the equally exhausted army of Philip IV. Later, in 1659, France and Spain made peace with a treaty under which the Catalan territory of Roussillon, around Perpignan, was given to France. After the revolt, Philip IV and his ministers were surprisingly magnanimous, allowing the Catalans to retain what was left of their institutions despite their disloyalty. This war, however, provided the Catalan national anthem, *Els Segadors*, 'The Reapers'.

Fifty years later came the second of the great national rebellions, in the War of the Spanish Succession, the last time Catalonia sought to regain its national freedoms by force. In 1700 Charles II of Spain died without an heir. Castile accepted the grandson of Louis XIV of France, Philip of Anjou, as King Philip V of Spain (1700-46). However, the alternative candidate, the Archduke Charles of Austria, promised to restore the traditional rights of the former Aragonese territories, and so won their allegiance. He also had the support, against France, of Britain, Holland

The 'Reapers' revolt at the gates of Barcelona, 1640.

and Austria. Once again, though, Catalonia backed the wrong horse, and was let down in its choice of allies. In 1713 Britain and the Dutch made a separate peace and withdrew their aid, leaving the Catalans stranded with no possibility of victory. After a 13-month siege in which every citizen was called to arms, Barcelona fell to the French and Spanish armies on 11 September 1714.

The most heroic defeat of all, this date marked the most decisive political reverse in Barcelona's history, and is now commemorated as Catalan National Day, the *Diada*. Some of Barcelona's staunchest resisters were buried next to the church of Santa Maria del Mar in the **Fossar de les Moreres** ('The Mulberry Graveyard'), now a memorial (*see chapter* **Sightseeing**).

In 1715 Philip V issued his decree of *Nova Planta*, abolishing all the remaining separate institutions of the Crown of Aragon and so, in effect, creating 'Spain' as a single, unitary state. Barcelona's own institutions, such as the *Consell de Cent*, were also dismantled, and local authority was vested in the military commander, the Captain-General. Large-scale 'Castilianisation' of the country was initiated, and Castilian replaced the Catalan language in all official documents.

In Barcelona, extra measures were taken to keep the city under firm control. The crumbling medieval walls and the castle on Montjuïc were refurbished with new ramparts, and a massive new Citadel was built on the eastern side of the old city, where the Parc de la Ciutadella is today.

To make space for it, thousands of people had to be expelled from La Ribera and forcibly rehoused in the Barceloneta, Barcelona's first planned housing scheme, with its barrack-like street plan unmistakably built by French military engineers. This citadel became the most hated symbol of Catalan subordination.

THE CITY BOUNCES BACK

Politically subjugated and without much of a native ruling class after the departure of many of its remaining aristocrats to serve the monarchy in Madrid, Catalonia nevertheless resuscitated in the eighteenth century. Catalans continued speaking their language, and went about developing their own, independent commercial initiatives. Barcelona began to grow again, as peasants flowed in from the war-devastated countryside.

Ironically, the Bourbons, by abolishing all legal differences between Catalonia and the rest of Spain, also removed the earlier restrictions on Catalan trade, especially with the colonies. In 1758 an independent Board of Trade (*Junta de Comerç*) was created in Barcelona to encourage commerce. The strength of the guild system of Barcelona had enabled it to maintain its artisan-oriented industries, and the city revived particularly following the official authorisation to trade with the Americas by King Charles III in 1778.

Shipping traffic picked up again, and during the last years of the century Barcelona had a booming export trade to the New World in wines and spirits from Catalan vineyards and textiles, wool and silk, especially the hand-stamped calicos called *Indianas*. In 1780 a merchant called Erasme de Gómina opened Barcelona's first true factory, a hand-powered weaving mill in C/Riera Alta with 800 workers. In the next decade Catalan trade with Spanish America quadrupled; Barcelona's population had grown from around 30,000 in 1720 to close to 100,000 by the end of the century.

This prosperity was reflected in a new wave of building in the city. A number of neo-classical mansions appeared, notably on C/Ample and the Rambla. The greatest transformation, though, was in the Rambla itself. Until the 1770s it had been no more than a dusty, dry riverbed where country people came to sell their produce, lined on the Raval side mostly with giant religious houses and on the other with Jaume I's second wall. In 1775 the Captain-General, the Marqués de la Mina, embarked on an ambitious scheme to demolish the wall and turn the Rambla into a paved promenade, work that would continue into the next century. Beyond the Rambla, the previously semi-rural Raval was rapidly becoming densely populated.

Barcelona's expansion was briefly interrupted by the French invasion of 1808. Napoleon sought to appeal to Catalans by offering them national recognition within his empire, but, curiously, met with very little response. After six years of turmoil, Barcelona's growing business class would resume their projects in 1814, with the restoration of the Bourbon monarchy in the shape of Ferdinand VII.

Factories, barricades & poets

The upheaval of the Napoleonic occupation ushered in 60 years of conflict and political disorder in Spain, as new and traditional forces in society – reactionaries, conservatives, reformists and revolutionaries – struggled with each other to establish a viable system of government. Even so, during this same era Barcelona was still able to embark upon the transformations of the industrial revolution, Catalonia, with Lombardy, being one of only two areas in southern Europe to do so before the last years of the nineteenth century.

On his restoration Ferdinand VII (1808-33) attempted to reinstate the absolute monarchy of his youth and reimpose his authority over Spain's American colonies, and failed to do either. On his death he was succeeded by his three-year-old daughter Isabel II (1833-68), but the throne was also claimed by his brother Carlos, who was backed by the most reactionary sectors in the country. To defend Isabel's rights the Regent, Ferdinand's widow Queen María Cristina, was obliged to seek the support of liberals, and so granted a very limited form of constitution. Thus began Spain's

Urban geometry

Once Barcelona's walls came down (*see page 23*), a plan was needed to develop the land beyond them and connect the city with Gràcia and the outlying towns. The Ajuntament held a competition for projects in 1859. The councillors actually preferred a scheme presented by the prestigious architect Antoni Rovira i Trias, for long straight streets radiating fan-like from Plaça Catalunya. Controversially, however, and for reasons that have never been explained, orders came from Madrid that the plan to be adopted was that of another Catalan engineer, Ildefons Cerdà (1815-75).

Cerdà had surveyed and drawn the city's first accurate plans in 1855. He was also a radical influenced by utopian socialist ideas, concerned with the cramped, unhealthy conditions of workers' housing in the old city. With its love of straight lines and uniform grid, Cerdà's plan is very much related to visionary rationalist ideas of its time, as was the idea of placing two of its main avenues along a geographic parallel and a meridian. His central aim was to alleviate overpopulation problems while fomenting social equality by using quadrangular blocks of a standard size, with strict building controls to ensure that they were built up on only two sides, to a limited height, leaving a garden in between. Each district would be of 20 blocks, containing all community necessities.

In the event, though, this idealised use of urban space was scarcely ever achieved, for the private developers who actually built the *Eixample* regarded Cerdà's restrictions on their property as pointless interference. Buildings went up to much more than the planned heights, and in practice all the blocks from Plaça Catalunya to the Diagonal have been enclosed, with very few inner gardens withstanding the onslaught of construction.

The most enduring feature of Cerdà's plan is the *xamfrà*, the bevelled corner of each block. The Ajuntament had disliked the scheme because it seemed to disregard the old centre of the city, and the principal *Modernista* architects initially railed against the project as a horror. Nevertheless, it would become the primary showcase for their imaginative feats, and an essential part of Barcelona's identity

Carlist Wars, in which Don Carlos' faction won a considerable following in conservative, rural Catalonia, in part because of its support for traditional, local rights and customs.

THE INDUSTRIAL CITY

While this see-saw struggle went on around the country, in Barcelona a liberal-minded local administration, freed from subordination to the military, was able to engage in some city planning, opening up the soon-to-be fashionable C/Ferran and Plaça Sant Jaume in the 1820s, and later adding the Plaça Reial. A fundamental change came in 1836, when the liberal government in Madrid decreed the *Desamortización* or disentailment of Spain's monasteries. In Barcelona, where convents and religious houses still took up great sections of the Raval and the Rambla, a huge area was freed for development.

The Rambla took on the appearance it roughly retains today, while the Raval, the main district for new industry in a Barcelona still contained within its defensive walls, rapidly filled up with tenements and textile mills, built several storeys high to maximise space. In 1832 the first steam-driven factory in Spain was built on C/Tallers, sparking resistance from the city's hand-spinners and weavers. Catalans who had made fortunes in the colonies invested back home, and industry developed apace.

Most of their factories, though, were still relatively small, and Catalan manufacturers were very aware that they were at a disadvantage with regard to the industries of Britain and other countries to the north. For decades, their political motto would not be anything to do with nationalism but protectionism, as they incessantly demanded of Madrid that the textile markets of Spain and its remaining colonies be sealed against all foreign competition.

Also, they did not have the city to themselves. Not only did the anti-industrial Carlists threaten from the countryside, but Barcelona soon became a centre of radical ideas. Its people were notably rebellious, and liberal, republican and even utopian socialist groups proliferated between sporadic bursts of repression. In 1842 a liberal revolt, the *Jamancia*, took over Barcelona, and barricades went up around the city. This was the last occasion Barcelona was bombarded from the castle on Montjuïc, as the army struggled to regain control.

The Catalan language, by this time, had been relegated to secondary status, spoken in every street but rarely written or used in cultured discourse. Then, in 1833 Bonaventura Carles Aribau published his *Oda a la Pàtria*, a romantic eulogy in Catalan of the country, its language and its past. Traditionally, this one poem is credited with initiating the *Renaixença* or rebirth of Catalan heritage and cul-

More turmoil: Gràcia riots against military service in 1870.

ture. Its early literature was lyrical and romantic rather than political, but also reflected the underlying energies of a renascent culture. The year 1848 was a high point for Barcelona and Catalonia, with the inauguration of the first railway in Spain, from Barcelona to Mataró, and the opening of the Liceu opera. Improved transport increased Barcelona's contacts with Paris, the mecca for all new ideas, and so augmented the city's cosmopolitan patina.

BARCELONA BREAKS ITS BANKS

The optimism of Barcelona's new middle class was counterpointed by two persistent obstacles: the weakness of the Spanish economy as a whole, and the instability of their own society, reflected in atrocious labour relations. No consideration was given to the manpower behind the industrial surge, the underpaid, overworked men, women and children who lived in increasingly appalling conditions in high-rise slums within the cramped city. Epidemics were frequent, and unrest multiplied. In 1855 the first general strike took place in Barcelona. The Captain-General, Zapatero, inaugurating a long cycle of conflict, refused to permit any workers' organisations, and bloodily suppressed all resistance.

One response to the city's problems that had almost universal support in Barcelona was the demolition of the city walls, which imposed a stifling restriction on its growth. For years, however, the Spanish state refused to contemplate relinquishing this hold on the city. To find space, larger factories were established in villages around Barcelona, such as Sants and Poble Nou. In 1854 permission finally came for the demolition of the citadel and the walls. The work began with enthusiastic popular participation, crowds of volunteers joining in at weekends. Barcelona at last broke out of the space it had occupied since the fourteenth century and spread outward into its new *Eixample*, the 'Extension', to a plan by Ildefons Cerdà (*see page 21* **Urban geometry**).

In 1868 Isabel II, once a symbol of liberalism, was overthrown by a progressive revolt. During the six years of upheaval that followed, power in Madrid would be held by a provisional government, a constitutional monarchy under an Italian prince and then a federal republic. Workers were free to organise, and in November 1868 Giuseppe Fanelli, an Italian emissary of Bakunin, brought the ideas of anarchism to Madrid and Barcelona, encountering a ready response in Catalonia. In 1870 the first Spanish workers' congress was held in Barcelona. The radical forces, however, were divided between multiple factions, while the established classes of society, increasingly threatened, called for the restoration of order. Carlist guerrillas reappeared in the countryside, sending refugees streaming into Barcelona. The Republic proclaimed in 1873 was unable to establish its authority, and succumbed to a military coup.

THE YANKEES OF EUROPE

In 1874 the Bourbon dynasty was restored to the Spanish throne in the shape of Alfonso XII, son of Isabel II. Workers' organisations were again suppressed. The middle classes, however, were ever more confident. The 1870s saw a frenzied boom in stock speculation, the *Febre d'Or* or 'Gold Fever', and the real take-off of building in the *Eixample*. From the 1880s *Modernisme*, the unique Catalan equivalent of art nouveau, became the preferred style of the new district, the perfect expression for the self-confidence, romanticism and impetus of the industrial class. The first modern Catalanist political movement was founded by Valentí Almirall.

Barcelona felt it needed to show the world what it had achieved. In 1885 an exhibition promoter named Eugenio Serrano de Casanova proposed to the city council, the Ajuntament, the holding of an international exhibition, such as had been held successfully in London, Paris and Vienna. Serrano was actually a dubious character who made off with large amounts of public funds, but by the time this became clear the city fathers had fully committed themselves. The Universal Exhibition of 1888 was used as a pretext for the final conversion of the Ciutadella into a park; giant efforts had to be made to get everything ready in time, including the building of an 'International Hotel' designed by Domènech i Montaner (which had to be demolished immediately after the exhibition) in only 100 days on the present-day Moll de la Fusta, a feat that led the Mayor, Rius i Taulet, to exclaim that 'the Catalan people are the yankee people of Europe'. The first of Barcelona's three great efforts to demonstrate that it was more than just a 'second city', the 1888 Exhibition signified both the consecration of the Modernist style, and the end of provincial, dowdy Barcelona and its establishment as a modern-day city on the international map.

The city of the new century

The 1888 Exhibition left Barcelona with huge debts, a new look and reasons to believe in itself as a paradigm of progress. The middle classes could see themselves as models of both taste and efficiency; radicals could feel they were at the centre of a hub of new ideas. As the year 1900 approached, in few cities was the new century regarded with greater anticipation than in Barcelona.

The Catalan *Renaixença* continued, and acquired a more political tone. In 1892 the *Bases de Manresa* were drawn up, a first draft plan for Catalan autonomy. Middle-class opinion was becoming more sympathetic to political Catalanism. A decisive moment came in 1898, when the underlying weakness of the Spanish state was abruptly made plain, despite the superficial prosperity of the first years of the Bourbon restoration.

Spain was manœuvred into a short war with the United States, in which it very quickly lost its remaining empire in Cuba, the Philippines and Puerto Rico. Catalan industrialists, horrified at losing the lucrative Cuban market, despaired of the ability of the state ever to reform itself. Many swung behind a conservative nationalist movement founded in 1901, the *Lliga Regionalista* or Regionalist League, led by Enric Prat de la Riba and the politician-financier Francesc Cambó. It promised both national revival and modern, efficient government.

Barcelona continued to grow, fuelling Catalanist optimism. The city incorporated most of the surrounding communities in 1897, reaching a population of over half a million, and in 1907 initiated the 'internal reform' of the old city with the cutting through it of the Via Laietana, intended to allow in more air and so make the streets less unhealthy.

Catalan letters were thriving: the *Institut d'Estudis Catalans* (Institute of Catalan Studies) was founded in 1906, and Pompeu Fabra set out to create the first Catalan dictionary. Literature had acquired a new maturity, and in 1905 Víctor Català (a pseudonym for Caterina Albert) shocked the country with *Solitud*, a darkly modern novel of a woman's sexual awakening that predated DH Lawrence on the subject. Barcelona had a vibrant artistic community, centred on *Modernisme*, from established, wealthy painters like Rusiñol and Casas to the penniless bohemians who gathered round them, like the young Picasso.

Barcelona's bohemians were also drawn to the increasingly wild nightlife of the Raval. The area had already been known for very downmarket entertainments in the 1740s, but cabarets, bars and brothels multiplied at the end of the nineteenth century. Looking back many years later from exile, the writer Lluís Capdevila wrote that one thing he missed about the Barcelona of his youth was that he had never known another city where there were so many places to eat at three in the morning.

Around the cabarets, though, there were also the poorest of the working class, whose conditions had continued to decline. Barcelona had some of the worst overcrowding and highest mortality rates of any city in Europe. Most exploited were the women and children, toiling for a pittance in dark, airless factories 15 hours a day. A respectable feminist movement, led by such figures as the writer Dolors Monserdà, undertook philanthropic projects aimed at educating the female masses. Barcelona, however, was more associated internationally with revolutionary politics and violence than with gradual reform.

In 1893 over 20 people were killed in a series of anarchist bombings, the most renowned of them when a bomb was thrown down into the stalls of the Liceu during a performance of *William Tell*. Those responsible were individuals acting alone, but the authorities took the opportunity to carry

A street in the Raval at the beginning of the 1930s.

out a general round-up of anarchists and radicals, several of whom, soon known as the 'Martyrs of Montjuïc', were tortured and executed in the castle above Barcelona. In retaliation, in 1906 a Catalan anarchist tried to assassinate King Alfonso XIII on his wedding day in Madrid.

Anarchism was then only a minority current among the workers of Barcelona, but in general rebellious attitudes, growing republican sentiment and a fierce hatred of the Catholic Church united the underclasses and predisposed them to take to the barricades with little provocation. In 1909 came the explosive *Setmana Tràgica*, the Tragic Week. It began as a protest against the conscription of troops for the colonial war in Morocco, but degenerated into a general riot and the destruction of churches by excited mobs. Suspected culprits were summarily executed, as was anarchist educationalist Francesc Ferrer, accused of 'moral responsibility' even though he had not even been in Barcelona at the time.

These events dented the optimism of the Catalanists of the *Lliga*, but in 1914 they secured from Madrid the *Mancomunitat* or administrative union of the four Catalan provinces, the first joint government in Catalonia in 200 years. Its first President was Prat de la Riba, succeeded in 1917 by the architect Puig i Cadafalch. However, the *Lliga*'s further projects for Catalonia were to be obstructed by a further inflammation of social tensions.

EXPLOSIVE TIMES

Spain's neutral status during World War I gave a huge boost to the Spanish, and especially Catalan, economy. Exports soared, as Catalonia's manufacturers made millions supplying uniforms to the French army. The economy was able to diversify, from textiles into engineering, chemicals and other more modern sectors. This provided the background to an extraordinary drama.

Barcelona also became the most amenable place of refuge for anyone in Europe who wished to avoid the war. It acquired an international refugee community, among them avant-garde artists Sonia and Robert Delaunay, Francis Picabia, Marie Laurencin and Albert Gleizes, and was a bolt-hole for all kinds of low life from around Europe. The nightlife of the lower Raval took on a newly exotic look, and a string of new cabarets and dance halls opened along the Rambla and C/Nou de la Rambla, each one more opulent than the last. All featured the required music of the era for a wild time, the tango. Gambling houses and drug dens appeared around the bars and brothels, and cocaine became widely available. Shortly afterwards this area would be dubbed the *Barrio Chino*, 'Chinatown', definitively identifying it as an area of sin and perdition, and the city acquired a reputation similar to that of Marseille in the 1970s, as the centre of drug trafficking and about every other kind of illegal trade in the Mediterranean.

Some of the most regular patrons of the lavish new cabarets were industrialists, for many of the war profits were spent immediately in very conspicuous consumption. This took place against a still more dramatic social background. The war also set off massive inflation, driving people in their thousands from rural Spain into the cities. Barcelona doubled in size in 20 years to become the largest city in Spain, and the fulcrum of Spanish politics.

Workers' wages, meanwhile, had lost half their real value. The chief channel of protest in Barcelona was the anarchist workers' union, the CNT, constituted in 1911, which gained half a million members in Catalonia by 1919. The CNT and the socialist UGT launched a joint general strike in 1917, roughly co-ordinated with a campaign of the *Lliga* and other liberal politicians for political reform. However, the politicians quickly withdrew at the prospect of serious social unrest. Inflation continued to intensify, and in 1919 Barcelona was paralysed for two months by a CNT general strike over union recognition. Employers refused to recognise the CNT, and the most intransigent of them hired gunmen to get rid of union leaders, especially a gang organised by an ex-German spy known as the 'Baron de Koening'. Union activists replied in kind, and virtual guerrilla warfare developed between the CNT, the employers and the state. Over 800 people were killed on the city's streets in the space of five years.

In 1923, in response both to the chaos in Barcelona and a crisis in the war in Morocco, the Captain-General of Barcelona, Miguel Primo de Rivera, staged a coup and established a military dictatorship under King Alfonso XIII. The CNT, already exhausted, was suppressed. Conservative Catalanists, longing for an end to disorder and the revolutionary threat, initially supported the coup, but were rewarded by the abolition of the *Mancomunitat* and a vindictive campaign by the Primo regime against the Catalan language and national symbols.

This, however, achieved the contrary of the desired effect, helping to radicalise and popularise Catalan nationalism. After the terrible struggles of the previous years, the 1920s were actually a time of notable prosperity for many in Barcelona, as some of the wealth recently accumulated filtered through the economy. Economic changes brought greater numbers of office and shop workers, who enjoyed new kinds of leisure like jazz, football and the cinema. The first signs of a tourist industry were seen, and a journalist named Ferran de Pol had coined the name *Costa Brava* for the coast around Palafrugell. This was also, though, a highly politicised society, in which new magazines and forums for discussion – despite the restrictions of the Dictatorship – found a ready audience.

A prime motor of Barcelona's prosperity during the 1920s was the International Exhibition of 1929, the second of the city's great showcase events. It had been proposed by Cambó and Catalan business groups, but Primo de Rivera saw that it could also serve as a propaganda event for his regime. In association with the Exhibition a huge number of public projects were undertaken, including the post office, the Estació de França and Barcelona's first Metro line, from Plaça Catalunya to Plaça d'Espanya. Thousands of migrant workers came from southern Spain to build them, many living in decrepit housing or shanties on the city fringes. By 1930, Barcelona was very different from the place it had been in 1910; it had over a million people, and its urban sprawl had crossed into neighbouring towns such as Hospitalet and Santa Coloma.

For the Exhibition itself the main architects of the day undertook the comprehensive redevelopment of Montjuïc and Plaça d'Espanya, in the style of the Catalan neo-classical architectural movement *Noucentisme*, an austere reaction to the excesses of Modernism. Their work, though, contrasted strikingly with the German pavilion by Mies van der Rohe (the **Pavelló Barcelona**), announcing the international trend toward rationalism.

THE REPUBLIC

Despite the Exhibition's success, in January 1930 Primo de Rivera resigned, exhausted. The King appointed another soldier, General Berenguer, as prime minister with the mission of restoring stability. The Dictatorship, though, had fatally discredited the old regime, and a protest movement spread across Catalonia against the monarchy. In early 1931 Berenguer called local elections, as a first step towards a restoration of constitutional rule. The outcome was a complete surprise, for republicans were elected in all of Spain's cities. Ecstatic crowds poured into the streets, and Alfonso XIII abdicated. On 14 April 1931, the Second Spanish Republic was proclaimed.

The Republic came in amid real euphoria. It was especially so in Catalonia, where it was associated with hopes for both social change and national reaffirmation. The clear winner of the elections in the country had been the *Esquerra Republicana*, a leftist Catalanist group led by Francesc Macià. A raffish, elderly figure, Macià was one of the first politicians in Spain to win genuine affection from ordinary people. He declared Catalonia independent, but later agreed to accept autonomy within the Spanish Republic.

The Generalitat was re-established as a government that would, potentially, acquire wide powers. All aspects of Catalan culture were then in expansion; for the first (and so far only) time a popular press in Catalan achieved a wide readership. Barcelona was a small but notable centre of the avant-garde. The ADLAN (*Amics de l'Art Nou*, Friends of New Art) group worked to promote art, and the GATCPAC architectural collective sought to bring rationalist architecture to Barcelona in association with the new authorities. Miró and Dalí had already made their mark in painting.

Prospects were still clouded by social conflicts. The CNT revived, and there were bitter strikes in some industries. By this time the anarchist

The militias leave for Aragón, 1936.

Confederation was only one of many leftist tendencies in the city – albeit the largest – for this was a time of enormous political effervescence. Social conflicts were slightly less intense in Catalonia than in the rest of Spain, in part because the *Esquerra* was able to follow its own reformist agenda. Its achievements in five years were more a matter of potential than realities, but tangible advances were made, particularly in primary education.

In Madrid, the Republic's first government was a coalition of republicans and socialists led by Manuel Azaña. Its goal was to modernise Spanish society through liberal democratic reforms, but as social tensions intensified the coalition collapsed, and a conservative republican party, with support from the traditional Spanish right, secured power after new elections in 1933. For Catalonia, the prospect of a return to right-wing rule prompted fears that it would immediately abrogate the Generalitat's hard-won powers. On 6 October 1934, while a general strike was launched against the central government in Asturias and some other parts of Spain, Lluis Companys, leader of the Generalitat since Macià's death the previous year, declared Catalonia independent. This, however, turned out to be something of a farce, for the Generalitat had no means of resisting the army, and the 'Catalan Republic' was rapidly suppressed.

The Generalitat was suspended, and over the next year fascism seemed to become a real threat, as the right called more and more frequently for authoritarian rule and political positions became polarised throughout Spain. Then, in February

Red city: anarchist Barcelona

One of Barcelona's many distinctions is that of being the only city in western Europe to have experienced a thoroughgoing social revolution within living memory. Another is that this revolution was to a great extent inspired by anarchists. Anarchism arrived in the city during the 1860s, and attained greater influence here than anywhere else in the world. Over the next 70 years the Catalan anarchist movement hit the depths and scaled the heights, from crude violence to the highest idealism, from euphoria to defeat.

The individual terrorist attacks of the 1890s were very untypical of Catalan anarchism. Rather, anarchists believed that an entirely self-managed society could be achieved through constant collective organisation, and a pugnacious intransigence before the ruling classes and the law. Anarchists set up co-operatives and workers' societies, schools and social centres, and were among the first to introduce progressive ideas on education and sexuality into Spain. During the 1930s, anarchist housing campaigns ensured that many of the poorest of the poor paid no rent, a feminist group, *Mujeres Libres* (Free Women), gained momentum, and a group called the 'Practical Idealists' planned a self-managed health service.

Anarchism gained its greatest strength in the 1910s and 1930s, after the creation of the union confederation the CNT. If the Passeig de Gràcia was the heart of the respectable city, the centre of anarchist Barcelona was the Paral.lel. On a corner of the small plaça by Paral.lel Metro station a Caixa bank office now occupies the site of the bar La Tranquilidad, which, as one veteran remembers 'had nothing tranquil about it', a regular meeting place of legendary militants such as Durruti and Ascaso, and frequently raided by the police. Opposite in C/Sant Pau, at number 116, an ornate iron awning still indicates the Pay-Pay, another favourite anarchist café, now sealed up and scheduled for demolition. Nearby in Avda Mistral, at number 17, was the base of the *Agrupación Faros*, largest of the anarchist clubs of the 1930s, which at one time had over 2,000 members.

In the first months of the Civil War, factories, public services, cinemas, the phone system and food distribution were all collectivised. Some collectives, such as those that took over public transport, worked very well; others met with more and more difficulties, especially as the war ground on, and morale was steadily worn down. Today, this world can seem to be just so many ghosts, less commemorated in modern Barcelona than events of the 1640s. Some groups keep the flame alive, though, such as the **Ateneu del Xino**, at C/Robadors 25, and the **Ateneu del Poble Sec**, at C/Elcano 48

1936, fresh elections were won by the Popular Front of the left. The Generalitat was reinstated, and in Catalonia the next few months were, surprisingly, relatively peaceful. In the rest of Spain, though, tensions were reaching bursting point, and right-wing politicians, refusing to accept the loss of power, talked openly of the need for the military to intervene. In July, the 1929 stadium on Montjuïc was to be the site of the Popular Olympics, a leftist alternative to the main Olympics of that year in Nazi Germany. On the day of their inauguration, however, 18 July, army generals launched a coup against the Republic and its left-wing governments, expecting no resistance.

WAR AND REVOLUTION

In Barcelona, militants of the unions and leftist parties, on alert for weeks, poured into the streets to oppose the troops in fierce fighting. In the course of 19 July the military were gradually worn down, and finally surrendered in the Hotel Colón on Plaça Catalunya. Opinions have always differed as to who could claim most credit for this remarkable popular victory: workers' militants have claimed it was the 'people in arms' who defeated the army, while others stress the importance of the police having remained loyal to the Generalitat. A likely answer is that they actually encouraged each other.

Tension released, the city was taken over by the revolution. People's militias of the CNT, different Marxist parties and other left-wing factions were marched off to Aragon, led by streetfighters such as the anarchists Durruti and García Oliver, to continue the battle. The army rising had failed in Spain's major cities but won a foothold in Castile, Aragon and the south, although in the heady atmosphere of Barcelona in July 1936 it was often assumed that their resistance could not last long, and that the people's victory was near-inevitable.

Far from the front, Barcelona was the chief centre of the revolution in Republican Spain, the only truly proletarian city. Its middle class avoided the streets, where, as Orwell recorded in his *Homage to Catalonia*, workers' clothing was all there was to be seen. Barcelona became a magnet for leftists from around the world, including writers such as Malraux, Hemingway and Octavio Paz. Industries and public services were collectivised. Ad-hoc 'control patrols' roamed the streets supposedly checking for suspected right-wing agents and sometimes carrying out summary executions, a practice that was condemned by many leftist leaders.

Tensions soon arose in the unstable alliance between the left-wing groups. The Communists, who had extra leverage because the Soviet Union was the only country prepared to give the Spanish Republic arms, demanded the integration of the loosely organised militias in a conventional army under a strong central authority. This was resisted by the anarchists and a radical-Marxist party, the

The Betlem church, bombed-out in 1938.

POUM, as a dilution of the revolution, and an attempt to sideline them. For weeks the Generalitat was inoperative before the workers' militias, but in September 1936 a new administration was formed with, remarkably, CNT ministers, who were also represented in the central republican government. The following months saw continual political infighting between the CNT, the POUM and the Communists, and co-operation broke down completely in May 1937, when republican and Communist troops seized the telephone building in Plaça Catalunya from a CNT committee, sparking off the confused war-within-the-civil-war witnessed by Orwell from the roof of the **Teatre Poliorama**. A temporary agreement was patched up, but shortly afterwards the POUM was banned, and the CNT excluded from power. A new republican central government was formed under Dr Juan Negrín, a Socialist allied to the Communists.

The war became more of a conventional conflict. This did little, however, to improve the Republic's position, for the Nationalists under General Francisco Franco and their German and Italian allies had been continually gaining ground. Madrid was under siege, and the capital of the Republic was moved to Valencia and then to Barcelona, in November 1937.

Catalonia received thousands of refugees, and food shortages and the lack of armaments ground down morale. Bombing raids were frequent, reaching a crescendo in the three days of terror caused by Italian bombers in March 1938. The Basque Country and Asturias had already fallen to Franco, and in the same month of March 1938 his troops reached the Mediterranean near Castellón, cutting the main Republican zone in two. The Republic had one last throw, in the Battle of the Ebro in summer 1938, when for months the Popular Army struggled to retake the river. After that, the Republic was exhausted. Barcelona fell to the Francoist army on 26 January 1939. Half a million refugees fled to France, to be interred in barbed-wire camps along the beaches.

Grey years

In Catalonia the Franco regime was iron-fisted and especially vengeful. Thousands of Catalan republicans and leftists were executed, Generalitat President Lluís Companys among them; exile and deportation were the fate of thousands more. Publishing, teaching and any other public cultural expression in Catalan, including even speaking it in the street, were rigorously prohibited, and every Catalanist monument in the city was dismantled. All independent political activity was suspended; censorship and the secret police were a constant presence, and the resulting atmosphere of fear and suspicion was to mark many who lived through it. The entire political and cultural development of the country during the previous century and a half was thus brought to an abrupt halt.

Barcelona was also impoverished, for the city would not regain its standard of living of 1936 until the mid-1950s. Food and electricity were rationed. Nevertheless, migrants in flight from the still-more brutal poverty of the south flowed into Barcelona, occupying precarious shanty towns that spread around Montjuïc and other areas on the city's edge. Reconstruction in post-war Barcelona of the nearly 2,000 buildings destroyed by bombing was slow, for the regime built little during its first few years other than monumental showpieces and the vulgarly ornate basilica on top of Tibidabo, completed to expiate Barcelona's 'sinful' role during the war. Later, cheap housing projects – standardised blocks – were undertaken to accommodate some of the city's mushrooming population.

Some underground political movements were able to operate. Anarchist urban guerrillas such as the Sabaté brothers attempted to carry on armed resistance, and March 1951 saw the last gasp of the pre-war labour movement in a general tram strike, the only major strike during the harshest years of the regime. It was harshly repressed, but also achieved some of its goals. Clandestine Catalanist groups began to make themselves known in small acts of resistance and rebellion, through underground publications or the performance in secret of

a new Catalan play. Some Catalan culture was tolerated: the poet Salvador Espriu promoted a certain resurgence of Catalan literature, and the young Antoni Tàpies held his first solo exhibition in 1949. For a great many people, though, the only remaining public focus of national sentiment was Barcelona football club, which acquired an extraordinary importance at this time, above all in its biannual meetings with the 'team of the regime', Real Madrid.

Years of international isolation and attempted self-sufficiency by the regime, which as a fascist survivor had been subject to a UN embargo, came to an end in 1953, when the United States and the Vatican saw to it that this anti-communist state was at least partially readmitted to the western fold. Even a limited opening to the outside world meant that foreign money began to enter the country, and the regime relaxed some control over its population. In 1959 the *Plan de Estabilización* (Stabilisation Plan), drawn up by Catholic technocrats of the Opus Dei, brought Spain definitively within the western economy, throwing its doors wide open to tourism and foreign investment.

Two years earlier in 1957 José María de Porcioles was appointed Mayor of Barcelona, a post he would retain until 1973. Porcioles has since been regarded as the personification of the damage inflicted on the city by the Franco regime during its 1960s boom, accused of covering it with drab high-rises and road schemes without any concern for its character. Barcelona grew chaotically, stretching in every direction and surrounded by polluting factories. Many valuable historic buildings – such as the grand cafés of the Plaça Catalunya – were torn down to make way for bland modern business blocks, and minimal attention was paid to collective amenities. Porcioles' most positive contribution was the creation of the Picasso Museum in 1970, following a donation from Picasso's Catalan friend and secretary Jaume Sabartès.

After the years of repression and the years of development, 1966 marked the beginning of what became known as *tardofranquisme*, 'late Francoism'. Having made its opening to the outside world, the regime was losing its grip, and labour, youth and student movements began to claim freedoms denied over the previous 25 years. Nevertheless, the Franco regime never hesitated to show its strength. Strikes and demonstrations were dealt with savagely, and just months before the dictator's death the last person to be executed in Spain by the traditional method of the garrotte, a Catalan anarchist named Puig Antich, went to his death in Barcelona.

In 1973, however, Franco's closest follower, Admiral Carrero Blanco, had been blown into the sky by a bomb planted by the Basque terrorist group ETA, leaving no one to guard over the core values of the regime. Change was in the air. The Catalans were getting feisty; agitation grew; they did not have long to wait.

When Franco died on 20 November 1975, the people of Barcelona took to the streets in celebration, and not a bottle of cava was left in the city by evening. However, no one knew quite what was about to happen. The Bourbon monarchy was restored, under King Juan Carlos, but his attitudes and intentions were not clear. In 1976 he made a little-known Francoist bureaucrat, Adolfo Suárez, prime minister, charged with leading the country to democracy.

The first months and years of Spain's 'transition' were still a difficult period. Nationalist and other demonstrations continued to be repressed by the police with considerable brutality, and far-right groups threatened less open violence. However, political parties were legalised, and June 1977 saw the first democratic elections to be held since 1936. They were won across Spain by Suárez' own new party, the UCD, and in Catalonia by a mixture of Socialists, Communists and nationalist groups.

It was, again, not clear how Suárez expected to deal with the demands of Catalonia, but shortly after the elections he surprised everyone by going to visit the President of the Generalitat in exile, a veteran pre-Civil War politician, Josep Tarradellas. His office was the only institution of the old Republic to be so recognised, perhaps because Suárez astutely identified in the old man a fellow conservative. Tarradellas was invited to return as provisional President of a restored Generalitat, and in October 1977 announced his arrival with the simple phrase '*Ja soc aquí*' ('Here I am!') from the balcony in the Plaça Sant Jaume.

The following year the first free local elections took place, won by the Socialist Party, with Narcis Serra as Mayor. They have retained control of the Barcelona Ajuntament ever since, presided over for most of this time by Pasqual Maragall, who replaced Serra when the latter left to join the Madrid government in 1982. Led by highly educated technocrats, they began, gradually at first, to 'recover' the city from its neglected state, enlisting the elite of the Catalan intellectual and artistic community in their support. No one epitomises this more than Oriol Bohigas, the architect and writer who was long the city's head of culture and chief planner. A rolling programme of urban renewal was initiated, from the public sculpture programme (*see chapter* **Art Galleries**) to the '*Barcelona, posa't guapa*' campaign, through which hundreds of historic façades were given an overdue facelift.

The year 1980 saw yet another set of elections, to the restored Generalitat, won by Jordi Pujol and his party Convergència i Unió. Again, they have kept power ever since. Imprisoned for Catalanist activities in 1960, Pujol represents a strain of conservative nationalism that goes back to Prat de la Riba. His very successful platform includes not only autonomy and the promotion of Catalan culture, language and identity, but also the consolidation of Catalonia as an economic hub within the European Union.

Style city

At the end of the 1970s, the inherent dowdiness of the Franco years was swept away by a new Catalan style for the new Catalonia: postmodern, high-tech, punkish, comic strip, minimalist and tautly fashionable. Innovative designers in all media added a new layer of sleek, chromed shine to a city whose Gothic and *Modernista* heritage had faded from years of neglect.

The design mania that struck the city in the 1980s can be attributed to newly released energy, a recuperation of Barcelona's artistic, artisan and architectural traditions, or another outbreak of that historic urge to remake the city in its own Catalan image, as in the preparations for the Exhibition of 1888. It can be experienced in every aspect of the city: from shopping arcades to shopping bags, discos to door handles, art galleries to ashtrays, no object escaped the Catalan designer's eye.

This emphasis on slick, fresh style began on a street and underground level, but the particularity of Barcelona was the extent to which it was taken up by public authorities, and above all the Ajuntament. Beginning with

Facing each other across Plaça Sant Jaume, Generalitat and Ajuntament are the two constants of modern Catalan politics. Relations between them have sometimes been uneasy, thanks to differences between the Pujolite national reconstruction project and the self-consciously modernising plans of the Socialists, and to straight personality clashes between Pujol and Maragall. Nevertheless, they needed to work together when Barcelona presented its candidacy for the 1992 Olympic Games, which it was duly awarded in 1986.

BARCELON-AAH

Far more than just a sports event, the Games were to be Barcelona's third great effort to cast aside any suggestion of second-city status and show the world its wares. The exhibitions of 1888 and 1929 had seen developments in the Ciutadella and on Montjuïc; now, the Olympics provided an opening to work on a city-wide scale. Taking advantage of the public and private investment they would attract, Barcelona planned an all-new orientation of itself toward the sea, in a programme of urban renovation of a scope unseen in Europe since the years after World War II.

The Olympic project formed the cornerstone of the Ajuntament's plans for the new city, but they went much further. The Games gave a pretext for the provision of an official umbrella and direction the open spaces programme of the first democratic city council, but with far greater focus once the Olympic bid was under way, sophisticated modernity became an essential part of the city's official image. Along with the creation of the new Barcelona in bricks and mortar went the city-sponsored promotion of Barcelona-as-concept, a seductive cocktail of architecture, imagination, tradition, style, nightlife and primary colours. This was perhaps the most spectacular – and certainly the most deliberate – of Barcelona's many reinventions of itself.

And it worked, for Barcelona was placed firmly on the map, even for people who just a few years earlier had thought of it as one more Spanish town with bullfights and flamenco. It did so in good part because behind all the PR there was a solid vision of the city, and the Catalan and international architectural and design community saw in Mayor Maragall and his colleagues not just more politicians but kindred spirits with shared aims. The city's leaders were not afraid to cast their net wide in incorporating every kind of trend and current into their great projects, and so a hand-to-mouth underground cartoonist like Javier Mariscal in a couple of years could find himself being given huge budgets to play with on style-palaces like the Torres de Avila bar (*right*), or the design of

Cobi, the first-ever hip Olympic mascot. The 'reinvention' also succeeded because the image of creativity and vivacity it generated corresponded to an idea many of Barcelona's citizens had always had of their city, as if the preceding drab decades had just been a bad dream.

Post-1992, it's been possible to look on all this with a bit more reserve. The cosy relationship between the artistic vanguard and public institutions has not always been seen to be good for creativity. Barcelona design has lost a lot of its impetus during the 1990s, and a good deal of it can now appear clichéd and facile. From the Ajuntament's point of view, though, it could be said to have served its purpose.

for a whole range of schemes and trends visible in the preceding years, in institutions and the street, bringing them together in a repackaging of the city for its own citizens and on an international stage.

Inseparable from all this was the figure of Mayor Maragall, a tireless 'Mr Barcelona' who appeared in every possible forum to expound his vision of the role of cities and intervened personally to set the guidelines for projects or secure the participation of major international architects. In the process Barcelona, like all Spanish cities a byword for modern blight only a few years before, became an international reference point in urban affairs. Many of the city's people responded to this vision, and Maragall established a personal popularity that went well beyond that of his Catalan Socialist Party.

From Tibidabo to the seafront, Barcelona spent six years *en obres* (under construction). Long-planned pieces of infrastructure such as ring roads were put in place along with strictly Games-related projects.

When the Games were finally held in July-August 1992, no one could quite say if they were worth it, but all agreed they were a great success. Once the parade had gone by, the city held its breath to see what happened next, and 1993 was a difficult year. The citizens had been assured many times that the Games would cost them next to nothing, but the next year they were presented with the highest local tax

increases in Barcelona's history. Bringing this off with charisma scarcely blemished was perhaps a greater demonstration of Pasqual Maragall's political skills than anything he'd done before.

From 1994 onwards, moreover, confidence picked up again, the city's relentless self-promotion seemed actually to be working in attracting investment, and Barcelona and Catalonia rode out Spain's post-1992 recession better than any other part of the country. Far from calling a halt to infrastructure development, the Ajuntament announced still more large-scale projects, concentrating this time on areas little touched in the run-up to 1992 such as the Old Port and the Raval. Maragall's own popularity was such that he was able to stand aside from the corruption scandals that dragged down his Socialist allies in the central government of Felipe González after 13 years in office, and enabled the right-wing *Partido Popular* to take power in Madrid after the elections of 1996.

Then, in 1997, having successfully won a fifth term, Maragall stood down by his own decision, apparently to prepare a challenge to his old rival Jordi Pujol as President of the Generalitat. He was succeeded by his rather anonymous deputy Joan Clos, who announced a modest agenda of administrative reforms, transport improvements and so on. Barcelona, though, is used to more bravura than discreet efficiency from its mayors.

Architecture

Barcelona's unique building styles are essential to the city's identity: classic Catalan combinations of solidity, ingenuity and wild imagination.

Architecture has always been particularly important among all the arts in Catalonia. It has emerged as the most appropriate medium – ahead of painting, music or any other art form – through which to express national identity. Periods when architecture flourished have paralleled eras of increased Catalan freedom of action, greater wealth and a reinforcement of collective civic pride.

A clear line of continuity, of recurring characteristics, can be traced between generations of Catalan architects. Ideas and attitudes are taken in from abroad, but are assimilated into this strong local culture. Catalan builders have always shown a desire to decorate surfaces, and a preoccupation with texture and the use of fine materials and finishes. This is combined with a simplicity of line and sense of sobriety often seen as distinguishing Catalan character from that of the rest of Spain. Other common elements are references to the traditional architecture of rural Catalonia – the large farmhouses or *masies*, with chalet-type tile roofs, massive stone walls and round-arched doorways, a style maintained by anonymous builders for centuries – and to the strong constructions of Catalan Romanesque and Gothic. There has also long been a close relationship between architects and craftsmen in the production of buildings, especially in the working of metal and wood.

Modern Catalans have a sense of contributing to their architectural heritage in the present day, rather than preserving it as a relic. Contemporary buildings are daringly constructed alongside (or even within) old ones, and this mix of old and new is a major characteristic of many spectacular projects seen in Barcelona over the last two decades.

The importance of architecture is also reflected in public attitudes. Barcelona's citizens cherish their buildings, and form a critical audience. One result of this is that a wide range of local architecture guides are available, some in English editions (*see p269* **Further Reading**). Informative free leaflets on different styles are provided (in English) at Generalitat tourist offices, such as *Discovering Romanesque Art in Catalonia*, *Routes of Gothic Art in Catalonia* and so on. They cover the whole country, but have sections on Barcelona. For details of buildings mentioned in this chapter, *see chapter* **Sightseeing**.

The old city

The old city of Barcelona, confined within its successive rings of walls, had become by 1850 – and remains today – one of the densest urban areas in Europe. Open space is at a premium here. Small squares and paved areas feel almost sculpted out of a solid mass of buildings. The Mediterranean sun, which rarely reaches some streets, fills these often modest spaces with light, giving an unequalled sense of drama. The spaces within buildings also sometimes seem hollowed out from the mass of the city fabric. The breathtaking beauty of **Santa Maria del Mar**, or the scale of the **Saló del Tinell**, contrast greatly with the tightly packed streets around them. This gives a feeling of luxury to even the simplest square or church, adding to their enchantment.

Roman to Romanesque

The Roman citadel of *Barcino* was founded on the hill of *Mons Taber*, just behind the Cathedral, which to this day remains the religious and civic heart of the city. It left an important legacy in the shape of the fourth-century first city wall, fragments of which are visible at many points around the old city (*see chapter* **Roman Barcino**).

Barcelona's next occupiers, the Visigoths, left little visible in the city, although a trio of fine Visigothic churches survives nearby in **Terrassa**. When the Catalan state began to form under the Counts of Barcelona from the ninth century onwards, the dominant architecture of this new community was massive, simple Romanesque. In the Pyrenean valleys there are hundreds of fine Romanesque buildings, notably at **Sant Pere de Rodes**, **Ripoll**, **Sant Joan de les Abadesses** and **Besalú** (*see chapter* **Trips Out of Town**). There is, though, relatively little in Barcelona. On the right-hand side of the Cathedral, looking at the main façade, is the simple thirteenth-century chapel of **Santa Llúcia**, incorporated into the later building, and in La Ribera there is the tiny travellers' chapel the **Capella d'en Marcús**. The greatest Romanesque monument in the city, though, is the beautifully plain church and cloister of **Sant Pau del Camp**, built in the twelfth century as part of a larger monastery.

Catalan Gothic

By the thirteenth century, Barcelona was the capital of a trading empire and its wealth and population were growing rapidly. The settlements called *ravals* or *vilanoves* that had sprung up outside the Roman walls were brought within the city by the building of Jaume I's second set of walls, which extended Barcelona west to the Rambla, then just an often-dry riverbed.

This growth and political eminence formed the background to the great flowering of Catalan Gothic, and the construction of many of Barcelona's most important civic and religious buildings, replacing Romanesque equivalents. The **Cathedral** was begun in 1298, in substitution of an eleventh-century building. Work commenced on the **Ajuntament** (*Casa de la Ciutat*) and **Palau de la Generalitat** (later subject to extensive alteration) in 1372 and 1403, respectively. Major additions were made to the **Palau Reial** of the Catalan-Aragonese kings, especially the **Saló del Tinell** of 1359-62, and the great hall of the **Llotja** or trading exchange was finished in 1380-92. Many of Barcelona's finest buildings were built or completed in the midst of the crisis that followed the catastrophe of the Black Death.

Catalan Gothic has very particular characteristics that distinguish it clearly from more northern, classic Gothic. It is simpler, and gives more prominence to solid, plain walls between towers and columns rather than the empty spaces between intricate flying buttresses of the great French cathedrals. Buildings thus appear much more massive. In façades, as much emphasis is given to horizontals as to verticals, and the latter and their octagonal towers end in flat roofs, not spires. Decorative intricacies are mainly confined to windows, portals, arches and gargoyles. Many churches have no aisles but only a single nave, the classic example being the beautiful **Santa Maria del Pi** in Plaça del Pi, from 1322-1453.

This style has provided the historic benchmark for Catalan architecture. It is simple and robust, yet elegant and practical. Innovative, sophisticated techniques were developed: transverse arches supporting timber roofs allowed the spanning of great halls uninterrupted by columns, a system used in the **Saló del Tinell**. Designed by Pere III's court architect Guillem Carbonell, it has some of the largest pure masonry arches in Europe, the elegance and sheer scale of which gives the space tremendous splendour. The **Drassanes**, built from 1378 like the royal shipyards (and now the **Museu Marítim**), is really just a very beautiful shed, but the enormous parallel aisles make it one of the most exciting spaces in the city.

La Ribera, also known as the *Vilanova del Mar*, had become the commercial centre of the city, and for its parish church would have the great masterpiece of Catalan Gothic, **Santa Maria del Mar**, built between 1329 and 1384. Its superb proportions are based on a series of squares imposed on one another, with three aisles of, unusually, almost equal height, and the interior is staggering for its austerity and spareness of structure.

The superb combination of delicacy and strength of **Santa Maria del Mar**.

Details are the essence of Modernisme.

Leading away from the church on one side is the **Carrer Montcada**, where the city's merchants built palaces to show their confidence and wealth. They all conform to a similar design of Mediterranean urban palace, presenting a blank exterior to the street, with heavy doors opening into a large, imposing patio. A grand external staircase on one side of the patio leads up to the main rooms on the first floor, which often have elegant open loggias. Several of these palaces now house some of Barcelona's most visited cultural institutions.

Forgotten centuries

By the beginning of the sixteenth century, political and economic decline meant there were far fewer patrons for new building in the city. In the next 300 years a good deal was still built in Barcelona, but rarely in any distinctively Catalan style, so that it has often been disregarded.

In the 1550s the **Palau del Lloctinent** was built for the royal viceroys on one side of Plaça del Rei, and in 1596 the present main façade was added to the **Generalitat**, in an Italian Renaissance style. The Church built lavishly, with baroque convents and churches along La Rambla, of which the **Betlem** from 1680-1729, at the corner of C/Carme, is the most important survivor. Later baroque churches include **Sant Felip Neri** (1721-52) and **La Mercè** (1765-75).

Another addition, after the siege of Barcelona in 1714, was new military architecture, since the city was encased in ramparts and fortresses. Examples remain in the **Castell de Montjuïc**, the buildings in the **Ciutadella** – one, curiously, the Catalan parliament – and the **Barceloneta**.

A more positive eighteenth-century alteration was the conversion of the Rambla into an urbanised promenade, begun in 1775 with the demolition of Jaume I's second wall. Neo-classical palaces were built alongside: thus, **La Virreina** and the **Palau Moja** (at the corner of Portaferrisa) both date from the 1770s. Also from that time but in a less classical style is the **Gremial dels Velers** (Candlemakers' Guild) at Via Laietana 50, with its two-coloured stucco decoration.

It was not, however, until the closure of the monasteries in the 1820s and 1830s that major rebuilding on the Rambla could begin. Most of the first constructions that replaced them were still in international, neo-classical styles. The site that is now the **Mercat de la Boqueria** was actually first remodelled in 1836-40 as Plaça Sant Josep to a design by Francesc Daniel Molina based on the English Regency style of John Nash, now buried beneath the 1870s market building, although its Doric colonnade can still be detected.

Molina was also responsible for the **Plaça Reial**, begun in 1848. Other fine examples from the same era are the collonaded **Porxos d'en Xifré**, the 1836 blocks opposite the Llotja.

The Eixample & the new city

In the 1850s, Barcelona was able to expand physically – with the long-awaited demolition of the walls – and psychologically, with economic expansion and the cultural reawakening of the Catalan *Renaixença*. The stage was set for it to spread into the great grid of Ildefons Cerdà's **Eixample** (*see p21* **History**).

While Cerdà's more visionary ideas were largely lost, the construction of the Eixample did see the refinement of a specific type of building: the apartment block, with large flats on the *principal* floor (first above the ground), often with large glassed-in galleries for the drawing room, and smaller flats above them. The growth of the area also provided perfect conditions for the pre-eminence of the most famous of Catalan architectural styles, *Modernisme*.

Modernisme

In the second half of the nineteenth century, there was uncertainty in the arts and architecture across Europe. The huge expansion of cities, dramatic social upheavals and new political pressures all created special tensions, while the introduction of new materials such as iron and steel demanded a new architectural language. As the end of the century approached, the movement known in French and English as art nouveau emerged, encompassing some of these concerns and contradictions.

International interest in Gaudí has often eclipsed the fact that the branch of art nouveau seen in Catalonia, *Modernisme* (always confusing, since 'modernism' in English usually refers to twentieth-century functional styles), was quite distinctive in its ideas and its products, and also that the style was perhaps more widely accepted in Barcelona than in any other city in Europe.

It developed out of the general renaissance of Catalan culture. Influenced, like other forms of art nouveau, by Ruskin, William Morris and the Arts and Crafts movement, French Symbolism and other international currents, *Modernisme* was also an indigenous expression that made use of its own Catalan traditions of design and craftwork. *Modernista* architects, as the name indicates, sought to function entirely within the modern world – hence their experimental use of iron and glass – but also to revive and express distinctly Catalan traditions – and so showed enormous interest in the Gothic of the Catalan Golden Age.

Modernisme was also a very wide-ranging and flexible movement. It admitted the coexistence of Gothic revivalism, floralising and decoration to the point of delirium, rationalist machine worship and the most advanced, revolutionary expressionism. *Modernistes* also sought to integrate fine and decorative arts, and so gave as much weight to furniture or glasswork as to painting or architecture.

Modernista architecture was given a decisive boost by the buildings for the Universal Exhibition of 1888, most of which were by Lluís Domènech i Montaner (1850-1923). Most no longer exist, notably the 'International Hotel' on the Moll de la Fusta that was built in under 100 days, but one that remains is the 'Castle of the Three Dragons' in the Ciutadella, built as the exhibition restaurant and now the **Museu de Zoologia**. It already showed many key features of Modernist style: the use of structural ironwork allowed greater freedom in the creation of openings, arches and windows, and plain brick, instead of the stucco previously applied to most buildings in Barcelona, was used in an exuberantly decorative manner. As further decoration there is an eclectic mix of neo-Moorish and medieval motifs in terracotta and glazed tiles.

Domènech was one of the main Modernist architects to develop the idea of the 'total work', working closely with craftsmen and designers on every aspect of a building – ornament, lighting, window glass. His greatest creations are the **Hospital de Sant Pau**, built as small 'pavilions' within a garden to avoid the depressing effect of a monolithic hospital, and the **Palau de la Música Catalana**, an extraordinary display of outrageous decoration.

After Domènech – and Gaudí – the third of the trio of leading Modernist architects was Josep Puig i Cadafalch (1867-1957), who showed a strong neo-

Gothic influence in such buildings as his *Casa de les Punxes* ('House of Spikes', officially the **Casa Terrades**) in the Diagonal, combined with many traditional Catalan touches. These are the famous names of *Modernista* architecture, but there were many others, for the style caught on with extraordinary vigour throughout Catalonia. Some of the most engaging are the least known internationally, such as Gaudí's assistant Josep Maria Jujol, who in his own name built some remarkable, sinuous buildings in Sant Joan Despí, west of Barcelona.

Catalan Modernist creativity was at its peak for about 20 years, from 1888 to 1908, during which time an extraordinary amount of work was produced, large and small. The Eixample is the style's foremost display case, with the greatest concentration of art nouveau in Europe (the Ajuntament's *Quadrat d'Or* book is a good architectural guide), but *Modernista* buildings and details can be found in innumerable other locations around Barcelona and Catalonia: in the streets behind the Paral.lel in Poble Sec or the villas on Tibidabo, in shop interiors or dark hallways, in country town halls or the cava cellars of the Penedès.

The twentieth century

By the 1900s *Modernisme* had become too extreme for the Barcelona middle class, and the later buildings of Gaudí, for example, were met with derision. The new 'proper' style for Catalan architecture was declared to be *Noucentisme*, which stressed the importance of classical proportions. However, it failed to produce anything of much note: the main buildings that survive are those of the 1929 Exhibition, which also brought with it some indeterminate monumental architecture, topped by the bizarre neo-baroque **Palau Nacional**.

The 1929 Exhibition also brought to Barcelona, though, one of the most important buildings of the century: Mies van der Rohe's German Pavilion, the **Pavelló Barcelona**. Even today it is modern in its challenge to conventional ideas of space, and its impact at the time was extraordinary. The famous Barcelona chair was designed for this building, which was rebuilt to its original design in 1986.

The major figure in Catalan architecture during the 1930s was Josep Lluís Sert, who with the GATC-PAC architecture collective struggled to introduce the ideas of his friend Le Corbusier and the 'International Style'. Under the Republic, he built a sanatorium off C/Tallers, and the **Casa Bloc**, a workers' housing project at Passeig Torres i Bages 91-105 in Sant Andreu. In 1937 Sert also built the Spanish Republic's pavilion for the Paris Exhibition, since rebuilt in Barcelona as the **Pavelló de la República** in Vall d'Hebron. His most important work, however, came much later, in the magnificent **Fundació Joan Miro**, built in the 1970s after he had spent years in exile in the US.

A hermit in the city: Antoni Gaudí

Seen as the genius of the *Modernista* movement, Antoni Gaudí was really a one-off, an unclassifiable figure. His work was a product of the social and cultural context of the time, but also of his own unique perception of the world, as well as a typically Catalan indulgence of anything specifically Catalan. Whereas his two great colleagues in Modernism, Domènech and Puig, were both public figures who took an active part in politics and many other fields, Gaudí, after being fairly sociable as a youth, became increasingly eccentric, leading a semi-monastic existence and enclosed in his own obsessions.

Born in Reus in 1852, he qualified as an architect in 1878. His first architectural work was as assistant to Josep Fontseré on the building of the **Parc de la Ciutadella** during the 1870s. The gates and fountain of the park are attributed to him, and around the same time he also designed the lampposts in the **Plaça Reial**. His first major commission was for the **Casa Vicens** in 1883-8. An orientalist fantasy, it is structurally fairly conventional, but his control of the use of surface material already stands out in its exuberant neo-Moorish decoration and the

superbly elaborate decorative ironwork on the gates. The **Col.legi de les Teresianes** convent school, undertaken a few years later (1888-9), is more restrained still, but the clarity and fluidity of the building, with its simple finishes and use of light, is very appealing.

An event of crucial importance in Gaudí's life came in 1878, when he met Eusebi Güell, heir to one of the largest industrial fortunes in Catalonia. Güell had been impressed by some of Gaudí's early furniture, and they also discovered they shared many religious ideas, on the socially redemptive role of architecture and (for Güell) philanthropy. Güell placed such utter confidence in his architect that he was able to work with complete liberty. He produced several buildings for his patron, beginning with the **Palau Güell** (1886-8), a darkly impressive, still-historicist building that established Gaudí's reputation, and including the crypt at **Colònia Güell**, one of his most original, structurally experimental and surprising buildings.

In 1883 Gaudí first became involved in the design of the temple of the **Sagrada Família**, begun the previous year. He would eventually devote himself entirely to this work. Gaudí was profoundly religious, and an extreme Catholic conservative; part of his obsession with the building was a belief that its completion would help redeem Barcelona from the sins of secularism and the modern era. From 1908 until his death he worked on no other projects, often sleeping on site, a shabby, white-haired hermit, producing visionary ideas that his assistants had to 'interpret' into drawings (on show in the museum alongside). If most of his modern admirers were to meet him they would probably say he was mad, but this strange figure would have an immense effect on Barcelona.

The Sagrada Família became the testing ground for his ideas on structure and form. However, he would see built only the crypt, apse and nativity façade, with its representation of 30 different species of plants. As Gaudí's work matured, he abandoned historicism and developed free-flowing, sinuous expressionist forms. His boyhood interest in nature began taking over from more architectural references, and what had previously provided external decorative motifs became the inspiration for the actual structure of his buildings.

In his greatest years, he combined other commissions with his cathedral. **La Pedrera** or **Casa Milà** (*pictured right*), begun in 1905, was his most complete project. Occupying a prominent position on a corner of Passeig de Gràcia, it has an aquatic feel about it: the balconies resemble seaweed, and the undulating façade the sea, or rocks washed by it. Interior patios are painted in blues and greens, and the roofscape is like an imaginary landscape inhabited by mysterious figures. The **Casa Batlló** (*left*), across Passeig de Gràcia, was an existing building remodelled by Gaudí in 1905-7, with a roof resembling a reptilian creature perched high above the street. An essential contribution was made by Gaudí's assistant Josep Maria Jujol, himself a very original *Modernista* architect, and more skilled than his master as a mosaicist.

Gaudí's later work has a dreamlike quality, which makes it unique and personal. His fascination with natural forms found full expression in the **Parc Güell**, of 1900-14. Here he

blurs the distinction between natural and built form in a series of colonnades winding up the hill. These seemingly informal paths lead to the surprisingly large central terrace projecting over the hall below, a forest of distorted Doric columns planned as the marketplace for Güell's proposed 'garden city'. The benches of the terrace are covered in some of the finest examples of *trencadís* or broken mosaic work, again mostly by Jujol.

In June 1926, Antoni Gaudí was run over by a tram on the Gran Via. Nobody recognised the down-at-heel old man, and he was taken to a public ward in the old Hospital de Santa Creu in the Raval. When it was discovered who he was, however, Barcelona gave its most famous architect an almost state funeral.

Gaudí in Barcelona

Gaudí left ten buildings in Barcelona. There are also buildings by him nearby at the **Colònia Güell** and **Garraf** (*see chapter* **Trips Out of Town**).
Casa Batlló *Passeig de Gràcia 43. Metro Passeig de Gràcia/bus 7, 16, 17, 22, 24, 28. See chapter* **Sightseeing**.
Casa Calvet *C/Casp 48. Metro Urquinaona/bus all routes to Plaça Urquinaona.* An apartment block from

1898-1900, quite conventional from the outside, but with a more radical interior and many fine details typical of Gaudí.
Casa Vicens *C/Carolines 22. Metro Fontana/bus 22, 24, 25, 28, 31, 32.* Not open to the public, but the exterior is very visible from the street.
Col.legi de les Teresianes *C/Ganduxer 95-105 (93 212 33 54). FGC Bonanova/bus 14, 16, 70, 74.* **Open** *Sept-June* 11am-1pm Sat. **Admission** free.
Palau Güell *C/Nou de la Rambla 3-5. Metro Liceu/bus 14, 18, 38, 59, 64, 91. See chapter* **Sightseeing**.
Parc Güell *C/d'Olot. Bus 24, 25. See chapter* **Sightseeing**.
Pavellons de la Finca Güell *Avda Pedralbes 7. Metro Palau Reial/bus 7, 74, 75, 114.* The spectacular, monstrous dragon gates in wrought iron from 1884-7 and the gatehouses on either side were the only parts of the Güell estate built by Gaudí.
La Pedrera *Passeig de Gràcia 92 (93 487 36 13). Metro Diagonal/bus 7, 22, 24, 28. See chapter* **Sightseeing**.
Temple Expiatori de la Sagrada Família *C/Mallorca 401 (93 455 02 47). Metro Sagrada Família/bus 19, 33, 34, 43, 50, 51, 54. See chapter* **Sightseeing**.
Torre Bellesguard *C/Bellesguard 16-20. Bus 22, 64, 75.* A more than usually Gothic-looking fantasy house built in 1900-2, not open to visitors but visible from the street. To find it, follow C/Sant Joan de la Salle straight up from the Plaça Bonanova.

Mediterranean sci-fi: the Montjuïc Olympic Ring and Calatrava's Communications Tower.

Barcelona's third style

The Franco years had an enormous impact on the city: as the economy expanded at breakneck pace in the 1960s, Barcelona received a massive influx of migrants, in a context of unchecked property speculation and minimal planning controls. The city was thus surrounded by endless high-rise suburbs. Another legacy of the era are some ostentatiously tall office blocks, especially on the Diagonal and around Plaça Francesc Macià.

Hence, when the new democratic city administration took over Barcelona at the end of the 1970s, there was a great deal that they could do. Budgets were limited, so it was decided that resources should initially be concentrated not on buildings as such, but the gaps in between, the public spaces, with a string of completely fresh, contemporary parks and squares. From this beginning, Barcelona placed itself in the forefront of international urban design (*see also p96* **Art Galleries**).

Barcelona's renewal programme accelerated and took on a much more ambitious shape with the award of the 1992 Olympics, helped by a booming economy in the late 1980s. The Games were intended to be stylish and innovative – a decision made clear by the choice of Javier Mariscal's Cobi as official mascot – and to provide a focus for a sweeping renovation of the city, centred on emblematic new buildings and infrastructure projects linked by clear strategic planning.

The three main Olympic sites – Vila Olímpica, Montjuïc and Vall d'Hebron – have quite different characteristics. The **Vila Olímpica** had the most comprehensive masterplan: it sought to extend Cerdà's grid down to the seafront, maintaining the continuity of the urban fabric. The main project on **Montjuïc** was the transformation of the existing 1929 stadium, but alongside it the city also acquired Arata Isozaki's **Palau Sant Jordi**, with its unusual space-frame roof. The **Vall d'Hebron** area is the least successful of the three sites, but the **Velòdrom** by Esteve Bonnell is one of the finest (and earliest) of the sports buildings, built before the Olympic bid in 1984.

A remarkable range of projects was completed in only a few years, and the city's modern architecture collection has continued to grow since 1992. Many striking buildings are by local architects such as Helio Piñón and Albert Viaplana, whose work combines fluid, elegant lines with a strikingly modern use of materials, from the controversial 1983 **Plaça dels Països Catalans** through daring conversions of historic buildings such as the Casa de la Caritat, now the **Centre de Cultura Contemporània**, and on to all-new major projects like the **Maremàgnum** mall in the old port. Others are by international names: Richard Meier's bold white **MACBA**, or Norman Foster's **Torre de Collserola** on Tibidabo, which, with the skyscrapers in the Vila Olímpica, has provided new emblems for Barcelona's skyline. The latest major project completed is Ricard Bofill's **Teatre Nacional**, with alongside it, still in the pipeline, the **Auditori** by Rafael Moneo. Barcelona's emphatically dynamic modern architecture has come to represent almost a 'third style' incorporated into the city's identity, alongside Gothic and *Modernisme* – but one that's far more diffuse and eclectic than either.

Barcelona Today

A change of look, a change of language: Barcelona is on a train of change that shows no sign of stopping.

When it joined the European Union in 1986 Spain received a tremendous input of funds, and began the process of transforming itself into a player equal to its European partners. Barcelona, though, was still a middling industrial city with ageing smokestack factories, a declining economy and no clear direction. It was beside the Mediterranean, true, but direct access to the sea was blocked by a long string of railroad tracks and warehouses. Barcelona, essentially, had the same economic woes as nineteenth-century, dirty-industrial cities in the UK and many other parts of the world.

Somewhere like Sheffield, for example, setting for the film *The Full Monty*, about a group of laid-off steelworkers who become male strippers in order to get some cash. The film impressed Barcelona's current mayor, Joan Clos, a doctor who spent years managing the city's public health service. 'I thoroughly enjoyed *The Full Monty*', Clos said in early 1998, 'it was an excellent portrait of a post-industrial city. Barcelona has been fortunate not to have had to show its *cul*, its arse, in order to transform itself into a post-industrial city.'

Mayor Clos' statement is a classic piece of official *Barcelon-ese*. On the one hand, it's smug as hell, and neatly sidesteps the fact that, as you can see in any copy of the *Guia del Ocio* listings magazine, there are plenty of male strip shows around Barcelona. At the same time, it has a core of truth that's impossible to deny. Barcelona does seem to have mapped out a future for itself that a hundred other industrial-revolution cities would die for.

MUNICIPAL VISIONS

Barcelona's 20-year transformation from an old textile, docks and engineering town into a design, fashion, style, services and leisure centre for the western Mediterranean – the kind of terms with which the city now describes itself – can be put down to many factors. Some arose by natural process: the explosion of fresh energies after decades of a sterile dictatorship, the city's enthusiastic rediscovery of its true nature and its cultural, architectural and craft traditions, or the Catalans' secret weapon, a phenomenal civic pride. Impossible to disregard is Barcelona's permanent paradox, that it has the awareness and ambitions of a capital city of a state without actually being one, and to compensate regularly feels a need to make a noise to demonstrate its importance to the world. Of vital importance, though, was very determined planning and intent on the part of the local authorities, especially the city council, the Ajuntament, under Pasqual Maragall, mayor from 1982 to 1997.

The 1992 Olympics conveniently provided Barcelona's Ajuntament with the perfect rationale for reinventing the city. It was Mayor Maragall's unreservedly ambitious vision of using the Games to highlight what Barcelona had to offer, of turning it into a world-class city, that, thus far, has managed to steer it past the fate of cities like Sheffield during the 1980s. A charismatic figure, Maragall also fitted in perfectly with a Catalan ideal of a man who gets things done. Since 1992, leaving the starting point of the Olympics projects well behind, Barcelona's concerted renovation of itself and its image has continued without a pause, and it now must be one of the most vigorously self-promoted cities in the world.

Consequently, Maragall's resignation smack in the middle of his fourth term in September 1997 came as a surprise to one and all. Assurances were given that his little-known deputy Clos would be able to take over without a hitch, and he is certain to be Socialist candidate for the mayoralty when elections are next due in 1999. The city's collective heart, though, skipped a beat as people wondered if a different hand at the helm might change their course for the worse.

Apparently not. Whatever Maragall's reasons for stepping down, it was not because the city was doing badly. In the wake of the Olympics plenty of sceptics had pointed to the deficit of 271.4 billion pesetas with which Barcelona closed the year of 1992, once the delegates from the competing countries had gone home. Mayor Maragall hiimself warned citizens that they should prepare themselves for a time of belt-tightening. However, things never grew that desperate. It hasn't been so bad. Barcelona weathered the recession years of 1993 and 1994 better than most Spanish cities, and much of the apparently superfluous office space that it had acquired during the Olympic years filled up during 1996-7. The deficit has gone down a little – to 240.5 billion pesetas by the end of 1997. At the same time, development has continued apace, and the convulsion of change that swept through Barcelona in the early 1990s has scarcely slackened.

Although the city council has been the strongest driving force, Barcelona's development projects also involve the Catalan government, the Generalitat (central governments in Madrid have generally little to say about them). Ajuntament and Generalitat do not always see eye to eye. This is commonly explained by the simple notion that the Ajuntament are Socialists while Jordi Pujol's nationalists are conservatives, but in postmodern Barcelona it's not clear what meaning these old left-right distinctions still have. For example, in the last few years the Ajuntament has negotiated a series of deals that would mean a huge facelift for the Plaça Catalunya, replacing its dowager-like 1950s image with a glitzy look for the new millennium. The Corte Inglés would be given a new façade, and joined by more office buildings, a gigantic Marks & Spencer, a Hard Rock and other trappings of global consumerism. It was, though, Jordi Pujol, as defender of traditional Catalan small businesses, who obstructed the scheme, imposing restrictions on the total area that could be used for mega-stores, shopping malls and the like. The project was held up for over a year. Where left and right fit in in all this would be a thing to study.

THE NEXT BIG IDEA

As the Olympics fade further into memory, and Barcelona keeps hearing of new projects designed to keep economic activity growing, extend the city infrastructure and further develop the idea of a post-industrial Barcelona, it's worth asking whether there will come a point when the Maragallian project of a 'city of services' has been achieved, or whether the city will continue to try out new schemes ad infinitum. At times it seems as if 'grand projects' could be an addiction to Barcelona Ajuntament just can't shake off.

Perhaps the most typically Barcelona – and most questionable – of all the current projects is the *Forum Universal de les Cultures*, the 'Universal Forum of Cultures', planned for 2004, with some support from UNESCO. It's actually an idea dreamed up entirely in Barcelona, after the international exhibitions office in Switzerland rejected the city's petition to hold a World Exhibition –a fourth Barcelona big event – sometime after the millenium. It certainly shows plenty of typical Barcelona chutzpah: lovely packaging and daring design, though what exactly the substance will be is hard to gauge.

According to the Ajuntament, the Forum will have the 'highly laudable but rather vague objective of 'cooperating in the construction of a culture of peace'. Officials go on to say the Forum 'is being designed to provide a location for meeting and celebrating the following three themes: the conditions of peace; the city and its sustainable development, and thirdly, cultural diversity'. They hope to attract 150,000 participants to the forums, workshops, debates, and so on – all from non-governmental organisations, since governments as such will not be invited. There is also to be a theme park built by the sea, the 2004 event's 'emblematic site'. It will stand on land reclaimed from the Mediterranean at the eastern end of town, near the Besós river. The Forum is also meant to be another of Barcelona's urbanising 'pretexts', this time for extending the Diagonal to the sea, creating a new district, lots of commercial space and a whole new stretch of beachfront (*see page 77*).

Linguistic politics

Catalonia is bilingual – Catalan and Spanish are both official languages, guaranteed to remain that way under the constitution. Catalan may have been reduced to a whisper during the Franco years, but the language is very much alive and well today. This is in large part due to the Generalitat's shaping of a linguistic policy which makes it effectively necessary to speak Catalan in many places and contexts, and the provision of large subsidies for Catalan books, TV, theatre, newspapers and radio.

Apart from the fact that street signs and many menus are printed in Catalan, the 'Catalan question' may not have much impact on most visitors. To locals, though, Catalan identity and its multiple manifestations are highly important. It could be called a user-friendly nationalism, in that there has never been significant support for an armed struggle for independence. The Catalan way has always been in the line of determined, businesslike, constructive activity.

In 1986 the Generalitat introduced its policy of 'Linguistic Normalisation', to re-establish Catalan language rights and promote the use of the language in every field. Primary school education is now conducted in Catalan, which will ensure that the children of immigrants from the rest of Spain will grow up speaking it. Catalonia, though, is not Quebec: Spanish-speakers sometimes chafe at pressure to speak Catalan in the workplace, but there are no laws requiring the use of both languages on labels, or in signage. And the programme has been remarkably successful, perhaps the greatest achievement of moderate nationalism since Spain's return to democracy: Generalitat statistics for 1998 showed that some 96 per cent of Catalonia's residents understood Catalan, 75 per cent could speak it, and almost all residents under 30 could speak, read, and understand it.

Catalonia's traditions are also flourishing, and its culture is in full bloom. In all-Spanish affairs, Catalans now have a powerful collective presence. Much of the credit for these successes goes to Jordi Pujol, president of the Generalitat since its full re-establishment in 1980. Since the early 1990s, years in which there have not been clear majorities in the Congress in Madrid, the deputies at state level of Pujol's party *Convergència i Unió* have held the balance of power. Pujol is a ruthless power broker, who determinedly plays the cards he holds to advance what he sees as Catalonia's interests. Accordingly CiU kept the Socialist Party in power from 1993-6, and since 1996 have done the same thing with the Partido Popular.

The price has been the same for both: a series of concessions on increased autonomy and funds for Catalonia. It is universally acknowledged that he has brought home just about as much of the bacon from Madrid as anyone could, and would be a hard person to beat in an election. Nevertheless, ex-mayor Pasqual Maragall may very possibly be preparing an attempt to do just that, as it is widely assumed that a desire to challenge for the presidency of the Generalitat was a prime motive behind his surprise resignation.

In 1997 the linguistic policy was modified and extended in new Generalitat legislation, which raised somewhat hysterical protests in the rest of Spain. The new regulations, though, are nothing too extreme. What people really like to do here with Catalan is speak it. The Catalans are a good people to be a foreigner among, since for many the guiding principle is to leave everyone to do what they want in whichever language they choose. They are, by and large, courteous, and to foreigners trying out their creaky Spanish, most people will still usually respond in slow, clear Castilian.

Construction is due to start in 2000, but it remains to be seen who and how many will turn up to celebrate. What the scheme's advertising omits is that the Olympics was automatically, naturally, a major international event, whereas the Forum is something nobody has ever heard of. Nor does it question whether Barcelona, the capital without a state, can find another model for its progress apart from putting on a big show every few years.

A more concrete development is the World Trade Center, due to open in late 1998 as the last piece of the Port Vell. Never a city to do things by halves, Barcelona is also due to have a high-speed train service to Madrid, Valencia, and on to France and the European network.

In the old centre of the city, change has also gone on apace in the Raval, where the Ajuntament has set about reclaiming dingy block after dingy block, turning the area into an attractive, diverse neighbourhood with a burgeoning population of students, yuppie couples, and artists, and a thriving gallery scene around the MACBA museum, commissioned by Pasqual Maragall himself. So, change or stagnate – that has been the favourite theme in Barcelona and, for the moment at least, there's plenty still going on.

Wishful thinking

Barcelona resident Matthew Tree goes on assignment.

Travel writers, what are they? A bunch of overseas operatives, that's what, hob-nobbing with the natives for no other purpose than to leave a few reams of finely crafted English prose in the dead-letter drop for the Station Controller: 'Barcelona, sir? It's all in the report.' Sir Anthony sits back in his creaking upholstery and peruses the contents: 'Splendid work, Foxtrot, puts me smack in the picture.'

Well, no it doesn't: the travel writer's usual trick of providing a supposed overview of a foreign spot, with a bit of mumbo jumbo about 'spirit of place' worked in for literary effect, rarely corresponds to reality as locals live it; locals like the Catalan writer Carles Puigdemont, who did a post-Olympic survey (*Cata...què?*, 1993) of 186 foreign press reports about his homeland from 12 different countries. He found only one – one – that was even reasonably accurate, a dossier from the French edition of *GEO* in March 1992. Its 54 pages covered the surrender of the city in 1714, bread with tomato, fiscal discrimination, the integration of the Andalusian and Galician influx of the 1960s, the local rock scene, human towers, the two language cultures, tortured separatists, salt cod, you name it. The remaining 185 reports turned out to be a familiar mix of impertinent clichés, cute impressions, wishful thinking and pig ignorance.

The kind of ignorance still being shown six years later by a British TV company when it called this writer to ask about the possibility of doing a programme in Barcelona with the aim of 'showing what typical Spaniards are like', leaving this writer gobstruck: hadn't they heard? That Barcelona is a city that has a 300-year history of rebellion (wars, riots, permanent grumbling) against the Spanish authorities, that its streets did not become truly bilingual until the 1950s, that the city has a football team whose supporters are driven into frenzies of rage when rivals insult them with the cry '*Viva España!*'? Does this still need to be explained?

It certainly does, but not here if for no other reason than that – much as he would like to roll back the siege of misrepresentation to which Barcelona is forever being subjected – this writer has lived here too long: its streets have become just streets, its people just people. The gawping at its marvels ceased long ago, as did any attempt to pigeonhole it for the folks back home.

For which Barcelona is to be written about? The one seen from cousin Pep's sunny modern flat,

1984, while Valencian singer Raimon howled out of the hi-fi? The Barcelona that lurked in the poorly lit student-free corridors of the school, 1985, run by onion-eating, Soberano-swilling Senyor Nicolàs from Bulgaria? Or the Barcelona spent sweating with the Vilafranca crowd in the Plaça Reial's Karma, 1986, before tottering home past sooty buildings six hours after dawn? Or that of the metro stations, 1987-89, the girls, girls, girls shut away forever by the sliding doors as the train pulled away with this tired, aching, hungover semi-erect writer carted off in it like a reluctant dog en route to English lessons with mechanics, schoolkids, cleaners, executives? Or the summer of 1992, a camera team on every corner guarded by police toting elephant guns while we long-term residents swelled with pride?

Or the Barcelona for which lucky stars have been thanked umpteen times over the last fourteen years? That would be the current one, 1998, glimpsed out of the window every night before bedtime, its green sky gracing shadowy buildings which have become work, routine, home. The indescribable, untransferable one, about which all attempted reports to the Station Controller have been carefully lit, and are now burning, quite rightly, in the bin.

Matthew Tree has lived in Barcelona since 1984, and been a regular contributor to Catalan-language magazines, newspapers and radio since 1990. In 1996 he became the first English-speaker to publish a novel written in Catalan, (*Fora de lloc*), which is now in its third edition. He is a member of the 'Germans Miranda' writers' collective, whose best-selling collection of erotic stories *Aaaahhhh*, hit the bookshops in April 1998. He is currently writing a novel in English.

Sightseeing

Sightseeing

From the Gothic archways and alleys of the old city to Modernista fantasies and spectacular contemporary creations, Barcelona offers a unique variety.

Time was when the only visitors who came to Barcelona were business people arriving for trade shows or day trippers in from the *costas* to the north and south on a rainy day. This all began to change in the 1980s, with the rise of Barcelona as a fashion city – and fashionable city – and the whole pre-Olympic promotion of the town. Today, some seven million people visit the city each year. In 1916 the great Dadaist Francis Picabia wrote on a painting *'Il n'est pas donné à tout le monde d'aller à Barcelone'*, not everyone has the fortune to go to Barcelona. Now it would seem near everyone wants to prove him wrong.

Barcelona is an easy city to explore, compact and with many of its major sights within easy walking distance of each other. Wandering around and soaking up the streetlife between stopovers in bars and cafés is as enjoyable a way of getting to know the city as visiting specific sights, and the best way to absorb quintessential Barcelona. When places are further afield, the

excellent city transport system makes it no problem to get to them (*see pages 256-60*).

Pick up any map of Barcelona and you will see a tightly-packed mass of narrow streets bordered by the Avda Paral.lel, the Ciutadella park, the Plaça Catalunya and the sea. This is the area that fell within the medieval walls and, until 150 years ago, made up the entire city. At its heart is the **Barri Gòtic** (Gothic Quarter), a body of interconnecting streets and buildings from Barcelona's Golden Age. Its twisting streets grew inside the original Roman wall, within which the city remained for hundreds of years. Then, as Barcelona grew wealthy in the Middle Ages, new communities developed around the Roman perimeter. These areas, La Mercè, **Sant Pere** and **La Ribera**, were brought within the city with the building of the second wall in the thirteenth century, and one of them, La Ribera, became the most dynamic part of the medieval city. The area south of this wall, on the other side of the river bed later

*Getting ready to start the show in **Plaça Catalunya**.*

to become the **Rambla**, was the **Raval**, the 'city outside the walls', but enclosed within a third city wall built in the fourteenth century. All of Barcelona's great medieval buildings are within this old walled city, with the exception of a very few – most notably the superb Gothic monastery of **Pedralbes** (*see page 75*) – which when built were in open countryside.

Barcelona grew little between 1450 and 1800. The old walls remained standing, and when industry developed in the nineteenth century it had to do so inside them, mostly in the Raval. Factories also appeared in small towns on the surrounding plain, such as **Gràcia**, **Sants**, and **Sant Andreu**. In the 1850s the walls finally came down, and Barcelona extended across the plain following the plan of Ildefons Cerdà for the **Eixample** ('Extension') to the city (*see also page 21*). With its long, long straight streets, this became Barcelona's second great characteristic district, and also the location for many of the greatest works of *Modernista* creativity between 1880 and 1914 – although there are others in many parts of the city. Beyond that are the city's traditional green lungs, the mountains of **Montjuïc** and, at the centre of the Serra de Collserola, **Tibidabo**, both towering above Barcelona and providing wonderful views.

Barcelona absorbed outlying districts such as Gràcia and Poble Nou in 1897, and then the quiet little towns of Sarrià and Pedralbes in 1921. Since then other surrounding towns such as L'Hospitalet de Llobregat have remained independent, even though they and Barcelona now form parts of one urbanised whole, officially united in a rather amorphous entity called the *Àrea Metropolitana*. For decades the mountain chain of Collserola provided a barrier to further expansion in that direction, but with the building of the Vallvidrera tunnel in the 1990s even Vallés towns like **Sant Cugat** (*see page 225*) are only a short drive from the city.

Each of Barcelona's traditional districts or *barris* has its own resilient, individual character. However, in the twentieth century Barcelona has often grown chaotically; then, in the last 20 years, it has undergone an unprecedented physical trans-

formation, in a burst of urban renovation unequalled in Europe, reaching a peak at the time of the 1992 Olympics. **Montjuïc** – with the main Olympic Stadium – and the **Port Olímpic** are the most important Games-related sites, but the old harbour or **Port Vell** is another area that has been spectacularly transformed, mostly after 1992, and there are many more examples of Barcelona's radical approach to urban renewal all around town. In the process the identities of individual *barris* have been altered, pushed and pulled in many different directions.

Barcelona has entered the post-industrial age, and change is one of the city's prime characteristics. Most of its factories are now in the Zona Franca, the industrial estate between Montjuïc and the airport. Within the city, old factories that had still not moved out have been encouraged to, while the shells of those that did have become open spaces, sports centres, artists' studios or clubs. The ultimate aim, according to former Mayor Maragall, has been 'for Barcelona to become a city of services'. Time will tell if it does.

For details of the museums and galleries mentioned below, *see chapters* **Museums** *and* **Art Galleries**.

Hubs of the city

Plaça Catalunya & Passeig de Gràcia

Map D4 The Plaça Catalunya is the city's centre, and the point at which the old, once-walled city meets Cerdà's nineteenth-century **Eixample** – the 525 square blocks above it. Most of the Plaça's statues and fountains date from the 1920s, but since the 1980s it's been repeatedly dug up and relaid to accommodate new traffic patterns. Surrounded by bank offices, it also houses the main branch of **El Corte Inglés** department store, a **Marks & Spencer** store due to open in 1999 and, opposite that, **El Triangle**, a new development also scheduled for opening in 1999. The Plaça Catalunya is an obvious city focal point, in that it's a transport hub: many bus routes stop here, including the airport bus; two Metro lines meet; the FGC lines to Tibidabo, Sarrià and the suburbs begin; and it has a main line (RENFE) railway station serving the airport, the coast to the North, the Montseny mountains and the Pyrenees. It also contains (underground) the very useful main city **tourist office**, the **Centre d'Informació Plaça Catalunya** (*see p251*). The Plaça's attractions have also increased thanks to the city's pavement-widening schemes, which have greatly expanded the space available for cafés. Gone however is a truly time-honoured vantage point, the Café Zurich at the top of the Rambla, where the Triangle is being built. We are told that when the new development is finished there will be a pavement café somewhere around it, but whether it will have any of the old Zurich's hang-out atmosphere is another thing.

Stretching away from the square on the side towards the sea are Barcelona's most famous avenue, the **Rambla**, and the **Portal de l'Angel**, a popular shopping street and another gateway to the **Barri Gòtic**. On the other side is the **Passeig de Gràcia**, the main artery of the Eixample. Along it are two of Gaudí's greatest works, **La Pedrera** and **Casa Batlló**, and on either side the long, straight streets are full of lesser-known *Modernista* gems. The Eixample also contains many of Barcelona's modish shopping haunts. Parallel to Passeig de Gràcia is **Rambla Catalunya**, the *Rambla* of the Eixample, with more cafés, and back on the

Miró's Woman and Bird. *See page 55.*

'The very spirit of a city' –

It is near-inevitable that one of the first things any visitor to Barcelona does is stroll along **La Rambla**, the magnificent mile-long walkway that cuts through the middle of the old city and leads down to the port. Neatly reversing the modern urban relationship between pedestrian and vehicle, it has often been described as the world's greatest street, and is certainly the definitive stroller's boulevard.

A Rambla is an urban feature unique to Catalonia, and there is one in most Catalan towns. Originally, the Rambla of Barcelona, like many of its smaller equivalents, was a seasonal river bed, running along the western edge of the thirteenth-century city, the name deriving from the Arabic word for riverbed, *ramla*. From the Middle Ages to the baroque era a great many churches and convents were built on the other

La Rambla took on its recognisable present form roughly between 1770 and 1860. The city wall came down in 1775, and the Rambla was gradually paved and turned into a boulevard. Seats were available to strollers for rent in the late eighteenth century. The avenue acquired its definitive shape after the closure of the monasteries in the 1830s, which made swathes of land available for new building. No longer on the city's edge, the Rambla became a wide path through its heart.

It used to be said that it was an obligation for every true Barcelona citizen to walk down the Rambla and back at least once a day. Nowadays, many locals are blasé about the place, and the street has been well-taken by the fast-food industry, but it remains one of Barcelona's essential attractions. There are many ways of *ramblejant*, going along the Rambla (a specific verb), from a

side of this riverbed, and some have given their names to sections of it: as one descends from Plaça Catalunya, it is successively called Rambla de Canaletes, Rambla dels Estudis, Rambla de Sant Josep, Rambla dels Caputxins and Rambla de Santa Mònica. Hence, it is often referred to in the plural – *Rambles*, or **Ramblas** in Spanish and English.

The Rambla also served as the meeting ground for city and country dwellers, for on the far side of these church buildings lay the still scarcely-built up Raval, 'the city outside the walls', and rural Catalonia. It thus became a natural market-place. From these beginnings sprang **La Boqueria**, Barcelona's largest market, still off the Rambla today.

saunter to a purposeful stride, but the best way to get a feel for it is to take one of the seats at the top of the avenue (for which you have to pay a few coins) or, more expensively, by heading for a café. The parade before your chair will be entertaining enough to keep you there for quite a while.

As well as having five names, the Rambla is divided into territories. The first part – at the top, by Plaça Catalunya – belongs by unwritten agreement to a group of elderly men who engage perpetually in a *tertulia*, a classic Iberian half-conversation, half-argument about anything from politics to football. This part of the Rambla also has the **Font de Canaletes** drinking fountain. Legend has it that if you drink from it, you'll return to Barcelona.

La Rambla

Below this, towards the mid-point of the Rambla, there are kiosks divided between those selling fauna and those selling flora. There's a brisk trade in birds of every variety, from hens and pigeons to brilliant parrots. Keep walking past the **Poliorama** theatre, and on the left C/Portaferrisa, a fashionable shopping street that leads to the Cathedral and the Barri Gòtic, opens on your left.

The boulevard's next and best-loved section is known as the *Rambla de les Flors*, because of its a string of magnificent flower-stalls, open well into the night. On the right, still looking downhill, and past the **Virreina** exhibition and information centre, is the great **Boqueria** market. Continue and you'll reach the **Pla de l'Os** (or **Pla de la Boqueria**), centre-point of the Rambla, with an entry to Liceu metro and a pavement mosaic created in 1976 by Joan Miró. On the left,

A brief detour along C/Nou de la Rambla will take you to Gaudí's **Palau Güell**, before you hit the stretch of the Rambla that has been a thriving prostitution belt. You may still see a few lycra-and-furred transvestites, but the authorities' clean-up efforts have greatly reduced the visibility (if not the existence) of street soliciting. Thanks to a new arts centre (the **Centre d'Art Santa Mònica**), and other renovations the sleaziness of this part of the Rambla has also been substantially diluted, although you should still be wary of pickpockets at all times. Towards the port, Rambla de Santa Mònica is where you'll find the **Museu de Cera** wax museum and, on Sundays, stalls selling bric-a-brac and craftwork of varying quality, alongside fortune-tellers and tarot-readers catering to the incorrigible local interest in all things astrological.

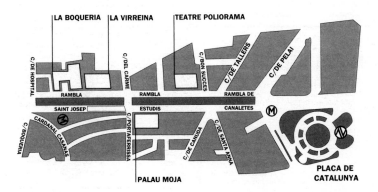

where more streets run off into the Barri Gòtic, is the extraordinary **Bruno Quadros** building (1883), with umbrellas on the wall and a Chinese dragon protruding over the street. Almost opposite is the façade of the Liceu opera, burned down in 1994 but scheduled to reopen in 1999. Behind it lies the *Barrio Chino* (*Xino*, in Catalan), 'Chinatown', traditional home of Barcelona's low-life, but now much changed (*see page 62*).

The Rambla de Caputxins is lined with mostly-expensive cafés. The **Café de l'Opera** (*see* *chapter* **Cafés & Bars**), opposite the Liceu, is the best, with a wonderful interior and reasonable prices. Further down on the left are C/Ferran, the most direct route to **Plaça Sant Jaume** and the **Plaça Reial**, with its cafés and budget hotels.

Other 'sights' of the Rambla are the 24-hour newsstands, offering the Spanish and international press and huge quantities of porn. This is where you come to buy a paper late-night or on Sundays. You'll also see buskers, clowns, human statues, puppeteers, dancers, and musicians working the length of the walkway, some licensed by the Ajuntament and 'Rambla regulars'. There's street theatre of another kind in the shape of the three-card sharpers or hustlers with three walnut shells and a pea under one of them, challenging you to a bet. There's the portrait painter and the caricature painter and the poet selling his wares. In short, all human life is there – along what Garcia Lorca called 'the very spirit of a city'.

Working the Rambla. See pages 46-7.

Passeig itself, halfway up, is Passeig de Gràcia RENFE station, stopping-point for long-distance trains and services to Castelldefels and Sitges. At the top, Passeig de Gràcia crosses the great avenue of the **Diagonal** then narrows to disappear into the attractive old town of **Gràcia**. From here the Diagonal, the longest single street in Europe, runs left up to Plaça Francesc Macià, the modern business centre of Barcelona and another fashionable shopping area, and to the right down to Plaça de les Glòries and the sea.

Plaça d'Espanya

Map A/B4 The Plaça d'Espanya is the main entrance route to the park of **Montjuïc** and the **Palau Nacional**, home of the **Museu Nacional d'Art de Catalunya (MNAC,** *see pp82-3*). Like the Palau the plaça itself was created for Barcelona's last great international jamboree before the Games of 1992, the Exhibition of 1929. Today most of the original Exhibition area is occupied by the **Fira de Barcelona**, the city's Trade Fair. Montjuïc was also the most important of the Olympic sites for 1992, with the main stadium and the giant **Palau Sant Jordi** indoor sports hall, and is the location of several more museums, theatres, attractions and cultural venues. From Plaça d'Espanya a 61 bus will take you up the hill to the **Olympic Ring**, the **Fundació Miró**, the **funfair** or, nearer the bottom, the **Poble Espanyol**. Giant escalators have also been installed alongside the steps leading to the Palau Nacional, giving easy access to the top of the hill, and another way up is to take the **Funicular** from another side of Montjuïc, by Paral.lel Metro. Not to be missed is a summer evening visit, when the **Font Màgica**, the giant illuminated fountain midway between Plaça d'Espanya and the MNAC, dances in changing pastel hues to Tchaikovsky's *Nutcracker*, Abba hits and other favourites while searchlights play over the palace dome (*23 June-23 Sept* 9-11.30pm, music 10-11pm, Thur-Sun only).

The Plaça d'Espanya also contains a railway station, for the FGC line to western Catalonia and Montserrat, and the airport bus stops here. Along the foot of Montjuïc, Avda Paral.lel leads back to the port area, while on the opposite side of the Plaça C/Tarragona – with, on one side, the **Parc de l'Escorxador**, containing a spectacular obelisk by Miró (*see p45 and p55*) – runs up to Barcelona's main rail station in Sants, and C/Creu Coberta leads straight into the *barri* of Sants.

Roman *Barcino*

Medieval Barcelona and all subsequent buildings in the Barri Gòtic were constructed on top of the Roman settlement of *Barcino*, founded in 15 BC, and many a local resident has set out to remodel a bathroom and turned up a bit of the Roman town. A good deal of it still lies undisturbed, but in the last few years the area excavated and opened up to public view has increased enormously.

As a second-rank outpost the original Roman city was small, covering only some 10 hectares (24 acres). Some of its perpendicular street plan can be seen in the remarkable remains underneath the **Museu d'Historia de la Ciutat**. Stretching all the way from the museum itself to beneath the Cathedral, this is the largest underground excavation of a Roman site in Europe, and very well-presented, even if labelling is only sometimes in English. There are numerous other Roman remains around the area: the museum's excellent pamphlet (in English), *Barcino Barcelona*, suggests a two-to-three-hour walk that takes you past all the main sites.

Most impressive are the many surviving sections of the Roman defensive wall, built in the fourth century. It's easy to follow their perimeter by walking, from in front of and facing the Cathedral, left down C/Tapineria, then past the large stretch of wall on Plaça Ramon Berenguer el Gran onto C/Sots-Tinent Navarro, right at the post office onto C/Ample, then right again onto C/Avinyó, C/Banys Nous and C/de la Palla to come back to the Cathedral, where the two drum towers on C/Bisbe Irurita are also of Roman origin, although much altered since.

On C/Sots-Tinent Navarro, turn right into Plaça dels Traginers, a small, shady plaça from which you can gaze on the circular tower that once defended Barcino's eastern corner. From here, if you walk straight on to C/Regomir and turn right, you will come to the **Pati Llimona**. Then, walk west to C/Avinyó, to the Pakistani restaurant at no 19: its rear dining room is a cave-like space incorporating a Roman wall. Further up, across C/Ferran at C/Banys Nous 16 there is a centre for disabled children which has inside it a large piece of Roman wall, with a relief of a pair of legs and feet (phone 93 318 14 81 to ask for a viewing time). Perhaps most striking of all Barcelona's Roman relics, however, are the four huge columns of the **Temple of Augustus**, on the site of the Forum and the centre of Barcino.

Pati Llimona

C/Regomir 3 (93 268 47 00). Metro Jaume I/ bus 17, 40, 45. **Open** 8am-10pm Mon-Fri; 10am-2pm Sat, Sun; *exhibitions* 10am-2pm, 4-8pm, Mon-Fri; 10am-2pm Sat, Sun. **Admission** free. **Map D5**
One of the oldest continually-occupied sites in Barcelona, incorporating part of a round tower that dates from the first Roman settlement, and later Roman baths. The excavated foundations are visible from the street, through large windows. Most of the building above is a fifteenth-century aristocratic residence, imaginatively converted into a social centre in 1988.

Temple of Augustus

C/Paradis 10 (Information Museu d'Historia de la Ciutat, 93 315 11 11). Metro Jaume I/bus 17, 40, 45. **Open** 10am-2pm, 4-8pm, Tue-Sat; 10am-2pm Sun, public holidays. **Admission** free. **Map D5**
The *Centre Excursionista de Catalunya* (a hiking club) contains the largest single Roman relic in the city, four fluted columns with Corinthian capitals from the eastern, rear, corner of the Temple of Augustus, built in the first century BC.

Plaça de les Glòries

Map F4 More a hub in potential than reality, although in Ildefons Cerdà's original plan for the Eixample it was intended that this should eventually become the centre of the city. At present an unlovely giant traffic junction, it is however of particular interest if you come into Barcelona by car, for it has a special **Metro-Park** car park that can be recommended as a place to leave your vehicle for the day (*see p260*). It is the location of the traditional **Els Encants** flea market, and recently has also begun to be redeveloped: one side contains a city business park, 'Barcelona Activa', and the vast **Barcelona Glòries** shopping mall, while on the other are three major cultural projects, the **Teatre Nacional**, the **Auditori** concert-hall and a historical archive, the **Arxiu de la Corona d'Aragó**. The Diagonal-Mar project to extending the Diagonal to the sea (*see p77*) will probably increase this area's importance in the future.

Barri Gòtic

In the first century BC Roman soldiers established a colony on a small hill called the *Mons Taber*, the precise centre of which is marked by a round millstone set into the paving of the Carrer Paradis, between the Cathedral and the Plaça Sant Jaume. The real centre of the Roman city, however, was a road crossing that occupied one part of the modern Plaça Sant Jaume. Large sections of the Roman wall can still be seen, and many other relics of *Barcino* can be found around the *barri* (*see opposite* **Roman Barcino**).

When Barcelona began to revive under the Catalan Counts, its social and political core remained where it had been under the Romans. As a result it became the site of what is now one of the most complete surviving ensembles of medieval buildings – from churches to private residences – in Europe.

The Gothic **Cathedral** is the third one built on the same site; the first was in the sixth century. Many buildings around here represent history written in stone, and deserve a visit. In C/Santa Llúcia, in front of the Cathedral, is the **Ca de l'Ardiaca**, housing the city archives, with a letterbox by the *Modernista* architect Domènech i Montaner showing swallows and a tortoise, said to symbolise the contrast between the swiftness of truth and 'the law's delay'. On the other side of the Cathedral in Plaça Sant Iu is the **Museu Frederic Marés**, with a courtyard café in summer that's one of the best places in the city on a hot day, the massive stone having a wonderfully cooling effect.

Alongside the cathedral the Catalan monarchs built the various sections of the Royal Palace, clustered around the **Plaça del Rei**. Most of the buildings of the palace now form part of the **Museu d'Història de la Ciutat**. Even after Catalonia lost its indigenous monarchy in the fifteenth century, this complex was still the seat of the Viceroys who governed the country. Local civil administration, meanwhile, was centred in the nearby **Generalitat** and **Ajuntament**, which before the opening of **Plaça Sant Jaume** in the last century faced onto the Carrers Bisbe and Ciutat.

The **Cathedral** square. See page 51.

The district's ancientness is very genuine, but the idea of it as a 'Gothic Quarter' is a fairly recent invention, from the 1920s. To help the image stick a few touches were made to enhance the area's Gothic-ness. Medieval buildings were rediscovered and restored, and one of the most-photographed features of the Barri Gòtic, the 'Bridge of Sighs' across C/Bisbe from the Generalitat, was actually a completely new addition, from 1928.

Apart from their historic buildings and official institutions, the Barri Gòtic-proper and the other areas between the Rambla and the Via Laietana are best-known today for a series of pretty, popular squares – of which Plaça Reial is the most important – their bars and restaurants, and the wonderful variety of their shops, from the oldest in Barcelona to the glitzy modern arcades on Portaferrisa.

The narrow streets bounded by Carrers Banys Nous, Call and Bisbe once housed a rich Jewish **Call** or ghetto (*see page 17*). Today it is best known for its antique shops. To walk around this area is to delight in what is perhaps the most satisfying and peaceful part of the Barri Gòtic. In the centre of the Call is the beautiful little square of **Sant Felip Neri**, with a fine baroque church and a soothing fountain in the centre. On C/Banys Nous, the old **Portalón** bodega still offers cheap meals in an increasingly expensive area.

*Home for low-life and now, increasingly, high-life, the **Plaça Reial**.*

Close by are the leafily attractive **Plaça del Pi** and **Plaça Sant Josep Oriol**, where there are some great pavement bars, and painters exhibit their work in the open air at weekends. The squares are separated by **Santa Maria del Pi**, one of Barcelona's most distinguished – but least visited – Gothic churches. The **C/Portaferrisa** is one of the city's most popular shopping streets, with some of its more street-trendy shops in places such as the **Gralla Hall** mini-mall.

Despite the expansion of Barcelona into the Eixample, the old centre has remained a centre of cultural, social and political life throughout this century. In a narrow street off Portal de l'Angel, C/Montsió, is the **Quatre Gats** café, legendary turn-of-the-century haunt of Picasso and other artists and bohemians. Between C/Portaferrisa and Plaça del Pi is C/Petritxol, one of the most charming streets of the Barri Gòtic, which contains several comfortable traditional *granges* offering coffee and cakes (*see chapter* **Cafés & Bars**), but which also has the **Sala Parés**, the city's oldest art gallery, where Rusiñol, Casas and the young Picasso all exhibited.

The area between C/Ferran and the port, properly called **La Mercè**, has a different atmosphere from the centre of the Barri Gòtic, shabbier and with much less prosperous shops. Its heart is the **Plaça Reial**, known for cheap hotels and also a favourite spot for a drink or an outdoor meal, provided you don't mind the occasional drunk. Another nineteenth-century addition, from the 1840s, it has the *Tres Gràcies* fountain in the cen-

tre and lampposts designed by the young Gaudí. On Sunday mornings a coin and stamp market is held here. The Plaça had a dangerous reputation in the past, and the atmosphere can still be heavy at times, but permanent policing now keeps things fairly under control. It has also been made safer by its revival in popularity, reflected in the opening or revamping of restaurants such as **Les Quinze Nits** and clubs like the **Jamboree**. Such are the fickle ways of Barcelona fashion that the **C/Escudellers**, the next street below the Plaça towards the port, once a deeply dubious and shabby prostitutes' alley well-known to visiting sailors from the US Sixth Fleet, is now a trendy place for grungy, hip socialising, with a string of new, cheap, studenty bars.

It can seem hard to imagine today, but the streets further towards the port, particularly C/Ample, were until the building of the Eixample the most fashionable in the city. The grand porticoes of some of the buildings –once wealthy merchants' mansions, now battered apartment blocks – still give evidence of former glories. Here too is the Church of the **Mercè**, home of Barcelona's patron Virgin. There are also the traditional cheap *tasca* tapas bars on C/de la Mercè, where there's a lively atmosphere on busy nights. Most of the surrounding area, however, has been becoming steadily more depressed and run down for most of this century. As usual, though, the local authorities have been making efforts to change the district's character, opening up new squares such as the one in front of the Mercè and another on

The Carrer Montcada

It's only a short walk from end to end, but along the C/Montcada you'll find a whole line of palaces, dating from the Middle Ages to the eighteenth century. Its history began in 1148, when the first houses were built here on land ceded to Guillem Ramon de Montcada. The street very soon became the centre of merchant life in La Ribera, and remained so throughout the Catalan Golden Age. Improbable though it might seem, this beautiful street, impassable to vehicles, was then the broadest thoroughfare in the district. Its merchant residences conform to a typical style of Mediterranean urban palace – elegant entrance patios with the main rooms on the first floor – and are closely packed together. Most have features from several periods, and in the last 30 years this old street has also become one of the great museum centres of Barcelona.

Beginning at C/Princesa and walking down Montcada, the first palace you reach is the **Palau Berenguer d'Aguilar**, main home of the **Museu Picasso**, part of which is thirteenth century. The museum also occupies the neighbouring **Palau Castellet** and **Palau Meca**, and in 1999 is due to expand into still more buildings along the street.

Opposite, at no. 12, is one of the finest and largest mansions, the **Palau dels Marquesos de Lió**, now the **Museu Tèxtil**, with a fine café where you can nurse a coffee protected by the palace's fourteenth-century walls. For a drink and a *tapa* it's hard to do better than go to no. 22, **El Xampanyet**, which has plied the public with bargain *cava* since 1929. Next door the Palau **Dalmases** (no. 20), re-built in the seventeenth century, deserves a visit not least for its eccentric bar (for both, *see chapter* **Cafés & Bars**). In 1640 rioting fishwives sacked the palace in front, the **Palau Cervelló-Giudice** (no. 25), now the **Galeria Maeght**, in protest at the profiteering activities of the Genoese banking family who then lived there, the Giudice, accused of manipulating prices in a time of famine and crisis.

On the left, just before Passeig del Born, is one of Barcelona's narrowest streets, the **Carrer de les Mosques** (Street of Flies), not wide enough for an adult to lie across. If it wasn't closed by barred gates, you could test this for yourself.

Carrer Montcada
Metro Jaume I/bus 17, 19, 40, 45. **Map D/E5**

C/Escudellers, named **Plaça George Orwell**. Another tactic is the siting of parts of the Universitat Pompeu Fabra on the lower Rambla, using the students as guinea pigs in urban renewal. Flats in this and other run-down areas of the old city are also popular with young foreigners, who don't object to their condition as much as local families do.

Beyond C/Ample and the Mercè you soon emerge out of narrow alleys onto the wide Passeig de Colom facing the port, where shipping offices and ships' chandlers still recall the dockside atmosphere of former decades, even though the quay opposite has been comprehensively transformed into the **Moll de la Fusta** (*see pages 58-60*). Monolithic in the centre of the Passeig is the army headquarters, the **Capitanía General**, with a façade that has the distinction of being the one construction in Barcelona directly attributable to the Dictatorship of Primo de Rivera.

Catedral de Barcelona
Pla de la Seu (93 315 15 54). Metro Liceu, Jaume I/bus 17, 40, 45. **Open** *Cathedral* 8am-1.30pm, 4-7.30pm, Mon-Fri; 8am-1.30pm, 5-7.30pm, Sat, Sun; *cloister* 9am-1.15pm, 4-7pm, daily; *museum* 10am-1pm daily. **Admission** *Cathedral/cloister* free; *choir* 300ptas; *museum* 100ptas. **No credit cards. Map D5**
The first cathedral on this site was founded in the sixth century, but the present one dates from between 1298 and 1430, except for its façade, finally finished in a rather un-Catalan Gothic-revival style in 1913 during the 'rediscovery' of medieval Barcelona (*see above*). In the far right corner of the Cathedral, looking at the façade, is the older and simpler Romanesque chapel of Santa Llúcia. The most striking aspect of the Cathedral is its volume: it has three naves of near-equal width. It contains many images, paintings and sculptures and an intricately-carved choir built

in the 1390s. The Cathedral museum, in the seventeenth-century Chapter-House, has paintings and sculptures with works by the Gothic masters Jaume Huguet, Bernat Martorell and Bartolomé Bermejo. In the crypt is the alabaster tomb of Santa Eulàlia, local Christian martyr and first patron saint of Barcelona. The cloister, bathed in light filtered through arches, palms and fountains, is the most attractive section of the Cathedral, and an atmospheric retreat from the city. It contains some white geese, for reasons that seem to have been lost in history, although the most common explanation is that they represent the purity of Santa Eulàlia. Inside there is also a lift to the roof, for a magnificent view of the city.
Wheelchair access.

Museu d'Història de la Ciutat
Plaça del Rei/C/Veguer 2 (93 315 11 11). Metro Liceu, Jaume I/bus 17, 19, 40, 45. **Open** *1 Oct-30 June* 10am-2pm, 4-8pm, Tue-Sat; 10am-2pm Sun, public holidays. *1 July-30 Sept* 10am-8pm Tue-Sat; 10am-2pm Sun, public holidays. *Guided tours* by appointment. **Admission** 500ptas; 300ptas under-16s, students, over-65s; free under-12s, 3-8pm first Sat of month. **No credit cards. Map D5**
The interest of the City History Museum lies more in the buildings it occupies than in the collections it holds. The basements of the fifteenth-century main building contain excavations of a large area of the Roman city, which extend like a complex cavern under the adjoining square (*see* **Roman Barcino**). Another part consists of several sections of the **Palau Reial**, especially the chapel of **Santa Agata**, and the Great Hall or **Saló del Tinell** – its massive, unadorned arches a classic example of Catalan Gothic. The chapel has a fifteenth-century altarpiece by Jaume Huguet that is one of the greatest Catalan medieval paintings. From the upper floors, there is access to the inside of the city wall, and from the chapel you can climb up the **Mirador del Rei Martí** watchtower. Another section, the Casa Padellàs, houses temporary exhibitions. Like others, the museum has been recently renovated, and has a well-stocked bookshop and information centre with several informative leaflets in English. *See also chapter* **Museums**.
Shop.

Plaça del Rei

Metro Liceu, Jaume I/bus 17, 19, 40, 45. **Map D5**
This wholly-preserved Medieval square is flanked on two sides by the **Palau Reial** (Royal Palace), most of it built in the thirteenth and fourteenth centuries for the Catalano-Aragonese 'Count-Kings', and now part of the **Museu d'Història de la Ciutat**. With additions from different periods piled on top of each other, the Plaça gives a vivid impression of the nature of life in the medieval city, particularly since the square, as well as receiving all the traffic of the court, also served as the main flour and fodder market. It has been fairly well-established that Ferdinand and Isabella received Columbus on his return from America either on the palace steps or in the **Saló del Tinell** behind, although miserable sceptics still place the story in doubt. To the left, looking into the Plaça, is the sixteenth-century Viceroys' palace, with its five-tiered watchtower, the **Mirador del Rei Martí**. The square, magnificently floodlit, is used for concerts each summer during the **Grec** festival (*see chapter* **Barcelona by Season**).

Plaça Sant Jaume

Metro Liceu, Jaume I/bus 17, 19, 40, 45. **Map D5**
The main square of the old city and still the administrative centre of modern Barcelona, the Plaça Sant Jaume contains both the City Hall (**Ajuntament**) and the seat of the Catalan regional government (**Palau de la Generalitat**), which stand opposite each other in occasional rivalry. They have not always done so: the square was only opened up in 1823, after which point the present neo-classical façade was added to the Ajuntament. That of the Generalitat is older, from 1598-1602. The greater part of both buildings, however, was built in the early fifteenth century, and both of their original main entrances give onto the street now called Bisbe Irurita on one side of the Plaça, and Ciutat on the other.
Ajuntament de Barcelona *Plaça Sant Jaume (93 402 70 00/special visits 93 402 73 64).* **Open** *office* 8am-3pm Mon-Fri; *visits* 10am-2pm Sat, Sun. **Admission** free.
Contrasting completely with the main façade, the old C/Ciutat entrance to the City Hall is entirely a work of Catalan Gothic. The centrepiece of the Ajuntament is the fifteenth-century **Saló de Cent** (Hall of One Hundred), site of all major municipal ceremonies. Visitors can see the main rooms at weekends, and you can also admire the Saló de Cent at weekly free concerts (*see chapter* **Music: Classical & Opera**). There is a tourist information office and gift shop just inside the Sant Jaume entrance.
Wheelchair access.
Palau de la Generalitat *Plaça Sant Jaume (93 402 46 17).* **Open** 23 April. **Admission** free.
Like the City Hall, the Generalitat has a Gothic side entrance, with above it a beautiful relief of Saint George, patron saint of Catalonia, made by master carver Pere Johan in 1418. Inside, the finest features are the raised patio, part of which is planted with orange trees, and the magnificent chapel of **Sant Jordi** of 1432-34, the masterpiece of Catalan architect Marc Safont. Unfortunately, the Generalitat is only regularly open to the public on Sant Jordi, 23 April (when queues are huge); at other times, call the information number to inquire if tours are being arranged, or ask at tourist offices.

Sant Pere & La Ribera

The *barris* contained within the second, thirteenth-century city wall are divided in two by the long, straight Via Laietana. On the right on the map below Plaça Urquinaona lies the district of **Sant Pere**, originally centred around the monastery of **Sant Pere de les Puelles**, which still stands, if greatly altered, in Plaça de Sant Pere. This used to

The **Plaça Sant Jaume**.

be a centre of textile production, and to this day streets like Sant Pere Més Baix and Sant Pere Més Alt contain many textile wholesalers and retailers. The district may be medieval in origin, but its finest monument is one of the most extraordinary works of *Modernisme*, the **Palau de la Música Catalana**, on C/Sant Pere Més Alt. Less noticed on the same street is a curious feature, unique in Barcelona, the **Passatge de la Indústria**, a long narrow arcade between C/ Sant Pere Més Alt and C/Ortigosa. Towards the Ciutadella, on the other side of the district, is another pleasant square, the **Plaça Sant Agustí Vell**. Sant Pere is currently in the process of being renovated, with whole blocks being razed to the ground, although plans to demolish the **Santa Caterina** market in the centre of the *barri* have (so far) been resisted.

The name of the area below Sant Pere, **La Ribera** (the waterfront), recalls the time before permanent quays were built, when the shoreline reached much further inland. One of the most attractive of all the districts of the old city, it has, though, fallen victim to two historic acts of urban vandalism. The first took place after the 1714 siege, when the victors razed one whole corner of the Ribera in order to construct the fortress of the Ciutadella, now the **Parc de la Ciutadella**. The second occurred when the Via Laietana was cut through the barri in the 1900s, in accordance with the theory of 'ventilating' insanitary city districts by driving wide avenues through them.

During Barcelona's Golden Age, from the thirteenth century onwards, La Ribera was both the favourite residential area of the city's merchant élite and the principal centre of commerce and trade. The main street is still the **C/Montcada**, with its extraordinary succession of palaces and the **Museu Picasso** (*see page 51* **The Carrer Montcada**). The streets around Montcada were filled with workshops supplying anything that the merchant owners might need, and these trades are still commemorated in the names of many of the streets.

On the corner of Montcada and C/Assaonadors is a small Romanesque chapel, the **Capella d'en Marcús**, which is occasionally open (for worship

Ways to see the city

Barcelona's highly active tourist authorities provide a whole assortment of facilities to help visitors see as much of their city as possible. For regular public transport, *see pages 256-60*. After all this, you can't say you couldn't get anywhere....

Barcelona Card

Rates *adults* 2,500ptas 24 hours; 3,000ptas 48 hours; 3,500ptas 72 hours. *Children 6-15* 2,000ptas 24 hours; 2,500ptas 48 hours; 3,000ptas 72 hours.

The latest in a series of Barcelona discount schemes organised by the city tourist authority: for the period stipulated this card gives you unlimited transport on Metro and buses, and discounts on the airport bus, on admission to most museums and at several shops and restaurants (the full current list is given with the card). It can be bought through travel agents outside Barcelona or at the **tourist offices** in Plaça Catalunya and Sants station (*see p251*). There are also two more discount schemes, the **Barcelona Pass** and **Barcelona BIP**, passes for which must be ordered in advance through travel agents and cannot be bought in Barcelona. Inquire when booking your trip.

Bus Turístic (Tourist Bus)

Dates Mar-Jan. **Frequency** *Mar-June, Oct-Jan* every 30 min, *June-Sept* every 15min, 9am-7.40pm daily. **Tickets** *1 day* 1,700ptas, 1,100ptas 4-12s; *2 days* 2,300ptas; free under-4s. **No credit cards.**

A special service that runs on a circular route through Plaça Catalunya and taking in all the main sights (including Vila Olímpica and Parc Güell). The full trip takes about two hours, and with one ticket you can get on and off the bus as many times as you like during the same day. You cannot use standard transport *targetes* (*see p257*) on the bus, but must buy tickets on board or at the Plaça Catalunya tourist office. All the single-deck buses are air-conditioned, adapted for wheelchairs (there are also open-top double-deckers which are not), and buses have guides on board. With the Bus Turístic ticket you also get discount vouchers for a very wide range of attractions (including the Sagrada Família, Tibidabo, Fundació Miró the Picornell swimming pool, and many others), which need not be used the same day.

Rodamolls

Dates & frequency *mid-Sept-Easter, Easter-mid June* hourly approx 11am-9pm, Sat, Sun, public holidays only; *Easter week, mid-June-mid-Sept* hourly approx 10am-midnight, daily. **Tickets** *single* 250ptas; 200ptas under-11s; *return* 400ptas; 300ptas under-11s. **No credit cards.**

The Rodamolls ('quay-wanderer') is another special bus service that follows a route around the harbour area, from the Colombus column around the Port Vell, past Maremàgnum and through Barceloneta to the Port Olímpic. Standard **Bus Turístic** ticket holders are entitled to a discount.

Tramvia de la Diagonal

At some time in the near future a tram line is planned to run along the Diagonal, from C/Entença through Plaça Francesc Macià to the edge of the city. So far the project is in the trial stage, and the start dates are undecided at time of writing. Inquire at tourist offices for current details of services.

Tours

Barcelona by Bicycle

C/Esparteria 3 (93 268 21 05). Metro Barceloneta/bus 14, 16, 17, 39, 45, 51. **Tours** 10am Sat, Sun; 8.30pm Tue, Sat. **Prices** *day tours* 2,000 ptas; *evening tours* (incl meal) 5,000ptas. **No credit cards. Map E5**

The **Un Cotxe Menys** cycle shop (*see p260*) runs bike tours starting in La Ribera and going through the Ciutadella, Sant Pere, the Barri Gòtic, the Raval, the Rambla, Barceloneta and Vila Olímpica. Day tours (stop for a drink included) last two and a half hours, evening trips (meal included) three and a half. There are English-speaking guides, and the cost includes hire of the bike. Prior booking is essential.

Bus tours

Julià Tours *Ronda Universitat 5 (93 317 64 54). Metro Universitat/bus all routes to Plaça Universitat.* **Tours** 9.30am-1pm, 3.30-7pm, daily. **Tickets** approx 4,500ptas. **No credit cards. Map C4**

Pullman Tours *Gran Via de les Corts Catalanes 635 (93 317 12 97/93 318 02 41). Metro Passeig de Gràcia/bus 7, 18, 50, 54, 56.* **Tours** 9.30am-1pm, 3.30-7pm, daily. **Tickets** approx 4,500ptas. **No credit cards. Map D4**

These two companies offer tours of the classic coach-and-multilingual-guide variety, both covering the same routes, which have changed little in decades.

L'Estiu al Museu/una Nit al Museu

Information: Museu d'Història de la Ciutat *Plaça del Rei/C/Veguer 2 (93 315 11 11). Metro Liceu, Jaume I/bus 17, 19, 40, 45.* **Tours** approx monthly. **Tickets** 850ptas; free under-7s. **No credit cards. Map D5**

This is a night tour around the buildings of the Museu d'Història de la Ciutat – wonderfully atmospheric at night –, including the different sections of the Plaça del Rei, with a glass of *cava* to round it off. There is roughly one organised each month, but there may be more frequent in summer; inquire at the museum for forthcoming dates.

Ruta del Modernisme

Information: *tourist offices & Centre del Modernisme, Passeig de Gràcia 35 (93 488 01 39). Metro Passeig de Gràcia/bus routes to Pg de Gràcia.* **Tickets** 1,500ptas; 900ptas students, over-65s; free under-10s. **Map D3**

This special multi-access ticket enables you to visit some 50 of the principal *Modernista* buildings in the city, including some such as the Palau de la Música that can otherwise be hard to get into. The ticket includes guided tours of several buildings and free public transport between them, plus discounts in some restaurants along the way.

Walking tours

Information: *Centre d'Informació Plaça Catalunya (906 30 12 82/93 304 31 35).* **Tours** 10am (English), noon (Catalan/Spanish), Sat. **Rates** 950ptas. 500ptas 4-12s. **No credit cards.**

Every Saturday at 10am professional English-speaking guides take visitors around the Barri Gòtic on foot in an informative tour of about two hours. Numbers are limited, so booking is very advisable.

only). It was paid for in the twelfth century by one Bernat Marcús, who is said to have organised the first postal service in Europe. It was from this chapel, then outside the city wall, that his riders set off for the north, and it also provided a refuge for travellers who arrived after the city gates had closed for the night. C/Carders, close by, is a continuation from C/Llibreteria of the Roman road that led eventually to Rome, and was for centuries the main road out of Barcelona to the north. Like many parts of the old city, this area has a declining, ageing population, as young people move out to newer housing. However, curiously – given that this is one of the oldest sections of the city – it has now acquired a significant immigrant population, and on Carders especially there's a clutch of bars run by Caribbean arrivals from the Dominican Republic, wafting salsa out into the Barcelona streets.

From C/Carders, C/Montcada leads across C/Princesa to the centre of the Ribera, the **Passeig del Born**. Its name originally meant 'joust' or 'list', and in the Middle Ages and for many centuries thereafter this was the centre for the city's festivals, processions, tournaments, carnivals and the burning of heretics by the Inquisition. At one end of the square is the old **Born** market, a magnificent 1870s wrought-iron structure that used to be Barcelona's main wholesale food market. It closed in the 1970s, when the market was transfered to the all-modern Mercabarna on the other side of Montjuïc. The building was saved from demolition, and current plans are that it should house a library.

At the other end of the Passeig from the market stands the greatest of all Catalan Gothic buildings, the magnificent church of **Santa Maria del Mar**. On one side of it a rather ugly new square was opened in 1989 on the site where it is believed the last defenders of the city were executed after the fall of Barcelona to the Spanish army in 1714. Called the **Fossar de les Moreres**, the 'Mulberry Graveyard', the square is inscribed with emphatic patriotic poetry, and nationalist demonstrations converge here on Catalan National Day, 11 September.

The closure of the Born market led initially to a certain decline in this area, but it has survived as the home of an old-established community, who have kept going as communities like this tend to do in Barcelona, and thanks to its inherent attractions for both tourism and nightlife. It has many good bars, from the **Café del Born** by the market and the irreplacable traditional **Xampanyet** in Montcada for daytime drinking to night-venues such as **Penúltimo**, and also excellent restaurants. Since the 1980s it has also been a centre for contemporary art. This is one of the hubs of Barcelona's alternative art scene, with venues such as **Metrònom** and **La Santa**.

From the Passeig and Santa Maria, tiny streets lead through sometimes precarious-looking, centuries-old arches to the main avenue along the harbourside and another symbol of the Ribera, the **Llotja** (Exchange), on the very edge of the port area. Its outer shell is a neo-classical building added in the eighteenth century, but its core is a

Building cranes have replaced dockside cranes in Barcelona's port.

Great parks

Barcelona is an intensely urban city, but fortunately there are many quiet green areas and even near-virgin woodland a short distance from the city centre, and since the 1980s the city authorities have also produced a large number of sometimes-spectacular new open spaces.

Parc de la Ciutadella

Metro Arc de Triomf, Barceloneta/bus 14, 16, 36, 39, 40, 41, 42, 51. **Open** *Oct-Mar* 8am-8pm; *April-Sept* 8am-9pm, daily. **Map E5**

Barcelona's main park, the Ciutadella occupies the site of the eighteenth century Citadel. Begun in the 1870s, the park was created as the site of the 1888 Exhibition. Just outside it stands the **Arc de Triomf** (Triumphal Arch), which formed the main Exhibition entrance. In the centre of the park is a lake where boats can be hired (200ptas per person, per half-hour); beside it is the great **Cascade** or ornamental fountain, on which the young Gaudí worked as assistant to Josep Fontserè, architect of the park. Although formally laid out, the Ciutadella makes an attractive change from the surrounding streets, and unusual statues – a life-sized model mammoth – increase its appeal. Surprisingly extensive, it also contains specific attractions: the **Zoo**, the **Museu d'Art Modern**, which shares the surviving buildings of the old Citadel with the Catalan Parliament, and two other museums, the **Museu de Geologia** and **Museu de Zoologia**. Not to be missed are the **Umbracle** or greenhouse, also from the 1880s, which has been beautifully restored to provide a mysterious pocket of tropical forest in the city, and the **Hivernacle** or winter garden, with an interesting bar (*see chapter* **Cafés & Bars**). Near the Ciutadella bikes can be hired to ride in the park (*see p260*).

Parc del Clot

C/Escultor Claperós. Metro Glóries/bus 56, 92. **Open** *Nov-Feb* 10am-6pm; *Mar, Oct* 10am-7pm; *April, Sept* 10am-8pm; *May-Aug* 10am-9pm, daily.

A few streets north of the flea market at Glóries and Clot metro, this is a park built on three levels full of flowering shrubs, palms and pines. A RENFE warehouse once stood here, and some sections of its curving brick walls still wind through the park.

Parc de la Creueta del Coll

C/Mare de Déu del Coll. Metro Vallcarca/bus 22, 25, 27, 28, 87. **Open** *Nov-Feb* 10am-6pm; *Mar, Oct* 10am-7pm; *April, Sept* 10am-8pm; *May-Aug* 10am-9pm, daily.

A new park created from an old quarry by Josep Martorell and David Mackay in 1987, and considered something of a model for the renovation of disused urban land. At its centre is a large lake with an artificial beach: visitors looking to appreciate the architectural features may find the number of kids enjoying it in summer overwhelming, but it's still an attractive place. Like other new parks in Barcelona, it contains modern sculpture: a piece at the entrance by Ellsworth Kelly, and a monumental work by Eduardo Chillida, *In Praise of Water*, sustained by cables.

Parc de l'Espanya Industrial & Plaça dels Països Catalans

Metro Sants-Estació/bus 27, 43, 44, 109. **Open** (Espanya Industrial) *Nov-Feb* 10am-6pm; *Mar, Oct* 10am-7pm; *April, Sept* 10am-8pm; *May-Aug* 10am-9pm, daily. **Map A3**

*The **Parc de l'Espanya Industrial**.*

The Espanya Industrial, by Basque architect Luis Peña Ganchegui, is the most post-modern of Barcelona's new parks. A line of 10 peculiar watchtowers, reminiscent of ship superstructures, look out over a boating lake: at night, lit up, they create the impression that some strange warship has managed to dock by the Sants rail station. There is sculpture by Anthony Caro and Andrés Nagel. On the other side of the station is the ferociously modern Plaça dels Països Catalans, created by Helio Piñón and Albert Viaplana in 1983 on a site where, the architects claimed, nothing could be planted due to the amount of industrial detritus in the soil. It's an open, concreted space, with shelter provided not by trees but steel ramps and canopies, the kind of architecture that you either find totally hostile or consider to have great monumental strength.

Parc de l'Estació del Nord

C/Nàpols. Metro Arc de Triomf/bus 40, 42, 54, 141. **Open** *Nov-Feb* 10am-6pm; *Mar, Oct* 10am-7pm; *April, Sept* 10am-8pm; *May-Aug* 10am-9pm, daily.

Behind the new bus station at Estació de Nord is a striking park from 1988. It's a big, open, grassy crescent with few trees or benches, just flat ceramic forms in turquoise and cobalt, which swoop and curve through the park: part of a specially-designed earthworks by Beverly Pepper.

Parc Joan Miró (Parc de l'Escorxador)

Metro Tarragona, Espanya/bus 27, 109, 127. **Map B3**

This park takes up four city blocks but feels like much more. Built on the site of a slaughterhouse, it's all stubby, *palmera* trees, but there's a surprising tranquility to the large dirt space, helped by Miro's phallic sculpture *Dona i Ocell*, rising out of the pool for which it was designed.

Parc del Laberint

C/Germans Desvalls (nr Passeig Vall d'Hebron). Metro Montbau/bus 27, 60, 73, 76, 85. **Open** *Nov-Feb* 10am-6pm; *Mar, Oct* 10am-7pm; *April, Sept* 10am-8pm; *May-Aug* 10am-9pm, daily. **Admission** *Mon, Tue, Thur-Sat* 275ptas; free over-65s, under-6s. *Wed, Sun* free.

One of the most atmospheric (and leafiest) parks is also most out-of-the-way, by the **Velòdrom** in Vall d'Hebron. Originally the grounds of a mansion (long demolished), it is surrounded by trees, and in the centre there is a formal garden with a strong element of fantasy, including the maze that gives the park its name. On Saturdays its secluded corners make it very popular for wedding photographs, so there's a good chance you'll be greeted by the sight of white bridal gowns flitting among the pines.

superb 1380's Gothic hall which, until the Barcelona exchange moved to Passeig de Gràcia in 1994, was the oldest continuously-functioning stock exchange in Europe. It also once housed the *Consolat del Mar*, the 'Consulate of the Sea', established to arbitrate in commercial disputes throughout the Mediterranean, and since then has equally accommodated a Customs Post and a School of Fine Arts, where Picasso and many others studied. Unfortunately it can be visited only if you attend a function organised through its owners, the Chamber of Commerce (*see pages 265-6*).

Palau de la Música Catalana

C/Sant Francesc de Paula 2 (93 268 10 00). Metro Urquinaona/bus 17, 19, 40, 45. **Guided tours** *Oct-May* 2pm, 3pm, Tue, Thur, 10am, 11am, noon, 1pm Sat; *June* 3pm Mon, Wed, Fri; 2pm, 3pm Tue, Thur; *July, Sept* varied times Mon-Fri. Closed Aug. **Admission** 500ptas. **No credit cards. Map D4**
Gaudí may be the best-known of Barcelona's turn-of-the-century architects, but the building that most truly represents

Hercules' seat: Montjuic

Whether the name means mountain of the Jews or the mountain of Jupiter, the huge, sprawling mass of Montjuïc, looming over the city from beside the port, is one of Barcelona's most loved features. This hill of 200 hectares (548 acres) is the largest area of open space within the city, a world of its own encompassing several different areas in a kind of up-and-down labyrinth. It's not a district, for hardly anyone lives there, but it is a delightful place for a stroll. From all over the hill, you get great views: they're particularly spectacular by the **Palau Nacional** above Plaça d'Espanya and at **Miramar**, next to the harbour.

According to one legend of the origins of Barcelona, it was founded by Hercules and populated by the crew of the ninth ship (*Barca nona*) that went with him on his labours. Hercules then sat on Montjuïc to admire his creation. But it also has other associations. The **Castell de Montjuïc** at the very top of the **Telefèric**, built in the seventeenth century, became with the Ciutadella one of the symbols of the suppression of Catalan liberties after 1714, and radicals were imprisoned and executed here. A place of fear, the castle was not handed over to the city by the army until 1960, since when it has housed the **Museu Militar**.

At the same time the rest of Montjuïc, wild and empty, was the city's favourite park, and when Barcelona was still confined in its walls people used to climb the hill to spend a day in the country. The military refused to allow much building on the mountain until well into this century, and it was not until the 1920s, and the run-up to the 1929 Exhibition, that Montjuïc was landscaped. Nowadays, though, as befits a favourite place for a day out, Montjuïc has several fun means of transport to help you to the top of the hill (*see page 59*).

Around the hill there are several distinct parks, and despite all the activity on the slopes it's always possible to find peaceful, shaded places. Below the castle, on the steep side of Montjuïc nearest the port, are the **Jardins Costa i Llobera**, which abound in exotic plants such as a Mexican cactus popularly known as *'el seient de la sogra'*, mother-in-law's seat. Not far above on the Montjuïc road, Avda Miramar, are the **Jardins del Mirador**, from where there is a spectacular view over the harbour. Carry on along this road away from the sea past the **Parc d'Atraccions**, one of Barcelona's two permanent funfairs, and you will reach the **Jardins Cinto Verdaguer**, with a beautiful pond, bridge, flowers and great view. The Avda Miramar continues to the municipal swimming pool, spectacularly rebuilt for the 1992 diving events, and the **Fundació Miró**. Continue straight on the main avenue up the hill from there and you will come to the **Anella Olímpica**, with all the main Olympic buildings and the **Bernat Picornell** swimming pool. Beyond there and away from the main landscaped areas Montjuïc is surprisingly full of still-wild, isolated, mysterious corners, while on the south side is Barcelona's largest cemetery.

If on the other hand from the Fundació Miró you head right and down the hill you will come upon a veritable orgy of monumentalist and *Noucentista* architecture from 1929 which now contains Montjuïc's other main cultural institutions. There are museums (the **MNAC**, the **Museu d'Arqueologia** and **Museu Etnològic**), and the **Teatre Grec** and **Mercat de les Flors** (*see chapter* **Theatre**), and plans have also been launched to bring these buildings together into a *'Ciutat del Teatre'* theatre complex. Further down there are the Trade Fair buildings (the **Fira**) leading down to Plaça d'Espanya, the **Mies van der Rohe Pavillion** and the ineffable **Poble Espanyol**. Carles Buïgas' water-and-light spectacular the **Font Màgica** by Plaça d'Espanya, however corny, never fails to round off a memorable walk.

the pure *Modernist*a style is Domènech i Montaner's 'Palace of Catalan Music'. Built in 1905-8, it's still the most prestigious concert hall in the city. The façade, with its combination of bare brick, busts and mosaic friezes representing Catalan musical traditions alongside the great composers, is impressive enough, but it is surpassed by the building's staggering interior. Decoration erupts everywhere: the ceiling centrepiece is of multi-coloured stained glass; 18 half-mosaic, half-relief figures representing the musical muses appear out of the back of the stage; and on one side, massive Wagnerian carved horses ride out to accompany a bust of Beethoven. The best way to see it is to go to a concert, but guided tours are available (booking is necessary; call ahead).

The old Palau virtually bursts under the pressure of the musical activity that goes on inside it, and a sensitive extension and renovation programmed carried out by architect Oscar Tusquets in the 1980s is shortly to be followed by yet more alterations, also by Tusquets. It also has an attractive souvenir shop (*see chapter* **Shopping**). *See also chapter* **Music: Classical & Opera.**
Wheelchair access.

Santa Maria del Mar
Plaça de Santa Maria (93 310 23 90). Metro Jaume I/bus 17, 19, 40, 45. **Open** 9am-1.30pm, 4.30-8pm, daily. **Admission** free. **Map D5**

L'Anella Olímpica (The Olympic Ring)
Passeig Olímpic. Metro Espanya, or Paral.lel, then Funicular de Montjuïc/bus 61. **Information**: *Estadi Olímpic (Catalan 93 481 00 92/Spanish 93 481 10 92); Palau Sant Jordi (Catalan 93 481 01 92/Spanish 93 481 11 92); Palau d'Esports, C/Lleida (Catalan 93 481 10 93/Spanish 93 481 10 93).* **Map A5**

The core area from the 1992 Games consists of a compact hub of monumental buildings in contrasting styles. The main **Estadi Olímpic** – now home to the city's 'second' football team Espanyol – although entirely new, was built within the façade of the existing 1929 stadium by a design team led by Federico Correa and Alfonso Milà. Next to it is the most original and attractive of the Olympic facilities, Arata Isozaki's **Palau Sant Jordi** indoor hall, with a vast metal roof built on the ground and raised into place by hydraulic jacks. It now regularly serves as a concert venue. In the plaça in front locals gather on Sunday afternoons for family walks and picnics, next to Santiago Calatrava's remarkable bow-like **Telefònica** tower. Further along is Barcelona's best swimming pool, the **Bernat Picornell** – predating the Games, but rebuilt for them – and the Sports University, designed by Ricard Bofill and Peter Hodgkinson in their neo-classical style. At the foot of Montjuïc by Plaça d'Espanya is another sports hall, the **Palau d'Esports**, built in the sixties but also rebuilt for 1992.

Pavelló Barcelona (Pavelló Mies van der Rohe)
Avda Marquès de Comillas (93 423 40 16). Metro Espanya/bus 9, 13, 38, 61, 65, 91. **Open** *Nov-March* 10am-6.30pm, *April-Oct* 10am-8pm, daily. **Admission** 300ptas; 200ptas students; free under-18s. **Credit** (shop only) MC, V. **Map A4**

The German Pavilion for the 1929 Exhibition, designed by Ludwig Mies van der Rohe, is also home to the Barcelona chair, since copied worldwide in millions of office waiting rooms. It was one of the most important founding monuments of modern rationalist architecture, with a revolutionary use of stone, glass and space. It was demolished after the Exhibition, but in 1986 a replica was built on the same site. Purists may regard this as a synthetic inferior of the original, but the elegance and simplicity of the design are still a striking demonstration of what rationalist architecture could do before it was reduced to production-line clichés.

Poble Espanyol
Avda del Marquès de Comillas (93 325 78 66). Metro Espanya/bus 9, 13, 38, 61, 65, 91, 109, N1. **Open** 9am-8pm Mon; 9am-2am Tue-Thur; 9am-4am Fri, Sat, eves of public holidays; 9am-midnight Sun. **Admission** 950ptas; 525ptas students, over-65s, 7-14s; free under-7s; group discounts. **Credit** not for admission; some shops only. **Map A4**

As part of the preparations for the 1929 Exhibition, someone had the bright idea of building, in one enclosed area, examples of traditional architecture from every region in Spain. The result was the Poble Espanyol or Spanish Village. Inside it, a Castilian square leads to an Andalusian church, then to replicas of village houses from Aragon, and so on. There are bars and restaurants of every kind, including vegetarian, and over 60 shops. Many of its businesses are workshops in which craftspeople hand-make and sell Spanish folk artefacts - ceramics, embroidery, fans, metalwork, candles and so on. Some of the work is quite attractive, some tacky, and prices are generally high.

A few years ago the village was given a facelift, with improved services and the installation of some quality (but expensive) restaurants. With the revamp came the 'Barcelona Experience': a half-hour audio-visual run-through of the city's life and history (with English commentary via headphones). Outside, street performers re-create bits of Catalan and Spanish folklore, and there are special children's shows. The Poble has an unmistakeable tourist-trap air, but it does have its fun side and, many of its buildings and squares are genuinely attractive. It also tries hard to promote itself as a night-spot, with karaoke bars, Cuban dinner-and-dancing restaurants, discos and a flamenco show, and dance bands perform regularly in the main square. Attached to the village is the bar that's the *summum bonum* of Barcelona design-bar-dom, **Torres de Avila** (*see chapter* **Nightlife**). This effort to make the village a happening night venue is not always successful, mainly because the space is so large that it's hard to get it full enough to create an atmosphere.

*Movement goes on in the **Raval** at night. See page 62.*

The Cathedral may attract more attention, but Santa Maria del Mar, known as 'the people's cathedral' because of its traditionally greater popularity, is undoubtedly the city's finest church, the summit of Catalan Gothic. Built remarkably quickly for a medieval building, between 1329 and 1384, it has an unusual unity of style. Inside, two ranks of slim, perfectly proportioned columns soar up to fan vaults, creating a wonderful atmosphere of space and peace. It's not so much a historical artefact as simply a marvellous building, somehow outside of time. There's also superb stained glass, particularly the great fifteenth-century rose window above the main door. Our ability to appreciate it is helped greatly by the fact that revolutionaries set fire to it in 1936, clearing out the wooden baroque images that clutter so many Spanish churches, and allowing the simplicity of its lines to emerge. From the outside, the especially Plaça Santa Maria, the church is equally impressive.

The Port Vell

At the foot of the Rambla Columbus, in Catalan **Colom**, points out to sea from atop his column, confusingly enough towards Italy. To his right are the fourteenth-century shipyards or **Drassanes**, now the **Museu Marítim**, and from near the foot of his column you can cross the harbour on the **Golondrines** trip boats (*see p59*). These are features that have been in place for years. However, had you made the ride up to the crown at Columbus' feet in, say, 1980, you would have seen the harbour beneath you thronged with cargo ships waiting to load or unload. Today, they have disappeared, and the scene has changed utterly. Commercial traffic has moved away to container terminals outside the main port. Simultaneously, Barcelona's inner harbour, rechristened the **Port**

Vell or Old Port, has undergone an extraordinary overhaul to turn it into a waterside leisure area, so much so that twenty years on a visitor simply would not know it. In only two or three years, since the mid-1990s, the former dockside has become one of Barcelona's foremost party zones.

At the end of the Rambla, if you cross the busy Passeig de Colom to the waterfront, you will come to the **Rambla de Mar**, a swivel-section wooden footbridge which opens to let boats enter and leave. It leads to the **Moll d'Espanya** quay, dominated by the **Maremàgnum** complex, a trademark work by ever-active Barcelona architects Helio Piñón and Albert Viaplana (*see also chapters* **Nightlife** *and* **Shopping**). As much of an entertainment as a shopping centre, it contains 50 shops, 25 restaurants and a dozen clubs and bars. A little slow to gain momentum when first opened in 1995, Maremàgnum has since become heavily successful, packed with young crowds on summer evenings, to the extent that it's now sometimes referred to as a new 'main square' of the city. Further along the same quay there's also an eight-screen cinema, the **IMAX** giant-format moviehouse and the **Aquàrium**.

If you've had enough of the mall and come back across the footbridge and turn right, you will come to the **Moll de la Fusta** or Wood Quay, the first part of the port to be redeveloped. Inaugurated in 1987, it contains a string of pavement bars and restaurants including Javier Mariscal's **Gambrinus**, topped by a giant fibreglass lobster that became an eighties' city landmark. As you

Taking a ride

Much-loved features of Barcelona are its special rides. Most offer special ways of getting around, up or down the city's three great fun-areas, Montjuïc, the Port and Tibidabo.

Horse-drawn carriages

Portal de la Pau (93 421 88 04/93 421 15 49).
Metro Drassanes/bus 14, 18, 38, 59, 64, 91.
Services *Mar-Nov* 11am-dark daily. **Charges** 6,000ptas per hour; rates negotiable for special parties.
No credit cards. Map C/D5
If you want the ultimate tourist experience and don't mind looking silly, ask a man for a ride behind his tired old nags. The usual route is up the Rambla from the port and back.

Montjuïc

Funicular de Montjuïc

Metro Paral.lel-Avgda Miramar (93 443 08 59).
Metro Paral.lel/bus 20, 36, 57, 64. **Open** *Nov-early June* 10.45am-8pm Sat, Sun, public holidays; *June-Sept* 11am-10pm daily; Oct 10.45am-8pm daily. Daily service also Christmas, Easter week, public holidays.
Tickets *single* 225ptas; *return* 375ptas. **No credit cards. Map C/B5**
Not much of a sightseeing trip, as for most of its route it runs underground, but this modern Funicular brings you out at a spot on Montjuïc convenient for the park, the **funfair**, the **Fundació Miró** and Miramar, and saves you a walk up the hill. It also connects with the **Teleféric**.

Montjuic Tourist Train

Departs from Plaça d'Espanya. Metro Espanya/bus all routes to Plaça d'Espanya. **Dates** *April-Sept* 10am-9pm Sat, Sun, public holidays. **Tickets** 200ptas; 150ptas under-16s. **No credit cards. Map A4**
Not so much a train as an open trolley pulled by a truck, which goes from Plaça Espanya to Miramar via the Palau Nacional, Fundació Miró, the Olympic Stadium and Poble Espanyol. It runs only on weekends and holidays.

Teleféric de Montjuïc (Montjuïc cable cars)

Estació Funicular, Avda Miramar (93 443 08 59).
Metro Paral.lel, then Funicular de Montjuic/bus 61.
Open *Nov-Mar* 11.30am-2.45pm, 4-7.30pm, Sat, Sun, public holidays; *April-May, mid-Sept-Oct* 11.30am-2.45pm, 4-7.30pm, daily; *June-mid-Sept* 11.30am-9.30pm daily. **Tickets** *single* 375ptas; *return* 575ptas; (under-12s) *return* 425ptas; group discounts. **No credit cards. Map B5-6**
Beginning outside the station of the Funicular, the Montjuïc cable cars run up to the castle at the top, with a stop at one side of the funfair. The four-seater cars are small and usually open, so vertigo sufferers might not enjoy it, but all along the route there are superb views over Montjuïc and the port.

The Port

Golondrines (swallow boats)

Moll de la Fusta (442 31 06). Metro Drassanes/bus 14, 18, 36, 38, 57, 64.

Drassanes-Breakwater & return (30min):
Departures *Nov-23 June* every 45min 11am-5pm Mon-Fri; every 25min 11.30am-7pm Sat, Sun. *24 June-Oct* every 25min 11.30am-7.30/8pm daily. Closed late Dec. **Tickets** 465ptas; 240ptas 4-10s; free under-4s.
Drassanes-Port Olímpic & return (2hrs):
Departures 11.30am, 1.15pm, 4.30pm Mon-Fri; 11.30am, 1.15pm, 4.30pm, 6.30pm, Sat, Sun, public holidays. Closed mid-Dec-mid-Feb. **Tickets** 1,250ptas; 875ptas over-65s, 11-18s; 525ptas 4-10s; free under-4s; group discounts. **Credit** MC, V. **Map C6**
The double-decker 'Swallow boats' will take you around the harbour to the end of the breakwater, where you can eat out, take in the sea air, go fishing, or come straight back. More solid, sea-going boats now run on a longer trip round to the **Port Olímpic**.

Transbordador Aeri (port cable cars)

Miramar, Parc de Montjuïc – Torre de Jaume I – Torre de Sant Sebastià, Barceloneta (93 317 55 27).
Metro Paral.lel, then Funicular de Montjuic/bus 61, or bus 17, 64 to Barceloneta. **Open** *Oct-June* noon-5.45pm Mon-Fri; noon-6.15pm Sat, Sun, public holidays; *June-Oct* 11am-9pm daily. **Tickets** (subject to confirmation) 675ptas round trip; 625ptas one way Miramar-Barceloneta; 600ptas round trip, 575ptas one way Barceloneta-Jaume I or Jaume I-Miramar.
No credit cards. Map C/D6
A product of the 1929 International Exhibition, the Transbordador cable car rattles its way across the harbour from Miramar on Montjuïc to Barceloneta, with a stopover in the middle on the Moll de Barcelona, beside the World Trade Center. The cars are large and windowed, and the views of Barceloneta and the Port area are spectacular.

Tibidabo

Funicular de Tibidabo

Plaça Doctor Andreu-Plaça del Tibidabo (93 211 79 42). FGC Av Tibidabo/bus 17, 22, 58, 73, N8, then Tramvia Blau. **Open** *Mar-May, Oct* 10.45am-8.30pm Sat, Sun, public holidays; *June-Sept* 10.45am-8.30-10.30pm Mon-Thur, Sun; 10.45am-1.30am Fri, Sat.
Tickets *single* 225ptas; *return* 375ptas.
No credit cards.
The Funicular that takes you from the end of the tramline to the very top of the mountain is art deco-esque, like much of the funfair. Each train has two halves, one pointing down and one pointing up, and if you secure a good seat at the bottom of the 'down' end, you'll get a panoramic view of the city.

Tramvia Blau (Blue Tram)

Avda Tibidabo-Plaça Doctor Andreu (93 441 29 99).
FGC Avda Tibidabo/bus 17, 22, 58, 73, N8. **Services** *mid Sept-22 June* 9.05am-9.35pm Sat, Sun, public holidays; (bus service 7.05am-9.45pm Mon-Fri); *23 June-mid-Sept* 9.05am-9.35pm daily. **Tickets** *single* 185ptas; *return* 325ptas. **No credit cards.**
The Blue Trams, beautiful old machines that have been running since 1902, clank their way along Avda Tibidabo between the FGC station and Plaça Doctor Andreu, passing many large *Modernista* houses en route. Once there, you can take in the view, have a meal or a drink, or catch the Funicular to the funfair on Tibidabo. Note that there's only a plain bus service on weekdays except in summer.

might expect, these bars are a little pricey, but the promenade has benches as well and makes a cool and pleasant place to mingle and watch the harbour lights on summer evenings. Later in the night some bars, such as **Distrito Marítimo** and **Octopussy** (*see chapter* **Nightlife**), become very happening harbourside club venues. At the north end of Moll de la Fusta, by the borders of La Ribera, is the giant 14-metre high mosaic sculpture, *Barcelona Head*, by the late Roy Lichtenstein.

If you carry on round the port to the right, you will reach the marina – with some very luxurious yachts – and a line of water-side restaurants. The *tinglados*, the huge dock storage sheds that once dominated Passeig Joan de Borbó, have nearly all been pulled down to open up an entirely new harbourside promenade on this side of Barceloneta. One exception is the **Palau de Mar**, a converted warehouse which now hosts several restaurants and the **Museu d'Història de Catalunya**. The only remaining commercial section is a small area for fishermen. Beyond there, if you continue walking you can go through the Barceloneta district to the Port Olímpic and the beach.

Returning to Columbus' feet, if, instead of walking across to Maremàgnum or along the Moll de la Fusta you head to the right, looking out to sea, you will come to the **Moll de Barcelona**, the view of which is dominated by the giant metal tower that is a stop for the **Transbordador Aeri** cable cars. This is still a working quay, the departure point for ferries to the Balearics (*see page 234*). At the end of the quay, though, there is another giant building scheme, still incomplete, labelled (in English) the **World Trade Center**. Work on this project was at a standstill for years through lack of finance, but it's now scheduled to open during 1998, although few believe this possible. One of its functions is to improve Barcelona's facilities for cruise traffic, even though the city has already become the Mediterranean's cruise capital.

The Center also aims for a wider role in post-millenium Barcelona. South of Montjuïc it is planned to extend the Zona Franca business area and the Port proper by occupying a triangular stretch of land taken over from the river Llobregat, which will be re-channelled southwards. The aim of all this is to consolidate Barcelona as the leading freight port in the western Mediterranean, and the World Trade Center is intended to be the logistics centre of this whole operation, with offices specialising in international trade as well as restaurants, shops and maybe a casino. The hope of Barcelona's ever-ambitious planners is that within a couple of years multinationals will be banging at its doors, all eager to make the building their Mediterranean headquarters.

Colom (Columbus Monument)

Plaça Portal de la Pau (93 302 52 24). Metro Drassanes/ bus 14, 18, 36, 38, 57, 59, 64. **Open** *end-Sept-Mar* 10am-1.30pm, 3.30-6.30pm, Mon-Fri; 10am-6.30pm Sat, Sun, public holidays. *April, May* 10am-1.30pm, 3.30-7.30pm, Mon-Fri; 10am-7.30pm Sat, Sun, public holidays. *June-end-Sept* 9am-9pm daily. **Admission** 250ptas; 150ptas over-65s, under-14s; group discounts. **No credit cards. Map C6**
Ride to the top of the Columbus column, built for the Universal Exhibition of 1888, for a panoramic view of the old city and the port from within the crown at the explorer's feet. The lift only holds four people plus an attendant at one time, so there may be a sizeable queue.

Smokeless chimneys

Off the Paral.lel, in Gràcia, in the Raval, in the Vila Olímpica, near the Mercat Sant Antoni… they stand singly or in twos or threes all over the city. Often with a thick cement base, these brown-brick chimneys narrow very gradually as they rise from the sites of old factories. The factories beneath them have closed, but the authorities have preserved their chimneys as mute monuments to an earlier age of frenetic industrial activity in Barcelona.

The workshops beneath these chimneys were centres of a political life in which generations of Barcelona's people were involved, and the Ajuntament has sought to give acknowledgement to some of the participants in these struggles, all now conveniently distant in time. There is a **Plaça Karl Marx** in Nou Barris, although Bakunin would have been more appropriate for this city. The Raval has its **Plaça Salvador** Seguí, after the great anarchosyndicalist leader murdered nearby in 1923, while **Plaça Angel Pestaña** in Nou Barris and **Plaça Joan Peiró** in Sants honour other leading figures of the CNT. Of foreigners, **George Orwell** has a square, or rather a triangle, named after him at the end of C/Escudellers. Andreu Nin, leader of the POUM organisation with which Orwell took part in the Civil War, murdered on the orders of Stalin, is recalled by an almost-illegible plaque on La Rambla 128, the last place he was seen alive, and **Passeig d'Andreu Nin** in Nou Barris. Finally, the greatest Barcelona revolutionary of them all, Buenaventura Durruti, is commemorated by a small plaça at the foot of Montjuïc, not far from where he was buried. It's reasonable to suppose that all of these people would have been appalled to see the tidy way in which their names are remembered.

Barceloneta

The triangular district known as Barceloneta ('Little Barcelona'), the part of the city between the harbour and the sea, was the product of an early example of authoritarian town planning. When after 1714 a large section of the Ribera (*see above*) was razed to the ground to make way for the new Citadel, the people thus displaced lived for many years in makeshift shelters on the beach, until in the 1750s the authorities decided to rehouse them in line with a plan drawn up by a French army engineer, Prosper Verboom.

The new district was built on land reclaimed from the sea. The street plan of Barceloneta, with long, straight narrow blocks, reveals its military origins. Its houses were initially of only one storey, but subsequently second, third and fourth storeys were permitted. In the nineteenth century this became the dockers' and fishermen's district, and the massive road and rail barrier that cut Barceloneta off from the rest of the city until the recent transformations helped it retain a distinctive atmosphere and identity. The local **Festa Major** is a riot of colour, with streets covered in paper garlands (*see chapter* **Barcelona by Season**).

Barceloneta has also traditionally been Barcelona's gateway to the beach. Until quite recently this was of interest only to a few devotees. Some may cavil at the water quality even today, but since the reconstruction of the city's beaches they have become much more pleasant. Consequently Barceloneta has become still more crowded on summer weekends as the throngs thread their way through its streets on their way to the Port Olimpic and the beaches of Poble Nou (*see pp75-7*).

Barceloneta has also been long associated with another pleasure, in its fine fish and seafood restaurants. There are any number of them in the district, but among the best are **Can Ros** and **Can Ramonet**. Away from the beach and the city Barceloneta leads into the Passeig de l'Escullera, the long road along the breakwater at the end of which is another restaurant and the landing point of the **Golondrines** trip boats.

A famous feature of Barceloneta was that it used to be possible to combine the district's two pleasures, in the traditional paella and seafood restaurants that lined the beach. These basic *chiringuitos* were closed down by city edict in 1991, but have (slightly) revived in smarter form. With regard to the Barceloneta, the city's massive reworking of the old port – and the transformation of the Passeig Joan de Borbó from dockyard service road to waterside promenade – has meant in effect a complete re-orientation of the area through 180°, from looking out to sea to overlooking the port. So, some former *chiringuito*-owners have been encouraged to reopen – together with all-new restaurants – on the new harbourside *passeig* and

On the beach

Until the 1980s, and before then for as long as anyone could remember, most of the sea frontage north-east of Barcelona harbour was an industrial wasteland. However, the city's planners like a challenge, and one of the key slogans of the whole pre/post-Olympic project has been that it should create a *Barcelona Oberta al Mar*, a 'Barcelona Open to the Sea'. As a major port Barcelona had obviously always been open to the sea in a grimy, workaday sort of way, but what was meant now was that the city should take on board, and enjoy, the fact that it lies on the Mediterranean. Beginning in the mid-1980s the seafront was transformed beyond recognition: over four kilometres of new beaches were created, with dikes to prevent erosion and thousands of tons of fresh sand, accompanied by stylish parks and palm-lined promenades; special measures were taken to improve water cleanliness; and, as a centrepiece, the **Port Olímpic** was built, one of Barcelona's most popular new amenities.

In the 1990s Barcelonans have caught on to their new beaches in a big way, and on any summer's day can be found in huge numbers along the sand, playing beach volleyball or rollerblading along the prom. The beaches have good new showers and safety facilities, plus ramps for wheelchair access. On some sunny days, they're positively too successful, and unless you're exceptionally gregarious, it's best to avoid the city beaches at weekends, especially in July.

Sun, sea and sand aren't the only attractions of Barcelona's renovated beachfront, for there's an enjoyable, leisurely walk between the beach and Colom. Centrepiece is the Port Olimpic, with its endless supply of bars and restaurants for when you come off the beach (*see chapter* **Restaurants**). Beyond the marina, looking towards the city, you'll see gleaming in the sunshine Frank Gehry's huge copper *Fish* sculpture, next to which there's a footbridge that will take you past more pleasant, clean beaches to Barceloneta.

Beaches of Barceloneta, Nova Icària, Bogatell & La Mar Bella
Metro Ciutadella-Selva de Mar, yellow line/bus 36, 41, 45, 59, 71, 92.

in the converted warehouse the **Palau de Mar**, while other old dock buildings have been torn down to open up a view of the harbour and Montjuïc that most Barceloneta residents had been unaware of all their lives.

The Raval

This is the name currently used for the area bounded by the Rambla, Paral.lel, Ronda Sant Pau and Ronda Sant Antoni, although it has been referred to by many different names in the past. 'Raval' is a revival of its original medieval name, referring to the part of the city outside the walls. The trades and institutions that confined here were those too dangerous or noxious to be allowed inside the city, such as brickmaking, slaughtering or tanning, or the huge **Antic Hospital de la Santa Creu**, which served the city from the fifteenth century until it finally closed in 1926. Other institutions located here were those that demanded too much space, such as the line of monasteries that once ran down one side of the Rambla. In the corner of the Raval next to the sea were the **Drassanes** or shipyards, now the **Museu Marítim**.

On the Paral.lel, near the port, there is still a large section of Barcelona's third wall, which brought the Raval within the city in the fourteenth century. However, Barcelona largely stagnated during the following centuries, and in 1800 much of the Raval had still not been built up, but consisted of small market gardens that supplied the city. A trace of this earlier Raval can still be seen in the name of one of the most beautiful pockets of peace in the *barri*, the ancient Romanesque church of **Sant Pau del Camp** (St Paul in the Field). Hence, when industry began to develop, it was in this area that most land was available. A great deal more land also came into use when liberal governments dissolved the monasteries in 1836, especially in the area around one of the great hubs of the district, the **Boqueria** market, built on the site of the former convent of Sant Josep.

Barcelona's first industry, mainly textile mills, thus had to grow within the cramped confines of the still-walled Raval, making use of every particle of space. Some of the strange, barrack-like factories from that time can still be seen, particularly in the narrow streets around C/Riereta. The workers from the factories lived alongside them, often in appalling conditions.

Then known to most people as the *Quinto* or 'Fifth District', this was the area where the dangerous classes of society hung out, and became the great centre of revolutionary Barcelona, a perennial breeding ground for anarchist and other radical groups. Conspiracies galore were hatched here, riots and revolts began on innumerable occasions and whole streets became no-go areas for the police after dark. In 1923, gunmen in the pay of employers murdered the great CNT leader Salvador Seguí on the corner of C/Cadena and C/Sant Rafael.

The other aspect of the area (or of that part of it between C/Sant Pau and the port) that made it notorious was its situation as a centre of low-life and the sex industry, with high-class brothels for the rich and cheap dives for the poor in the so-called *Barrio Chino* (*Xino*, in Catalan) or Chinatown. This label was given to the area (which had no Chinese connections) in the twenties by a local journalist, Francesc Madrid, after he saw a film about vice in San Francisco's Chinatown, and swiftly caught on. Barcelona had always had an underworld, centred in the Raval, but it really took off during World War I (*see page 25*). The two elements of the district, workers and drifters, co-existed side by side, and its narrow streets were crowded 24 hours a day with people coming and going, buying and selling.

Here people on the run from the police found it easy to live clandestinely. The decadent life of the *Barrio Chino* has often been romanticised, particularly by foreign writers like Jean Genet. Its heyday was in the twenties and thirties, but it managed to survive to a certain extent under Franco. Hundreds of bars and cheap hostals lined streets like Nou de la Rambla, catering to a floating population.

Today the whole district has changed enormously. It still has an industrial flavour, but its surviving industry consists of small, old-fashioned workshops in trades like printing, furniture repair or building supplies. The Hospital now houses cultural and academic institutions. Radical politics has failed to revive under the new democracy. The biggest change has been in the *Barrio Chino*, which has been a prime target of the Ajuntament's urban renewal schemes.

Serious problems began for the *Chino* at the end of the seventies, with the arrival of heroin. The area's old, semi-tolerated petty criminality became much more threatening, affecting both the morale of Barcelona residents and the tourist trade. The authorities set about dealing with the problem with their customary clean-sweep approach. Between 1988 and 1992 most of the area's cheapest *hostals* were closed, and whole blocks associated with drug dealers or prostitution demolished to make way for new squares. The people displaced were often transferred to newer flats on the outskirts of town, out of sight and so perhaps out of mind. Another element in what the authorities aptly call the *esponjament* (mopping up) of the Raval has been gentrification, with the construction of a students' residence, a new police station and office blocks on the razed sites. Some of the changes have undeniably been for the best, but their cumulative effect has been to leave one of the more unique parts of the city looking rather empty. Another, unpredicted, change in the Raval, though, has been the appearance of a sizeable Moslem

*The tower of Domènech's Casa Lleó Morera, part of the **Mansana de la Discòrdia**. See page 71.*

community, mostly of Maghrebi immigrants, who have taken over flats no longer wanted by Spaniards. This is now one of the city's most multicultural areas, where Moslem *halal* butcher shops serving North Africans sit alongside *carnisseries* selling every part of the pig to Catalans.

The main thoroughfare of the lower Raval, **C/Nou de la Rambla**, today has only a fraction of its earlier animation, but retains a surreal selection of shops – theatrical costumiers where strippers could buy all the sequins they could ever need, alongside fashion shops that bizarrely specialise in demure bridal wear. It also contains a peculiar addition from the 1880s, the **Palau Güell**, built by Gaudi for Eusebi Güell. It was an extremely eccentric decision by Güell to have his new residence located in what was already a deeply unfashionable area, and he often had trouble persuading dinner guests to take up their invitations.

It is the upper Raval, towards Plaça Catalunya, that has seen the largest-scale official projects for the rejuvenation of the area, with the building of the giant cultural complex that includes both the **Museu d'Art Contemporani (MACBA)** and the **Centre de Cultura Contemporània (CCCB)**, in what was once the workhouse, the *Casa de la Caritat*. A clutch of new contemporary art galleries have sprung up around them, as well as laid back but fashionable restaurants like **Silenus** or bohemian bars like the **Fortuny**.

As well as acquiring a completely new association with sophisticated culture, parts of the old district have enjoyed a new lease of life thanks to their bars having been rediscovered as places for slightly grungy socialising. The **London Bar** on C/Nou de la Rambla and **Marsella** on C/Sant Pau are both forever popular with the local foreign community. For a relaxing drink the open-air bar on Plaça Vicenç Martorell is great, and new bars have appeared, such as the Irish **Quiet Man** on C/Marqués de Barberà.

Antic Hospital de la Santa Creu

C/Carme 47-C/Hospital 56 (no phone).
Metro Liceu/bus 14, 18, 38, 59.
Open 9am-8pm Mon-Fri; 9am-2pm Sat. **Map C5**
A hospital was founded on this site in 1024: the present buildings are a combination of a fifteenth-century Gothic core – including a beautifully shady colonnaded courtyard – with baroque and classical additions. It remained the city's main hospital until 1926, and Gaudi died here.Today it houses Catalonia's main library, an arts school and, in the chapel, **La Capella** exhibition space (*see chapter* **Art Galleries**).

Palau Güell

C/Nou de la Rambla 3-5 (93 317 39 74). Metro Liceu/bus 14, 18, 38, 59. **Open** 10am-2pm, 4-8pm, Mon-Sat. Closed public holidays. **Admission** 300ptas; 150ptas under-16s, over-65s; free under-6s. **No credit cards. Map C5**
This medievalist palace was built in 1886-88 as a residence for Gaudi's patron Eusebi Güell, on one of the less prepossessing streets in the *Barrio Chino*. It was Gaudi's first major commission for Güell, and also one of the first buildings in which he revealed the originality of his ideas. Once

past the fortress-like facade, one finds an interior in impeccable condition, with lavish wooden ceilings, dozens of snake-eye stone pillars, and original furniture – like a dressing table whose mirror looks like its about to fall off. The roof terrace is a garden of decorated chimneys, each one different from the other.

Sant Pau del Camp

C/Sant Pau 101 (93 441 00 01). Metro Paral.lel/bus 20, 36, 57, 64, 91. **Open** 11am-1pm, 5-7pm, Mon, Wed-Sun. **Admission** free.
Barcelona's oldest church was built in the twelfth century, when the surrounding Raval was just open fields, as part of a monastery. The Romanesque structure has none of the towering grandeur of the Cathedral or Santa Maria del Mar: it is a squat, hulking building, rounded in on itself to give a sense of intimacy and protection to worshippers. On either side of the portal are columns made from material from seventh- and eighth-century buildings.

Paral.lel & Poble Sec

If you stand by the old city walls at Santa Madrona and look across the broad street towards Montjuïc, you will see a *barri* lining the side of the hill. The street is Avinguda Paral.lel, a curious name that derives from the fact that it coincides exactly with 41° 44' latitude north, one of Ildefons Cerdà's more eccentric conceits. The barri is Poble Sec. The avenue was the prime centre of Barcelona nightlife – often called its 'Montmartre' – in the early decades of this century, full of theatres, night clubs and music halls. A statue on the corner with C/Nou de la Rambla commemorates Raquel Meller, a legendary star of the street who went on to equal celebrity around the world. She stands just outside the live-porn show the **Bagdad**. Apart from this one live show, while there are still plenty of theatres and cinemas along the Paral.lel, most of its cabarets have disappeared. There was a real ending of an era in 1997 when El Molino, most celebrated of the avenue's traditional, ultra-vulgar old music halls, finally and suddenly shut up shop. One other, the **Arnau**, precariously survives, but more as a theatre than a real music hall.

The name Poble Sec means 'dry village', fitting testimony to the fact that as late as 1894 this *barri* of poor workers celebrated with dancing the installation of the area's first street fountain, which still stands, in C/Margarit. By 1914 some 5,000 people lived in shanties up where the district meets Montjuïc. During the *Setmana Tràgica* in 1909, more religious buildings had been destroyed here than in any other part of the city (*see page 25*).

On the stretch of the Paral.lel opposite the city walls three tall chimneys stand incongruously in the middle of modern office blocks. They are all that remains of the Anglo-Canadian electricity company known locally as *La Canadenca*, ('The Canadian'), which was the centre of the great general strike of 1919. Beside the chimneys an open space has been created, the **Parc de les Tres Xemeneies**, now popular with rollerbladers.

An amiable symbol of Barcelona, Gaudí's dragon from the **Parc Güell**. *See page 73.*

Today Poble Sec remains a friendly working class *barri* of quiet, relaxed streets and squares. It has plenty of cheap bars, most of whose clientele are football-crazy, and a number of reasonable restaurants such as **La Tomaquera** or **La Bodegueta**. Towards the Paral.lel there are some distinguished *Modernista* buildings, which local legend has maintained were built for *artistas* from the cabarets by rich sugar-daddies. At C/Tapioles 12 there is a beautiful, extremely narrow wooden Modernist door with typically writhing ironwork, while at C/Elkano 4 don't miss *La Casa de les Rajoles*, with a very unusual white mosaic façade that gives an impression of weightlessness. As you penetrate further into the barri the streets grow steeper, some becoming narrow lanes of steps that eventually provide a superb view of the city.

The Eixample

A fateful decision was taken in the 1850s when, after Barcelona was finally given permission to expand beyond its medieval walls, the plan chosen (by the government in Madrid) was the regular grid-iron of Ildefons Cerdà. Opinion in Barcelona was much more favourable to the fan-shaped design of the municipal architect Antoni Rovira i Trias, which can be seen at the foot of a sculpture of the man in Plaça Rovira i Trias, in Gràcia (*see also page 21*).

With time, though, the 'Extension' (*Eixample/Ensanche*) has become as much – if not more – of a distinctive feature of Barcelona as the medieval city. With its love of straight lines, parallels and meridians, Cerdà's plan is a monumental example of nineteenth-century rationalism. The more utopian features of the plan, though – building on only two sides of each block, and gardens in the middle of each block – have largely been forgotten. Today, most of the interior courtyards are car parks, workshops or shopping centres. The garden around the **Torre de les Aigües** water tower at C/Llúria 56 is one of the only courtyards in the *barri* where one can get a glimpse of how attractive and humane Cerdà's plan could have been.

The Eixample was built up between 1860 and 1920, mostly after 1890. This coincided with – and vitally encouraged – the great flowering of *Modernisme*, the distinctive Catalan variant of art nouveau. The equal weight *Modernistes* gave to decorative and fine arts is reflected throughout the district, in countless shop fronts, hallways, and small gems of panelling or stained glass, as well as in the great buildings of major architects such as Puig i Cadafalch or, of course, Gaudí.

The Eixample is the economic and commercial core of Barcelona, with banks and insurance companies, fashionable shops and arcades, any number of restaurants, good cinemas and the best art galleries and bookshops, as well as its world-famous architecture. However, as a residential area it also has an ageing population, and the long one-way streets have been ever-more dominated by traffic in recent years. The Ajuntament has set up a Pro-Eixample project to revitalise the area, one aim of which is to recover for communal use the inner courtyard of each block.

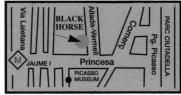

When the district was first built and until the 1920s the rail line to Sarrià (now the FGC) went overground up C/Balmes, effectively cutting the Eixample in two. Ever since, the grid has been regarded as having two halves. The *Dreta* (right – to the right of Balmes looking uphill) contains most of the more distinguished architecture, museums and main shopping avenues. The *Esquerra* (left – to the left of Balmes) was built slightly later, and is a little more residential. Together they have formed the centre of Catalan middle-class life for most of the last hundred years. To newcomers unused to such straight lines they can be disorientating, but they form a very special urban environment with an atmosphere all of its own.

The Dreta

The great avenue of the Passeig de Gràcia is the centre of the district. It is famous for its architectural masterpieces, built as elegant residences, such as the **Mansana de la Discòrdia**, with buildings by Gaudí, Puig i Cadafalch and Domènech i Montaner, and Gaudí's **La Pedrera**. The Passeig and parallel Rambla Catalunya are fashionable shopping streets, a centre for both stylish arcades like **Bulevard Rosa** and design emporia like **Vinçon**. Window shopping for art has traditionally been concentrated close by in C/Consell de Cent between Balmes and Rambla Catalunya, and nearby there is too one of the most impressive of all Barcelona's art spaces, the **Fundació Tàpies**.

Toros

Plaza de Toros Monumental
Gran Via de les Corts Catalanes 743 (93 245 58 04). Metro Monumental/bus 6, 7, 18, 56, 62. **Open** (visits & museum) *April-Sept* 10.30am-2pm, 4-7pm, Mon-Sat; 10.30am-1pm Sun. (Bullfights) *April-Sept* approx 5-6pm Sun. **Admission** *visits & museum* 375ptas; 275ptas under-16s. **No credit cards. Map F4**
If you're set on seeing a bullfight, carry on to Madrid or Seville – this archetypally Spanish activity has never had a strong following in Barcelona, and in recent years one of the city's two bullrings has closed down. The other, the Monumental, holds fights every Sunday during the season, and has a small bullfighting museum.
Ticket office: *C/Muntaner 24 (93 453 38 21). Metro Universitat/bus all routes to Plaça Universitat.* **Open** *April-Sept* 11am-2pm, 4-8pm, Wed-Sat. Closed public holidays. **No credit cards. Map C4**

The cafés on Rambla Catalunya are pleasant, but pricey, and a favourite meeting place for affluent local residents on summer evenings. Cheaper possibilities for a stopover on a walk around the area are **La Bodegueta** and the **Bracafé**. This part of the Eixample is also the place to find some of the most famed 1980s' design bars and clubs, some of which, though, have been sliding down the pinnacle of fashion for a few years. Notable from a design

*Taking in Barcelona from a **Tibidabo** café. See page 73.*

point of view are **Nick Havanna**, **Velvet** and **Zsa Zsa**, all near the corner of Balmes and Rosselló.

As well as the most renowned *Modernista* buildings, the streets around Passeig de Gràcia are full of other extraordinary examples of work from that time, whether whole buildings or details. Since the end of the 1980s the section of the Eixample between C/Muntaner and C/Roger de Flor has been labelled the *Quadrat d'Or* or 'Golden Square' of *Modernisme*, and plaques have been placed on 150 protected buildings that are considered of special merit. A guidebook to them is available, in English, from the **Llibreria de la Virreina** (*see page 251 and chapter* **Shopping**) and other bookshops.

Particularly of note are the hallway and exuberant overall decoration of the **Casa Comalat**, designed by Salvador Valeri in 1906 (Avda Diagonal 442-C/Còrsega 316). On Avda Diagonal are two characteristic buildings of Puig i Cadafalch, the **Casa Vidal Quadras** (number 373), now the **Museu de la Música**, and the **Casa Terrades** (416-420), an extraordinary neo-Gothic fantasy with pointed towers that have gained it the alternative name of *Casa de les Punxes* ('House of Spikes'). Not far away – in the block on the corner of C/València and C/Bruc – there is a small market designed by Rovira i Trias, the **Mercat de la Concepció**, now undergoing repairs but with flower stalls outside that normally remain open 24 hours a day.

The outer Eixample to the north of the Diagonal is mainly a residential area, for the most part built after 1910, but with some striking Modernist buildings such as Puig i Cadafalch's 1901 **Casa Macaya**, now the cultural centre of the **Fundació La Caixa** (*see chapter* **Art Galleries**). The area is dominated, though, by the towering mass of the **Sagrada Família**. Not far away is another great Modernist project, Domènech i Montaner's **Hospital de Sant Pau**, begun in 1902 as a long-overdue replacement for the old hospital in the Raval, but not completed until 1930. It and Gaudí's creation stand at opposite ends of Avda Gaudí, made into a pleasant walkway in 1985.

Hospital de la Santa Creu i Sant Pau

C/Sant Antoni Maria Claret 167 (93 347 31 33). Metro Hospital de Sant Pau/bus 15, 19, 20, 25, 45, 47, 50, N1, N5. **Map F2**

Built on the garden-city principle, Domènech's hospital became the most useful of *Modernista* projects for Barcelona's citizens, as well as one of the most beautiful. Begun in 1901 and finished by the architect's son in 1929, it consists of 48 pavilions separated by gardens and linked by underground tunnels. A wealth of sculptures, murals and mosaics strikes the eye everywhere, each pavilion having its own ornamental identity. As a place for a patient suffering from a not-too-distressing illness, it is wonderful, though not, alas, for much longer, as plans are afoot to move several medical services elsewhere. While it is a working hospital visitors are free to wander through the courtyards and gardens.

La 'Mansana de la Discòrdia'

Passeig de Gràcia 35-45. Metro Passeig de Gràcia/bus 7, 16, 17, 22, 24, 28. **Map D3**

The 'Block of Discord', between Carrers Consell de Cent and Aragó, is so-called because on it, almost alongside each other, stand buildings by the three greatest figures of Catalan Modernist architecture, all constructed between 1900 and 1907, in wildly clashing styles. At number 35 is Domènech i Muntaner's **Casa Lleó Morera**, a classic Modernista building of exuberantly convoluted, decorative forms. Three doors up at number 41 is Puig i Cadafalch's Gothic-influenced **Casa Amatller**; next to that is Gaudí's unclassifiable **Casa Batlló**, rising like a giant fish out of the pavement (*see also chapter* **Architecture**).

La Pedrera

Passeig de Gràcia 92-C/Provença 261-5 (93 484 59 95/93 484 59 00). Metro Diagonal/bus 7, 16, 17, 18, 22, 24, 28. **Open** 10am-8pm daily; *mid-June-mid-Sept* also 9pm-1am Fri, Sat. *Guided tours* (in English) 6pm Mon, Wed, Fri; 11am Sat, Sun, public holidays. **Admission** 500ptas; 300ptas students under 25, over-65s; free under-12s. **No credit cards. Map D3**

The last building Gaudí worked on before succumbing to the Sagrada Família represents his most radical departure from a recognisably *Modernista* style. Built entirely on columns and parabolic arches, with no supporting walls, and supposedly without a single straight line or right-angled corner, this curving, globular apartment block, also known as the Casa Milà, contrasts strikingly with the angularity of much of the Eixample. Its revolutionary features were not appreciated by the Milà family – who paid for it – nor by contemporary opinion, which christened it *La Pedrera* ('The Stone Quarry') as a joke. It is now owned by the **Fundació Caixa de Catalunya**, which has beautifully restored the building and uses one floor as a separate exhibition space, while on another there is a permanent exhibition on the architect and *Modernisme*, the **Espai Gaudí** (*see chapters* **Museums** *and* **Art Galleries**). With the ticket you can also go on the informative guided tours (in English, Spanish or Catalan), which let you see some of its main features and especially the roof, with its extraordinary semi-abstract sculptures (actually ventilation shafts and chimneys). Note that in winter tours may not continue after dark, even though the exhibition space stays open.
Shop.

Temple Expiatori de la Sagrada Família

Plaça Sagrada Família-C/Mallorca 401 (93 455 02 47). Metro Sagrada Família/bus 19, 33, 34, 43, 50, 51, 54. **Open** *Oct-Feb* 9am-6pm; *Mar, Sept* 9am-7pm; *April-Aug* 9am-8pm, daily. **Admission** 800ptas; 550ptas over 65s; free under-10s; group discounts. *Lifts to the spires* 200ptas. **Credit** (groups only) V. **Map F3**

Gaudí's masterpiece or monsterpiece, to which he dedicated himself for the last 18 years of his life, often sleeping on the site – although the project had in fact been initiated by another architect, Francisco del Villar, in 1882. Only the crypt, the apse and the four towers of the Façade of the Nativity, along C/Marina, were completed in his lifetime. Every element in the decoration, much of it carved from life, was conceived by Gaudí as having a precise symbolic meaning, and he was deeply opposed to the idea of anyone appreciating the building outside of its religious context. An essential part of any visit is an attempt to climb the towers beyond the level that can be reached by lift: this gives the remarkable sensation of walking out into space. Descent via the spiral staircase is not recommended for those suffering from vertigo. The **museum** in the crypt contains models and a history of the project and other information on Gaudí (*see chapter* **Museums**). Work on the cathedral was resumed in 1952 by some of Gaudí's assistants, who drew up plans based on some of his sketches and what they remembered of the great man's ideas (he never used detailed plans), and has accelerated in the last few years. The new towers of the Façade of the Passion are completed, with sculptures by Josep Maria Subirachs that horrified many Gaudí admirers.

The second sculptor now working on the building is Japanese, Etsuro Sotoo, who seems to be adhering more faithfully to Gaudí's intentions, with six musicians, adorning the rear of the cathedral, that are flowing and modest. No one would hazard a guess as to when it will be finished. *Museum. Shop.*

The Esquerra

This side of the Eixample quickly became the new area for some activities of the city that the middle classes did not want to see on their doorsteps. A huge slaughterhouse was built in the extreme left of the area, and was only knocked down and replaced by the **Parc Joan Miró** in 1979. The functional **Hospital Clínic** was sited on two blocks between C/Còrsega and C/Provença, and further out still on C/Entença is the city's 1905 **Modelo** prison. There are two great markets, the **Ninot**, just below the hospital, and the **Mercat de Sant Antoni**, designed by Rovira i Trias and touching onto the Raval, which is taken over by a great **second-hand book market** every Sunday morning. This is also an area for academic institutions, from the enormous **Escola Industrial** on C/Comte d'Urgell to the original **Universitat Central** building on Plaça Universitat, from 1842.

Modernista architecture does extend over into this side of the Eixample (as the *Quadrat d'Or* concept recognises), with some wonderful examples such as superb façade of the **Casa Societat Torres Germans** (C/París 180-2), by Jaume Torres i Grau, from 1905. There are some fine bars, such as the **Velòdrom** on C/Muntaner. Beyond the hospital and the Escola Industrial the outer Eixample contains no great sights or monuments, but leads up to the Plaça Francesc Macià, developed since the sixties as the centre of the new business district and the more expensive shopping areas, and the main crossroads of affluent Barcelona. Beyond the office blocks and smart cafés of the Plaça itself lie the fashionable business and residential areas of the Zona Alta.

Gràcia

'Gràcia – independència' and even *'Freedom for Gràcia'* can occasionally be seen on T-shirts here. This isn't a demand for the *barri* to become perhaps the smallest state in the world but a half-serious petition to be separated from Barcelona, to which it was annexed in 1897. Fiercely protective of their own identity, *Graciencs* still refer to outsiders as *'barcelonins'*, as if they did not really belong here.

Little more than a village in 1820 with about 2,500 inhabitants, Gràcia had become the ninth-largest city in Spain by 1897. when it had 61,000 people. It was also known as a radical centre, of Catalanism, republicanism, anarchism and, to a certain extent, feminism. Place names such as Mercat de la Llibertat, Plaça de la Revolució and C/Fraternitat tell their own story.

As you enter the district, and the rigid blocks of Cerdà's grid give way to narrow streets arranged haphazardly, the change in atmosphere is striking. Many streets consist of small, two-storey buildings, and a series of attractive small squares provide space to pause and talk. The most important of them are **Plaça Rius i Taulet**, site of the pre-1897 town hall and a magnificent clock tower designed by Rovira i Trias, **Plaça Virreina**, the peaceful and relaxing **Plaça Rovira i Trias**, with an appealing bronze statue of this great-but-unappreciated architect himself, and **Plaça del Sol**. It acquired a new one in 1993, not elegant but unpretentious and designed for kids, the **Plaça John Lennon**.

Gràcia contains one of Gaudí's earliest and most fascinating works, the **Casa Vicens** of 1883-88, hidden away in C/Carolines. And of course the most visited place in the whole municipal district is his **Parc Güell**, on the Tibidabo side of the area above Plaça Lesseps, across the busy Travessera de Dalt. *Modernisme* is also represented by Domènech's **Can Fuster** (1908-11) at C/Gran de Gràcia 2-4, and above all by the work of Francesc Berenguer, Gaudí's assistant, who designed the **Mercat de la Llibertat**.

Gràcia's independent attitude is also reflected in a strong attachment to traditions like the **Festa Major**, the biggest in Barcelona, which for a few days in August makes the *barri* a centre for the whole city (*see chapter* **Barcelona by Season**). The district contains many small factories and workshops, and also has a sizeable Catalan-speaking Gypsy community. Gràcia is also home to a large number of students, and a substantial creative community – photographers, actors, designers – who contribute much to its atmosphere.

Coffee in Plaça del Sol is a relaxing alternative to busier places in the centre of the city, though the area is at its best after dark. The **Café del Sol** itself is an old favourite but the streets below contain many more. A few years ago, Gràcia also had its turn as the most in-vogue area for night-time wandering – becoming known as *Gràcia divina* – and acquired an additional crop of bars, although the centre of fashion has now moved on, towards the Eixample and lately back to the old city.

The educated nature of local residents is seen in the number of cultural venues in the district, such as the **Centre Artesà Tradicionarius** for folk music and dance, and theatres such as the **Regina** children's theatre, the experimental **Sala Beckett** and especially the **Teatre Lliure**. There are also two of the most enterprising cinemas in the city, the **Verdi** and **Verdi Park**.

Parc Güell

C/d'Olot. Bus 24, 25. **Open** *Nov-Feb* 10am-6pm; *Mar, Oct* 10am-7pm; *April, Sept* 10am-8pm; *May-Aug* 10am-9pm. **Map E1**

In 1900 Gaudí's patron Eusebi Güell commissioned him to oversee the design of a garden city development on a hill on the edge of the city, which he envisaged would become a fashionable residential area. Gaudí was to design the basic structure and main public areas; the houses were to be designed by other architects. The wealthy families of the time, however, did not appreciate Gaudí's wilder ideas, scarcely any plots were sold, and eventually the estate was taken over by the city as a park. Its most complete part is the entrance, with its Disneylandish gatehouses and the mosaic dragon that's become another of Barcelona's favourite symbols. The park has a wonderfully playful quality, with its twisted pathways and avenues of columns intertwined with the natural nature of the hillside. At the centre is the great esplanade, with an undulating bench covered in *trencadís*, broken mosaic – much of it not the work of Gaudí but of his assistant Josep Maria Jujol. Gaudí lived for several years in one of the two houses built on the site (not designed by himself), now the **Casa-Museu Gaudí** (*see chapter* **Museums**). The park stretches well beyond the area designed by Gaudí, away into the wooded hillside. *Café-restaurants.*

Sants

The official municipal district of Sants, meaning 'Saints', includes three *barris*, Sants proper, La Bordeta and Hostafrancs. When Barcelona's gates shut at 9pm every night, hostels, inns and smithies grew up around the city to cater for latecomers. Such was the origin of Sants, but by the 1850s it had also become a major industrial centre.

Centred around an old Roman road called for centuries *Camí d'Espanya* ('the Road to Spain') and now C/Creu Coberta-C/de Sants, by 1850 Sants had already become the site for giant textile factories such as the Muntades brothers' *Espanya Industrial*. It was also a centre of labour militancy. In 1855 the first general strike in Catalonia broke out here, and the CNT held a major Congress in Sants in 1918.

Today Sants remains, like Gràcia, one of the areas of Barcelona with a strongest sense of its own identity, but practically all of these industrial centres have disappeared. The huge **Espanya Industrial** site, long disused as a factory, became a futuristic park in 1985 after a long neighbourhood campaign for more open spaces. One of the 1980s Barcelona parks most liked by the public, it has a lovely lake where boats can be hired and Andrés Nagel's *Gran Drac de Sant Jordi*, a huge dragon for kids to play on (*see page 55*). Other old factories have become workshops, libraries and schools.

The **Estació de Sants**, alongside the park, also dominates the *barri*. In front of it is the **Plaça dels Països Catalans**, a square of granite and grim metal that's as much loathed by local residents as it is admired by design critics. On the other, southern, side of the station are the more appealing *Places* of **Sants** and **Peiró**. In the latter the first-ever Catalan film was shot, *'Baralla en un café'* ('Cafe Brawl'), in 1898. Near the Plaça de Sants is a complex called **Les Cotxeres**, an old tram depot converted into a multi-functional community and arts centre. From there, C/Creu Coberta runs into Plaça d'Espanya, where C/Tarragona, to the left, sharply marks the end of Sants and the beginning of the Eixample. This street has changed beyond recognition through pre- and post-Olympic projects, with high-rise office towers that have led it to be dubbed – perhaps in hope – the 'Wall Street' of Barcelona.

Tibidabo & the Zona Alta

Local dignitaries have customarily taken official visitors to the top of **Tibidabo**, the giant peak towering up behind the city, for an overview of Barcelona. The name *Tibi dabo* comes from the Latin for 'to thee I shall give', the words used by the Devil during his temptation of Christ. The view is certainly magnificent, even when there's smog down below, and the clean air a welcome change. Since it was made accessible by the building of the rail line to Avinguda Tibidabo and the wonderful **Tramvia Blau** ('Blue Tram') in the 1900s Tibidabo has joined Montjuïc as one of Barcelona's two 'pleasure mountains', visited at least a few times each year by just about everyone in town.

Getting there, by train, tram and **Funicular**, is part of the fun (*see page 59*). The square between the tram and the funicular is one of the best places in the city for an al fresco drink or meal: try the **Mirablau** bar or **La Venta** (*see chapters* **Restaurants** *and* **Cafés & Bars**). From the square, tracks lead along the city-side of the Serra de Collserola which are great for jogging. Further down the flanks of the hill there are more elegant, airy bars, such as **Partycular** and **Rosebud** (*see chapter* **Nightlife**), and also the **Museu de la Ciència**. At the very top of the funicular is the city's best **funfair** (*see page 77*), and, for a completely limitless view, the giant needle of Norman Foster's **Torre de Collserola**. Next to the funfair is a church, built in an extravagantly bombastic style and completed in 1940 to 'atone' for Barcelona's revolutionary role in the Spanish Civil War. To the left of it, on the other side of the ridge, there are stunning views over the Vallès to the north, while down the hillside are tracks where you can easily lose yourself for an afternoon among near-virgin pinewoods. For more on walks nearby, *see page 75* **Exploring Collserola**.

Below Tibidabo are the districts of the **Zona Alta** (literally 'Upper Zone', or simply Uptown). This is the name collectively given to a series of *barris* – among them Sant Gervasi, Sarrià, Pedralbes, Putxet – that fan out across the area above the Diagonal and to the left of Gràcia on the map. They are 'upper' both literally, in that they are at a higher elevation than most of the city and so enjoy cleaner air, and in social standing, as these are the most expensive residential areas of Barcelona. In the Zona Alta the streets are cleaner, quieter and have markedly fewer small shops than in other areas of the city.

*A uniquely preserved monument, the **Monestir de Pedralbes**.*

This is the home of the *pijos* and *pijas*, the city's pampered upper-middle class youth, who throng the area's many bars and cafés. As well as luxury apartment blocks it is common to see large, individual houses with gardens, many of which have been turned into elegant restaurants and bars. **Tres Torres** is a good example. These areas have few major sights other than the remarkable **Museu-Monestir de Pedralbes**, now home of the Barcelona branch of the **Museu Thyssen**. However, the centre of **Sarrià** and the area of **Pedralbes** around the monastery still retain an appreciable flavour of what were quite sleepy country towns until well into this century.

The Zona Alta has dotted around it several works by Gaudí. From wealthy Pedralbes a walk down Avda de Pedralbes leads to his wonderful gate house and gates, the **Pavellons de la Finca Güell** at no 15, with a bizarre wrought-iron dragon. In the garden of the **Palau de Pedralbes** on Avda Diagonal, a former Güell residence, there is a delightful Gaudí fountain, and back on the other side of the Zona Alta off the Plaça Bonanova, near Tibidabo FGC station, is the remarkable Gothic-influenced **Torre Figueres**, or **Bellesguard**.

The Palau de Pedralbes contains two interesting museums, the **Museu de Ceràmica** and **Museu de les Arts Decoratives**. Around it, on either side of the Diagonal, is the Zona Universitària, chosen as the area for the expansion of Barcelona's main university in the 1950s. Some 100,000 students pass through it every day, but this doesn't make its buildings any less bleak and impersonal. At the very end of the Diagonal at the city's edge, is the **Parc Cervantes**, with a magnificent rose garden that's a must for the visitor.

From there, turn back along the Diagonal toward Plaça Maria Cristina and Plaça Francesc Macià to enter the fastest-growing business district of modern Barcelona. It is just as fast-growing a shopping area, with stores, fashion malls and especially the 'horizontal skyscraper', **L'Illa** (*see chapter* **Shopping**). This also houses the modish club and music venue **Bikini** (*see chapter* **Nightlife**).

Close to Plaça Francesc Macià itself there is a small, popular park, the **Turó Parc**. To the right of it on the map is **Sant Gervasi**. This area had its moment of glory as the most fashionable night-time meeting-point in Barcelona, especially the streets around the junction of C/Marià Cubí and C/Santaló, site of bars and clubs such as **Mas i Mas** and **Universal**. The revival of the old city has taken the crowds away a little, which can mean that at least it's easier to get a drink. Also in Sant Gervasi, but closer to Gràcia, is one of the great survivors of the Barcelona club scene, the **Otto Zutz**.

Monestir de Pedralbes (Col.lecció Thyssen-Bornemisza)

Baixada del Monestir 9 (93 280 14 34).
FGC Reina Elisenda/bus 22, 63, 64, 75. **Open** 10am-2pm Tue-Sun. **Admission** *Monastery only* 400ptas; 250ptas students under-25, over-65s; group discounts; free under-12s. *Col.lecció Thyssen only* 400ptas; 250ptas students under-25, over-65s; group discounts; free under-12s. *Monastery & Col.lecció Thyssen* 700ptas; 400ptas students under 25, over-65s; group discounts; free under-12s. **Credit** (shop only) AmEx, MC, V.

Exploring Collserola

t's a much-repeated local cliché to say that Barcelona, until the Ajuntament decided to build it a beach, lived with its back to the sea, but it's at best only half-true. One is on steadier ground in saying that, with the exception of Tibidabo, and despite the hiking vogue of the last century, the city has long cold-shouldered the Collserola mountain chain to its north and west.

Tibidabo is at the centre of Collserola, with its funfair, bars, restaurants and fabulous views, especially from the huge Torre de Collserola. The 6,550-hectare (16,000 acre) park of the Serra de Collserola proper is however more easily reached by FGC trains on the Terrassa-Sabadell line from Plaça Catalunya, getting off at **Baixador de Vallvidrera** station.

A ten-minute walk from the station into the woods along Carretera de l'Església takes you to the **Centre d'Informació** (93 280 35 52), where some information about the mountain range is available in English, and maps can be bought. This very helpful Centre also has an exhibition area and bar. There are five suggested itiner-

aries, ranging from a walk of a mere 20 minutes to an excursion to the Serra d'en Cardona of over two hours. Other, longer hikes have also been signposted. The great thing however is to explore for oneself, because the Collserola is a wonderful natural reserve, with the trees providing delicious shade on a hot day. Walking is easy, as paths and climbs are well maintained. You occasionally comes upon abandoned *masies*, traditional Catalan farmhouses. Picnic spaces are clearly indicated, but it is strictly forbidden to light fires following a devastating conflagration in 1994.

Holm oak and pines predominate among the trees, squirrels and rabbits are everywhere, and the scents and colours of herbs and wild flowers are exhilarating. A Collserola trip can be rounded off by a visit to the quiet hill town of **Vallvidrera**, where an old bar in the main plaça, **Can Trampa**, will provide rest and refreshment for the weary traveller. From there, a ride down a funicular takes you to **Peu de Funicular** station, from where the FGC will return you to Plaça Catalunya.

Founded in 1326 by Queen Elisenda, wife of Jaume II of Aragon, this monastery still houses a community of 24 nuns. With the installation of the Col.lecció Thyssen-Bornemisza art collection in part of the cloister the rest of the monastery that is on view has also been thoroughly reorganised. A tour of the building now provides a fascinating glimpse of life in a medieval cloister: visitors can see the pharmacy, the kitchens, and the huge refectory with its vaulted ceiling. The main attraction, though, is the convent itself, and above all, the magnificent, entirely intact three-storey Gothic cloister. To one side is the tiny chapel of Sant Miquel, covered with striking murals from 1343 by Ferrer Bassa, a Catalan painter who was a student of Giotto. The Thyssen collection occupies a former dormitory on one of the upper floors (*see also chapter* **Museums**). *Disabled: wheelchair access to art collection only. Shop.*

Torre de Collserola

(93 406 93 54). FGC Av Tibidabo/bus 17, 22, 58, 73, N8; then Tramvia Blau and Funicular. **Open** (subject to confirmation) 11am-2pm, 4-8pm, Mon-Fri; 11am-8pm Sat, Sun, public holidays. **Admission** 550ptas. **No credit cards.**
Incredibly, this ride was closed to the public for some two years, with no information facilitated to poor souls waiting for the doors to open. It should, though, reopen in summer 1998. Norman Foster's 288-metre (800-ft) communications tower, built to take TV signals to the world in 1992, stands atop Collserola like some mutant insect poised to swoop on the city. A glass lift takes you to an observation deck 115m up. On a decent day, it's a staggering eagle's view of Barcelona: a couple of times a year, it's clear enough to see Mallorca, at other times, you might just see an endless haze. Free transport should be provided from the Funicular to the tower.

Les Corts

The rural origin of this barri can still be heard in the name, 'The Farmsheds', although there rarely seems much that's rustic in it any more. In among its apartment blocks, though, there is the area around **Plaça del Carme**, the surviving core of the old village of Les Corts, annexed to Barcelona in 1867, which can still evoke the atmosphere of an entirely different era.

For most Barcelona residents, though, Les Corts means **Fútbol Club Barcelona**, whose massive sports complex takes up a lot of the district's space. Curiously, the area around the stadium becomes the haunt of prostitutes, transvestites and cruising drivers when darkness falls.

Nou Camp

Avda Aristides Maillol, access 9 (93 330 94 11/ 93 496 36 00). Metro Collblanc/bus 15, 52, 53, 54, 56, 57, 75. **Open** *Nov-Mar* 10am-1pm, 3-6pm, Tue-Fri; 10am-2pm Sat, Sun, public holidays. Closed Mon. *April-Oct* 10am-1pm, 3-6pm, Mon-Sat; 10am-2pm public holidays. Closed Sun. **Admission** 475ptas; 350ptas under-13s; group discounts. **No credit cards.**
The largest football stadium in Europe, the shrine of Barcelona FC. First built in 1954, the Nou Camp has been added to since to accommodate ever more of the club's 100,000-plus members. It also contains the club museum, visitors to which can tour the stadium (*see also chapters* **Museums** *and* **Sport & Fitness**).

The Vila Olímpica

In 1986 Barcelona was elected Olympic City for 1992, and the whole population seemed to pour into the streets to celebrate. Then the job began of preparing to build what would soon be called the city's last *barri*, the Olympic Village, most ambitious of all the 1992 projects. It was a local cliché to say that Barcelona had turned its back to the sea, with industrial barriers that since the 1850s had effectively cut its citizens off from their abandoned, refuse-strewn beaches. Now, the plan was to open out.

Not since Cerdà or Gaudí has anyone had such an impact on the physiognomy of Barcelona as the architects Oriol Bohigas, Josep Martorell, long-time resident Scot David Mackay and Albert Puigdomènech, who were entrusted with the over-

There are many ways of taking the air along Barcelona's new seafront.

all design of the all-new district, to be built on reclaimed industrial land. Constructed in the space of two years, it was officially named *Nova Icària* to recall the utopian socialist community that briefly existed in this area in the last century, but the name has never stuck. As well as a range of services some 2,000 apartments were built, which it was hoped would provide low-cost housing once the athletes had vacated them after the Games, although harsh economic facts have since dictated otherwise.

Those who have paid the price and acquired flats in the village have at their disposal an impressive range of new leisure areas and seafront parks. Taken as a whole the project is spectacular. Cerdà's original concept for the Eixample was taken as an inspiration, with semi-open blocks built around services and garden areas. Every stop had to be pulled out to get the project completed for July 1992 – some sections, such as the skyscraper **Hotel Arts**, missed the date and were not inaugurated until a good while later. The final effect of the Vila, however, is bleak, although the waterway parallel to C/Moscou and the red brick of **Plaça Tirant lo Blanc** go some way to softening the harshness. The gateway buildings to the *barri*, all glass and stone, create a forbidding impression; there are few corner shops or cafés; the spiky metal pergolas on Avda Icària look like a grim parody of trees, and even the jokey sculpture in the **Parc de Carles I**, *David i Goliat*, leaves one with the feeling that this is one world in which the Goliaths usually slay the Davids. Complaints have also begun from residents about the poor quality

of some of the buildings, suggesting that corners were cut in the race to meet the deadline.

The effect is of a rather cold, un-Mediterranean suburb, but as in many suburbs its open spaces are colonised by cyclists and rollerbladers at weekends. Most successful part of the Vila by far is the **Port Olímpic**, the 743-mooring space leisure marina built from nothing since 1988, now packed with young (and older) crowds every weekend night throughout the year (*see chapters* **Restaurants** *and* **Nightlife**). During the day, it's also possible to hire sailing boats (*see chapter* **Sports & Fitness**).

Poble Nou, Clot, Sagrera

These three districts, north of the old city along the coast, once formed part of one large independent municipality, **Sant Martí de Provençals**. Originally a farming and fishing community, it was, like Sants, one of the areas chosen by manufacturers as they sought to expand, and became the centre of heavy industry of Barcelona, disputing with Sabadell the title of *la Manchester Catalana*.

This brought the usual problems – child labour, diseases, overcrowding, noise, smells, smoke – and the usual responses: cooperatives, unions, strikes and other conflicts. In 1897 it was absorbed into Barcelona, and split into three *barris*, Poble Nou, Clot and La Sagrera.

Poble Nou contained the greater part of Sant Martí's industry, and so continued to be a centre of radicalism and conflict. As a result it would pay dearly after 1939. Francoist troops carried out frequent executions in the *Camp de la Bota*, on the very northern edge of the city by the sea, where a sombre monument to the victims now stands. Then, in the 1960s, the *barri* began to change its character. Entire factories folded, moved to the Zona Franca or got out of the city altogether. The departure of the most historic, Can Girona, in 1992 marked the end of an epoch.

Today Poble Nou has become a laboratory for post-industrial experiments. The old factories have become schools, civic centres, workshop centres, open spaces for public use. Many artists have moved in, attracted by the greater working space and lower rents compared with Ciutat Vella. One entire former section of the barri is now the Vila Olimpica. From a hive of dirty industry it has become one of the city's gateways to the beach. In the middle of it there are still parts of the old Poble Nou, and even earlier Sant Martí: the lovely **Rambla del Poble Nou** compares favourably with the one in the city centre, while the area around **Plaça Prim** has kept its own village atmosphere. At night some old disused factory buildings have been recycled as clubs and music venues, the best known of which is **Zeleste**. And Poble Nou still has – looking distinctly odd amid some of the recent developments – Barcelona's oldest and most atmospheric cemetery, the **Cementiri de l'Est**.

The north of Poble Nou and the whole north side of the city along the coast is yet another area that is due to come under the attention of the planners. Centrepiece of the scheme is a plan to extend the Diagonal all the way to the sea from Plaça de les Glòries. This, however, is supposedly going to be underpinned by a very controversial project, the *Fòrum Universal de les Cultures*, the 'Universal Forum of Cultures', scheduled for 2004 (*see chapter* **Barcelona Today**). How much interest (and so money) this 1992-style festival will generate internationally, though, is as yet a very open question. Cynicism is rife, but for the moment most people are reserving judgment on the project – the feeling being that if this area can be rejuvenated even a little, the effort will be worthwhile. If it all comes to fruition, this will be another part of Barcelona that will change out of all recognition.

Clot and **La Sagrera**, both small *barris*, experienced much the same history as Poble Nou. Clot boasts one of the most intimate and friendly of Barcelona's food markets in the **Plaça Font i Sagué**, and the **Parc del Clot**, an old railway station-site transformed with a very effective waterfall design. Nearby is **Plaça de les Glòries** (*see page 49*), centrepiece of plans to upgrade this incorrigibly shabby area. In La Sagrera, meanwhile, the huge Pegaso truck factory has been recycled into a school and the **Parc Pegaso**, with a boating lake, and the area has one of the finest pieces of recent architecture in Barcelona, the **Pont de Calatrava** linking it to Poble Nou via C/Bac de Roda, about

Funfairs

Parc d'Atraccions de Montjuïc (Montjuïc Funfair)

Avda Miramar (93 441 70 24).
Metro Paral.lel, then Funicular de Montjuic/bus 61.
Open mid-Sept-23 June noon-9pm Sat, Sun, public holidays; *24 June-early Sept* 6pm-11pm Tue-Fri; 11am-midnight Sat, Sun, public holidays.
Admission *entrance only* 700ptas; individual rides approx 300-400ptas; pass with unlimited number of rides 2,000ptas; free under-3s. **Credit** AmEx, DC, MC, V. **Map B6**
The newer of the city's two funfairs, this one lacks the period charm of its Tibidabo competitor, but is still packed on warm nights. It also has an open-air theatre, where Spanish singing stars of the traditional variety exercise their ample lungs each summer. Best way to get there is by **Telefèric** to the top of the funfair, and then walk down (*see p59*).

Parc d'Atraccions de Tibidabo (Tibidabo Funfair)

Parc d'Atraccions del Tibidabo, Plaça del Tibidabo 3-4 (93 211 79 42). FGC Av Tibidabo/bus 17, 22, 58, 73, N8; then Tramvia Blau and Funicular to park.
Open end-Mar-early May noon-8pm Sat, Sun, public holidays; *Easter week* noon-8/9pm daily; *early May-June* 10am-6pm Wed-Fri; noon-9pm Sat, Sun, public holidays; *July-Aug* noon-10pm Mon-Thur, Sun; noon-1am Fri, Sat; *Sept* noon-8pm Mon-Fri; noon-10pm Sat, Sun, public holidays. *Oct* noon-8pm Sat, Sun, public holidays. **Admission** *entrance only* 1,000ptas; 600ptas over-65s; free under-5s. Pass & unlimited number of rides 2,400ptas; 600ptas under-5s. **Credit** AmEx, DC, MC, V.
The funfair at the top of Tibidabo opened in 1901, and some rides date from the twenties: the giant model plane that takes you slowly out into space on a revolving arm; the wonderfully silly, unfrightening *Castillo Misterioso* (Haunted Castle); and the **Museu d'Autòmates** (*see chapter* **Museums**). A major effort has been made since the 1980s to pep up the park, now dubbed *Tibidabo, la Muntanya Màgica* ('The Magic Mountain'), with dynamic new rides, such as a 'Tunnel of Terror'. Its greatest asset, though, is the soaring view, which adds to the impact of any ride. *See also chapter* **Children**.

the only new building to be popularly known by the name of its architect, Santiago Calatrava. La Sagrera has also been chosen as the site of a new main station – yet more renovation – for the high-speed train (TAV) linking Madrid with France, due to come into service early in the new century.

Horta, Guinardó, Vall d'Hebron

The area north of Gràcia, above and to the right of it on the map, is made up of contrasting *barris*, traditionally of rich and poor, the former in valleys and the latter on hillsides. Until the building of the **Túnel de la Rovira**, which begins near the Plaça d'Alfons el Savi, many of these areas were relatively isolated from the city.

Joined to Gràcia by the long Avda Mare de Déu de Montserrat, **Guinardó** above all means two big parks. One, the **Parc de les Aigües**, contains a fun sculpture of a buried submarine by Josep Maria Riera, and Barcelona's most eccentrically beautiful municipal district headquarters, the **Casa de les Altures**, a neo-Arabic fantasy from 1890. The other, **Parc del Guinardó**, is one of the city's older parks, opened in 1920. The *barri* of **El Carmel** has its own **Parc del Carmel**, but also the extraordinary **Parc de la Creueta del Coll**, an old quarry turned into a swimming pool. Escalators have been installed in some of the district's (very) steep streets to make climbing easier.

Incorporated into Barcelona in 1904, the aptly-named **Horta**, 'Market Garden', has managed to retain many rural features, and in particular some very well-preserved *masies* or traditional Catalan large farmhouses. The medieval **Can Cortada**, in C/Campoamor, shows at a glance that these patriarchal houses also served as fortresses, while **Can Mariner** in C/d'Horta is said to date back to 1050. Another is now a great restaurant, **Can Travi Nou**. Horta's abundant water supply once made it the great laundry centre for respectable Barcelona, with a whole community of *bugaderes* or washerwomen, as the open-air stone tanks along the lovely C/Aiguafreda attest.

The **Vall d'Hebron**, just above Horta along the Ronda de Dalt ring road on the flanks of Collserola. was one of the city's four main venues for Olympic events, and so has inherited centres for tennis, archery and cycling, at the **Velòdrom**. Around the sports venues there are some very striking examples of street sculpture, such as Joan Brossa's *Visual Poem* near the Velòdrom and Claes Oldenburg's very popular *Matches*, near the tennic centre. There is also a reconstruction of Josep Lluís Sert's **Pavelló de la República**. One of the area's most distinctive assets, though, is much older, the wonderful, semi-concealed **Parc del Laberint** from 1791, while for many locals the Vall d'Hebron means above all the **Ciutat Sanitària**, the largest hospital in the city.

Pavelló de la República

Avda Cardenal Vidal i Barraquer (93 428 54 57).
Metro Montbau/bus 45, 85, 102. **Open** 9am-8pm Mon-Fri. **Admission** free.
The Spanish Republic's pavilion for the 1937 Paris Exhibition, designed by Josep Lluis Sert, was the building in which Picasso's *Guernica* was first exhibited, and also an emblematic work of rationalist architecture. It was completely demolished after the exhibition, but in 1992, following the recreation of that other flagship building the **Pavelló Barcelona** (*see p57*), the controversial decision was taken to create a facsimile of Sert's building, even though it had no direct connections with Barcelona. The pavilion, austerely functionalist, now forms a curious pair with Oldenberg's *Matches* across the street. It houses a research library, but visitors can see the greater part of the building.

Sant Andreu & Nou Barris

Leaving Barcelona along the Meridiana, which like the Paral.lel derives its name from solar coordinates, **Sant Andreu** is to the right, and **Nou Barris** to the left. Sant Andreu was another of the industrial and working class hubs of the city. Much altered in the 1960s, it has seen three recent renovations: on Passeig Torres i Bages, at nos 91-105, Sert's **Casa Bloc**, one of the main contributions of the Republican era to Barcelona, has been restored. Just off the Meridiana a lovely wine press has been installed in Plaça d'en Xandri, and in Plaça Mossèn Clapés an ivy-covered modern pergola provides relief from the sun.

Nou Barris (Nine Neighbourhoods) has a different make-up. In the 1950s, when the flow of migration into the city was at its height, ramshackle settlements were built here, followed by tower blocks. Parks, sculptures and services have been provided to make it more humane – the **Can Dragó** sports complex – but this is still the poorest part of town.

The outer limits

As well as Barcelona proper, the *Area Metropolitana* is made up of a ring of smaller cities. Until this century, all were still rural, but beginning in the 1920s they have acquired industrial estates and large migrant populations from the rest of Spain, and in some cases become dormitory towns for Barcelona.

North of Barcelona, **Badalona** is famous above all for its basketball team, **Joventut**, which has won the European Basketball Cup, something that its rival FC Barcelona has never managed. **Santa Coloma de Gramenet** has a large Andalusian population and organises the **Feria de Abril**, a ten-day *fiesta* (*see chapter* **Barcelona by Season**). It is said to be visited by three million people, which might be an Andalusian exaggeration.

On some cars in the city you may sees the sticker *'L'H'*. This assertion of identity is a reminder that **L'Hospitalet de Llobregat**, just south west, is the second city of Catalonia, even though it is completely integrated into Barcelona's transport network. With a big Andalusian-born population, it is also Catalonia's centre for flamenco. There are several flamenco *peñas*, or clubs, among them **A.C.A.**, C/Clavells 2-4, (93 437 55 02), for dancing, and **Tertulia Flamenca**, C/Calderon de la Barca 12 (93 437 20 44), which runs guitar classes. A Flamenco festival is held on the Saturday before Christmas at **Teatre Joventut**, C/Joventut 10, when *villancicos*, strange Flamenco carols, are sung. Equally, Hospitalet has plenty of bars and restaurants with Andalusian specialities – try **Andalucia Chiquita**, Avda Isabel la Catòlica 89 (93 438 12 67). In summer, the area around C/Severo Ochoa becomes a huge outdoor café, offering tapas of all types at much more reasonable prices than in Barcelona.

Museums

As befits the city's character, Barcelona's museums cover a diversity of cultural interests – refined, eccentric, erotic and esoteric.

Barcelona has many fascinating, high-quality museums, but only a few that can really be considered world class. The primary reason is historical: while state capitals like London, Paris or Madrid have had responsibility for creating representative national collections, Barcelona, denied such political status, has pieced its museums together by other means. The fruit of private initiatives and individual energies, Barcelona's museums tend to be more partial than comprehensive, more idiosyncratic than conventional, full of innumerable wonderful objects, but with only a handful of recognised masterworks.

Barcelona awoke late to the pleasures of museum culture. Its first public museum – now the **Museu de Geologia** – was set up just before the 1888 Universal Exhibition, and many more were born following the 1929 Exhibition on Montjuïc. Only since the most recent restoration of the Catalan government, the Generalitat, in 1980 has there been a drive to create 'national' museums,

with the aim of representing present-day and historical art (**MACBA** and the **MNAC** respectively), Catalan history (the **Museu d'Història de Catalunya**) or Catalonia's scientific legacy, in the **Museu Nacional de la Ciència i la Tècnica** in Terrassa (*see page 225*).

Apart from these official projects, the richness of Barcelona's museums is largely the result of an impressive level of individual effort, especially in the early part of this century. Scientists and academics gathered material for research purposes (as in the older science museums). Wealthy specialised collectors like Rocamora (in the **Museu Tèxtil**) or Plandiura and Cambó (most of whose holdings are now in the **MNAC**) accumulated fine art and objects for pure pleasure, later ceding or selling them to public institutions. Equally, artists such as Picasso and Miró, late in life, favoured the city with legacies of their work, while the sculptor Frederic Marès was given an entire building not for his own work but to display an incredible

*Miró's subversive spirit lives on at the **Fundació Joan Miró**. See page 81.*

FRA ANGELICO DA FIESOLE

collection of sculpture and other oddities (the **Museu Frederic Marès**). In most cases these holdings have passed into public ownership, and especially to the City of Barcelona.

Barcelona has had the good sense to house its collections in the best of its architecture, from the **Museu d'Història de la Ciutat** (the city history museum), literally within the ruins of the Roman city, to the **Museu Picasso** in its Gothic palace and the **Museu Marítim** in the inspiring medieval shipyard of the Drassanes. Purpose-built and equally impressive are Josep Lluis Sert's impeccable **Fundació Miró**, and the luminous **MACBA** museum of contemporary art, designed by Richard Meier. The extraordinary settings of many museums can be sufficient compensation for the limitations they might have in other areas.

In contrast to these more spectacular examples, there's a rambling selection of private, small museums hidden away in the oddest of places, like the **Museu d'Autòmates** on Tibidabo, the **Museu del Perfum** with its thousands of scent bottles, the **Museu de Carrosses Fúnebres** with its old hearses or the **Museu del Calçat**, the shoe museum. Plans are under way to create a motorcycle museum in Poble Nou, while the pastrycooks' guild is concocting a chocolate museum, which hopefully will be 'interactive', if not a bit fattening.

Opening days, information & discounts
Most museums, and all public ones except the MACBA, are closed on Mondays. They are open, with Sunday hours, on most public holidays, but there are some holidays when virtually all museums close, namely: New Year's Day; 6 January; Christmas Day; 26 December. When it comes to working out what is being shown, most labelling is in Catalan, Spanish or both. Many museums, however, now try to provide some labelling in English, or offer free brochures or translations that can be consulted while touring the galleries. Some museums offer occasional guided tours, but, again, they are rarely in English. Many museums give discounts to holders of **Bus Turístic** tickets or the **Barcelona Card** (*see chapter* **Sightseeing**).

Gaudí & Miró

Casa-Museu Gaudí
Parc Güell, Carretera del Carmel (93 219 38 11). Bus 24, 25. **Open** *Nov-Feb* 10am-6pm, *Mar-Oct* 10am-7pm, daily. **Admission** 300ptas; group discounts. **No credit cards. Map E1**
One of few houses actually completed in the **Parc Güell**, this modest residence was designed by Gaudí's colleague Francesc Berenguer. Gaudí himself designed the graceful pergola in the garden, and lived here from 1906 to 1926, although in his final years he mostly slept in the workshop at the Sagrada Família. The simple interior, in tune with Gaudí's spartan religiosity, offers examples of the beautiful and outlandish furniture designed by him and his disciples such as Josep Maria Jujol. Also on show are memorabilia of Gaudí and his collaborators, and drawings for some of his wilder, unfinished projects.

Fra Angelico's Madonna of Humility, *part of the* **Col.lecció Thyssen Bornemisza**. *See page 84.*

Espai Gaudí
La Pedrera, C/Provença 261-265 (93 484 59 95). Metro Diagonal/bus 7, 16, 17, 18, 22, 24, 28. **Open** 10am-8pm daily; *mid-June-mid-Sept* also 9pm-1am Fri, Sat. *Guided tours* (in English) 6pm Mon, Wed, Fri; 11am Sat, Sun, public holidays. **Admission** 500ptas; 300ptas students under 25, over-65s; free under-12s. **No credit cards. Map D3**
In the large attic of Gaudí's **La Pedrera** (*see chapter* **Sightseeing**), beneath an inspiring sequence of brick arches, we find the city's only systematic overview of Gaudí's œuvre. Drawings, photographs, maquettes and audio-visual displays give a simple yet thorough idea of the master's creative evolution, with special emphasis on La Pedrera itself. The recently restored space was once used to hang residents' washing, and there even used to be some small apartments occupying the floor. Above is the building's marvellous roof terrace. On the lower floor the **Fundació Caixa de Catalunya**, which owns the building, has a space for temporary exhibitions (*see chapter* **Art Galleries**). *Shop.*

Fundació Joan Miró
Plaça Neptú, Parc de Montjuïc (93 329 19 08). Metro Paral.lel then Funicular de Montjuïc/bus 61. **Open** *Oct-June* 10am-7pm Tue, Wed, Fri, Sat; 10am-9.30pm Thur; 10am-2.30pm Sun, public holidays. *July-Sept* 10am-8pm Tue, Wed, Fri, Sat; 10am-9.30pm Thur; 10am-2.30pm Sun, public holidays. **Admission** 700ptas; 400ptas students, over-65s; group discounts. **Credit** (shop only) MC, V. **Map B5**
Joan Miró died in 1983, but not before creating the foundation that bears his name, which opened to the public in 1975. Designed by his friend Josep Lluis Sert, it is one of the world's great museum buildings: white walls, rustic tile floors, open airy galleries, and an elegant system of roof arches to let in natural light. Expanded in the 1980s, it houses a collection of over 200 paintings, 150 sculptures, all of Miró's graphic work, and some 5,000 drawings, though not all is shown at once. The permanent collection occupies over half of the exhibition space, while the galleries nearest the entrance are reserved for temporary shows. The basement **Espai 13** shows young contemporary artists. The collection begins with large paintings from Miró's late period, giving an idea of his trademark use of primary colours and simplified organic forms symbolising stars, the moon and women. There is also a huge tapestry. On the way to the sculpture gallery is the reconstructed *Mercury Fountain* by Miró's great friend Alexander Calder, originally built for the Spanish Republic's pavilion at the 1937 Paris Exhibition; a number of other Calder works, including a mobile, are dotted about the building. Next there are some of Miró's sculptures, made with great technical virtuosity, such as the bronze *Man and Woman in the Night* (1969). His transition from youth to maturity is seen in donations from his wife, Pilar Juncosa, and his dealer, Joan Prats. The **Sala Joan Prats** shows Miró as a cubist (*Street in Pedralbes*, 1917), naïve (*Portrait of a Young Girl*, 1919) or surrealist, culminating in the ominous *Man and Woman in Front of a Pile of Excrements* (1935). From the **Sala Pilar Juncosa** upstairs a ramp leads to newer paintings. Larger and simpler in form, many use thick black outlining, like *Catalan Peasant by Moonlight* (1968). The large *Sunbird* (1968) sculpture is of Carrara marble, and more sculpture is found on the roof terrace, with a fine view of the city. An excellent selection of drawings is found in a large windowless gallery. The collection ends with works by twentieth-century masters – Moore, Léger, Balthus, Ernst, Oldenburg – donated to the foundation. The Miró hosts many other activities, especially in contemporary music (*see chapter* **Music: Classical & Opera**) and has a good research library. *Café-restaurant. Children's theatre, weekends Oct-May. Concerts. Disabled: toilets, wheelchair access. Guided tours (12.30pm Sat, Sun). Library. Shop.*

The MNAC

In the late 1980s work began on creating the **Museu Nacional d'Art de Catalunya**, the National Museum of Catalan Art or MNAC, which is intended to bring together work from every era of the country's rich visual heritage up to the early twentieth century in one comprehensive museum, housed in the giant **Palau Nacional** on Montjuïc. This project still has years to run, but since the reopening of the Romanesque collections at the end of 1995, and the addition of the Gothic sections in 1997, some of its main elements have at last taken shape. When the renovation of the building is finally complete the idea is to install the rest of the national collections century by century, perhaps even moving the works of *Modernisme* up the hill from the **Museu d'Art Modern** in the Ciutadella (*see page 85*).

The museum's beginnings

In the first decades of this century a handful of art historians realised that scores of solitary churches in the Pyrenees were falling into ruin, and with them the extraordinary Romanesque mural paintings that adorned their interiors. Entire chunks of some buildings were 'saved' by private collectors to be set up elsewhere (as in the Cloisters in New York), but in Catalonia the laborious task was begun of removing murals intact from church apses and remounting them on new supports. Since the 1930s, the Palau Nacional has been the haven for this rare legacy, unique in the world, now shown in an updated installation from 1995.

The Palau looks down over the city from a regal perch on Montjuïc, presiding over the long boulevard leading up from Plaça Espanya. Although it may look like the baroque palace of some absolute monarch, it was built only as a 'temporary pavilion' for the 1929 Exhibition. If that clash of times and styles does not make it enough of a pastiche, then its renovation under architect Gae Aulenti, famous for the Musée d'Orsay in Paris, helps provide the ultimate postmodern touch. Underneath the dome is the **Sala Oval**, a vast hall that is used for occasional public and corporate events.

Some proud locals call the MNAC the 'Catalan Louvre', but its only resemblance with the Parisian museum is in square metres of galleries. Where the collection really stands out – the Romanesque murals – neither the Louvre nor any other museum can compare. Yet the MNAC makes no attempt to represent major international tendencies in art as truly great world museums like the Louvre, New York's Metropolitan or the National Gallery in London do. The Gothic section, however superb, exclusively presents Catalan art and its influences. Not even the large private collection left to Catalonia by the Cambó family, which includes a few non-Spanish masters (Tintoretto, Rubens, De la Tour) mixed in with national figures (Zurbarán and Goya), can make up for this.

The Romanesque murals

None of this takes anything away from the undisputed star of the MNAC, the Romanesque, a style long disdained as rough and primitive, lacking the perspective and masterly technique of Renaissance art. Curiously enough, if the

Romanesque is now admired, it is partly due to the avant-garde, with its search for abstract forms and eagerness to shake up classical harmony. Whatever our reasons for enjoying it today, however, the Catalan Romanesque was developed in other times and for quite other motives. As eleventh-century Christendom pushed the Moors southward out of Catalonia, small churches and monasteries were founded along the way, serving as beacons for beleaguered pilgrims and monks. Inside, unsophisticated depictions of the *Pantocrator* (Christ in Majesty), the Virgin, biblical stories and the sufferings of the saints served to instruct doubting villagers in the basics of the faith, turning church walls into a picture book.

The result is a series of images of extraordinary, timeless power. The new display comprises 21 sections in loose chronological order, with the murals set into free-standing wood supports or reconstructed church interiors. For each group there is a photo and model of the original church, and a map of its location. One of the highlights is the tremendous *Crist de Taüll*, from the twelfth-century church of Sant Climent de Taüll in the Pyrenean valley of Boí, in section five. The massive figure of the Pantocrator holds a book with the words *Ego Sum Lux Mundi*, 'I am the Light of the World'. On the left, near a smaller apse, there is a figure of a monk, meditating. Section seven reveals another treasure, from the church of Santa Maria de Taüll (in the same village as Sant Climent), with an apse of the Epiphany and Three Kings and a wall of the Last Judgement, packed with images of demons and the unrighteous being tossed into the flames of Purgatory. On some columns original 'graffiti' has been preserved, scratchings – probably by monks – of animals, crosses and labyrinths.

Other sections, including sculptures and carvings, focus thematically on dramatic angels, strange seraphim with wings covered in eyes (from the apse of Santa Maria d'Aneu, *left*), the Lamb of God, or the transition from the expressionless early figures of the Virgin and Child to the more tender renderings that emerged later. After 1200 (section 13) greater fluidity and sophistication was evident in painting, with details personalised for each particular figure, their eyes more alive. The last section, 21, has some non-Catalan murals that were saved from the burning-out during the Civil War of the monastery of Sigena in Aragon, and show a remarkable mix of thirteenth-century influences from across Europe.

Barcelona viewed from the **MNAC**.

Gothic & Renaissance galleries

The Gothic collection is also impressive, although the strong Italian and Flemish influences that can be traced in the different works make it clear that the styles on display were not unique to Catalonia. Visitors can follow the evolution of Catalan Gothic painting, with many great altarpieces on wood panels and alabaster sculptures pulled out of parish churches in Barcelona itself. One section even points up how anti-Semitic iconography made its way into some painting (section three).

The highlights are the works of the indisputable Catalan masters from the Golden Age, such as Bernat Martorell (section 11), and the tremendously subtle work of Jaume Huguet (section 12), including a series dedicated to St Vincent (*see page 14*) and a lovely depiction of *St George Escorting a Princess*. The tail-end of the Gothic galleries are being used to show the odd Renaissance and baroque piece, while the Cambó Collection, with an international mix of works from the Gothic era up to the eighteenth century, has been tucked downstairs. High-quality temporary shows are presented at the MNAC, including some on the Spanish baroque with works lent by the Prado, and others on early photography. Guidebooks and extensive labelling are provided in English.

Museu Nacional d'Art de Catalunya
Palau Nacional, Parc de Montjuïc (93 423 71 99). Metro Espanya/bus 13, 55, 61. **Open** 10am-7pm Tue, Wed, Fri, Sat; 10am-9pm Thur; 10am-2.30pm Sun, public holidays. **Admission** 800ptas; 400ptas under-21s, over-65s; *temporary exhibitions* prices vary; *combined ticket* 900ptas, 30% discount under-21s, over-65s. Group discounts (by appointment). **Credit** (shop only) V. **Map A5**
Café. Disabled: toilets, wheelchair access. Shop.

Nice museum, shame about the pictures? Richard Meier's **MACBA**.

Museu del Temple Expiatori de la Sagrada Família

C/Mallorca 401 (93 455 02 47). Metro Sagrada Família/bus all routes to Sagrada Família.
Open *Oct-Feb* 9am-6pm daily; *Mar, Sept* 9am-7pm daily; *Apr-Aug* 9am-8pm daily. **Admission** 800ptas; 550ptas groups with guide; free under-10s. *Lifts to spires* 200ptas.
Credit (shop only) MC, V. **Map F3**

In the crypt of the Sagrada Família is a rather piecemeal display dedicated to the design and ongoing construction of Gaudí's interminable cathedral. Perhaps the most fascinating discovery is that Gaudí's drawings for the project were largely creative expressions of his ideas, rather than detailed plans that could be followed. Photos trace the long history of the temple, while models and decorative details bring the construction process closer to visitors. There are also images from other Gaudí buildings. *See also chapter* **Sightseeing**.

Art museums

Col.lecció Thyssen-Bornemisza – Monestir de Pedralbes

Baixada del Monestir 9 (93 280 14 34).
FGC Reina Elisenda/bus 22, 63, 64, 75, 114. **Open** 10am-2pm Tue-Sun. **Admission** *Monastery* 400ptas; 250ptas students under 25, over-65s; group discounts; free under-12s, first Sun of month. *Col.lecció Thyssen* 400ptas; 250ptas students under 25, over-65s; group discounts. *Combined ticket* 700ptas; 400ptas students under 25, over-65s; group discounts; free under-12s.
Credit (shop only) AmEx, MC, V.

The Pedralbes Monastery was a fascinating place to visit even before the Thyssen Collection moved in, and together they make medieval religious life all the more vivid. Much the greater part of Baron Hans-Heinrich von Thyssen-Bornemisza's collection, acquired for Spain in 1993, is in the Museo Thyssen in Madrid, but the 90 works brought to Barcelona were chosen to harmonise with the setting, with religious images such as the Virgin predominant. Occupying

a former nuns' dormitory on one side of the convent's magnificent fourteenth-century cloister, the collection specialises in Italian painting from the thirteenth through to the seventeenth century – an important influence in Catalonia – and European baroque works. There is one true masterpiece, Fra Angelico's *Madonna of Humility*, painted in Florence in the 1430s. Other notable works include a small *Nativity* (c1325) by Thaddeus Gaddi, and a subtle *Madonna and Child* by Titian (1545). German painting is well represented, with a series of saints by Lucas Cranach the Older. There is also a Rubens *Virgin with Child* from 1618. Spanish baroque works include a Velázquez portrait of Mariana of Austria, Queen of Spain (1655-7). Other thematically related paintings are regularly lent from Madrid. Still a convent of the 'Poor Clares', the monastery, with its enormous three-floor Gothic cloister, is one of the best-preserved in Europe. In one of the day cells there are extraordinary mural paintings attributed to the Catalan master Ferrer Bassa (1346), influenced by the school of Siena. It's also possible to visit the chapterhouse, refectory and many other parts of the convent, for which *see chapter* **Sightseeing**.
Disabled: wheelchair access to art collection only. Shop.

Museu d'Art Contemporani de Barcelona (MACBA)

Plaça dels Àngels 1 (93 412 08 10).
Metro Catalunya/bus all routes to Plaça Catalunya.
Open noon-8pm Mon, Wed-Fri; 10am-8pm Sat; 10am-1pm Sun, public holidays. *Guided tours* 6pm Mon, Wed-Sat; 11am Sun; groups 10am-noon (by appointment).
Closed Tue. Admission 700ptas; 500ptas students under 25, over-65s; free under-16s. *Wed only* 350ptas.
Credit AmEx (shop only), MC, V. **Map C4**

The pristine white MACBA, obstreperously landed in the middle of the old Raval, is more than a museum: it is the shiniest symbol of Barcelona's ongoing project to revitalise this working-class quarter with culture. While all around it the city is tearing down large tracts of housing, speculators begin to pounce on what's left, and this contemporary art museum, designed by internationally fashionable US architect Richard Meier and opened in late 1995, stands out on its own, as if dropped from the sky. Meier has associated the whiteness of the building with Mediterranean light and sensibility, although this doesn't explain why he has used the same white in Des Moines, Iowa, and the City Hall in The Hague as well. Like many of his buildings, the MACBA has a perky geometry: horizontal sun screens break the glass façade; the entrance, marked by a jutting balcony, is like a constructivist puzzle. Most Barcelonans were happy with the results until Frank Gehry's stunning Guggenheim Museum in Bilbao came along to awaken all their old insecurities about cultural inferiority, amplified by general dissatisfaction with the MACBA's content. One of the most glaring problems is its permanent collection, dominated by an inexplicably poor selection of work by name artists who seem to shine everywhere but here, almost as if Barcelona had set out to put together a collection of leftovers. Thirsty for the blood of someone who could be held responsible for such mediocrity, Barcelona's Leviathan-like art bureaucracy has already devoured two directors (one just before the MACBA opened, the other in early 1998). Those who have been waiting decades for a contemporary art showcase in Barcelona have been left to grind their teeth, while the MACBA turns up constantly in the media as a subject of debate, backbiting and polemic.

Like the Raval's other major cultural acquistion, the neighbouring **CCCB** (*see chapter* **Art Galleries**), the MACBA has a lot of excess space, with an entrance hall, lobby, interminable hallways and long ramps all eventually leading to the shows, which are hidden away behind free-standing walls. The museum normally shows a part of its permanent collection in combination with temporary exhibits. Since the MNAC and Museu d'Art Modern are supposed to take us up to the Civil War, the MACBA begins with the 1940s, although earlier works by Paul Klee, Alexander Calder and Catalan sculptor Leandre Cristòfol can be seen. The work from the 1940s to the 1960s is mostly painting, with Spanish artists of the *art informel* style (Millares, Tàpies, Guinovart), a sister movement to abstract expressionism. Holdings from the last 30 years feature more international artists, with examples of work by Rauschenberg, Beuys, Anselm Kiefer, Mario Merz, Christian Boltanski and photographer Hannah Collins complementing a Spanish collection that includes a thorough review of Catalan painting (Ràfols Casamada, Xavier Grau, Miquel Barceló) and Spanish sculpture (Miquel Navarro, Susana Solano, Sergi Aguilar), with fine Basque abstract work (Oteiza and Chillida). Temporary shows are a real mixed bag, from small solo shows and collaborations with other museums to the MACBA's own productions. The museum also has a very good gift-and-design shop (*see also* chapter **Shopping**) and a website at *www.macba.es*.
Café-restaurant. Disabled: toilets, wheelchair access. Library. Shop.

Museu d'Art Modern

Edifici del Parlament, Parc de la Ciutadella (93 319 57 28). Metro Ciutadella/bus 14, 39, 40, 41, 42, 51, 141. **Open** 10am-7pm Tue-Sat; 10am-2.30pm Sun. *Guided tours* by appointment. **Admission** 500ptas; 350ptas students under 25, over-65s; group discounts; free under-7s; *temporary exhibitions* 400ptas; 300ptas students under 25, over-65s; *combined ticket* 600ptas, 550ptas students under 25, over-65s. **Credit** (shop only) V. **Map E5**
This museum, which shares one of the eighteenth-century citadel buildings in the Parc de la Ciutadella with the Catalan Parliament, should not be confused with museums that go by similar names in other countries. Its theme is not contemporary art, but Catalan art from the early nineteenth century to the 1930s. It is therefore the prime showcase for the great burst of creativity – leaving aside architecture – associated with *Modernisme*, the Catalan art nouveau. It is now administratively part of the MNAC, and it could end up being moved into the Palau Nacional, but it's hard to imagine it all fitting. The museum galleries begin with the Romantic painter Marià Fortuny, whose liking for oriental exoticism

and ostentatious detail led to his *Odalisque* (1861) and telling *La Vicaria* (1870). After the realism of the Olot school (the Vayreda brothers) there is impressionist-influenced work by the main *Modernista* painters, Ramon Casas and Santiago Rusiñol. Casas' beloved image of himself and Quatre Gats-owner Pere Romeu riding tandem gives a vivid sense of the vibrant spirit of the close of the last century, and there is a large collection of drawings and graphic work. *Modernisme* always sought not to discriminate between fine and decorative arts, and a major attraction here is the superb selection of furniture and decorative objects in different media, indicating as well as can the movement's painting and architecture the creative freedom and new-found wealth of the time. There is masterful work by Gaudí and Puig i Cadafalch, and exquisite marquetry tables and other pieces by the superb furniture-maker Gaspar Homar. Figurative sculpture is represented by Josep Llimona and the neoclassicist Josep Clarà, who formerly had his own museum in the city. In painting, the collection carries on with the dark, intense gypsy portraits by Isidre Nonell, which influenced Picasso's Blue Period, the blurry, lavishly coloured landscapes of Joaquim Mir, and the eerie tones of Josep de Togores. The collection trickles off at the end with just two paintings by Dalí – one a 1925 portrait of his father – and work by two avant-garde sculptors from the 1930s, Julio Gonzalez and Pau Gargallo. González' welded head (*The Tunnel*, 1932-3) points to the roots of contemporary abstract sculpture. There is also a gallery for very well-done temporary exhibits corresponding to the museum's period.
Disabled: toilets, wheelchair access. Shop.

Museu Diocesà (Diocesan Museum)

Avda de la Catedral, Pla de la Seu (93 315 22 13). Metro Jaume I/bus 17, 19, 40, 45. **Open** 10am-2pm, 4-8pm Tue-Sat; 10am-2pm Sun. **Closed** sometimes Aug. **Admission** 200ptas (varies, depending on exhibition). **Credit** (shop only) V. **Map D5**
The best of Catalan religious art is in the MNAC on Montjuïc, but this space run by the Diocese of Barcelona has a few strong works, such as a group of sculpted Virgins on the top floor, and Gothic altarpieces by Bernat Martorell and other medieval masters. There are also temporary exhibits. The building itself is worth seeing, though, as it includes the Pia Almoina, a former alms house, which is stuck on to a Renaissance canon's residence that, in turn, was built inside a Roman tower. The architectural mishmash, so typical of Barcelona, is topped off by the effects of a recent renovation.
Shop.

Museu Frederic Marès

Plaça Sant Iu 5-6 (93 310 58 00). Metro Jaume I/ bus 17, 19, 40, 45. **Open** 10am-5pm Tue-Sat; 10am-2pm Sun. *Guided tours* by appointment. **Admission** 300ptas; 150ptas students under 25, under-12s; 250ptas groups (by appointment). **No credit cards. Map D5**
The son of a customs agent in Port Bou on the French border, Frederic Marès possibly began his career in the arts by 'collecting' from travellers unable to pay import duties in cash. Trained as a sculptor (his figurative bronzes and marbles are found all over Barcelona), Marès dedicated his 97-year-long life to gathering every imaginable type of object. Created for him by the city in the 1940s, his museum contains his personal collection of religious sculpture, and the stunning 'Sentimental Museum'. Legions of sculpted virgins, crucifixions and saints on the lower floors (the first floor Romanesque, the upper Gothic, Renaissance and baroque) testify to an intense interest in the history of his own profession. Quantity reigns over quality, although there is work by the odd master (Alejo de Vahía, Room 21). Marès even collected clothing for saints. The **Museu Sentimental** is on the top floor, an extraordinary testimony to a collector's kleptomania, with everything from iron keys, ceramics and old carpenters' tools to Havana cigar labels, pocket watches, early Daguerrotypes, Torah pointers... Especially beautiful

The Picasso Museum

When his father José Ruiz Blasco was hired to teach at Barcelona's art school in 1895, 13-year-old Pablo Ruiz Picasso was a budding young artist whose drawings suggested a firm academic training. By the time of his definitive move to Paris in 1904 he had already painted his great-est Blue Period works, and was on his way to becoming the most acclaimed artist of the century. Barcelona's Picasso Museum is testimony to these vital formative years, spent in the city in the company of Catalonia's nascent avant-garde.

The museum arose out of a donation to the city by Picasso's private secretary and friend Jaume Sabartès, complemented by holdings from the artist's family. It graces a row of elegant medieval courtyard-palaces on C/Montcada, beginning with the mostly fifteenth-century Palau Berenguer d'Aguilar, with a courtyard almost certainly by Marc Safont, architect of the patios of the Generalitat. Since it first opened in 1963 it has expanded to incorporate two adjacent mansions, the later but also impressive Palaus Meca and Castellet, each with its own courtyard. In order to add another 3,500sq m the City of Barcelona has now begun further extensions in the next pair of buildings along the street (the baroque Casa Mauris and the early Gothic Casa Finestres, Nos. 21 and 23) and into a large courtyard behind them, which should be ready by late 1999. All to show as much of the collection of over 3,000 paintings, drawings and other work as possible, complemented by temporary shows on early twentieth-century masters and Picasso-related themes.

Two things stand out in the museum. The seamless presentation of Picasso's development from 1890 to 1904, from schoolboy doodlings – he was a constant, and very skilful, doodler – to art school copies to intense innovations in blue, is unbeatable. Then, in a flash, one jumps to a gallery of mature cubist paintings from 1917, and

---

is the *Sala Femenina*, in a room once belonging to the medieval royal palace: fans, sewing scissors, nutcrackers, and perfume flasks give a charming image of nineteenth-century bourgeois taste. There is a great summer café in the museum's medieval courtyard (*see chapter* **Cafés & Bars**). *Café (mid-Mar-late Sept).* Shop.

Decorative & performing arts

Museu de Ceràmica/
Museu de les Arts Decoratives

Palau Reial de Pedralbes, Avda Diagonal 686 (Ceràmica 93 280 16 21/Arts Decoratives 93 280 5024). Metro Palau Reial/bus 7, 67, 68, 74, 75. **Open** 10am-3pm Tue-Sun. **Admission** *both museums* 700ptas; 400ptas students under 25, over-65s; free under-12s; *one museum* 400ptas; 250ptas students under 25, over-65s. **No credit cards**.
The Palau Reial on the Diagonal was originally built as a residence for the family of Gaudi's patron Eusebi Güell, and in one corner of the gardens is a famous iron gate designed by Gaudi. It became a royal palace and was greatly expanded

in the 1920s, when it was ceded to King Alfonso XIII. The building briefly returned to royal use in 1997, when it was used for the wedding banquet of King Juan Carlos' daughter Cristina. The rest of the time the palace houses two separate museums, which can both be entered on the one ticket. The **Ceramics Museum** has a fine collection of Spanish historical ceramics, organised by regional styles, which vary sharply. Especially beautiful are the medieval dishes, mostly for everyday use, particularly those from Manises near Valencia. Catalan holdings include two wonderful tile murals from the early eighteenth century: *la xocolatada* depicts chocolate-drinking at a garden party, while the other gives a graphic image of a chaotic baroque bullfight. An entire section is dedicated to the famous Valencian manufactury of Alcora, which from 1727 to 1895 satisfied the tastes of the world's aristocracies. Upstairs, along with temporary shows, there is a fine collection of twentieth-century ceramics: highlights include the refined simplicity of Catalan master Josep Llorens Artigas, and excellent work by Picasso and Miró. The **Decorative Arts Museum** occupies the other wing of the building. The palace's original painted walls provide a handsome setting for furniture and decorative objects from completes the hopscotch with a leap to oils from the late 1950s, based on Velázquez' famous *Las Meninas* in the Prado in Madrid. This veritable *vistus interruptus* could leave the visitor itchy for more. The culmination of Picasso's early genius in *Les Demoiselles d'Avignon* and the first cubist paintings (1907 and beyond) is completely absent.

So, there's nothing one can do but accept the collection's gaps as twists of history, and enjoy its many strengths. After some wonderful ceramics – donated by his widow Jacqueline – the chronological galleries begin in 1890, when young Pablo still lived in his native Málaga, sketching pigeons like his father (who painted them incessantly). Already at the age of nine his drawing was sure and inventive. After he had painted some perceptive portraits of old people and sailors in La Coruña (1895), Picasso and his family came to Barcelona, living on the nearby C/de la Mercè. Work from Picasso's student years includes portraits of his family, life drawings and landscapes, including some of Barceloneta beach. Pressured by his father to attract patrons, he did some large realist paintings, one of which, *Science and Charity* (1897), won a prize in Madrid. Only in the late 1890s did he begin to sign his bawdy nightlife scenes and caricatures with Picasso, his mother's last name. There are fascinating sketches of Barcelona 'decadents', letters-in-cartoons done on his first trip to Paris, and his menu cover from Els Quatre Gats, his first paid commission.

As he gained in artistic independence, his taste for marginal types intensified, with perversely

beautiful paintings like *Margot* and *La Nana* (1901). The intense Blue Period is well represented by *El Loco* (1904) and *Dead Woman* (1903), as well as an azure oil of Barcelona rooftops recently donated by the Picasso heirs. The chronology is broken with the works from 1917 – the last extended period Picasso spent in Barcelona – including one titled *Passeig de Colom*, before you arrive at the many works inspired by *Las Meninas* and a series done in Cannes in 1957. Finally, the museum has an extensive collection of his impressive limited-edition lithographs and lino cuts.

Museu Picasso

C/Montcada 15-19 (93 319 63 10). Metro Jaume I/ bus 17, 40, 45. **Open** 10am-7.30pm Tue-Sat, public holidays; 10am-3pm Sun. **Admission** *museum only* 600ptas; 300ptas students under 25, over-65s; 225ptas student groups (by appointment); *temporary exhibitions* prices vary; free under-12s, 1st Sun of month; 3-7.30pm Wed for groups with appointment. **Credit** (shop only) AmEx, MC, V. **Map E5**
Café-restaurant. Library. Shop.

---

the Middle Ages onward, with styles from Gothic through to romanticism and Catalan *Modernisme*, ending with art deco. Quality is high, although not a lot is shown at any one time, even though the museum has large, first-class holdings of decorative clocks, Catalan glasswork and other items. Visitors can also look down into the palace's sumptuously decorated oval throne room. One section is dedicated to Catalan industrial design in the twentieth century, a gesture to Barcelona's ambitious design community. Key works from the 1950s and 1960s include Antoni Bonet's BKF chair, and designs by Barba Corsini and André Ricard. The 1980s are represented by Oscar Tusquets and Javier Mariscal's 'duplex stool'. In a building in the gardens there is a collection of old carriages, which has been closed to visitors for some time. *Disabled: wheelchair access to Decorative Arts Museum only. Shop.*

Museu del Calçat (Shoe Museum)

Plaça Sant Felip Neri 5 (93 301 45 33). Metro Liceu, Jaume I/bus 17, 19, 40, 45. **Open** 11am-2pm Tue-Sun. **Admission** 200ptas; 100ptas over-65s; free under-7s; group discounts. **No credit cards. Map D5**

Run by a shoemakers' guild founded in 1203, this museum is in a tiny building on one of the city's most enigmatic squares. On view is only a small part of a collection that goes from original Roman sandals to present-day footwear: especially fine are the women's embroidered satin dress shoes from the last century. Shoes worn by the famous include pairs donated by cellist Pau Casals and celebrated Catalan clown Charlie Rivel, or the boots of the first Catalan on Everest. There's also seamless footwear, traditional shepherds' shoes, baby booties, and an enormous shoe made from the mould for the Columbus statue at the foot (where else) of La Rambla.

Museu de la Música

Avda Diagonal 373 (93 416 11 57). Metro Diagonal/ bus all routes to Passeig de Gràcia/Diagonal. **Open** *mid-June-mid-Sept* 10am-2pm Tue-Sun; *mid-Sept-mid-June* 10am-2pm Tue, Thur, Thur-Sun; 10am-8pm Wed. **Admission** 400ptas; 250ptas students under 25, over-65s; free under-12s. **No credit cards. Map D5**

This museum occupies the beautiful *Modernista* Casa Vidal-Quadras, completed by Puig i Cadafalch on the basis of an existing building in 1902. Its collection does a good job contrasting European examples of string, wind, keyboard and percussion instruments with parallel versions from other continents. An excellent example is a display linking African percussion with modern jazz drumming, while the cross-cultural mix of instruments as diverse as wood flutes, bagpipes and sitars is fascinating. Particularly well presented is the modern classical guitar, from its origins 200 years ago in Andalusia. The collection also testifies to an instrument industry that has been thriving in Barcelona for over 200 years. Temporary shows are presented on the top floor. *Shop.*

Museu Tèxtil i de la Indumentària (Textile & Fashion Museum)

C/Montcada 12 (93 319 76 03/93 310 45 16).
Metro Jaume I/bus 17, 40, 45. **Open** 10am-8pm Tue-Sat; 10am-3pm Sun. *Guided tours* by appointment.
Admission 400ptas; 250ptas students under 25, over-65s; group discounts; free under-12s, 3-8pm 1st Sat, 3rd Wed of month. *Combined ticket with Museu Barbier-Mueller* 700ptas; 400ptas students under 25.
Credit (shop only) AmEx, MC, V. **Map D5**
Even if clothing is not your thing, the sight of café tables might draw you into the handsome courtyard of this medieval palace, just across from the Picasso Museum. It occupies two side-by-side buildings, the Palau Nadal and the Palau dels Marquesos de Llió; the latter still retains some of its thirteenth-century wooden ceilings. It brings together items from a number of collections, including medieval Hispano-Arab textiles and the city's lace and embroidery collection. The real highlight is the collection of historical clothing – from baroque to twentieth century – that Manuel Rocamora donated in the 1960s, one of the finest of its kind. The museum has also received donations from Spanish designer Cristóbal Balenciaga, famous for the 1958 'baby doll' dress, just the thing for breakfast at Tiffany's. Contemporary textile art and a smart selection of small temporary shows are offered on the ground floor. For the very popular café, *see chapter* **Cafés & Bars**.
Café-restaurant. Shop.

History & Archaeology

Museu d'Arqueologia de Catalunya

Passeig de Santa Madrona 39-41 (93 423 21 49/ 93 423 56 01). Metro Poble Sec/bus 55. **Open** 9.30am-7pm Tue-Sat; 10am-2.30pm Sun. Closed public holidays.
Admission Tue-Sat 200ptas; free students, over-65s, under-16s. **No credit cards. Map B5**
In the attractively renovated Palace of Decorative Arts, built for the 1929 Exhibition on Montjuïc, this is one of the city's better scientific museums, and the art deco centre section has been imaginatively refurbished. With pieces mostly from digs in Catalonia and Mediterranean Spain, it begins with the palaeolithic period, and moves on through subsequent eras, including relics of Greek, Punic, Roman and Visigoth colonisers, taking us right up to the early Middle Ages. There are curious objects related to early metallurgy, along with models of neolithic and Iron Age burial sites. A few galleries are dedicated to the Mallorcan Talaiotic cave culture, and the Carthaginian presence in the Balearics is recalled by lovely terracotta goddesses and beautiful jewellery from a huge dig on Ibiza. A large gallery is dedicated to Empúries, a source of extensive holdings (for Empúries itself, *see chapter* **Beaches**). Roman work includes original floor mosaics (curators argue these are better preserved when walked upon), and a reconstructed Pompeian palace room. The centre section has monumental Greek and Roman pieces, including a sarcophagus showing the rape of Proserpine, while the exterior rotunda is dedicated to the native Iberians. Upstairs there are Roman funerary stiles and fine mosaics, one of a woman wearing a grotesque comic mask. For some reason an enormous statue of a sexually charged Priapus

cannot be visited up close (it was formerly hidden from view completely, and they are still unsure what to do with it). The museum also hosts occasional temporary shows.
Disabled: toilets, wheelchair access. Library. Shop.

Museu Barbier-Mueller d'Art Precolombí

C/Montcada 14 (93 319 76 03). Metro Jaume I/bus 17, 19, 40, 45. **Open** 10am-8pm Tue-Sat; 10am-3pm Sun.
Admission 500ptas; 250ptas students under 25; group discounts. *Combined ticket with Museu Tèxtil* 700ptas; 400ptas students under 25. **No credit cards. Map D5**
Though Columbus' famed voyage took place in 1492, the Barbier-Mueller Museum makes clear that the 'pre-Columbian' era extended well beyond that date, as the subjugation of indigenous cultures by the *conquistadores* lasted for decades. In 1996 the Barbier-Mueller museum in Geneva agreed to show around 170 pieces from its superb collection of ancient American art in Barcelona, meticulously selected and displayed on a rotating basis. To house them, the city spent several million pesetas renovating a medieval palace across from the Picasso Museum. A minus is its overly theatrical lighting, a cliché of 'tribal art' presentation, but nevertheless the museum treats us to many extraordinary pieces from Mexico, Central America, the Andes and the lower Amazon, some of which date as far back as the second millennium BC. Among its treasures are a large, hollow, ceramic female figure from the pre-Mayan Olmec period, an expressive sculpture of the fire god Hueheuteotl (Veracruz, AD500-800) and rare holdings from the little-known Caviana and Marajó islands at the mouth of the Amazon, stylistically close to present-day Brazilian indigenous patterns. Gold and silver objects from Peru and Bolivia complete this good short introduction to pre-Columbian art. The museum also has a very good bookshop.
Café. Shop.

Museu Egipci (Egyptian Museum)

Rambla Catalunya 57-59 (93 488 01 88).
Metro Passeig de Gràcia/bus 7, 16, 17, 22, 24, 28.
Open 10am-2pm, 4-8pm Mon-Sat; 10am-2pm Sun.
Admission 700ptas; 500ptas under-15s, students, over-65s. **Credit** (shop only) MC, V. **Map D3**
This small private museum is due to move into more spacious premises a few blocks away early in 1999 (C/València 284, between Passeig de Gràcia and C/Pau Claris). It is run by the Fundació Arqueològica Clos, whose founder Jordi Clos owns a hotel chain that includes the nearby Hotel Claris (*see chapter* **Accommodation**). Clos has collected Egyptian artefacts since he was a young man, and his foundation is reputable enough to do official digs in Egypt. Almost all finds from these excavations stay in Egypt, but Clos also buys pieces from auctions and museums. Most of the objects, from pre-dynastic ceramics (3,500 BC) to a sarcophagus from the 'decadent' Ptolemaic period (third century BC), are related to burial rites. A small ancient-empire carved goods carrier and a lower-epoch mummy are among the most important works, and there are also dramatic re-creations of tombs, beautiful examples of ornamentation and impressive x-rays of mummified animals. The new space will house temporary exhibits organised in collaboration with major world museums in the field, and there will be a terrace café.
Library. Shop.

Museu Etnològic

Passeig de Santa Madrona (93 424 68 07).
Metro Poble Sec/bus 55. **Open** 10am-7pm Tue, Thur; 10am-2pm Wed, Fri-Sun, public holidays. **Admission** 400ptas; 250ptas students under 25, over-65s; group discounts; free under-12s. **No credit cards. Map A5**
Extensive holdings from non-European cultures, totalling over 30,000 pieces, are shown in Montjuïc's Ethnology Museum on a rotating basis. Shows change every few years, and are designed to give an idea of different cultures and not just display objects out of context. The museum is especially

A new port of call by the harbourside, the **Museu d'Història de Catalunya**.

strong in certain, very varied areas: pre-Columbian artefacts, Afghan carpets, religious sculpture from India and Nepal, Australian Aboriginal bark painting. Part of the first floor has been made into a permanent space for the top-notch collection of Japanese *Mingei*, or popular crafts, and Japan-related temporary shows and activities are also organised. *Library. Shop.*

Museu d'Història de Catalunya

Plaça Pau Vila 3 (93 225 47 00). Metro Barceloneta/ bus all routes to Barceloneta. **Open** 10am-7pm Tue-Thur; 10am-8pm Fri, Sat; 10am-2.30pm Sun. *Guided tours* by appointment. **Admission** 500ptas; 250ptas under-15s, students under 25, over-65s; group discounts; free under-7s, disabled. Temporary exhibitions 500ptas; 250ptas under-25s, over-65s; *combined ticket* 800ptas.
Credit (shop only) MC, V. **Map D6**

The only example in Barcelona of a museum that consciously sets out to explain something thoroughly from start to finish opened in 1996 in the Palau de Mar by the old port. The relative shortage of museum-quality objects inside has led detractors to call it a theme park, but its visually dynamic displays offer a pretty complete overview of Catalan history from pre-history to the restoration of the Generalitat in the 1980s. All kinds of different materials are used to keep us alert, in state-of-the-art museum fashion – texts, photos, real objects, reproductions, videos, animated models and re-creations of domestic scenes. There are hands-on exhibits, such as a waterwheel and wearable armour. The eight sections are given titles like 'Roots', 'Birth of a Nation' (the consolidation of Catalonia in the Middle Ages) and so on, coming into the contemporary era with 'The Electric Years', including the Civil War (with a recreated bomb shelter), and 'Undoing and New Beginnings' on life under Franco and beyond. Large temporary shows hosted by the museum deal with just about everything imaginable, from the history of the Liceu opera to the presence of the Moors in medieval Catalonia. Despite being a Generalitat project, the museum manages to avoid overbearing flag-waving. It is labelled in Catalan, but a guidebook is available in English. A *Mediateca*

on an upstairs floor has photos, texts and videos on screen, consultable in English, and the top-floor restaurant has an unbeatable view over the Port and Barceloneta. *Café-restaurant. Shop.*

Museu d'Història de la Ciutat

Plaça del Rei (93 315 11 11). Metro Jaume I/ bus 17, 40, 45. **Open** *1 Oct-30 June* 10am-2pm, 4-8pm, Tue-Sat; 10am-2pm Sun. *1 July-30 Sept* 10am-8pm Tue-Sat; 10am-2pm Sun, public holidays. *Guided tours* by appointment. **Admission** 500ptas; 300ptas under-16s, students under 25, over-65s; group discounts; free under-12s, 3-8pm 1st Sat of month. **No credit cards. Map D5**

The City History Museum had a chance beginning: when the medieval Casa Padellàs was being transferred to this site in 1931, remains of the Roman city of Barcino were uncovered while digging the new foundations. They now form a giant labyrinthine cellar beneath the museum, with Roman streets and villas still visible, a visit to which takes you underneath the Plaça del Rei and winds as far as the Cathedral itself, beneath which there is a fourth-century baptistery. There are also sculpted busts and funerary monuments that were found in the excavations. The admission fee also gives access to a series of wonderful medieval buildings: parts of the medieval royal palace, the Santa Àgata chapel (with Gothic altarpieces by Jaume Huguet), the stern Rei Marti tower and the superb fourteenth-century Saló del Tinell banqueting hall. The Casa Padellàs itself holds long-term exhibitions, but no effort is made to represent all historical periods. The museum's concise *Barcino Barcelona* brochure lists other evidence of Rome – such as the Temple of Augustus – around the Gothic quarter. *See also chapter* **Sightseeing**. *Shop.*

Museu Marítim

Avda de les Drassanes (93 318 32 45/93 301 18 71). Metro Drassanes/bus 14, 18, 38, 57, 59, 64. **Open** 10am-6pm Tue-Sat; 10am-2pm Sun. **Admission** 800ptas; 400ptas over-65s, under-16s; free under-7s. **No credit cards. Map C6**

*The **Museu de la Ciència** – with antique submarine – stands amid the fresh air of Tibidabo.*

The oft-stated remark that Barcelona has lived with its back to the sea is belied by the building this museum occupies – the impressive **Drassanes** or medieval shipyards, the finest of their kind in the world. Since a 1990s facelift and the addition of attractive 'temporary' exhibits (which may be in place for years), the museum has become one of the most visited in the city. The highlight is the full-scale reproduction of the Royal Galley that was the flagship of Don Juan de Austria at the battle of Lepanto against the Turks in 1571. This battle and the subsequent history of Barcelona's port are now presented in 'The Great Sea Adventure', a series of unashamedly audience-pleasing historical simulations, accompanied by headphone commentaries (also in English). Visitors get caught in a storm on a nineteenth-century trader, take a steamer to Buenos Aires, and go underwater in the *Ictineo*, the prototype submarine of Catalan inventor Narcis Monturiol. Another display is 'From the Boat to the Company', with recreated dockside-life scenes from the last century. There is lots of space for temporary shows under the austere Gothic arches, such as a recent production dedicated to Robinson Crusoe. The museum has a prolific collection of paintings and drawings that allow you to see how the port of Barcelona has changed, as well as real traditional fishing craft, pleasure boats, fishing paraphernalia, explanations of boat-building techniques and a section on map-making and navigation. A full visit takes a good hour and a half. There is also an unusually good café-restaurant, **La Llotja** (*see chapters* **Restaurants** *and* **Cafés & Bars**).
Café-restaurant. Library. Shop.

Museu Militar

Castell de Montjuïc, Parc de Montjuïc (93 329 86 13). Metro Paral.lel then Funicular and Telefèric de Montjuïc. **Open** 9.30am-8pm Tue-Sun. **Admission** 200ptas; group discounts. **No credit cards. Map B6**
The military museum occupies the eighteenth-century fortress overlooking the city from the top of Montjuïc. Used to bombard the city in past conflicts, and as a prison and place of execution after the Civil War (a monument in the moat to Catalan President Lluis Companys recalls his death here in 1940), the castle has strongly repressive associations,

and is the only place in Barcelona where you still find a statue of Franco. However, its diverse selection of historic armaments – including non-European – is truly excellent: armour, swords and lances; muskets – especially beautiful are the Moroccan *moukhala* – rifles and pistols; and menacing crossbows. Other highlights include 23,000 lead soldiers that represent a Spanish division of the 1920s, a room of Scottish uniforms, and the display of Jewish tombstones from the medieval cemetery discovered nearby, the only direct reminder of death in the entire museum.
Bar. Library. Shop.

Science & natural history

Museu de la Ciència

C/Teodor Roviralta 55C/Cister 64 (93 212 60 50). FGC Tibidabo then Tramvia Blau/bus 17, 22, 73. **Open** 10am-8pm Tue-Sun. **Admission** 500ptas; *additional exhibits* 250ptas extra; 350ptas students under 25, over-65s; *additional exhibits* 200ptas extra; group discounts; free under-7s and 1st Sun of month. **Credit** (shop only) MC, V.
Barcelona's Science Museum – fitted into an out-of-the-way but attractively restored factory building at the foot of Tibidabo – is run by the cultural foundation of the ever-active La Caixa savings bank. Oriented especially towards school groups and young people, it is designed to teach basic scientific principles in the most engaging way possible. Fortunately, the quality of the displays is such that there's plenty to interest visitors of all ages. The permanent section uses lively interactive apparatus and hands-on displays to explain optical phenomena, quirks of perception, mechanical principles, meteorology, the solar system – there's a planetarium – and other topics, even including AIDS. Highlights include the prisms, lasers and holograms in the optics section; the inclusion of live fish and plants to explain biological habitat; and the re-creation of a tornado in miniature. For very small children there's the special *Clik dels Nens* interactive section. Temporary presentations last at least a

year, but the separate building for them, across the garden, will undergo renovation well into 1999. A good place to visit with a packed lunch. *See also chapter* **Children**. *Café. Shop.*

Museu de Geologia

Passeig dels Tilers/Passeig Picasso, Parc de la Ciutadella (93 319 68 95). Metro Arc de Triomf/bus 14, 39, 40, 41, 42, 51, 141. **Open** 10am-2pm Tue-Sun. *Guided tours* by appointment. **Admission** 400ptas; 250ptas under-16s, students under 25, over-65s; group discounts; free under-12s, 1st Sat of month. **No credit cards. Map E5**

Once known as the Museu Martorell, the oldest museum in Barcelona was opened in 1882 in this same building to house the private holdings of Francesc Martorell. In one wing there is a rather dry display of minerals, painstakingly classified, complementing explanations of various geological phenomena found in Catalonia. More interesting is the other wing, with a selection from the museum's over 300,000 fossils, including imprints of flora and fauna – even dinosaurs – and fossilised bones from all geological periods. Many fossils were found locally on Montjuïc or inside caves on the site of the Parc Güell. *Library. Shop.*

Museu de Zoologia

Passeig Picasso, Parc de la Ciutadella (93 319 69 12). Metro Arc de Triomf/bus 14, 39, 40, 41, 42, 51, 141. **Open** 10am-2pm Tue, Wed, Fri, Sun; 10am-6pm Thur, Sat. *Guided tours* by appointment. **Admission** 400ptas; 250ptas under-16s, students under 25, over-65s; group discounts; free under-12s, 1st Sat of month. **No credit cards. Map E5**

Another of the city's older museums in the Ciutadella, the Zoology Museum occupies the much-loved 'Castle of the Three Dragons', built by Domènech i Muntaner as the Café Restaurant for the 1888 Universal Exhibition. In the basement, there's a Whale Room with, yes, a whale skeleton, where very popular, temporary shows are organised, such as one on bats or another on endangered species. The upper floor has a fine collection of dissected and preserved animals – mammals, reptiles, birds – displayed just as they were at the turn of the century, along with thousands of invertebrates. A very thorough guidebook is available in English. *Disabled: wheelchair access. Library. Shop.*

Specialities & oddities

Galeria Olímpica

Estadi Olímpic, Parc de Montjuïc (93 426 06 60). Metro Paral.lel then Funicular de Montjuïc/bus 61. **Open** *Oct-May* 10am-1pm, 4-6pm Tue-Fri; 10am-2pm Sat, Sun, public holidays. *Apr-June* 10am-2pm, 4-7pm Tue-Fri; 10am-2pm Sat, Sun, public holidays. *July-Sept* 10am-2pm, 4-8pm Tue-Sat; 10am-2pm Sun, public holidays. **Admission** 390ptas; 340ptas under-12s, students; 160ptas over-65s; group discounts. **Credit** AmEx, MC, V. **Map A5**

Barcelona's great event of 1992 deserves a better monument than this, for it has little of the kind of thing real sports fans want to see. Would it really be so difficult to get 1,500m-winner Fermín Cacho's shoes, a Michael Jordan Dream Team kit, or the swimsuit of some gold-medal Australian crawler? The small space is chock-full of photos and video fragments, but the large video library is open only to researchers, a shame for anyone who'd like to relive their favourite event. There's a lot of peripheral paraphernalia: a huge inflatable Cobi mascot, a recreation of an Olympic Village room, designer volleyball holders. The best part is a section of costumes, props and scenery – some by theatre group la Fura dels Baus – from the opening and closing ceremonies. A spectacular big-screen film on the Games is rather uninformative but serves to give a feel for the event. *Library. Shop.*

Museu d'Autòmates del Tibidabo (Tibidabo Automata Museum)

Parc d'Attraccions del Tibidabo (93 211 79 42). FGC Av Tibidabo/bus 17, 22, 73 then Tramvia Blau and Funicular de Tibidabo. **Open** as funfair (*see chapter* **Sightseeing**). **Admission** 200ptas plus funfair entry.

The first automata belonged to the mechanical age, operating without the constant intervention of external energy. In contrast, this collection of electrified toys from the early twentieth century, found inside the funfair on Tibidabo, contains some of the finest examples of coin-operated fairground machines in the world. Still in working order, some date as far back as 1909. The entertaining scenarios include a 1924 mechanic's workshop and the saucy *La Monyos* (1913), named after a famed eccentric who cruised the Rambla: she claps her hands, shakes her shoulders and winks, her pigtails flying. Best of all is the depiction of hell (*El Infierno*): look through a small glass hole into a fireball and, to the sound of roaring flames, repentant maidens slide slowly into the pit prodded by naked devils. Admission is pricey if you aren't touring the amusement park as well.

Museu de Carrosses Fúnebres (Hearse Museum)

C/Sancho de Avila 2 (93 484 17 00). Metro Marina/bus 6, 40, 42, 141. **Open** 4-6pm Mon-Fri; 10am-1pm Sat. **Admission** free. **Map F4**

Mysteriously invisible from the street (ask the security guard at the desk to see it), this incredible collection of historical funeral carriages is a big hit with retired folk. Whatever morbid motives there might be for this, the charm of these 20 horse-drawn carriages and three motorised vehicles is that they actually were used in Barcelona, from the eighteenth century up to the 1970s. The carriages vary from delicately ornate white hearses reserved for children and 'single people' (presumably virgins) to a windowless black velour mourning carriage that carried the unfortunate 'second wife' (mistress) to the cemetery gates. Model horses and funeral officials dressed in costume complete the scene, with images of the carriages as originally used. The Studebaker used to bury Generalitat President Francesc Macià in 1933 and a hefty Buick Special round off the collection.

Museu del Clavegueram (Sewer Museum)

Passeig de Sant Joan, corner Avda Diagonal (93 457 65 50). Metro Verdaguer/bus 15, 20, 21, 45, 47, 55. **Open** 9am-2pm Tue-Sun. **Admission** 200ptas. **No credit cards. Map E3**

The olfactory antipode of the Perfume Museum. The aromas of the sewer museum waft all the way up to the entrance, in a small free-standing structure in the middle of the pavement just off the Diagonal. A sequence of ramps takes you well below street level to rooms full of photos, drawings and texts that trace the history of sewers from ancient Babylonia, Rome and Crete up to modern versions in London, Paris and Barcelona. An excessively detailed section on the Barcelona system closes the exhibition part. Only at weekends are visitors taken in to see the monumental water collectors and sewers below, all recently constructed, accompanied by the communal flow of rushing flushes and, sometimes, the sound of some of the city's six million rats.

Museu de l'Eròtica

C/Bergara 3 (93 318 98 65). Metro Catalunya/bus all routes to Plaça Catalunya. **Open** 10am-10pm daily. **Admission** 975ptas; 775ptas students, over-65s; group discounts. **Credit** MC, V. **Map D4**

A visit to the Erotic Museum could be as good as foreplay. Opened in 1997 by a private consortium, the rather chaotic collection is offered up with a healthy dose of kitsch, entirely appropriate given the section on Barcelona's 'T & A' music-hall tradition, or the intimidating replicas of antique S & M

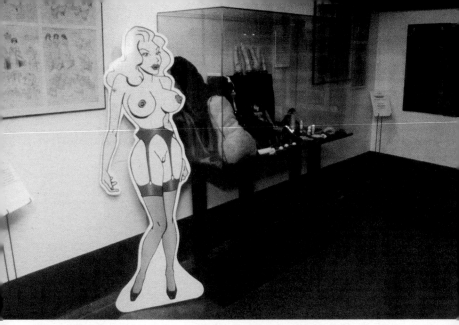

Had enough high culture? Then go for smut. The **Museu de l'Eròtica.**

contraptions. Suggestive initials apart, the museum gets down to business on the first floor with loads of Kama Sutra illustrations and Japanese erotic drawings, mixed in with images from turn-of-the-century French girly magazines and cheap replicas of African phallic sculpture. Upstairs there are some excellent nineteenth-century engravings by German Peter Fendi, as well as other extravagant early illustrations and postcards. The photos of brothels and transvestites in Barcelona's *Barrio Chino* in the decadent 1930s are rare and wonderful. Another highlight is the chance to get off on telephone sex in different languages, including English. The Eròtica is Barcelona's most expensive museum – so now what will you say if you're asked whether you've ever paid for sex? *Shop.*

Museu del FC Barcelona

Nou Camp, Avda Aristides Maillol, access 7 (93 496 36 00/93 496 36 08). Metro Collblanc/bus 15, 52, 53, 54, 56, 57, 75. **Open** 10am-6.30pm Mon-Sat; 10am-2pm Sun, public holidays. **Admission** 475ptas; 350ptas under-13s; group discounts. **No credit cards**.

A must-see for soccer fans, vying with the slightly higher-brow Picasso as the city's most visited museum. Even the less fanatical might find a certain charm in the historical paraphernalia and photos accumulated since the club was founded in 1899. The shiniest silver in the trophy case belongs to the European Cup Winners' Cups of 1979, 1982, 1989 and 1997, and the club's greatest treasure, the 1992 European Cup, won at Wembley against Sampdoria. Anything goes in the chronological arranged collection, even a display of old entrance tickets, players' boots, maquettes of former stadiums, and a ref's whistle. We also discover the origin of the *Barça* fans' nickname, *culés* ('bums', as in rear-ends): spectators used to sit on the high perimeter wall surrounding the old field, their overhanging backsides offering a singular view to those outside. A visit to the museum also gives you a look at the cavernous Nou Camp stadium (capacity 114,000) but to catch the real atmosphere you have to go to a game. The museum has recently been expanded to accommodate large temporary shows and new displays, including a major exhi-

bition planned to mark the club's centenary in 1999. Upstairs there is *Barça's* rather embarrassing art collection. *Café (Apr-Oct). Shop.*

Museu del Perfum

Passeig de Gràcia 39 (93 215 72 38).
Metro Passeig de Gràcia/bus 7, 16, 17, 22, 24, 28.
Open 10.30am-1.30pm, 4.30-7.30pm Mon-Fri; 11am-1.30pm Sat. **Admission** free. **Map D3**

Thousands of people walk past the Regia perfumery (*see chapter* **Shopping**) every day without realising that the 'Museu del Perfum' sign is no promotional gimmick. Entering through a narrow corridor at the back, one comes into a room full of thousands of scent bottles, dating from pre-dynastic Egypt to the present. The museum began when owner Ramon Planas moved his shop here in 1960, and began gathering what is now one of the world's finest collections. Hundreds of bottles trace the period before perfumes were labelled, including Egyptian, Greek, Roman and baroque examples. The rest are shown by brands: examples from the late eighteenth century onwards of Guerlain, Dior and 4,711 limited-edition bottles, such as a Dali creation for Schiaparelli and a prized art-nouveau flask by René Lalique for the Coty Cyclamen brand. The aromas of other lands – India, Turkey, Iran, even countries in the former Soviet Union – can also be seen, if not sniffed.

Museu Verdaguer

Vil.la Joana, Carretera de les Planes, Vallvidrera (93 204 78 05). By train FGC from Plaça Catalunya to Baixador de Vallvidrera. **Open** 10am-2pm Tue-Sun. **Admission** free.

Jacint Verdaguer (1845-1902) was the foremost poet of the nineteenth-century Catalan *Renaixença*. His neo-romantic poetry, often on nature or spiritual themes, was enormously popular, and even though he was a priest his funeral brought thousands onto the streets in anti-clerical Barcelona. This old stone farmhouse where he spent his last days has a sparse collection of his belongings, but even if you can't understand the nuances of Catalan poetry, its setting in the hills above the city makes this an attractive outing, with enticing views on a clear day. *Library. Shop.*

Art Galleries

With a tremendous visual heritage, Barcelona's art scene has a tendency to dwell on past glories, but fresh galleries and a dynamic alternative scene are pumping new life into the city's creative heart.

As proud capital of the Catalan art scene, Barcelona lives a perpetual tug-of-war between the vivid memory of past grandeur and the compulsive need to get on with being a seedbed of contemporary art in the here and now. This dilemma is sharpened by the fact that the icons of Catalan art – Picasso, Miró, Dalí – were eminently modern, with wide international popular appeal, a flattering reality for a city so anxious to offer an image that's culturally hip. Even though Picasso moved here as a teenager, Miró left to set up his studio in Mallorca, and Dalí was driven more by the maddening winds of his native Figueres than by any Barcelona breeze, all these artists, plus Gaudí, testify to the vitality of visual culture in the city in the first decades of the century. Living up to such standards in the present is no easy task.

If Barcelona was a minor hot spot of the early twentieth-century avant-garde, it was in great part because it had a liberal bourgeoisie willing to tolerate and even promote the radical ideas of artists and architects. This vitality was knocked back under the Franco dictatorship, and attempts to revive its spirit had to be made semi-clandestinely. In the late 1940s the *Dau al Set* (Dice on Seven) group, which included painter Antoni Tàpies and poet-artist Joan Brossa, published their surrealist-inspired magazine virtually underground.

Tàpies was the only internationally relevant artist who emerged in this period, his abstract style – still highly influential – evolving from surrealism to *art informel*, a continental version of abstract expressionism. By the 1960s, Catalan artists were hooked into other international currents, *arte povera* – with its sculptural use of rough, rudimentary materials – and conceptual art. Artists like Francesc Torres and Antoni Muntadas (who both made the leap into the international arena, moving to New York) rose to prominence in the last years of the Franco era by combining conceptualism with new media.

When democracy returned, the Barcelona art world was convinced that simply by invoking the mood of the pre-war years, and adding in a hefty dose of chauvinistic self-promotion, the city would be able to offer another generation of top-flight artists to the world. Some who fitted the art-star formula – like the spectacular Mallorcan-born painter Miquel Barceló – were hyped to the heavens, while other excellent artists, including some successful elsewhere, were virtually ignored. Even now the city has problems grasping the difference between quality culture within its midst and mere hyperbole.

Fortunately, however, Barcelona is coming back to its cosmopolitan senses. In private galleries, the bonds of nationalistic sentiment have been broken when it comes to showing and buying art. In turn, the ample public funding provided to bring in quality international exhibitions has helped to override the remaining clichés of local aesthetic tradition. The only blot on the landscape is the **Museu d'Art Contemporani (MACBA)**, opened to fanfares in 1995, but as yet floundering in its role as flagship of Catalan contemporary art (*see chapter* **Museums**).

FRINGE ADVENTURES

With so many big institutions patronising contemporary art, the Catalan art scene has a tendency to get 'top-heavy', with super-productions overshadowing more modest endeavours. Fortunately, post-Olympic Barcelona has been inundated by a wave of fresh alternative projects, many run by artists themselves. Not all of these new fringe spaces, short-term projects and festivals have managed to survive, but those that have provide a respite from the staid nature of official shows and much of the commercial gallery scene. A younger generation of artists has used these outlets to break with the abstract gestural painting and austere minimalist sculpture that has dominated official Catalan art. Video, film, fashion and music can play just as big a part in making art as oil paint or chipped stone. Finding what's on offer in this alternative art world can be difficult, but it has given Barcelona a much more varied and enjoyable art scene (*see page 100*).

There is no definitive guide to Barcelona galleries and artistic activities. Listings appear in the *Guia de Ocio* and some papers, but they are rarely comprehensive (*see chapter* **Media**). It can be just as easy to go to a gallery district and do the rounds. Almost all galleries are closed on Mondays. Show openings typically take place at around 8pm on Tuesdays and Thursdays, and are open to anyone. Curious visitors will also find that most gallery-owners are happy to show their 'backroom' collections on request.

Many museums, particularly the **Fundació Miró** and the **MACBA**, also host temporary exhibitions. For these, *see chapter* **Museums**.

La Capella (Capella de l'Antic Hospital de la Santa Creu)

C/Hospital 56 (93 442 71 71). Metro Liceu/bus 14, 18, 38, 59. **Open** noon-2pm, 4-8pm, Tue-Sat; 11am-2pm Sun. **Admission** free. **Map C5**

Administered by the Ajuntament, this exhibition space is modelled on the **Sala Montcada** of La Caixa and the Espai 13 of the **Fundació Miró** (*see chapter* **Museums**). Curators seek out younger artists to create new work. The impressive Gothic building was once the chapel of the medieval hospital next door, and the choir balcony and side chapels add character to the space. As well as exhibiting young Barcelona-based artists, the gallery displays work from local art schools and exchanges exhibits with similar foreign galleries.

Centre d'Art Santa Mònica

La Rambla 7 (93 316 28 10). Metro Drassanes/bus 14, 18, 38, 59. **Open** 11am-2pm, 5-8pm, Mon-Sat; 11am-3pm Sun. **Admission** normally free. **Map C5**

In the 1980s the Catalan government undertook the renovation of this seventeenth-century monastery as a centre for contemporary art. The polemical result, by Maremàgnum-architects Piñón and Viaplana, is hard enough for installation artists to work with, and almost unusable when it comes to showing paintings (observe the extravagantly tiled lower cloister, or the ridiculously narrow corridors that pass for galleries upstairs). After playing host to some very fine contemporary shows in the early 1990s (including work by Joseph Beuys, Hannah Collins, and media artist Antoni Muntadas), it has taken on more modest projects, as the Generalitat's art budget is being absorbed by the MACBA. *Bookshop. Disabled: wheelchair access.*

Centre de Cultura Contemporània de Barcelona (CCCB)

C/Montalegre 5 (93 306 41 00). Metro Catalunya/bus all routes to Plaça Catalunya. **Open** *mid-June-mid-Sept* 11am-8pm Tue-Sat; 11am-7pm Sun, public holidays; *mid-Sept-mid-June* 11am-2pm, 4-8pm, Tue, Thur, Fri; 11am-8pm Wed, Sat; 11am-7pm Sun, public holidays.

Admission *One exhibition* 600ptas; 400ptas students under 25, over-65s, *Wed only* 400ptas; *two exhibitions* 900ptas; 700ptas students under 25, over-65s; *three exhibitions* 1,200ptas; 1,000ptas students under 25, over-65s; free under-12s. **Credit** MC, V. **Map C4**

This lavishly equipped centre makes a duo of recent major cultural projects in the Raval with the adjacent **MACBA**. It occupies part of the Casa de la Caritat, which was built at the beginning of the last century on the site of a medieval monastery to serve as the city's main workhouse. The massive façade and impressive courtyard remain from the 1802 building, but beginning in 1988 the rest was rebuilt wholesale (by Piñón and Viaplana) to transform it into a 'multi-disciplinary, multi-functional' cultural centre. The result is a dramatic combination of the original building with Piñón and Viaplana's favoured glass curtain walls. The guiding focus of the centre is on cities in all their aspects – an idea meant to keep Barcelona's architectural community happy. The CCCB offers very solid exhibitions on twentieth-century art, architecture and urban themes and a whole gamut of other activities, including a festival of video art, an alternative cinema festival, the **Sonar** music festival in June, dance performances, concerts, film screenings and inter-disciplinary urban studies courses (*see also page 100 and chapter* **Music: Rock, Roots & Jazz**). Visitors must descend a ramp on one side of the courtyard, pass underneath it through a wide hall, pay, and then take

Martí Llorens

As a generation of emerging Barcelona artists make a name for themselves in international circles, it is surprising how tardy their hometown can be in proffering them the recognition they deserve. No better example can be found than the case of photographer Martí Llorens, who was born and still lives in the port-side *barri* of Barceloneta. Llorens' anonymity is all the more bewildering given that his intelligent and witty images make constant reference to Barcelona.

His remarkable series on the demolition of factories in Poble Nou before the building of the Olympic Village, taken with an old pinhole camera, won the 1991 European Photography Award in Berlin, but has yet to seen in his home city. Since then Llorens has explored the history of photography as a medium by creating historical falsifications of Barcelona's past, often using old cameras and subtle photomontage techniques: in one series, *Columbus and Barcelona* (1992, *right*), a Zeppelin flies over the Columbus Monument, while in another he 'created' air-to-ground photos of the city that seemed to come from an era predating the invention of both photography and flight. In *Revolutionary Memoirs*, shown in 1997-8 in the USA and several European countries (but not in Spain), Llorens presented photos of the extras in *Libertarias*, Vicente Aranda's 1996 film about women anarchist militia members in the Civil War.

The wrinkled edges and discoloured sepia tones of the photos, along with handwritten dedications as if they actually had been sent from the bloody Ebro front, made them seem strangely like real snapshots from the period. Martí Llorens' shining talent – and frequent successful exhibitions in New York and Berlin – have not kept him from being an unknown artist in Catalonia.

escalators up to the galleries – a circuitous route that shows off the architecture while for some reason associating 'contemporary culture' with long, vacuous preludes. *Bookshop. Café. Disabled: toilets, wheelchair access.*

Col.legi d'Aparelladors i Arquitectes Tècnics de Barcelona

C/Bon Pastor 5 (93 209 82 99). Bus 6, 7, 15, 27, 33, 34, 58, 64. **Open** 10am-8pm Mon-Fri. Closed afternoons Aug. **Admission** free. **Map C2**

This professional body for building engineers has a well-run gallery showing all kinds of work by designers, architects and urban planners, Contemporary artists and photographers exhibit work on related themes. *Disabled: wheelchair access.*

Col.legi d'Arquitectes

Plaça Nova 5 (93 301 50 00). Metro Jaume I/bus 17, 19, 40, 45. **Open** 10am-9pm Mon-Fri; 10am-2pm Sat.
Admission free. **Map D5**
The College of Architects, opposite the Cathedral, hosts interesting exhibitions related to twentieth-century architecture. The façade murals were designed by Picasso in the 1950s, but executed by other artists, since he was not then able to enter Spain. *Bookshop. Café. Disabled: wheelchair access.*

Fundació Antoni Tàpies

C/Aragó 255 (93 487 03 15). Metro Passeig de Gràcia/bus 7, 16, 17, 22, 24, 28. **Open** 11am-8pm Tue-Sun; *Aug only* 11am-8pm Tue-Sat; 11am-3pm Sun.

Admission 500ptas; 300ptas students, over-65s; free under-7s. **No credit cards**. **Map D3**
Antoni Tàpies is Catalonia's best-known living artist, and his foundation in the heart of the Eixample is a must-see, if not for obvious reasons. Tàpies had the good sense to do more than simply create a shrine to himself: he set up a foundation, with solid exhibition programming in a handsome, idiosyncratic gallery. It is housed in a renovated *Modernista* publishing house built in the 1880s by Domènech i Muntaner, and the main space, including the labyrinthine basement, is usually set aside for international contemporary art. Opened in 1990, it presents some of the best exhibitions in the city: thematic shows (the idea of the museum, the Fluxus movement) alternate with retrospectives of artists such as Hans Haacke or Brazilian Lygia Clark. A selection of Tàpies' own

work can usually be seen on the upper floor, and sometimes throughout the entire space. The incredible winding tube sculpture on the roof, titled *Núvol i Cadira* (Cloud and Chair), reflects his fascination with eastern mysticism. The library contains a fine collection of books on oriental art.

Disabled: wheelchair access. Library (restricted access).

Fundació La Caixa

Centre Cultural de la Fundació La Caixa, Passeig de Sant Joan 108 (93 458 89 07). Metro Verdaguer/bus 6, 15, 19, 34, 43, 50, 51, 55. **Open** 11am-8pm Tue-Sat; 11am-3pm Sun, public holidays. Closed Aug. **Admission** *Tue-Fri, Sun* 300ptas; 175ptas students, over-65s; group discounts. *Sat* free. **No credit cards. Map E3**
All Spain's *caixes* (*cajas*, in Spanish), or savings banks, are obliged to spend part of their earnings on social and cultural activities. The foundation set up by the largest, the Caixa de Pensions or just *La Caixa*, has since the 1980s built up one of the most important collections of international contemporary art in Spain. More recently the foundation has been shifting its focus towards fields such as ethnology, archaeology and cultural heritage, but it still presents some of the best art exhibits in Barcelona. Until at least late 1999 the main centre will be at this address, in the Palau Macaya, a magnificent *Modernista* building by Puig i Cadafalch from 1901 that creatively mixes Moorish and Gothic styles; however, another even larger cultural centre is planned near Plaça d'Espanya. The Macaya centre usually offers one large

or two smaller exhibits, one of them often of photography. The same building houses the **Mediateca** arts library (*see p264*), and an excellent music and arts bookshop. The foundation also runs one of Barcelona's most reputable spaces for more daring contemporary art, the **Sala Montcada** by the Picasso Museum. Emerging Spaniards and high-riding foreigners yet to be seen in Barcelona are invited to create new work especially for the gallery.

Bookshop. Café. Library.

Branch: **Sala Montcada** C/Montcada 14 (93 310 06 99).

Fundació Caixa de Catalunya

Passeig de Gràcia 92 (93 484 59 79). Metro Diagonal/bus 7, 16, 17, 22, 24, 28. **Open** 10am-8pm daily. **Admission** 500ptas; 300ptas students, over-65s; free under-12s. **Credit** (shop only) MC, V. **Map D3**
This Caixa foundation has the advantage of owning Gaudí's masterpiece the Casa Milà (**La Pedrera**, *see chapter* **Sightseeing**) which it has been systematically restoring as a cultural centre. Access to the gallery space is via the spectacular main entrance and stone staircase. The gallery itself is an excellent example of a Gaudí interior: plaster reliefs in the ceiling recall the building's marine-life themes, and none of the walls are straight. Shows mainly feature high-quality international twentieth-century art and modern Barcelona artists, but are also worth visiting just to get a full look at Gaudí's work. On the floor above is the **Espai Gaudí** (*see chapter* **Museums**).

Street art

At the end of the 1970s the new, democratic socialist administration of Barcelona set out with a will to renovate their long-neglected city, to an extent that few citizens could then imagine. Beginning before the 1992 Olympics were even a vague project, they embarked on a remarkably ambitious programme to develop new public space in the city, with nearly 100 entirely new squares and parks.

Typified by hard surfaces and creatively designed benches and lamp-posts, these squares were also conceived to incorporate dozens of public sculptures specially commissioned by the city, in the largest programme of its kind in the world. Artists were offered a modest flat fee, with costs born by the Ajuntament; major Spanish and international artists, among them Joan Miró, Antoni Tàpies, Eduardo Chillida, Richard Serra, Roy Lichtenstein, Jannis Kounellis and Rebecca Horn, responded. Their works, together with many older sculptures pulled out of the city's store rooms, are now distributed across Barcelona. A special effort was made to establish visual landmarks in the outlying neighbourhoods that had sprung up chaotically in the 1950s and 1960s – what one of the prime movers of the scheme, architect Oriol Bohigas, called 'monuments on the periphery'. The result is truly impressive – if now stylistically a bit dated, as the initiative was stalled in 1993.

Many of the squares could be described as 'sculptures' in their own right. One of the first to be completed is one of the most polemical: Albert Viaplana and Helio Piñón's 1983 **Plaça dels Països Catalans** in front of Sants station. Heavily criticised for its lack of greenery and excessive use of stone and metal, it is nonetheless impressive for its flowing lines and risky design. The same architects also created the **Rambla de Mar**, the footbridge and decking that leads to their **Maremàgnum** shopping and leisure pier. The graduated sloping of the wooden boardwalk down to the unrailed edge imitates a sandy shore, an innovative 'installation' that would be near-inconceivable in countries where local administrations fear civil suits for accidents in public places. Also worth seeing are Santiago Calatrava's **Bac de Roda** bridge and **Telefònica** tower on Montjuïc; Norman Foster's **Torre de Collserola**, and the overdone deconstructionist sun-shields on **Via Icària** in the Vila Olímpica, by Enric Miralles and Carme Pinós. For these, and more on each area, *see chapter* **Sightseeing**.

Sculpture around the city

Barceloneta & Port Vell *Metro Barceloneta or Drassanes/bus 14, 17, 18, 36, 57, 59, 64.* **Map D6**.
Sculptures related to harbour themes by Rebecca Horn (Barceloneta beach), Jannis Kounellis (C/Almirall Cervera), Lothar Baumgarten (the names of the winds

Palau de la Virreina

*La Rambla 99 (93 301 77 75) Metro Liceu/bus 14, 38,
59.* **Open** 11am-8.30pm Tue-Sat; 11am-2.30pm Sun.
Admission 500ptas; 250ptas students, over-65s; free
under-16s. **No credit cards. Map D5**
This neo-classical palace takes its name from the wife of a
Viceroy of Peru, who lived there after it was built in the 1770s.
The beautiful upstairs rooms still have some original wall and
ceiling paintings, although they cannot always be seen. It is
now the Ajuntament's main exhibition space, hosting shows
that vary from selections from the city collection to travelling
exhibits. The lower floor is used mostly to show the work of
mid-career Catalan artists, but it has been suggested to turn
the space into a restaurant. The courtyard is often used for
installations. In the same building is the city's cultural information centre and bookshop (*see chapter* **Shopping** *and p251*).
Disabled: wheelchair access.

Off-Barcelona

Tecla Sala Centre Cultural

*Avda Josep Tarradellas 44, Hospitalet de Llobregat (93
338 57 71). Metro Torrassa/bus L12 from Plaça Maria
Cristina.* **Open** 11am-2pm, 5-8pm, Tue-Sat; 11am-2pm
Sun. Closed Aug. **Admission** normally free.
The magnetism of Barcelona tends to mean that suburban
artistic endeavours are condemned to obscurity. In

Hospitalet, actually Catalonia's second city and still on the
Metro system, the Tecla Sala has begun to make a dent in
the metropolitan cultural scene. Belying the problems it faces
in attracting a public, this converted factory is one of the
most attractive gallery spaces in the city. It presents its own
shows of top-level Spanish artists, such as Rogelio López
Cuenca, and important international figures (sculptor Barry
Flanagan, or avant-garde photographer Emmanuel Sougez).
The space also hosts several other cultural activities.

Commercial galleries

C/Consell de Cent and the Barri Gòtic are
Barcelona's longest-established gallery areas, but
in recent years new clusters of contemporary galleries have developed around the MACBA in the
Raval and in La Ribera, near the Born market.

Uptown & Gràcia

There is no defined gallery district in the city's
Zona Alta, although a few good spaces are dotted
around the areas above and below Diagonal.
Gràcia has few galleries, in spite of the many artworks gracing the walls of its bars.

of the Catalan coast, set into the paving of Passeig Joan
de Borbó), and Juan Muñoz (end of Passeig Joan de
Borbó). Roy Lichtenstein's unmissable *Barcelona Head*
is on Passeig de Colom, across from the post office.
Parc de la Creueta del Coll *Metro Penitents/bus
19, 25, 28.* Giant sculptures by Ellsworth Kelly and
Eduardo Chillida.
Parc de l'Espanya Industrial *Metro Sants-
Estació/bus 43, 44, 109.* **Map A3.** Small sculptures by
Anthony Caro, Pablo Palazuelo and others.
Parc de l'Estació del Nord *Metro Arc de
Triomf/bus 40, 42, 141.* **Map E4.** A large landscape
sculpture by Beverly Pepper.
Plaça de la Palmera *Metro La Pau/bus 33, 40, 43,
44.* Richard Serra's *Wall*, a brilliantly conceived

double-curving wall, divides this square in the far-east
of Barcelona, created out of a former factory site.
Vall d'Hebron *Metro Montbau/bus 27, 60, 73, 85,
173.* Near the former Olympic tennis site are works by
Susanna Solano and Claes Oldenburg (his giant
Matches, see above). Joan Brossa's disintegrating
Visual Poem is nearby, by the Horta Velodrome. Much
older, but also fascinating, is the **Parc del Laberint**.
Via Júlia *Metro Roquetes/bus 11, 32, 50, 51,
76, 81.* Sculptures by Catalans Sergi Aguilar and
Jaume Plensa.
Vila Olímpica *Metro Ciutadella-Vila Olímpica/bus
36, 41, 45, 49, 71.* **Map F6.** Sculptures including
Frank Gehry's *Fish* (at the Hotel Arts) and *Cometa*
(Kite) by Antoni Llena (Parc de les Cascades).

Galeria Alejandro Sales

*C/Julián Romea 16 (93 415 20 54). FGC Gràcia/bus 16,
17, 22, 24, 27, 28, 127.* **Open** 11am-2pm, 5-8.30pm,
Tue-Sat. Closed Aug. **No credit cards**. **Map D2**
Alejandro Sales is one of the city's most successful young
dealers. As well as hosting impeccable shows by name artists
in his main space, he has 'Blackspace', a room where young
Spanish and foreign artists present small-scale exhibitions –
often installations – with little commercial pressure.

Galeria Estrany-de la Mota

*Passatge Mercader 18 (93 215 70 51). FGC Provença/bus
7, 16, 17.* **Open** 10.30am-1.30pm, 4.30-8.30pm, Mon-Sat.
Closed Aug. **No credit cards**. **Map E1**
Former Gràcia-based dealer Àngels de la Mota has recently
teamed up with prestigious dealer Antoni Estrany. They use
this cavernous iron-columned basement to show Spanish
neo-conceptualists such as Pep Agut, Barcelona photographer Montserrat Soto and foreign artists such as Thomas
Grunfeld. A good place for serious collectors.

Galeria H₂0

C/Verdi 152 (93 415 18 01). Bus 24, 31, 32, 74.
Open 11am-1pm, 5.30-8pm, Tue-Fri; 11am-1pm Sat.
Closed Aug. **No credit cards**. **Map E1**
A space run by industrial designers on one floor of a small
Gràcia house, showing design, photography, architectural
projects and contemporary art. Performance art and literary
readings are often presented in the charming back garden.

Galeria Metropolitana de Barcelona

C/Torrijos 44 (93 384 31 83). Metro Fontana/bus 39.
Open 11am-1.30pm, 5-9pm, Mon-Fri. Closed last half
July, 1st half Aug. **No credit cards**. **Map E2**
This small gallery on a lively Gràcia street has come up with
some of the city's freshest, most innovative recent shows. A
show on painting and the cinema and a visiting exhibit of
Japanese artists are examples of the mixed bag offered here.

Around C/Consell de Cent

Historically Barcelona's most prestigious gallery
district, but some galleries have closed in recent
years and those taking their place are not quite of
the same calibre. Other galleries of interest are
Galeria María José Castellví, C/Consell de
Cent 278 (93 216 04 82), **Galeria Joan Gaspar**,
Plaça Dr Letamendi 1 (93 323 07 48) and **Ignacio
de Lassaletta**, Rambla de Catalunya 47, pral (93
488 00 06), with a stunning *Modernista* interior.

Edicions T

C/Consell de Cent 282 (93 487 64 02).
Metro Passeig de Gràcia/bus 7, 16, 17. **Open** 10am-2pm,
4-8pm, Tue-Fri; 11am-2pm, 5-8.30pm, Sat. Closed Aug.
Credit MC, V. **Map D3**
Founded to produce and show fine art prints, Edicions T has
begun to show some of the best of Spanish and foreign art,
including Catalan sculptor Jaume Plensa and Czech-born
Jana Sterbak. Prints by Tàpies, Austrian painter Arnulf
Rainer and Sol Lewitt are available, among others.

Galeria Carles Taché

*C/Consell de Cent 290 (93 487 88 36). Metro Passeig de
Gràcia/bus 7, 16, 17, 63.* **Open** 10am-2pm, 4-8.30pm,
Tue-Sat. Closed Aug. **Credit** V. **Map D3**
One of the few dealers to emphasise Spanish artists. Taché
has the good fortune to represent some of the best, includ-
ing senior painters Eduardo Arroyo and Miguel Angel
Campano and the young Barcelona sculptor Jordi Colomer.
The prices are pretty steep.
Disabled: wheelchair access.

Galeria Joan Prats

*Rambla Catalunya 54 (93 216 02 84). Metro Passeig de
Gràcia/bus 7, 16, 17.* **Open** 10.30am-1.30pm, 5-8.30pm,
Tue-Sat. Closed Aug. **Credit** V. **Map D3**
This gallery has its origins in an encounter in the 1920s
between Joan Prats, son of a fashionable hatmaker, and Joan
Miró. The only remnant of the original business is the name
and the hat motifs on the façade – Prats' collection of Miró
is now in the **Fundació Miró**. 'La Prats' represents senior
Catalan painters such as Ràfols Casamada and Hernández
Pijoan, presenting individual shows in a winding interior
designed by Josep Lluis Sert. The gallery also shows important mid-career artists, including Catalonia's most brilliantly original creator, Perejaume. A wide selection of prints by
internationally renowned artists can be viewed and bought
at the **Artgràfic-Joan Prats** space, a block away.
Branch: Artgràfic-Joan Prats C/Balmes 54 (93 488 13 98).

Galeria Senda

*C/Consell de Cent 292 (93 487 67 59). Metro Passeig de
Gràcia/bus 7, 16, 17, 63.* **Open** 11am-2pm, 5-8.30pm,
Tue-Sat. Closed Aug. **Credit** MC, V. **Map D3**
In this upstairs space above a blacksmith's workshop, deal-
er Carles Duran shows Spanish and international painting,
and exhibits and sells work on paper by blue-chip artists like
Peter Halley. The roof terrace is often used for installations.

Gothsland Galeria d'Art

*C/Consell de Cent 331 (93 488 19 22). Metro Passeig de
Gràcia/bus 7, 16, 17, 63.* **Open** 10am-1.30pm, 4.30-
8.30pm, Mon-Sat. Closed Aug. **No credit cards**. **Map D3**
The dynamism of Catalan *Modernisme* in architecture and
decorative arts was rarely matched by contemporary painting and sculpture, as a visit to this gallery, Barcelona's principal specialist in original Modernist work, makes clear. If
you're fortunate, though, you can find work by major figures
of the era on its walls – impressionist landscapes by the Olot
school or Joaquim Mir, portraits by Isidre Nonell or minor
works by Santiago Rusiñol and Ramon Casas. Gothsland
also has a spectacular collection of original *Modernista* furniture and antiques (*see also chapter* **Shopping**).

The upper Raval/MACBA area

Since the opening of the MACBA galleries have
sprouted up all around the upper Raval, in anticipation of an art boom. Some are new, others have
moved in from elsewhere, and the quality of only a
few is proven. Plans to move the FAD (*Foment de
les Arts Decoratives*) design foundation into the
Convent dels Àngels across from the museum in
1999 are leading to a design boom as well. Other
venues worth a look are **Galeria dels Àngels**,
C/Àngels 16 (93 412 54 54), New York-based **BAI**,
C/Ferlandina 25 (no phone) and **Cotthem Gallery**,
C/Dr Dou 15 (93 270 16 69), associated with a name-
sake gallery in Belgium and showing work by Bram
Bogart, Kenny Scharf and Robert Longo.

Galeria Carles Poy

*C/Dr Dou 10 (93 412 59 45). Metro Catalunya/bus all
routes to Plaça Catalunya.* **Open** 11am-2pm, 5-8pm, Tue-
Sat. Closed Aug. **Credit** AmEx, DC, MC, TC, V. **Map C4**
Since Poy first opened in the Gothic Quarter in the 1980s he
has been one of the city's most refreshing young dealers.
Now in the Raval, he has no problem in showing Madrid
artists, or top-level Canadians like Colette Whitten. A
Richard Wentworth show is planned for late 1998. The great
design shop next door, **Dou Deu**, sells artist-made objects
(*see chapter* **Shopping**).

Galeria Ferran Cano

Plaça dels Àngels 4 (93 310 15 48). Metro Catalunya/ bus all routes to Plaça Catalunya. **Open** 5-8pm Tue-Fri; 11am-2pm Sat. **No credit cards**. **Map C4**
One of the most successful dealers in Spain, Mallorca-based Ferran Cano has opened a small gallery on the square facing the MACBA. He shows a tremendous number of different artists, often young, commercially viable painters.

Urània

C/Dr Dou 19 (93 412 23 45). Metro Plaça Catalunya/ bus all routes to Plaça Catalunya. **Open** 11am-1.30pm, 5-8.30pm, Tue-Sat. **Credit** MC, V. **Map C4**
Run by a team of exhibition organisers, this gallery is used as a showcase for a range of projects in graphic design, architecture and photography. Some work is for sale, but the idea is not directly commercial. Regular gallery artists include Cuban photographer Juan Pablo Ballester and Madrid-based Amparo Garrido.

Barri Gòtic

The Gothic Quarter has held its own in spite of the fuss made about MACBA across the Rambla. Its galleries are very varied: on C/Petritxol and C/Portaferrisa you'll find mostly figurative painting; Palla and Banys Nous are the home of historic painting, antiques and book dealers; below Plaça Sant Jaume is mainly for contemporary art. Also interesting are **Galeria Miguel Marcos**, C/Jonqueres 10, 1° 1ª (93 319 07 57), who represents Joan Brossa and Ferran Garcia Sevilla; **Galeria Pergamon**, C/Duc de la Victòria 12 (93 318 06 35); **Galeria Tres Punts**, C/Avinyó 27 (93 315 03 57) and alternative spaces **L'Angelot** and **Studio Meyetta** (*see below* **The fringe scene**).

Antonio de Barnola

C/Palau 4 (93 412 22 14). Metro Liceu, Jaume I/bus 14, 17, 18, 38, 40, 45, 59, 91. **Open** 5-9pm Tue-Fri; noon-2pm, 5-9pm, Sat; *July* 5-9pm Tue-Sat. Closed Aug. **Credit** AmEx, MC, TC, V. **Map D5**
This handsome gallery presents impeccable shows of the best of Spanish contemporary art. Dozens of artists, including young Catalan painter Mireya Masó and sculptor Begoña Montalbán, have passed through the space, along with national photography prize-winner Humberto Rivas. Barnola also shows an interesting variety of work related to architecture and design.
Disabled: wheelchair access.

Sala d'Art Artur Ramon

C/Palla 23 (93 302 59 70). Metro Liceu/ bus 14, 17, 18, 38, 40, 45, 59, 91. **Open** 5-8pm Mon; 10am-1.30pm, 5-8pm, Tue-Sat; 11am-2pm Sun. Closed Aug, some Sats June-Sept. **No credit cards**. **Map D5**
The best of the local dealers in historic art, Artur Ramon is a real expert in putting together intelligent exhibits of Catalan and European painters and thematic shows (from Chinese snuff bottles to Catalan ceramics), spending years searching through private collections. His gallery shop is on a street brimming with antique furniture- and book-dealers.

Sala Parés

C/Petritxol 5 (93 318 70 08). Metro Liceu/ bus 14, 18, 38, 59, 91. **Open** 10.30am-2pm, 4.30-8.30pm, Mon-Sat; *Oct-May only* 11am-2pm Sun. Closed two weeks Aug. **Credit** AmEx, V. **Map D5**
The Sala Parés opened in 1840 and is now owned by a branch of former Mayor Pasqual Maragall's family. It promoted *Modernista* painters (Rusiñol, Mir, Nonell) `t the turn of the century, and it was here that Picasso had his first one-man show. Now renovated, the spacious gallery specialises in figurative and historical painting. Across the street, the associated **Galeria Trama** offers more contemporary work, such as the popular Perico Pastor.
Branch: Galeria Trama C/Petritxol 8 (93 317 48 77).

Art Larson's Titanic, *a 1998 installation in* **Espai 22A**. *See* **Hangar**, *page 100.*

La Ribera & the Born

The Born district was the hub of Barcelona's 1980s art boom, but the last few years have seen many galleries close. However, the proximity of the **Museu Picasso** and reopening of **Metrònom** have assured the district's continuity. Also worth a look is **Tristan Barberà**, C/Fusina 11 (93 319 46 69), which specialises in limited-edition prints.

Galeria Berini

Plaça Comercial 3 (93 310 54 43). Metro Jaume I/bus 14, 39, 51. **Open** *Sept-June* 10.30am-2pm, 5-8.30pm, Tue-Sat; *July* closed Sat. Closed Aug. **No credit cards. Map E5**
Dealer Toni Berini owns one of the few prestige Born galleries to have resisted the MACBA fanfare. She showcases the work of sculptors and painters from Spain and the USA, and also fine Latin American figurative painters.
Disabled: wheelchair access.

Galeria Maeght

C/Montcada 25 (93 310 42 45). Metro Jaume I/bus 17, 40, 45. **Open** 10am-2pm, 4-8pm, Tue-Sat. **Credit** AmEx, DC, MC, V. **Map D5/E5**
The Paris-based Maeght gallery opened this extraordinary space in the 1970s. In a Renaissance palace on C/Montcada with a lovely courtyard and noble staircase, it shows hot Spanish and European painters and sculptors, and has the work of many first-class artists in its holdings. It also promotes and sells the fine prints and books produced by France-based Éditions Maeght.
Disabled: wheelchair access.

Metrònom

C/Fusina 9 (93 268 42 98). Metro Jaume I/bus 39, 51. **Open** 10am-2pm, 4.30-8.30pm, Tue-Sat. Closed July-Aug. **Map E5**
Run by collector Rafael Tous, this was Barcelona's most vital art space in the 1980s. After closing briefly, it has steadily won back its original impetus, focusing on photography and multimedia installations. Beneath a glorious *belle époque* domed ceiling, Tous also organises concerts of experimental music, and upstairs there is a performance and video space.
Bookshop. Disabled: wheelchair access.

The fringe scene

Perhaps the oddest aspect of the Barcelona art scene before the 1992 Olympics was the scarcity of independent initiatives on the part of artists, who tended to let public bodies and private dealers set the artistic agenda. While in other cultural sectors the 1980s were a boom time for individual innovation, the speculative international market of the time, with its search for saleable stars straight out of art school, and the bonanza of official patronage available in pre-Olympic Barcelona seduced many artists into an aggressive quest for commercial success.

A new type of politicised art activism has emerged since 1992. Some initiatives imitate 1970s models (art parties, performance art, open studios), while others hook up with the city's squatters' movement. In some fields – performance, video art – there is a distinctly iconoclastic Catalan style, influenced by Dada and the theatre of the absurd (also a forte of the **Espai Escènic Joan Brossa**,

see chapter **Theatre**). The result is a multifarious range of art activities, many well organised and/or with institutional backing, others short-term and poorly presented. Venues that welcome the best work include **Metrònom** and the **CCCB**, which hosts an international multimedia festival, the **Mostra de Video Independent**, and part of the **Sonar** new music festival each June (*see chapter* **Music: Rock, Roots & Jazz**). Another event to follow is the **Marató de l'Espectacle** performance jamboree in May/June (*see chapter* **Barcelona by Season**), which now generally coincides with **Drap Art**, a festival of art and design using recycled materials.

On a smaller scale, there's a string of places that stage art parties and performance evenings – the **Cafè del Sol**, or clubs like the **Apolo** – while other artists prefer a nomadic life, finding new locations for every event. This kind of thing blends into frontier Barcelona nightlife, and semi-legal or one-off venues that come and go. For more on all this, and more venues, *see chapter* **Nightlife**.

L'Angelot

C/Correu Vell 10, baixos 3 (93 345 05 25). Metro Jaume I/bus 17, 40, 45. **Open** 5-8pm Tue-Fri. Closed Aug. **Map D5**
Run by video specialist Claudia Gianetti and her artist husband Thomas Nölle, this is a small gallery in the Barri Gòtic specialising in video art, photography and new technologies. It's only open when there's something on, so call ahead.

Centro Cultural La Santa

C/Rec 58, corner of C/Guillem (93 268 11 56). Metro Barceloneta/bus 14, 39, 51. **Open** 5.30-8.30pm Tue, Thur. **Map E5**
In a ramshackle old workshop just off the Born, this is the 'showcase' for an association with an international membership of over 100 artists. As much a part of the exhibit is the place itself, with a kitsch/surreal décor of post-Gaudíesque mirrors and tiles. There are also extravagant chairs, jewellery and other items for sale. The Tuesday and Thursday events have a party atmosphere; there may also be something going on there at other times, but it's best to check first.

Studio Meyetta

C/Jupí 4 (93 935 91 31). Metro Jaume I/bus 17, 40, 45. **Open** by appointment. Closed Aug. **No credit cards. Map D5**
Architect Mirko Meyetta and former gallerist Benet Costa do small shows of first-rate artists' work. Exhibits can be viewed on opening night, or afterwards by appointment.
Disabled: wheelchair access.

Hangar

Passatge del Marqués de Santa Isabel 40 (93 308 40 41). Metro Poble Nou/bus 40, 42. **Open** 24hrs daily; *information* 9am-2pm Mon-Fri.
The availability of inexpensive empty factory space in Poble Nou has given rise to an exodus of artists from the Raval to this sprawling working-class neighbourhood. Besides being a multi-disciplinary production centre with studios and other services for artists, Hangar is the headquarters of the influential Catalan visual artists' association. Other artist-run spaces in Poble Nou include **Espai 22A**, C/Llull 226, local 22A (93 442 26 84) and the gallery of the **Centre Civic Can Felipa**, C/Pallars 277 (93 266 44 41). Poble Nou artists also organise an open studio project in the summer.

Eat, Drink, Sleep, Shop

Accommodation

Lodging logistics for the Mediterranean metropolis.

A mention for the 1992 effect is still obligatory when looking at hotels in Barcelona. The need for accommodation in the lead-up to the Olympics sparked off a frenetic burst of hotel building and renovation: nearly 30 new hotels were built, mostly in the three- to five-star brackets, and many more received a complete face-lift. Consequently Barcelona acquired something of a glut of luxury options, and a wide choice of mid-range hotels. Even so, the local authorities consider that there is still a shortage of hotel rooms in the city, given Barcelona's burgeoning popularity as a trade fair and conference venue, and plans are in hand to construct an additional 15 or so, most of them in the medium price range.

Some foreign (mostly northern) visitors think that Barcelona's post-1992 accommodation lacks character, especially the new mid-range hotels with their uniform glowing marble reception areas. However, marble is cool and clean in a Mediterranean city, and these hotels do guarantee visitors reasonable comfort at reasonable prices; also, in among the functional business hotels there is still a selection of more individual places to stay.

At the same time as hotel-building was proceeding apace for business and middle-bracket travellers, though, the Ajuntament pre-1992 also closed many of the cheapest *pensions* in the old city, deeming them too run down to be acceptable. For a time it became noticeably more difficult to find a really cheap room in Barcelona. However, in the last few years there have been signs of a re-opening of some old budget locations, still at low prices but with much-improved facilities.

In the last century, Barcelona's first real hotels were all built along the Rambla, and a large number of hotels can still be found concentrated in the old city – also still the best area for cheaper accommodation. The other main hotel area is the Eixample, where there are many mid-range places and some good-value *hostals*. This is the best area to stay if you need easy vehicle access, preferably in a hotel with its own parking, as on-street parking is risky and inconvenient (*see page 260*).

STARS, HOTELS, *HOSTALS* & PRICES

All accommodation in Catalonia is regulated by the Generalitat. Years ago, accommodation in Spain included a bewildering mix of *fondas, residencias, pensions* and hotels. Today, there are officially only two categories, hotels (H) and *hostals*

(HS), although many places continue to use the old names, which can be confusing. To be a hotel, star-rated one to five, a place must have bathrooms in every room. Ratings are given on the basis of overall quality and services rather than price. *Hostals*, star-rated one to three and usually cheaper than hotels, do not have to have en suite bathrooms throughout, nor do many have restaurants. They have been hit by renovation as well, though, and so many have bathrooms in at least some rooms. In short, star ratings are not an automatic guide to cost or facilities, and even four-star hotels can throw up pleasant surprises in their prices.

The prices quoted are the official weekday rates for the Easter and mid-summer high season. They should be taken as **guidelines** only, though, for prices at individual hotels are also very variable. Mid- and upper-range hotels, especially, frequently offer reductions of up to 40 per cent at weekends or outside the busiest periods, as well as company and other discounts, and so can provide remark-

The **Hotel Catalunya Plaza**. *See page 105.*

ably good deals; at the other end of the scale, when a trade fair or special event is in town, prices tend to soar. It's always worth checking current prices and inquiring about discounts, offers and so on. All hotel bills are subject to seven per cent IVA (value-added tax) on top of the basic price. Breakfast is not included in rates given below unless stated. Many hotels overcharge for light breakfasts, and it is often better just to go to a café. If you want to leave a car in a hotel car park, this will also usually add to your bill, and you should reserve parking when booking the room.

There is a hotel booking office (with no commission, but a deposit is requested against the bill) at the main tourist office, the **Centre d'Informació Plaça Catalunya** (*see page 251; Map D4*), and a private office, **Ultramar**, inside Sants rail station. Both take bookings in all categories, but their lists are selective, not exhaustive of all accommodation in Barcelona. Tourist offices do, though, have a full list. When booking, to be sure of light or a view, ask for an outside room (*habitación exterior*); many Barcelona buildings are built around a central patio or air shaft, which can be gloomy. Inside (*interior*) rooms, however, may gain in quietness what they lack in light.

Ultramar Express

Vestibule, Estació de Sants (93 491 44 63). Metro Sants-Estació/bus 27, 43, 44, 109. **Open** 8am-10pm daily. Closed 26 Dec. **Map A3**
When booking you will be asked to pay a deposit (around 2,000ptas), which will be added into your hotel bill, and a small fee (about 100ptas), and will be given a map and directions.

Real luxury (over 30,000ptas)

Barcelona Hilton

Avda Diagonal 589-591, 08014 (93 495 77 77/fax 93 495 77 00). Metro Maria Cristina/bus 6, 7, 33, 34, 63, 66, 67, 68. **Rates** *single* 27,000ptas; *double* 70,000-90,000ptas. **Credit** AmEx, DC, JCB, MC, TC, V.
Opened in 1990, Barcelona's 288-room Hilton was designed by Helio Piñón and Albert Viaplana – architects of the Plaça dels Paisos Catalans in Sants, and more recently of Maremàgnum in the port – in a minimalist steel-and-glass style. It lacks the range of facilities of some of its competitors, but some of its rooms are a little more intimate. In the heart of Barcelona's modern main business area, it concentrates particularly on providing business services.
Hotel services *Air-conditioning. Babysitting. Bar. Business/conference facilities. Car park. Currency exchange. Disabled: rooms (4) adapted for the disabled, wheelchair access. E-mail. Fax. Gym. Interpreters. Laundry. Lifts. Limousine service. Multilingual staff. Non-smoking rooms. Restaurants. Safe. Terrace.* **Room services** *Hairdryer. Minibar. Radio. Room service (24hrs). Telephone. TV (satellite).*

Hotel Arts

C/Marina 19-21, 08005 (93 221 10 00/fax 93 221 10 70/reservations from UK freephone 0800 234 0000/ from US freephone 0800 241 3333). Metro Ciutadella/ bus 36, 41, 92. **Rates** *standard room* 40,000ptas; *suite* 45,000ptas. **Credit** AmEx, DC, MC, V. **Map F6**.
A monument of Olympic Barcelona, the giant 455-room Arts tower by the Port Olímpic is an interloper built by American

Best pools

Hotel Arts – the only seafront pool in Barcelona.
Hotel Ambassador – a rooftop pool and whirlpool.
Hotel Balmes – a ground-floor pool for those afraid of heights.
Hotel Onix – a small rooftop pool, but with a great feeling of space.
Hotel Plaza – a rooftop pool with unbeatable views.
Hotel Regente – small pool, but, then, a rooftop bar at sunset…

architects (the Skidmore, Owings and Merrill practice). It's also the first hotel in Europe run by the Ritz-Carlton chain, and has a unique beach-front location and a matchless range of services. The views are staggering, there are specially-commissioned contemporary artworks scattered around the hotel, and the waterfall-lined lobby and garden areas are really magnificent. On the three top floors is 'The Club', a separate area for guests desiring still more privacy and service. As well as its standard rates the Arts offers a range of special weekend and other price packages, making a few days' spree in this most opulent symbol of the new Barcelona a possibility even if you don't have an expense account.
Hotel services *Air-conditioning. Babysitting (24hrs max). Bar. Beauty salon. Car park. Conference facilities. Currency exchange. Disabled: rooms (3) adapted for the disabled, wheelchair access. Dry cleaning. E-mail. Fax. Fitness centre (gym/sauna/massage). Garden. Hairdresser. Interpreters. Laundry. Lifts. Limousine service. Multilingual staff. Non-smoking floor. Restaurants. Shops. Swimming pool (outdoor). Ticket agency.* **Room services** *Hairdryer. Minibar. Radio. Room service (24hrs). Safe. Telephone. TV (satellite). Video.*

Hotel Claris

C/Pau Claris 150, 08009 (93 487 62 62/fax 93 215 79 70). Metro Passeig de Gràcia/bus 20, 21, 39, 43, 44, 45, N4, N5. **Rates** *single* 27,300ptas; *double* 34,100ptas; *suite* 42,000ptas; *suite duplex* 45,000ptas; *breakfast* 2,400ptas. **Credit** AmEx, DC, EC, JCB, MC, TC, V. **Map D3**.
A unique 121-room hotel in the heart of the Eixample, well located for Passeig de Gràcia and the best shopping areas. Discreet and refined, for lovers of ancient art, modern design, new technology and *la dolce vita*, the Claris has a special feature that stems from the archaeological interests of owner Jordi Clos, who also maintains the **Museu Egipci** of Egyptian relics (*see chapter* **Museums**). His collections originated in Rome, India and Burma as well as Egypt; some of them are housed in a small hotel museum, the rest are scattered around the hotel, including in the bedrooms.
Hotel services *Air-conditioning. Bar. Business services. Car park. Child-minding service. Conference facilities. Currency exchange. Disabled: rooms (4) adapted for the disabled, wheelchair access. Fitness centre (gym/sauna). Garden. Interpreters. Lifts. Limousine service. Multilingual staff. Non-smoking floor. Restaurants. Swimming pool (outdoors). Ticket agency.* **Room services** *Hairdryer. Minibar. Room service (24hrs). Safe. Telephone. TV (satellite). Video (some).*

Hotel HUSA-Palace

Gran Via de les Corts Catalanes 668, 08010 (93 318 52 00/fax 93 318 01 48). Metro Passeig de Gràcia/ bus 7, 18, 47, 50, 54, 56, 62, N1, N7. **Rates** *single* 28,000ptas; *double* 35,000ptas; *suite* 80,000. **Credit** AmEx, DC, EC, JCB, MC, TC, V. **Map D4**.

Since 1995, when this hotel was taken over by the HUSA chain – owners of many other hotels – Barcelona has no longer officially had a Ritz, even though the famous name is actually built into the façade (and taxi-drivers still call it that). However, the nineteenth-century ex-Ritz was extensively and tastefully renovated in the early 1990s, and despite the change of title still qualifies as the most elegant hotel in town, offering old-fashioned style that its rivals can only envy. Its no. 108 royal suite has been a favourite of Woody Allen, Orson Welles and the Duke and Duchess of Windsor, but the old Ritz's most regular celebrity guest was Salvador Dali, who spent months there at a stretch. The 150 large rooms have luxurious bathrooms, and despite redeco-

ration have kept their classical furnishings and atmosphere. The sumptuous restaurant is open to the public.
Hotel services *Air-conditioning. Babysitting. Bar. Conference facilities. Currency exchange. Disabled: rooms (3) adapted for the disabled, wheelchair access. Fax. Garden. Interpreting services. Laundry. Lifts. Limousines. Multilingual staff. Non-smoking floor. Restaurant. Ticket agency.* **Room services** *Hairdryer. Minibar. Radio. Room service (24hrs). Safe. Telephone. TV.*

Hotel Le Meridien Barcelona

La Rambla 111, 08002 (93 318 62 00/fax 93 301 77 76). Metro Liceu/bus 14, 38, 59, N6, N9. **Rates** *single 26,000ptas; double 32,000ptas; suite 73,000ptas.* **Credit** AmEx, DC, TC, JCB, MC, V. **Map D5**.
Part of the French Meridien chain, this 209-room hotel couldn't be more central, although nowadays the Rambla is not the place you expect to find a luxury hotel of this calibre. Thanks in part to its heart-of-things location, though, it's popular with celebrities and has a certain hip status: Bruce Springsteen, Michael Jackson, the Stones and Oasis have all stayed here. The restaurant, Le Patio, serves Mediterranean cuisine. Good 'Winter-Passport' and 'Summer-Passport' rates are available in December-February and July-August.
Hotel services *Air-conditioning. Babysitting. Bar. Car park. Conference facilities. Currency exchange. Disabled: rooms (4) adapted for the disabled, wheelchair access. Fax. Fitness centre (gym). Interpreting services. Laundry. Lifts. Limousine. Multilingual staff. Non-smoking rooms. Restaurant. Safe. Ticket agency.* **Room services** *Hairdryer. Minibar. Radio. Room services (24hrs). Telephone. TV (satellite). Video.*

Rooms with a view

Opulent cascades at the **Hotel Arts**.

Hostal Jardí – people-watching views of leafy Plaça Sant Josep Oriol with its artists and outdoor cafés.
Hotel Arts – hard-to-beat views of sea and city
Hotel Catalunya Plaza – relaxing views from elegant interiors.
Hotel Colon – the Cathedral and its wide open *plaça*.
Hotel Onix – the Parc Joan Miró just isn't the same from ground level.
Hotel Plaza – hypnotising; you may never leave your room.
Hotel Triunfo – the Ciutadella park and the glass and iron frame of the Hivernacle.

Smooth comfort (20-30,000ptas)

Hotel Ambassador

C/Pintor Fortuny 13, 08001 (93 412 05 30/reservations 93 318 91 33/fax 93 302 79 77). Metro Liceu/bus 14, 38, 59, N6, N9. **Rates** *single 22,000ptas; double 28,000ptas.* **Credit** AmEx, DC, EC, JCB, MC, TC, V. **Map D4**.
Excellently located just off the Rambla, near **Le Meridien** (*see above*), this modern hotel has a plain façade that belies its elegant interior. Completely rebuilt pre-Olympics, it was consciously planned on a smaller scale than other hotels of this standard, with only 105 rooms. Exterior rooms overlook one of three streets, one of which can be a bit gloomy; if you want direct sunlight, ask for an upper-floor room to the rear. There is an attractive ground-floor lounge bar where drinks are served from a turn-of-the century newspaper kiosk, a rooftop pool, jacuzzi and sun lounge with panoramic views of the city – a big plus – an underground car park and prices that make it a real find for a hotel with this kind of facilities.
Hotel services *Air-conditioning. Bar. Car park. Conference facilities. Currency exchange. Disabled: rooms (4) adapted for the disabled, wheelchair access. Fax. Fitness centre (gym/massage/sauna). Interpreters. Laundry. Lifts. Limousine service. Multilingual staff. Non-smoking rooms. Restaurant. Swimming pool (outdoors). Terrace. Ticket agency.* **Room services** *Hairdryer. Minibar. Room service (7am-11pm daily). Safe. Telephone. TV (satellite).*

Hotel Catalunya Plaza

Plaça Catalunya 7, 08002 (93 317 71 71/fax 93 317 78 55). Metro Catalunya/bus all routes to Plaça Catalunya. **Rates** *single 17,000ptas; double 20,000ptas; triple 23,000ptas.* **Credit** AmEx, DC, JCB, MC, V. **Map D4**.
Not to be confused with the bigger, modern-style **Plaza** (*see below*), this gracious 46-room hotel, renovated in 1992, is housed in a nineteenth-century building with beautiful stained-glass windows and ornate ceilings representing the four seasons. It's one for those who enjoy old-world ele-

*Cutting-edge design, or a cartoon? The **Plaza** is much nicer inside. Really. See page 108.*

gance but don't want to break the bank. The rooms at the front of the hotel have the best views, and are double-glazed. A generous breakfast is also served, in a delightful dining room from which you have a full view of the fountains in Plaça Catalunya. The hotel also serves a good lunchtime set menu for 1,600ptas.
Hotel services *Air-conditioning. Bar. Conference facilities. Currency exchange. Fax. Laundry service. Lifts. Multilingual staff. Restaurant. Ticket agency.* **Room services** *Hairdryer. Minibar. Room service (7am-11pm). Safe. Telephone. TV.*

Hotel Colón

Avda de la Catedral 7, 08002 (93 301 14 04/fax 93 317 29 15). Metro Jaume I/ bus 17, 19, 40, 45. **Rates** *single* 15,500ptas; *double* 23,000ptas; *suite* 36,500-41,500ptas.
Credit AmEx, DC, EC, MC, TC, V. **Map D5**.
This 147-room hotel has a prime position opposite the Cathedral in the heart of the Barri Gòtic, so that from its front rooms you have a matchless position for watching the *sardana* dancing on Sundays, or the antique market on Thursdays. The piano bar is a relaxing corner, and there is a good restaurant; hotel furnishings have touches of old-world luxury, and staff are friendly and efficient. The sister hotel the **Regencia Colón**, just around the corner, is also comfortable, with cosy breakfast room, but lacks the view, and is another price-bracket cheaper. Guests staying there can use the facilities at the main Colón.
Hotel services *Air-conditioning. Babysitting. Bar. Conference facilities. Currency exchange. Disabled: rooms (2) adapted for the disabled, wheelchair access. Fax. Laundry. Lifts. Limousines. Multilingual staff. Restaurant.* **Room services** *Hairdryer. Minibar. Radio. Room service (24hrs). Safe. Telephone. TV (satellite).*
Branch: Hotel Regencia Colón C/Sagristans 13-17, 08002 (93 318 98 59 /fax 93 317 28 22).

Hotel Condes de Barcelona

Passeig de Gràcia 75, 08008 (93 488 33 00/fax 93 487 14 42). Metro Passeig de Gràcia/bus 7, 16, 17, 22, 24, 28, N4, N6. **Rates** *single* 19,500ptas; *double* 20,500ptas.
Credit AmEx, DC, EC, MC, V. **Map D3**.
The 1891 Hotel Condes was fully renovated in the 1980s, and is beautifully floodlit at night. Its marble-floored lobby has retained the features of the original courtyard, right up to the pentagonal skylight, and rooms are decorated in keeping with the style of the building. It also has a rooftop terrace overlooking Passeig de Gràcia, with fine views. One of Barcelona's more popular hotels, it has recently expanded into an adjacent building which, while pleasant, doesn't have the charm of the original; when booking, – well in advance – state a preference for the original building.
Hotel services *Air-conditioning. Babysitting. Bar. Car park. Conference facilities. Currency exchange. Disabled: rooms adapted for the disabled, wheelchair access. Fax. Laundry. Lifts. Limousines. Multilingual staff. Non-smoking rooms. Restaurant. Swimming pool (outdoor).* **Room services** *Hairdryer. Minibar. Room service (7am-11pm). Safe. Telephone. TV (satellite). Video.*

Hotel Duques de Bergara

C/Bergara 11, 08002 (93 301 51 51/fax 93 317 34 42). Metro Catalunya/bus all routes to Plaça Catalunya. **Rates** *single* 16,900ptas; *double* 20,900ptas.
Credit AmEx, DC, MC, TC, V. **Map D4**.
A luxury hotel created in 1987 from an 1898 *Modernista* edifice by Gaudí's teacher Emili Sala, and located just off Plaça Catalunya. The original style has been kept in hall and stairways, while communal rooms are very modern. The 149 guest rooms are spacious and well furnished, and double rooms often have a small seating area as well. Most rooms are light and look onto the street or a quiet courtyard, but check when booking, as a few rooms are dark.

Hotel services *Air-conditioning. Babysitting.*
Conference facilities. Currency exchange. Disabled: rooms
(7) adapted for the disabled, wheelchair access. Fax.
Laundry. Lifts. Limousine. Multilingual staff. Restaurant.
Swimming pool. Terrace. Ticket agency. **Room services**
Hairdryer. Minibar. Radio. Room service (24hrs). Safe.
Telephone. TV (satellite).

Hotel Plaza

Plaça Espanya 6-8, 08014 (93 426 26 00/fax 93 426 04
00). Metro Espanya/bus 9, 38, 65, 91, 109, N1. **Rates**
single 18,900ptas; *double* 22,900ptas; *suite* 35,000-
50,000ptas; *breakfast* 1,500ptas. **Credit** AmEx, DC, EC
(25,000ptas max), JCB, MC, TC, V. **Map A4.**

Many new arrivals in Barcelona experience a double-take
when they see this huge building, right on Plaça d'Espanya,
but give it time, for its bunker-like façade belies the splendour and charm of the hotel's interior. With 338 rooms, the
Plaza has been overshadowed by another modern 'giant', the
Arts (*see above*), built at the same time, but in the hotel-with-
a-view stakes it can certainly hold its own, with breathtaking vistas from its front towers across Plaça d'Espanya to
Montjuïc, the MNAC museum and the fountains. The nine
suites in the upper tower all offer heady 360° views. It also
has very high-quality facilities: the breakfast room with its
draped ceilings is ritzily palatial, while on a more mundane
level there's a fully-fitted gym, beauty salon and great
rooftop pool. Booking a room can be difficult at times, but
November-December and July-August should be no problem, and there are also low-season rates.
Hotel services: *Air-conditioning. Babysitting. Bar. Car*
park. Conference facilities. Currency exchange. Disabled:
rooms (4) adapted for the disabled, wheelchair access.
Fax. Fitness centre (gym/sauna/massage). Interpreting
services. Laundry. Lifts. Limousines. Multilingual staff.
Restaurant. Swimming pool (outdoor). Terrace. **Room**
services *Hairdryer. Minibar. Room service (24hrs).*
Safe. Telephone. TV (satellite).

Hotel Regente

Rambla Catalunya 76, 08008 (93 487 59 89/
fax 93 487 32 27). Metro Passeig de Gràcia/FGC
Provença/bus 20, 21, 43, 44, N7. **Rates** *single* 14,900-
19,500ptas; *double* 17,500-24,500ptas.
Credit AmEx, DC, EC, JCB, MC, TC, V. **Map D3.**

The Regente occupies the Casa Juncosa, a *Modernista* mansion designed by Salvador Viñals and constructed in 1913.
It has recently been entirely renovated, and the façade
restored to its original state. Stained-glass decoration in the
interior gives this 79-room hotel a distinctive charm: rooms
on the sixth and seventh floors all have large terraces – those
to the front somewhat larger – with stunning views, while
lower rooms give on to gracious wrought-iron balconies.
Double-glazed windows shield out street noise. A more modern asset is the rooftop pool area, which, with stunning views
over Montjuïc, Tibidabo, and just about all of Barcelona, is
a perfect place to enjoy the sunset. Other extras include exercise bikes in several rooms. An excellent Eixample choice.
Hotel services *Air-conditioning. Babysitting. Bar.*
Conference facilities. Currency exchange. Disabled: rooms
(2) adapted for the disabled, wheelchair access. Fax.
Fitness facilities. Interpreting services. Laundry. Lifts.
Limousines. Multilingual staff. Restaurant (only
breakfast). Swimming pool (outdoor). Terrace. Ticket
agency. **Room services** *Hairdryer. Minibar. Radio.*
Room service (7am-11pm daily). Safe. Telephone. TV
(satellite).

Hotel Rivoli Ramblas

La Rambla 128, 08002 (93 302 66 43/
reservations 93 412 09 88/fax 93 317 50 53). Metro
Catalunya/bus all routes to Plaça Catalunya. **Rates** *(incl*
breakfast) single 23,600ptas; *double* 29,900ptas. **Credit**
AmEx, DC, JCB, MC, TC, V. **Map D4/D5.**

An elegant and luxurious hotel rebuilt in the early 1990s, the
Rivoli is a world apart from the bustle on the Rambla outside, but still just a few minutes' walk from Plaça Catalunya.
The 90 rooms have interesting colour schemes, and the Blue
Moon piano bar is a relaxing place to end the evening, mak-
ing the hotel a popular stop-over for both Spanish business
people and international visitors.
Hotel services *Air-conditioning. Babysitting. Bar. Car*
park. Conference facilities. Currency exchange. Fax.
Fitness facilities (gym/sauna/solarium). Interpreting
services. Laundry. Lifts. Limousines. Multilingual staff.
Restaurant. Terrace. Ticket agency. **Room services**
Hairdryer. Minibar. Room service (7am-11pm). Safe.
Telephone. TV (satellite).

Upper-mid (13-20,000ptas)

Hotel Balmes

C/Mallorca 216, 08008 (93 451 19 14/fax 93 451 0049).
FGC Provença/bus 7, 16, 17, 20, 21, 43, 54, 58, 64, 66,
N3. **Rates** *single* 12,600ptas; *double* 18,500ptas; *suite*
21,000ptas. **Credit** AmEx, DC, EC, MC, TC, V. **Map D3.**
A pleasant 1990-vintage 100-room hotel in the middle of the
Eixample. Rooms are comfortable: those at the rear get the
morning sun and look out onto an interior garden, solarium
and pool, and some ground-floor rooms have their own outside terraces. All-round comfort and service above the norm
for this grade of hotel.
Hotel services *Air-conditioning. Babysitting. (24hrs'*
notice). Bar (Mon-Fri). Car park. Conference facilities.
Currency exchange. Fax. Garden. Interpreting services.
Laundry. Lifts. Limousine. Multilingual staff. Restaurant
(Mon-Fri). Swimming pool. Ticket agency. **Room**
services *Hairdryer. Minibar. Radio. Room service (8am-*
11pm Mon-Fri). Safe. Telephone. TV (satellite).

Hotel Oriente

La Rambla 45-47, 08002 (93 302 25 58/
fax 93 412 38 19). Metro Drassanes/bus 14, 18, 38, 59,
N6, N9. **Rates** *single* 8,800ptas; *double* 14,300ptas.
Credit AmEx, DC, EC, MC, TC, V. **Map D5.**
Still one of the most atmospheric hotels in this price bracket,
the Oriente was Barcelona's first 'grand hotel', inaugurated
in 1842 and incorporating sections of an old Franciscan
monastery built two centuries earlier. It once played host to
such illustrious personalities as Washington Irving, Hans
Christian Anderson, General Grant, screen stars such as Mary
Pickford or Errol Flynn and – due to its proximity to the Liceu
– a catalogue of musicians: Toscanini, Maria Callas, Casals
and many others. Reminders of its glorious past can be seen
in its old-world dining room and elegant ballroom, which
retains parts of the old monastery cloister. The hotel, however, has definitely seen better days, and today is a far cry
from what it must have been like in its heyday. Its 142 rooms
are spacious, but quite spartan: many overlook the noisy
Rambla, while the rooms on the C/Unió side face the site of
the under-reconstruction opera house, making them especially noisy during work hours. Service is patchy. However,
there are often good weekend and low-season rates.
Hotel services *Bar. Conference facilities. Fax. Lifts.*
Multilingual staff. Restaurant. **Room services** *Room*
service (7am-10pm). Safe. TV. Telephone.

Hotel Royal

La Rambla 117, 08002 (93 301 94 00/reservations 93
318 73 29/fax 93 317 31 79). Metro Liceu/bus 14, 38,
59, N6, N9. **Rates** *single* 11,500ptas; *double* 18,500ptas;
triple 22,000ptas. **Credit** AmEx, DC, MC, V. **Map D4.**
While not overflowing with personality, this 20-year-old
hotel is modern and functional, and a bargain given its location. Another attraction are the staff, who are especially helpful. Its 108 rooms are tastefully decorated, and the view from
front rooms over the tree-lined Rambla is unique.

Hotel services *Air-conditioning. Babysitting. Bar. Car park. Conference facilities. Currency exchange. Disabled: wheelchair access. Fax. Interpreting services. Laundry. Lift. Limousine. Multilingual staff. Non-smoking floor. Restaurant. Ticket agency.* **Room services** *Hairdryer. Minibar. Radio. Room service (7am-11pm). Safe. Telephone. TV (satellite). Video.*

Nouvel Hotel

C/Santa Ana 18-20 (93 301 82 74/fax 93 301 83 70). Metro Catalunya/bus all routes to Plaça Catalunya. **Rates** (incl breakfast) *single* 8,300ptas, *double* 13,200ptas, *triple* 15,750ptas. **Credit** AmEx, MC, V. **Map D4**
Very near Plaça Catalunya and the Rambla, in a carefully refurbished *Modernista* building, this cosy hotel has 69 spacious rooms, with high ceilings and tall doors. The larger front rooms conserve their original tiled floors, non-fitted wardrobes and beautiful wrought-iron balconies, overlooking a pedestrian street. Decoration in the rear rooms is more modern, but they are quieter. There are several comfortable, elegant sitting rooms and TV rooms to let you feel at home.
Hotel services *Air-conditioning. Disabled: room (1) adapted for the disabled, wheelchair access. Fax. Laundry. Lift. Multilingual staff.* **Room services** *Safe. Telephone. TV (satellite).*

Park Hotel

Avda Marquès de l'Argentera 11, 08003 (93 319 60 00/ fax 93 319 45 19). Metro Barceloneta/bus 14, 16, 17, 39, 45, 51. **Rates** (incl breakfast) *single* 9,350ptas; *double* 14,600ptas. **Credit** AmEx, DC, JCB, MC, V. **Map E5.**
Despite its resemblance to a shabby seaside apartment block, the Park Hotel, opposite the Estació de França, has been refurbished with style. Public areas and the 87 rooms are comfortably decorated in pale yellow, and the hotel has kept its kitschy seventies art deco turquoise mosaic bar, a place you might go to even if you weren't staying here. Service is friendly, and there are particularly good facilities for disabled visitors.
Hotel services *Air-conditioning. Bar. Car park. Conference facilities. Currency exchange. Disabled: rooms (5) adapted for the disabled, wheelchair access. Fax. Laundry. Multilingual staff. Non-smoking rooms. Restaurant. Terrace.* **Room services** *Hairdryer. Minibar. Radio. Room service (7am-midnight). Safe. Telephone. TV (satellite).*

Lower-mid (6-13,000ptas)

Hostal Jardí

Plaça Sant Josep Oriol 1, 08002 (93 301 59 00/fax 93 318 36 64). Metro Liceu/bus 14, 18, 38, 59, N6, N9. **Rates** older (interior) rooms *single* 4,000ptas; *double* 5,500ptas; new (exterior) rooms *single or double* 6,600-7,500ptas. **Credit** AmEx, DC, MC, V. **Map D5.**
One of the most popular lower-range hotels in Barcelona, overlooking the quiet, leafy Plaça del Pi in the Barri Gòtic, the Jardí post-renovation has rooms with different levels of facilities, and hence varying prices. The fully renovated outer rooms are more expensive, but still a bargain, and have great views of the streetlife in the plaça. All rooms have bathrooms, but the inner rooms are more basic, and the inside patio can be noisy. Book well in advance.
Hotel services *Refreshments available from reception (24hrs). Safety deposit box.* **Room services** *Telephone. TV (some).*

Hostal-Residencia Ramos

C/Hospital 36, 08001 (93 302 07 23/fax 93 302 04 30). Metro Liceu/bus 14, 18, 38, 59, N6, N9. **Rates** *single* 3,500-4,000ptas; *double* 5,000-6,500ptas; *triple* 7,500-9,000ptas. **Credit** AmEx, DC, EC, MC, TC, V. **Map C5.**
Ideally situated off the Raval-side of theRambla, overlooking Plaça Sant Agusti, this hotel occupies the first floor of a

charming old building with a black and white tiled entrance and elegant wide staircase – but no lift. All rooms have bath, telephone, TV, central heating and air-conditioning, and those at the front have a view of the tree-filled *plaça*.
Hotel services *Air-conditioning. Fax. Multilingual staff (reception). Refreshments available. Safe. Terrace.* **Room services** *Room service (10am-6pm). Telephone. TV.*

Hostal Rey Don Jaime I

C/Jaume I 11, 08002 (tel/fax 93 310 62 08). Metro Jaume I/bus 17, 40, 45. **Rates** *single* 4,100ptas; *double* 6,200ptas. **Credit** AmEx, DC, EC, JCB, MC, V. **Map D5**.
This long-established *hostal* is handy for the Barri Gòtic and La Ribera, but it sits on the Via Laietana, main artery for traffic through the old city. Basic but clean, the 36 rooms all have balconies and bathrooms, and it's popular with a young clientele.
Hotel services *Currency exchange. Lift. Lounge. Multilingual staff. Safe. TV. 24-hour reception.* **Room services** *Telephone.*

Hotel España

C/Sant Pau 9-11, 08001 (93 318 17 58/ fax 93 317 11 34). Metro Liceu/bus 14, 18, 38, 59, N6, N9. **Rates** (incl breakfast) *single* 5,400ptas; *double* 10,300ptas. **Credit** AmEx, DC, MC, V. **Map C5.**
The Hotel España, in the Raval just off the Rambla, is a landmark of *Modernista* architecture, ranking almost with the Palau de la Música in renown. The lower floors were designed by Domènech i Montaner in 1902: the main restaurant, in which a good lunch menu is available, is decorated with floral motifs in tile and elaborate woodwork, while beyond it is a larger dining room, with extravagant murals of river-nymphs by Ramon Casas, also in tiles. In the adjoining bar, there is a huge fireplace by sculptor Eusebi Arnau. After these rooms, the more modern guest rooms can be a disappointment, but several open on to a bright interior patio. Book well in advance, as it is regularly full.
Hotel services *Bar. Fax. Conference facilities. Lifts. Multilingual staff. Restaurant. Safe. TV.* **Room services** *Safe (some). Telephone.*

Hotel Gaudí

C/Nou de la Rambla 12, 08001 (93 317 90 32/ fax 93 412 26 36). Metro Drassanes/bus 14, 18, 38, 59, N6, N9. **Rates** (incl breakfast) *single* 8,000ptas; *double* 11,000ptas. **Credit** AmEx, DC, EC, JCB, MC, TC, V. **Map C5.**
The Gaudí's great selling point has been its status as the main mid-level hotel in a central, convenient and much-visited area that's within the old Barrio Chino, its well-equipped rooms contrasting with the shabbiness nearby. Directly opposite is Gaudí's **Palau Güell** (*see chapter* **Sightseeing**). Accordingly the hotel has acquired an all-new, Gaudí-inspired reception area, and the 73 rooms are good for this area and price-bracket. Service is undynamic.
Hotel services *Air-conditioning. Babysitting. Bar (noon-midnight). Car park. Conference facilities. Currency exchange. Disabled: rooms (2) adapted for the disabled, wheelchair access. Fax. Fitness centre (gym). Interpreting services. Lifts. Multilingual staff. Restaurant.* **Room services** *Hairdryer. Radio. Room service (noon-midnight). Safe. Telephone. TV (satellite).*

Hotel Internacional

La Rambla 78-80, 08002 (93 302 25 66/ fax 93 317 61 90). Metro Liceu/bus 14, 18, 38, 59, N6, N9. **Rates** *single* 5,600ptas; *double* 9,000ptas. **Credit** AmEx, DC, EC, MC, V. **Map D5.**
An institution on the Rambla, the 1894 Internacional has been extensively refurbished during the 1990s, and all its 60 high-ceilinged rooms have new bathrooms. With an outside balcony room you're ideally placed to watch the action on the Rambla come and go, and it's always full (so that it's

necessary to book at least a week in advance), but be warned that it's also very noisy, and that with such a ready audience the staff don't exactly strive to be helpful.
Hotel services *Bar. Currency exchange. Fax. Lift (from 1st floor). Multilingual staff. Safe (for hire). TV. Meals for groups.* **Room services** *Telephone.*

Hotel Mesón Castilla

C/Valldonzella 5, 08001 (93 318 21 82/fax 93 412 40 20), Metro Universitat/bus all routes to Plaça Catalunya.
Rates *single* 8,900ptas; *double* 12,600ptas. **Credit** AmEx, DC, MC, V. **Map C4**.
A favourite with northern visitors, who enjoy the hearty buffet breakfasts served in the cosy dining room or on the newly decorated patio terrace. Founded in 1930, the hotel retains an old-world look. In its 56 impeccably clean rooms there is antique, hand-made furniture, and some rear rooms have balconies with views of the nearby **MACBA** (*see chapter* **Museums**). It also has three large rooms with up to four beds, ideal for families with children. Despite the central location, all rooms are quiet.
Hotel services *Air-conditioning. Car park. Disabled: wheelchair access. Fax. Laundry. Lifts. Multilingual staff. Safe. Terrace.* **Room services** *Minibar. Telephone. TV (satellite).*

Hotel Metropol

C/Ample 31, 08002 (93 310 51 00/fax 93 319 12 76). Metro Jaume I/bus 14, 17, 36, 40, 45, 57, 59, 64.
Rates *single* 10,500ptas; *double* 12,900ptas.
Credit AmEx, DC, MC, V. **Map D5**.
Another nineteenth-century hotel given a make-over in 1992, although its reception area still has its old charm. Half the 68 rooms look on to C/Ample, which is unusually quiet for a street in the old city very near the port. The Metropol offers good weekend deals, and also has reservation agreements with several local restaurants.
Hotel services *Air-conditioning. Disabled: wheelchair access. Fax. Laundry. Lift. Multilingual staff.* **Room services** *Minibar. Safe. Telephone. TV (satellite).*

Hotel Oasis

Pla del Palau 17, 08003 (93 319 43 96/ fax 93 310 48 74). Metro Barceloneta/bus 16, 17, 36, 40, 45, 59, 64. **Rates** *single* 4,850ptas; *double* 6,955ptas; *triple* 9,095ptas; *quadruple* 11,770ptas.
Credit AmEx, DC, MC, V. **Map D5**.
An unusually well-equipped near-budget-range hotel conveniently located near Estació de França and the Port Vell. All rooms have bathrooms and TV; most are external, with balconies, and can be noisy. Downstairs, the restaurant offers a decent menu for 1,000ptas, and there's also a café-bar that's open all day.
Hotel services *Bar. Lift (from first floor). Multilingual staff. Restaurant. Safe.* **Room services** *Air-conditioning (some rooms). Safe (some rooms). Telephone. TV (satellite).*

Hotel Onix

C/Llançà 30, 08015 (93 426 00 87/fax 93 426 19 81). Metro Espanya/bus 9, 13, 27, 109, 127. **Rates** *single* 9,600ptas; *double* 12,000ptas; *breakfast (buffet)* 1,000ptas.
Credit AmEx, DC, MC, V. **Map B4**.
A comfortable hotel near the Plaça d'Espanya area, with good access to Sants train station and the airport. All rooms have balconies, and those on the front (still quite quiet) face the now-disused Arenas bullring, while those at the back on the C/Diputacio side have great views over the **Parc Joan Miró** (*see chapter* **Sightseeing**) especially from the fifth floor. A relaxing alternative to city-centre hotels, it also has a rare asset in this price-bracket – a small rooftop pool and sun deck, with views of Montjuïc and the Palau Nacional.
Hotel services *Air-conditioning. Bar. Babysitting (24hrs' notice).Conference facilities. Car park. Disabled: rooms (3) adapted for the disabled, wheelchair access.*

Old-world charm

Hostal Girona – turn-of-the-century grace without going broke.
Hotel Catalunya Plaza – the lower floors ooze with charm.
Hotel Colón – comfort in a gracious environment.
Hotel España – a *Modernista* monument.
Hotel HUSA-Palace – the Ritz is still the most elegant place in town.
Hotel Mesón Castilla – beamed ceilings and rustic furniture offer a warm atmosphere.
Hotel Regente – a 1913 *Modernista* building with a distinctive feel.

Fax. Laundry. Lifts. Multilingual staff. Restaurant (for groups only). Swimming pool (rooftop). Ticket agency. **Room services** *Hairdryer. Minibar. Radio. Refrigerator. Room service (8am-11pm). Safe. Telephone. TV (satellite).*

Hotel Peninsular

C/Sant Pau 34-36, 08001 (93 302 31 38/ fax 93 412 36 99). Metro Liceu/bus 14, 18, 38, 59, N6, N9. **Rates** (incl breakfast) *single* 4,300ptas; *double* 6,300ptas. **Credit** EC, MC, TC, V. **Map C5**.
Like its grander neighbour the **Oriente** (*see p108*), the Peninsular was built (in the 1880s) in the remains of a former monastery, and its best feature is its tiled, plant-lined patio. It was modernised in the early 1990s, and all 80 rooms are clean and comfortable, with baths or showers. For a room with a view, secure one that looks over the courtyard.
Hotel services *Lift. Multilingual staff. Patio. Safe. TV lounge.* **Room services** *Air-conditioning (some). Telephone.*

Hotel Principal

C/Junta de Comerç 8, 08001 (93 318 89 74/fax 93 412 08 19). Metro Liceu/bus 14, 38, 59, N4, N6. **Rates** *single* 6,500ptas; *double* 8,500ptas. **Credit** AmEx, DC, EC, MC, TC, V. **Map C5**.
One of several hotels and *hostals* on this quiet street near the Rambla, the Principal has some distinctive features of its own – notably some ornate furniture in the bedrooms. All 60 rooms have recently modernised bathrooms. The same management also runs the cheaper Joventut along the street.
Hotel services *Air-conditioning. Babysitting. Bar. Currency exchange. Fax. Lifts. Multilingual staff. Restaurant.* **Room services** *Minibar. Safe. Telephone. TV (satellite)*
Branch: Hotel Joventut C/Junta de Comerç 12 (93 301 84 99).

Hotel San Agustin

Plaça Sant Agusti 3, 08001 (93 318 16 58/fax 93 317 29 28). Metro Liceu/bus 14, 38, 59, N6, N9.
Rates (incl breakfast) *single* 7,000ptas; *double* 10,500ptas. **Credit** AmEx, MC, TC, V. **Map C5**.
A traditional hotel that's been going well over 100 years, but underwent a 1992 refit, with a new reception area, lifts, bathrooms, full air-conditioning and TVs in every room. Some would say it's lost character, but its rooms are comfortable and still have some charm; the top floor offers attic-style rooms with oak-beamed ceilings and romantic views of old Barcelona. Lower rooms have balconies overlooking the tree-lined square and Sant Agusti church, or a less attractive side street. It has three very large rooms – with two bathrooms – which sleep up to six, ideal for families or groups. With all

*A welcoming corner in the Raval, the **Hotel Mesón Castilla**. See page 111.*

the renovation, it hasn't lost one of its most attractive features, a pleasant lounge-bar overlooking Plaça Sant Agusti. One of the best-value hotels in the area.
Hotel services *Air-conditioning. Babysitting. Bar. Conference facilities. Currency exchange. Disabled: rooms (2) adapted for the disabled, wheelchair access. Fax. Interpreting services. Laundry. Lifts. Multilingual staff. Restaurant. Ticket agency.* **Room services** *Hairdryer. Radio. Room service (9am-6pm). Safe. Telephone. TV (satellite).*

Hotel Triunfo

Passeig Picasso 22, 08003 (tel/fax 93 315 08 60) Metro Arc de Triomf/bus 39, 51. **Rates** *single* 5,500ptas; *double* 8,500ptas. **No credit cards. Map E5.**
The great attraction of this small, intimate hotel is its location, since most of its 15 rooms have balconies overlooking the Ciutadella Park and the zoo, and it is also very handy for the rest of La Ribera. All rooms have been recently renovated and are clean and bright, with good bathrooms. A change from more congested areas of the old city.
Hotel services *Air-conditioning. Lift. Refreshments available. Safe.* **Room services:** *Telephone. TV (satellite).*

Budget (6,000ptas and under)

Long-established as the favourite place to look for those in search of an inexpensive room in Barcelona is the Plaça Reial, just off La Rambla. Other good areas to find cheap hotels in the old city are the Raval, on the other side of La Rambla, and in La Ribera, near the Estació de França. The Eixample also has some rather more tranquil, but still good-value, budget hotels and *hostals*. Note that some budget places do not have someone on the door 24 hours a day, so check before going out.

Hostal Ambos Mundos

Plaça Reial 10, 08002 (93 318 79 70/fax 93 412 23 63). Metro Drassanes/bus 14, 18, 38, 59, N6, N9. **Rates** *single* 3,000ptas; *double* 4,000ptas. **Credit** AmEx, MC, V. **Map D5.**
One of the most popular of the Plaça Reial *hostals*, above a bar of the same name. The Ambos Mundos' 12 simple, tiled rooms are quite large, and all have baths. Outside rooms have small balconies overlooking the square, and in the cavernous reception area you can relax, play pool or watch TV.
Hotel services *Safe. TV.* **Room services** *Telephone.*

Hostal Girona

C/Girona 24, 1° 1ª, 08010 (93 265 02 59) Metro Urquinaona/ bus 19, 18, 39, 40, 41, 42, 47, 55. **Rates** *single* 3,000ptas; *double* 6,000ptas. **Credit** AmEx, DC, MC, V. **Map E4.**
A white marble stairway leads up to this family-run eight-room pension on the first floor of a magnificent turn-of-the-century Eixample building. The reception area has original *Modernista* furniture, huge doors and high ceilings, and the atmosphere is cosy and refined. The four double rooms have brand-new en suite bathrooms; single rooms are without baths, but all have central heating and TV. Most are outside rooms with balconies, and some interior rooms are a bit dark. There is a tiny breakfast area where coffee and refreshments are served. The surrounding streets house some of the finest *Modernista* architecture in the city, but although quite central the area goes unnoticed by most Barcelona visitors.
Hotel services *Laundry. Lounge. Lift. Refrigerator. Safe.* **Room services** *Telephone. TV.*

Best value for money

Hostal Maldà – no frills attached, but comfort and even charm at budget prices.
Hostal Windsor – treat yourself to 'living in style' without going broke.
Hotel Mesón Castilla – centrally located yet quiet, relaxing, comfortable.
Hotel San Agustín – 100-year-old former convent offers charm and comfort a stone's throw from the Rambla.
Hotel Onix – a fine inexpensive hotel with rooftop pool and great views.

Hostal Lausanne

Avda Portal de l'Àngel 24, 08002 (93 302 11 39) Metro Plaça Catalunya/bus All routes to Plaça Catalunya. **Rates** *single* 2,000ptas; *(with shower)* 5,000ptas; *(with bath)* 6,000ptas.
No credit cards. Map D4.
This 17-room, family-run *hostal* is on the first floor of a beautiful old building with a magnificent entrance, and inside there are high ceilings and spacious rooms, some with balconies overlooking the busy pedestrian strip between Plaça Catalunya and the Cathedral. It's clean and bright, with a large sitting room, and the owners are helpful and friendly.
Hotel services *Lift (from 1st floor). Lounge. Multilingual staff. Safe. Telephone. TV. Terrace. 24hr reception.*

Hostal Layetana

Plaça Ramon Berenguer el Gran 2, 08002 (tel/fax 93 319 20 12). Metro Jaume I/bus 17, 40, 45. **Rates** *single* 2,300ptas; *double* 3,600ptas; *(with shower)* 5,200ptas. **Credit** MC, V. **Map D5**.
A view right along the Roman wall and a stunning hall and lift give this *hostal* loads of character. Service is friendly, most of its 20 rooms have been renovated and given bathrooms, and the other, communal bathrooms are well-kept. Noise from Via Laietana is the major drawback.
Hotel services *Lift. Refreshments available (24hrs). Safe. Terrace. TV.*

Hostal Maldà

C/del Pi 5, 1° 1ª, 08002 (93 317 30 02). Metro Liceu/bus 14, 18, 38, 59, N6, N9. **Rates** *single* 1,500ptas; *double* 2,500ptas. **No credit cards. Map D5**.
Quite a find in every sense; access to the hotel is through one of the entrances to a shopping arcade, which makes finding it a bit of a quest, but even the hike up to the second floor (no lift) is forgotten when you meet the friendly lady who runs this small, comfortable place. There are no en suite bathrooms, just washbasins, but the bathrooms down the hall are impeccably clean and bright, and the apartment is exceptionally well-lit considering the narrow street. The stairway leading to the hostel was the service entrance of the mansion of an eighteenth-century aristocrat, the Marquès de Villalonga; its main entrance is now the grand staircase that leads up to the Maldà cinema, while the gardens were converted into the Galeries Maldà, Barcelona's oldest shopping arcade. The arcade entrance is open until 12.30am, after when a night porter comes on duty.
Hotel services *Laundry. Lounge. Refrigerator. Telephone. TV (satellite).*

Hostal Noya

La Rambla 133, 1°, 08002 (93 301 48 31). Metro Catalunya/bus all routes to Plaça Catalunya. **Rates** *single* 1,800ptas; *double* 3,400ptas. **No credit cards. Map D4**.
This modest *hostal* is in an excellent position on the Rambla, and good value for its location. All 15 rooms have balconies overlooking the crowds, but bathrooms are communal. No breakfast, but there's a good café-restaurant below.
Hotel services *Telephone.*

Hostal Orleans

Avda Marquès de l'Argentera 13, 08003 (93 319 73 82/ fax 93 319 22 19) Metro Barceloneta/bus 16, 17, 36, 40, 45, 51, 57, 59. **Rates** *single (with bath)* 2,500ptas; *double (with shower, one person)* 3,500ptas; *double (with shower, two people)* 5,500ptas; *double (with bath)* 6,500ptas. **Credit** AmEx, DC, MC, V. **Map E5**.
This family-run *hostal* near the Port and the Ciutadella has 17 good-sized rooms with balconies, most of which look on to a wide but noisy avenue or a quieter side-street. All rooms are spotless, but the upper-floor accommodation is more modern. There are special rates for triple or quadruple occupancy, and weekly rates can be negotiated for all rooms.
Hotel services: *Fax. Laundry. Lounge. English-speaking staff. Telephone.* **Room services**: *Telephone (some rooms). TV (satellite).*

Hostal Palermo

C/Boqueria 21, 08002 (tel/fax 93 302 40 02). Metro Liceu/bus 14, 18, 38, 59, N6, N9. **Rates** *single* 2,200-2900; *double* 3,600-4,600ptas; *triple* 5,000-6,000. **Credit** DC, MC, TC, V. **Map D5**.
Twenty-eight impeccably clean rooms, only two of which have bathrooms, but all recently refurbished. A stone's throw from the Rambla, this is a cheerful budget place to stay.
Hotel services *Dining room. Lounge. Safe. Telephone. TV.*

Hostal Paris

C/Cardenal Casañas 4, 08002 (tel/fax 93 301 37 85). Metro Liceu/bus 14, 18, 38, 59, N6, N9. **Rates** *single* 2,400-2,800ptas; *double* 4,000ptas; *(with shower)* 4,500ptas; *(with bath)* 5,500ptas. **Credit** AmEx, MC, V. **Map D5**.
Between the Rambla and the Plaça del Pi, this 45-room *hostal* was given a well-needed face-lift for the Olympics. It has a welcoming entrance and reception area, with a very large sitting room overlooking the Rambla. The exterior rooms are fine, but the interior ones, while quieter, receive very little natural light. Not for claustrophobics.
Hotel services *Multilingual staff.* **Room services** *Safe (some rooms).*

Hostal Parisien

La Rambla 114, 08002 (93 301 62 83). Metro Liceu/ bus 14, 18, 38, 59, N6, N9. **Rates** *single* 2,000ptas; *double* 3,500ptas; *(with shower)* 4,000ptas, 4,500ptas. **No credit cards. Map D5**.
A friendly young couple run this 13-room *hostal* which is a student favourite, with a great mid-Rambla location opposite the Palau Virreina. The rooms are well-kept, and four have en suite bathrooms. The ones overlooking the Rambla are noisy, but atmospheric, while others are darker but quieter.
Hotel services *Air-conditioning. Lounge. Multilingual staff. Safe. Telephone. TV (satellite).*

Hostal Plaza

C/Fontanella 18, 08010 (tel/fax 93 301 01 39l). Metro Urquinaona/bus all routes to Plaça Catalunya. **Rates** *single* 3,000-3,500ptas; *double* 4,500-5,500ptas; *triple* 6,500-7,500ptas. **Credit** AmEx, DC, MC, V. **Map D4**.
Remodelled and run by eager-to-please friendly Americans, the Plaza is an out-of-the-ordinary budget hotel with all-new high-standard plumbing and a veritable glut of services for

guests – including laundry (5kg, 1,000ptas), sitting room with TV, the use of a fridge, freezer and microwave, loads of information on the city and even, they say, discounts at local restaurants and clubs. All 14 rooms have showers and fans. A change from more traditional Spanish cheap hotels. You can even book by e-mail to plazahostal@mx3.redestb.es

Hotel services *E-mail. Fax. Kitchen facilities. Laundry. Lift. Multilingual staff. Safe. TV (satellite) room. Vending machine. Ventilators.* **Room services** *Fan. Radio.*

Hostal Rembrandt

C/Portaferrissa 23, 08002 (tel/fax 93 318 10 11). Metro Liceu/bus 14, 38, 59, N6, N9. **Rates** *single* 2,700ptas; *(with shower)* 3,500ptas; *double* 4,000ptas; *(with shower)* 4,500ptas; *(with bath)* 5,000ptas. **No credit cards. Map D5.**

A cheerful 29-room *hostal* centrally located on the main shopping street of the Barri Gòtic. Refurbished a few years ago, it's kept spotlessly clean, with pleasantly decorated rooms. The foyer opens onto a tiled patio, sometimes used as an eating area. Popular with backpackers, and the owners will put up to five people in one room at very reasonable prices.

Hotel services *Multilingual staff. Safe. Telephone. TV room.*

Hostal Santcarlo

Plaça Urquinaona 5, 3°, 08002 (93 302 41 25) Metro Urquinaona/bus all routes to Plaça Urquinaona. **Rates** *single* 2,000ptas; *(with bath)* 2,500ptas; *double* 3,500ptas *(with bath)* 4,500ptas. **No credit cards. Map D4.**

A no-frills *hostal*, centrally located on the third floor (yes, there's a lift) of a pleasant building just off Plaça Catalunya. It could have benefitted from pre-Olympic renovation: rooms are clean but spartan, and the only concessions to luxury are central heating and hot water. Outside rooms have balconies overlooking the busy *plaça*, which can be quite noisy, so they're a better bet for cool weather when the balcony doors can be closed. Otherwise, inside rooms are better and, as the interior patio is quite large, are quite bright.

Hotel services *Lift. Lounge. Telephone. TV.*

Hostal San Remo

C/Ausiàs Marc 19-C/Bruc 20, 1° 2°, 08010 (93 302 19 89/ fax 93 301 07 74). Metro Urquinaona/bus 18, 19, 39, 40, 41, 42, 47, 55, 141. **Rates** *(incl breakfast) single* 3,500ptas; *double* 5,200ptas. **Credit** MC, V. **Map E4.**

Another relaxing alternative to the bustle of the Rambla, but still conveniently central, this friendly, family-run hotel on the first floor of an old Eixample building has been completely remodelled. All rooms have central heating, air-conditioning, new bathrooms and double-glazing. Outside rooms have south-facing balconies, and there are two interior rooms which are also bright. The owner, Rosa, takes good care of her guests, many of whom are regulars, and her son speaks a little English. Breakfast is served in a sitting-room with big bay window, TV and even a piano. Guests are provided with keys to the street door and to the flat and room doors, so there's no need to worry about being locked out.

Hotel services *Air-conditioning. Fax. Lift. Safe. Telephone.* **Room services** *TV (cable).*

Hostal La Terrassa

C/Junta de Comerç 11, 08001 (93 302 51 74/fax 93 301 21 88). Metro Liceu/bus 14, 18, 38, 59, N6, N9. **Rates** *(incl breakfast) single* 2,100ptas; *(with shower)* 3,200ptas; *double* 3,600ptas; *(with shower)* 4,200ptas; *triple* 4,800ptas; *(with shower)* 5,400ptas. **Credit** AmEx, DC, MC, V. **Map C5.**

One of the most likeable of Barcelona's cheap *hostals*, and great value. Around half the rooms have bathrooms, and the best have balconies overlooking the street or an attractive

You may not get a room with a view in Barcelona, but you'll always get a room. The Carrer Sant Pau.

Best for children

Barcelona hotels are not especially well geared for children, and no play areas as such are provided.

Hotel Arts – expensive, yes, but there's a superb ground-level pool and a great big beach-front

Hotel Balmes – safe, ground-level pool and small garden.

Hotel Colon – child-minding facilities and cots available.

Hotel Mesón Castilla – family rooms, some rooms with well-protected terraces, and a breakfast patio perfect for kids.

Hotel San Agustin – large adjoining rooms with only one entrance door for safety, ideal for families .

---

interior patio, where breakfast is served in summer. The owner also runs Hostal Jardi.

Hotel services *Lounge. Multilingual staff. Safe. Telephone. Terrace. TV.*

Hostal Victória

C/Comtal 9, 1° 1a, 08002 (93 318 07 60/93 317 45 97). Metro Catalunya/bus all routes to Plaça Catalunya. **Rates** *single* 2,500ptas; *double* 4,000ptas; *(with bathroom)* 4,500ptas. **No credit cards. Map D4.**

A spacious 30-room *hostal* in the heart of the old town, ideal for budget travellers as it has communal cooking and washing facilities. The owner can be a bit authoritarian and the rooms are basic, but they're clean and light, and most have balconies. There's also a patio, rare for a one-star *hostal*.

Hotel services *Dining room. Kitchen. Laundry. Lift. Lounge. Refreshments available (24hrs). Terrace. TV. Telephone.*

Hostal Windsor

Rambla Catalunya 84, 08008 (93 215 11 98). Metro Passeig de Gràcia/bus 7, 50, 54, 56, N7. **Rates** *single* 3,500ptas; *(with shower)* 4,300ptas; *double* 5,900ptas; *(with shower)* 7,100ptas. **No credit cards. Map D3.**

A cheap and cheerful way of enjoying the *fin de siècle* splendour of the Eixample, the Windsor occupies a stylish *Modernista* building in a thriving, well-connected area. It's small, and can get crowded, so book ahead.

Hotel services *Lift. Multilingual staff. Telephone. TV.*

Hostal-Residencia Oliva

Passeig de Gràcia 32, 4°, 08007 (93 488 01 62/ 93 488 01 62). Metro Catalunya or Passeig de Gràcia/bus 7, 16, 17, 22, 24, 28, N6, N9. **Rates** *single* 3,100ptas; *double* 5,700ptas; *(with bath)* 6,700ptas. **No credit cards. Map D4.**

A 16-room *hostal* on the fourth floor of a massive old Eixample apartment block with two lifts, one brand new and the other a much-photographed museum piece. It's a relaxed, family-run place, and most rooms are light and well-aired: doubles with bathrooms are especially comfortable. The six rooms facing Passeig de Gràcia have splendid views, but as there's no double-glazing they can be noisy in summer.

Hotel services *Lounge. Lifts. Telephone.* **Room services** *: TV (some).*

Hosteria Grau

C/Ramelleres 27, 08001 (93 302 31 30//fax 93 301 81 35). Metro Catalunya/bus all routes to Plaça Catalunya. **Rates** *single* 3,300ptas; *double* 4,750-6,250ptas. **Credit** AmEx, DC, EC, V. **Map D4.**

On a corner of C/Tallers, a short walk from the Rambla, this pleasant *hostal* is ideal if you're likely to get the munchies: it offers breakfast until noon for 325ptas, either downstairs in their very likeable café (open until 9pm) or in the truly tiny first-floor sitting room. The rooms are clean and pleasant, but the inside singles are gloomy. In reception, they provide a variety of information on what's on in the city.
Hotel services *Fax. Multilingual staff. Telephone. TV lounge. 24-hour reception.*

Hotel Call

C/Arc de Sant Ramon del Call 4, 08002 (93 302 11 23/fax 93 301 34 86). Metro Liceu/bus 14, 18, 38, 59, N6, N9. **Rates** *single* 3,200ptas; *double* 4,500ptas; *triple* 5,700ptas; *quadruple* 6,400ptas. **Credit** MC, V. **Map D5**.
Situated between the Rambla and Plaça Sant Jaume in what was once the medieval Jewish quarter – the Call – this hotel, refurbished for 1992, is a clean, modern, functional place to stay. Rooms are air-conditioned and have modern bathrooms. It's in a corner building, and most rooms overlook one of the narrow adjoining pedestrian streets which are very quiet at night, while some give on to a darkish inside patio. There is a sitting area with TV in reception.
Hotel services *Air-conditioning. English spoken. Fax. Lift. Lounge.* **Room services** *Telephone. TV.*

Hotel Toledano

La Rambla 138, 08002 (93 301 08 72/ fax 93 412 31 42). Metro Catalunya/bus all routes to Plaça Catalunya. **Rates** *single* 2,600-3,600ptas; *double* 4,100-5,900ptas. **Credit** AmEx, DC, MC, V. **Map D4**.
Very near to Plaça Catalunya on the upper stretch of the Rambla, the Toledano can be noisy, but is certainly convenient. The 28 rooms are plain, but 18 have renovated bathrooms, and there's a chintzy communal sitting area looking out over the Rambla.
Hotel services *Disabled: wheelchair access. Lift. Multilingual staff. Safe.* **Room services** *Telephone. TV (satellite).*

Pensión-Hostal Mari-Luz

C/Palau 4, 2° 1a, 08002 (tel/fax 93 317 34 63). Metro Jaume I/bus 17, 40, 45. **Rates** *per person* 1,300-1,500ptas. **No credit cards. Map D5.**
A spotlessly clean *hostal* a few streets' walk from the main Plaça Reial-drag, where Mari-Luz takes great care of her lodgers. The patio and staircase of the old building could do with some paint, but it's atmospheric, likeable, and affordable. The 18 rooms, five of which have their own showers, are plain but quiet.
Hotel services *Laundry. Multilingual staff. Refreshments available from reception (24hrs). Safe.*

Pensión Vitoria

C/de la Palla 8, pral, 08002 (93 302 08 34). Metro Liceu/bus 14, 38, 59, N6, N9. **Rates** *single* 1,500ptas; *double* 2,500ptas; *(with bath)* 3,000ptas. **No credit cards. Map D5.**
Very close to the Plaça del Pi, the Vitoria has 12 clean, light and airy rooms, all of which have balconies. Ten rooms share one bathroom, but there are also two doubles that have en suite showers and toilets. Despite the basic facilities they have a loyal bunch of repeat guests, so book early, especially to get the rooms with showers.
Hotel services *Multilingual staff. TV. Telephone.*

Apartment Hotels

Apartment hotels comprise self-contained small flats, with cooking facilities, plus maid service. They are good for slightly longer stays, and usually offer reduced monthly or longer-term rates.

Apartamentos Mur-Mar

La Rambla 34, 08002 (93 318 27 62/fax 93 412 50 39). Metro Drassanes/bus 14, 18, 38, N6, N9. **Apartment rates per night** Nov-Mar *one person* 5,000ptas; *two people* 7,500ptas; *three people* 9,500ptas; *four people* 11,500ptas; Apr-Oct, Christmas & Easter *one person* 6,000ptas; *two people* 8,500ptas; *three people* 10,500ptas; *four people* 12,500ptas. **Credit** $TC. **Map D5**.
Near the bottom of the Rambla, these 33 apartments are relatively basic, but still a bargain. Each sleeps up to four, and has a small but well-equipped kitchen, lounge, double bedroom and bathroom. Interior apartments are quiet but dark.
Hotel services *Air-conditioning. Bar. Fax. Laundry. Lift. Multilingual staff. Restaurant. Safe.* **Room services** *Kitchen with refrigerator. Radio. Telephone. TV.*

Apartaments Calàbria

C/Calàbria 129, 08015 (93 426 42 28/93 426 74 85/fax 93 426 76 40). Metro Rocafort/bus 9, 41, 50, 56, N1, N2. **Apartment rates per night** *one person* 7,750ptas; *two people* 9,500ptas; *each additional person* 3,250ptas extra. **Per month** 160,000ptas; *two months or more* 145,000ptas/month. **Credit** AmEx, MC, V. **Map B4**.
An Eixample apartment block, well placed between the centre and Plaça d'Espanya, converted into 72 short-term apartments. They don't overflow with character, but all have good kitchen and bathroom facilities and separate lounge areas, and the reception has efficient office services. Its rates are also more competitive than other *aparthotels* and it needs to be booked well in advance.
Hotel services *Air-conditioning. Car park. Currency exchange. Disabled: wheelchair access. Fax. Laundry. Lifts. Multilingual staff.* **Room services** *Refrigerator. Room service (8am-3pm Mon-Fri; 8am-1pm Sat, Sun). Safe. Telephone. TV (satellite).*

Aparthotel Atenea

C/Joan Güell 207-211, 08028 (93 490 66 40/fax 93 490 64 20). Metro Les Corts/bus 6, 7, 15, 33, 34, 43, 59, 63, 66, 67, 68, 70, 72. **Apartment rates per night**: *single studio* 14,000ptas; *double studio* 16,000ptas; *single apartment* 15,200ptas; *double apartment* 17,000ptas; *third person supplement* 4,000ptas; 20% discount at weekends; group discounts. **Per month** 270,000ptas, single or double studio or aparment. **Credit** AmEx, DC, EC, JCB, MC, TC, V.
With all the services of a four-star hotel, including a bar, large restaurant, meeting rooms and car park, this large (105 apartments), brand new *aparthotel* is ideally located in the heart of Barcelona's modern business area, just a few blocks from the Hilton and a branch of El Corte Inglés department store. True to Barcelona trends in modern design, the apartments are highly efficient and the small kitchens are fine for light cooking. Food shopping service available on request.
Hotel services *Air-conditioning. Bar. Car park. Conference facilities. Currency exchange. Disabled: rooms (4) adapted for the disabled, wheelchair access. Fax. Lift. Multilingual staff. Photocopiers. Restaurant.* **Room services** *Hairdryer. Refrigerator. Room service (7am-11pm). Safe. Telephone. TV (satellite). Video on request.*

Aparthotel Senator

Via Augusta 167, 08021 (93 201 14 05/fax 93 202 00 97). FGC Muntaner/bus 58, 64, N8. **Apartment rates per night** *one person* 11,500ptas; *two people* 13,500ptas; *three people* 15,500ptas; *four people* 17,500ptas. **Per month** *one person* 205,000ptas; *two people* 245,000ptas; *three people* 260,000ptas. **Credit** AmEx, DC, MC, V. **Map C1**.
Comfortable white-walled apartments with bamboo furniture and plants, in the Sant Gervasi area of the Zona Alta. There's no restaurant or bar, but the kitchen is fine for preparing light meals.
Hotel services *Air-conditioning. Fax. Laundry. Lift. Multilingual staff. Safe.* **Room services** *Minibar. Kitchen with refrigerator. Safe. Telephone. TV (satellite).*

Youth Hostels

Albergue Kabul

*Plaça Reial 17, 08002 (93 318 51 90/
fax 93 301 40 34). Metro Drassanes/bus 14, 18, 38, 59,
N6, N9.* **Open** 24 hours daily. **Rates** *per person*
1,200ptas. **No credit cards. Map D5.**
A welcoming private youth hostel on the Plaça Reial. There
is a reception/TV room with tables, benches and a soft-drinks
dispenser; it has rooms that house from two to 12 people, and
vary from cramped dormitories with mattresses on the floor,
to light and airy doubles with views onto the Plaça. There
are no private bathrooms, but the communal showers and
toilets are well-kept and clean.
Hotel services *Billiard table. Kitchen. Laundry. Lift.
Lounge. Multilingual staff. Refreshments. Safe. Telephone.
TV (satellite). Video.*

Alberg Mare de Déu de Montserrat

*Passeig de la Mare de Déu del Coll 41-51, 08023 (93 210
51 51/fax 93 210 07 98). Metro Vallcarca/bus 22, 25,
27, 28, 87, N4.* **Open** *reception* 8am-midnight daily.
Rates (under 25) *full board* 2,675ptas; *half board*
2,250ptas; *b&b* 1,700ptas; (over 25) *full board* 3,600ptas;
half board 2,950ptas; *b&b* 2,275ptas. *Sheet/towel hire*
350ptas. **Credit** MC, V
This giant, 183-bed official youth hostel is in a pleasant old
house surrounded by gardens, some way from the centre up
the hill at the back of Barcelona in Vallcarca, but it's not far
from a Metro. Most rooms are for six people, although there
are some for up to 12, and lots of facilities. IYHF cards are
required.
Hotel services *Auditorium. Car park. Dining room.
Disabled: room (1) adapted for the disabled, wheelchair access.
Fax (receive only) and photocopy service. Laundry.
Multilingual staff. Refreshments. Safe. Slide projector.
TV/video room.*

Alberg Pere Tarrés

*C/Numància 149-151, 08029 (93 410 23 09).
Metro Les Corts/bus 15, 43, 59, 63, 67, 68.* **Open** 8.30-
11am (until noon in summer), 3-11pm daily (front door is
open until 1am). **Rates** (per night, incl breakfast)
1,500ptas; sheets extra. **Credit** MC, V
This renovated official hostel has 94 places (four to ten beds
per room) and five shared bathrooms. There's an attractive
roof terrace, but regulations are strict: no cigarettes or alcohol in dorms; no eating or drinking outside the dining room.
IYHF cards are required, and you need to book in summer.
Hotel services *Car park. Kitchen. Laundry. Multilingual
staff. Meals cooked for groups. Patio. Refreshments. TV
lounge.*

Hostal de Joves

*Passeig Pujades 29, 08018 (tel/fax 93 300 31 04).
Metro Arc de Triomf/bus 40, 41, 42, 141, N6.*
Open 7-10am, 3pm-midnight daily. **Rates** (incl
breakfast) *under-25s* 1,500ptas; *over-25s* 1,700ptas.
No credit cards. Map E5.
This hostel, renovated a few years ago, looks out over the
Ciutadella. Most of the 68 beds are in non-smoking dormi-
tories, but there are a few double rooms. IYHF cards are
needed, and five nights is the maximum length of stay.
Hotel services *Dining room. Kitchen. Laundry.
Lockers. Multilingual staff. Refreshments. Telephones.*

Campsites

There are 13 campsites within a short radius of
Barcelona. For more comprehensive information,
get the *Catalunya Campings* brochure from the
Palau Robert tourist office (*see page 251*).

Cala Gogó

*Carretera de La Platja, 08820 El Prat de Llobregat (93
379 46 00/fax 93 379 47 11). Bus 65 from Plaça
d'Espanya/by car C-246 to Castelldefels, then Airport
exit to Prat beach (7km/4 miles).* **Open** *15 Mar-15 Oct*
(reception) 9am-10pm, (office) 9am-2pm daily. **Rates**
(per plot per night) *Mar-Jun, Oct* 1,040ptas; *with light*
1,360ptas; plus *adults* 400ptas; *children 2-9* 310ptas;
June-Sept: 1,460ptas; *with light* 1,900ptas; plus *adults*
580ptas; *children 2-9* 440ptas. **Credit** EC, MC, TC, V.
The nearest campsite to the city, Cala Gogó is large, well-
equipped and has capacity for 4,500 people. It's 7km (four
miles) to the south near the beach at Prat, which is, though,
also near the airport, so noise can be a problem. There's a
supermarket, restaurant, bar and swimming pool on-site, and
campers can fish, play tennis, or use diving facilities.

Camping Albatros

*Autovia de Castelldefels, km 15, 08850 Gavà
(tel/fax 93 633 06 95). Bus L95 from Barcelona (Ronda
Universitat), stops 250m from the camp entrance/by car
C-246 to Gavà (15km/9 miles).* **Open** *1 May-27 Sept* 7am-
midnight (campsite); 8am-10pm (reception). **Rates** (per
person per night) 2,000ptas; *under-10s* 400ptas; plus extra
charges for cars, motorbikes, caravans, tents & light.
No credit cards.
An extensive campsite on the beach in Gavà south of
Barcelona, between the airport and Castelldefels. It has a first
aid centre, shopping, hairdresser, laundry, bar and restaurant all on site. There are also mobile homes for hire, and
nearby there is a sports centre with tennis, minigolf and
water sports. Videos in English are shown free in the video-
cinema, and during the main July and August season there
are also city excursions and free children's entertainment
and activities.

Masnou

*Carretera N-II, km 633, 08320 El Masnou
(tel/fax 93 555 15 03). Bus CASAS from Passeig Sant
Joan to Rambla de Prim, corner of C/Guipúzcoa/by car N-
II to Masnou (11km/7 miles)/by train RENFE to Masnou
from Plaça Catalunya.* **Open** (campsite) 8am-9pm daily;
(campsite) *Oct-May* 24hrs; *June-Sept* 7am-11pm daily.
Rates (per person per night) 650ptas; *under-10s* 550ptas;
plus extra charges for cars, motorbikes, caravans, tents,
& light. **No credit cards.**
The closest campsite north of Barcelona, tucked under a
range of hills and offering pleasant respite from the city.
Unlike the big sites along the beach south of town it's relatively small, with only 120 plots. You can pitch a tent under
the trees, or hire a bungalow (2,000ptas per person per day,
minimum four people). Showers are included in the price and
there's a bar, restaurant, supermarket, kids' playground and
pools on site. The nearby beach is sandy, and has diving and
sailing facilities.

El Toro Bravo

*Autovia de Castelldefels, km 11, 08840 Viladecans
(93 637 34 62/fax 93 637 21 15). Bus L95 from
Barcelona (Ronda Universitat)/by car C-246 to Viladecans
(11km/7 miles).* **Open** *mid-June-Aug* 8am-8pm;
Sept-mid-June 8.30am-1.30pm, 4-6pm. **Rates** (per person
per night) *Sept-mid-June* 625ptas; *under-10s* 465ptas; *mid-
June-Aug* 675ptas; *under-10s* 490ptas; plus extra charges
for vehicles, tents, caravans & light.
Credit AmEx, EC, MC, TC. V.
It is nearly 10km (6 miles) from the main-road bus stop to
the site, but we're assured that lifts are often given to puffed-
out campers. Open all year, it has space for 3,500 campers
and services that include an on-site hairdresser. They also
rent out 2-4-berth caravans and bungalows (Sept-Jun
4,850ptas; Jun-Aug 7,250-12,700ptas per day), rates varying
according to size and season. The site has lots of shade,
swimming pools and tennis courts, and is by the sea.

Restaurants

Subtle modern dishes, punchy country cooking, bargain platters of fine seafood: Barcelona's sophisticated restaurant scene has many pleasures to explore.

Barcelona can justifiably boast of serving up some of the best food in Europe. This is true not only of the city's most expensive restaurants, but also of many others down the line. People here consider the enjoyment of food one of life's clear priorities. According to the statistics, there are nearly 2,500 eating establishments in town, which means by the law of averages you're going to find at least one place to eat on every other street.

Out of this huge selection, most places serve one form or another of Catalonia's own rich and varied cuisine (*see pages 122-3* **The Catalan Menu**). Contrary to what foreigners often assume, there is no such thing as a generic 'Spanish national' cuisine, once you get away from a few universal basics such as potato omelette and grilled hake. In Barcelona, as well as Catalan restaurants, there are many others, that serve the mainly seafood-based cooking of Galicia in north-west Spain, plus several more which offer the food of the Basque Country, Castile, Andalusia, or other Spanish regions. Foreign restaurants have multiplied in the city in recent years, adding Brazilian, Indonesian, Mexican, Japanese, Peruvian, Pakistani, Syrian and more cuisines to the standard Chinese fare that has been around for decades (*see page 130* **International**). Non-meat-eaters fare less well, but there are some decent vegetarian restaurants to choose from (*see page 132* **Vegetarian**).

As well as the restaurants listed here, many bars also provide food, from snacks to full meals, so for more places to eat, *see chapter* **Cafés & Bars**. For restaurants welcoming a gay clientele, *see chapter* **Gay & Lesbian Barcelona**. For places to eat in the small hours, *see chapter* **Nightlife**.

Restaurant practicalities

When to set your clock, and book Catalans eat late. Lunchtime is at what they call 'midday' – around 2pm. In the evening you won't get a full meal before 8.30pm in most places; 9-9.30pm is the average time for dinner. It's always a good idea to book in restaurants from mid-range upwards, and in every kind of restaurant on Fridays and Saturdays.
Children Most restaurants welcome children, but few have specific children's menus, and they're not often seen in top-flight dining rooms (*see also chapter* **Children**).
Prices, tips & taxes The lunchtime *menu del día* is one of Barcelona's great bargains, with plenty of places offering three courses for around 1,000ptas. It's best to make this your main meal if you want to eat cheaply, and several very cheap restaurants open for lunch only. Evening prices will usually be higher, although some restaurants now offer

a menu for dinner as well. There is no percentage rule for tipping: it's common in mid- or upper-range restaurants to leave around 200-300ptas – rarely over 500ptas – but many locals leave no tip at all, or just a nominal 25ptas. Bills include seven per cent IVA tax (VAT), which is usually, but not always, incorporated into the prices shown on the menu.
Sundays & holidays Despite growing flexibility in opening times, there are relatively few places open on Sunday evenings, and those that are often fill up. Many restaurants close for Easter (usually Good Friday through Easter Monday, sometimes longer) as well as for some time during August; we've listed annual closing dates where possible, but at holiday times it's a good idea to phone first to avoid a wasted journey.
*The average prices listed are based on the average cost of a starter, a main course and dessert, **without** drink. Set menus, however, do often include beer, wine or water.*

Top flight

Agut d'Avignon

C/Trinitat 3 (93 302 60 34). Metro Liceu/bus 14, 18, 38, N6, N9. **Lunch served** 1-3.30pm, **dinner served** 9-11.30pm, daily. **Average** 4,000-4,500ptas. **Credit** AmEx, DC, EC, JCB, MC, TC, V. **Map D5**
Down a small alleyway, one of Barcelona's finest restaurants offers comfort and service belying the shabbiness of much of the surrounding area. The menu is based on classic Catalan dishes (excellent *farcellets de col*, stuffed cabbage leaves), others from various Spanish regions, such as Castilian roasts, and some creations of their own like wild boar with strawberry sauce, duck with figs, or oyster soup. *Air-conditioning. Booking essential.*

Beltxenea

C/Mallorca 275 (93 215 30 24). Metro Diagonal or Passeig de Gràcia/bus 7, 16, 17, 18, 20, 21, 22, 24, 28, 39, 43, 44, 45, N4, N6. **Lunch served** 1.30-3.30pm Mon-Fri. **Dinner served** 8.30-11.30pm Mon-Sat. Closed four weeks Aug. **Average** 6,000ptas. **Credit** AmEx, DC, MC, V. **Map D3**
The foremost outpost of new Basque cuisine in Barcelona. In a first-floor Eixample flat with a pretty interior garden, it's very discreet, so much so that a small brass plaque is the only sign of the restaurant's existence on the street. As in all Basque cooking, the basis is seafood: specialities include a melon and lobster salad and *tronc de lluç Ondarroa* (hake). *Air-conditioning. Booking essential. Tables outdoors (interior patio).*

Botafumeiro

C/Gran de Gràcia 81 (93 218 42 30). Metro Fontana/bus 22, 24, 28, N4, N6. **Meals served** 1pm-1am daily. Closed three weeks Aug. **Average** 6,000ptas. **Credit** AmEx, DC, JCB, MC, TC, V. **Map D2**
This spacious Gràcia restaurant specialises in the best of Galician food, which means, above all, quality seafood. The lobster, langoustines, scallops, oysters and other shellfish selected by chef-proprietor Moncho Neiras are unbeatable,

and it stays open late. There are also two singers, one with guitar, playing only if you want them to, or so they claim. *Air-conditioning. Booking essential.*

Ca l'Isidre

C/es Flors 12 (93 441 11 39/93 442 57 20). Metro Paral.lel/bus 20, 36, 57, 64, 91, N4, N6. **Lunch served** 1.30-4pm, **dinner served** 8.30-11.30pm, Mon-Sat. Closed public holidays, Easter, four weeks July/Aug. **Average** 6,000ptas. **Credit** AmEx, MC, V. **Map C5**
A small family-run restaurant near the Paral.lel that receives regular visits from King Juan Carlos. Chef César Pastor's regular dishes include artichoke hearts stuffed with wild mushrooms and duck liver, and loin of lamb broiled English-style. Desserts are made by the daughter of the family, master *pastissera* Núria Gironès. English and French are spoken. *Air-conditioning. Booking essential.*

La Dama

Avda Diagonal 423 (93 202 06 86/93 202 03 22). Metro Diagonal, FGC Provença/bus 6, 7, 15, 27, 33, 34, 127. **Lunch served** 1-3.30pm, **dinner served** 8.30-11.30pm, daily. Closed 25 Dec. **Average** 7,000ptas. **Gourmet menus** 5,975ptas, 7,950ptas. **Credit** AmEx, DC, EC, MC, TC, V. **Map C2**
On the first floor of an ornate *Modernista* building from 1915 by Manuel Sayrach, this is one of Barcelona's dining power-houses, serving a well-dressed clientele of local and foreign elites and wielders of the expense account. It maintains its status with superbly prepared classic and contemporary dishes, including delicacies such as gratinated sea urchins with cava, grilled goat kidneys with selected herbs or loin of venison seasoned with five different kinds of peppers. The only hitch is that it's also one of the most expensive in town. The wine list is ample, and service utterly smooth. *Air-conditioning. Booking essential.*

Gaig

Passeig Maragall 402 (93 429 10 17). Metro Vilapicina/bus 19, 45, N5. **Lunch served** 1.30-4pm Tue-Sun. **Dinner served** 9pm-11pm Tue-Sat. Closed public holiday evenings; Easter, Aug, 25, 26 Dec. **Average** 5,500ptas. **Gourmet menu** 5,450ptas (no drinks); 8,650ptas (includes wine). **Credit** AmEx, DC, EC, MC, V.
Founded in 1869 as a café for cart drivers, this famous restaurant has been in the Gaig family for four generations. Specialities include *arròs de colomi amb ceps* (young pigeon in rice with wild mushrooms) and stuffed pigs' trotters. A favourite dessert is the *pecat de xocolata* ('chocolate sin', a thick mousse). The wine cellar is a sight in itself. *Air-conditioning. Booking essential. Disabled: wheelchair access. Tables outdoors (summer).*

Jaume de Provença

C/Provença 88 (93 430 00 29). Metro Entença/bus 41, 43, 44. **Lunch served** 1-4pm Tue-Sun. **Dinner served** 9-11.30pm Tue-Sat. Closed Easter, Aug, Christmas week. **Average** 7,000ptas. **Gourmet menu** 7,000ptas. **Credit** AmEx, DC, MC, V. **Map B3**
This small restaurant tucked away in the Eixample is one of the most prestigious in Barcelona. Its reputation is due entirely to the quality and originality of the cuisine of chef Jaume Barguès: menus are a mixture of traditional Catalan recipes and ideas of his own, such as crab lasagne, or salad of wild mushrooms with prawns and clams. Again, a superlative wine list. *Air-conditioning. Disabled: wheelchair access.*

Neichel

C/Beltrán i Rózpide 16 bis (93 203 84 08). Metro Maria Cristina/bus 7, 63, 67, 68, 74, 75, 114. **Lunch served** 1.30-3.30pm Mon-Fri. **Dinner served** 8.30-11.30pm Mon-Sat. Closed Easter, Aug, first week Sept, 25 Dec. **Average** 9,500ptas. **Gourmet menu** 7,700ptas. **Credit** AmEx, DC, MC, V.

Worth a trip

A short journey by road or rail will take you to two of the most impressive restaurants in Catalonia. For information on transport, *see page 224.*

Fonda Europa

C/Anselm Clavé 1, Granollers (93 870 03 12). By car A7 or N-152 (35km/22 miles)/ by train RENFE to Granollers. **Lunch served** 1-3.30pm, **dinner served** 9-11.15pm, daily. Closed 25 Dec. **Average** 4,000ptas. **Credit** AmEx, DC, EC, JCB, MC, $TC, V.
First opened in 1714, this inn-restaurant serves very traditional Catalan food such as pork *a la llauna*, *cap i pota* (tripe, cheeks and trotters)and cod with *samfaina*, plus equally hearty desserts. A 'cart-driver's breakfast' (smoked herring, wine and *torrades*) is served on market days (Thursdays). *Air-conditioning. Booking essential.*

El Racó de Can Fabes

C/Sant Joan 6, Sant Celoni (93 867 28 51/38/61). By car A7 or C-251 (60km/37 miles)/by train RENFE to Sant Celoni. **Lunch served** 1.30-3.30pm Tue-Sun. **Dinner served** 8.30-10.30pm Tue-Sat. Closed first two weeks Feb, end June-first week July, 25 Dec, 6 Jan. **Average** 10,000ptas. **Credit** AmEx, DC, EC, JCB, MC, TC, V.
In a small town at the foot of the Montseny mountains, the Racó has all of three Michelin stars, and presiding figure Santi Santamaria is acclaimed as the greatest of all Catalan chefs. Specialities include scallop salad, cold vegetable stew with truffles and a superlative grill of Mediterranean seafood. Desserts and cheeses are superb too. A gourmet pilgrimage, and for all its prestige service is unpretentiously welcoming. *Air-conditioning. Booking essential. Disabled: wheelchair access.*

In a modern block in the best part of town, Neichel serves an exquisite array of Mediterranean dishes, meticulously prepared and presented in high style. Owner-chef Jean-Louis Neichel, from Alsace, is the foremost representative of classic French culinary tradition in Barcelona, and his Michelin-starred restaurant is one of the city's very best. His cooking reveals a combination of his French training and influences picked up during long residence in Barcelona. Dishes offered à la carte change with the seasons and might include a fine puzzle-like arrangement of foie gras marinated with muscatel and accompanied by figs and rhubarb jelly; mushroom soup with black truffles and Corsican meatballs, or fillet of sea bass with a sauce of light mustard, tomato and capers, served with fresh young fennel. As well as the six-course gourmet menu there is a separate menu, also of six courses, devoted entirely to dishes made with black truffles from the valleys of Huesca. The wine list, cheeses and desserts are all equally remarkable. *Air-conditioning. Booking essential.*

Ot

C/Torres 25 (93 284 77 52). Metro Verdaguer/bus 15, 20, 45, 47, N5. **Lunch served** 2-3.30pm Mon-Fri. **Dinner served** 9-11pm Mon-Sat. Closed Easter, two weeks July-Aug, 25 Dec. **Set menu** 4,100ptas. **Credit** MC, V. **Map E2**.

The city's magazine in English

BARCELONA METROPOLITAN
Pick up your free copy
www.web-show.com/metropolitan

This small restaurant on a quiet street in Gràcia has been praised by high-ranking gourmets as one of the Spanish culinary surprises of recent years. Run by two young chefs, it serves daringly original variations on classic Catalan and Mediterranean cuisine: one example is fillet of sole lightly fried with crushed hazelnut, garlic and parsley, which is then layered with a purée of peas and topped by semi-sweet ravioli stuffed with cinnamon and milk. The finely tuned ingredients of their *carn d'olla*, the traditional Catalan Christmas dish, are a real treat. Ot offers a set menu of five courses, served in a coquettishly modest manner and changed once a fortnight. Wines and cheeses are also excellent.
Air-conditioning. Booking essential.

Passadís del Pep

Pla del Palau 2 (93 310 10 21). Metro Jaume I/bus 14, 16, 17, 36, 40, 45, 51, 57, 59, 64. **Lunch served** 1.30-3.30pm, **dinner served** 9-11pm, Mon-Sat. Closed public holidays, three weeks Aug. **Average** 9,000ptas (incl drink). **Credit** AmEx, DC, MC, V. **Map D5.**
An eccentric restaurant that's impossible to find unless you know where to look (go down the long, unmarked corridor next door to a Caixa office). There is no menu, just some of the best seafood in Barcelona, with a superb first-course buffet and cava included in the price. *Fideus amb llamàntol* (noodles with lobster) is recommended. For a cheaper alternative, try **Cal Pep** (*see below* **Seafood**), run by the same family. *Air-conditioning. Booking advisable.*

Roig Robí

C/Sèneca 20 (93 218 92 22/93 217 97 38). Metro Diagonal/bus 7, 15, 22, 24, 27, 28, 33, 34, 127, N4, N6. **Lunch served** 1.30-4pm Mon-Fri. **Dinner served** 9-11.30pm Mon-Sat. Closed public holidays, two weeks Aug. **Average** 6,000ptas. **Gourmet menu** 6,000ptas. **Credit** AmEx, DC, MC, V. **Map D2.**
Roig Robí is run by self-taught chef Mercè Navarro and two of her children – an unusual set-up for a top restaurant that counts businessmen, writers and artists as its regulars, including Antoni Tàpies, who designed the menu. Specialities include an *amanida de foie* (foie gras salad), lobster with rice, and Palamós prawns with crispy leeks and garlic sauce.
Air-conditioning. Booking essential. Tables outside (garden terrace, June-Sept). Vegetarian dishes on request.

Catalan

Agut

C/Gignàs 16 (93 315 17 09). Metro Jaume I/bus 17, 40, 45. **Lunch served** 1.30-4pm Tue-Sun. **Dinner served** 9pm-midnight Tue-Sat. Closed Aug, 25 Dec. **Average** 2,300ptas. **Set Lunch** 1,275ptas Tue-Fri. **Credit** MC, V. **Map D5**
Agut is known throughout Barcelona for its appetising traditional Catalan food, and, despite being located in a narrow street near the port, all kinds of people make the pilgrimage to its doors. Applauded for its cannelloni, steak with Roquefort and home-made profiteroles, among other dishes. *Air-conditioning. Booking advisable. Disabled: wheelchair access.*

L'Antic

C/Riereta 8 (93 442 81 79). Metro Sant Antoni/bus 20, 64, 91, N6, N9. **Meals served** 10am-5pm Mon-Fri; 8.30pm-1am Mon-Sat. Closed public holidays & about ten days Aug. **Average** 2,000ptas. **Set lunch** 900ptas Mon-Fri. **Set dinner** 1,500ptas Mon-Thur; 2,000ptas Fri-Sat. **Credit** AmEx, MC, V, DC. **Map C5**
A small, comfortable restaurant in the Barrio Chino, L'Antic is run by a Catalan-Argentinian couple who serve up an assortment of grilled meats *al estilo argentino*. Other specialities are more Catalan, such as a range of *torrades* (*see page xxx*). There is a very decently-priced lunch menu. *Air-conditioning. Booking essential.*

Le Bistrot

Avda Diagonal 640 (93 405 92 00). Metro Maria Cristina/bus 6, 7, 33, 34, 63, 66, 67, 68. **Lunch served** 1-4pm Mon-Fri. **Dinner served** 9pm-midnight Mon-Sat. Closed Aug. **Average** 3,500ptas. **Credit** MC, V.
A fashionable, nay chic, warehouse-with-contemporary-art styled joint with pricey but good Catalan and French food. At the monied end of Diagonal, it caters to media people, actors, businessmen, models and other well-heeled urban fauna. Your menu might include ravioli stuffed with foie gras, or duck in mushroom sauce; for dessert, the chestnut sorbet coated with hot chocolate will make better, happier individuals of one and all. Downstairs there's a comfortable bar with small dancefloor, which draws down factions of the after-dinner crowd.
Air-conditioning. Booking essential.

Café de l'Acadèmia

C/Lledó 1 (93 319 82 53/93 315 00 26). Metro Jaume I/bus 17, 40, 45. **Breakfast served** 9am-noon Mon-Fri. **Lunch served** 1.30-4pm Mon-Fri, **dinner served** 9pm-midnight, Mon-Fri. Closed public holidays. **Average** 3,000ptas. **Set lunch** 1,000-1,200ptas. **Credit** AmEx, MC, V. **Map D5**
Perhaps the best of a clutch of quality restaurants near the Catalan government and City Hall, the Acadèmia serves some 50-odd dishes that range from Catalan classics such as *rossejat* (rice and fish broth) with prawns to a delicious brochette of chicken and quail with sesame and soy sauce.
Air-conditioning. Booking essential. Tables outdoors (Easter-Oct).

El Cafetí

C/Hospital 99, end of passage (93 329 24 19). Metro Liceu/bus 14, 18, 38, 59, N6, N9. **Lunch served** 1.30-4pm Tue-Sun. **Dinner served** 9-11.30pm Tue-Sat. Closed Easter weekend, last three weeks Aug. **Average** 2,500ptas. **Set menu** 1,100ptas Tue-Fri, Sat lunch (not public holidays). **Credit** DC, MC, TC, V. **Map C5.**
This small restaurant at the end of an alleyway has perfected a series of Catalan-French dishes over the last 15 years, and built up a regular local clientele. Specialities include house paté, several cod dishes, goulash, and a range of home-made desserts. The staff speak English, French and German.
Air-conditioning. Booking essential at weekends. Disabled: wheelchair access. Vegetarian dishes.

Cala Sila/Madrid-Barcelona

C/Aragó 282 (93 215 70 26). Metro Passeig de Gràcia/bus 7, 16, 17, 22, 24, 28, N4, N6. **Lunch served** 1-4pm Mon-Sat. **dinner served** 8.30pm-midnight, Mon-Sat. **Average** 1,500ptas. **Credit** AmEx, DC, MC, V. **Map D3**
This café-restaurant opened in the 1940s as a station café, in the days when the railway line from Madrid ran as an open trench along C/Aragó – hence the name Madrid-Barcelona, built into the stylish façade. A recent takeover has transformed the old place into a somewhat cute, definitely trendy hangout for pretty young Catalans. Menus feature enjoyable, well-priced modern Catalan and international dishes.
Air-conditioning. Disabled: wheelchair access.

Can Culleretes

C/Quintana 5 (93 317 30 22). Metro Liceu/bus 14, 18, 38, 59. **Lunch served** 1.30-4pm Tue-Sun. **Dinner served** 9-11pm Tue-Sat. Closed three weeks July, 25 Dec. **Average** 3,000ptas. **Set menu** 1,600ptas Tue-Thur; 2,000ptas Tue-Fri. **Seafood menu** 3,500ptas. **Credit** MC, V. **Map D5**
The oldest restaurant in Barcelona, founded 1786, with a rambling interior covered in old photos of local celebrities. The lengthy main menu includes rich traditional dishes such as *civet de porc senglar* (wild boar stew) and *cuixa d'oca amb pomes* (goose leg with apples), while the new, lighter seafood menu is highly recommended. House policy is to undercharge for wine, and there are good Raïmats at 650ptas and vintage Riojas for 1,300ptas. Go early to avoid queuing.
Air-conditioning. Booking essential (Fri-Sun).

The Catalan menu

Catalan food is not just a matter of a few regional dishes, but a complete cuisine clearly distinguishable from its neighbours in France and the rest of Spain. Much use is made of four basic elements: the *sofregit*, chopped tomato and onion lightly fried together in olive oil; *samfaina*, a mix of onion, peppers, ripe tomatoes, aubergines and garlic similar to ratatouille, used as an ingredient and an accompaniment; and most distinctive of all the *picada*, for thickening and seasoning, a variable combination of ingredients mixed in a mortar, perhaps garlic, parsley, saffron, ham, bread and crushed nuts. Last is *all i oli*, garlic mayonnaise, best of all made fresh just with wild garlic pounded together with olive oil (and occasionally an egg yolk), and served on the side with meats or seafood.

Grilled meat (with *all i oli*) is a mainstay of traditional Catalan country cooking, especially lamb, pork, sausages and rabbit, usually prepared on an open charcoal grill (*a la brasa*). There's also a vegetarian variant, *escalivada*, of aubergines, red peppers and onions grilled almost black, then peeled and cut into strips. Catalan cuisine is not afraid to mix flavours, such as meat, fruit and nuts. Casserole-like dishes, cooked in a broad earthenware bowl (a *cassola*), include fairly conventional things such as chicken with *samfaina*, but also surprises such as the *mar i muntanya* ('sea and mountain') dishes from the Empordà region around Figueres, mixing meat and seafood surf-and-turf style in subtle combinations such as a stew of prawns, chicken and wild mushrooms, or pork with crayfish. The many fish and seafood dishes include several made with the big frying pan called a paella. The world-famous rice paella hails from Valencia, but the range of similar Catalan variants includes *arròs negre* ('black rice', cooked in squid ink), and *fideuà*, made with noodles instead of rice.

Other features of Catalan cuisine are its rich variety of salads, and other interesting vegetable-based dishes such as the beautifully simple *espinacs a la catalana*. Cannelloni (*canelons*), introduced from Italy in the last century, are surprisingly another standard, used in sufficiently distinctive ways (with no tomatoes in the sauce) to count as a real local speciality. Catalan cooking, moreover, has not stood still, and many Barcelona restaurants now present inventive modern Catalan food, incorporating a range of international influences and lighter, more subtle ingredients. For a note on wines, *see*

chapter **Shopping**; for drinks and types of coffee, *see chapter* **Cafés & Bars**.

Words and phrases below are given in Catalan, Spanish and English, respectively.

Useful basic terminology

una cullera	*una cuchara*	a spoon
una forquilla	*un tenedor*	a fork
un ganivet	*un cuchillo*	a knife
un tovalló	*una servilleta*	a napkin
una ampolla de	*una botella de*	a bottle of
una altra	*otra*	another (one)
més	*más*	more
pa	*pan*	bread
oli d'oliva	*aceite de oliva*	olive oil
sal i pebre	*sal y pimienta*	salt and pepper
amanida	*ensalada*	salad
truita	*tortilla*	omelette
(note: truita can also mean trout)		
la nota	*la cuenta*	the bill
un cendrer	*un cenicero*	an ashtray
vinagre	*vinagre*	vinegar
vi negre/rosat/	*vino tinto/rosado*	red/rosé/
blanc	*blanco*	white wine
bon profit	*aproveche*	enjoy your meal
sóc vegetarià/ ana	*soy vegetariano/a*	I'm a vegetarian
sóc diabètic/a	*soy diabético/a*	I'm a diabetic

Cooking terms

a la brasa	*a la brasa*	charcoal-grilled
a la graella/ planxa	*a la plancha*	grilled on a hot metal plate
a la romana	*a la romana*	fried in batter
al forn	*al horno*	baked
al vapor	*al vapor*	steamed
fregit	*frito*	fried
rostit	*asado*	roast
ben fet	*bien hecho*	well-done
a punt	*medio hecho*	medium
poc fet	*poco hecho*	rare

Catalan specialities

amanida catalana/*ensalada catalana* mixed salad with a selection of cold meats

bacallà a la llauna/*bacalao 'a la llauna'* salt cod baked in garlic, tomato, paprika and wine

botifarra/*butifarra* Catalan sausage: variants include *botifarra negre*, blood sausage; *blanca*, mixed with egg

botifarra amb mongetes/*butifarra con judias* sausage with haricot beans

calçots a specially sweet variety of large spring onion (scallion), available only from November to spring, and eaten char-grilled, on its own except for *romesco* sauce

carn d'olla traditional Christmas dish of various meats stewed with *escudella*, then served separately.

conill amb cargols/*conejo con caracoles* rabbit with snails

crema catalana cinnamon-flavoured custard dessert with burnt sugar topping, similar to crème brûlée

escalivada/*escalibada* grilled and peeled peppers, onions and aubergine

escudella thick winter stew of meat and vegetables

espinacs a la catalana/*espinacas a la catalana* spinach quick-fried in olive oil with garlic, raisins and pine kernels

esqueixada summer salad of marinated salt cod with onions, olives and tomato

fideuà/*fideuá* paella made with noodles

pa amb tomàquet/*pan con tomate* bread prepared with tomato, oil and salt (*see pxxx*)

peus de porc/*pies de cerdo* pigs' trotters

romesco a spicy sauce from the coast south of Barcelona, made with crushed almonds and hazelnuts, tomatoes, oil and a special type of red pepper (the *nyora*)

sarsuela/*zarzuela* fish and seafood stew

sípia amb mandonguilles/*sepia con albóndigas* cuttlefish with meatballs

suquet de peix/*suquet de pescado* fish and potato soup

torrades/*tostadas* toasted *pa amb tomàquet*

Carn i aviram/Carne y aves/Meat & poultry

ànec	*pato*	duck
bou	*buey*	beef
cabrit	*cabrito*	kid
conill	*conejo*	rabbit
faisà	*faisán*	pheasant
fetge	*higado*	liver
llebre	*liebre*	hare
llom	*lomo*	loin of pork
llengua	*lengua*	tongue
ous	*huevos*	eggs
perdiu	*perdiz*	partridge
pernil	*jamón serrano*	dry-cured ham
pernil dolç	*jamón york*	cooked ham
pollastre	*pollo*	chicken
porc	*cerdo*	pork
porc senglar	*jabali*	wild boar
ronyons	*riñones*	kidneys
vedella	*ternera*	veal
xai/be	*cordero*	lamb

Peix i marisc/Pescado y mariscos/Fish & seafood

anxoves	*anchoas*	anchovies
bacallà	*bacalao*	salt cod
besuc	*besugo*	sea bream
calamarsos	*calamares*	squid
cloïsses	*almejas*	clams
cranc	*cangrejo*	crab
escamarlans	*cigalas*	crayfish
escopinyes	*berberechos*	cockles
gambes	*gambas*	prawns
llagosta	*langosta*	spiny lobster
llagostins	*langostinos*	langoustines
llenguado	*lenguado*	sole
llobarro	*lubina*	sea bass
lluç	*merluza*	hake
musclos	*mejillones*	mussels
pop	*pulpo*	octopus
rap	*rape*	monkfish
salmó	*salmón*	salmon
sardines	*sardinas*	sardines
sípia	*sepia*	cuttlefish
tonyina	*atún*	tuna
truita	*trucha*	trout

(note: truita *can also mean an omelette*)

Verdures/Legumbres/Vegetables

all	*ajo*	garlic
alvocat	*aguacate*	avocado
bolets	*setas*	wild mushrooms
ceba	*cebolla*	onion
cigrons	*garbanzos*	chickpeas
col	*col*	cabbage
enciam	*lechuga*	lettuce
endivies	*endivias*	chicory
espinacs	*espinacas*	spinach
faves	*habas*	broad beans
mongetes blanques	*judias blancas*	haricot beans
mongetes verdes	*judias verdes*	French beans
pastanagues	*zanahorias*	carrots
patates	*patatas*	potatoes
pebrots	*pimientos*	peppers
pèsols	*guisantes*	peas
tomàquets	*tomates*	tomatoes
xampinyons	*champiñones*	mushrooms

Postres/Postres/Desserts

flam	*flan*	crème caramel
formatge	*queso*	cheese
gelat	*helado*	ice-cream
iogur	*yogur*	yoghurt
mel i mató	*miel y mató*	cottage cheese with honey
pastís	*pastel*	cake
postre de músic	*postre de músico*	nuts and raisins with muscatel
tarta	*tarta*	tart

Fruïta/Fruta/Fruit

figues	*higos*	figs
maduixes	*fresas*	strawberries
pera	*pear*	pear
plàtan	*plátano*	banana
poma	*manzana*	apple
préssec	*melocotón*	peach
raïm	*uvas*	grapes
taronja	*naranja*	orange

A newly fashionable venue for eating on the once-disreputable Plaça Reial, the **Quinze Nits**.

Can Travi Nou

C/Jorge Manrique (93 428 03 01). Metro Horta/ bus 45, 85, 102. **Lunch served** 1.30-4pm daily. **Dinner served** 8.30-midnight Mon-Sat. **Average** 3,500ptas. **Credit** AmEx, DC, JCB, MC, TC, V.

Occupying a huge, beautiful old *masia* or traditional Catalan farmhouse, with garden, on a hill above Horta, this feels more like a country restaurant than somewhere within a city. Food is traditional Catalan, with speciality *mar i muntanya* dishes such as *sípia amb mandonguilles* and *cueta de rap amb all torrat* (monkfish tail with toasted garlic). Difficult to reach by public transport, so take a cab, but it's well worth finding. *Air-conditioning. Booking advisable. Disabled: wheelchair access. Tables outdoors (garden, Easter-Sept).*

Los Caracoles

C/Escudellers 14 (93 302 31 85). Metro Liceu/bus 14, 18, 38, 59, N6, N9. **Open** 1pm-midnight daily. **Average** 3,500ptas. **Credit** AmEx, DC, JCB, MC, V. **Map D5**.

With its chickens roasting on spits outside, the Caracoles has been in every guidebook for about 50 years, and is consequently packed with tourists. The menu features local standards: better, cheaper food can now be found elsewhere.

Citrus

Passeig de Gràcia 44 (93 487 23 45). Metro Gràcia/FGC Gràcia/bus 7, 16, 17, 22, 24, 28, N4, N6. **Lunch served** 1-4.30pm daily. **Dinner served** 8pm-1am Mon-Sat; 8pm-midnight Sun. Closed dinner 25, 31 Dec. **Average** 2,900ptas. **Credit** AmEx, DC, MC, V. **Map D3**

On a second floor, with great views over Passeig de Gràcia, Citrus is the latest in a series of big, well-designed, affordable eating places that have appeared in central Barcelona, catering to a crowd who savour the surroundings as much as the food served. The emphasis is on light Catalan dishes like potato stuffed with smoked salmon or *bacallà al vapor amb picada d'olives* (steamed cod with crushed olives), and well-spaced tables and the view make for an agreeable meal. *Air-conditioning. Booking advisable. Disabled: wheelchair access.*

El Convent

C/Jerusalem 3 (93 317 10 52). Metro Liceu/bus 14, 18, 38, 59, 91, N4, N6, NS. **Lunch served** 1-4pm, **dinner served** 8-midnight, daily. Closed 25 Dec. **Average** 2,800ptas. **Set lunch** 985ptas Mon-Sat. **Credit** AmEx, DC, EC, JCB, MC, V. **Map C5**

Go before the queue arrives. See page 128.

Until 1998 this rambling old four-storey building housed the main **Egipte** (*see below*), many people's favourite Barcelona restaurant. Fortunately the new management have chosen to keep it much as it was, and serve the same long menu of traditional Catalan dishes (the chef and kitchen crew have remained on board). With its antique fittings, bustling atmosphere, good food and service it remains a convivial standby. As in its previous identity, it's very crowded at peak times. *Air-conditioning.*

Egipte
La Rambla 79 (93 317 95 45). Metro Liceu/bus 14, 18, 38, 59, N4, N6. **Lunch served** 1-4pm, **dinner served** 8pm-midnight, daily. **Average** 2,800ptas. **Set lunch** 985ptas Mon-Sat. **Credit** AmEx, DC, EC, JCB, MC, V. **Map D5**
After years of serving around the corner at their well-known location on C/Jerusalem (*see* **El Convent**), the Egipte has consolidated into a three-floor location on the Rambla. Apart from the move, not much has changed, and it still offers an extensive menu with 30 choices for each course.
Branch: Petit Egipte C/Floristes de la Rambla 14 (93 318 60 86)
Air-conditioning.

Estevet
C/Valldonzella 46 (93 302 41 86). Metro Universitat/bus all routes to Plaça Universitat. **Lunch served** 1.30-4pm, **dinner served** 9pm-midnight, Mon-Sat. Closed public holidays, two weeks Aug. **Average** 2,500-3,000ptas. **Set lunch** 1,200ptas. **Credit** AmEx, DC, MC, V. **Map C4**
One of the oldest restaurants in town, run for the last 48 years by Jordi Suñé. The food is enjoyable and carefully prepared – the langoustines, grilled asparagus and *filet Café de Paris* are particularly good – but it's worth coming here almost as much for the warm atmosphere, with striking paintings, photos of celeb diners such as Maradona and Gary Lineker and regulars who treat the place a bit like a family dining room. *Air-conditioning. Booking essential (lunch). Disabled: wheelchair access.*

El Glop
C/Sant Lluís 24 (93 213 70 58). Metro Joanic/bus 21, 39, 55, N4. **Lunch served** 1-4pm, **dinner served** 8pm-1am, daily. **Average** 2,000ptas. **Credit** MC, V. **Map D2**
El Glop ('The Sip') is a long-running success, serving chargrilled meat and seasonal vegetables at good prices. Specialities include snails cooked *a la llauna* and *xoriço al vi*

Dockside dining

Once upon a time it was possible to sit with your toes in the sand and sample a paella at a string of slightly ramshackle seafood restaurants on the beach in the Barceloneta. The Olympic revamp and EU regulations did away with those places, but one of the foremost themes of Barcelona's great reconstruction has been to 'open up the city to the sea', and so new places have been created where you can dine al fresco with a seafront view.

Within the **Port Vell**, by the new marina at the eastern end of the port and Barceloneta Metro, there is the well-restored **Palau de Mar**, lined with restaurants with outside tables such as **Llevataps** (93 221 24 33) and the **Merendero de la Mari** (93 221 31 41). Most present similar mainly-seafood menus, and are relatively expensive, but on a warm evening you get a superb view of the city back across the harbour. Behind the Palau, the Barceloneta may have lost its beach-front paella-bars but still has the city's largest concentration of good seafood restaurants (*see page 129* **Seafood**). It's possible to find a table outdoors all year long at the many places along Passeig Joan de Borbó, such as the cheap **La Oficina** (*see page 137*) or **El Rey de la Gamba** (93 221 75 98).

Carry on through Barceloneta and you'll eventually come to the **Port Olímpic**, most attractive of the Olympic areas and most successful in establishing a post-games life for itself, above all on summer weekends (*see also chapter* **Sightseeing**). It's big, modern, and surrounded by the parasoled terraces of some 200 bars and restaurants. Some are overpriced, but it's also by the sea, busy, smells of fresh-cooked fish, democratic – with fast-food chains vying for space with luxury restaurants – and open late, with plenty of places serving food until 2am. It can even have some of the atmosphere of the old Barceloneta beach.

There's a whole range of fast food on offer, from Mexican to the Catalan sandwich chain **Pans & Company**, and for a more expensive kind of burger there's the local satellite of **Planet Hollywood** (*see page 135*), just outside

At **Tinglado Moncho's**.

the Port by Frank Gehry's golden fish. It's fish restaurants that predominate, though, and a quick wander around the Port leaves you spoilt for choice. For cheap seafood, try the branch of **El Rey de la Gamba** (93 221 00 12). **Tinglado Moncho's** (93 221 83 83) and **El Cangrejo Loco** (93 221 05 33) are pricier but serve superb fresh seafood, and in summer the Cangrejo has a terrace upstairs with a view of the sea and a midday menu at 1,000ptas. More upmarket is **La Galerna** (93 221 27 74; average 3,500ptas), while the smaller **El Celler del Rocxi** (93 225 19 65) is the most refined of all, with excellent food at 5,000ptas. Leaving the Port, a longish walk along the beachside boardwalk will take you to **Catamaran** (93 221 01 75), a good-quality, low-priced fish restaurant with a choice of self-service or (more expensive) table service.

(chorizo in wine). One of few restaurants in Barcelona to serve the strong *vi de Gandesa*, a good table wine from western Catalonia. In summer the ceiling is opened up to create a kind of indoor patio. It's often very crowded, but the more spacious Nou Glop is nearby, a few streets away.
Air-conditioning. Booking essential. Disabled: wheelchair access.
Branches: El Glop Jardi C/Albert Llanas 2 (93 218 21 43); **El Nou Glop** C/Montmany 49, torre (93 219 70 59).

La Llotja

Museu Maritim, Avda Drassanes (93 302 64 02). Metro Drassanes/bus 14, 18, 36, 38, 57, 59, 64, N6, N9.
Lunch served 1-3.45pm, **dinner served** 9pm-midnight, Tue-Sun. **Average** 3,000ptas. **Set lunch** 1,200ptas. **Credit** MC, V. **Map C5**
Set inside the wonderfully-restored fourteenth-century Drassanes, amid 12m high, perfectly rounded arches, La

Llotja is the recent creation of Josep Maria Blasi, a well-known gourmet and food critic. The excellent selection of Catalan food includes a medieval dish or two, such as roast chicken with saffron, in homage to the ancient stone edifice. At midday, there's a very interesting two-course lunch menu, and courtyard is always a delicious place to sit. *See also chapter Cafés & Bars: Pavement tables.*
Tables outdoors (patio).

Mastroqué

C/Codols 29 (93 301 79 42). Metro Drassanes/bus 14, 18, 36, 38, 57, 59, 64, N6, N9. **Lunch served** 1.30-3.30pm Mon-Fri. **Dinner served** 9-11.30pm Mon-Sat. Closed Aug. **Average** 3,000ptas. **Set lunch** 1,200ptas. **Credit** DC, MC, V. **Map D5**
One thing Catalan restaurateurs might learn from their French neighbours is the art of mellow lighting. Many places in Barcelona are over-lit, but this is not the case with French-run Mastroqué. On one of the narrowest streets in the city, the nevertheless-roomy restaurant, upscale without being pretentious, offers an interesting selection of fine French, Catalan and other Spanish regional dishes, such as a hot goat cheese starter with cooked peppers and tomatoes. The set lunch is generous and excellent.
Air-conditioning. Booking advisable weekends.

Els Ocellets

Ronda Sant Pau 55 (93 441 10 46). Metro Sant Antoni or Paral.lel/bus 20, 64, 91, N6, N9. **Lunch served** 1.30-4pm Tue-Sun. **Dinner served** 8.30-11.30pm Tue-Sat. Closed public holidays, Easter. **Average** 2,000ptas. **Set lunch** 950ptas Tue-Fri (not holidays). **Credit** AmEx, DC, JCB, MC, V. **Map C5**
This comfortable restaurant and its older, more picturesque parent Can Lluís, a little way up a narrow street across the Ronda Sant Pau, share the same menu and the same popularity, but lately the Ocellets has had the edge in cooking. Try the spicy *romescada*, the *esqueixada* or the *filet de vedella al cabrales* (veal fillet with a powerful goat's cheese sauce). Note that bookings are only taken for large groups, so it's necessary to get there early to avoid queueing. Menu prices do not include tax.
Air-conditioning at Els Ocellets. Booking advisable.
Branch: Can Lluís C/de la Cera 49 (93 441 11 87).

La Parra

C/Joanot Martorell 3 (93 332 51 34). Metro Hostafrancs/bus 52, 53, 56, 57, N2. **Lunch served** 2-4.30pm Sat-Sun. **Dinner served** 8.30pm-12.30am Tue-Fri; 8.30pm-midnight Sat. Closed public holidays, Easter, Aug (phone to check). **Average** 3,500ptas. **Credit** MC, V. **Map A3**
A great outlet for stout Catalan country cooking *a la brasa* within the city asphalt. You pass a giant wood-fired grill as you enter this 180-year-old ex-coaching inn, which has a menu offering one of the best *escalivades* in town and hefty portions of leg of lamb, rabbit, pork, beef steaks and spare ribs, served on wooden slabs with freshly made *all i oli*. Other specialities include roast duck and an unbeatable *orada a la sal* (gilt-head bream baked in salt), and from November to March there are *calçots*, specially cultivated spring onions from the Valls area (*see p122* **The Catalan Menu**), eaten on their own, charcoal-grilled, with *romesco* sauce. Well-priced wines are served, and rare *orujos* (fierce Galician spirits), but they happily refuse to stock Coca-Cola.
Air-conditioning. Booking advisable. Disabled: wheelchair access. Tables outdoors.

Les Quinze Nits

Plaça Reial 6 (93 317 30 75). Metro Liceu/bus 14, 18, 38, 59, N6, N9. **Lunch served** 1-3.30pm, **dinner served** 8.30-11.30pm, daily. Closed 25 Dec. **Average** 2,000ptas. **Set lunch** 950ptas Mon-Fri. **Credit** AmEx, DC, MC, V. **Map D5**
This small chain caused a minor sensation in the Barcelona restaurant world by offering a combination of sophisticated modern Catalan food in light, elegant surroundings at prices significantly lower than the norm at this level, and, in the case of two branches, in formerly down-at-heel locations in Plaça Reial and C/Escudellers where nobody thought restaurants like this could work. Defying the doubters, they've been hugely successful. Menus are all similar: try the *civet de conill* (rabbit stew), *parillada de peix* (seafood mixed grill) or the succulent *arròs negre*. Their popularity is such that food quality and service can get pressured at busy times, and they have an annoying no-bookings policy, which often means lengthy queues. One consolation is that this can favour foreigners, who tend to eat earlier than locals do.
Air-conditioning. Disabled: wheelchair access. Tables outdoors (Quinze Nits only).
Branches: La Fonda C/Escudellers 10 (93 301 75 15); **Hostal de Rita** C/Aragó 279 (93 487 33 60); **L'Hostalet de la Mamasita** Avda Sarrià (93 321 92 96).

El Salón

C/Hostal d'en Sol (93 315 21 59). Metro Jaume I/bus 17, 40, 45. **Lunch served** 2-5pm, **dinner served** 8.30pm-midnight, Mon-Sat. **Average** 2,500ptas. **Credit** AmEx, MC, V. **Map D5**
With antique couches, mirrors and high-backed chairs, El Salón has the feel of an elegant bohemian living room. The cuisine has French overtones, with a fair amount of creamy sauces, but the base is Catalan and very good. Try roast guinea-fowl with chestnut comfit and creamy clove sauce, or aubergine tart with goat's cheese and pesto.
Air-conditioning. Booking advisable. Disabled: wheelchair access.

Senyor Parellada

C/Argenteria 37 (93 310 50 94). Metro Jaume I/bus 17, 40, 45. **Lunch served** 1-3.30pm Mon-Sat, **dinner served** 9-11.30pm, Mon-Sat. Closed public holidays. **Average** 3,000ptas. **Credit** AmEx, DC, MC, V. **Map D5**
The atmosphere is relaxed, and the décor a stylish combination of modern touches with the centuries-old walls of a stone building in La Ribera. As well as the pillared main dining room, there are attractive rooms upstairs. Specialities include thyme soup, cod with honey and cinnamon ice-cream, *crema catalana* and delicious modern variations on Catalan standards such as *escalivada*. Service is courteous, and it's a place where it's easy to settle in for several hours.
Air-conditioning. Booking essential.

Set Portes

Passeig Isabel II 14 (93 319 29 50). Metro Barceloneta/bus 14, 17, 36, 40, 45, 57, 59, 64. **Meals served** 1pm-1am daily. **Average** 4,000ptas. **Credit** AmEx, DC, EC, JCB, MC, £$ptasTC, V. **Map D5**.
Founded in 1836 and a historic institution in itself, the huge 'Seven Doors' is another restaurant that's on every tourist list and so regularly packed with foreigners, but it also maintains standards and serves good paella and fish dishes. The speciality is *paella de peix*: for maximum flavour ask for the shells to be left on the seafood. Despite the frilly fittings and the piano player, prices are generally reasonable. Bookings are taken only for meals between 1.30-2.30pm and 8-9.30pm; expect long queues, especially on Sunday evenings.
Air-conditioning. Booking advisable.

Silenus

C/Angels 8 (93 302 26 80). Metro Catalunya/bus all routes to Plaça Catalunya. **Lunch served** 1-4pm Mon-Sat. **Dinner served** 9-11.30pm Tue-Thur; 9-11.45pm Fri-Sat. Closed 25, 31 Dec. **Set lunch** 1,100ptas Tue-Fri; 1,500ptas Sat. **Set dinner** 3,000ptas. **Credit** DC, MC, V. **Map C4**
A short walk from the MACBA, Silenus is a recent addition to a neighbourhood undergoing re-vitalisation. Run by artist Andrés Cobo and his wife, the restaurant feels laid-back and

fresh, with comfy sofas lining the walls and minimalist décor that highlights the open, high-ceilinged nature of the space. Food is a market-fresh offering of Catalan and Spanish regional dishes, with set menus only. Silenus is popular with a varied, young crowd, service is friendly and there are regular exhibits of quality paintings by local artists.
Booking advisable for dinner. Disabled: wheelchair access. Tables outdoors (May-Oct).

La Tomaquera
C/Margarit 58 (no phone). Metro Paral.lel/bus 20, 36, 57, 64, N6, N9. **Lunch served** 2-4.30pm Tue-Sun. **Dinner served** 8.30-11.30pm Tue-Sat. Closed eves of holidays, Easter, Aug, 25 Dec. **Average** 2,000ptas. **No credit cards. Map B5**
Despite owner Manel's refusal to have a phone or put an entry into local listings guides, people from all over town visit this enjoyable Poble Sec restaurant, above all for its specialities: *caracoles* (snails) and *a la brasa* meat, with fabulous *all i oli*. In quality, quantity and preparation the meat is the best in town, and there are also good salads and desserts.

La Venta
Plaça Dr Andreu (93 212 64 55). FGC Avda Tibidabo/bus 17, 22, 73, 75, N8, then Tramvia Blau. **Lunch served** 1.30-3.30pm Mon-Sat, **dinner served** 9-11.30pm, Mon-Sat. Closed 25, 31 Dec. **Average** 5,000ptas. **Credit** AmEx, DC, EC, MC, V.
In the square at the foot of the funicular on Tibidabo, La Venta has an outside terrace that's a lovely place to enjoy a meal in the fresh mountain air. It's also attractive indoors, and in winter a glass conservatory maintains the open-air atmosphere. Regulars on the sophisticated, imaginative menu include sea urchins au gratin and cod tail with vegetables, and there are also interesting, morish desserts. Service is friendly and efficient.
Air-conditioning. Booking essential. Disabled: wheelchair access. Tables outdoors.

Seafood

Any number of restaurants in Barcelona serve seafood, but those listed here are notable fish and crustacean specialists. There are a great many more good seafood restaurants clustered around the Port Vell and Port Olímpic (*see page 127* **Dockside dining**).

Bar Mundial
Plaça Sant Agusti Vell 1 (93 319 90 56). Metro Arc de Triomf/bus 39, 40, 41, 42, 51, 141. **Bar open** 9am-11pm Mon, Wed-Sat; 9am-5pm Sun. **Meals served** 1.30-11pm Mon, Wed-Sat; 1.30-5pm Sun. Closed two weeks Aug. **Average** 2,500ptas. **No credit cards. Map E5**
A small, unpretentious bar-restaurant in La Ribera specialising in freshly cooked seafood, mainly plain-grilled. A single *parrillada* (mixed seafood grill) platter is ample for two, and costs just 2,200ptas. Fish soups are also recommended.
Air-conditioning. Booking essential (evenings).

Cal Pep
Plaça de les Olles 8 (93 310 79 61). Metro Jaume I/ bus 14, 16, 17, 39, 41, 51. **Lunch served** 1-4.30pm Tue-Sat. **Dinner served** 8pm-midnight Mon-Sat. Closed Easter, Aug, public holidays.
Average *bar* 2,500ptas; *restaurant* 5,000ptas. **Credit** AmEx, DC, MC, V. **Map D5/E5**
There are more seats at the bar than in the restaurant, a brick-lined room decorated with a boar's head and antique cash registers. At bar, Pep himself grills most of the exceptional fish and seafood, keeping up a constant stream of chat. He also runs the costlier **Passadis del Pep** (*see p121*).
Air-conditioning. Booking essential for restaurant.

Can Ramonet
C/Maquinista 17 (93 319 30 64). Metro Barceloneta/bus 17, 39, 45, 57, 59, 64. **Meals served** *Mar-Dec* 10am-4pm, 8pm-midnight, daily. *Jan-Apr* 10am-4pm, 8pm-midnight, Mon-Sat; 10am-4pm Sun. Closed mid-Aug-mid-Sept. **Average** 4,500ptas. **Credit** V. **Map E6**
Reportedly the oldest building in Barceloneta, opened as a tavern in 1763 and run since 1956 by the Ballarin family. A spectacular display of fresh seafood greets you at the entrance, and if you're not sure what anything is called you can just point to it. Eat tapas at the bar, or larger *racions* at one of the tables, perhaps lobster with clams, cod with *romesco*, *serrano* ham or some of the best anchovies in town.
Air-conditioning. Booking advisable. Disabled: wheelchair access. Tables outdoors.

Can Ros
C/Almirall Aixada 7 (93 221 45 79). Metro Barceloneta/bus 17, 39, 45, 57, 59, 64. **Lunch served** 1-5pm daily. **Dinner served** 8pm-midnight Mon, Tue, Thur-Sun. **Average** 2,500ptas. **Set lunch** 1,025ptas Mon-Fri. **Gourmet menu** 1,800ptas Mon-Fri. **Credit** AmEx, V. **Map D6**
The best value in Barceloneta. A good way to order is to pick a mixture of mussels, clams, *peixets* (whitebait in batter), salted prawns and so on while waiting for the main course, which can take up to 40 minutes for paella or *arròs negre*.
Air-conditioning. Booking advisable weekends.
Branch: La Marsalada Passeig Joan de Borbó 58 (93 221 21 27).

Els Pescadors
Plaça Prim 1 (93 225 20 18). Metro Poble Nou/bus 36, 71, 92, 141, N6. **Lunch served** 1-3.45pm, **dinner served** 8pm-midnight, daily. Closed Easter, Christmas period (phone to check), public holidays. **Average** 5,000ptas. **Credit** AmEx, DC, JCB, MC, TC, V.
A very attractive restaurant in a small old square back from the beach area, with a beautiful outside terrace. The specialities are refined Catalan fish and seafood dishes, and the oven-cooked fish specials, using the pick of the same day's catch from ports on the coast, are superb. Vegetarian options include a subtle *amanida d'herbes de marge* (watercress salad) and vegetables in batter with *romesco* sauce.
Air-conditioning. Booking essential. Disabled: wheelchair access. Tables outdoors (Apr-Oct).

El Salmonete
Space 108, Maremàgnum, Moll d'Espanya (93 225 81 43). Metro Drassanes/bus 14, 18, 36, 57, 59, 64. **Lunch served** 1-5pm, **dinner served** 8pm-midnight, daily. **Average** 3,500ptas. **Credit** AmEx, MC, V. **Map D6**
Once one of the best-known traditional beach restaurants in Barceloneta, the Salmonete has been resurrected on the first floor of the Maremagnum complex (*see chapter* **Shopping**). Specialities include a range of different paellas and *suquet de peix*, and it offers a spectacular panoramic harbour view.
Air-conditioning. Disabled: wheelchair access. Tables outdoors (balcony).

Pica-pica & llesqueries

It's possible to be here a while before the realisation hits you that the famous Spanish *tapa* is not actually prominent in local eating habits. There are some great tapas bars in Barcelona (*see chapter* **Cafés & Bars**), but thicker on the ground is the local equivalent – places that serve *pica-pica*, more substantial assortments of cheeses, cold meats, anchovies and so on with slices (*llesques*) of toasted tomato bread (*see page 131* **The great** tomato bread). A place that specialises in tomato bread (*pa amb tomàquet*) with different toppings is a *llesqueria*. Restaurants providing food *a la brasa* (*see above* **Catalan**) offer similar dishes, as first courses or on their own. This can be a cheap or expensive way of eating, depending on the main ingredients.

La Bodegueta

C/Blai 47 (93 442 08 46). Metro Poble Sec/ bus 20, 57, 64, N6, N9. **Lunch served** 1.30-4pm Tue-Sun, **dinner served** 8.30pm-midnight, Tue-Sun. Closed Easter, late Aug, 25 Dec. **Average** 2,000ptas. **Credit** AmEx, DC, MC, V. **Map B5**

A pleasant local *llesqueria* with enjoyable *escalivada* with anchovies and *bacallà amb samfaina*. Decent house wine, fast service and reasonable prices.
Air-conditioning. Booking essential weekends. Disabled: wheelchair access.

Café del Centre

C/Girona 69 (93 488 11 01). Metro Girona/ bus 6, 7, 18, 19, 45, 50, 51, 54, 55, 56, N1, N2, N5. **Meals served** 8am-2am Mon-Fri; 7.30pm-2am Sat. Closed public holidays, three weeks Aug. **Average** 1,500ptas. **Credit** MC, V. **Map E4**

This turn-of-the-century marble and wood bar offers fine cheeses (try the Maó), patés, cold meats, smoked herring and salmon, and ten different salads until the small hours, with live (and untacky) piano music on Thursday, Friday and Saturday nights. A genuine local bar that's well worth a visit.

Flash Flash

C/La Granada del Penedès 25 (93 237 09 90). FGC Gràcia/bus 16, 17, 22, 24, 27, 28, 127, N4, N6. **Meals served** 1pm-1.30am daily. Closed 25 Dec. **Average** 2,500ptas. **Credit** AmEx, DC, MC, V. **Map D2**

Not a *llesqueria* but a *sandwicheria*. It's 1960s through and through, all white with silhouettes of Twiggy-esque models around the walls. House speciality is tortilla, in many varieties, and there are good burgers and sandwiches, with lots of vegetarian options.
Air-conditioning. Disabled: wheelchair access.

Pla de la Garsa

C/Assaonadors 13 (93 315 24 13). Metro Jaume I/bus 17, 40, 45. **Lunch served** 1.30-4 pm Mon-Sat. **Dinner served** 8pm-1am daily. Closed midday 25, 31 Dec. **Average** 2,500ptas. **Set lunch** 1,200ptas. **Set dinner** 2,000ptas. **Credit** AmEx, EC, MC, V. **Map E5**

Antique-dealer Ignasi Soler transformed a sixteenth-century stables and dairy near the Picasso museum into a beautiful restaurant serving high-quality cheeses, patés and cold meats. At midday there's an excellent, good-value set menu with larger dishes as well as *torrades*.
Air-conditioning. Booking essential at weekends. Disabled: wheelchair access.

Qu Qu (Quasi Queviures)

Passeig de Gràcia 24 (93 317 45 12). Metro Passeig de Gràcia/bus 7, 16, 17, 22, 24, 28, 50, 54, 56, N4, N6, N9. **Meals served** 8am-1am daily. Closed from 10pm 24, 31 Dec. **Average** 2,000ptas. **Credit** AmEx, DC, MC, V. **Map D4**

One of a crop of new-style snack restaurants that have opened on Passeig de Gràcia, the Qu Qu is ahead of the rest, with a wide range of high-quality salads, cheeses and Catalan charcuterie, including *llonganisses*, *bull*, *secallona*, *somaia* and other kinds that are otherwise hard to find in Barcelona. There's also a deli counter selling the same food to take away.
Air-conditioning. Disabled: wheelchair access. Tables outdoors (Easter-Oct).

Around Spain

Amaya

La Rambla 20-24 (93 302 10 37). Metro Liceu/bus 14, 18, 38, 59. **Lunch served** 1-5pm, **dinner served** 8.30pm-midnight, daily. **Average** 4,000ptas. **Set menus** 950ptas Mon-Fri. **Credit** AmEx, DC, EC, JCB, MC, V. **Map D5**

A big, central Basque restaurant, traditionally popular with actors, writers, opera singers and politicians. Basque specialities include *angulas* (elvers, baby eels), *lubina* (sea bass) and *besugo* (sea bream), cooked in several different ways. The extensive wine list includes Txakoli, a good, light, dry Basque white wine. Livelier for lunch than dinner.
Air-conditioning. Car park. Tables outdoors (Apr-Nov).

El Asador de Burgos

C/Bruc 118. (93 207 31 60). Metro Verdaguer/bus 20, 21, 39, 45, 47. **Lunch served** 1-4pm Mon-Sat. **Dinner served** 9-11pm Mon-Thur; 9-11.30pm Fri-Sat. Closed Aug. **Average** 5,000ptas. **Credit** AmEx, DC, MC, V. **Map E4**

Castilian food is for confirmed carnivores, with only a very little vegetable relief. First courses at this restaurant include *morcilla* blood sausage, roast chorizo, sliced marinated pork, and baby peppers. Typical main courses are roast lamb, roast piglet, grilled ribs of lamb, and a veal steak that looks like it could kick sand in the face of the standard entrecôte served elsewhere. Booking is essential, as the roasts are prepared fresh three hours in advance, in a traditional tiled oven.
Air-conditioning. Booking essential. Disabled: wheelchair access.

Casa Lorca

C/Laforja 8 (93 415 81 94). FGC Gràcia/ bus 16, 17, 27. **Meals served** 1pm-2am daily. **Average** 2,500ptas. **Set lunch** 1,000ptas. **Set dinner** 1,200ptas. **Credit** AmEx, DC, EC, JCB, MC, TC, V. **Map D2.**

With 68 dishes on its main menu, Casa Lorca mixes purely Andalusian food – fish or chickpeas *a la andaluza*, or in summer cold soups like gazpacho and *ajoblanco* (cold white garlic soup) – with more Catalan-orientated cannelloni, pigs' trotters or *pa amb tomàquet* with cheese or ham.

El Mallorquí

C/Francisco Giner 21 (93 217 06 05). Metro Diagonal/ bus 22, 24, 28, N4, N6. **Lunch served** 1-4pm Mon-Fri. **Dinner served** 8.30-11pm Mon-Sat. Closed Easter, Christmas week. **Average** 2,200ptas. **Set lunch** 975ptas Mon-Fri. **Credit** EC, MC, V. **Map D2**

A restaurant in Gràcia with a tasty assortment of Mallorcan dishes such as *sobrassada*, a spicy meat paste, with honey, or *tumbet*, fried aubergine, potato, and red pepper baked in tomato sauce and served with lamb – or without, for a vegetarian alternative. There are also excellent cheeses from Menorca and island goods for sale, from Menorcan gin to Mallorcan glassware. There's a pleasant outdoor dining area in summer.
Booking advisable. Tables outdoors (garden, May-Sept).

International

For more Asian restaurants, *see below* **Budget**.

La Bella Napoli

C/Margarit 14 (93 442 50 56). Metro Paral.lel/bus 20, 57, 64, N6. **Lunch served** 1.30-4pm, **dinner served** 8pm-midnight, daily. Closed midday Aug. **Average** *pizza* 1,000ptas; *à la carte* 2,500ptas. **Credit** MC, V. **Map B5**

For many, the best pizzas in Barcelona (ask for the owner's own invention, pizza primavera). Other delights include *arancino* (rice, ham, peas and parmesan) and *berenjena a la parmigiana* (aubergine, mozzarella, *ragú* and parmesan).
Air-conditioning.
Branch: C/Villarroel 101 (93 454 70 56).

The great tomato bread

According to the head chef of the Set Portes (*see p128*) *pa amb tomàquet* (bread with tomato, *pan con tomate* in Castilian) is made as follows: 'Rub the open side of a very ripe tomato, cut in half, against the surface of the bread, so that the tomato pulp is evenly spread over the bread. Add salt and a drop of oil.' If the slices of bread have been toasted, then they're called *torrades*. All very simple, but this basic invention has become one of the most universally appreciated creations of Catalan cooking, with a mystique attached to it all of its own.

Although tomatoes first appeared in Catalonia in the sixteenth century, they didn't become well known until the eighteenth, but their application to bread seems to have started early, and the first written reference appeared in 1884. Leopold Pomés, author of the definitive *Theory and Practice of Bread with Tomato* (1984), claims *pa amb tomàquet* was invented by a painter who wanted to combine the colours of the sunset on an edible base, but it most probably originated as a way of using up the previous day's bread.

The 'secret' is that the tomatoes have to be good, and very ripe. Both sweet and savoury, tomato bread is delicious with just about anything, but goes especially well with strong hams, cold meats, anchovies and cheeses. For Catalans it's an immediate, strong symbol of home, especially, perhaps, because it's perversely ignored in the rest of Iberia

Bunga Raya

C/Assaonadors 7 (93 319 31 69). Metro Jaume I/ bus 17, 40, 45. **Dinner served** 8pm-1am Tue-Sun. Closed Sept (usually). **Average** 2,000ptas. **Set dinner** 1,795ptas. **No credit cards**. **Map E5**
The set dinner at this Malaysian-Indonesian restaurant, a single-plate *rijstafel*, is good value. It's a bit cramped and service could be quicker, but you can't have everything.
Book Fri, Sat. Disabled: wheelchair access.

Cantina Mexicana I & II

C/Encarnació 51 (93 210 68 05) & C/Torrent de les Flors 53 (93 213 10 18). Metro Joanic/bus 21, 39, N4. **Lunch served** 1-4pm Mon-Sat. **Dinner served** 8pm-12.30am Tue-Sun. Closed Easter week, part of Aug (phone to check), 24, 31 Dec. **Average** 2,500ptas. **Credit** MC, V. **Map E2**
Both Cantinas, very close to each other on a street corner, offer the same food – *enchiladas*, *machaca*, guacamole, *frijoles*

– but CM II, in Torrent de les Flors, has a larger, more comfortable space. Ingredients are imported from Mexico, and dishes are much more authentic than standard Tex-Mex. If one of them closes for a holiday, the other one will be open. *Air-conditioning. Booking advisable. Vegetarian dishes.*

Conducta Ejemplar – El Rodizio

C/Consell de Cent 403 (93 265 51 12). Metro Girona/bus 6, 19, 50, 51, 55, N1, N4, N5. **Lunch served** 1-4pm Mon-Sat. **Dinner served** 8.30pm-midnight Mon-Thur; 8.30pm-1am Fri, Sat. **Set lunch** 950ptas. **Lunch buffet** 1,800ptas Mon-Fri; 2,300ptas Sat. **Evening buffet** 2,300ptas. **Credit** MC, V. **Map E3**
An original; one of very few places in Barcelona to offer a *rodizio*, a Brazilian meat buffet. Eat as much as you like from a hot and cold buffet followed by 12 different types of meat including Castilian sausage, steak, turkey, lamb, Brazilian-cut beef, veal and marinated pork. Vegetarians beware. *Air-conditioning. Disabled: wheelchair access.*

Den

C/Quintana 4 (93 302 49 69). Metro Liceu/bus 14, 18, 38, 59, N6, N9. **Lunch served** 1.30-4pm daily, **dinner served** 9-11.30pm, daily. **Average** 1,500ptas. **Set lunch** 900-1,000ptas Mon-Sat. **Set menus** 1,560-1,850ptas. **No credit cards. Map D5**

A small restaurant with a Japanese chef who prepares sushi, sashimi, tempura and a variety of rice dishes and soups. Fixed-price menus include *yakiniku*: meat barbecued by diners themselves at gas grills installed at the tables.
Air-conditioning. Booking advisable (Fri, Sat).
Branch: Yellow (sake bar) C/Xuclà 7 (no phone).

Fu Li Yuan

C/Viladomat 73 (93 325 10 48). Metro Sant Antoni/bus 13, 41, 55, 91, 141. **Lunch served** noon-4.30pm daily, **dinner served** 8pm-midnight, daily. **Average** 1,500ptas. **Set lunches** 795ptas, 995ptas Mon-Fri. Set dinner 1,350ptas. **Credit** MC, V. **Map B4.**

One of the few good budget Chinese restaurants, which serves a number of dishes such as Beijing duck that are normally only found on the menus of its more upmarket competitors. Popular with locals, and service is friendly and fast.
Air-conditioning. Booking advisable.

Paradís

C/Paradís 4 (93 310 72 43). Metro Jaume I/ bus 17, 40, 45. **Dinner served** 8.30pm-midnight Mon-Sat. Closed 25 Dec. **Set menus** 1,500ptas daily. **Credit** MC, V. **Map D5**

African and vegetarian food in an unlikely setting – an elegant, old, wood-panelled restaurant smack next door to the Generalitat. The African part hails from Senegal and includes such specialities as *mafe*, veal in peanut sauce with potatoes, carrots and cassava. Reggae is the background sound of choice, and on weekend nights the place transforms into a dance club (*see chapter* **Nightlife**).
Air-conditioning. Booking advisable at weekends.

Peimong

C/Templaris 6-10 (93 318 28 73). Metro Jaume I/bus 17, 40, 45. **Lunch served** 1-4.30pm Tue-Sun, **dinner served** 8pm-midnight, Tue-Sun. Closed Aug. **Average** 1,200ptas. **No credit cards. Map D5**

If there's another Peruvian restaurant in town, it hasn't had the success of this small place. No-frills décor is made up for by the food, mainly from the northern part of Peru, which includes such things as *ceviche*, grouper fish marinated in lemon and spices, and *pato en ají*, duck stewed with peas, potatoes and white rice. It's popular with a mixed, local and foreign crowd.
Air-conditioning. Booking essential (Fri-Sun).

Shalimar

C/Carme 71 (93 329 34 96). Metro Liceu/bus 14, 38, 59, N6, N9. **Lunch served** 1-4pm Mon, Wed-Sun. **Dinner served** 8-11.30pm daily. Closed 25 Dec. **Average** 2,500ptas. **Credit** DC, MC, V. **Map C5.**

One of the best mid-price Pakistani restaurants in town, the Shalimar serves a selection of South Asian standards, with good tandoori dishes, in unpretentious surroundings.
Air-conditioning. Booking essential (Fri, Sat).

Vegetarian

Visitors ordering 'vegetarian' sandwiches should not be surprised to find they include ham or tuna, and that bean or lentil stews can contain meat stock, so check when ordering (ask *¿lleva tocino?* to see if it's made with pork fat). Asian restaurants also usually offer decent vegetarian choices.

Biocenter

C/Pintor Fortuny 25 (93 301 45 83). Metro Liceu/bus 14, 18, 38, 59, N6, N9. **Meals served** 9am-5pm Mon-Sat. Closed public holidays. **Average** 1,500ptas. **Set menu** 1,125ptas Mon-Fri; 1,500ptas Sat. **No credit cards. Map C4**

In a large, well-lit space, across the road from the health-food shop of the same name. There's a wide range of salads and filling set menu, and vegans are catered for. Beer is served.
Air-conditioning.

La Buena Tierra

C/Encarnació 56 (93 219 82 13). Metro Joanic/bus 21, 39, N4. **Lunch served** 1-4pm, **dinner served** 8pm-midnight, Mon-Sat. Closed Easter, Jul/Aug (phone to check). **Average** 2,000ptas. **Set lunch** 900ptas Mon-Fri. **Credit** AmEx, MC, V. **Map E2**

This pleasant restaurant in a little old house in Gràcia, with pretty garden at the back, has some of the best vegetarian food in town. Specialities include *canelons de bosc* (cannelloni and wild mushrooms), vol-au-vent with cream of asparagus and refreshing gazpacho and melon soups in summer.
Booking essential (Fri, Sat). Tables outdoors (garden).

Comme Bio

Via Laietana 28 (93 319 89 68). Metro Jaume I/bus 17, 19, 40, 45. **Lunch served** 1-4pm, **dinner served** 8-11pm, daily. **Average** 2,500ptas. **Set lunch** 1,275ptas Mon-Fri; 1,400ptas Sat; 1,600ptas Sun. **Credit** AmEx, DC, MC, V. **Map D5**

An ambitiously large, stylish place that combines an extensive health-food shop and boutique of artist-made products with a full vegetarian restaurant. Maybe it's a vision of the future, but at any rate the food is good and reasonably priced, with a varied listing of 40-odd dishes.
Air-conditioning. Booking essential.
Branch: Gran Via de les Corts Catalanes 603 (93 301 03 76).

Govinda

Plaça Vila de Madrid 4-5 (93 318 77 29). Metro Catalunya/bus all routes to Plaça Catalunya. **Lunch served** 1-4pm daily. **Dinner served** 8.30-11.45pm Tue-Sat. Closed dinner public holidays. **Average** 2,500ptas. **Set lunch** 1,250ptas. **Set menu** 1,700 Fri night-Sun. **Credit** AmEx, DC, MC, V. **Map D4-5**

Indian vegetarian restaurant in a quiet, attractive square near the Rambla. An excellent salad bar, home-made bread, a choice of two hot dishes and home-made desserts make up a lunch menu of outstanding value. No alcohol or coffee.
Air-conditioning. Booking advisable.

L'Hortet

C/Pintor Fortuny 32 (93 317 61 89). Metro Liceu/ bus 14, 18, 38, 59, N6, N9. **Lunch served** 1-4pm daily. Closed public holidays. **Set lunch** 975ptas Mon-Fri; 1,200ptas Sat, Sun. **No credit cards. Map C4**

Only open at lunchtime, this homey little place is one of the more imaginative vegetarian restaurants, offering a different set menu every day. Cheap, too. No alcohol.
Disabled: wheelchair access.

L'Illa de Gràcia

C/Sant Domènec 19. (93 238 02 29). Metro Fontana/bus 22, 24, 28, N4, N6. **Lunch served** 1-4pm Tue-Fri; 2-4pm Sat, Sun. **Dinner served** 9pm-midnight Tue-Sun. Closed Easter, late Aug, 25 Dec, public holidays. **Average** 1,500ptas. **Set lunch** 800ptas Mon-Fri. **Credit** DC, MC, V. **Map D2**

An unusual place – at least for northern European sensibilities: while serving solely vegetarian food, L'Illa allows smoking and serves beer, wine and coffee. Specialities include *crep illa de Gràcia* (pancake with mushrooms, cream, and pepper), and home-made cakes. Prices are very reason-

able, with the most expensive dish on the menu at just 675ptas, and the set lunch is excellent value.
Booking essential (Fri, Sat)

Juicy Jones

C/Cardenal Casañas 7 (93 302 43 30). Metro Liceu/bus 14, 18, 38, 59, N6, N9. **Meals served** noon-midnight Tue-Sun. **Set menu** 975ptas. **No credit cards.** **Map D5**
This funky, colourful place could be the original veggie voodoo lounge, with a freaky-streaky paint job and long thin bar where at least 17 different fresh juices are served. The well-prepared all-veg food is excellent and cheap. Food is served late and all the way through the opening times, and it's one of the best places open on Sundays.
Air-conditioning.

Self Naturista

C/Santa Anna 11-17 (93 318 23 88/93 318 26 84). Metro Catalunya/bus all routes to Plaça Catalunya. **Meals served** 11.30am-10pm Mon-Sat. Closed public holidays. **Average** 1,250ptas. **Set menu** 910ptas. **No credit cards.** **Map D4**
The best-known vegetarian restaurant in Barcelona looks like a college self-service canteen, only cleaner. The good-value set menu includes stews and soups, most made without dairy products, and Catalan dishes such as *escalivada*, plus special local ingredients such as wild mushrooms, when in season. Popular, so there are long queues for lunch.
Air-conditioning.

Budget

Bar-Restaurante Romesco

C/Arc de Sant Agustí 4 (93 318 93 81). Metro Liceu/bus 14, 18, 38, 59, N6, N9. **Meals served** 1pm-midnight Mon-Sat. Closed Aug, 25 Dec. **Average** 1,200ptas. **No credit cards.** **Map C5/D5**.
Even closer to the Rambla, and nearly always full, the Romesco is enshrined as a favourite with young foreigners, and many locals too. House speciality is *frijoles*, a Spanish-Caribbean dish of black beans, mince, rice and fried banana, a bargain at just over 500ptas. Noisy and convivial, this is one of the city's best cheap eating houses. To find it, just head down C/Sant Pau and look to the right.
Disabled: wheelchair access.

Ca l'Abuelo

C/Providència 44 (93 284 44 94). Metro Fontana/bus 39. **Lunch served** 1.15-4pm Mon-Sat. **Dinner served** 9-11.30pm Fri, Sat. Closed Aug-Sept (phone to check). **Set lunch** 975ptas. **Set dinner** 1,175ptas. **Credit** MC, V. **Map E2**
In Gràcia, this friendly, well-run place offers one of the best deals in town: an open buffet of over 40 different dishes for a mere 975ptas. You can gorge yourself on prawns, chicken, veal, pork, various fish dishes, stews or salads, and a good choice of desserts. Fridays and Saturdays it's a little more expensive and these, alas, are the only days dinner is served.
Air-conditioning. Booking essential (Fri, Sat).

Cafè de la Ribera

Plaça de les Olles 6 (93 319 50 72). Metro Barceloneta/bus 14, 16, 17, 45, 51. **Open** Apr-Oct 8am-10pm, Nov-Mar 8am-5pm, Mon-Sat. **Lunch served** 1-4.30pm Mon-Sat. **Set lunch** 975ptas. **No credit cards.** **Map E5**
Dishes at this very popular, ever crowded place include *revueltos de espinaca* (scrambled eggs with spinach), veal with goat's cheese, and fish soups. The set lunch menu changes daily, and from spring to autumn there are tables outside, with salads, pizzas and fresh juices available all day.
Air-conditioning. Tables outdoors (April-Oct).

Cervantes

C/Cervantes 7 (93 317 33 84). Metro Jaume I/bus 14, 18, 38, 59, N6, N9. **Lunch served** 1.30-4.30pm Mon-Fri. Closed Easter, three weeks Aug, public holidays. **Set menu** 1,100ptas. **No credit cards.** **Map D5**
A friendly lunch restaurant run by three sisters. The food is strictly Catalan, with *botifarra*, paella and *escudella* and amenably priced. Popular with tie-wearing city-hall workers and green-haired students from the nearby art school.

Elisabets

C/Elisabets 2-4 (93 317 58 26). Metro Catalunya/bus all routes to Plaça Catalunya. **Lunch served** 2.45-3.30pm Mon-Sat. Closed three weeks Aug. **Set lunch** 975ptas. **No credit cards.** **Map C4/D4**
A classic little lunchtime eating house with a long history of serving good cheap Catalan food to the neighbourhood and anyone else who wanders in. The menu gives a wider-than-average choice, often with good lamb with *all i oli*.
Air-conditioning. Booking advisable.

Escondite del Pirata

C/de la Cera 23 (93 443 04 34). Metro Sant Antoni/bus 20, 64, 91, N4, N6. **Meals served** 1pm-midnight Mon-Sat. Closed Aug (phone to check). **Set menus** 950ptas Mon-Fri lunch; 1,250ptas Fri evening, Sat. **No credit cards.** **Map C5**
The 'Pirate's Hideout' serves decent versions of Catalan dishes such as rabbit stew or grilled fresh tuna, and a variety of original salads. The clientele is a mixture of noisy, alternative-ish locals, chain-smoking artists, and the odd foreigner.
Booking essential Fri-Sat.

La Fragua

C/Cadena 15 (93 442 80 97). Metro Liceu/bus 14, 38, 59, N6, N6, N9. **Meals served** 8pm-1am Tue-Sun. Closed public holidays, some days in Aug. **Average** 1,500ptas. **Set menu** (for groups) 1,650ptas. **No credit cards.** **Map C5**
This large, dark bar-restaurant – still part-owned by the CNT anarchist trade union – has a barn-like atmosphere, with paved stone floor, high ceiling and the remains of the old forge (*fragua*) it once was. The food is simple, with dishes such as grilled rabbit with *all i oli*, grilled fish and salads.
Booking advisable (Fri, Sat).

Garduña

C/Morera 17-19 (93 302 43 23). Metro Liceu/bus 14, 38, 59, N6, N9. **Lunch served** 1-4pm daily. **Dinner served** 8pm-midnight Mon-Sat. **Average** 3,000ptas. **Set menus** 975ptas (lunch, incl 1 drink), 1,375ptas (lunch and dinner). **Credit** AmEx, MC, V. **Map C5**
Located inside the Boqueria market, the Garduña preserves a good deal of the feel of the nineteenth-century inn it once was. It was converted into strictly eating quarters in the 1970s, and the good, inexpensive Catalan food is guaranteed fresh, with the superb market right at the door. Get a table on the quieter upstairs floor to better appreciate the charm of the place.
Air-conditioning.

Marcelino 2000

C/Consell de Cent 236 (93 453 10 72). Metro Universitat/bus 54, 58, 64, 66, N3, N8. **Meals served** 1-5pm, 8pm-midnight, Mon-Sat. Closed two weeks Aug, Christmas period (phone to check). **Average** 1,500ptas. **Set menu** 1,000ptas Mon-Thur; 1,100ptas Fri, Sat. **Credit** AmEx, MC, V. **Map C3-4**
The Bodegas Marcelino are a chain of 17 bar-restaurants found across the Eixample, with a straightforward Galician-oriented menu of first-course stews, soups and salads, and mainly meat and seafood grills. The best way to find others is to visit one and pick up a napkin, which gives a full list.
Air-conditioning. Tables outdoors.

Packaged eating

Putting paid to the bland old idea that a place to eat should be distinguished by the food, the theme/concept restaurant has gained a firm foothold in the urban culinary landscape. In the post-Olympic years Barcelona has become especially appealing to international franchisers, eager to capitalise on the city's attraction as a hub of culture, leisure and tourist-inspired consumption, leading to a sudden glut of themed eateries.

There was a time when enticing 'concepts' linked to eating had to do with the origin of the food itself, the choice of Chinese, Mexican or Thai determining décor and much of the experience. This outmoded model, stemming from cities like Amsterdam, London or San Francisco, has always been much weaker in Barcelona, where minority groups are far smaller. Instead, the conceptualisation of lunch, dinner and drinks is easily bound to music, fashion, film and sport.

Stamped out of standard moulds for easy mastication, outlets like the **Hard Rock**, **Fashion Café**, **Planet Hollywood**, **Replay** and the inevitable local equivalent **Magic Barça**, dedicated to the football team, point up the contrast between Barcelona's subtle design values of the 1980s and their kitschification in the 1990s. Most have merchandising counters vending backpacks and T-shirts, sun-visored waitresses, pricey menus of American/Mediterranean cuisine and – with the exception of Magic Barça – that certain *je ne sais quoi* that helps you forget you're in Barcelona.

Every theme restaurant strives for its own brand image. Since the first Hard Rock opened in London in 1971 they have rarely strayed from their Far West barnyard ambience, which in Barcelona sticks out like a banjo player's sore thumb. The converted office space where Fashion Café struts its stuff is distinguished by elegant green and white marble walls, proudly preserved – only to have photos of Elle, Naomi and Claudia tackily tacked on to them (in the upstairs lounge the original décor is treated more tastefully). Both insist on distinguishing motifs: Hard Rock's huge 'Save the Planet' sign shines eco-hypocrisy over Plaça Catalunya, while a horrendous neon-outlined camera lens is the focal point of Fashion Café.

Planet Hollywood leaps to further themed heights, mimicking the rock 'n' roll paraphernalia in Hard Rock with an even finer collection of movie costumes and bric-a-brac. The interior is now split between Indiana Jones and the Titanic.

Understated by comparison is Replay, part Italian casualwear store, part café-restaurant. Apart from a fake rustic Roman mosaic, Replay's renovation of the cavernous Santa Eulàlia store on Passeig de Gràcia is respectable, and the union of fashion and food handled with tact, however sticky the prices.

Proof that Barcelona doesn't always have to import its concept atmospheres can be found in **Sub 34.3** in Maremàgnum, initially opened as 'Steven Spielberg's Dive' but now bought back by a local investor. As the name implies this day-and-night club is inspired by submarine motifs, with a suitably claustrophobic excess of hatches, portholes and radar screens topped off by periscopes offering views of the city. The interior, by designer Paco Luque, compensates for a chaos of colour with some one-off detailing, not least in the toilets (in the fine tradition of the city's design bars). Magic Barça, for its part, first opened at the Port Olímpic but is due to move to a location closer to the club's heart, by the Nou Camp stadium. A sports bar, it suffers from the unavoidable team colour scheme of claret and blue, perfect on the backs of Cruyff or Ronaldo but resembling a topless-bar paint job when extended wall to wall.

Locations

Fashion Café *Passeig de Gràcia 56 (487 34 06). Metro Passeig de Gràcia/bus 7, 16, 17, 22, 24, 28, N4, N6.* **Lunch served** 1-4pm daily. **Dinner served** 8pm-midnight Mon-Thur, Sun; 8pm-1am Fri, Sat. **Average** 2,500ptas. **Set menus** 1,990ptas Mon-Fri, set dinner and fashion show 3,500ptas Tue-Thur. **Credit** AmEx, DC, JCB, MC, V. **Map D3** *Air-conditioning. Booking advisable. Disabled: wheelchair access. Tables outdoors.*

Hard Rock Café *Plaça Catalunya 21 (270 23 05). Metro Catalunya, FGC Catalunya/bus all routes to Catalunya.* **Meals served** 12.30pm-2am daily. **Average** 2,000ptas. **Set menu** 1,500-2,000ptas. **Credit** AmEx, DC, JCB, MC, V. **Map D4** *Air-conditioning. Disabled: wheelchair access. Tables outdoors (May-Sept).*

Magic Barça *Passeig Marítim 36 (93 225 92 00). Metro Barceloneta/ bus 45, 59.* **Meals served** *Jan-Mar* 8pm-1am Thur, Fri; 1pm-1am Sat; 1-4pm Sun; *Mar-Dec* 1pm-midnight Mon-Thur; 1pm-2am Fri-Sun. **Average** 2,000ptas. **Set lunch** (summer) 1,250ptas Mon-Fri. **Credit** V. **Map E6** At some point the restaurant will move to the Nou Camp. *Air-conditioning. Booking advisable. Disabled: wheelchair access. Tables outdoors (Easter-mid-Sept).*

Planet Hollywood *Marina Village, C/Marina 19-21 (93 221 11 11). Metro Ciutadella/bus 36, 41, 92.* **Meals served** 1pm-midnight Mon-Thur, Sun; 1pm-1am Fri, Sat. Closed 25 Dec. **Average** 2,500ptas. **Credit** AmEx, JCB, MC, V. **Map F6** *Air-conditioning. Disabled: wheelchair access. Tables outdoors (June-Sept).*

Replay *Passeig de Gràcia 60 (93 467 72 24/93 488
22 15). Metro Passeig de Gràcia/bus 7, 16, 17, 22, 24,
28, N5, N6.* **Lunch served** 1-4pm daily. **Dinner
served** 8.30pm-midnight Mon-Wed; 8.30pm-12.30am
Thur-Sat. **Average** 2,700ptas. **Set menu** 1,250ptas.
Credit AmEx, MC, V. **Map D3**
*Air-conditioning. Booking advisable at weekends.
Disabled: wheelchair access. Tables outdoors.*

Sub.34.3 *Maremàgnum (93 225 81 58). Metro
Drassanes/bus 14, 36, 57, 59, 64.* **Lunch served**
1-4.30pm Mon-Thur; 1-5pm Fri-Sun. **Dinner
served** 8.30pm-midnight Mon-Thur; 8.30pm-
12.30am Fri-Sun. **Average** 2,250ptas. **Credit**
AmEx, DC, MC, V. **Map D6**
*Air-conditioning. Booking advisable. Disabled:
wheelchair access.*

Enjoy delicately prepared Mediterranean cuisine in this Renaissance house, with modern décor and glass ceiling.

Passatge de la Concepció, 5, Barcelona.
Tel. 93 487 01 96

Quality food and friendly staff in informal surroundings, just metres from the beach (next to the Hotel Arts). Enjoy our rice specialities prepared in a coal-fired oven.

AGUA
bar · tapas · restaurant

Pº Marítim de la Barceloneta, 30, Barcelona.
Tel. 93 225 12 72

ACONTRALUZ
restaurant

Mediterranean cuisine in an elegant restaurant with minimalist décor and interior garden.

Milanesat, 19, Barcelona.
Tel. 93 203 06 58

Mercè Vins

C/Amargós 1 (93 302 60 56). Metro Urquinaona/bus 17, 19, 40, 45. **Breakfast served** 8am-noon Sat. **Lunch served** 1.30-4pm Mon-Fri. **Dinner served** 8-11pm Wed, Fri, Sat. Closed public holidays, some days in Aug. **Set lunch** 1,095ptas. **Credit** V. **Map D5.**
Mercè Vins offers short set menus (no à la carte) with dishes such as *llom amb ametlles i prunes* (pork with almonds and prunes) or *estofat* (beef stew). It's tiny, and always packed – and note the individual opening times. In the evenings, there's a *llesqueria* service *(see page xxx)* only. *Air-conditioning (upstairs). Booking advisable.*

Mesón Jesús

C/Cecs de la Boqueria 4 (93 317 46 98). Metro Liceu/ bus 14, 38, 59, N6, N9. **Lunch served** 1-4pm Mon-Fri. **Dinner served** 8-11.30pm Mon-Sat. Closed Easter, Aug, public holidays. **Average** 2,500ptas. **Set lunch** 1,100ptas. **Set dinner** 1,250ptas. **Credit** MC, V. **Map D5**
Small, cosy and clean, this family-run restaurant off Plaça del Pi feels like it hasn't changed much since the last century. The hard-working team provides good Catalan and Spanish dishes, and it's popular with locals and foreigners. *Air-conditioning.*

La Oficina

Passeig Don Joan de Borbó 30 (93 221 40 05). Metro Barceloneta/bus 17, 39, 45, 57, 59, 64. **Lunch served** 1-4.30pm, **dinner served** 8.30-11.30pm, Mon, Wed-Sun. Closed 20 days Sept, midday 25 Dec. **Average** 2,000ptas. **Set menus** 1,150ptas Mon-Sat; 1,300ptas Sun. **Credit** AmEx, DC, MC, V. **Map D6**
With tables outside all year round, and great views of the city and Port Vell, La Oficina provides one of the best deals on this heavily touristed harbourside strip. The set menus give a wide choice of dishes, usually including paella. *Air-conditioning. Tables outdoors.*

Punjab Restaurante

C/Joaquin Costa 1B (93 443 38 99). Metro Liceu/bus 14, 38, 59, N6, N9. **Meals served** noon-midnight daily. **Average** 1,500ptas. **Set menu** 500ptas. **No credit cards. Map C4**
When this small Pakistani restaurant first opened it daringly posted a sign offering 25,000ptas to anyone who found a cheaper place to eat. Its own offer was a set three-course meal for 495ptas. Months later most of the sign remains, but the figure of 25,000ptas has been blanked out. Has someone actually come up with a cheaper place? Not that we know of. The menu features basics like chicken tikka or samosas, and the food isn't bad. *Air-conditioning. Booking advisable.*

Restaurante Económico – Borrás

Plaça Sant Agustí Vell 13 (93 319 64 94). Metro Arc de Triomf/bus 39, 40, 41, 42, 51, 141. **Meals served** 12.30-4.30pm Mon-Fri. Closed public holidays, Easter, Aug. **Average** 1,100ptas. **Set lunch** 950ptas. **No credit cards. Map E5**
A pretty restaurant looking on to a quiet square. The good set lunch gives a choice of around nine first courses and ten seconds, regularly including *fideuà*, baked potatoes, macaroni and *arroz a la Cubana*, rice with tomato sauce a fried egg, and a fried banana, if you ask for one.

Restaurante Pakistani

C/Carabassa 3 (93 302 60 25). Metro Drassanes/bus 14, 18, 38, 59, N6, N9. **Meals served** 1pm-1am daily. **Average** 1,500ptas. **No credit cards. Map D5.**
Central, just off Plaça George Orwell, this clean, green-walled little place serves good cheap dishes such as chicken with couscous (550ptas) or veggies with rice (425ptas). *Air-conditioning.*

Restaurante Xironda Orense

C/Roig 19 (93 442 30 91). Metro Liceu/bus 14, 18, 38, 59, N6, N9. **Lunch served** 1-4pm, **dinner served** 8.30pm-2am, Mon-Sat. Closed Aug. **Average** 900ptas. **No credit cards. Map C5**
Walk past the narrow crowded bar to the narrow crowded dining room, where you can choose from a decent variety of salads and mainly meat-based Galician dishes served in surprisingly generous quantities. A Catalan salad costs 350ptas, and a plate of lamb chops just 500ptas. There is no set menu.

Rodrigo

C/Argenteria 67 (93 310 30 20). Metro Jaume I/bus 17, 40, 45. **Lunch served** 8am-5pm Mon-Wed, Fri-Sun. **Dinner served** 8.30pm-1am Mon, Tue, Fri-Sun. Closed Aug. **Average** 1,100ptas. **Set lunch** 1,050ptas; 1,300ptas Sat, Sun, holidays. **Set dinner** 1,300ptas. **Credit** MC, V. **Map D5**
Home cooking and bargain prices attract huge crowds to Rodrigo's jumble of tables, especially on Sundays. Full meals are not served in the evening, but there is a wide choice of hot and cold sandwiches. Note the unusual closing days.

Los Toreros

C/Xuclà 3-5 (93 318 23 25). Metro Catalunya/bus 14, 38, 59, N6, N9. **Lunch served** 1-4pm Tue-Sun. **Dinner served** 8pm-midnight Tue-Sat. Closed two weeks Aug/Sept. **Average** 1,100ptas. **Set lunch** 875ptas Tue-Fri; 975ptas Sat; 1,075ptas Sun. **Set dinner** 1,750ptas. **No credit cards. Map D4/D5**
Long-established low-price restaurant serving *ternera* and chips, potato tortilla, salads and other standards, and with walls plastered with bullfight photos. *Air-conditioning. Booking essential dinner (Thur-Sat).*

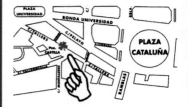

Cafés & Bars

Bocadillos and beer on a sunny square, or hot chocolate at a cosy granja – Barcelona can suggest many different ways to slake a thirst.

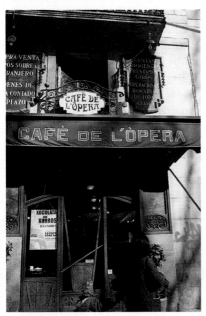

The Cafè de l'Opera. See page 141.

An eminently social city, Barcelona is home to an enormous number of bars and cafés, and you won't get a real taste of what the city's about without paying some of them a visit. Some places are the meeting points around which neighbourhood life turns, others old-fashioned bodegas with an ageing clientele sampling wine from the barrel. There are outdoor cafés on sunny squares, designer spots with imported beer, and small *granges* for afternoon coffee and cream cakes. Most recently the city has acquired a string of quasi-Italian coffee shops that bear an uncanny resemblance to places dotting the West Coast of the US.

Tapas in Barcelona are generally not as varied as in some other parts of Spain, but great examples can be found, and most bars offer food of some kind, from sandwiches to a full lunch menu. The listing that follows can only be one selection from all the cafés and drinking-holes around the city. In the same way that it's near-futile to try to categorise some of them, it's just as hard to draw a sharp distinction in Barcelona between places you might visit during the day or evening to talk over a drink or a coffee, and places where you'd call in as part of a night on the town. For bars that are more clearly oriented to night-time socialising, *see* chapter **Nightlife**, and for some more bar-restaurants, *see* chapter **Restaurants**.

Opening times, especially in more traditional cafés, can be variable (many close earlier or later at night, according to trade), and those given below should be taken as **guidelines** *rather than fixed hours. Except where indicated, the bars listed do not accept* **credit cards**.

Barri Gòtic

L'Ascensor
C/Bellafila 3 (93 318 53 47). Metro Jaume I/bus 17, 40, 45. **Open** 6pm-3am daily. **Map D5**.
An old wooden *ascensor* (lift) provides the entrance to this relaxed and tastefully appointed bar near the Ajuntament. Inside there's always an up-for-it, friendly crowd.

The Bagel Shop
C/Canuda 25 (93 302 41 61). Metro Plaça Catalunya/bus all routes to Plaça Catalunya. **Open** 9.30am-8.30pm Mon-Sat. Closed three weeks Aug. **Map D4**.
This small café run by a Canadian from Montreal is the only place in Barcelona where you can find fresh bagels in a range of varieties. Other hard-to-find goodies you may be gagging for are available, such as fudge brownies and carrot cake.

Bar Celta
C/Mercè 16 (93 315 00 06). Metro Drassanes/ bus 14, 18, 38, 59, N6, N9. **Open** 10am-1am Mon-Sat; 10am-midnight Sun. **Map D5**.
One of the best of the string of *tascas* (traditional bars, popular for a drinks-and-tapas crawl) on C/Mercè, near the port, this Galician bar is also a place that doesn't warm its tapas by microwave. Huge trays of (mostly) seafood line the bar. Particularly recommended are the *patatas bravas* and *rabas* (deep-fried chunks of squid), washed down with Galician white wine served, as is traditional, in white ceramic cups.

Boadas
C/Tallers 1 (93 318 95 92). Metro Catalunya/ bus all routes to Plaça Catalunya. **Open** noon-2am Mon-Thur; noon-3am Fri-Sat. **Map D4**.
One of Barcelona's institutions, a genuine 1933 art deco cocktail bar opened by Miguel Boadas after he learned the trade in the famed Floridita Bar in Havana. It's now run by his daughter. Boadas staff can mix a huge variety of cocktails, and the wood-lined walls are strung with mementos from their most famous patrons – including a sketch or two by Miró.

A great art deco café-billiard hall-place to read the paper, **El Velòdrom**. *See page 149.*

Café La Cereria

C/Baixada Sant Miquel 3-5 (no phone). Metro Liceu/bus 14, 18, 38, 59, N6, N9. **Open** 7am-9pm daily. **Map D5.**
Amid the invasion of multinational chains such as Il Caffè di Roma, this new, quiet, friendly café is very welcome. In a very attractive *Modernista* former wax shop, and run as a co-op, La Cereria offers home-made cakes and tarts and a large assortment of teas, herbal and traditional. The wooden tables are home-made, as are, of course, the various *bocadillos* you may order while seated at them.

Cafè de l'Opera

La Rambla 74 (93 317 75 85/93 302 41 80). Metro Liceu/bus 14, 38, 59, N6, N9. **Open** 8am-2am Mon-Thur, Sun; 8am-2.45am Fri-Sat. **Map D5.**
Another institution, the last real nineteenth-century grand café in the city, and by far the best of the cafés on the Rambla. With genuine *Modernista*-era décor, L'Opera continues to be enormously popular, with a contentedly mixed clientele – locals, foreigners, a large gay contingent and anyone else. An unbeatable place for people-watching on the Rambla. *Tables outdoors.*

Jamaica Coffee Shop

C/Ferran 6 (no phone). Metro Liceu/ bus 14, 38, 59, N6, N9. **Open** 7am-midnight Mon-Thur, Sun; 7am-3am Fri-Sat. **Map D5.**
A large coffee shop that's part of a locally-based chain. The range of excellent-quality coffees is more expensive (150ptas) than in your normal joint, but coffee connoisseurs will enjoy such treats as the exotic, powerful Baronhill Peaberry bean from Jamaica. The Jamaica Shops are friendlier and generally better-run than similar new-style coffee houses in the city. Good quality teas (again expensive) are also available. *Air-conditioning. Disabled: wheelchair access*
Branches: 12 more branches around Barcelona.

Kikes

C/Rauric 3 (no phone). Metro Liceu/bus 14, 38, 59, N6, N9. **Open** 6pm-midnight daily. **Map D5.**

Billing itself as a cultural association rather than a bar, this small, mellow and hip hole in the wall serves only beer and wine, apart from non-alcoholic drinks. It's run by the people who operate **Shanghai** and **Oviso's** (*see chapter* **Nightlife**) and caters to much the same crowd of young alternative folk.

Margarita Blue

C/Josep Anselm Clavé 6 (93 317 71 76). Metro Drassanes/bus 14, 18, 38, 59, N6, N9. **Open** 10am-1am Mon-Wed, Sun; 10am-3am Thur-Sat. **Credit** MC, V. **Map D5.**
A roomy, colourful bar/restaurant that serves very good Mexican food at all hours at moderate prices. On Thursday and Sunday evenings, short original performances are held; on Friday and Saturday nights a varied crowd gathers for drinks, nachos and guacamole. As you sip your blue drink, be sure to observe the remarkable winged lightbulbs that serve as lamps, and the lovely tiled artwork of nude, flying women. If you're in need of a pick-me-up, try the special Ibizan energy cocktail, the *'turbital'*.

Mesón del Café

C/Llibreteria 16 (93 315 07 54). Metro Jaume I/bus 17, 40, 45. **Open** 7am-11pm Mon-Sat. **Map D5.**
A charming hole-in-the-wall café that's regularly packed. It's reckoned to have the best coffee in town, served by some of the city's fastest moving waiters.

Món Obert

Passatge d'Escudellers 5 (93 301 72 73). Metro Liceu/bus 14, 38, 59, N6, N9. **Open** 9am-9pm Mon-Thur; 9am-midnight Fri-Sat. **Credit** MC, V. **Map D5.**
Art and culture have found a home in this large, new space, a co-op organised by six women. It combines a café (with full lunchtime menu, home-made bread and pastries, and sandwiches and light dishes available until closing time), bookshop, a small library, a gallery for art shows, a children's area, a music room and a private room for parties and special dinners. Check out flyers announcing poetry readings, art openings, tango classes, and many other events.

Café customs

Basic etiquette

The civilised and rarely abused system of pay-as-you-leave is the norm in Barcelona bars, except in very busy night bars and some outdoor terraces, such as those in the Plaça Reial, where you will often be asked to pay as soon as drinks are served. If you're having trouble getting a waiter's attention, a loud but polite '*Oiga*' (literally, 'hear me'), or, if you're trying your Catalan, '*Escolti*' should do the trick. As in restaurants, tipping is entirely discretionary, but it's common to leave something if you've had table service, and food as well as a drink. Most people just round up the bill to the nearest 100ptas, or leave some of the change. Some people also leave a few coins (rarely over 25ptas) even when served at the bar, more an old-fashioned courtesy than a real tip.

In most local and more traditional bars paper napkins (*servilletas*), olive stones, toothpicks, cigarette butts and other disposables are customarily dropped on the floor, but this is not done in smarter places. Check what local patrons are doing. One other point is that Spaniards are the biggest consumers of low-alcohol drinks in the world (a curious fact). Catalans, in particular, do not drink to get drunk, and it's not unusual for people to sit on a drink for an hour or more.

Coffee & tea

A large, milky coffee is a *café amb llet* (Catalan) or *café con leche* (Spanish), which locals generally only have with breakfast, although you can order it at any time of day. After mid-morning people are more likely to have a small coffee with a dash of milk, a *tallat* (Catalan)/*cortado* (Spanish), or a black espresso (*café sol/café solo*). A *café americano* is a *solo* diluted with twice the normal amount of water, and a *carajillo* is a *solo* with a shot of spirits. If you just ask for a *carajillo* it will normally be with brandy (*carajillo de coñac*), but you can also order a *carajillo de ron* (rum), whisky or whatever takes your fancy. Decaffeinated coffee (*descafeinado*) is widely available, but if you don't want just instant decaf with hot milk, ask for it *de máquina* (espresso).

Tea, except in cafés that specialise in it, is a bit of a dead loss, but herbal teas (*infusiones*) are always available. Very popular are *menta* (mint) or *manzanilla* (camomile).

Beer

The Damm beer company reigns supreme in Catalonia. Their most popular product is Estrella, a good, standard lager. Voll-Damm is a stronger, heavier brew; interesting, but not that widely distributed, is their dark beer Bock-Damm. Also a common brand, but well behind in local

sales, is San Miguel. Bottled beers can be ordered in *medianas* (the standard bottle of a third of a litre) or smaller *quintos* (a quarter-litre). Bars with draught beer serve it in *cañas* (about the same as a *mediana*) or *jarras* (about half a litre). Imported beers are increasingly available (especially Guinness) but they are considerably more expensive than local brands.

Wines, spirits & other drinks

All bars stock a basic red (*negro* or *tinto*), white (*blanco*) or rosé (*rosado*). If a red wine is a bit on the acid side, try it with lemonade (*gaseosa*). Except in bars that specialise in wines, good wines tend to be expensive, and the selection limited: for a wider choice, go to a *bodega*. Most bars stock popular brands of *cava*, but 'Champagne bars' will have a wider variety, and traditional specialists such as the **Xampanyet** and **Can Paixano** have their own cheaper 'house' brands.

Spirit mixes such as *gin-tonic*, *vodka-tónica* or a *cuba-libre* (white rum and coke) are very popular for night-time social drinking. Both Catalonia and Andalusia produce high-quality brandies, more full-bodied than French brandies but still subtle; of Catalan brandies, Torres 5 and Torres 10 are two of the best. Fruit-flavoured schnapps drinks are also popular here. Drunk icy-cold, in peach, lemon or apple varieties, a schnapps is a pleasant way to finish a meal.

Non-alcoholic drinks

Ver popular alternatives to alcohol are the Campari-like but booze-free Bitter Kas, and tonic water (*una tónica*), drunk with just ice and lemon. Mineral water is *aigua/agua mineral*: ask for it *amb gas/con gas* (fizzy), or *sense gas/sin gas* (still).

Food

Most bars have some kind of *bocadillos*, hefty, crusty bread rolls filled with *llom/lomo* (pork), *jamón serrano*, potato tortilla, tuna, cheese and other ingredients; some bars use long, thin rolls called *flautes*. When you order a *bocadillo* the waiter will usually check that you want it *amb tomàquet?* or *con tomate?*, spread with tomato Catalan-style (*see chapter* **Restaurants**: **The great tomato bread**). A *sandwich* is made with white sliced bread, and a *bikini* is a toasted ham and cheese sandwich.

Most Barcelona tapas bars offer a fairly standard choice, although some, such as the Basque **Euskal Etxea**, have a wider range. Some Catalan bars have a *llesqueria*-type selection (*see chapter* **Restaurants**). The following are some of the most common tapas varieties (names given in Spanish only).

Albóndigas meatballs; **Anchoas** salted anchovies; **Berberechos** cockles; **Boquerones** pickled fresh anchovies; **Chipirones en su tinta** small squid cooked in their ink; **Croquetas** (**de pollo, de bacalao**, etc) croquettes (with chicken, salt-cod, etc); **Empanadas** large flat pie, usually with tuna filling; **Empanadillas** (**de atún**) small fried pastries, usually with tuna filling; **Ensaladilla Rusa** mixed 'Russian' salad; **Gambas al ajillo** prawns fried with garlic; **Habas a la Catalana** broad beans, onions and *botifarra* blood sausage cooked in white wine; **Mejillones** mussels; **Olivas** olives; **Patatas bravas** deep-fried potatoes with hot pepper sauce; **Pincho moruno** peppered pork brochette; **Pulpo a la gallega** octopus with paprika and olive oil.

La Palma

C/Palma de Sant Just 7 (93 315 06 56). Metro Jaume I/bus 17, 40, 45. **Open** 7.30am-3.30pm, 7-10.30pm Mon-Sat. Closed three weeks Aug. **Map D5**.
One of the better old *bodegas*, with wine from the barrel and great *torrades* of hams and cheeses. Décor is suitably aged.

La Plata

C/Mercè 28 (93 315 10 09). Metro Drassanes/bus 14, 18, 38, 59, N6, N9. **Open** 9am-1pm Mon-Sat. Closed some weeks Aug. **Map D5**.
The most charming of the C/Mercè *tascas* (*see above* **Bar Celta**), this ceramic-lined bar serves only deep-fried whitebait, tomato and onion salads, anchovies and wines from the barrel. Its hours are erratic (they tend to pull the shutters down once the night crowds have poured in).

El Portalón

C/Banys Nous 20 (93 302 11 87). Metro Liceu/bus 14, 18, 38, 59, N6, N9. **Open** 9.30am-midnight Mon-Sat. Closed some days Aug. **Map D5**.
Probably the best example of a traditional Barcelona *bodega*, opened in the 1860s, this cavernous barrel-lined bar has kept its rustic charm despite recent renovation. Fine-value food and wine are served from a long wooden bar on to simple old marble tables, while regulars chat and play dominoes.

Els Quatre Gats

C/Montsió 3-bis (93 302 41 40). Metro Catalunya/bus all routes to Plaça Catalunya. **Open** 8am-2am Mon-Sat; 5pm-2am Sun. Closed three weeks Aug.
Credit AmEx, DC, JCB, MC, V. **Map D5**.
Not so much an institution as a monument. In 1897 a figure-about-town called Pere Romeu opened this café in a *Modernista* building by Puig i Cadafalch, and for the next few years it was the great meeting-point of bohemian Barcelona. Major *Modernista* artists such as Rusiñol and Casas painted pictures especially for it, and the menu illustration was Picasso's first paid commission. It closed in 1903, and was used for decades as a textile warehouse, until in the early 1980s it was finally restored and reopened, with reproductions by contemporary artists of the original paintings. Under the current management, it's more smart than bohemian, but it's an attractive place for a coffee, with good if pricey tapas. In the room at the back, where Pere Romeu presented avant-garde performances, is the restaurant, which has the attraction of the full menu being available throughout opening times. There's a good set lunch menu for 1,500ptas.

Schilling

C/Ferran 23 (93 317 67 87). Metro Liceu/bus 14, 18, 38, 59, N6, N9. **Open** 10am-2.30am Mon-Sat; noon-2.30am Sun. **Credit** V. **Map D5**.
Indisputable proof of Barcelona's membership in the major leagues of European café society, Schilling could almost be a sleek modern-day heir of the sort of grand café that thrived when the Austro-Hungarian empire was still intact (though in fact the place only opened up in 1997). Spacious, elegant, hip and very popular, Schilling serves a variety of *bocadillos*, desserts and teas, as well as other refreshments and alcohol. *See also* chapter **Gay & Lesbian Barcelona**.

Les Tapes

Plaça Regomir 4 (93 302 48 40). Metro Jaume I/bus 17, 40, 45. **Open** 9am-11pm Mon-Sat. Closed some weeks Aug. **Map D5**.
The sign 'We rip off drunks and tourists' above the bar shouldn't worry you, for this place specially welcomes English-speakers. Run by Santi, who worked in Birmingham

as a chef, and his English wife, Les Tapes has English football on the TV on Saturday afternoons, shelves of English books to browse through and a noticeboard for foreigners looking for contacts, rooms, jobs and the like. They also do the occasional special dish, such as roast pork or a curry.

Taverna Basca Irati

C/Cardenal Casañas 17 (93 302 30 84). Metro Liceu/bus 14, 18, 38, 59, N6, N9. **Open** noon-midnight daily. Closed three weeks Aug. **Credit** AmEx, MC, V. **Map D5**.
An extremely busy place serving Basque-style tapas, with a long, long bar to displays the wealth of Basque imagination when it comes to designing delicious bite-size combinations. Note: the selection dwindles dramatically the later it gets. There's also a good, full-service restaurant at the back.

Thiossan

C/Vidre 5 (93 317 10 31). Metro Liceu/bus 14, 38, 59, N6, N9. **Open** 7pm-2am Mon-Thur, Sun; 7pm-2.30am Fri, Sat. **Map D5**.
A comfortable, laid-back African bar-cum-cultural centre just off Plaça Reial. It features exhibitions, some light West African edibles, and regular reggae music sessions.

Venus Delicatessen

C/Avinyó 25 (93 301 15 85). Metro Jaume I/bus 17, 40, 45. **Open** noon-midnight daily. **Map D5**.
Two sisters run this recently opened and innovative place, serving decent deli-style food with a wide selection of pâtés and cheeses, nine different salads, many types of *bocadillos*, and dishes such as vegetable lasagne and chilli con carne. The atmosphere is relaxed and international.

La Ribera

Bar Hivernacle

Parc de la Ciutadella (93 268 01 77). Metro Arc de Triomf/bus 39, 40, 41, 42, 51. **Open** 10am-10pm daily. **Map E5**.
A bar inside the beautiful iron-and-glass *Hivernacle*, or greenhouse, of the Ciutadella park, built by Josep Amargós in 1884. With three parts (one shaded room, one unshaded room and a terrace), it hosts exhibitions and occasional jazz and classical concerts, and as well as plants around the bar there's a display of tropical plants in one of the rooms alongside. *Tables outdoors (all year).*

Cafè del Born Nou

Plaça Comercial 10 (93 268 32 72). Metro Jaume I/bus 14, 16, 17, 39, 45, 51. **Open** 9am-10pm Mon; 9am-2.30am Tue-Fri; 9.30am-2.30am Sat; 9.30am-10pm Sun. **Map E5**.
A big, airy café opposite the old Born market. With a soothing interior and music, interesting food selection and the odd exhibition from a local artist, this new café makes one of the most relaxing places in the area to enjoy a coffee or two. *Tables outdoors (May-Sept).*

Café Kafka

C/Fusina 7 (93 310 05 26). Metro Jaume I/bus 39, 51. **Open** noon-1am Mon-Wed; noon-2am Thur; noon-3am Fri; 7pm-3am Sat. **Credit** V. **Map E5**.
The modern, all white, hard-edged design of this place successfully masks all traces of Franz. The author may not be around, but there's bound to be a few fine groovers and Born locals in sight, perhaps sampling some of the good value, good quality North African food that is served here until late.

Euskal Etxea

C/Montcada 1-3 (93 310 21 85). Metro Jaume I/bus 16, 17, 40, 45. **Open** *restaurant* 1-3.30pm, 9-11.30pm; *bar* 8.30am-11.30pm Tue-Sat; 8.30am-4pm Sun. **Credit** MC, V. **Map D/E5**.
Catalonia may not be famous for its tapas, but the Basque

Awaiting the arrival of the great Basque tapas at the Euskal Etxea on C/Montcada .

Pavement tables

At times it's debatable whether thirst draws you to one of Barcelona's shaded outdoor café *terrazas* or just a desire to stop and admire the world around you. No matter, they make great places in which to write a postcard, read a book, meditate on the scenery, or just join in the great Mediterranean sport of people-watching.

In the last few years several of Barcelona's older museums have realised that their stone courtyards make ideal locations for cafés. One such is the **Tèxtil Cafè** (*see* **La Ribera**), another the delightful **Cafè d'Estiu** ('Summer Café' – as it's only open part of the year) in the Gothic courtyard of the **Museu Frederic Marès**. Also in Barri Gòtic is **L'Antiquari** in Plaça del Rei, with an excellent view of one of the area's finest medieval squares, while in La Ribera **Vascelum** is the perfect place from which to contemplate the majestic counterposition of verticals and plain space in the façade of Santa Maria del Mar. By the port, but staying in the medieval world, is the little-known **La Llotja**, inside the vast old shipyard that houses the **Museu Marítim**. As well being a very pleasant and peaceful café it also serves excellent food.

On a different note, in the Plaça Reial, **Glaciar** is a perennially hip spot from which to observe the *plaça*'s melting-pot of streetlife, and in the more peaceful Plaça Sant Josep Oriol the **Bar del Pí** offers a front-row seat for the art market and the buskers that appear there. Staying on the streets, it's impossible not to mention the legendary Café Zurich, which for decades served drinks to the world from the top of the Rambla on Plaça Catalunya. Destroyed in 1997 to make way for a shopping centre (*see chapter* **Sightseeing**), the word is that it will be reborn in one form or another. Back at the port end of the Rambla, by the statue of Columbus pointing the way to the New World, **Cava Universal** is a landmark bar with optimum viewing of the crowds heading back and forth from the new new world of Maremàgnum.

From the tables of **Gambrinus** on Moll de la Fusta, meanwhile, it's possible to admire a characteristic product of the 1980s Barcelona design boom, Javier Mariscal's giant fibreglass prawn on top of the bar. There are good, if expensive, tapas, and you can survey the scene around the port. For a real view, though, the best places are the mountains that overlook the city. The oddly little-known **Miramar** on Montjuïc, at the end of the road from the Fundació Miró past the funfair, offers a sweeping vista over the port and the Mediterranean. The most breathtaking panorama of all, though, is the one from the **Mirablau** at the end of the tram line on Tibidabo (opposite the Funicular) on Montjuïc. It has both an outside

Country certainly is, and this bar has the best Basque tapas in Barcelona, a mouth-watering array of small *pinchos* (from chunks of tuna and pickles to delicately deep-fried crab claws and complicated mixed tapas) that make a grand entrance at midday and at 7pm. Get there early for the best selection and be prepared to stand up. At the back there's a full restaurant with a good Basque menu, and the Barceloneta branch, **Txakolín**, has a larger dining room and bar.
Branch: Txakolín C/Marquès de l'Argentera 19 (93 268 17 81).

Palau Dalmases

C/Montcada 20 (93 310 06 73). Metro Jaume I/bus 17, 40, 45. **Open** 8pm-2am Tue-Sat; 6-10pm Sun. **Credit** AmEx, V. **Map D5/E5.**
Not a bar, they say, but a 'baroque space' on the ground floor of one of the most beautiful courtyard palaces of C/Montcada, the seventeenth-century Palau Dalmases. Its promoters aim to provide an 'aesthetic experience' that will 'satisfy all five senses': walls are adorned with period paintings, the ornate furniture and semi-religious accoutrements are to match; spectacular displays of flowers, fruit and aromatic herbs give it the look of an Italian still life, and suitably baroque music plays in the background. Fresh fruit drinks are provided as well as alcohol, and there are occasional music recitals. Deeply eccentric, decadent, a tad pretentious, but soothing to ear, nose and eye, and worth the elevated prices.
Tables outdoors.

Tèxtil Cafè

C/Montcada 12-14 (93 268 25 98). Metro Jaume I/bus 17, 40, 45. **Open** 10am-midnight daily Closed Mon in July & Aug. **Credit** AmEx, MC, V. **Map D5/E5.**
Another special bar on C/Montcada, in the beautiful, tranquil courtyard of the fourteenth-century Palau dels Marquesos de Lió, now home to the **Museu Tèxtil** and **Museu Barbier-Mueller** (*see chapter* **Museums**). Very popular, and a great place to stop over while sightseeing. *See also chapter* **Gay & Lesbian Barcelona**.
Tables outdoors.

El Xampanyet

C/Montcada 22 (93 319 70 03). Metro Jaume I/bus 17, 40, 45. **Open** noon-4pm, 6.30-11.30pm Tue-Sat; noon-4pm Sun. Closed some days Aug. **Credit** V. **Map D5/E5.**
Forget art and great museums for a while, this 'little champagne bar' is one of the eternal attractions of C/Montcada. It's lined with coloured tiles, barrels and antique curios, has a few marble tables, and there are three specialities: anchovies, cider and 'Champagne' (a pretty plain *cava*, if truth be told, but very refreshing), served by the glass or bottle. Other good tapas – particularly good tortilla – are available, too. Owner Sr Esteve – born above the shop in 1930, one year after his father opened the bar – and his family are unfailingly welcoming, and it's one of the best places on the entire planet to while away an afternoon, or a day, or a week. Opening times can vary unpredictably.

terrace and giant floor-to-ceiling windows seemingly suspended in space, from where you can admire Barcelona laid out below you by day and by night.

Locations

L'Antiquari de la Plaça del Rei *C/Veguer 13 (93 310 04 35). Metro Jaume I/bus 17, 40, 45.* **Open** 5pm-2am daily. **Map D5.**
Bar del Pi *Plaça Sant Josep Oriol 1 (93 302 21 23). Metro Liceu/bus 14, 18, 38, 59, N6, N9.* **Open** 9am-11pm Mon-Fri; 9.30am-11pm Sat; 10am-3pm, 5-10pm Sun. **Map D5.**
Café d'Estiu *Museu F Marés, Plaça de Sant Iu 5 (93 310 30 14). Metro Jaume I/bus 17, 40, 45.* **Open** *Easter-Sept* 10am-10pm Tue-Sun. **Map D5.**
Cava Universal *Plaça Portal de la Pau 4 (93 302 61 84). Metro Drassanes/bus 14, 18, 36, 38, 57, 59, 64, N6, N9.* **Open** 7am-3pm, 3pm-11pm daily. **Map C6.**
Gambrinus *Moll de la Fusta (93 221 96 07). Metro Drassanes/bus 14, 36, 57, 59, N6, N9.* **Open** 11am-1am Mon, Tue, Thur-Sun. **Map D6.**
Glaciar *Plaça Reial 3 (93 302 11 63). Metro Liceu/bus 14, 18, 38, 59, N6, N9.* **Open** 4pm-2.15am Mon-Fri; 4pm-2.45am Sat; 9am-2.15am Sun. **Map D5.**
La Llotja *Museu Maritim, Avda Drassanes (93 302 64 02). Metro Drassanes/bus 14, 18, 36, 38, 57, 59, 64, N6, N9.* **Open** 12.30pm-2am Tue-Wed; 12.30pm-5am Thur-Sun. **Map C5.**
Mirablau *Plaça Doctor Andreu (93 418 58 79) FGC Tibidabo/bus 17, 22, 58, 73, 75, then Tramvia Blau.* **Open** 11am-4.30am Mon-Thur, Sun; 11am-5am Fri, Sat.
Miramar *Avda Miramar (93 442 31 00/NB: phone number liable to change). Metro Paral.lel, then Funicular de Montjuic/bus 61.* **Open** 10am-3am Mon, Tue, Thur-Sun. Closed Nov. **Map D5.**
Vascelum *Plaça Santa Maria del Mar (93 319 01 67). Metro Jaume I/bus 17, 40, 45.* **Open** 9am-1am Tue-Sun. **Map D5.**

Port Vell/Barceloneta

Can Paixano

C/Reina Cristina 7 (93 310 08 39). Metro Barceloneta/bus 14, 39, 57, 59, 64. **Open** 9am-10.30pm Mon-Sat. **Map D5.**
A cavernous hole-in-the-wall bar in a street down by the port packed with cheap electronics shops – not in Barceloneta proper – with very drinkable no-label *cava* and an enormous range of toasted *bocadillos*. Dead cheap, and packed with workers during the day and young foreigners at weekends.

Jai-ca

C/Ginebra 13 (93 319 50 02). Metro Barceloneta/bus 17, 39, 45, 57, 59, 64. **Open** 10am-midnight daily. **Credit** V. **Map E6.**
High-quality, no-nonsense Basque tapas bar in the heart of the Barceloneta, specialising in fried and grilled seafood. *Tables outdoors (May-Oct).*

El Vaso del Oro

C/Balboa 6 (93 319 30 98). Metro Barceloneta/bus 17, 39, 45, 57, 59, 64. **Open** 8.30am-midnight daily. Closed Sept. **Map E6.**
A very narrow *cerveceria* (beer-bar), one of few in Barcelona that makes its own (excellent) brew. Don't go expecting a table (there aren't any). There is, though, a long, often crowded bar that will test your dexterity as you try not to elbow your neighbour's *patatas bravas*. Tapas-lovers' heaven.

Raval

Bar Almirall

C/Joaquim Costa 33 (93 412 15 35). Metro Universitat/bus 24, 41, 55, 64, 91, N4, N6. **Open** 7pm-2.30am daily. **Map C4.**
Opened in 1860, the Almirall has the distinction of being the oldest continuously functioning bar in the city, and still has its elegant wooden early *Modernista* décor, albeit now charmingly unkempt. It's no ageing relic, but remains fashionable in a laid-back way. Old travel posters and knick-knacks line the walls, and the vintage sofas and armchairs that fill the large room are great for settling into with groups of friends.

Bar Fortuny

C/Pintor Fortuny 31 (93 317 98 92). Metro Plaça Catalunya/bus 14, 38, 59, N6, N9. **Open** 10am-midnight Tue-Sun. **Map C4.**
A subtle stroke of genius transformed this one-time neighbourhood hangout for chess-playing elderly men into a science-fiction tinged arena where various generations of the culturally hip now sit and smoke together. The former *bodega*'s oak wine barrels are still in place, as are a few of the chess players, now overseen by a collection of toy robots. It's particularly popular with gay women. The music in the background tends towards contemporary, ambient and experimental. Also, good, wholesome home-cooking is available throughout the day and evening. *See also chapter* **Gay & Lesbian Barcelona**.

Bar Kasparo

Plaça Vicenç Martorell 4 (93 302 20 72). Metro Catalunya/ bus all routes to Plaça Catalunya. **Open** *summer* 9am-midnight, *winter* 9am-10pm, daily. Closed Jan. **Map C4.**
A small bar in the arcades of one of the city's more peaceful squares, taken over (and renovated) by three Australian sisters, who offer more varied fare than just basic tapas. The terrace is a great spot for sitting out on a sunny day. *Tables outdoors.*

Bar Pastís

C/Santa Mònica 4 (93 318 79 80). Metro Drassanes/bus 14, 18, 38, 59, 64, 91, N6, N9. **Open** 7.30pm-2.30am Mon-Thur; 7.30pm-3.30am Fri-Sat. **Map C5.**
Down a tiny alley off the bottom end of La Rambla, this is another of Barcelona's 'bar-institutions'. It was opened in the 1940s by Quimet and Carme, a Catalan couple who'd lived in Marseilles, and the pictures around the walls were painted by Quimet himself, apparently always when drunk. They began the tradition of playing exclusively French music, and serving only pastis, and the bar became a favourite of boxers, French sailors, Barrio Chino-types and the Franco-era intelligentsia. Quimet died in 1963, and for years the bar became more eccentric still, as his wife made it a monument to his memory. Under its current management the drinks menu has expanded, but you're unlikely to hear any music from south of the Pyrenees except for the occasional live acoustic gig. Small, dark, quirky, and, with Piaf, Montand or Charles Trenet in the background, a unique atmosphere.

Els Tres Tombs

Ronda Sant Antoni 2 (93 443 41 11/93 442 29 98). Metro Sant Antoni/bus 20, 24, 38, 41, 55, 64. **Open** 6am-12.30am daily. **Map C4.**
A perennially busy bar/restaurant on the border between the Raval and the Eixample. Its year-round outdoor tables are perfectly oriented to the sun, and the bar is especially crowded midday on Sunday, after the book market closes at the nearby Mercat de Sant Antoni. Also, because of early opening hours, it's a fuelling stop for after-hours clubbers. *Tables outdoors (all year).*

*Shady, peaceful tables in the middle of the Raval at **Bar Kasparo**. See page 147.*

Raval

C/Doctor Dou 19 (93 302 41 33). Metro Catalunya/bus all routes to Plaça Catalunya. **Open** *8pm-2.30am Mon-Thur; 8pm-3am Fri, Sat. Closed some days Aug.* **Map C4.**
Well-known as a post-performance watering-hole for the theatrical set, Raval has a wide clientele who appreciate its elegant design, comfy sofas and late (often spontaneous) opening hours. The perfect place for a late-night chat.

Poble Sec

Bar Primavera

C/Nou de la Rambla 192 (93 329 30 62). Metro Paral.lel/ bus 20, 36, 57, 64, 91, N4, N6. **Open** *Sept-June 8am-until dark daily; July-Aug 8am-1am daily.* **Map C5.**
At the very end of Nou de la Rambla, halfway up Montjuïc, this peaceful outdoor bar/café feels well away from the urban activity bubbling down below. In the summer grapevines provide shade, there's always a dog lying around, and it's a great place to stop on the way up or down the hill. Rudimentary *bocadillos* are served as well as drinks.
Tables outdoors (Easter-Sept).

Cervecería Jazz

C/Margarit 43 (93 443 05 60). Metro Paral.lel/bus 20, 57, 64, N4, N6. **Open** *6pm-2am Mon-Sat.* **Map B5.**
German and Belgian beers, a long wooden bar and a rustic-meets-baroque interior make this one of the more original bars in the area. The sandwiches are great – from a standard 'club' to *frankfurt a la cerveza* (Frankfurter in beer) – and the music (mixed jazz) is never so loud as to inhibit conversation.

Quimet & Quimet

C/Poeta Cabanyes 25 (93 442 31 42). Metro Paral.lel/bus 20, 36, 57, 64, N4, N6. **Open** *11.30am-4pm, 6.30-10.30pm, Mon, Tue, Thur-Sun. Closed Aug.* **Credit** *MC, V.* **Map B5.**
A small, top-quality bodega with wines stacked in pyramids behind the bar and a very healthy selection of tapas on display. It gets overwhelmingly crowded around mealtimes.

Taverna Noray

C/Concòrdia 42 (93 442 12 86).
Metro Poble Sec/bus 20, 57, 64, N4, N6. **Open** *7pm-2am Mon-Thu & Sun; 7pm-3am Fri-Sat.* **Map B5.**
Eccentric, neighbourhood bohemian bar, crammed with old photos of musicians and film-stars, chandeliers, fish tanks, clocks and anything else you'd find in a mad granny's attic. Its small front terrace gets lively during the summer, inducing the odd angry neighbour to throw things on to it – the response from the nonchalant owner being a bemused shrug.
Tables outdoors (May-Sept).

The Eixample

See also **Zona Alta** *for* **Mas i Mas.**

La Bodegueta

Rambla de Catalunya 100 (93 215 48 94). FGC Provença/bus 20, 21, 43, 44, N7. **Open** *8am-2am Mon-Sat; 6.30pm-2am Sun.* **Map D3.**
A straightforward bodega-bar slap in the middle of chicdom. Old wooden barrels line the walls and small marble tables add a classy-intimate feel. There's a great choice of tapas at reasonable prices, and a good lunch menu for 1,150ptas.
Tables outdoors (May-Oct).

Bracafé

C/Casp 2 (93 302 30 82). Metro Catalunya/bus all routes to Plaça Catalunya. **Open** *7am-midnight daily.* **Map D4.**
A popular café patronised by Passeig de Gràcia shoppers, known for its Brazilian coffee which has made it on to the 'best in Barcelona' list.
Tables outdoors (all year).

El Café de Internet

Gran Via de les Corts Catalanes 656 (93 412 19 15/e-mail: cafe@cafeinternet.es). Metro Catalunya/bus 7, 18, 50, 54, 56, 62, N1, N2, N3, N9. **Open** *10am-midnight Mon-Wed; 10am-2am Thur-Sat.* **Map D4.**

The place to keep in touch with cyberspace if you didn't bring your laptop. Downstairs there's a fairly nondescript bar/restaurant with pool tables, while upstairs the patient terminals await. Price per half hour of surfing (or e-mailing) is 600ptas. You can receive e-mail here if you open an account; it's free, but you will have to pay the minimum half-hour rate to access your mail. There is another Internet café in Maremágnum, the **Insòlit Internet Bar/Café** (93 225 81 78), but it only allows you to send mail, not receive it.

La Gran Bodega

C/València 193 (93 453 10 53). Metro Universitat, Passeig de Gràcia/bus 20, 21, 43, 44. **Open** 7am-1am daily. **Credit** MC, V. **Map C3.**

Bustling tapas bar, a first stop for students and office workers before a night out. Adventurous tourists acquaint themselves here with the *porrón* (the Catalan drinking jug that has you pour wine down your throat from a long glass spout). It takes several goes to master the art – but it's fun trying. *Tables outdoors (May-end Sept).*

Laie Llibreria Café

C/Pau Claris 85 (93 302 73 10). Metro Urquinaona/ bus all routes to Plaça Urquinaona. **Open** *café* 9am-1am Mon-Fri; 10.30am-1am Sat; *bookshop* 10am-9pm Mon-Fri; 10.30am-9pm Sat. **Credit** AmEx, DC, MC, V. **Map D4.**

Barcelona's bookshop-café, an enormously successful concept. The upstairs café has its own entrance (and hours), but is popular with a literary set and anyone looking for a comfortable bar in which to sit and read. It has great cakes and coffees, magazines for browsing and a good lunch menu for 1,650ptas; there are also outside tables on a patio, and live jazz some evenings. *See also chapter* **Shopping**. *Tables outdoors (May-Oct).*

El Velòdrom

C/Muntaner 213 (93 430 51 98). Metro Hospital Clínic/bus 6, 7, 15, 33, 34, 58, 64, N8. **Open** 6am-1.30am Mon-Thur; 6am-2.30am Fri-Sat. Closed some weeks Aug. **Map C2.**

A much-loved two-storey art deco bar from 1933 that attracts a complete mix of people, from office workers during the day to a younger crowd at night. Billiard tables, long leather sofas and an upper balcony give it a real 'café society' feel. A great place to go with a group, or just to write a letter alone in one of its many comfortable corners.

Gràcia

Bar Canigó

C/Verdi 2 (93 213 30 49). Metro Fontana/bus 22, 24, 28, 39, N4, N6. **Open** 10am-1am Mon-Fri; 8pm-3am Sat. Closed some days late Aug. **Map E2.**

One of the last old-style bodega-bars in Gràcia that hasn't been thoughtlessly modernised, with wooden bar and old mirrors on the walls. No tapas, but great *bocadillos* and *flautas*. There's also a pool table, and the outside tables look out onto the wonderfully named Plaça de la Revolució. *Tables outdoors (Apr-Sept).*

Cakes & coolers

One of Barcelona's symbolic links to the countryside is the *granja* – literally 'farm' in Catalan – small family-run, slightly quaint cafés. Originally direct outlets for fresh dairy products in the city, they've developed into a genre of café/shop all their own. Most serve alcohol, but that's not the point of going there. Instead, they specialise in coffee, cakes, pastries, dairy products and such things as *suizos* (thick hot chocolate topped by a mountain of whipped cream) and *batidos* (milkshakes). Built to satisfy Catalans' traditional sweet tooth, they're especially popular for afternoon call-ins while shopping.

Some of the best are in C/Petritxol, between Plaça del Pi and C/Portaferrisa. The **Granja Dulcinea** boasts traditional wooden fittings and white-jacketed waiters who cater swiftly for the Saturday evening crowds. **La Pallaresa** nearby has a more antiseptic 1960s look, but its *suizos* are rated among the best. In a narrow street on the Raval side of La Rambla, the **Granja M Viader** has done a roaring trade since 1870. If you're in the Eixample, try the 1960s **Granja Camps**.

These places can seem pretty heavy in the summer heat, but then other drinks are available. *Orxateries/ horchaterias* serve *Orxata* (Spanish *horchata*), a delicious, milky drink made by crushing a nut called a *chufa*. It may not be appreciated on first tasting, but once you're used to it, it's wonderfully refreshing on a hot day. *Orxata* curdles quickly once made, and so has to be bought fresh from a specialised producer. They also sell home-made ice-creams and *granissats/granizados* (fruit or coffee drinks sipped through crushed ice). Two fine *horchaterias* very close to one another share the same name, although they rigorously deny any connection: the **Orxateria-Gelateria Sirvent** has outside tables that are a fine place to sit out late, while **Horchatería Sirvent** has none – but on summer nights, crowds of people drink standing around the door. Poble Nou boasts the famous **El Tío Che**, open since 1912, and the only place in town that still does a malt-flavoured *granizado*.

Locations

Granja Camps *Rambla Catalunya 113 (93 215 10 09). Metro Diagonal, FGC Provença/bus 22, 24, 28.* **Open** 7.15am-9pm Mon-Fri; 7.15am-2pm, 5-9pm Sat. **Map D3.**
Granja Dulcinea *C/Petritxol 2 (93 302 68 24). Metro Liceu/bus 14, 18, 38, 59, 64, 91.* **Open** 9am-1pm, 4.30-9pm, Mon-Fri; 9am-1pm, 4.30-9.15pm, Sat, Sun, public holidays **Map D5.**
Granja La Pallaresa *Calle Petritxol 11 (93 302 20 36). Metro Liceu/bus 14, 18, 38, 59, N6, N9.* **Open** 9am-1pm daily; 4-9pm Mon-Fri, 4-10pm Sat, Sun. **Map D5.**
Granja M Viader *C/Xuclà 4-6 (93 318 34 86). Metro Liceu/bus 14, 18, 38, 59, 64, 91.* **Open** 5-8.45pm Mon; 9am-1.45pm, 5-8.45pm Tue-Sat. **Map D4/D5.**
Horchatería Sirvent *C/Parlament 56 (93 441 27 20). Metro Poble Sec/bus 20, 24, 64, 91, N4, N6.* **Open** *Easter-mid Oct* 10am-1.30am daily. **Map C5.**
Orxateria-Gelateria Sirvent *Ronda Sant Pau 3 (93 441 76 16). Metro Paral.lel/bus 20, 36, 57, 64, 91, N4, N6.* **Open** *Easter-mid-Oct* 9am-2.30am daily. **Map C5.**
El Tío Che *Rambla del Poble Nou 44-46 (93 309 18 72). Metro Poble Nou/bus 36, 71, 92, 141, N6.* **Open** *Oct-May* 9am-2pm, 5-9pm Mon, Tue, Thur-Sun; *May-mid-Oct* 9/10am-1am Mon-Thur, Sun; 9/10am-3am Fri-Sat.
Closing times for all the above places vary as the summer season progresses.

Culture shock: pubs

Revealing, perhaps, an underlying attraction for the peoples of northern European isles, Catalans have opened their arms, wallets, and tastebuds to a growing contingent of 'authentic' Irish, Scottish and English pubs. While a red-faced group of foreigners will always be found propping up these bars, natives – despite Catalan reservations about a night spent drinking for the sake of it – have also become regular patrons, much to the pleasure, one suspects, of the Guinness corporation.

First to arrive was **Kitty O'Shea's**, at the upper end of town off Avda Sarrià, a branch of the Paris-based Irish pub chain. A little further into town, in the Eixample near Plaça Francesc Macià, is **Flann O'Brien's**, which shows English league football, and across town from there is the huge **Michael Collins Irish Pub** by the Sagrada Familia, with Irish food, live Irish music four days a week, and more satellite TV sports. Perhaps most popular of all is Seamus Farrell's **The Quiet Man**, ideally located (for a bar) in the old *Barrio Chino*, and which looks like it's been lifted lock, stock and Guinness barrel from the streets of Dublin, as parts of it may have been. It has some of the best live Irish music of any of the pubs.

Even the Maremàgnum centre has got in on the act, and houses the interestingly-named **Irish Winds**, an Irish pub with an outside *terraza*. Moving on from theme-Ireland to theme-Britain, Barcelona's first Scottish pub

The Clansman in La Ribera is wetting whistles with Gillespie's Scottish Stout, and the English, not to be outdone, have mounted their very own **Black Horse** at the other end of C/Princesa as well as the **Sherlock Holmes** uptown near Santaló, a place which claims to have been 'founded in the 1900s'.

Locations

The Black Horse *C/Vermell 16 (93 268 33 38).* *Metro Jaume I/bus 39, 51.* **Open** 6pm-3am Mon-Thur; 3am-morning Fri-Sun. **Map D5/E5.**

The Clansman *C/Vigatans 13 (93 319 71 69).* *Metro Jaume I/bus 17, 40, 45.* **Open** 6pm-2.30am Mon-Thur; 6pm-3am Fri; 3pm-3am Sat; 3pm-2.30am Sun. **Map D5.**

Flann O'Brien's *C/Casanova 264 (93 201 16 06).* *Bus 6, 7,14, 15, 33, 34, 59, 66, N8.* **Open** 6pm-3am daily. **Map C2.**

Kitty O'Shea's *C/Nau Santa Maria 5 (93 280 36 75).* *Metro Maria Cristina/bus 6, 33, 34, 66, 67, 68.* **Open** 11am-2.30am Mon-Thur; 11am-3pm Fri; noon-3pm Sat; noon-2.30am Sun.

Irish Winds *Maremàgnum, Moll d'Espanya (93 225 81 87). Metro Drassanes/bus 14, 18, 36, 57, 59, 64, , N6, N9.* **Open** 1.30pm-4.30am Mon-Thur, Sun; 1.30pm-5am Fri, Sat. **Credit** V. **Map D6.**

The Michael Collins Irish Pub *Plaça Sagrada Família 4 (93 459 19 64). Metro Sagrada Família/bus 19, 33, 34, 43, 50, 51, 54, N7, N9.* **Open** noon-3am daily. **Credit** MC, V. **Map F3.**

The Quiet Man *C/Marquès de Barberà 11 (93 412 12 19). Metro Liceu/bus 14, 18, 38, 59, N6, N9.* **Open** 6pm-2am Mon-Thur, Sun; 6pm-3am Fri, Sat. **Map C5.**

The Sherlock Holmes *C/Copérnic 42-44 (no phone). FGC Bonanova/bus 16, 58, 64, 74.* **Open** 7pm-2.30am Mon-Thur, Sun; 7pm-3am Fri, Sat. **Credit** MC, V. **Map C1.**

Bodega Manolo

C/Torrent de les Flors 101 (93 284 43 77). Metro Joanic/bus 39, 55, N4. **Open** *bar* 9am-9pm Tue-Fri; 11.30am-9pm Sat; 10.30am-4pm Sun. **Dinner served** 9-11.30pm Thur-Sat. **Map E2**.

Another old Gràcia bodega, this time with peeling paint as well as the requisite wall of oak wine barrels. Manolo's speciality, apart from wine, is high-quality anchovies from Cantabria. There's also a well-priced (900ptas) lunch menu; dinner (Thur, Fri, Sat only) is à la carte and more expensive, but with such things as goat ribs with wild mushrooms or monkfish in creamy onion sauce, is definitely worth it.

Café del Sol

Plaça del Sol 16 (93 415 56 63). Metro Fontana/bus 22, 24, 28, N4, N6. **Open** Open 1pm-2.30am Mon-Thur, Sun; 1pm-3am Fri-Sat. **Map D2**.

The Plaça del Sol is lined with bars with tables outside, but this remains the most popular terrace. A great place to spend a warm evening, watching the parade of jugglers, fire-eaters and musicians that turn the *plaça* into an impromptu stage.
Tables outdoors (all year).

Casa Quimet

Rambla del Prat 9 (93 217 53 27). Metro Fontana/bus 16, 17, 22, 24, 28, N4, N6. **Open** 6.15pm-2am Tue-Sun, Mon if public holiday. Closed Feb, Aug. **Map D2**.

Strange but true: Also known as the 'guitar bar', Casa Quimet is just that: over 200 guitars line the walls and ceiling of this faded old bar, and you're welcome to grab one and join in the ongoing 'jam session'. You might be able to distinguish a song, or you might just hear a lot of people playing and singing at once, and you can also wear one of their very large stock of silly hats. The drink range is more limited, though. Don't expect a friendly chat with the owner, for his detachment as he presides over the scene is legendary, and adds one more surreal touch to the place.

El Roble

C/Lluís Antúnez 7 (93 218 73 87). Metro Diagonal/bus 16, 17, 22, 24, 27, 28, N4, N6. **Open** 7am-1am Mon-Sat. Closed Aug. **Map D2**.

Large, bright, old-style tapas bar, with a great selection of fresh seafood tapas, well-filled Galician *empanadas* and a wide range of tortillas. One of the better places to eat tapas in Barcelona, and often bustling.

Salambó

C/Torrijos 51 (93 218 69 66). Metro Joanic/bus 21, 39, N4. **Open** noon-2.30am Mon-Thur, Sun; noon-3am Fri-Sat. **Credit** MC, V. **Map E2**.

An elegant two-storey café, opened in 1992 but which deliberately echoes the large literary cafés of the 1930s, with plenty of tables, billiard tables and an unusual selection of fragrant teas, sandwiches and salads. Extremely popular, especially with the crowds from the Verdi cinemas.
Tables outdoors (May-Oct).

Sol Solet

Plaça del Sol 13 (93 217 44 40). Metro Fontana/bus 22, 24, 28, 39, N4, N8. **Open** 7pm-3am daily. Closed late Aug. **Map D2**.

The only bar in town with wholefood tapas – tabouleh, guacamole, feta and tomato salads, and a selection of tortillas – and so a Godsend for vegetarians. Marble tables, wood-lined walls and intimate lighting add to its appeal. Tapas are all 275ptas.
Tables outdoors (all year).

Tetería Jazmín

C/Maspons 11 (93 218 71 84). Metro Fontana/bus 22, 24, 28, N4, N6. **Open** 7pm-2am Tue-Thur; 7pm-2.30am Fri-Sat; 7pm-midnight Sun. Closed three weeks Aug/Sept. **Map D2**.

A relaxed, comfortable, North African-styled tea parlour, with low tables and pillowed sofas conducive to extended evenings of chat. Along with tea, it's possible to order light North African dinners featuring couscous with a variety of vegetarian accompaniments.

Virreina Bar

Plaça de la Virreina 1 (93 237 98 80). Metro Fontana/bus 21, 39, N4. **Open** noon-2.30am daily. **Map E2**.

Friendly bar/meeting place on one of the smaller Gràcia squares, with outside tables that fill up quickly on hot summer nights. Known for a good range of imported beers such as Mexican Desperado and Belgian Chimay, the Virreina also serves a wide variety of *bocadillos* and sandwiches.
Tables outdoors (all year).

Zona Alta

Bar Tomàs

C/Major de Sarrià 49 (93 203 10 77). FGC Sarrià/bus 34, 66, 94. **Open** 8am-10pm Mon, Tue, Thur-Sun.

It's not easy to maintain a reputation for serving 'the best *patatas bravas* in the city', but this bar in the old village of Sarrià manages to do just that. Students flock here not only for the excellent *bravas* but also for *empanadilla de atún* and great anchovies.

Casa Fernández

C/Santaló 46 (93 201 93 08). FGC Muntaner/bus 14, 58, 64, N8. **Open** *restaurant* 1pm-1.30am Mon-Thur, Sun; 1pm-2am Fri-Sat; *bar* 12.30pm-2.30am Mon-Thur, Sun; 12.30pm-3am Fri-Sat. **Credit** AmEx, DC, MC, V. **Map C1**.

An elegant variation on the tapas bar, and a regular stop-off on the fashionable bar circuit around C/Santaló, Casa Fernández serves a fine array of tapas, desserts and homemade soups, and their (very good) own-brand beer as well as imported beers. A rather expensive full restaurant menu is also available: particularly good are the meats and steaks.
Tables outdoors (May-Oct).

Mas i Mas

C/Marià Cubí 199 (93 209 45 02). FGC Muntaner/bus 14, 58, 64, N8. **Open** 7.30pm-2.30am Mon-Thur, Sun; 7.30pm-3am Fri, Sat. **Map C2**.

The Mas brothers have made a splash with their string of music/club venues (**La Boîte, Jamboree, Moog**: *see chapters* **Nightlife** *and* **Music: Rock, Roots & Jazz**). They began with this tapas bar-café, and on the C/Santaló route, an evergreen favourite with the young uptown set. Defying the slightly pretentious image, the tapas are actually very good, and not especially expensive. In the Eixample, on C/Còrsega near the junction of Passeig de Gràcia and Diagonal, the Mases have a similarly stylish café-restaurant, with fine tapas and a good, fair-value lunch menu.
Branch: **Mas i Mas Café** C/Còrsega 300 (93 237 57 31).

Vila Olímpica/Port Olímpic

Port Olímpic has bars one after the other (*see also* chapter **Restaurants**), but worth singling out is:

Cafè & Cafè

Moll del Mistral 30 (93 221 00 19). Metro Ciutadella/bus 36, 41, 92, N8. **Open** 4pm-2am Mon-Wed; 4pm-3am Thur; 4pm-4am Fri; 4pm-5am Sat; 3pm-2am Sun. **Credit** MC, V. **Map F6**.

Relaxed coffee house/cocktail bar in the Port Olímpic with a mind-boggling range of coffees to choose from. Particularly good is the 'Royal', sweetened with cane sugar.
Tables outdoors (all year).
Branch: Plaça Universitat 11 (93 317 86 13).

Nightlife

Britpop, hip hop, trip hop or sip-pop – whatever gets you through the night, it's here.

At times it can seem that there are more people on Barcelona's streets by night than by day. Roving bands of revellers, post-midnight traffic jams and an array of crowded bars give the impression of a city in the throes of a major celebration. But no, it's simply that in this town people like to go out, they like to go out in groups, and they like to go out late.

Waterfront cafés that stay open until 5am, elegant design bars, the occasional underground party and clubs galore are all part of the mix. Many places have been the same for years, but the nocturnal terrain has also altered a good deal –especially after the pivotal summer of 1992 – and, as with any vibrant city, keeps on evolving. The scene now encompasses huge entertainment zones in the **Port Vell** (Maremàgnum) and the **Port Olímpic**. With no sleeping neighbours to worry about, these areas, especially in summer, are heaving with gleeful revellers until dawn.

Shifts in geography aside, Barcelona's night crowd has always been fad-conscious and now, more than ever, is receptive to the latest global trends. This means the hippest new nightspots are firmly in the hands of an international techno-clan. The techno crowd may be the biggest element, but you can find near-anything you desire in this city: funk and soul clubs, cocktail bars, hip young hangouts or open-air clubs. In music, salsa and Latin music have lately been enjoying one of the revivals they go through every few years in Barcelona.

Apart from the booming waterside areas, there are other recognisable night-time zones. The old town, the **Ciutat Vella**, is in a state of flux as it regains its popularity. The **Plaça Reial** is always full of activity and any night of the week you'll find something going on in the bars there, as the centre of a black-clad 'alternative' scene. Nearby C/Escudellers, once the domain of Felliniesque tarts, now draws hordes of students, attracted by its old-world grunginess (and cheapness). Across Via Laietana **La Ribera** – around Passeig del Born – continues to be popular, with elegant bars, techno hang-outs and local dives all within a stone's throw of one another. Another area of interest is **Poble Nou**, inland from the Vila Olímpica, which has its own nightspots and, like many of the city's *barris*, is very much party to its own scene.

The no-man's land of the **Eixample** is worth a visit to check out its famous but now passé design bars, or visit some rejuvenated clubs. The area

near **Plaça Francesc Macià** and C/Santaló has a slew of bars and clubs that cater to a young, affluent crowd. In **Gràcia**, the atmosphere is more relaxed: its bars are mostly full of regulars. The two main squares, Plaça del Sol and Plaça Rius i Taulet, are good places from which to orient yourself before exploring the area. Many of Barcelona's wealthy folk, meanwhile, live on or near **Tibidabo**, and the hill is where you'll find some of the most elegant bars and clubs, often with staggering vistas.

The Anglo-Saxon concept of a 'club', based on restrictive licencing laws, doesn't entirely apply here. Obviously, there are places that are very much clubs, with door policy and so on, but there are also loads of places that are really just bars, don't charge admission (except maybe at peak times) but have a dance floor. Bars and clubs, naturally, also open and close all the time, so look out for flyers, and check the local press (*see chapter* **Media**). Below is a sample of what to expect as you make a journey through to the end of night. *Unless otherwise stated, admission is free to the places listed, and they do not accept credit cards.*

Mostly bars

Andy Capp
C/Bonavista 13 (no phone). Metro Diagonal/bus 6, 15, 22, 24, 28, 33, 34, 39, N§, N6. **Open** 6pm-2.30am Mon-Thur, Sun; 6pm-3am Fri, Sat. **Map C2**
A shabby, amiable rock 'n' roll bar named after Reg Smythe's hero. A picture of Andy covers one wall, a graffiti-like mural another. No dance space, but there is music, from mainstream rock and reggae to occasional heavy metal. Regulars are a mix of old hippies, students and aspiring musicians.

Ciutat Vella
C/Sant Rafael 11 (93 442 5358). Metro Liceu/bus 14, 38, 59, N6, N9. **Open** 8pm-3am daily. **Map C5**
A friendly little bar buried deep in the back streets of the *Barrio Chino*, Ciutat Vella is a regular hangout for resident foreigners and a mixed alternative crowd. There are regular art exhibitions and, on Thursday nights, Irish music.

Distrito Marítimo
Moll de la Fusta (93 221 55 61). Metro Drassanes/bus 14, 36, 57, 59, 64, N6, N9. **Open** noon-4.30am Tue-Sat; 11am-4.30am Sun. **Map D6**
Committed fun-seekers like to start here, at this modern outdoor bar overlooking the old port. At 1am on a Friday or Saturday, the place is jammed to the walls. Inside, it's steamy and tight, but there's a good-sized terrace outside where you can walk and watch the lights reflected in the water of the harbour. It generally serves as a crossroads for those gearing up for further dancing later on at such places as **Fellini**, **Apolo-Nitsaclub** or **La Terraza** (*see below* **Clubs**).

*So, your name's **Dot** too, eh? Cool.*

Dot

C/Nou de Sant Francesc 7 (93 302 70 26).
Metro Drassanes/bus 14, 18, 38, 59, N6, N9.
Open 9pm-2.30am Mon-Thur, Sun; 9pm-3am Fri-Sat.
Closed some days Aug. **Map D5**
A new dance-bar in the dark and alley-like back streets
around the Plaça Reial, with a coolness that has made it one
of the most popular in the old city. Calling itself a 'light club',
Dot consists of two spaces, a red-lit bar area for chat, and,
through a futuristic door to the back, a small but functional
dancefloor. The sound system is top, as is the music – drum
'n' bass, lounge, space funk and club/dance.

Eldorado Bar Musical

Plaça del Sol 4 (93 237 36 96). Metro Fontana/bus 22,
24, 28, N4, N6. **Open** *café* 6-10pm daily (*winter* 7-10pm);
bar 10pm-2.30am Mon-Thur, Sun; 10pm-3am Fri, Sat;
terrace 6pm-2.30am daily. **Map D2**
Noisy, welcoming Gràcia dance and billiards bar, across the
plaça from the **Cafè del Sol** (*see chapter* **Cafés & Bars**).
Like other bars on the square and around the *barri* it's popular with a variety of ages and types. The walls are painted
with comic heroes, while videos flash on the screens next to
the bar, though they're nothing to do with the music, which
is mostly mainstream rock.

La Fira

C/Provença 171 (989 78 10 96).
Metro Hospital Clínic, FGC Provença/bus 7, 16, 17, 22,
24, 28, N4, N6. **Open** 10pm-3am Tue-Thur; 7pm-4.30am
Fri, Sat; 6pm-1am Sun. **Map C3**
Large, airy space that calls itself a 'bar museum' – possibly
the wackiest museum in town. It's furnished entirely with
old fairground equipment: dodgems, waltzers, or swings provide the seating, and the several bars and food stands are
designed like stalls. One of the liveliest of Barcelona's more
extravagant bars.

Heaven

C/Escudellers 20 (93 412 25 36). Metro Drassanes/bus 14,
18, 38, 59, N6, N9. **Open** 9.30pm-3am daily. **Map D5**
This large, recently renovated Escudellers bar may not be
everyone's vision of the eternal reward, but as a place to
drink and slouch around on a couch it's fine. The crowd tends
towards college age; the music is Britpop and trip-hop, and
in the back room there's a pool table for those of you in need
of redemption.

Kentucky

C/Arc del Teatre 11 (93 318 28 78).
Metro Drassanes/bus 14, 18, 38, 59, N6, N9.
Open 7pm-3am Mon-Sat. Closed Aug. **Map C5**
An old red-light American bar left over from the 1960s, when
Barcelona was a port of call for US Navy ships. The bar looks
essentially unchanged since then: a long, narrow space with
an old juke-box, which has a surprisingly large selection of
music. The Kentucky is popular among an assortment of
foreigners, Raval locals and slumming uptowners.

Al Limón Negro

C/Escudellers Blancs 3 (no phone).
Metro Liceu/bus 14, 18, 38, 59, N4, N6. **Open** 8pm-
2.30am Mon-Thur; 8pm-3am Fri, Sat. **Map D5**
World music, contemporary art and pastel orange paint on
100-year-old walls give this bar near C/Escudellers a cheerful modern feel. It calls itself a 'multi-bar' and hosts exhibitions, live music and theatre. Food is served upstairs.

London Bar

C/Nou de la Rambla 34 (93 318 52 61). Metro Liceu/
bus 14, 18, 38, 59, N6, N9. **Open** 7pm-4am Tue-Sun.
Admission free. **Credit** MC, V. **Map C5**
With its 1910 bar and wall mirrors, the London doesn't look
much like an English pub, but is reminiscent of England in
that people tend to arrive and then stay for the rest of the
evening. Once a hangout for Catalan hippies, it was taken
over a few years back by a livelier management who have
kept it popular among young expat residents and a mixed
bunch of partying natives. There are regular jazz concerts,
for which there's no entrance fee but drink prices are raised
accordingly (*see chapter* **Music: Rock, Roots & Jazz**).

Malpaso

C/Rauric 20 (93 412 60 05). Metro Liceu/bus 14, 18, 38,
59, N6, N9. **Open** 9.30pm-2.30am Mon-Thur, Sun;
9.30pm-3am Fri, Sat, eves of public holidays. **Map D5**
Down a back alley from Plaça Reial is this busy little bar,
replete with alternative rock sounds and a buzzy, young
crowd. As you sip your Carlsberg, check out the model train
that runs the length of the glass-covered bar counter…

Marsella

C/Sant Pau 65 (93 442 72 63). Metro Liceu/
bus 14, 18, 38, 59, N6, N9. **Open** 5pm-2.30am Mon-
Thur, Sun; 5pm-3am Fri, Sat. **Map C5**

A survivor of the *Barrio Chino*'s colourful past, the Marsella is a well-loved bar that's been in the same family for five generations. Dusty, untapped 100-year-old bottles sit in tall glass cabinets (they still have locally made absinthe, *absenta*, here), old mirrors line the walls, and motley chandeliers loom over the invariably cheerful clientele. It's one for the expat crowd, and attracts many gays too. The bar gets crowded late night on weekends, so it's wise to come a bit earlier if you want to secure a comfortable spot at one of the old wooden tables.

Miami Bar

C/Assaonadors 25 (93 319 25 92). Metro Jaume I/bus 17, 40, 45. **Open** 10pm-3am daily. **Map D5**
Painted lizards on a sheet-metal ceiling look down on the dark décor of this one-time girlie bar, currently owned and run by a young English DJ and his Basque wife. The excellent selection of music ranges from soul and funk all-nighters with heavy doses of reggae, to dance/house and drum 'n' bass, with some Latin lines and speed garage thrown in to keep your pulse up.

Network

Avda Diagonal 616 (93 201 72 38). Bus 6, 7, 15, 27, 33, 34, 67, 68. **Open** *breakfast* 8am-1pm Mon-Fri; *lunch* 1-4pm Mon-Sat; *dinner* 8pm-1am Mon-Thur; 8pm-2am Fri, Sat; *tapas* 8am-4pm daily. **Set menus** *lunch* 1,200ptas Mon-Fri; *lunch & dinner* 2,500ptas Mon-Fri. **Credit** AmEx, MC, V.
A classic on Barcelona's 1980s design-bar circuit, this high-tech bar/restaurant owes a hell of a lot to *Blade Runner*. From the street, there's little to see: the big underground main space is entered via a spiral staircase. Downstairs, designers Eduard Samsó and Alfredo Arribas took the 1950s juke-box a tad further by installing video monitors on every table; below that there's a third level with pool tables. It attracts a yuppyish clientele, and is still a place to be seen. Its 'international' food, though is often disappointing.

Nick Havanna

C/Rosselló 208 (93 215 65 91). Metro Diagonal, FGC Provença/bus 22, 24, 28, N4, N6. **Open** 11pm-4am Mon-Thur, Sun; 11pm-5am Fri, Sat. **Admission** free Mon-Thur, Sun; 1,100ptas (incl one drink) Fri, Sat, nights before public holidays. **Credit** MC, V. **Map D3**
Waiters from a postmodern fantasy, a bank of TV screens, bar stools like saddles, and a pendulum swinging over the dancefloor are just some features of this cavernous club-like space, designed in 1987 by Eduard Samsó. Weekends after 1am there's little room to dance and the DJ plays everything from Spanish rock to techno. During the week it's a spacious, friendly place, despite all the design.

Octopussy

Moll de la Fusta (93 221 40 31). Metro Drassanes/ bus 14, 36, 57, 59, 64. **Open** midnight-3am Thur-Sat. **Credit** V. **Map D6**
Not quite as popular as nearby Distrito Marítimo (*above*), but definitely a waterfront party at the weekend. The music is

Under the stars

Come warm weather, there's nothing most Barcelona natives like to do more than spend an evening in the open air, drinking cool drinks, strolling, dancing, chatting, or just plain observing. Conscious of this desire to be outside, bar and club owners have opened up more and more *terrasses* (outdoor bars), mainly around the Port Vell and Port Olimpic, but also in the old city.

The culmination of the outdoor bar boom, however, are the *carpas*: gigantic summer dance-and-dance parties held under circus-like tents. Occupying areas as vast as 15,000 square metres, they're like huge night-time amusement parks. You pay an entrance fee (which includes a drink) and then can visit any of the 20 or so clubs that have spaces within the area. The crowd is mainly of young, energetic clubbers, though the events are big enough to draw a cross-section of the populace. Inside, dance to salsa, soul, funk, or the ever present techno. They usually function Thursday to Saturday, June to August; they can change each summer, so check for any new openings.

Firestiu

Plaça de l'Univers, Fira de Barcelona area (93 322 03 26/ 93 410 89 17). Metro Espanya/bus 9, 38, 51, 53, 65, 91, N1. **Open** *June-Aug* 10pm-4.30am Thur-Sat. **Admission** (incl one drink) 1,000ptas Thur, Fri; 1,200ptas Sat . **Map A4**
In one of the Trade Fair areas near Plaça d'Espanya, this is probably the largest *carpa*. Participating clubs include

Up & Down, La Boîte, Antilla Cosmopolita and 15 or so others. And there are other things to do – bunjee-jumping, mini-golf, live music and karaoke are all part of the show.

Gran Terrassa d'Amèrica

Avda Montanyans (no phone). Metro Espanya/bus 61. **Open** check press for details. **Map A4**
Not really a *carpa* but a summertime stage and open-air club behind Poble Espanyol on Montjuic that opens up each year. In the past it was distinguished by the fact that only Latin American or African music was played, but now the Terrassa has veered toward trendier electronic sounds, with programming by the popular Vots club promoters.

Pyramid

C/Tirso de Molina/Avda de la Fama, Fira de Cornellà area, Cornellà de Llobregat (93 322 03 26). FGC Almeda. **Open** *June-Aug* 10pm-4.30am Thur-Sat; 9pm-3am Sun. **Admission** 1,000ptas (incl one drink).
On the outskirts of greater Barcelona in the unappreciated dormitory suburb of Cornellà de Llobregat, Pyramid not only has its posse of participating clubs but also lists bunjee-jumping, live concerts, human football games and pocket bike races among its attractions. Should you need to sit for a while, there is also an outdoor cinema.

Torre Melina

Camí de la Torre Melina & C/Oviedo, off Diagonal next to Hotel Juan Carlos I (93 414 63 62). Metro Zona Universitària/bus 7, 67, 68, 74, 75. **Open** *June-early Oct* 10pm-5am Mon-Sat. **Admission** 1,000ptas (includes one drink). **Credit** V.
Classiest of the carpas, in a very smart part of town by the Polo Club. Participating clubs include Jimmy'z (*see* **Clubs**) and several other upmarket venues.

You may feel like this when leaving **Octopussy**, *but be careful, or you'll fall in the dock.*

varied, with the emphasis on dance and house, and the mixed crowd is less frantic, making it actually possible to sit outside at a table and enjoy a drink. The terrace is open all year.

El Otro

C/València 166 (93 323 67 59). Metro Hospital Clínic/bus 20, 21, 43, 44, 63, N8. **Open** 10.30pm-3am daily. Closed Aug. **Map C3**
A lively place in the Eixample, El Otro, unlike some design bars, feels genuinely relaxed, and is regularly packed with a chatty young crowd. In shape, it's the same as most Eixample bars: a long bar on one side with small dancefloor at the end.

Ovisos

C/Arai 5 (907 26 47 26). Metro Liceu/bus 14, 18, 38, 59, N6, N9. **Open** 10pm-3am daily. **Map D5**
A deep recess of a grunge bar in Plaça George Orwell on C/Escudellers that attracts a young, hip, down-and-out crowd. The music, though excellent in range (ambient, garage, sip-hop) is often barely audible, coming as it does from a battered cassette deck placed on one corner of the main bar. Nearby on the narrow C/Aglà it has a sister bar, **Shanghai**, which is smaller, more refined but still gets packed at weekends.

Partycular

Avda Tibidabo 61 (93 211 62 61). No public transport. **Open** 7pm-3am Tue-Sun. **Credit** AmEx, MC, V.
Not grungy at all. Pleasant all year, this enormous bar located in an enormous house on the hill up to Tibidabo really comes into its own in summer. It has rambling gardens sprinkled with bars, from where you can look across to the lights of the funfair: there's lots of space, beautiful people to look at, dance areas, tables to chat at and dark corners to be romantic in. When the weather's cold, the grandeur of the rooms makes it a good place for an after-dinner drink. Don't bother trying to get there by public transport, take a cab.

Penúltimo

Passeig del Born 19 (93 310 25 96). Metro Jaume I/bus 14, 16, 17, 39, 45, 51. **Open** 10pm-2.30am Mon-Wed, Sun; 10pm-3am Thur-Sat. **Credit** MC, V. **Map E5**

'Cleopatra's milkbar' might be a better name for this dancebar; with its bizarre hotchpotch of kitsch and modern design. Dance parties featuring soul, funk, acid jazz, latin and reggae mixes are staged at the weekend by DJ, Marta. The atmosphere is infectious, the crowd is an eclectic mix and, on a good night, the place is an oasis of funky fun.

Rosebud

C/Adrià Margarit 27 (93 418 88 85). No public transport. **Open** 7pm-4am Mon-Thur, Sun; 7pm-5am Fri, Sat. **Admission** usually free. **Credit** MC, V.
On the way up to Tibidabo, in front of the Museu de la Ciéncia, is this huge two-level bar. The garden and pond area have views over Barcelona that make it worth a visit, even if décor is a tad characterless. It's jammed at weekends; there's no dancefloor, but punters shuffle as much as space allows.

Sidecar

C/Heures 4-6 (93 302 15 86). Metro Liceu/bus 14, 18, 38, 59, N6, N9. **Open** 10pm-3am daily. **Closed** Aug. **Map D5**
In a corner of the Plaça Reial, this bar has been here for years. Early evening it's a quiet place to play pool or read comics. Later it gets livelier, mostly with a student crowd, and it can be difficult to move on the basement dancefloor, let alone see bits of memorabilia such as a petrol pump and yes, a sidecar. There's a terrace bar in summer. It's also a laid-back music venue (*see chapter* **Music: Rock, Roots & Jazz**).

Snooker Club Barcelona

C/Roger de Llúria 42 (93 317 97 60). Metro Passeig de Gràcia/bus 7, 18, 39, 45, 54, 56, 62, N1, N2, N3, N9. **Open** 6pm-3am Mon-Thur; 6pm-4am Fri, Sat; 6pm-2am Sun. **Admission** free; snooker tables 1,000ptas per hour. **Credit** MC, V. **Map D4**
A novel concept – the designer billiard hall – this impressive space was an early product of the Barcelona design-bar boom. The bar areas, in peach and silver grey with arched roof and a lot of open space, are striking. The tranquility of the place is enjoyed by a 30-something clientele. There are pool and Spanish *carambola* tables, but snooker is the centre of attraction.

Texaco

*C/Pere IV 164 (93 309 92 64). Metro Llacuna/
bus 6, 40, 42, 141, N6.* **Open** 10pm-3.30/4am Fri, Sat,
eves of public holidays.

An authentic piece of hard-driving rock 'n' roll America,
miraculously transplanted to the old *barri* of Poble Nou. The
walls are littered with images of American archetypes: cow-
boys, bikers and rockers; you can even get American-style coffee. There's a small stage where bands sometimes play, but
live music or not, the place gets crowded at weekends.

Torres de Avila

*Avda Marquès de Comillas, Poble Espanyol
(93 424 93 09). Metro Espanya/bus 13, 61.* **Open** *music
bar* 11pm-2am Thur-Sat; *disco* 2am-6am Thur-Sat.
Admission *disco* 1,500ptas. **Credit** V. **Map A4**

The peak of Mariscalism, ultimate product of the Barcelona
design-bar phenomenon. There are actually seven bars
inside this building, inside the main entrance to the **Poble
Espanyol** (*see chapter* **Sightseeing**). The entrance is a
copy of one of the gates to the medieval city of Avila – hence
the name. The main theme of the design, by Javier Mariscal
and architect Alfredo Arribas, was day and night, and the
whole edifice is full of symbols. Only the best materials were
used in the construction and fittings, and the whole thing
cost over three million pounds; whatever you say, the result
is beautiful, at times magical. At one time it was more of a
monument than a bar, but in the last couple of years the stiff
drink prices have been lowered to a more moderate 600ptas
(beer) and 1,000ptas (spirits), and it now functions as a
trance-techno disco. When the rooftop terrace bar opens in
summer, it's a stunning city vantage point. In July and
August, it may also be open on Tuesdays and Wednesdays.

Tres Torres

*Via Augusta 300 (93 205 16 08). FGC Tres Torres/bus
66, 94.* **Open** 5pm-3am Mon-Sat. **Credit** V.

As you go up the hill towards Tibidabo, you also go upmarket. Tres Torres is quite a long way up, and its garden is a
favourite spot with Barcelona's more affluent citizens. It's
worth a visit to see the building, built in the last century as
a private house, with a courtyard and small upstairs terrace.

Underworld

*C/Almogàvers 122-C/Pamplona 88 (93 309 12 04). Metro
Marina/bus 6, 40, 42, 141, N6.* **Open** 1-5am Fri, Sat.
Admission *disco* 700-900ptas (incl one drink). **Map F5**

Located in what was the private lounge of **Zeleste** (*see chapter* **Music: Rock, Roots & Jazz**), Underworld has plenty
of room to dance. Fridays, it's electronic avant-garde with
elements of techno and jungle; Saturdays, it's pure electronic dance. Being out of the centre, it depends on people in the
know and walk-ins from Zeleste. Downstairs is the Pop Bar,
administering strictly to the needs of pop-music fans.

Universal

*C/Marià Cubi, 182 bis-184 (93 201 35 96). FGC
Muntaner/bus 14, N8.* **Open** 11pm-3.30am Mon-Wed;
11pm-4am Thur-Sat. **Credit** AmEx, MC, V. **Map C2**

Divided over two floors, Universal has two distinct atmospheres. Downstairs, the music is loud, the décor dark, and
away from the bar there's plenty of space for dancing.
Upstairs is a light, high-ceilinged bar-room, big enough to
seat diners and quiet enough for conversation.

Velvet

*C/Balmes 161 (93 217 67 14). FGC Provença/
bus 7, 16, 17.* **Open** 7.30pm-5am Mon-Thur, Sun;
7.30pm-6.30am Fri, Sat. **Map D3**

A design bar with a 1950s theme that features a larger-than-
usual dancefloor, dramatic toilets, deafening, naff music and
bar staff sporting the shortest skirts and widest epaulettes
in town. The affluent young and very young things who fill
the place are far less dramatic than the surroundings.

Zimbabwe

*C/Mozart 13 (no phone). Metro Diagonal, Fontana/
bus 22, 24, 28, N4, N6.* **Open** 7pm-2.30am Mon-Thur,
Sun; 7pm-3am Fri, Sat. **Map D2**

In the bosom of Gràcia, this friendly place plays excellent non-
stop reggae and Afro-Latin music. Naturally brewed 'rasta' ginger beer is available, while shawarmas and falafels are served
until 3am at the Bar Bosforo, directly across the road.

Zsa Zsa

*C/Rosselló 156 (93 453 85 66). FGC Provença/bus 14,
54, 58, 59, 63, 64, 66, N3, N8.* **Open** 7pm-3am Mon-
Thur; 7pm-3.30am Fri, Sat. **Credit** V. **Map C3**

A chic, elegant design bar patronised mainly by a conventional
bunch, who go to talk and sample the sophisticated range of
drinks. The particular innovation of designers Dani Freixes
and Vicente Miranda are the lighting, which changes continuously and subtly, so the mirrored wall appears sometimes
completely black and at other times ablaze with colour. Bar
staff are greatly appreciated by regulars for their cocktail skills.

Clubs

Antilla Cosmopolita

*C/Muntaner 244 (93 200 77 14). Bus 6, 7, 15, 33, 34, 58,
64, N8.* **Open** 9pm-4.30am Mon-Thur; 11pm-6am Fri, Sat,
eves of public holidays; 11pm-4.30am Sun. **Admission**
1,500ptas (incl one drink); members free. **Map C2**

A relaxed, friendly, firey salsa club with a regular live programme (*see chapter* **Music: Rock, Roots & Jazz**). Its
location just above Diagonal ensures a healthy mix including star dancers and uptown girls in short, swirly skirts.

Bikini

*C/Déu i Mata 105 (93 322 08 00). Metro Les Corts/bus 15,
43, 59.* **Open** (three rooms) *Cockteleria/Dry* midnight-
4.30am Tue, Wed, Sun; midnight-5am Thur; midnight-6am
Fri, Sat; *Rock* 11.30pm-5am Tue-Thur, Sun; 11.30pm-6am
Fri, Sat; *Salsa* same hours as Rock room, Tue-Sat; 11.30pm-
4.30am Sun. **Admission** 1,000ptas (Tue-Thur, Sat);
1,400ptas (Fri, Sat). **Credit** AmEx, V.

If there were such a thing as a state disco, it would probably
be like Bikini. Its institutional feel can be explained from its
past: dating from the 1950s, the original Bikini called itself
a 'multi-space' and had rooms for concerts and activities.
After being the focus of late-1980s revels it closed when a
huge mall, L'Illa, was built on the site. In 1996 the new Bikini
opened underground within the mall. True to its origins it
still offers three distinct spaces (*see chapter* **Music: Rock,
Roots & Jazz**): a club, a Latin room and a cocktail lounge.

La Boîte

*Avda Diagonal 477 (93 419 59 50). Bus 6, 7, 15, 27, 33,
34, 63, 67, 68, N8.* **Open** 11pm-5.30am Mon-Thur, Sun;
11pm-6am Fri, Sat. **Admission** (incl one drink) 1,200-
3,000ptas, depending on the band. **Map C2**

One of a handful of clubs uptown that pulls in people from
across the city, owned by the Mas brothers (of **Jamboree**
and **Moog**), and also a music venue. They work hard to create a good atmosphere: the long bar hugs the curved walls,
and mirrored columns make the space surprisingly intimate.
The resident DJ plays mainly soul, funk and old Motown
favourites, and the smallish dancefloor can get crowded at
weekends. *See also chapter* **Music: Rock, Roots & Jazz**.

Club Apolo/Nitsaclub

*C/Nou de la Rambla 113 (93 441 40 01/93 442 51 83).
Metro Paral.lel/bus 36, 57, 64, 91, N6, N9.* **Open** *club*
midnight-6am Thur-Sat; *gigs* times vary. **Admission**
club (incl one drink) 1,200ptas; *gigs* prices vary. **Map C5**

This elegant old ballroom has changed hands many times
over the years, but has always drawn a crowd. The most
recent management has put it to good use with a programme

Twisting by the port

No area in Barcelona has more bars per square metre than the **Port Olímpic**. Between Easter week and October, the 50 or so bars and restaurants lining the lower level of the port are utterly packed; after 11pm, the pocket-sized dance bars pump up the music and by 1am, most of the restaurants have converted into dance spaces as well. Mid-summer, it can take an hour to push your way from one end of the strip to the other. Almost all the Port bars are similarly small, and differences in décor are minimal. Every bar has a big outdoor *terrassa*. Music runs from Spanish techno to salsa to rock to disco, but the same bar that plays salsa at 1am may play techno at 2am – it depends what the crowd is into.

Since it's some way from the centre, most people who start a night out at the Port Olímpic end up staying there, moving from one bar to another until closing time at 5am. A few bars, such as **Panini**, **Mar i Cel** and **Els Argonautes** are a bit bigger – and so less packed – than the rest, and **Salsa Art Bar** plays only salsa, but generally, since they're all so close and venues change so often, you're best off just walking along the strip and choosing for yourself. *See also chapter* **Restaurants**.

Still by the water but closer to the centre of things is **Maremàgnum**, the huge entertainment palace in the middle of the Port Vell. All year round, but above all in summer, Maremàgnum at night is one massive teen party and, as such, has significantly redefined the city's nocturnal landscape. Catering strictly to the masses, the area offers a strip of Latin-American music bars and clubs on its lower level.

Provocatively dressed dancers' hips wiggle to salsa, rumba, and other heated sounds at the **Tropicana Bar** (93 225 80 46), the **Caipirinha Bar** (93 225 80 03), or, the club best liked by dedicated *salseros*, **Mojito Bar** (93 225 80 14). Upstairs on the third (top) level, meanwhile, the younger and even more provocatively dressed masses squeeze together in the open-air techno/machine-driven roof-top patio, with a mini-golf course, **Central Golf** (no phone). The deal here is to go around the large square (the golf course is in the middle) and check out the four clubs that each command one side. Techno dominates all, even seeping into the **Irish Winds**, a sort-of traditional-looking Irish pub with its own outdoor terrace (*see chapter* **Cafés & Bars**). Maremàgnum stays bopping until 5am.

of techno-oriented dance parties and concerts. On Fridays, Saturdays and eves of public holidays, the place becomes the **Nitsaclub**, a very popular, very young techno/house/drum 'n' bass dance-a-thon. On other nights the venue often hosts live concerts (*see chapter* **Music: Rock, Roots & Jazz**).

Costa Breve

C/Aribau 230 (93 414 27 78). FGC Provença/ bus 6, 7, 15, 33, 34, 58, 64, N8. **Open** midnight-6am Thur-Sat. **Admission** usually 1,000ptas (incl one drink). **Credit** V. **Map C2**
Costa Breve has a long history of attracting a varied (largely uptown) clientele. Low ceilings, dim lights and curved bar help create an atmosphere for unwinding, and people really get into it on the dance floor, mainly to funk and popular dance tunes. There are also weekly live acts under the venue's other identity, **La Tierra** (*see chapter* **Music: Roots, Rock & Jazz**).

Fellini

Estació de França, Avda Marquès de l'Argentera (no phone). Metro Barceloneta/bus 14, 39, 51. **Open** 1.30am-5.30am Fri, Sat. Closed some days Aug. **Admission** (incl one drink) 1,500ptas. **Map E5**
In the basement of Estació de França, this subterranean darkland consists of three spaces, a very large cement dancefloor, a medium-sized cement dancefloor, and a small lounge in which cement is not as visible (and with disco instead of

Jamboree

Plaça Reial 17 (93 301 75 64). Metro Liceu/bus 14, 18, 38, 59, N6, N9. **Open** 8.30pm-4.30am Mon-Thur, Sun; 8.30pm-5am Fri, Sat. **Admission** *gigs* (incl one drink) 1,200ptas; *disco* free. **Map D5**
Live acts here end around 1am, and the club, famed for black soul and dance music, begins. This subterranean brick vault is hugely popular, and gets very cramped. Total gridlock is averted by a steady stream of people going upstairs (for free) to Tarantos, where they can chill to Latin and Spanish music. *See also chapter* **Music: Roots, Rock & Jazz**.

Jazzmatazz

Passatge Domingo 3 (93 211 88 97). Metro Passeig de Gràcia/FGC Provença/bus 20, 21, 22, 24, 28, 43, 44. **Open** 9pm-4am Tue-Thur; 9pm-5am Fri, Sat; 8pm-midnight Sun; *gigs* midnight Tue-Sat; 8.30pm Sun. **Admission** free. **Map D3**
Without a doubt one of the most interesting places to have opened up in the Eixample in recent memory. Lit only by glowing orange squares encased in the bar and stage area,

techno). Not long ago this place was a mecca for untold numbers of clubbers caught up in international techno-thump. The crowds have dwindled, but the thump lives on… and on. When you leave, don't forget to stop in at the station's café/bar (*see below* **Late/early eating**).

Going underground

Scattered among the ruins and renovations of the Barrio Chino and Raval are a handful of private, 'underground' spaces where artistico-cultural events are staged, which occasionally bloom into full-grown parties. These parties are private in the sense that they're not held in a bar or club, but in a space that's been taken over by a group of active, artistic-minded individuals, who every so often open up their uniquely-fashioned environments to anybody who has managed to find out about them. They may not charge admission, but will probably need a contribution to the costs.

Some places call themselves 'cultural associations' and have regular events programmes – theatre workshops and performances, tai-chi classes, art exhibitions or rummage sales. Others stage imaginatively cool dance parties with the latest electronic sounds accompanied by original visual projections. On a good night, these parties are the place to be. The best way to find out about this kind of event is to keep your eyes peeled for flyers announcing them in bars and shops in the neighbourhood (such as **Aurora**, the **Escondite del Pirata** (*see chapter* **Restaurants**), **Bar Fortuny** (*see chapter* **Cafés & Bars**), or Divine clothes and music shop (*see chapter* **Shopping**).

There's also a select band of semi-legal, clandestine bars in town which, for obvious reasons, can't be listed here. One with a tad more

visible existence is the **Marx Bar** near Plaça George Orwell. To find it, ask around in the trendier bars on the plaça, but note that it's a fairly tight underground scene, and not everyone's cup of hemlock.

L'Atelier – Art de Vivre Total

C/Cadena 49 bajos (93 441 07 16). **Map C5**
A huge, remarkable 'life-art' space that in another era was a laundry and bath house. There are four perfectly preserved ten-metre-long stone washrooms, which now serve as performance spaces and chill-out rooms whenever there's the occasional experimental drum 'n' bass electro-music party or DJ session.

Conservas

C/Sant Pau 58 bajos (93 302 06 30/e-mail: conservas@ mail.sendanet.es). **Map C5**
A medium-sized, well-kept space with excellent, sporadic programming of contemporary theatre performances, poetry readings and comedy acts. Extremely popular with those in the know.

Simbiosis

C/Riereta 5 (93 443 10 71). **Open** Thur-Sat from 11pm. **Map C5**
Exhibiting highly original metalwork and sculptures as well as funky wall-paintings and projections, Simbiosis also hosts regular theatre performances, live concerts, DJ sessions and more.

Yasta

C/Tallers 45, interior bajos, local 8 (93 317 96 99). **Map D4**
An experimental, multipurpose cultural association offering a wide range of programming, including tai-chi workshops, exhibitions, jumble sales, and far-out parties.

Jazzmatazz is a cool venue for funk, hip-hop, soul, and jazz fusion gigs, as well as a late-night club at the weekend. There's no cover, but you have to order at least one drink (beer on tap is remarkably reasonable at 400ptas a *tubo*). Monthly art exhibitions are also staged in a unique, glassed-off area. *See also chapter* **Music: Roots, Rock & Jazz**.

Jimmy'z

Hotel Princesa Sofia, Plaça Pius XII 4 (93 414 63 62). Metro Maria Cristina/bus 7, 67, 68, 74, 75, 114. **Open** 11pm-4am Wed; 11pm-5am Thur-Sat. **Admission** 1,000ptas (incl one drink). **Credit** V.
In the palatial bowels of high-rise Hotel Princesa Sofia, the decor of Jimmy'z is just what you'd expect. Like many larger discos it has four areas, including an 'ethnic' room for salsa; a big central techno dancefloor; and a private lounge, where you need to know Jimmy to get in. The crowd is young and monied.

Karma

Plaça Reial 10 (93 302 56 80). Metro Liceu/ bus 14, 18, 38, 59, N6, N9. **Open** 11.30pm-5am Tue-Sun; *bar* 9.30pm-2.30am Tue-Sun. **Admission** free-1,000ptas (incl drink). **Map D5**
Right on Plaça Reial and with a guard-boys at the door, Karma is impossible to miss. It has a long history of serving tourists and a cross-section of locals, although the young student crowd dominates. Intense competition from clubs nearby has lowered attendances, but this bomb-shelter of a club remains crammed at weekends. The doormen let you walk in if they like the look of you; if not, you pay. Music is mainstream rock.

KGB

C/Alegre de Dalt 55 (93 210 59 06). Metro Joanic/bus 21, 39, 55, N4. **Open** *gigs* 9pm-midnight; *disco* midnight-5am Thur-Sat. **Admission** *gigs* depends on the band; *disco* (incl one drink). **Map E2**
The best time to go to this stark, industrial-style warehouse is 2am or later. The crowd are a lively alternative bunch. Despite its residential Gràcia location, KGB stays open late enough to attract hardcore insomniacs: by 5am,

the place is thick and thumping. The drill-hammer techno gets harder and faster the later it gets. Frenetic live concerts are held here sometimes, and international DJs pass through. *See also chapter* **Music: Roots, Rock & Jazz**.

Luz de Gas

C/Muntaner 246 (93 209 77 11/93 209 73 85). Bus 6, 7, 15, 33, 34, 58, 64, N8. **Open** 11pm-4.30/5.30am daily. **Admission** (incl one drink) approx 1,800ptas. **Credit** AmEx, DC, MC, V. **Map C2**
Elegant red velvet with a touch of kitsch sets the tone for this live venue (*see chapter* **Music: Rock, Roots & Jazz**), which doubles as a disco after 2am. Very popular with an uptown, middle-of-the-road clientele.

Moog

C/Arc del Teatre 3 (93 301 72 82). Metro Liceu, Drassanes/bus 14, 18, 38, 59, N6, N9. **Open** 11.30pm-5.30am Mon-Thur, Sun; 11.30pm-6.30am Fri, Sat. **Admission** (incl one drink) 1,200ptas. **Map C5**
Moog expands the Mas i Mas family's empire (*see* **Jamboree, La Boîte**) to encompass techno and electronic dance. An excellent programme of name DJs keeps this place perennially popular with a happy, young, lively crowd. The dancefloor is smallish and can get tight, but the upstairs chill-out offers some relief. International DJs usually guest on Wednesday nights.

New York

C/Escudellers 5 (93 318 87 30). Metro Liceu/ bus 14, 18, 38, 59, N6, N9. **Open** midnight-4.30am Thur-Sat, eves of public holidays. **Admission** *midnight-1.15am* 500ptas; *1.15am-close* 1,000ptas. **Map D5**
Students and teenagers thrash it out to Britpop and similar in this former sex club, which metamorphosed overnight into a hang-out for Barcelona's home-grown version of Generation X. It's big, with a mezzanine above the dancefloor and couches that date from the club's licentious origins in the late 1970s, but with no air-conditioning, the air becomes a sweaty soup. **Panams**, at La Rambla 27, is a similar sex-club venue (which still has a live show) that hosts similar club nights.

Chilling out at **Fellini**. *See page 158.*

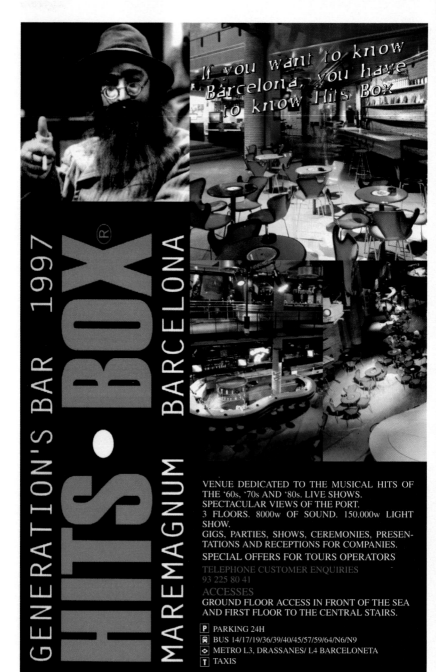

Otto Zutz Club

C/Lincoln 15 (93 238 07 22). FGC Gràcia/bus 16, 17, 25, 27, 127. **Open** 11pm-6am Tue-Sat. **Admission** 1,500-2,000ptas. **Credit** AmEx, DC, MC, V. **Map D1-2**

A landmark among the city's nocturnal offerings, Otto offers three levels of hard-edged but elegant décor, with galleries overlooking the dancefloor. In times past it was the hottest club in town, but has lost its trendy cachet lately and moved inexorably towards the mainstream. On an average weekend night the place fills up with wannabes and expensive clothing labels, and door policy tends to be snooty. Even so, when a good DJ is visiting, it's a great place to dance. The Hot Club, a new space on the second floor, has recently been inaugurated and the tone there is softer and funkier. There's also live music, usually jazz, several nights of the week.

Paradís

C/Paradís 4 (93 310 72 43). Metro Jaume I/ bus 17, 40, 45. **Open** 6pm-2.30am daily. **Map D5**

A reggae, Afro-Latin music club in the vaulted basement of a restaurant next door to the local government palaces. It doesn't gets going until after 2 or 3am, when other places have closed. Occasional live gigs are held, and reggae-dub rap sessions. A limited selection of West African food is also served earlier in the evening (*see chapter* **Restaurants**).

Salsa Latina

C/Bori i Fontesta 25 (93 209 88 24). Bus 6, 7, 33, 34, 64, 66, 67, 68. **Open** midnight-6am daily. **Admission** 1,500ptas men; 1,200ptas women (incl one drink).

The music is hot and jumping salsa – swinging hips and fancy footwork in abundance – but the décor's far from exotic, just a few parrots on the walls. The crowd is mixed and friendly.

Up & Down

C/Numància 179 (93 205 51 94). Metro Maria Cristina/bus 63, 67, 68. **Open** *restaurant* 9.30pm-2am Tue-Sat; *Up* midnight-5am Tue-Sat; *Down* midnight-5am Thur-Sat. **Admission** *Up* 3,000ptas; *Down* 2,000ptas; (each incl one drink). **Credit** AmEx, DC, MC, V.

Barcelona's classic disco for socialites and their entourages, with two levels: the 'Up'stairs, where an older crowd congregates for dinner and live music, and 'Down'stairs, where their well-dressed offspring dance to disco numbers. It used to be notoriously snooty and claimed to be members-only, but now just anyone can get in.

Walden Eight

Avda Indústria 12, Sant Just Desvern (93 499 03 42). No public transport. **Open** midnight-5.30am Fri-Sat Closed some days Aug. **Credit** MC, V.

So the design-bar phenomenon isn't quite dead. In the suburb/town of Sant Just Desvern on the western edge of metropolitan Barcelona, Walden Eight is a post-industrial sci-fi fantasy in a defunct cement factory, with a crystal-ceilinged, flying saucer-like restaurant 30m up the factory's chimney. It was designed by Alfredo Arribas, architect of **Network** and the **Torres de Avila**, and sits next door to Ricard Bofill's famous Walden building. Walden Eight is a techno/house club with a wide range of programming, including concerts by international groups such as Female and Regis, performances by bizarre circus people and a bevy of very skilled go-go dancers. At the very top of the chimney there's a viewing area from where you can gaze down on the city's twinkling lights. Wow.

After-hours

Venues may stay open after their stated closing times.

Aurora

C/Aurora 7 (93 442 30 44). Metro Paral.lel, Liceu/bus 14, 20, 38, 59, 64, N6, N9. **Open** 10pm-2.30am daily; also 6am-noon Sat, Sun, public holidays. **Map C5**

A small, red-walled bar in the Barrio Chino with eclectic music that attracts the perkier, more artistic elements of the neighbourhood. On Fridays and Saturdays it's not clear if the bar ever shuts; on Sunday at any rate, it's open at dawn, and steadily fills up with restless types until about noon.

Circus

Camí de la Fuxarda, Poble Espanyol (no phone) Metro Espanya/bus 13, 61, N1, N2. **Open** midnight-7am Fri, Sat. **Map A4**

A large basilica-like techno dance club that stays open late enough to attract the all-night crowd. The place is spacious and modern, with various levels and a large, comfortably carpeted chill-out room.

La Terraza

Avda Marquès de Comillas, behind Poble Espanyol (93 423 12 85). Metro Espanya/bus 13, 61, N1, N2. **Open** 11pm-6am Fri-Sun. **Admission** 1,000ptas, incl one drink. **Map A4**

In the semi-open-air Sotaventa disco, this is a spacious after-hours club that functions in the warmer months – although be prepared for it to have a different name, for the management changes each season. The best time to arrive is around 7am, to enjoy the dawn in a cool, elegant garden setting.

Cabaret & dance halls

An era came to a close in 1997 when the owners of the Molino, last and most famous of the music halls on the Paral.lel, suddenly declared bankruptcy and closed the place down. However, efforts may well be made to revive it. Thankfully, other great institutions of old Barcelona like **La Paloma** are still going strong.

Bodega Bohèmia

C/Lancaster 2 (93 302 50 61). Metro Drassanes/bus 14, 18, 38, 59, 91. **Open** 10.30pm-4am Mon-Thur; 5-8.30pm, 10.30pm-4am, Fri-Sun. **Admission** free, but with one compulsory drink (min 1,000ptas). **Map C5**

Something out of a David Lynch film, the Bodega Bohèmia is stranger than fiction. To a tiny audience, or even nobody at all, Catalan cabaret stars of yesteryear run through their repertoire, accompanied by an out-of-tune piano. At times it can be heartbreaking, but rather than let it affect you, sit back and enjoy what's good, laugh with the worst, and talk during the stand-up comics.

El Cangrejo

C/Monserrat 9 (93 301 85 75). Metro Drassanes/bus 14, 18, 38, 59. **Open** 7pm-3am Mon-Wed; 11pm-3am Thur; 11pm-3.30am Fri, Sat. **Admission** free. **Map C5**

In the heart of the *Barrio Chino*, El Cangrejo (the Crab) is pure sleaze, a leftover from the neighbourhood's days of fame as a district of forbidden fruits. People come here to be entertained by an over-the-top troupe of drag queens doing Liza Minelli, but the regular clients and ageing (like, 70 years old) camp barmen are as strange as anything on the small stage. The clientele runs from local devotees who know all the performers, to tourists trying out the Barrio Chino experience. An old woman sits in silence by the door; she's probably the one who keeps track of how many drinks you have; beware, because, while there's no cover charge, drink prices are hefty.

Cibeles

C/Còrsega 363 (93 457 38 77). Metro Diagonal/bus 20, 21, 39, 45, 47. **Open** Open 11.30pm-4am Thur; 11.30pm-5am Fri; 6-9.30pm, 11.30pm-5am Sat; 6-9.30pm Sun. Closed Aug. **Admission** (incl one drink) *Thur* 1,000ptas; *Fri, Sat night* 1,500ptas; *Sat afternoon, Sun* 800ptas (women), 900ptas (men). **Map D3**

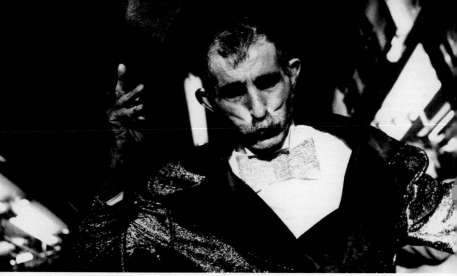

All manner of folk can be found around Barcelona at night. Morning at **Pinocho's**.

Built in the 1940s and revamped in the 1980s, Cibeles is a large galleried dance hall similar to **La Paloma** (*see below*), but without the rococo decoration. It's usually packed with a good-humoured crowd that gets younger as the evening goes on, and the orchestra play everything from foxtrots to cha-cha-cha, mambo and rock 'n' roll. With bars upstairs and in the main hall, and soft bench seats round the gallery ideal for romantic tête-à-têtes, the mood becomes infectious and it's hard not to have a good time.

La Paloma

C/Tigre 27 (93 301 68 97). Metro Universitat/bus 24, 41, 55, 64, 91, 141, N6. **Open** 6-9.30pm, 11.30pm-5am, Thur-Sat; 6-9.30pm Sun; 6-9.30pm public holidays. **Admission** *Thur, Fri afternoons* free (women), 500ptas (men); *Fri, Sat nights* 800ptas; *Sat afternoon, Sun* 500ptas (women), 600ptas (men). **Map C4**
A complete mix of people frequents this magnificent 1902 dance hall, where clubbers mix with pensioners, many of them practised dancers who have been coming here for years. The band gives you a chance to try anything from cha-cha-cha to jive, passing through tango, *paso doble* and even flamenco-ish *Sevillanas*. Anyone who likes kitsch will fall in love with the exuberant, galleried interior, and the atmosphere virtually ensures a fun night out.

Late/early eating

Bar-Kiosko Pinocho

Stand 67-68, Mercat de la Boqueria (93 317 17 31). Metro Liceu/bus 14, 18, 38, 59, N6, N9. **Open** 6am-35pm Mon-Sat. **Map D5**
A bar-stall inside the Boqueria market that's a popular breakfast spot for night-birds on their way home. During the day, it's also good for lunch, if not as cheap as it looks.

Cafè Arnau

Avda Paral.lel 62 (93 329 21 04). Metro Paral.lel/bus 36, 57, 64, 91, N6, N9. **Open** 10am-3am Tue-Sun. **Credit** MC, V. **Map C5**
Next door to Teatre Arnau and close to many bars and clubs, this café-restaurant stays open all night every night, closing for just a few hours. You can order from a standard Spanish menu. After the 'official' closing time, don't be put off by the metal shutters; ring the bell beside the metal door.

Churreria Aguilar

Escorial 1 (93 219 35 53). Metro Joanic/bus 21, 39, 55, N4. **Open** 11am-3pm, 5-10pm, Thur; 11am-3pm, 5-10pm, midnight-7am Fri, Sat; 8am-10pm Sun. **Map E2**
A small *churreria* in Gràcia that caters for the late-night crowd. Snacks and hot chocolate are served to revellers doing the rounds. Opening times are more than usually erratic.

Granja de Gavà

C/Joaquim Costa 37 (93 317 58 83). Metro Universitat/bus 24, 41, 55, 64, 91, 141, N6. **Open** *Sept-May* 8am-10pm daily; *May-early Sept* 8am-10pm Mon-Fri; 8am-3pm Sat. **Map C4**
A clean, well-run, *Modernista granja* (milk bar) in the middle of the Raval; here, you can get hot chocolate, fruit juices, sandwiches and, of course, coffee, from very bright and early at weekends.

Midnight Express

Estació de França, Avda Marquès de l'Argentera (93 310 14 78). Metro Barceloneta/bus 14, 39, 45, 51, 57, 59, 64, N6, N10, N11. **Open** 6.45am-9pm Mon-Fri; 5am-9pm Sat, Sun, public holidays. **Map E5**
The grand, spacious and early-opening station bar inside the Estació de França is a breakfast favourite for revellers (especially with those turning out of **Fellini** downstairs. A great place for end-of-the-night relaxation.

Roxi

C/Torrent de l'Olla 141 (no phone). Metro Fontana/bus 22, 24, 28, 39, N4, N6. **Open** 8.30pm-2.30am Tue-Thur, Sun; 8.30pm-3am Fri, Sat. **Map D2**
In the heart of Gràcia, Roxi is a clean, mercifully dimly lit after-hours bar that opens (semi-officially) on weekend mornings for early-birds and up-all-nighters. There's a pool table in the back, a well-stocked bar, and very good *bocadillos* to replenish lost nutrients and alleviate the munchies.

Zoo

C/Escudellers 33 (93 302 77 28). Metro Liceu/bus 14, 18, 38, 59, N6, N9. **Open** 6pm-2am Mon-Thur, Sun; 6pm-2.30am Fri, Sat. **Credit** MC, V. **Map D5**
A central night café with restaurant service. Endangered animals and their incarcerated mates are not on the menu, but you will find such dishes as 'penguin' toast with spinach, pine nuts, raisins, and cream cheese. Also great salads.

Shopping

Mall-cruising, hole-in-the-wall fashion houses or the personal touch as you choose your cheese: Barcelona's shops cover all the options.

The shape of things to come looms over Plaça Catalunya. See page 165.

Tradition and innovation are two elements that characterise Barcelona's shopping scene. They have coexisted here harmoniously for decades – which may be the secret of the city's success. Big everything-under-one-roof mixed spaces were slow to arrive, but since the 1980s Barcelona has taken to them with typical verve, first in the shape of fashion *galeries* such as **Bulevard Rosa**, and then with the appearance of full-scale, massive shopping malls on the Diagonal (*see page 169*). It seems, though, that the city centre is ready to go to war to justify its status: as **Marks & Spencer** are frantically readying their new Plaça Catalunya branch, work is also in full swing on an all-new complex at the top of the Rambla, **El Triangle**.

Meanwhile, the small, individual, downright quirky shops that are one of the glories of Barcelona have been struggling on for years – capacity for survival is one of their characteristics – but so far at least have always managed to co-exist alongside the expansion in retail space. The biggest concentration of traditional shops is in the old city (*see page 180* **Small is beautiful**). The most prestigious fashion stores are to be found on Passeig de Gràcia, Rambla Catalunya and around and above Plaça Francesc Macià on Diagonal, but there are trendy fashion outlets in the old city as well, especially around Portaferrissa.

Sundays

Most shops close in the afternoon, from about 1.30pm to 4.30pm, and traditionally Sunday and holiday opening has been closely regulated: the only shops always open on Sundays have been cake shops, *pastisserias* (*see page 252*). However, 'large spaces' – which means big stores and malls – are now allowed to stay open through the day, and on eight Sundays each year, including all four Sundays prior to Christmas. The other four 'Sunday shopping' days are spread around the year, and widely advertised in the local press. On Saturdays, many shops open in the morning only. The city tourist authorities have also tried out a plan for late opening on Thursdays, but it's failed to catch on, as small shopkeepers sensibly preferred to keep their leisure time.

Sales & tax refunds

Sales run from the second week in January to the end of February, and during July and August. VAT (IVA) depends on the classification of the product – 7% on food, 16% on items classified as luxury – but note that in many larger stores non-European residents can request a Tax-Free

Open all hours

There are no 24-hour shops as such here, except at some 24-hour petrol stations (*see page 260*), but the ones listed below are open most hours that you're likely to be awake.

Late-night standbys

Depaso *C/Muntaner 14 (93 454 58 46).*
*Metro Universitat/bus all routes to Plaça
Universitat.* **Open** 6am-2.30am Mon-Thur; 6am-3am Fri-Sun. **Credit** MC, V. **Map C4**
General store for non-sleepers or those in dire straits. There are smaller branches around the city, attached to petrol stations.

Drugstore David *C/Tuset 19-21 (93 200 47 30).*
FCG Gràcia/bus 6, 7, 15, 16, 17, 27, 33, 34, 58,64.
Open 7.30am-5am daily. **Credit** V. **Map C2**
This pioneer in out-of-hours stores. It incorporates a tobacco shop, bookshop, newsstand, restaurant, foodstore, delicatessen and wine shop, as well as some clothing and toys.

7-11 *Plaça Urquinaona (93 318 88 63). Metro
Urquinaona/bus all routes to Plaça Urquinaona.*
Open 7am-3am daily. **Credit** MC, V. **Map D4**
The familiar franchise has 50 branches around Barcelona, many at petrol stations. This branch is the most central.

Vip's *Rambla de Catalunya 7-9 (93 317 48 05).*
Metro Catalunya/bus all routes to Plaça Catalunya.
Open 8am-2am Mon-Thur; 8am-3am Fri; 9am-3am Sat-Sun. **Credit** AmEx, DC, $TC, V. **Map D4**
Vip's houses a restaurant, a supermarket, a fairly good bookshop (some books in English), a newsstand and a toy-gift section.

cheque on purchases of more than 15,000ptas, which can be cashed at the airport to reclaim VAT charges. Stores within the scheme have a 'Tax-Free' sticker on the shop front.

One-stop

El Corte Inglés

*Plaça Catalunya 14 (93 302 12 12). Metro Catalunya/bus
all routes to Plaça Catalunya.* **Open** 10am-9.30pm Mon-Sat. **Credit** AmEx, DC, MC, V. **Map D4**
The bulldozer of retailing in the whole of Spain, with a department-store monopoly since it swallowed up its only competitor, Galerías Preciados, in 1995. The former Galerías store in Avda Portal de l'Angel, left to gather dust for years, is to reopen as a megastore specialising in music, audio equipment and books. Not only does El Corte Inglés provide all the goods you expect to find in a department store, you can also have keys cut, shoes re-heeled, hair and beauty treatments carried out, and meals or drinks in the rooftop café. The air-conditioning offers respite from a hot August day. Should there be anything you can't find in the main stores (and you have a car) the company also has a giant hypermarket, **Hipercor**, in Sagrera on the north side of the city.
Branches: Avda Diagonal 617-619 (93 419 28 28); Avda Diagonal 471-473 (93 419 20 20); **Hipercor** Avda Meridiana 350-358 (93 346 38 11).

Marks & Spencer

*Plaça Catalunya 32 (phone unavailable at time of writing).
Metro Catalunya/bus all routes to Plaça Catalunya.* **Open**
10am-9.30pm Mon-Sat. **Credit** AmEx, DC, MC, V. **Map D4**

Due to the extent of rebuilding required in what was previously one of the long-established main bank branches on the Plaça, a fierce pace has had to be adopted to get everything ready for the opening of Europe's biggest M&S, planned for May 1999. Barcelona already has a two-floor M&S in **L'Illa** mall (*see p196*), but the plans for this six-floor megastore on the corner of the Rambla are much, much grander. And it's almost directly opposite El Corte Inglés… there's a challenge.
Branch: L'Illa, Avda Diagonal 557.

Antiques

The streets around C/de la Palla, in the Barri Gòtic, are crowded with small, idiosyncratic antique shops. Antiques are also found around C/Consell de Cent and C/Dos de Maig in the Eixample, and there are some less expensive shops near **Els Encants** (*see page 179*).

L'Arca de l'Àvia

*C/Banys Nous 20 (93 302 15 98). Metro Liceu/bus 14,
18, 38, 59.* **Open** 10.30am-2pm, 5-8pm, Mon-Fri.
Credit AmEx, DC, EC, MC, TC, V. **Map D5**
The antique cottons, linens and silks at this shop are always beautifully displayed. Unfortunately, they're not cheap, but the patchwork eiderdowns, dresses (from 20,000ptas) and antique beaded bags (from 18,000ptas) are lovely to behold.

Bulevard dels Antiquaris

*Passeig de Gràcia 55 (93 215 44 99). Metro Passeig de
Gràcia/bus 7, 16, 17, 22, 24, 28.* **Open** Sept-May
9.30am-1.30pm, 4.30-8.30pm Mon-Sat; *June-Sept* Mon-Fri.
Map D4
Beside the main **Bulevard Rosa** fashion mall (*see p173*), this antiques arcade houses 73 shops under one roof. Wares on sale range from fine paintings to ivory, religious artefacts and porcelain dolls. In **Turn of the Century**, you'll find miniature musical instruments from the 1930s, old jewellery and furniture for dolls' houses.

Galuchat

*C/València 261 (93 487 58 55). Metro Passeig de Gràcia/
bus 7, 16, 17, 22, 24, 28.* **Open** 11am-2pm, 5-8pm Mon-Fri. **Credit** AmEx, DC, JCB, MC, V. **Map D3**
A shop that's after Pedro Almodóvar's heart, filled with kitsch furniture and curiosities. Prices can vary from about 800ptas for a 1940s metal-and-glass cup, to 145,000ptas for a 1950s armchair.

Gothsland Galeria d'Art

*C/Consell de Cent 331 (93 488 19 22). Metro Passeig de
Gràcia/bus 7, 16, 17, 22, 24, 28.* **Open** 10am-1.30pm,
4.30-8.30pm Mon-Sat. **No credit cards**. **Map D3**
A near-unique specialist: a magnificent art and antiques gallery-shop that deals in original Catalan *Modernista* art, furniture and decoration. As well as a large selection of fine furniture – sometimes including pieces by Gaspar Homar –, you can find polychrome terracotta sculptures by Casanovas, Pau Gargallo or Lambert Escaler, others in alabaster by Cipriani, beautiful *Modernista* vases and mirrors, or a marble sculpture by Frederic Marés. There are also paintings from the same period. *See also chapter* **Art Galleries**.

La Llar del Col.leccionisme

*C/Llibreteria 13 (93 268 32 59). Metro Jaume I/bus 17,
40, 45.* **Open** 10am-1.30pm, 4.30-8pm Mon-Fr; 10am-1.30pm Sat. **No credit cards**. **Map D5**
More a bric-a-brac than an antique shop, the 'Home of Collecting' has lots of small items such as old postcards, posters, medals, watches… Owner Jesús Torriente seems to enjoy the company of visitors as much as doing business.

Bookshops

General

Crisol
C/Consell de Cent 341 (93 215 31 21). Metro Passeig de Gràcia/bus 7, 16, 17, 22, 24, 28. **Open** 10am-10pm Mon-Sat. **Credit** AmEx, DC, MC, V. **Map D3**
A bookshop with a bit of everything, from gifts to records, along with a book-finding service. It has well-stocked English-language, foreign press and record sections too, and the basement photography department has high-standard cameras and equipment. Sections of the Rambla Catalunya branch, including the news stand, stay open till 1am.
Branch: Rambla Catalunya 81 (93 215 27 20).

Laie Llibreria Café
C/Pau Claris 85 (93 302 73 10). Metro Urquinaona/bus all routes to Plaça Urquinaona. **Open** *bookshop* 10am-9pm Mon-Fri; 10.30am-9pm Sat; *café* 9am-1am Mon-Fri; 10.30am-1am Sat. **Credit** AmEx, DC, MC, V. **Map D4**
An international, arts-based bookshop-café; the staff are extremely helpful, and the selection of books is imaginative. Upstairs is the splendid and relaxing café. *See also chapter* **Cafés & Bars**.

Llibreria Francesa
Passeig de Gràcia 91 (93 215 14 17). Metro Diagonal/bus 7, 16, 17, 22, 24, 28, N4, N6. **Open** 9.30am-2.30pm, 4-8.30pm Mon-Fri; 9.30am-2pm, 5-8.30pm Sat. **Credit** AmEx, MC, V. **Map D3**
A long-established bookshop with Catalan, Spanish, French and English books and a big selection of travel books.

Llibreria de la Virreina
Palau de la Virreina. La Rambla 99 (93 301 77 75). Metro Liceu/ bus 14, 18, 38, 59. **Open** 10am-8.30pm Mon-Sat. **Credit** AmEx, MC, V. **Map D5**
The bookshop in the city information centre on the Rambla (*see p251*) has an unbeatable selection of books on everything to do with Barcelona, from architectural guides to beautifully-illustrated table editions, plus ideas for souvenirs.

El Lokal
C/de la Cera 1, bis (93 329 06 43). Metro Sant Antoni/bus 20, 64, 91. **Open** 5-9pm Mon; 10am-1.30pm, 5-9pm Tue-Fri; 5-9pm Sat. **No credit cards. Map C5**
More than a bookshop – an anarchists' hideout. The shop has over 1,000 titles on anarchism, anti-militarism, history, ecology, feminism and so on; general subjects are available in the ground-floor *Amanecer* shop, while in the *Distri* section you can find comics, fanzines, magazines, CDs, videos, pins and T-shirts. Cool.

Tartessos
C/Canuda 35 (93 308 81 81). Metro Catalunya/bus all routes to Plaça Catalunya. **Open** 10am-2pm, 4.30-8pm, Mon-Sat. **Credit** AmEx, MC, V. **Map D4**
Tartessos sells all types of books to survive, but their reason for being is a love of photography. Most of their collection of photography books are specially imported from France, Germany, the UK or USA: find classics like Henri Cartier-Bresson, or vanguard names such as Joel Peter Wilkin. The shop also hosts an annual exhibition of works by young photographers resident in Barcelona.

Comics

Norma Comics
Passeig de Sant Joan 9 (93 245 45 26). Metro Arc de Triomf/bus 19, 39, 40, 41, 42, 51, 55, 141. **Open** 10.30am-2pm, 5-8.30pm Mon-Sat. **Credit** AmEx, MC, V. **Map E4**

The largest comic shop in Barcelona, with one floor dedicated to European and American comics, another to Japanese Manga, and special sections for Star Wars, Star Trek, model kits and the like. They also have their own publishing house. Saturday afternoons it can be so crowded it's difficult to see the shelves. Next door, Norma has opened Tintin Barcelona, geared exclusively to the boy and related paraphernalia. Norma also runs an art gallery, showing original drawings of Prince Valiant by Harold Foster and selling prints.

English-language bookshops

BCN Books
C/Aragó 277 (93 487 31 23). Metro Passeig de Gràcia/bus 7, 16, 17, 22, 24, 28. **Open** 9am-2pm, 4-8pm, Mon-Fri; 10am-2pm Sat. **Credit** AmEx, V. **Map D3**
Everything from computer-instruction books and teaching materials to the latest best-sellers. There is also a large selection of language dictionaries and reference books.

Come In
C/Provença 203 (93 453 12 04). Metro Hospital Clínic, FGC Provença/bus 7, 54, 58, 64, 66. **Open** 9.30am-2pm, 4.30-8pm Mon-Sat. Closed Aug. **Credit** MC, V. **Map C3**
Barcelona's largest English bookshop, with a selection that includes teaching books and general material, from Chaucer to Joan Collins. Check the noticeboard if you're looking for Spanish or Catalan classes, or private English classes.

English Bookshop
C/Entença 63 (93 425 44 66). Metro Rocafort/bus 9, 27, 41, 50, 56, 109, 127. **Open** 9am-2pm, 4-8pm Mon-Fri; 10am-1.30pm Sat. **Credit** V. **Map B4**
A wide variety of themes and titles, with a good stock of educational aids for teacher and student. If, though, all you want is a book for beach or train, though, then it's also got a decent choice of general paperbacks.

Second-hand & rare books

Angel Batlle
C/Palla 23 (93 301 58 84). Metro Liceu/bus 14, 18, 38, 59. **Open** 9am-1.30pm, 4-7.30pm Mon-Fri. **No credit cards. Map D5**
Despite the second-hand paperbacks in the window, this is a venerable antiquarian bookshop. Inside, as well as books, there's an enormous and diverse collection of prints: English fox-hunting scenes, botanical studies of Catalan wildlife, old maps, and much more. Prints cost from 1,500ptas.

Travel specialists

Altaïr
C/Balmes 69-71 (93 454 29 66). Metro Passeig de Gràcia, FGC Provença/bus 7, 16, 17, 20, 21, 43, 44. **Open** 10am-2pm, 4.30-8pm Mon-Sat. **Credit** AmEx, DC, MC, V. **Map D3**
A travel bookstore that publishes a magazine of the same name, in Spanish. Books are classified by country or region rather than language. There's an excellent selection on Catalonia and Spain, sections on anthropology, photography, world music, guidebooks, dictionaries, and a big stock of maps.

Llibreria Quera
C/Petritxol 2 (93 318 07 43). Metro Liceu/bus 14, 18, 38, 59. **Open** 9.30am-1.30pm, 4.30-8pm Mon-Fri; 10am-1.30pm, 5-8pm Sat. **No credit cards. Map D5**
If you're planning a trip to the Catalan countryside or the Pyrenees this is the ideal place to find walking maps of every part of the country. Staff also have information on mountaineering and all kinds of outward-bound adventures.

Women

Pròleg

*C/Dagueria 13, baixos (93 319 24 25). Metro Jaume I/
bus 17, 40, 45.* **Open** 5-8pm Mon; 10am-2pm, 5-8pm
Tue-Fri; 11am-2pm, 5-8pm Sat. *Aug* 5-9pm Mon-Fri.
Credit MC, V. **Map D5**

Barcelona's only feminist bookshop, Pròleg has faced the
economic problems of any minority-interest bookshop, but
still has the best range of women's writing in Barcelona. The
shop also organises poetry readings and discussions.

Children

Clothes

Generally, children's clothes are expensive in
Spain. Some adult chains, such as **Zara** (*see page
173*), also have imaginative children's lines.

Cache Cache

*Passeig de Gràcia 62 (93 215 40 07).
Metro Passeig de Gràcia/bus 7, 16, 17, 22, 24, 28.* **Open**
10am-8.30pm Mon-Sat. **Credit** V. **Map D3**

Cache Cache design and make everyday, casual clothing in
natural fibres – mostly cotton – for children aged from
nought to 12. They have 20 shops throughout Barcelona.

Prénatal

*Gran Via de les Corts Catalanes 611 (93 302 05 25).
Metro Passeig de Gràcia/bus 7, 16, 17, 18, 22, 24, 28,
50, 54, 56, 62.* **Open** 10am-8pm Mon-Sat. **Credit**
AmEx, DC, MC, V. **Map D4**

French-owned chain with everything from clothes for the
pregnant mum to clothes for kids up to about eight years old.
Prams and pushchairs, cots, feeding bottles and toys are
sold, too, and all are made from quality materials. There are
several branches, including a large, central one in **Galeries
Maldà** (*see p169*).

Toys

Joguines Monforte

*Plaça Sant Josep Oriol 3 (93 318 22 85). Metro Liceu/bus
14, 18, 38, 59.* **Open** 9.30am-1.30pm, 4-8pm Mon-Sat.
Credit AmEx, DC, MC, V. **Map D5**

A traditional toy shop that's one of the oldest in Barcelona.
The owner tells how she once got rid of 'all those old toys in
the back room', only to find them later sold as antiques.

Xalar

*Baixada de la Llibreteria 4 (93 315 04 58). Metro Jaume I/
bus 17, 40, 45.* **Open** 10am-2pm, 4.30-8.30pm, Mon-Sat.
Credit AmEx, DC, MC, V. **Map D5**

Traditional wooden and educational toys, and dolls' houses.

Cosmetics & perfumes

Perfumeria Anna de Lis

*Rambla Catalunya 61 (93 487 61 13).
Metro Passeig de Gràcia/bus 7, 16, 17, 22, 24, 28.*
Open 9.30am-8.30pm Mon-Fri; 10am-2pm, 5-8.30pm, Sat.
Credit AmEx, DC, MC, V. **Map D5**

A traditional cosmetics shop that stocks well-known brands
of creams and potions, numerous perfumes, and make-up.
Branch: C/Aribau 54 (93 454 19 00).

Regia

*Passeig de Gràcia 39 (93 216 01 21).
Metro Passeig de Gràcia/bus 7, 16, 17, 22, 24, 28.* **Open**
10am-8.30pm Mon-Fri; 10.30am-2pm, 5-8.30pm Sat.
Credit AmEx, DC, EC, JCB, MC, V. **Map D3**

Since 1928, Regia has been serving a very select Barcelona
clientele at its main shop and beauty salon. It stocks over 60
types of scent, plus all the best beauty potions, in a world
apart where every last detail is attended to. For those interested in nasal nostalgia, there's also the **Museu del Perfum**
at the back of the shop (*see chapter* **Museums**).

A shop-museum for perfumery connoisseurs, **Regia**.

Temporary Exhibitions
Cinema, Seminars & Festivals
The FIRST EUROPEAN CENTRE
dedicated to city themes.

Centre de Cultura Contemporània
de Barcelona
Montalegre, 5
Telephone: 34 93 306 41 00

Down at the mall

Despite the fact that Barcelona acquired its first everything-under-one-roof space as early as 1942, in the **Galerias Maldà**, the city was slow to pick up on the idea. During the 1990s, though, it has certainly caught up, as relatively modest local fashion *galerias* have been followed by some of the largest malls you'll ever see, at either end of the Diagonal. More *centres comercials* are in the pipeline.

Barcelona Glòries

Avda Diagonal 208 (93 486 04 04). Metro Glòries/bus 56, N2. **Open** *shops* 10am-10pm Mon-Sat. **Map F4**
The largest shopping centre in Spain – a huge, drive-in mall with over 200 shops, including international names such as C&A and even Dr Marten's – has a positively Californian look to it. Located by the Plaça de les Glòries, near **Els Encants** flea market (*see* **Markets**) and the Teatre Nacional de Catalunya, it's built around an open-air plaça with bars and restaurants, and a multiplex cinema (not VO, *see chapter* **Film**). The mall has several good coffee shops and some quite high-quality stores specialising in Spanish ham and other food products. For cut-price produce, there's also a hypermarket.

Galerias Maldà

C/del Pi 5-Portaferrissa 22 (no phone). Metro Liceu/bus 14, 38, 59. **Open** 10am-1.30pm, 4.30-8pm, Mon-Sat. **Map D5**
The first shopping centre in Barcelona, bang in the centre of the old town with access from Plaça del Pi and Portaferrissa, has a bit of everything: from a small shop that specialises in clothes hangers to chain shoe shops and a big furniture store. It also houses a cinema and a very popular *pension*.

L'Illa

Avda Diagonal 557 (93 444 00 00). Metro Maria Cristina/ bus 6, 7, 33, 34, 63, 66, 67, 68. **Open** 10am-9pm Mon-Fri; 10am-9.30pm Sat; *supermarkets* 9.30am-9.30pm Mon-Sat.
Thanks to its prime location in the fashionable business area on the upper Diagonal, L'Illa attracts a more upmarket clientele than its Glòries counterpart. It has many trendy-ish fashion shops, and a well-stocked **Caprabo** supermarket, as well as **Marks & Spencer**. Don't miss the **Decathlon** sportswear specialists or the newest addition, **Fnac**, the French music and books giant, which also presents concerts and photographic exhibitions beside its coffee shop.

Maremàgnum

Moll d'Espanya (93 225 81 00). Metro Barceloneta/bus 14, 17, 36, 39, 40, 45, 57, 59, 64. **Open** 11am-11pm daily. **Map D6**
A mall, or what? Maremàgnum is intended to be an all-round leisure complex, with restaurants, games, cinemas and nightclubs, and so far has pretty much succeeded. It's unique because of its Old Port *locale*, because of its having been designed by two of the lead-architects of modern Barcelona, Viaplana and Piñón, and because the main access to it is a bridge linking it with the Rambla. For those who find normal malls claustrophobic, it's a delight, and the giant mirror-wall above the main entrance creates spectacular visual effects. You can get a whiff of sea air while browsing in designer gift shop **D-Barcelona**, and one of Barcelona's most in-vogue current designers, **Armand Basi** has an outlet here. **Colomer** make beautiful silver jewellery, and football fans will get a kick out of **La Botiga del Barça**, with every possible kind of football-related merchandise. For other facilities in the mall *see chapters* **Restaurants** *and* **Nightlife**.

Aspectos

C/Rec 28 (93 319 52 85). Metro Jaume I/bus 14, 39, 51. **Open** 4.30-8pm Mon-Fri; 10.30am-2pm Sat. Closed Aug. **Credit** V. **Map E5**
Opened in 1991 by Camilla Hamm, this shop houses the work of well-known international furniture and product designers such as Mendini, Grawunder, Kima, Garouste-Bonetti, Carolyne Quartermain, Lowenstein, Forasetti and Eckhart, as well as being a showcase for young unknowns. It also runs periodic exhibitions of design work.

BD Ediciones de Diseño S.A.

C/Mallorca 291 (93 458 69 09). Metro Passeig de Gràcia/bus 20, 21, 39, 43, 44, 45, 47. **Open** 10am-2pm, 4-8pm Mon-Fri; 10am-2pm, 4.30-8pm Sat. **Credit** AmEx, DC, MC, V. **Map D3**
One of the institutions of Barcelona's design world, BD stocks an impressive array of (reproduction) furniture by design gurus such as Macintosh and Gaudí, as well as more contemporary designers – Ricard Bofill, Mariscal, Oscar Tusquets and the Memphis group. Exclusive designs by Alessi, Wittman, Celcotti and Owo are also on display in this magnificent *Modernista* house, the Casa Thomas by Domènech i Montaner. Well worth wandering round for inspiration, even if you can't afford so much as a chairleg.

Dos i Una

C/Rosselló 275 (93 217 70 32). Metro Diagonal/bus 7, 16, 17, 22, 24, 28. **Open** 10.30am-2pm, 4.30-8pm Mon-Fri; 10.30am-2pm, 5-8pm Sat. **Credit** AmEx, DC, JCB, MC, V. **Map D3**
The first design shop to open in Barcelona, and an early patron of Mariscal, Dos i Una has now grown up (it was 20 in 1997) and turned into a high-class gift shop, selling design crockery, embroidered cacti, wacky lamps and accessories, plus postcards, earrings, shirts and T-shirts.

Dou Deu

C/Doctor Dou 10 (93 301 29 40). Metro Catalunya/bus all routes to Plaça Catalunya. **Open** 10am-2pm, 4.30-8.30pm Tue-Sat. Closed Aug. **Credit** AmEx, DC, MC, V. **Map C4**
A wonderful shop associated with the **Galeria Carles Poy** (*see chapter* **Art Galleries**), which sells only artist-made objects – but still usable, from T-shirts to watches and glassware, and at reasonable prices. The stable includes familiar names such as Mariscal and Toni Miru and the less exposed such as Imma Jansana and Nina Pawlowsky.

Ici et Là

Plaça Santa Maria del Mar 2 (93 268 11 67). Metro Jaume I/bus 17, 40, 45. **Open** 4.30-8.30pm Mon; 10.30am-2.30pm, 4.30-8.30pm Tue-Sat. **Credit** MC, V. **Map D5**

Noténom *may not have a name but it does have style. See page 172.*

The brainchild of three women – two French, one Spanish – who believe that original furniture and accessories shouldn't be limited to the well-heeled. They offer a range of contemporary creations and exotic craftwork (which they source themselves around Barcelona, Europe and the world, avoiding middle-men and agents), at deliberately reasonable prices. It's full of wacky and interesting ethnic objects, in line with their multicultural philosophy.

Insòlit

Avda Diagonal 353 (93 207 49 19).
Metro Verdaguer/bus 6, 15, 33, 34. **Open** 10am-1.30pm, 4.30-8pm, Mon-fri; 11am-2pm, 5-8pm, Sat. **Credit** AmEx, DC, MC, V. **Map E3**
One of the few shops of its kind to stock entirely original work, and most of owners Juma and Mun's witty, innovative designs are sold only through this outlet. For 20,000ptas, you can pick up a star-shaped table in wood and iron, and there is also tableware, bizarre lamps and colourful kitsch furniture. The shop also contains a few examples of other people's work too.

MACBA

Plaça dels Angels 1 (93 412 08 10).
Metro Catalunya/bus all routes to Plaça Catalunya. **Open** noon-8pm Mon-Wed-Fri; 10am-8pm Sat; 10am-1pm Sun. **Credit** AmEx, MC, V. **Map C4**
Whatever your opinion of the bright white MACBA as a museum, it has a stylish souvenir shop, with artist-made items and original artwork as well as more nick-nacky pieces. There are also periodic shows by young artists.

Matarile

Passeig del Born 24 (93 315 02 20). Metro Jaume I/bus 14, 39, 51. **Open** 4.30-8pm Mon-Fri; 10.30am-2pm Sat. Closed Aug. **Credit** V. **Map E5**
Owner Mauricio, an interior decorator and lamp-maker, has opened this place to sell his own 'lamps and other light objects'. He uses unusual materials, recycled and otherwise, and also has restored lamps from the 1970s, some for sale.

Vinçon

Passeig de Gràcia 96 (93 215 60 50). Metro Diagonal/ bus 7, 16, 17, 22, 24, 28. **Open** 10am-2pm, 4.30-8.30pm Mon-Sat. **Credit** AmEx, JCB, MC, V. **Map D3**
Barcelona's most renowned design palace, with everything for the home down to the smallest accessory. If you find the stock of superbly extravagant furniture a tad expensive, browse round the lighting, kitchen, bathroom and fabric departments for something affordable. It often feels, though, that as Vinçon has got bigger and more corporate the stock has become steadily less innovative. Each December it houses **Hipermerc'art**, an 'art supermarket' selling paintings en masse: astute buyers can pick up originals by rising young artists for as little as 9,000ptas. Art and architecture buffs will also be tickled to know that Vinçon's upper floor is the former apartment of Santiago Rusiñol, one of the greatest *Modernista* artists.

Fashion
Designers

Adolfo Domínguez

Passeig de Gràcia 32 (93 487 41 70). Metro Passeig de Gràcia/bus 7, 16, 17, 22, 24, 28. **Open** 10am-8.30pm Mon-Sat. **Credit** AmEx, DC, MC, V. **Map D4**
One of the foremost names in Spanish fashion, Galician Adolfo Dominguez deserves his reputation as a designer of well-made, timeless clothes for men and women, usually in stylishly austere colours. A suit (male or female) will set you back around 80,000ptas.
Branches: Passeig de Gràcia 89 (93 215 13 39); Diagonal 490 (93 416 17 16); C/Pau Casals 5 (93 414 11 77).

Groovy threads in the **Gralla Hall** *on Portaferrisa. See page 173.*

Eccentric but slick second-hand and recycled objects at **Corrosiu**. *See page 173.*

Armand Basi

Passeig de Gràcia 49 (93 215 14 21).
Metro Passeig de Gràcia/bus 22, 24, 28. **Open** 10am-
8.30pm Mon-Sat. **Credit** AmEx, DC, MC, V. **Map D3**
One of the Spanish designers with the highest hipness rat-
ing, and his main shop is suitably in the centre of things.
This is the only place where you can find everything in Basi's
men's and women's collections, from his brightly coloured
shirts to more timeless suits, classic knitwear, evening dresses and a wide variety of accessories.

David Valls

C/València 235 (93 487 12 85).
Metro Passeig de Gràcia/bus 20, 21, 43, 44. **Open** 10am-
2pm, 5-8.30pm Mon-Fri; 10.30am-2pm, 5-8.30pm Sat.
Credit AmEx, DC, MC, V. **Map D3**
Original upmarket knitwear for new bohemians. David Valls
is known for using the newest technology to create unique
textures and fabrics. In his shop he sells an extensive collection for women – his dresses are something really special
– and a stylish yet classic selection of sweaters for men.

Groc

Rambla Catalunya 100 (93 215 01 80).
*Metro Diagonal, FGC Provença/bus 7, 16, 17, 20, 21, 43,
44.* **Open** 10am-8.30pm Mon-Sat.
Credit AmEx, DC, JCB, MC, V. **Map D3**
The place to find men's and women's clothing by the best-
known Catalan designer, Toni Miró. His clothes are designed
with flair, and beautifully made in irresistible materials.
Shoes by Miró and jewellery by Chelo Sastre also feature.
Branch: C/Muntaner 385 (93 202 30 77).

Jean-Pierre Bua

*Diagonal 469 (93 439 71 00). Bus 6, 7, 15, 27, 33, 34,
63, 67, 68.* **Open** 10am-2pm, 4.30-8.30pm Mon-Sat.
Credit AmEx, DC, MC, V. **Map D3**
First and for many years the only Barcelona shop to sell
avant-garde and top international designer fashion to a loyal
upmarket clientele. There are great exclusive selections from

Dries van Noten, Yohji Yamamoto and personal friend Jean-
Paul Gaultier, and this is also the place to go for modern
bridalwear. The friendly staff, Luis and Adolfo, make everyone welcome, and it's worth checking for special sales.

Josep Font

*Passeig de Gràcia 106 (93 415 65 50). Metro
Diagonal/bus 7, 16, 17, 22, 24, 28.* **Open** 10am-8.30pm
Mon-Sat. **Credit** AmEx, MC, V. **Map D2**
As soon as you walk through the door what strikes you is
this Catalan designer's draw upon all things Mediterranean.
Particularly outstanding in his work are his minimalist
designs and pale colours for women's day suits and evening
dresses.

Noténom

*C/Pau Claris 159 (93 487 60 84). Metro Passeig de
Gràcia/bus 7, 16, 17, 22, 24, 28, 39, 45.* **Open** 10.30am-
2pm, 4.30-8.30pm Tue-Sat. **Credit** AmEx, MC, V. **Map D3**
Opened in 1997, Noténom ('It has no name') has become a
must among stylists and the city's fashion-conscious. Owner
Mario's experience in the fashion world has made it a focal
point for all the newest trends and lines, carefully selected
from around the world (labels such as Exté, NN Studio, So
and D2). The two-level store sells both men's and women's
wear, and a selection of fashion jewellery and accessories.

Designer bargains

Contribuciones

C/Riera de Sant Miquel 30 (93 218 71 40).
*Metro Diagonal/bus 6, 7, 15, 22, 24, 27, 28, 33, 34,
127.* **Open** 11am-2pm, 5-9pm, Mon-Sat. **Credit** AmEx,
DC, MC, V. **Map D2**
Labels vary, depending on what's available, and there's a
tendency to stock the previous year's collections, but the
great bonus-point is that everything in this spacious fashion
store is sold at half-price. The shop also has its own in-house
designer, Miguel de Otos, who creates a wonderful range of
reasonably-priced silks.

Preu Bo

C/Comtal 22 (93 318 03 31). Metro Urquinaona/bus 17, 19, 40, 45. **Open** 10am-8.30pm Mon-Fri; 10.30am-2.30pm, 4.30-8.30pm Sat. **Credit** AmEx, DC, MC, V. **Map D4**
Preu Bo translates as 'good price', and considering they stock designer clothes, prices are great, with up to 65% off marked prices for end-of-lines by Roberto Verinno, Jordi Cuesta, Purificación García, Joaquim Verdú, Maria Encarnación and C'ést Comme Ça. Staff are very friendly.
Branches: C/Balmes 308 (93 414 44 57); C/Craywinckel 5 (93 418 81 74).

Fashion malls

Galeries of individual small shops have sprouted apace since the early 1980s, some occupying the interiors of whole Eixample blocks, and they are the most popular places for fashion browsing.

Bulevard Rosa

Passeig de Gràcia 55 (93 309 06 50).
Metro Passeig de Gràcia/bus 7, 16, 17, 20, 22, 24, 28, 43, 44. **Open** 10.30am-8.30pm Mon-Sat. **Map D3**
A major 1980s success story, this arcade began the *galeria* boom and has attracted some of the most interesting designers of clothes, shoes and jewellery. It has more than 100 shops, including luxury men's underwear outlet **Oltre Intimo**. It's popular with fairly well-heeled browsers, and the Diagonal branch is classier still.
Branch: Avda Diagonal 474 (93 309 06 50).

Gralla Hall

C/Portaferrisa 25 (93 412 32 72). Metro Liceu/bus 14, 38, 59. **Open** 10.30am-2pm, 4.30-8.30pm, Mon-Sat. **Map D5**
In the middle of the Portaferrisa shopping area, the Gralla is one of Barcelona's favourite places for clubwear and street fashion. For (relatively expensive) club fashion **Fantasy**, which has a great range of jewellery, bags and accessories, and **Loft Avignon** are two of the best shops in town. Round the corner is **Club**, home to two local talents; you won't find the same design twice. Downstairs, **Mayday** is the place where young clubbers get geared up for a Saturday night.

El Mercadillo

C/Portaferrisa 17 (no phone). Metro Plaça Catalunya/bus 14, 18, 38, 59, 91. **Open** 11am-9pm Mon-Sat. **Map D5**
It's hard to miss the entrance to the Mercadillo, Barcelona's grungier fashion mall – as well as the neon striplights scattered around this former palace, there's a life-sized fibreglass camel. Clothes include PVC jackets, tartan trousers, Gothic jewellery, tie-dyed jeans, lacy bodices, suede thigh-length boots and nylon bomber jackets. The wonderful bar at the back opens onto an old terrace.

High-street stores

Mango

Passeig de Gràcia 65 (passatge) (93 215 75 30). Metro Passeig de Gràcia/bus 7, 16, 17, 22, 24, 28. **Open** 10.15am-8.30pm Mon-Sat. **Credit** AmEx, DC, EC, JCB, MC, V. **Map D3**
With over 80 branches in Spain, Mango is a store with international appeal. Prices are not cheap compared to its foreign equivalents (the UK's Jigsaw or Warehouse), but fabrics used are good-quality and the clothes are well made.
Branches: C/Mar 44, Badalona (93 384 23 53); C/Portaferrisa 16 (93 301 84 83); Avda Portal de l'Àngel 7 (93 317 69 85).

Zara

C/Pelai 58 (93 301 09 78). Metro Catalunya/bus all routes to Plaça Catalunya. **Open** 10am-9pm Mon-Sat. **Credit** AmEx, DC, MC, V. **Map D4**

A highly successful store with over 100 branches throughout Spain, and which has now spread to Paris, New York and London. Whatever top designers produce each season, Zara copies at a fraction of the price. Also no-nonsense clothes for men, women and children at reasonable prices.
Branches: Avda Portal de l'Àngel 24 (93 317 65 86); C/València 245 (93 488 29 49).

Second-hand

There has never been too much of a second-hand clothes culture in Barcelona. Your best bet may be **Els Encants** market, where some stalls specialise in different types of clothes like old Levi's, 1970s leather jackets or flowery 1940s dresses.

Corrosiu

C/Magdalenes 14 (93 412 55 93). Metro Urquinaona/bus all routes to Plaça Urquinaona. **Open** 5-8pm Mon; 11am-2pm, 5-8pm, Tue-Sat. **No credit cards. Map D5**
The place where second-hand turns into style. Newly decorated with a 1970s feel, Corrusiu stocks good-quality second-hand clothes, dolly-wear, jewellery and a camp, often bizarre collection of 'recycled' objects and accessories.

Humana

Travessera de Gràcia 85 (93 415 78 88). FCG Gràcia/bus 16, 17, 27, 127. **Open** 10am 2pm, 4.30-8pm, daily. **No credit cards. Map C2**
Good-quality clothes for men and women. There's usually a fair choice of silk shirts at about 2,000ptas, and denim shirts around 1,000ptas. Profits go towards aiding Third World countries. Several more branches around the city.

Street style

Most street fashion shops are located around C/Portaferrissa and the narrow streets near La Rambla. Malls like **El Mercadillo** and **Gralla Hall** (*see above*) offer a good choice, and it's worth strolling down C/Avinyó to find work by young local designers and interesting new small shops.

Divine

C/Ramelleres 24 (93 412 61 70). Metro Catalunya/bus all routes to Plaça Catalunya. **Open** noon-9pm Mon-Sat. **Credit** AmEx, DC, JCB, MC, V. **Map D4**
An eccentric shop. Clothes by young local designers are techno-inspired, recycling garments with a twist. In the back room Divine turns into **Tasmanian** music shop, where you can find the latest in techno. Shop staff are also well-armed with info about upcoming raves, should you be interested.

Tribu

C/Avinyó 12 (93 318 65 10). Metro Jaume I/bus 17, 40, 45. **Open** 10.30am-2pm, 4.30-8.30pm, Mon-Fri; 10.30am-8.30pm Sat. **Credit** AmEx, DC, MC, V. **Map D5**
More than just a fashion store, Tribu is the hippest place for modern urban trendies to shop. Clothes for both sexes come from a range of fresh labels, international and local. Paulinha Rio falls into the latter category, and Barcelonans can't seem to get enough of her clothes. The shop also has spaces for art shows, and local DJs take turns at the decks on Saturdays.

Zsu-Zsa

C/Avinyó 50 (93 412 49 65). Metro Jaume I/bus 17, 40, 45. **Open** 11am-2pm, 5-8.30pm, Mon-Sat. **Credit** AmEx, MC, V. **Map D5**
Original, well-designed clothes for younger women, mainly one-off pieces – especially knitwear. Also a small but choice selection by young local designers.

Marketing

There are over 40 food markets in Barcelona, and every *barri* has its own. **La Boqueria** is deservedly the most famous, but there are others worth visiting: **Santa Caterina**, off Via Laietana near the Cathedral, has some of the best prices; **Sant Antoni**, near the Paral.lel, has a clothes market around the edge and food stands in the middle; and **Mercat de la Llibertat** in Gràcia has a local village atmosphere. The **Mercat del Ninot** in C/Mallorca-C/Casanova has everything you could think of, while the **Mercat de la Concepció** at València/Bruc (which has just undergone renovation) is famous for flowers. Markets open early (from 8am or earlier) and most close up at around 2-3pm, depending on each stall. Monday is not a good day to go, as stocks are low. Don't expect stalls to take credit cards, and for a note on queueing, *see page 253.*

La Boqueria (Mercat de Sant Josep)
La Rambla 91 (93 318 25 84). Metro Liceu/bus 14, 18, 38, 59. **Open** 8am-8pm Mon-Sat. **Map D5**
One of the greatest markets in the world, and certainly the most attractive and comprehensive in Barcelona. The Boqueria is always full of tourists, locals and gourmands. Even amid all the bustle, it's possible to appreciate the orderliness of its structure: fruit and vegetables around the edge, meat and chicken kept apart, and fish and seafood stalls in the centre, arranged in a circle. Enter through the main gates, set back from the Rambla, amid great colourful heaps of red peppers, cucumbers and fruit. Don't buy here, though: the stalls by the entrance are more expensive than those further inside. They do, however, offer delights such as *palmitos* (palm roots), *higos chumbos* (Indian figs) or *caña dulce* (sugar cane sticks). **J Colomines** (stall 477), on the right-hand side of the entrance, specialises in fresh herbs, tropical fruit and African food. It's one of the few places selling fresh coriander, tarragon, ginger, limes and okra throughout the year. At the back of the market, there's a stall that's a monument in itself, **Llorenç Petras** (stall 869-870) (*see* **Mushroom marvels**). On the way, admire the glistening meat and fish stalls, kept firmly in order by perfectly made-up ladies in spotless white overalls. Nothing is wasted: heads, trotters and tripe are all laid out on marble slabs. Or stop at one of the cheese stalls offering selections of the 81 types of Spanish cheeses with a *denominación de origen*: try pungent *cabrales*, dry *mahón* from Menorca, or the delicious *garrotxa*, a Catalan cheese made from goat's milk, not to mention the many delicious lamb's milk *manchegos*. Specialised stalls selling over 40 varieties of olives are dotted all over the market.

Fashion accessories
Jewellery

Forum Ferlandina
C/Ferlandina 31 (93 441 80 18). Metro Universitat/bus 24, 41, 55, 64, 91, 141. **Open** 10.30am-2pm, 5-8.30pm, Mon-Sat. **Credit** AmEx, MC, V. **Map C4**
Near the MACBA, this space features all trends in contemporary jewellery. Exclusively designed pieces are made in a variety of materials, from precious stones to plastic. There are also temporary shows by leading artists in jewellery.

Hipòtesi
Rambla Catalunya 105 (93 215 02 98). FGC Provença/bus 7, 16, 17, 20, 21, 43, 44. **Open** 10am-1.30pm, 5-8.30pm, Mon-Sat. **Credit** AmEx, DC, MC, V. **Map D3**
A wonderful place to see fine original work by Spanish and foreign designers of gold and silver jewellery, and striking costume pieces.

Joaquín Berao
C/Rosselló 277 (93 218 61 87). Metro Diagonal/bus 7, 16, 17, 22, 24, 28. **Open** 10.30am-2pm, 4.30-8pm, Mon-Fri; 11am-2pm Sat. **Credit** AmEx, DC, JCB, MC, V. **Map D3**

Mushroom marvels

Catalonia has as much of a passion for wild mushrooms as any part of the Mediterranean. There's a great deal of culture attached to funghi (*bolets* in Catalan, in Spanish *setas*). The prime season for them is the autumn, when families take to the hills on *bolet* hunts, but there are varieties available at other times of year. Few Catalan *bolets* have English names (or sometimes Spanish ones). Many fruit and vegetable shops sell woodland mushrooms each autumn – especially the highly valued, sweet *rovellons*. Lesser-known but equally tasty are *llenegues*, and nutty-flavoured *girgoles* and *reig bord* are other favourites.

If you don't trust in your ability to collect them yourself – many kinds are poisonous, after all – the best bet is to visit *bolet* specialist **Llorenç Petras** at stalls 869 and 870 in the Boqueria (*see left* **Marketing**), who stocks nothing but them, – up to 30 varieties at any time. While the best season is still autumn, he can provide *bolets* all year round: when a variety is not available locally, he gets them from other parts of Spain, Portugal, Turkey, or even Pakistan or Afghanistan if necessary.

From the baskets displayed at the stall you can choose bitter-tasting Japanese *matsutakes* for about 2,000ptas per kilo, or a mixed kilo of eight to ten varieties of local *bolets* for 1,100ptas. Petras also freezes, dries and tins mushrooms; dried varieties include *ceps* and *moixarnons*, while *llanega blanca* and *rovellons* are available in tins, as is a mixed assortment called *barretxa*. A 300gram jar of pickled *bolets* costs about 400ptas. He even grinds mushrooms to make seasonings for soups and stews. Some tips from the master: break *bolets* up by hand, not with a knife; contact with water should be kept to a minimum, as they get spongy; use olive oil in cooking, and avoid overcooking – if grilling, keep heat low. Chopped garlic, *serrano* ham and parsley can be added to them, but not much else, so as not to drown their natural flavour.

One of the most avant-garde jewellery designers in Barcelona, Berao works with titanium and aged bronze as well as gold and silver. Certainly not cheap, but he is very good. Berao also has shops in Milan and Tokyo.

Magari
C/Elisabets 18 (93 301 86 76). Metro Catalunya/bus all routes to Plaça Catalunya. **Open** 10.30am-2pm, 4.30-8.30pm, Tue-Sat. **Credit** AmEx, MC, V. **Map C4**
Less of a shop than a jewellery gallery, a space to discover the passionate world of contemporary jewellery, to understand, enjoy and wear it. Magari has a permanent collection of original and exclusive pieces and hosts temporary exhibitions of international jewellery.

Leather & luggage

A clutch of relatively inexpensive shops along C/Ferran sell leather bags, cases, belts and purses. Leather goods can also be found in most shoe shops, as well as in the department stores.

Calpa
C/Ferran 53/Call 22 (93 318 40 30). Metro Liceu, Jaume I/bus 14, 18, 38, 59. **Open** 9.30am-8pm Mon-Fri; 10am-2pm, 5-8.30pm, Sat. **Credit** AmEx, DC, JCB, MC, V. **Map D5**
Bags for every taste, from 3,000ptas lightweight carry-alls to beautifully finished leather cases for 30,000ptas. **Branch:** C/del Pi 5 (93 412 58 22).

Casa Antich SCP
C/Consolat del Mar 27-31 (93 310 43 91). Metro Jaume I/bus 17, 40, 45. **Open** 9am-8pm Mon-Sat. **Credit** AmEx, DC, MC, V. **Map D5**
A huge family-owned shop that stocks a vast range of bags, briefcases, suitcases and enormous metal trunks. This part of the Ribera has dealt in luggage and baggage literally for centuries, and Antich is one of a clutch of shops that keeps up the tradition. If they haven't got what you want, they'll make it for you. Prices are very reasonable.

Loewe
Passeig de Gràcia 35 (93 216 04 00). Metro Passeig de Gràcia/bus 7, 16, 17, 22, 24, 28. **Open** 9.30am-2pm, 4.30-8pm, Mon-Sat. **Credit** AmEx, DC, JCB, MC, TC, V. **Map D3**
Loewe, one of the most celebrated leather companies in the world, occupies the Lleó Morera building in the **Mansana de la Discòrdia**, and earned condemnation in the 1960s when they modernised the façade. They have since been obliged to restore it. Inside there are high-priced bags and suitcases of superb quality. Some foreign currencies are accepted. **Branches:** Avda Diagonal 570 (93 200 09 20); C/Johann Sebastian Bach 8 (93 202 31 50).

Lingerie & underwear

Casa Ciutad
Avda Portal de l'Àngel 14 (93 317 04 33). Metro Catalunya/bus all routes to Plaça Catalunya. **Open** 10am-8.30pm Mon-Fri; 10.30am-9pm, Sat. **Credit** AmEx, DC, MC, V. **Map D4/D5**

This charming shop opened in 1892, and sells some of the prettiest women's underwear you can find. The sign at the door says 'manufacturers of combs and articles for the dressing-table', and its collection of combs, in every shape, size and material – including virtual antique models – is truly something to behold. Opening times are variable, and some Saturdays it may stay open at midday.

Janina

Rambla Catalunya 94 (93 215 04 21). Metro Diagonal/ FGC Provença/bus 22, 24, 28. **Open** *Oct-May* 10am-2pm, 4.30-8pm Mon-Sat; *May-Sept* 10am-2pm, 4.30-8.30pm Mon-Sat. **Credit** AmEx, DC, MC, V. **Map D3**
A well-established shop that sells its own exclusive underwear in beautiful silks and satins, as well as stocking designs by Risk and La Perla – a luxurious set of silk pyjamas can cost 23,000ptas, and an still more sumptuous matching dressing-gown 24,000ptas. They also have a big selection of swimsuits and bikinis.
Branch: Santacana Via Augusta 180 (93 209 00 00).

WC – Susana Riera

C/Avinyó (93 201 58 75). Metro Jaume I/ bus 17, 40, 45. **Open** 11am-2pm, 5-8.30pm, Mon-Sat. **Credit** AmEx, MC, V. **Map D5**
Susi and best mate Raul C are the moving spirits of this tiny shop selling Susana Riera's collection of pretty, trendy cotton underwear and women's swimwear.

Scarves & textiles

Rafael Teja Atelier

C/Santa Maria 18 (93 315 20 86). Metro Jaume I/bus 17, 40, 45. **Open** 11am-2pm, 4.30-8pm Tue-Sat. **Credit** MC, V. **Map D/E5**
A specialist scarf shop by Santa Maria del Mar with wares that range from cashmere shawls from Nepal to hand-painted silk foulards made by artisans round the corner. Prices suit all purses: from 3,000ptas to a more luxurious 15,000ptas. There's also a small fashion jewellery section.

Shoes

Muxart

C/Rosselló 230 (93 488 10 64). Metro Diagonal/bus 7, 16, 17, 22, 24, 28. **Open** 10am-2pm, 4.30-8.30pm, Mon-Fri; 10am-2pm, 5-8.30pm, Sat. **Credit** AmEx, MC, V. **Map D3**
Started in the Balearics in the 1980s and now one of the most fashionable shoe brands, Muxart links design with traditional hand-made manufacturing, using exquisite leather combined with other rare materials. Irresistible sandals, bags and other accessories, and a small, tasteful range for men.

Noel Barcelona

C/Pelai 46 (93 317 86 38).
Metro Plaça Catalunya/bus all routes to Plaça Catalunya. **Open** 9.45am-2pm, 4.30-8.30pm Mon-Fri; 9.45am-8.30pm Sat. **Credit** MC, V. **Map D4**
Funky, trendy shoes in bright colours with spiky heels; knee-high red (or, if you prefer, green or silver) boots with platform soles – Noel Barcelona's footwear is not for the shy.

Tony Mora

Passeig de Gràcia 33 (93 487 65 64) Metro Passeig de Gràcia/bus 7, 16, 17, 22, 24, 28. **Open** 10.15am-2pm, 5-8.30pm, Mon-Sat. **Credit** AmEx, DC, EC, MC, $TC, V. **Map D3-4**
Nothing but boots – ankle-high or knee-high numbers; cowboy boots with an urban look, and classic Spanish *camperas*.

Traditional shoes

The traditional Catalan shoe (*espardenyes/alpargatas*) is a type of espadrille with ribbons attached. It's now used as leisurewear, and by performers of the *sardana* – Catalunya's national dance.

La Manual Alpargatera

C/Avinyó 7 (93 301 01 72). Metro Liceu/bus 14, 18, 38, 59. **Open** 9.30am-1.30pm, 4.30-8pm, Mon-Sat. **Credit** AmEx, DC, JCB, MC, V. **Map D5**

Liquid assets

The prime Catalan wine area, the Penedés, produces good reds, whites and rosés: the Torres and René Barbier labels are reliable, and Bach whites have a great dry tang. The most famous of Spanish wines, Rioja, can be found everywhere, but quality is pretty variable. Red Cune is always good, and can cost as little as 600ptas. In recent years the Ribera del Duero and Navarra regions have been as highly regarded as Rioja for reds.

Catalan *cava*, sparkling wine, also hails from the Penedès. *Caves* are labelled, according to quality and sweetness, *Brut Nature*, *Brut*, *Seco* and *Semi-Seco*, the latter of which can be not *seco* at all but very sweet, and is the cheapest. Prices range from 500ptas: expect to pay around 900ptas for a decent *Brut*. For more on Catalan wines, *see pages 242-4*.

El Celler de Gèlida

C/Vallespir 65 (339 26 41). Metro Plaça del Centre/bus 54. **Open** 9am-2pm, 5-8.30pm Mon-Fri; 9.30am-2.30pm, 5-8.30pm Sat. Closed Aug. **Credit** MC, V.
A little way off the beaten track in Sants, but this modern cellar has over 3,000 labels and an unbeatable selection of Catalan wines. Staff are knowledgeable, and advise many restaurants on their lists.

Lafuente

C/Johann Sebastian Bach 20 (201 25 21). FGC Bonanova/bus 14. **Open** 9am-2pm, 4.30-8.30pm, Mon-Fri; 9am-2pm Sat. **Credit** MC, V. **Map C1**
A smart wine store with another huge selection, covering wines, *cavas* and spirits. A good choice of non-Spanish wines.

Vila Viniteca

C/Agullers 7-9 (310 19 56/268 32 27). Metro Jaume I/bus 17, 40, 45. **Open** 8am-3pm, 5-9pm, Mon-Sat. **Credit** AmEx, DC, MC, V. **Map D5**
Joaquim Vila continues the work of his grandfather, who opened this shop in 1932. From outside it looks like a normal grocery store, but inside there's a huge selection of wine and *cava*, all explained in a monthly broadsheet.

Vins i Caves La Catedral

Plaça de Ramon Berenguer el Gran 1 (319 07 27). Metro Jaume I/bus 17, 40, 45. **Open** 4.30-8.30pm Mon; 10.30am-2.45pm, 4.30-8.30pm ,Tue-Sat. **Credit** AmEx, DC, JCB, MC, V. **Map D5**
A good supply of wines from all over Spain, and a particularly good choice of Catalan wines and *cavas*.

*Yum. Some of **Escribà**'s creations.*

In business since 1910, and today Sr Tasies continues the tradition of individually-made espadrilles. He's an expert on this kind of footwear, knowing everything from the types of hemp or jute used for the sole to the hundreds of traditional variations in colour and style. His expertise doesn't go unnoticed: regulars include Michael Douglas, Jack Nicholson and the Pope. Espadrilles can be made to order: your template is stored for future orders. Prices range from 600 to 6,000ptas.

Florists

Flower and plant shops can be found everywhere; many offer Interflora delivery service. As well as the flower stalls on the Rambla, there are stalls at the **Mercat de la Concepció** (corner of C/València-C/Bruc, **Map E3**) open all night.

Arte Japonés
C/Tamarit 168, baixos (93 442 64 85). Metro Sant Antoni/ bus 24, 41, 55, 64, 91. **Open** 8.30am-8.30pm Mon-Sat; 8.30am-3pm Sun, public holidays. **Credit** MC, V. **Map C4**
Near the Sant Antoni market, this shop offers more than the traditional bunch of roses or gladioli – from bonsai to bouquets of exotic origin, it's all blooming here.

Food
Chocolate, cakes & bread
Escribà Pastisseries
Gran Via de les Corts Catalanes 546 (93 454 75 35). Metro Urgell/bus 9, 14, 24, 50, 56. **Open** 8am-9pm Mon-Sun. **Credit** V. **Map C4**

A traditional chocolate shop famous for its victories in the Easter cake competition (*see chapter* **Barcelona by Season**). Every year larger and more ambitious creations are produced, such as the huge chocolate woman who languished in the shop for several months. Antoni Escribà, author of these extravaganzas and champion *pastisser* of Barcelona, is a local celebrity. His most delectable cakes are the *rambla*, made from biscuit, truffle and chocolate (250ptas). The Rambla branch is installed in the Antigua Casa Figueras, and has a beautiful mosaic façade.
Branch: La Rambla 83 (93 301 60 27).

Forn de Pa Sant Jordi
C/Llibreteria 8 (93 310 40 16).
Metro Jaume I/bus 17, 40, 45. **Open** 7am-9pm Mon-Sat.
No credit cards. Map D5
There's nearly always a queue outside the Sant Jordi bread shop – testimony to the delicious cakes on sale inside. The bread is good, and the *xuxos/chuchos* (cream doughnuts) are particularly tasty, but the speciality is *tortellet de cabell d'àngel*, a pastry filled with 'angel's hair' (spun-candied fruit).

La Mallorquina
Plaça de les Olles 7 (93 319 38 83). Metro Barceloneta/ bus 16, 17, 45. **Open** 8am-2pm, 5-8.30pm Tue-Sat; 8am-3pm Sun. Closed Aug. **No credit cards. Map E5**
The smell of baking *carquinyolis* (a Catalan biscuit made with almonds) hits you as you walk past La Mallorquina. The chocolate croissants are also worth tucking into.

Pastisseria Maurí
Rambla Catalunya 102 (93 215 10 20/09 98).
Metro Diagonal, FGC Provença/bus 7, 16, 17, 22, 24, 28.
Open 8am-9pm Mon-Sat; 9am-3pm, 5-9pm, Sun, public holidays; Closed *July-Aug* Sun afternoon.
Credit MC, V. **Map D3**
Granja Mauri opened in 1885 as a grocery specialising in cakes, and the elaborate painted ceiling is a relic from that time. Enjoy delicate sandwiches or lunch in the tea room, or take away a ready-to-eat meal from what remains of the grocery store. The nearby branch sells home-made chocolates.
Branch: Rambla Catalunya 103 (93 215 81 46).

Colmados/general food stores
Colmado Murrià
C/Roger de Llúria 85 (93 215 57 89). Metro Passeig de Gràcia/bus 39, 43, 44, 45. **Open** 10am-2pm, 5-9pm Mon-Sat. **Credit** AmEx, DC, MC, V. **Map D3**
Two blocks away from Passeig de Gràcia you'll find this magnificent *Modernista* shop with tiled decoration designed by Ramon Casas, stocking a wonderful range of food stuffs and over 300 wines, including their own *Cava Murrià*.

Colmado Quilez
Rambla Catalunya 63 (93 215 23 56/93 215 87 85). Metro Passeig de Gràcia/bus 7, 16, 17, 22, 24, 28. **Open** 9am-2pm, 4.30-8.30pm, Mon-Fri; 9am-2pm Sat; *Oct-Dec* 9am-2pm, 4.30-8.30pm, Mon-Sat. **Credit** AmEx, MC, V. **Map D3**
A classic in its own right, one of the monuments of the Eixample. The walls of this store are lined with cans and bottles from all over the world: there are huge quantities of hams and cheeses, and it stocks every type of alcohol: saké, six types of schnapps, a wall of whiskies, and *cava* from over 55 bodegas, including one, Cava La Fuente, sold exclusively in this shop. The excellent own-brand coffee, Cafe Quilez, is imported from Colombia – and ground for you on the spot.

Food specialities
As well as selling Spanish dry-cured ham (*jamón serrano*) ham shops offer other cold meats such as chorizo, *salchichón*, Catalan *botifarra* and spicy

Mallorcan *sobresada*. The quality of *jamón* varies a lot, and you can expect to pay up to 14,000ptas a kilo for the best, traditionally cured *jabugo* ham. All cheese shops in Spain have classic *manchego* – *seco* (or even *seco añejo*) for fans of strong, dry cheeses, *semi* or *tierno* for something milder – but it's also easy to find other, more unusual varieties.

Cafés el Magnífico

C/Argentería 64 (93 319 60 81). Metro Jaume I/bus 17, 40, 45. **Open** 8.30am-1.30pm, 4-8pm, Mon-Fri; 9.30am-1.30pm Sat. Closed *July-Sept* Sat. **No credit cards. Map D5**
Since 1919 the Sans family has imported, prepared and blended coffees from around the world. Prices vary from 1,200ptas per kilo for a simple blend, to 12,000ptas per kilo for the especially smooth Jamaican coffee. They also stock over 150 cases of tea, including blends from Taiwan, Nepal, India, Sri Lanka, China, Japan and Sikkim.

Casa Gispert

C/Sombrerers 23 (93 319 75 35). Metro Jaume I/bus 17, 40, 45. **Open** 9am-1.30pm, 4-7.30pm, Mon-Fri; 10am-2pm, 5-8pm, Sat. Closed *July-Aug* Sat. **Credit** MC, V. **Map D5**
Founded in the 1850s, Casa Gispert is a wholesale outlet famous for its top-quality nuts, dried fruit and coffee. Both nuts and coffee (there are two blends, sold under the trade name of Sabor) are roasted on site in the magnificent original wood-burning stove. A kilo (the minimum order) of Iranian pistachios costs 900ptas. Delve into enormous baskets of almonds and hazelnuts, still warm from the oven.

Formatgeria Cirera

C/Cera 45 (93 441 07 59). Metro Sant Antoni/bus 20, 64, 91. **Open** 9am-2pm, 5.30-8.30pm, Mon-Fri; 9am-2pm Sat. **Credit** MC, V. **Map C5**
As well as home-made cheesecakes – suitable for diabetics – this shop has a great selection of Spanish cheeses, including some from small dairies. There's also fine *sobresada* from Mallorca, and pâtés, hams and cavas from all over Spain.

Jamón Jamón

C/Mestre Nicolau 4 (93 209 41 03).
Bus 6, 7, 33, 34, 66, 67, 68. **Open** 8am-midnight Mon-Sat. **Credit** AmEx, DC, MC, V. **Map C2**
Nothing but the best quality *jabugo* ham. Buy half a kilo, or invest in a whole leg. Like many of these places, Jamón Jamón combines shop with café, and upstairs a restaurant of sorts offers *pa amb tomàquet*, ham and cheese, and wine.

Magatzem de Pernils, Formatges i Embotits

C/Enric Granados 22 (93 453 19 53). Metro Passeig de Gràcia/bus 20, 21, 43, 44. **Open** 8am-2pm, 5-8.30pm, Mon-Sat. **Credit** AmEx, MC, V. **Map C3**
An endless selection of different *serrano* and *jabugo* hams, and an equally superb choice of Spanish charcuterie and cheeses.

Mantequerías Puig

C/Xuclà 21 (93 318 12 84). Metro Catalunya/bus all routes to Plaça Catalunya. **Open** 8.30am-2pm, 4.30-8pm, Mon-Fri; 8.30am-2pm Sat. **Credit** MC, V. **Map D5**
As well as serving the public this traditional cheese shop supplies many local hotels and restaurants. If you don't see what you want, ask: there are dozens more cheeses out back.

Mel Viadiu

C/Comtal 20 (93 317 04 23). Metro Catalunya/bus17, 19, 40, 45. **Open** 10am-2pm, 4.30-8.30pm Mon-Sat. **Credit** AmEx, DC, MC, V. **Map D4**
Specialists in local honey – most of it from Caldes de Montbui, just outside Barcelona. Try their honey sweets to soothe the throat, and there's a large fridge of pots of pure

royal jelly. Sr Viadiu, who exports honey to Fortnum & Mason, also stocks an array of jams and foreign cereals.
Branch: C/Creu Coberta 85 (93 431 65 11).

Health foods

Herbolari Ferran

Plaça Reial 18 (93 304 20 05). Metro Liceu/bus 14, 18, 38, 59. **Open** 9.30am-2pm, 4.30-8pm Mon-Sat. **Credit** MC, V. **Map D5**
Herbolari Ferran has been serving a faithful public since the 1940s, and the large, recently-inaugurated basement area is divided between an old-fashioned herb shop, a modern self-service store, coffee/teashop, bookshop and area for exhibitions, talks and the like. A very all-round health service.

Macrobiòtic Zen

C/Muntaner 12 (93 454 60 23). Metro Universitat/bus 9, 14, 24, 41, 50, 55, 56, 64, 91, 141. **Open** 9am-8pm Mon-Fri; *Aug* times vary, phone to check. **No credit cards. Map C4**
All kinds of cheeses suitable for macrobiotic, diabetic and vegetarian diets, and a self-service canteen in the back.

Supermarkets

Caprabo is a small chain with at least one branch in every district. With a car, the hypermarkets of **Glòries** and **Hipercor** (*see* **One-stop**) become accessible; **Pryca** hypermarkets are near the north and southern exits to Barcelona on the ring road.

Gifts & crafts

Ceràmica Villegas

C/Comtal 31 (93 317 53 30). Metro Urquinaona/bus 17, 19, 40, 45. **Open** 9.30am-1.30pm, 5-8.30pm, Mon-Fri; 10am-2pm, 5-8.30pm, Sat. **Credit** AmEx, DC, MC, V. **Map D4**
Worldwide distributors of ceramics. The three-floor building houses a wide selection, from one-off or limited-series art pieces to more popular rustic styles. There's a small selection of antique water jugs and ceramic jewellery, too.

Coses de Casa

Plaça Sant Josep Oriol 5 (93 302 73 28). Metro Liceu/bus 14, 18, 38, 59. **Open** 9.45am-1.30pm, 4.30-8pm, Mon-Fri; 10am-2pm, 5-8.30pm, Sat. **Credit** AmEx, DC, MC, V. **Map D5**
The rolls of beautiful woven fabric for sale at Coses de Casa are traditional, Moorish influenced Mallorcan work. Cushions and bedcovers abound, and curtains or cushions can be made to order by the staff.

2 Bis

C/Bisbe Irurita 2 bis (93 315 09 54).
Metro Jaume I/bus 17, 40, 45. **Open** 10am-2pm, 4.30-8.30pm, Mon-Fri; 10am-2pm, 5-8.30pm Sat. **Credit** AmEx, DC, MC, V. **Map D5**
Quirky objects for everyone – toys for kids and adults, tin planes, life-sized Tintin characters, and lots of other items in wood, paper and papier mâché. A great place to explore, with an upper floor that's almost as packed as the main shop.

Germanes García

C/Banys Nous 15 (93 318 66 46). Metro Liceu/14, 18, 38, 59. **Open** 4.30-7.30pm Mon; 9.30am-1.30pm, 4.30-7.30pm, Tue-Sat. **Credit** MC, V. **Map D5**
There's no name on the shop-front, but it's impossible to miss this wickerwork outlet from the number of baskets hanging

*Lose yourself among the junk at **Els Encants***.

in the entrance. Inside, browse through wickerware of every description – from fruit baskets at 800ptas, to laundry baskets for 3,500ptas. Much of the furniture, which includes screens and chests of drawers, is made in the workshop.

Kitsch

Placeta de Montcada 10 (93 319 57 68). Metro Jaume I/bus 17, 40, 45. **Open** *Oct-Easter* 11am-3pm, 5-8pm Tue-Sat; *Easter-Sept* Mon-Sat. **Credit** AmEx, MC, V. **Map E5**
Guadalupe Bayona, sister of twins Pili & Mili, a comedy duo popular in Spanish 1960s films, combines being a lawyer with a passion for making objects in papier mâché. Most of her creations are inspired by paintings, by Klimt, Botero, Dalí or Picasso, but she also recreates famous living personalities. *La Rocío*, a life-sized lady in flamenco dress who stands at the entrance, is the symbol of the shop. Prices from 3,000ptas to 100,000ptas, if you wish to be immortalised.

Les Muses del Palau

C/Sant Pere Més Alt 1 (93 268 31 95) Metro Urquinaona/bus 17, 19, 40, 45. **Open** 10am-8pm Mon-Sat. **Credit** AmEx, V. **Map D5**
This recently inaugurated and tastefully decorated shop just beside the Palau de la Música has some original ideas for gifts inspired by Dalí, Gaudí and others, and makes a welcome change from the standard kitsch souvenir shop.

Markets: flea, art & antique

Barri Gòtic antique/art markets

Antique Market *Avda de la Catedral 6 (93 291 61 00). Metro Jaume I/bus 17, 19, 40, 45.* **Open** *Jan-Nov* 10am-10pm Thur. **No credit cards**.
Art Market *Plaça Sant Josep Oriol (93 291 61 00). Metro Liceu/bus 14, 18, 38, 59, 91.* **Open** *first weekend each month* 10am-10pm Fri-Sat; 10am-3pm Sun. **No credit cards. Map D5**
Bric-a-brac and antique stalls are spread attractively in front of the Cathedral every week. Few bargains, but it's always

enjoyable to rummage through the lovingly displayed religious artefacts, pipes, watches, lace hankies and old telephones. Before Christmas, it transfers to the Plaça del Pi. An **art market** of variable quality is held in Plaça del Pi/Plaça Sant Josep Oriol one weekend each month through the year.

Book & Coin Market

Mercat de Sant Antoni, C/Comte d'Urgell 1 (93 423 42 87). Metro Sant Antoni/bus 20, 24, 41, 55, 64, 141. **Open** 9am-2pm (approx) Sun. **No credit cards. Map C4**
This Sunday morning second-hand book market is an institution in Barcelona and at times can get very crowded. Rummage through boxes of dusty tomes, old magazines and video games, and admire the collections of old coins. If it becomes too much, look for a table at the nearby bar **Els Tres Tombs** and watch the bargain-hunters pass by.

Brocanters del Port Vell

Portal de la Pau (93 317 01 12). Metro Drassanes/bus 14, 18, 36, 38, 57, 59. 64. **Open** 10am-8pm Sat, Sun. **No credit cards. Map C6/D6**
A relatively new bric-a-brac and antique market – inaugurated 1997 – held near the bottom of the Rambla beside the Maremàgnum bridge. Because of its ideal location it has already established itself as a hide-out for the many Barcelona people on the look-out for that extra piece to add to their collection – ceramics, china, coins, old records, holy water fonts, costume jewellery, mantillas, toys, fountain pens, you name it – while going for a Sunday morning stroll along the seafront.

Els Encants – Flea Market

C/Dos de Maig, corner C/Consell de Cent (93 246 30 30). Metro Glòries/bus 62, 92. **Open** *June-Sept* 7am-8pm, *Oct-May* 8am-6pm Mon, Wed, Fri, Sat. **No credit cards. Map F4-3**
Despite modernisation all around it, Els Encants (also known as the *Mercat de Bellcaire*) remains the most authentic of flea markets – from its fringes, where old men lay out battered shoes and toys on cloths on the ground, to the centre, where

a persistent shopper can snaffle up bargains to furnish a whole flat. Here, you'll find earthenware jugs and country furniture from La Mancha, second-hand clothes, some good new clothes and textiles, and loads and loads of fascinating junk. If possible avoid Saturdays, as it can get very crowded, and watch out for short-changing, and pickpockets. It's officially open in the afternoons, but many stalls pack up at midday. For bargains, get there first thing in the morning.

Stamp & Coin Market

Plaça Reial (no phone). Metro Liceu/ bus 14, 18, 38, 59, 91. **Open** 9am-2pm (approx) Sun. **No credit cards. Map D5**
A market for enthusiasts, this somewhat incongruous gathering blends surprisingly well with the sometimes unsalubrious goings-on in Plaça Reial. Having inspected the coins, stamps and rocks, you can take an aperitif in the sun and watch the experts poring over each other's collections.

Records & music

Casa Luthier

C/Balmes 73 (93 454 15 78)
Metro Passeig de Gràcia/bus 7, 16, 17, 20, 21, 43, 44.
Open 9.30am-1.30pm, 4.30-8pm, Mon-Fri; 10am-2pm Sat.
Credit AmEx, MC, V. **Map D3**
Nothing but guitars, in all shapes and sizes. They also stock books and magazines on the subject, and have a school where guitar classes are given.

Discos Castelló

C/Tallers 3 (93 318 20 41). Metro Catalunya/bus all routes to Plaça Catalunya. **Open** 10am-2pm, 4.30-8.30pm, Mon-Sat. **Credit** AmEx, DC, MC, V. **Map D4**
Discos Castelló is a chain of small shops all with a slightly different emphasis. This one specialises in classical music. The others – all nearby – sell more pop, and the Nou de la Rambla branch has a big selection of ethnic music and flamenco. The staff know their stuff.
Branches: C/Nou de la Rambla 15 (93 302 42 36); C/Sant Pau 2 (93 302 23 95); C/Tallers 7 (93 302 59 46); C/Tallers 9 (93 412 72 85); C/Tallers 79 (93 301 35 75).

Ethnomusic

C/Bonsuccès 6 (93 301 18 84). Metro Catalunya/bus all routes to Plaça Catalunya. **Open** 5-8pm Mon; 11am-2pm, 5-8pm, Tue-Sat. **Credit** AmEx, MC, V. **Map C4**
This ethnic music shop in the Raval is a far cry from Barcelona's designer shops. It has finds in music from any place on the planet, with the Americas, Africa and Asia all well-represented. However, what most foreign visitors seem to be hunting is something unique in flamenco. Staff know their business and are extremely helpful.

Jazz Collectors

Passatge Forasté 4 bis (93 212 7478). FGC Tibidabo/bus 17, 22, 73. **Open** 10.30am-2pm, 4.30-8.15pm, Mon-Fri; 11am-2pm Sat. **Credit** MC, V.
Make the pilgrimage up to Jazz Collectors, known all over Spain for its eclectic collection ranging from be-bop to swing. Enthusiasts from abroad come here to find deleted American and Japanese jazz records, which can cost up to 150,000ptas.

Virgin Megastore

Passeig de Gràcia 16 (93 412 44 77). Metro Plaça Catalunya/bus all routes to Plaça Catalunya. **Open** 10am-9.30pm Mon-Thur; 10am-10.30pm Fri-Sat. **Credit** AmEx, MC, V. **Map D4**
The arrival of Virgin in Barcelona was received with as much excitement as you would expect from a visit by a rock star. The three-floor megastore seems to be living up to expectations, with all kinds of Spanish and international music, and a healthy stock of videos in English.

Tobacco & cigars

L'Estanc de Laietana

Via Laietana 4 (93 310 10 34). Metro Jaume I/bus 17, 40, 45. **Open** 8.30am-2pm, 4-8pm, Mon-Fri; 9am-2pm Sat. **Credit** (for gifts, not cigarettes) MC, V. **Map D5**
The busiest and most famous of the tobacco shops in Barcelona is run with zest and enthusiasm by Señor Porta. One hundred brands of cigarettes and 100 types of rolling tobacco are on sale. He has built a *humidor* at sea level in his underground cellar to store his clients' cigars.

Gimeno

Passeig de Gràcia 101 (93 237 20 78). Metro Diagonal/ bus 7, 16, 17, 22, 24, 28. **Open** 10am-2pm, 4-8.30pm, Mon-Sat. **Credit** AmEx, DC, JCB, MC, V. **Map D3**
Packed with Catalans having their lighters repaired, Gimeno has anything and everything to do with smoking. The wooden walls are lined with hundreds of pipes and lighters. Plus, there's an interesting collection of ornate walking sticks.

Small is beautiful

Until recently, shops in Barcelona kept to a specific trade, and sought to know it well. As a result, the city has about the most eccentric range of specialists you'll find anywhere.

Almacenes del Pilar

C/Boqueria 43 (93 317 79 84). Metro Liceu/ bus 14, 18, 38, 59. **Open** 10am-1.30pm, 4.30-8pm, Mon-Sat. **Credit** MC, V. **Map D5**
This quaint shop exhibits *Mantones de Manila* (fringed embroidered silk shawls) in its window, and inside there are shawls, *mantillas* and a huge range of materials used in traditional costumes in all the regions of Spain – see the fantastic brocades used in Valencian outfits. If a red woollen sash is what you've been searching, look no more.

Aureliano Monge

C/Boters 2 (93 317 94 35). Metro Liceu/bus 14, 38, 59. **Open** 9am-1.30pm, 4-8pm, Mon-Sat. **Credit** AmEx, DC, MC, V. **Map D5**
Even if old stamps and coins are not your thing, this *Modernista* shop is worth a look through the window. Designed in 1904 by Calonge, a disciple of Gaudi, it has walls covered in neo-Gothic dark mahogany and four seats which beat classification. The business deals in stamps and coins.

La Casa del Feltre

C/Canvis Vells 8 (93 319 39 00). Metro Jaume I/ bus 17, 40, 45. **Open** 9.30am-1.30pm, 4-8pm, Mon-Fri; 10am-1.30pm Sat. Closed Aug.
Credit AmEx, DC, MC, V. **Map D5**
A shop that's been selling nothing but felt since 1795, initially mostly for sailors' uniforms. On the ground floor there are over 120 different shades of material, which can be bought in small squares for school projects or by the metre for card tables. They also manufacture fancy-dress suits, in felt of course, which are on sale from Christmas to Carnival.

Casa Moreli

C/Banys Nous 13 (no phone). Metro Liceu/ bus 14, 18, 38, 59. **Open** 5.30-8pm Mon-Fri. Closed Aug. **No credit cards. Map D5**
A shop devoted to feathers, wrapped carefully in tissue paper and stored in white cardboard boxes stacked up high around the room. There are some rather dusty but beautifully made feather masks in the window; inside, old ladies try to flog their mangy goose feathers to Sra Moreli.

Cereria Subirà

*Baixada de Llibreteria 7 (93 315 26 06). Metro Jaume I/
bus 17, 40, 45.* **Open** *9am-1.30pm, 4-7.30pm, Mon-Fri;
9am-1.30pm Sat.* **Credit** AmEx, JCB, MC, V. **Map D5**
The oldest shop in Barcelona opened in 1761 as a ladies' fashion store, but for many decades has been a candle shop.
Apart from the extraordinary range of candles, it's worth a
visit for the original décor alone, with steps swirling down
from the gallery, and two black maidens holding up torch-
like lights at the foot of the stairs.

Collector's Club

*Baixada de Llibreteria 8 (93 315 11 05/fax 93 310 26
46). Metro Liceu/bus 14, 38, 59.* **Open** *11.30am-1.30pm,
5-8pm, Mon-Sat.* **Credit** V. **Map D5**
Run by a young French woman, this tiny shop is crammed
ceiling-high with thousands of collectors' items relating to the
world of perfume, miniature bottles, mostly old but some new,
and old posters, labels, adverts…. She also buys and sells
costume jewellery from the nineteenth century to the 1950s.

La Cubana

*C/Boqueria 26 (93 317 18 40). Metro Liceu/bus 14, 38,
59.* **Open** *9.30am-1.30pm, 4.30-8pm, Mon-Sat.* **Credit**
AmEx, MC, V. **Map D5**
Founded 1824, this quaint shop is of little interest from an
architectural point of view, but it's an institution in the old
part of town, where it has supplied ladies with fans, silk
shawls, gloves, *mantillas* and the like. Demand for such
things is not what it was, but they seem to be holding out in
the hope that the changing winds of fashion might blow back
in their direction…

Drap

*C/del Pi 14 (tel/fax 93 318 14 87). Metro Liceu/bus 14,
38, 59.* **Open** *9.30am-1.30pm, 4.30-8.30pm, Mon-Sat.*
Credit AmEx, DC, MC, V. **Map D5**
The name means rag (dolls), and Drap is the place to find
anything you could dream of related to the world of dolls'
houses. Some articles are designed and made by owner, Pilar
Durán herself. The selection of bathroom accessories, including perfumes and soaps, is incredible. You can buy a chair
for 2,000ptas; an empty house for around 100,000ptas.

Herboristeria del Rei

*C/del Vidre 1 (93 318 05 12). Metro Liceu/bus 14, 18,
38, 59.* **Open** *10am-2pm, 5-8pm Mon-Sat.* **Credit** MC, V.
Map D5
In an archway between C/Ferran and Plaça Reial, this unique
shop was founded in 1818 by Josep Vilà, and originally called
La Lineana after the great botanist Linnaeus. It was decorated by the theatre designer Francesc Soler i Rovirosa with
an ornate interior combining a neoclassical structure and
Gothic details. Inside, around the shop at second-floor level
there is a grand balcony, while the walls belows are lined
with what seem to be hundreds of tiny specimen drawers all
individually worked in marquetry or decorated with miniature watercolours. In 1858 the shop was made official herbal-
ist to Queen Isabel II, and changed its name to *Herboristeria
del Rei*. It went back to *La Lineana* in the two republican
periods, and these name changes are still visible today in the
gold lettering on the door.

El Ingenio

*C/Rauric 6 (93 317 71 38). Metro Liceu/bus 14, 18, 38,
59.* **Open** *10am-1.30pm, 4.15-8pm, Mon-Fri; 10am-2pm,
5-8.15pm, Sat.* **Credit** AmEx, MC, V. **Map D5**
Ingenio lives up to its name with a truly ingenious collection
of paper, cardboard, feather and papier mâché masks and
party accessories. There are fancy-dress outfits, carnival
clothes, poppers, decorations, puppets, tricks and jokes to
choose from, and stick-on Dali moustaches are 200ptas each,
and can be twisted into exactly the right shape. The shop,
naturally, does booming business at Carnival time.

El Rei de la Màgia. *Weird.*

Merceria i Novetats – Manel Mogas Puig

*C/Llibreteria 5 (93 310 57 46). Metro Jaume I/bus 17,
40, 45.* **Open** *9.30am-1.30pm, 4.30-8pm, Mon-Fri; 10am-
2pm Sat.* **No credit cards**. **Map D5**
Buttons, lace, tassles and all you might need in sewing,
embroidering or decorating in a beautiful old shop a stone's
throw from the Ajuntament, where the owner seems to sit
for hours presiding over the cash register.

Perfumeria Prat

*La Rambla 68, (93 317 71 39). Metro Liceu/
bus 14, 18, 38, 59.* **Open** *10am-2pm, 4-8.30pm, Mon-Sat.*
Credit AmEx, DC, MC, V. **Map D5**
This beautiful perfumery, which until 1997 occupied part of
the Liceu building, has been transported pillar by pillar to a
new site across the Rambla. This undertaking was justified
by the history of the place: the first *perfumeria* established
in all Spain, by a certain Renaud Germain in 1847. Its owners never rested on their laurels, and today it continues to
thrive, with a fine selection of perfumes and cosmetics.

El Rei de la Màgia

*C/Princesa 11 (93 319 39 20). Metro Liceu/bus 14, 18,
38, 59.* **Open** *10am-2pm, 5-8pm, Mon-Fri, 10am-2pm Sat.*
Credit MC, V. **Map D5**
Many a magician's training ground, founded in 1881, this is
anything but an ordinary retail outlet. Starting with the decoration, it forms a small stage with a delicately carved
counter, behind which is a theatrical black curtain. Walls are
covered with autographed photos of magicians. There are
no pre-established prices and one doesn't go there to buy a
specific item, but rather develop an idea or concept which
might require the use of a special chair, box or mechanism,
specially made for the purpose. Ritual is perhaps the key to
describing the way everything happens here.

Solingen Paris-Barcelona (Ganiveteria Roca SA)

*Plaça del Pi 3 (93 302 12 41/fax 93 412 53 49).
Metro Liceu/bus 14, 18, 38, 59.* **Open** *9.45am-1.30pm, 4.15-
8pm, Mon-2pm, 5-8pm, Sat. Closed two weeks
Aug.* **Credit** AmEx, DC, MC, V. **Map D5**
Every cutting instrument under the sun is available here.
Knives and scissors for all thinkable purposes, and of all
shapes and sizes, are wrapped in green felt and brought forth
for inspection by sombre salesmen. Seriously weird.

Sombrereria Obach

*C/Call 2 (93 318 40 94). Metro Liceu/
bus 14, 18, 38, 59.* **Open** *9.30am-1.30pm, 4-8pm, Mon-
Sat.* **Credit** MC, V. **Map D5**
Hats of all varieties are for sale in Sr Obach's traditional
establishment, from nylon pom-poms through top-quality
felt berets, to formal headgear for men and women.

Services

Places to have your hair cut, hire an outfit, buy a ticket to a show or get a ticket out of town.

Services in Barcelona show the same contrast between old-world and ultra-modern as so much else in the city. In recent years change has been especially radical in the area of all-day services, as big stores, supermarkets and shopping malls have fostered the idea of quick service with same-day cleaners, shoe repairers, opticians and other franchise-style businesses. At the same time there are still plenty of quirky old businesses around, so that Barcelona now offers very wide customer choice.

Apartment/room rentals

Habit Servei
C/Muntaner 206, entlo 1º (93 209 50 45). Metro Hospital Clínic/bus 54, 58, 64, 66. **Open** 10am-2pm, 4-8pm, Mon-Fri. **Credit** MC, V. **Map C2**
Josep, who runs this service, can solve your accommodation problems if you're looking for a room in a flat for at least two weeks. It's often used by foreign Erasmus students and universities and business schools, but is open to anybody. Payment is made direct to the agency, and depending on area can be around 50,000ptas a month for a shared flat or 40,000ptas for a room in a private house. He also rents whole flats. There's no agency fee, but a 40,000ptas deposit, which will be returned at the end of the period. English spoken.

Body & hair care
Beauty treatments

Instituto Francis
Ronda de Sant Pere 18 (93 317 78 08).
Metro Catalunya/bus all routes to Plaça Catalunya.
Open 9am-8pm Mon-Fri; 9am-4pm Sat (varies in summer). **Credit** DC, MC, V. **Map D4**
If you want the full works, the Francis has eight floors dedicated to making you look and feel better. Make-up and make-overs are on the first floor, and you can work your way up through hairdressing, waxing, facials, slimming and massages. Not cheap, but a real treat.

Hairdressers

Clear
C/del Pi 11 (93 317 08 22). Metro Liceu/bus 14, 38, 59. **Open** 10am-8pm Mon-Sat. **Credit** MC, V. **Map D5**
Welcome to the hair salon for the year 2000: the place where the stylish go for pure, simple minimalist cuts or the craziest extensions. Even if you're not looking for a makeover, the all-white futuristic décor can be worth a visit.

Llongueras
C/Balmes 162 (93 218 61 50). Metro Diagonal/FGC Provença/bus 6, 7, 15, 16, 17, 27, 33, 34, 127. **Open** 9.30am-6.30pm Mon-Sat; *July, Aug* 9.30am-6.30pm Mon-Fri; 9.30am-2pm Sat. **Credit** AmEx, DC, V. **Map D3**

The best-known hairdressing chain in Spain, with over a dozen branches in Barcelona. They're quite expensive, but at the Balmes shop there is a cheaper hairdressing school.

La Pelu
C/Argentería 70-72 (93 310 48 07). Metro Jaume I/bus 17, 40, 45. **Open** 9.30am-7pm Mon-Wed; 9.30am-9pm Thur, Fri; 10am-7pm Sat. **Credit** MC, V. **Map D5**
Groovy cuts for men (from 2,500ptas, wash and cut), women (from 3,900ptas) and children. On the night of the full moon each month they also open 11pm-2am, with magic and other entertainments while you have your midnight trim.
Branch: C/Tallers 35 (93 301 97 73).

Peluquería Vicente
C/Tallers 11 (no phone). Metro Catalunya/bus all routes to Plaça Catalunya. **Open** 9am-1pm, 4-8pm, Mon-Fri; 9am-1pm Sat. **No credit cards**. **Map D4**
So you don't want to be trendy. For a no-nonsense haircut, try this small barber's shop. To be adventurous, have what is one of the closest shaves in the world.

Polo-pelo
Gralla Hall, C/Portaferrisa 25 (93 412 38 42). Metro Liceu/bus 14, 38, 59. **Open** 10.30am-8.30pm Tue-Sat. **Credit** MC, V. **Map D5**
A hip hairdressers in the **Gralla Hall** (*see pxxx*), run with flair by French-Argentinian Eric. One of the best places for fun highlights and for those who want something different.
Branch: Passeig del Born 14 (93 268 18 45).

Clothes & accessories

A wide range of services, including shoe repairs and key-cutting, are also available at **El Corte Inglés** department store (*see chapter* **Shopping**).

Cleaning, repairs, shoe repairs

One-hour cleaners are a growth industry in Barcelona, with prices often lower than those of older dry cleaners. There are still plenty of the latter around, though, and many of the old street-corner repairers that make it possible to have virtually any piece of clothing altered or restored. Look for any shop offering '*Arreglos*' or '*Brodats/Bordados*'. For shoe repairers, look for the sign *Rápido*.

5 a Sec
L'Illa, Avda Diagonal 557 (93 444 00 34). Bus 6, 7, 33, 34, 63, 66, 67, 68. **Open** 9am-9pm Mon-Fri; 9.30am-9.30pm Sat. **Credit** AmEx, MC, V. **Map C2**
An efficient, modern dry cleaners offering a one-hour service at reasonable prices. Five branches, and plans for more.

Jaimar
C/Numància 91-93 (93 322 78 04). Metro Plaça del Centre/bus 15, 43, 54, 59. **Open** 9.30am-1.30pm, 4.30-8pm, Mon-Fri; 10am-1.30pm Sat. **No credit cards**
A traditional repair shop that will take up, take apart, or put back together almost any piece of clothing, in virtually any material from wool to leather.

Mr Minit

Centre Barcelona Glòries, Avda Diagonal 208
(tel/fax 93 486 03 52). Metro Glòries/bus 56.
Open 10am-10pm Mon-Sat. **Credit** V. **Map F4**
On-the-spot shoe repairs and key cutting: heels will cost
about 700ptas, a straightforward key a mere 150ptas. Several
more branches around the city.

Qualitat Servei

C/Amargós 10 (93 318 31 47/93 301 36 87).
Metro Urquinaona/bus 17, 19, 40, 45. **Open** 8am-9pm
Mon-Sat. **Credit** MC, V. **Map D4**
Near the Barri Gòtic, this shop will wash and iron or dry-
clean clothes and deliver them to you within 24 hours; how-
ever, there is no pick-up service. Also minor repairs.

Dress & costume hire

Casa Peris

C/Junta de Comerc 20 (93 301 27 48) Metro Liceu/bus
14, 18, 38, 59. **Open** 9am-2pm, 3.30pm-6.30pm, Mon-
Fri. **No credit cards. Map C5**
A family firm that has been flourishing since 1840. It has
supplied both the Liceu and Madrid operas, and its wardrobe
stock numbers close to one million theatrical costumes. A
walk through the warehouse is an experience, with a Don
Juan outfit from the Liceu, or the many costumes used in
films. More mundanely, men's formal wear hires for
8,000ptas; a Louis XV outfit rents out for around 250,000ptas.

Menkes

Gran Via de les Corts Catalanes 642 & 646 (93 412 11
38). Metro Passeig de Gràcia/bus 7, 18, 50, 54, 56, 62.
Open 9.30am-1.30pm, 4.30-7.45pm, Mon-Fri; 10am-
1.30pm, 5-8pm, Sat. **Credit** AmEx, DC, MC, V. **Map D4**
Kit yourself out for Carnaval or that special *festa* at this magnificent theatrical costumiers and dress hire store. No 646 is
for sales, with a vast selection of ballet shoes (also made to
measure); no 642 has over 800 sumptuous designs available
for rental for children and adults, from the inevitable Catalan
peasant and flamenco outfits to chicken suits and Carnival
queen regalia worthy of Carmen Miranda. Any design can
be made to order. Also jokes, false noses and other silly
things, and dinner jackets for the more discreet.

Faxes & photocopies

A great many local *papereries* (stationers) have
photocopiers, and also fax machines.

Central Fotocopia

C/Pelai 1, pral (tel/fax 93 412 61 02). Metro
Universitat/bus all routes to Plaça Universitat. **Open** 9am-
2.30pm, 4-8pm, Mon-Fri. **Credit** MC, V. **Map D4**
Good-value photocopiers much used by students: some of
the best rates in town for large numbers of copies, but long
queues in term time. Also a fax sending/receiving service.

Copisteria Miracle

C/Dr Joaquim Pou 2 (93 317 12 26/fax 93 412 18 12).
Metro Jaume I/bus 17, 19, 40, 45. **Open** 9am-1.30pm, 4-
7.30pm, Mon-Fri. **Credit** MC, V. **Map D5**
The best in the city for high-quality copying of all kinds, at
reasonable prices. Again, queues are long. The other bran-
hes do not close at midday.
Branches: C/Rector Ubach 6 (93 200 85 44/fax 93 209 17
82; Passeig Sant Joan 57 (93 265 52 94/fax 93 265 30 70.

Food delivery

Few places specifically offer takeaway meals or
food delivery except for pizzerias. However, many
restaurants will provide a takeaway service if you
make an arrangement in advance.

Pizza World

C/Diputació 329 (93 487 85 85). Metro Girona/bus 7, 18,
39, 45, 47, 50, 54, 56, 62, N1, N9. **Open** 1-4pm, 7pm-
midnight, Mon-Thur; 1pm-midnight Fri-Sun, holidays. **No**
credit cards. Map E4
Probably the handiest pizza delivery service, with 16 branches. This one is in the central Eixample; from 7-11pm, daily,
phone the free line 902 30 53 05 to ask for your nearest
branch. You will be asked the address where you're staying,
and be told the number of the right branch; you then have
to ring it yourself. At other times call any branch and ask
the same question. Deliveries are made until midnight.

Caixes don't only have cash

Catalonia's savings banks (*caixes d'estalvis*) are
among its most characteristic institutions,
involved in many other fields as well as loans
and deposit accounts. In keeping with Catalans'
love of all things modern, they have embraced
electronics in a big way to expand into ticket
sales. Most theatres and many other venues now
release tickets through one or other *caixa*: to find
out tickets currently sold by each one, check at
any branch, or in listings magazines (*see*
chapter **Media**). No booking fees are charged.

La Caixa

Next to the cash machines at many branches of the
biggest of them all, the Caixa de Pensions, better known
simply as *La Caixa*, you will find a machine called a *Servi-
Caixa*, through which you can with a Caixa account or a
credit card obtain T2 and T50/30 travel cards, local infor-

mation and tickets to a wide range of attractions and
events, including **Port Aventura** and the **Liceu** season,
24 hours a day. You can also order tickets by freephone
(**902 33 22 11**).

Caixa de Catalunya

Central desk *Plaça Catalunya (no phone).*
Open 6-10pm Mon-Wed, Fri; 4-10pm Thur, Sat;
3-6pm Sun. **Map D5**
La Caixa's eternal competitor sells tickets for many
theatres (never the same ones as the *Servi-Caixa*) over
the counter at all its branches. You can reserve tickets
by phone with a credit card through their *Tel-Entrades*
freephone line (**902 10 12 12**, 8am-1am daily); you
then collect them at the venue. Also, you can get
tickets half-price by buying them (cash only) within
three hours of a performance at the Caixa de Catalunya
ticket desk next to the main tourist office, the **Centre
d'Informació Plaça Catalunya** (*see p251*), in an
underground location beneath the plaça.

Musical instrument rental

La Lonja del Instrumento – la casa de la musica

C/Gran de Gràcia 206 (93 415 77 77) Metro Fontana/bus 22, 24, 28. **Open** 10am-2pm, 4-8.30pm, Mon-Sat. **Credit** AmEx, MC, V. **Map D2**
A rare service for renting, selling, exchanging or repairing musical instruments, specialising in second-hand instruments. Renting an electric guitar for a weekend can cost from 1,500ptas plus a deposit (10% of the value of the instrument). A saxophone will cost around 20,000ptas.

Opticians

Grand Optical

Lower level, Centre Barcelona Glòries, Avda Diagonal 208 (93 486 02 77). Metro Glòries/bus 56. **Open** 10am-10pm Mon-Sat. **Credit** AmEx, MC, V. **Map F4**
If you lose or break your glasses in Barcelona you can now have them replaced or repaired while you wait. Grand Optical can provide an eye-test and new glasses within two hours; one hour if you have your prescription. English-speaking staff are on hand and lense prices begin at about 4,000ptas (plus frames).

Optipolis

Rambla de Catalunya 75 (93 215 29 39). Metro Passeig de Gràcia/bus 20, 21, 22, 24, 28, 43, 44. **Open** 10am-8.30pm Mon-Sat. **Credit** AmEx, DC, MC, V. **Map D3**
The same speed, type and price of service as Grand Optical, but closer to the centre of the city. English-speaking staff. **Branch**: Centre Glòries, Avda Diagonal 208 (93 486 04 28).

Photographic

Film developing is expensive, and unless you need pictures immediately you might prefer to wait until you get home.

Arpi Foto Video

La Rambla 38-40 (93 301 74 04). Metro Drassanes/bus 14, 18, 38, 59, 91. **Open** 9.30am-2pm, 4.30-8pm, Mon-Sat. **Credit** AmEx, DC, MC, V. **Map D5**
A giant specialist camera store with a wide range of professional-standard cameras and accessories and a good basic repair department; opening times vary from section to section. Service has improved lately, but can still be snail-like at times; however, they do know what they are doing. Stock ranges from happy-snappers to studio Hasselblads.

Fotoprix

C/Pelai 6 (93 318 20 36/information 93 451 10 43). Metro Universitat/bus all routes to Plaça Universitat. **Open** 9.30am-2pm, 4.30-8.30pm, Mon-Fri; 10am-2pm, 4.30-8.30pm, Sat. **Credit** V. **Map D4**
A chain with over 100 branches in the city offering one-hour film developing, photocopying and fax services.

Ticket agents

Tickets for a wide range of concerts and events are sold through savings banks (*see* **Caixes don't only have cash**). Otherwise, the best places to get tickets in advance are the venues themselves. Concert tickets for smaller venues may be sold in record shops (*see chapter* **Shopping**); look out for details on posters. The bullring has its own ticket office (*see chapter* **Sightseeing**); tickets to *Barça* football games can only be bought from the club.

Sharp cuts at **La Pelu**. *See page 182.*

Bulevard Rosa ticket desk

Bulevard Rosa, Passeig de Gràcia 53. Metro Passeig de Gràcia/bus all routes to Passeig de Gràcia. **Open** 10am-8.30pm Mon-Sat. **No credit cards. Map D3**
Within the Bulevard Rosa shopping centre, this desk has bigger-scale concert and some theatre tickets.

Taquilles Gran Via/Aribau

Plaça Universitat, corner Gran Via de les Corts Catalanes & C/Aribau (no phone). Metro Universitat/ bus all routes to Plaça Universitat. **Open** 10am-1pm, 4.30-7.30pm, Mon-Sat. Closed public holidays. **No credit cards. Map C4**
This booth in one corner of Plaça Universitat has tickets to large-scale pop concerts in any of the local sports arenas, and also Espanyol football games and other events in the Olympic buildings (stadium, Palau Sant Jordi, Velòdrom).

Travel services

Travel agents have become more competitive here, and it pays to shop around to find good deals.

Halcon Viajes

C/Aribau 34 (93 454 59 95/information 902 30 06 00). Metro Universitat/bus all routes to Plaça Universitat. **Open** 9.30am-1.30pm, 4.30-8pm, Mon-Fri; 10am-1.30pm Sat. **Credit** AmEx, DC, MC, V. **Map C4**
This giant with 500 offices throughout Spain is more than just a travel agency. Part of the same group is the airline Air Europa, and there are bargain deals on its Spanish domestic and European flights available only through the agency. They also have well-priced weekend packages to hotels in Spain, France and Portugal, and good deals on car rental.

Nouvelles Frontières

C/Balmes 8 (93 304 32 33/reservations 902 21 21 20). Metro Universitat, FGC Plaça Catalunya/bus all routes to Plaça Catalunya. Open 9.30am-8pm Mon-Fri; 10am-6pm Sat. **Credit** AmEx, DC, MC, V. **Map D4**
A no-nonsense agency with very competitive prices, sometimes offering savings of over 10,000ptas on European flights compared to many larger agencies.

Viatges Wasteels

Inside vestibule, Plaça Catalunya RENFE station (93 301 18 81). Metro Catalunya/bus all routes to Plaça Catalunya. **Open** 8.30am-8.30pm Mon-Fri; 10am-1pm Sat Oct-Nov 10am-2pm, 5-8pm, Mon-Fri; 10am-1pm Sat. **Credit** AmEx DC, MC, V. **Map D4**
Discounts on national and (especially) international rail tickets, and many flights, for students and under-25s. An ISIC student card or similar youth document (Euro 26) is required for flight discounts; for trains a passport (to confirm your age) is sufficient. Students over 25 are not eligible for rail discounts on trains within Spain.

Arts & Entertainment

Children

Beaches, funfairs, sharks, parks and dragons, and fun museums: there should be something to catch the little dears' attention.

Barcelona is an easy place to negotiate for families with children. Forget any reputation Catalans might have for being a little cold: they are in general very friendly and, like good Mediterraneans, adore children. Kids here generally play a more welcome part in everyday life than further north in Europe, and are allowed to be as noisy and loud as the mood takes them. Children follow their parents' timetable, and when Anglo-Saxon children are tucked in for the night these kids are having dinner with their parents, enjoying an ice-cream on the Rambla or just charging around city squares on their bikes. This relaxed general attitude, however, translates into a lack of child-specific concessions and services, particularly in restaurants and on public transport. Baby-changing facilities are few and far between, and taxis rarely have seatbelts in the back. Public transport is only free for children under four and a half.

Owing to the city's compact layout getting around and finding interesting itineraries for the whole family should pose no problem. Cobbled streets of the old city can prove tricky with pushchairs, though, and take care with traffic: cars rarely stop completely at street crossings, and even when the green man tells you it's fine to cross, something may come speeding around the corner.

Eating out

Special children's menus are almost non-existent in Barcelona restaurants, but they're very used to having children running around, and there are few places where children aren't welcome; restaurants will often supply small portions or simple dishes on request. The chain theme restaurants that have made an explosive entrance into Barcelona (*see pages 134-6*) cater very much to the younger audience with high chairs, children's menus, play packs and so on. For something not wholly multinational, try **Magic Barça**.

Sights & museums

With a little planning many of Barcelona's sights can be seen happily with children in tow. Many museums have pleasant cafes, some in idyllic courtyards, and many of its most famous landmarks have something to offer the young. They can let off steam in the park with a newly installed mini-lake by the **Sagrada Família**; run riot on the rooftop of Gaudí's **Pedrera**, and coo at the white geese in the **Cathedral** cloister. The **Rambla** is a playground in itself, loud and colourful. An especially good museum for kids is the **Museu Marítim**, which has

life-sized models of boats and captains' cabins to explore, plus a fabulous full-sized oared galley and an audio-visual exhibit in which visitors experience life at sea through the ages. Even children who may not have heard of Catalan history a day or so before can have their imagination taken by the high-tech audio-visuals and interactive exhibits at the **Museu d'Història de Catalunya**. Young football fans will have to be taken to the **Museu del FC Barcelona**. For details of places mentioned *see chapters* **Sightseeing** *and* **Museums**.

Museu de Cera (Wax museum)

Passatge de la Banca 7 (93 317 26 49). Metro Drassanes/bus 14, 18, 38, 59. **Open** *end Sept-late June* 10am-1.30pm, 4-7.30pm, Mon-Fri; 10am-1.30pm, 4.30-8pm Sat, Sun, public holidays; *23 June-23 Sept* 10am-8pm daily. **Admission** 900ptas; 550ptas over-65s, 5-11s; free under-5s. **No credit cards. Map D5**
Over 300 wax figures inhabit this impressive but gloomy nineteenth-century former bank at the foot of the Rambla. There's the usual collection of heroes and villains from past and present; good costumes make up for some rather approximate artistry. In the square outside is an eccentric bar, **El Bosc de les Fades**, with intriguing fairy-grotto décor. Go early before the magical atmosphere vanishes in the smoke. *Café. Disabled: toilets, wheelchair access.*

Museu de la Ciència

C/Teodor Roviralta 55-C/Cister 64 (93 212 60 50). FGC Tibidabo, then Tramvia Blau/bus 17, 22, 73. **Open** 10am-8pm Tue-Sun. **Admission** 500ptas; *additional exhibits* 250ptas extra; 350ptas students under-25, over-65s; *additional exhibits* 200ptas extra; free under-7s, *additional exhibits* 200ptas extra; *Clik dels Nens* 300ptas. **Credit** (shop only) V.
The science museum on Tibidabo is the most child-oriented of Barcelona museums, teaching everything from mechanics to the human body through hands-on fun and gadgetry. Budding Einsteins can become scientists for a day, creating experiments and trying out touchy-feely tests. The museum has a special section for children aged three to seven, the *Clik dels Nens*, and a planetarium. There are also regular, very good temporary exhibitions. *See also chapter* **Museums**. *Café. Shop.*

Attractions & rides

Most children's attractions are on the two mountains overlooking Barcelona, or in the Port Vell. There is a whole range of fun rides for getting around these areas, as well as the **Bus Turístic** tourist bus. The **Poble Espanyol** 'model village' on Montjuïc is a bit of a tourist trap but offers arts and crafts demonstrations and magic and circus shows for children. For the Poble and Montjuïc and

It's all good clean fun: the festa *of* **Sant Joan.** *See page 190.*

Tibidabo rides, *see chapter* **Sightseeing.** For a rainy day a good (expensive) standby can be the **IMAX** giant-format cinema (*see chapter* **Film**).

L'Aquàrium de Barcelona

Moll d'Espanya, Port Vell (93 221 74 74). Metro Barceloneta/bus 14, 17, 36,40, 57, 59, 64. **Open** *Sept-June 9.30am-9pm Mon-Fri; 9.30am-9.30pm Sat, Sun, public holidays. July, Aug 9.30am-11pm daily.* **Admission** 1,400ptas; 950ptas 4-12s; over-65s; *group discounts; free under-4s; advance sales* Caixa de Catalunya. **Credit** MC, V.

Pricey, but a good place to wind down as well as being educational. Its 21 tanks have been designed to reproduce habitats of the Mediterranean and tropical marine creatures they house. Most spectacular is a huge circular tank teeming with Mediterranean fish and sharks: an 80-metre glass tunnel allows you to walk through it to admire the shark's teeth, inches from your face. Young children prefer the interactive installation upstairs by the café, where they can enter different marine environments and play with the fish. The aquarium is supervised by English-speaking staff.

Font Màgica de Montjuïc

Plaça d'Espanya. Metro Espanya/bus 9, 13, 38, 61, 65, 91. **Fountains** *23 June-23 Sept 9-11.30pm, music 10-11pm, Thur-Sun.*

Barcelona's most outrageously tacky monument, the giant dancing fountain at the foot of Montjuïc, never fails to enthrall anyone who sees it, and kids love it. Sit in one of the terrace bars while it works its magic, dancing in time to popular tunes and showing off a kaleidoscope of colours.

Montjuïc funfair

Parc d'Atraccions de Montjuïc, Avda Miramar (93 441 70 24). Metro Paral.lel then Funicular de Montjuïc/bus 61. **Open** *mid-Sept-23 June noon-9pm Sat, Sun, public holidays; 24 June-early-Sept 6pm-11pm Tue-Fri; 11am-midnight Sat, Sun, public holidays.* **Admission** *entrance only* 700ptas; *individual rides* approx 300-400ptas; *pass*

with unlimited number of rides 2,000ptas; free under-3s. **Credit** AmEx, DC, MC, V. **Map B6**

Loud and brash, this funfair is simpler and cheaper than its Tibidabo competitor, and lacks the other's charm. In its favour, besides spectacular views, is the fact that other Montjuïc attractions can be worked into the same trip. To get there take the **Funicular** up the mountainside, then the soothing **Telefèric** chair lifts, swinging you up through the tree tops. To be more adventurous go on from Montjuïc on the renovated but still dubious-looking **Transbordador** across the port: after dangling you menacingly over the water, it arrives at a tower in Barceloneta. Children love it.

New Park

La Rambla 88 (93 412 51 78). Metro Liceu/bus 14, 18, 38, 59. **Open** *10am-11pm Mon-Thur, Sun; 10am-1am Fri, Sat.* **No credit cards. Map D5**

Modern kids will welcome this giant amusement arcade on the Rambla, with three floors of rides, slides, video games, and a special area for young children with bouncy castles. Attractions are paid for individually, and cost 100-200ptas.

Tibidabo funfair

Parc d'Atraccions del Tibidabo, Plaça del Tibidabo (93 211 79 42). FGC Av Tibidabo/bus 17, 22, 58, 73, N8 then Tramvia Blau, Funicular. **Open** *end Mar-early May noon-8pm Sat, Sun, holidays. Easter week noon-8/9pm daily. May-June 10am-6pm Wed-Fri; noon-9pm Sat, Sun, holidays. July-Aug noon-10pm Mon-Thur, Sun; noon-1am Fri, Sat. Sept noon-8pm Mon-Fri; noon-10pm Sat, Sun, holidays. Oct noon-8pm Sat, Sun, holidays.* **Admission** *entrance only* 1,000ptas; 600ptas over-65s; *free under-5s. Pass with unlimited number of rides* 2,400ptas; 600ptas under-5s. **Credit** AmEx, DC, MC, V.

It'll be hard to keep this one a secret for long, as the huge ferris wheel is visible all over the city. Make a day of it by taking the **Tramvia Blau** up the hill to the beginning of the **Funicular**, which takes you through the woods to the top of the mountain and the funfair. Few amusement parks can compete with its spectacular mountain-top views. The park was comprehensively renovated a few years ago, but has managed to keep good old-fashioned attractions like bumper cars and a hall of mirrors. Its most recent addition is Hotel Krueger, a much acclaimed house of horrors where actors try to scare the wits out of you. Also worth a visit is the **Museu d'Automates**, a wonderful collection of amusement arcade machines (*see chapter* **Museums**). If the kids are not too tired, ramble back down to the tram stop on the well sign-posted path through the woods.

Zoo de Barcelona

Parc de la Ciutadella (93 221 25 06). Metro Barceloneta, Ciutadella/bus 14, 39, 40, 41, 42, 51. **Open** *Nov-Feb* 10am-5.30pm; *Mar, Oct* 10am-6pm; *Apr, Sept* 10am-7pm; *May-Aug* 9.30am-7.30pm daily. **Admission** 1,400ptas; 950ptas under-12, over-65s; group discounts; free under-3s. **Credit** MC, V. **Map E5**
Campaigners want to move the zoo out of Barcelona and reclaim the section of the Ciutadella it occupies. This would be a welcome break for its sad-looking animals, as current space limitations mean that enclosures are small and sparse. It's well designed for humans, though, with plenty of green, shady picnic areas and short distances between enclosures. There are regular shows at the Dolphinarium, and Barcelona's celebrity *Copito de Nieve* (Snowflake), only albino gorilla in captivity. Young kids love the farm area, where they can play with the small and people-friendly critters.

Parks & playgrounds

Easily the best park in the city centre for children is the **Ciutadella**. Lush and green, it's a great place for a picnic, and you can also take a boat out on the small lake, or hire bikes or roller skates nearby. Gaudí's fairy-land **Parc Güell** also appeals to kids, who can clamber around the bright ceramic sculptures and follow paths winding through the woods. Be warned that areas shown on maps as green can be no more than dusty squares. For details of parks, *see chapter* **Sightseeing**.

Parc del Castell de l'Oreneta

Camí de Can Caralleu & C/Montevideo (93 424 38 09). Bus 22, 64, 75. **Open** *Nov-Feb* 10am-6pm; *Mar, Oct* 10am-7pm; *Apr, Sept* 10am-8pm; *May-Aug* 10am-9pm, daily.
One of Barcelona's largest parks, a short walk from the **Monestir de Pedralbes**, this is a great favourite with local children. Main attractions include the *poni club* where kids can take short pony rides and a little train pulled by a model steam loco. Also a play area, sports circuit and snack bar.

Parc del Laberint

C/Germans Desvalls (near Passeig Vall d'Hebron). Metro Montbau/bus 27, 60, 73, 76, 85. **Open** *Nov-Feb* 10am-6pm; *Mar, Oct* 10am-7pm; *April, Sept* 10am-8pm; *May-Aug* 10am-9pm, daily. On days with paid admission, last admission one hour before closing. **Admission** *Mon, Tue, Thur-Sat* 275ptas; *Wed, Sun* free; free under-6s, over-65s. **No credit cards**.
Created for a local aristocrat, these beautiful gardens have been open to the public since 1971 and contain a maze, ornamental pool and play area. Have a snack in the specially designated area near the entrance, but picnicking is not allowed anywhere else in the park. *See also chapter* **Sightseeing**.

Turó Parc

Avda Pau Casals. Bus 6, 7, 14, 15, 27, 30, 33, 34, 66. **Open** *Nov-Feb* 10am-6pm; *Mar, Oct* 10am-7pm; *Apr, Sept* 10am-8pm; *May-Aug* 10am-9pm, daily. **Map C2**
A small, shady park that's a good place for a break from shopping in the Diagonal, and has a play area and a mini-theatre that on Sundays hosts children's shows.

Beaches

Barcelona's 4km (2½ miles) of beaches (*see cı apter* **Sightseeing**) have lifeguards, showers and play areas. The sea is safe to swim in, and the sands are pretty clean. There are very few toilets at the beach, and no baby-changing facilities. Most restaurant toilets are for clients only, but waiters will probably be lenient if your kid looks desperate. *See also chapter* **Sport & Fitness**.

Entertainment

Film

Barcelona is having a *VO* (original version) movie boom, with over 20 screens showing films undubbed in the original language. The **Verdi** has one screen that shows only children's films in VO, and the **Filmoteca** has a children's session Sundays at 5.30pm. For details *see chapter* **Film**.

Music

The **Auditori del Centre Cultural de La Caixa** (*see chapter* **Music: Classical & Opera**) presents top-notch family concerts designed to appeal to even the youngest children, complete with entertainers to act out the 'story'. They're usually on Saturday mornings or Sunday afternoons from September to May. Also worth checking out is the **Classics als Parcs** cycle in June and July, when bands and orchestras play in the city's parks in the evenings.

Theatre

Barcelona hosts some excellent children's theatre, but a basic understanding of Catalan or Spanish is essential. Plays and puppet shows can be seen at the **Jove Teatre Regina**, C/Sèneca 22 (93 218 15 12); **El Llantiol** C/Riereta 7 (93 329 90 09) and **Teatre Malic** C/Fusina 3 (93 310 70 35) and the **Teatre de l'Eixample** and **Artenbrut** (*see chapter* **Theatre**). Sundays there are children's shows at **Casa Elizalde** (*see chapter* **Music: Classical & Opera**), **Turó Parc**, **Poble Espanyol** and the **Fundació Miró**. Recent years have also seen a big increase in English-language theatre in Barcelona, including productions suitable for children. Details of any coming up will be posted in any of the English bookshops, and *Barcelona Metropolitan* magazine.

Festivals & seasons

See also chapter **Barcelona by Season**.

December: Christmas

In the run up to Christmas the **Santa Llúcia** market invades the Cathedral square. Very pretty, this is where Barcelonans buy their Christmas trees and crib figures. Children traditionally get their presents on 6 January, **Reis**, and the excitement begins on the evening of the 5th with the *Cavalcada*, the parade that follows the arrival of the Three Kings in the harbour on a *Golondrina*. Worth visiting is the annual exhibition *Els Pessebres del Monestir* at the **Monestir de Pedralbes**, when the finest craft specialists in the art of crib-making show their creations.

February: Carnaval

Carnaval is wonderful for kids, as the week before Lent sees the streets of Barcelona filled with miniature Batmen, fairies and bumble bees. Colourful parades are held along the Rambla with King Carnestoltes as grand protagonist.

March, April: Easter

Less of a children's celebration, but you'll probably have to treat them to a *mona*, the elaborate chocolate sculptures traditionally bought by Godparents for their Godchildren.

May: La Tamborinada

An event on a Saturday in May, when for a whole day the Ciutadella is taken over by street performers, puppet shows, magicians, circus acts and other entertainers.

June: Sant Joan

The biggest shows of the summer, Sant Joan makes its noisy entrance on 23 June, Midsummer Night's Eve, when bonfires appear around the city and fireworks are set off in every corner. Hectic for small children, but very much a teen favourite.

September: La Mercè

A huge street party: every afternoon for a week and through the day at the weekend, squares fill with clowns, puppets, concerts and theatre. The spectacular *Correfoc*, a procession of fire-breathing dragons and other bizarre creatures through the streets of Barcelona, is a frenzy of flying sparks. This one can be pretty hair-raising even for adults.

Out of town/waterparks

For a day at the seaside, the best place is **Sitges**, with pleasant, safe beaches. For a more hectic day it would be perverse for kids not to make the trip to **Port Aventura**, one of Europe's largest theme parks. *See chapter* **Trips Out of Town: Beaches**.

Aqualeón Safari

Finca les Basses, Albinyana (977 68 76 56). By car A2, then A7 via Vilafranca, or N340 to El Vendrell, then right to Albinyana (65km/40 miles). **Open** *late-Mar-late May, mid-Sept-Oct* 10am-6pm Sat, Sun, *late-May-mid-Sept* 10am-6pm daily. **Admission** *late-Mar-late May, mid-Sept-Oct* 1,575ptas; 875ptas under-12s; free under-3s. *late-May-mid-Sept* 2,075ptas; 1,150ptas under-12s; free under-3s. **Credit** AmEx, DC, MC, V.

An all-in-one water park and safari park between Barcelona and Tarragona with tigers, birds of prey and parrots as well as water slides and wave machines. Captive dolphins too.

Catalunya en Miniatura

C/Disseminats, Torrelles de Llobregat (93 689 09 60). By Bus Oliveras from Plaça d'Espanya/by car N-II to Sant Vicens dels Horts, then left (10km/6 miles). **Open** *Oct-Mar* 10am-6pm, *April-Sept* 10am-7pm, daily. **Admission** 1,000ptas; 800ptas over-65s; 600ptas under-14s; free under-3s. **No credit cards.**

A model village with over 170 accurate miniatures of monuments and buildings from all over Catalonia. There's also a miniature train to take you around the park.

Illa de Fantasia

Finca Mas Brassó, Vilassar de Dalt (93 751 45 53). By car A19 or N11 north, left at Premià de Mar (24km). **Open** (*waterpark*) *June-mid-Sept* 10am-7pm Mon-Fri, Sun; 10am-4am Sat; (*disco*) all year 10pm-6am Sat. **Admission** *waterpark* 1,400ptas; 1,000ptas 3-11s; free under-3s. **No credit cards.**

Ideal for cooling off overheated kids, this great waterpark has a big open-air pool, slides, wave machines and play pools. After the kids have left it reopens as a water-disco.

Parc de les Aus

Carretera de Vilassar de Mar a Cabrils, Vilassar de Mar (93 750 17 65). By car A19 or N11 north to Vilassar, then left (24km/15 miles)/by train RENFE from Sants or Plaça Catalunya to Vilassar, then taxi. **Open** 10am-8pm Tue-Sun. **Admission** 900ptas; 650ptas under-7s; free under-3s. **No credit cards.**

Over 300 local and exotic bird species are contained in this bird sanctuary with extensive gardens, picnic and play areas.

Vintage trains

Steam trains **Information & reservations** *(93 302 48 16)*. **Dates** Sept-June. **Departures** from Martorell 11.10am; return from Monistrol 12.45pm; arrives Martorell 1.30pm. **Tickets** 1,600ptas return; 1,000ptas return 3-14s; free under-3s. **No credit cards.**

For train fans there are two choices, both from the FGC railways. To travel on a steam train, first take an ordinary FGC train from Plaça d'Espanya to Martorell-Enllaç any Sunday at 10.17am. There you will find a steam train waiting to take you to Monistrol de Montserrat, returning an hour later. If you prefer a 1920s electric train, the first Sunday of any month the FCG line from Plaça Catalunya to Reina Elisenda gets out vintage rolling stock for the day. Trains are wood-panelled, charming and there is live jazz laid on. Unfortunately, both services do not run in July or August. Railways buffs also enjoy the **Museu del Ferrocarril**, Catalonia's railway museum, in **Vilanova i la Geltrú** (Plaça Eduard Maristany (93 815 84 91). What's more, it's near a beach and can be combined with a trip to Sitges.

Babysitting/childcare

The growing number of working women has led to an increase in childcare facilities in the city. The agencies below employ qualified childminders, and can supply an English-speaker if necessary.

Cangur Serveis

C/Aragó 227, 1° (93 487 80 08/24-hour mobile 908 22 01 77). Metro Passeig de Gràcia/bus 7, 16, 17, 22, 24, 28. **Open** *office* 9am-7pm Mon-Thur; 9am-2pm Fri; calls answered on mobile 24 hours daily. **No credit cards.**

A specialised childcare agency that can provide babysitters at two hours' notice every day of the year. Charges begin at 850ptas per hour, or 6,000ptas for a special all-night service; there are discounts for longer-term arrangements.

Cinc Serveis

C/Pelai 11, 5C (93 412 56 76/24-hour mobile 908 59 97 00). Metro Catalunya/bus all routes to Plaça Catalunya. **Open** *office* 9.30am-1.30pm, 4.30-8.30pm, Mon-Fri; calls answered on mobile 24 hours daily. **No credit cards.**

The basic rate after 9pm is 1,100ptas per hour; day and longer-term rates are less.

Global Kids

Centre Barcelona Glòries, Avda Diagonal 208 (93 486 01 49). Metro Glòries/bus 56, 92. **Open** 10am-9pm Mon-Fri; 11am-10pm Sat; noon-9pm Sun, public holidays. **Admission** 750ptas Mon-Fri; 950ptas Sat, Sun, public holidays. **No credit cards.**

An educational activity centre for children aged one to ten. Building a house, acting in the mini-theatre, working out in the children's gym or getting their hands dirty in the crafts corner are just some ways they can pass the time here. There is a 'Drop & Shop' service for children aged three and over.

Happy Parc

C/Comtes de Bell-lloc 74-78 (93 490 08 35). Metro Sants-Estació/bus 44, 109. **Open** 5-9pm Mon-Fri; 11am-9pm Sat, Sun; 11am-2pm, 5-9pm, public holidays. **Admission** 500ptas per hour; 125ptas each subsequent 15mins. **No credit cards.**

An indoor fun park with running, jumping, bouncing and sliding equipment for kids from 2-12. The main branch is by Sants station. All activities are included, but note the increase in cost if you stay more than an hour.
Branch: C/Pau Claris 97 (93 317 86 60).

Dance

Sponsors may be scarce, but Barcelona's dance companies show their strength in creativity.

In Spain, while Madrid is the great centre of traditional Spanish dance and has the most solid ballet programme, Barcelona has clearly established itself as the most vibrant centre for contemporary dance. There are no big, institutional companies presiding over the scene, but the city is the base for a diverse range of small- to medium-sized groups producing exciting original work.

This situation emerged out of the cultural exuberance of late-1970s Barcelona, when new freedoms encouraged new departures in all the arts. The freedom to experiment was especially evident in dance, since Barcelona had never really had any recognised dance groups, nor even a classical ballet school. Unhindered by set tradition, young dancers were free to try anything and everything. At the same time, dancers who had studied and worked abroad such as Cesc Gelabert or Angels Margarit returned to lend their refined skills to the development of a Catalan dance movement.

Today, Catalan dance groups have won widespread international acclaim, yet enthusiasm remains an essential element in keeping the dance scene going. Many Barcelona venues now feature dance in their programmes, but the dance world still suffers from a lack of funding, schools and a central location where dancers can study, practise and perform. The Institut del Teatre dance school plays a major role, but apart from that only a few private schools carry on the work of nurturing serious contemporary dancers. During the 1980s Cesc Gelabert, most admired of Catalan dancers, ran his own school, La Fàbrica, which became the most important dance location in the city. Internal problems and Gelabert's wish to concentrate on choreography led to its closure. A recent development is that several newer companies have joined together to rent a building in Gràcia called La Caldera (The Boilerhouse), as a shared rehearsal space.

The sponsorship that is available for dance tends to go into performances rather than development of new talents and productions, and dance groups find it hard to prevent talented young stars from going abroad to further their careers. This concentration on performance over preparation can result in well-dressed but hurried pieces with undernourished content; nevertheless, in Barcelona's dance programme it's still common to come across fine, inventive performances in which the power of imagination makes the lack of resources a minor consideration.

NON-CONTEMPORARY DANCE

If contemporary dance, for all its problems, has become an integral part of the local arts scene, opportunities to see other kinds of dance (except folk dancing, for which *see chapter* **Barcelona by Season**) are relatively few. Barcelona still does not have a classical ballet school, nor will there be a ballet company in the city until the rebuilding of the Liceu is completed. In the meantime, the itinerant Liceu programme occasionally features visiting productions – often, unfortunately, by tired touring companies from eastern Europe – at its various venues (*see chapter* **Music: Classical & Opera**).

As for true Spanish dance and flamenco, it's not often that the best of the genre can be seen here. There have always been nightclubs in the city presenting flamenco shows mostly for tourists, rarely with first-rate performers–although even middling flamenco can, if you're lucky, provide a memorable evening. Since about 1995, in addition, there has actually been something of a vogue for flamenco in Barcelona, with venues like **Tarantos** sprucing up décor and programmes. This has had more effect in music and singing than dance, but, again, you may be lucky and find that a top-flight artist is in town. For venues, *see chapter* **Music: Rock, Roots & Jazz**.

Information

Associació dels Professionals de Dansa de Catalunya *Via Laietana 52, pral 12 (93 268 24 73).*
Acts as a clearing-house for the various companies, with information on who is doing what in Barcelona dance at any time. For immediate programme information, check the *Guia del Ocio* and the free monthly *Barcelona en Música*, available in record shops and at venues. These and other leaflets for public theatres such as **L'Espai** are also available at **La Virreina** information centre in the Rambla (*see page 251*).

Dance groups

Other groups worth looking out for include **Búbulus**, **Satsumas**, **Increpación Danza**, **Hamilton/Renalias** and the excellent **Trànsit**.

Danat Dansa

This company has experimented continually ever since it first performed in 1985. Choreography is by Sabine Dahrendorf, from Germany, and Alfonso Ordóñez, from León, in collaboration with a core group of five dancers. The extensive research behind each piece, and the varied backgrounds of the directors, ensure works with complex content and an original, dynamic language. Recent work includes the acclaimed *La Japonesa o la impossible llegada a Dèdalo*, a piece for seven dancers based on the myth of the minotaur.

Erre Que Erre

Made up of former members of Danat Dansa, this young company won immediate acclaim from critics and public for its dense, fast-paced work for five dancers, *Vaivén*, presented at **L'Espai** in early 1998.

Gelabert-Azzopardi Companyia de Dansa

In the 1970s Cesc Gelabert travelled to the USA to study architecture. Once there, though, he changed track into dance, at the Cunningham School in New York. When he returned home he became the most influential figure in Catalan contemporary dance, helping develop a particular style concentrating more on form than emotion, and forming a crop of new dancers at his school La Fàbrica. He also began working with Lydia Azzopardi, previously at The Place in London, who contributed a more sophisticated level of traditional dance knowledge. Recently their company has toured in Germany, Belgium and France, but also performs frequently in the **Teatre Lliure**. It will perform at the 1998 Edinburgh Festival with a piece for seven dancers called *Zumzum.ka*, and also in the repertoire is a solo piece choreographed by Gerhard Bohner for Gelabert himself, titled *Im (Goldenen) Schnitt* (The [Golden] Section).

Lanònima Imperial Companyia de Dansa

With choreography by Juan Carlos García, another dancer who had worked with Cesc Gelabert, Lanònima also gains much from the time he spent with Galotta in France and Cunningham in America. Since he founded the company in 1986 García has used his extensive training to develop a rich and very physical language, with philosophical content. At its best, it's exhilarating. At the 1997 Grec festival the company premièred *Landschaft mit Schadden* (Landscape with Shadows), a joint production with Berlin's Tanztheater group, which has been presented in Germany during 1998. Also in 1998 Lanònima will present *Cuerpo y Luz* (Body and Light), a work for eight dancers exploring sensuality and eroticism.

Mal Pelo

The name means 'bad hair', implying a rebellious spirit. Formed in 1989 by two well-respected dancers, Pep Ramis and Maria Múñoz, this group has performed across Europe and in the US, where it received excellent reviews for *Dol*, presented in Philadelphia and New York in 1995. Its choreography attempts to combine abstract dance with a strong storyline. Mal Pelo is preparing a new piece for seven dancers to present at the Grec festival in summer 1998, and Muñoz herself recently teamed up with Mudances director Angels Margarit in a piece for two dancers called *SAO*.

Mudances

Angels Margarit has been gaining in stature as a choreographer over the last decade, producing highly structured, complex work. The group features two male dancers and four women, and has had considerable international success, beginning in 1991 with *Atzavara*. In 1994 and 1995 they toured several countries with *Corol.la*, a solo piece for Margarit. Any piece by this company is worth seeing. Recently, Margarit has danced in *SAO* with Maria Múñoz, while the company has been preparing a piece for the 1998 Grec called *Oraché, Un Vent de Terra*, featuring three extra dancers, from Venezuela, Cuba and the Netherlands.

Roseland Musical

Roseland was formed in 1983 by Marta Almirall to bring exciting, original dance to children, although its work is complex enough to satisfy adults as well. Storylines and choreography are all original, and the style a combination of theatre, dance and music. The company has toured widely, gaining an international reputation. Its latest piece, *La Casa per la Finestra*, tells the story of a house abandoned by its owners, and a love affair between a notebook and a toothbrush that have been left behind.

Venues

Barcelona has only one venue with a consistent dance programme, the Generalitat's **L'Espai**, but several more that include dance in with theatre and/or music menus. Dance performances feature regularly at the **Mercat de les Flors**, the **Teatre Lliure**, the Institut de Teatre's **Teatre Adrià Gual** and **Teatre de l'Eixample** all present dance with reasonable frequency, and the **Sala Beckett** hosts a range of more small-scale, fringe events (for all, *see chapter* **Theatre**). There are dance seasons at the **Casa Elizalde** (*see chapter* **Music: Classical & Opera**), and an eclectic range of fairly experimental dance shows also feature in the programme at the **Centre de Cultura Contemporània** (*see chapter* **Art Galleries**).

L'Espai

Travessera de Gràcia 63 (93 414 31 33).
FGC Muntaner/bus 27, 58, 64, 127. **Box office** 6.30-10pm Tue-Sat; 6.30-9pm Sun *advance sales* box office & Servi-Caixa. **Performances** *Sept/Oct-June* usually 10pm Thur-Sat, 7pm Sun. **Tickets** 1,000-2,000ptas.
No credit cards. Map C2
A regional government showcase, this venue's full title is 'L'Espai de Dansa i Música de la Generalitat de Catalunya'. Hence it's still not entirely for dance, but combines a dance programme with contemporary and other music of various kinds. The companies presented are nearly always contemporary, although in the dance world the complaint is heard that it still doesn't welcome the most experimental companies.

Lanònima's Landscape with Shadows.

Film

Moviegoing is booming in Barcelona, with audiences rising for local creations as well as Hollywood product.

This is a city of film-lovers, where queues for the latest Hollywood blockbuster stretch around the block. In fact, against the grain of the pattern seen in many other European countries, moviegoing is increasing in popularity. A string of new cinemas has opened in recent years, including multiplexes such as the six-screen **Renoir** in Les Corts, the eight-screen **Maremàgnum** centre in the port, and the 15-screen **Icària** in the Vila Olímpica. Alongside Maremàgnum is an example of the cinema's current technological toy, a giant-format **IMAX** screen. Recent additions are the delightful **Méliès Cinemes**, with two screens in the heart of the Eixample showing Hollywood classics.

Most first-run films are dubbed into Castilian Spanish, or sometimes Catalan. Fortunately, though, there are many people in the city who want to see films in the language in which they were made, with Castilian subtitles, and the number of cinemas showing pictures in this format has increased steadily in the last few years. There are currently about 30 screens regularly showing films undubbed, and demand is still growing.

The biggest crowds may be for Hollywood movies, but Spanish and Catalan films are not shunned by Barcelona audiences. One consequence of the current boom in cinemagoing in Spain has been to give new encouragement to domestic production. In 1997, 13 per cent of film tickets bought in Spain were for Spanish productions, up from 9.3 per cent in 1996. The quirky melodramas of Pedro Almodóvar have been an international cult, and his 1997 *Carne Tremula* (Live Flesh) played well abroad. Very popular at home have been the post-Almodóvarian comedies of Alex de la Iglesia, such as the 1995 *El Día de la Bestia*. His 1997 follow-up *Perdita Durango*, adapted from a Barry Gifford novel, won a lukewarm reception from critics, but did well at the box office.

Despite these successes and the international plaudits received by a few pictures such as Fernando Trueba's 1993 Oscar-winner *Belle Epoque*, though, production overall in Spain is still lower than in the 1960s. However, the central government provides large subsidies in an effort to maintain Spain's film industry, and the current expansion in production may be an indication that this effort is finally bearing fruit.

CATALAN CINEMA

In the first part of this century, Barcelona was a major film centre. By the 1960s, though, Madrid had begun to exert its influence more and more, and is now the unquestioned centre of Spain's film industry. The Catalan government offers its own subsidies to local productions, on condition that the film be shown in Catalan inside Catalonia. This incentive has not been able to halt Barcelona's slow decline as a production centre for Spanish-language films.

Fortunately, Barcelona's failure to bolster its film production industry has not dampened individual talent. Several recent Catalan films have been shown internationally, and one curious feature of them is that some have been made all or partly in English. One to watch out for is Marta Balletbó-Coll's delightfully funny lesbian romance *Costa Brava (Family Album)*, made on a shoestring but well received in London and the US; another is Isabel Coixet's *Coses que no et vaig dir mai* (Things I Never Told You), filmed in Oregon.

Not in English but also interesting were two Catalan films released in 1997, *Un Cos al Bosc* (Something in the Woods), a mystery story starring Almodóvar regular Rossy de Palma that had a highly successful Barcelona run, and *Actrius* (Actresses), directed by Ventura Pons, whose previous *Carícies* (Caresses), was well-received at the 1998 Berlin festival. *La Camarera del Titànic* (The Waitress of the Titanic) is the latest offering from Catalan director Bigas Luna, whose torrid, hormone-packed Spanish-language melodramas *Jamón, Jamón* (Ham, Ham) and *Huevos de Oro* (Golden Balls) caused a certain international stir. Finally in production is *La Ciutat dels Prodigis*, an adaptation of Eduardo Mendoza's great Spanish-language Barcelona novel *La Ciudad de los Prodigios* (City of Marvels), which after years of delays is set to begin shooting in June 1998.

FILMS UNDUBBED

Independent movies are almost always shown in their original language, and it's also now common for Hollywood releases to be shown in English on at least one screen in the city. Films shown undubbed with Spanish/Catalan subtitles are called *versió original* or VO films, and identified by the letters VO. We list specialised VO cinemas below. The official film theatre, the **Filmoteca**, shows varied programmes virtually always in VO.

So this isn't the one with Leonardo in: Bigas Luna's La Camarera del Titànic.

Tickets & Times

Current programme details are found in the *Guía del Ocio* and daily papers (*see chapter* **Media**). Like most things in Barcelona, filmgoing tend to happen later than in more northerly countries, and the most popular sessions are those that start around 10.30pm, when there are big queues at weekends. On Sundays, it's advisable to buy tickets in advance or at least arrive at the cinema in very good time for 8pm and 10.30pm shows. Real 'late' shows are after midnight on Fridays and Saturdays. There are good VO weekend late shows at the **Casablanca, Icària, Renoir,** and **Verdi.** Of non-VO cinemas, the **Club Capitol, Glòries, Savoy** and **Lauren** also have late shows.

All cinemas have a cheap day (*día del espectador*), nearly always on Monday or Wednesday. Few take phone bookings, but getting a ticket is rarely a problem except on weekend evenings. For information on films for children, *see chapter* **Children.**

Mega-Screen Movies

IMAX Port Vell

Moll d'Espanya (902 33 22 11). Metro Barceloneta/ bus 14, 17, 36, 40, 45, 57, 59, 64. **Open** *box office* 30 min before first performance, until 1am. *Reservations and advance sales* through Servi-Caixa, and at box office until one hour before performance time. **Tickets** *before 3pm* 850ptas Mon-Fri, 1,000ptas Sat, Sun, public holidays; *3-8pm* 1,300ptas, *after 8pm* 1,500ptas, daily. **Credit** MC, V. **Map D6.**

Opened in 1995, Barcelona's IMAX cinema in the port has drawn large audiences, but how many filmgoers bother to see 'large format' cinema more than once is unknown. It offers a choice of mega-formats, with films on a wrap-around, dome-like OMNIMAX screen and on a towering flat IMAX screen in 3-D, with polarised glasses for each customer. The problem is that there aren't many films made for these screens, so programmes rarely stray from a repetitive round of nature films like *Life in the Deep,* and other documentaries like *New York-3D* and the IMAX chestnut *The Rolling Stones live at the Max.* Once you've been amazed by Mick Jagger's 30-foot nostrils once, a fairly big so-what factor comes into play. One feature film has been made for IMAX, an aviation adventure called *Wings of Courage* with Tom Hulce, but vast costs and uncertain rewards discourage large-scale productions. *Disabled: toilet, wheelchair access.*

VO Cinemas

Alexis

Rambla Catalunya 90 (93 215 05 06). Metro Passeig de Gràcia/FGC Provença/bus 20, 21, 22, 24, 28, 44. **Open** *box office* 4-11pm daily. **Tickets** 500ptas Mon; 725ptas Tue-Fri; 750ptas Sat, Sun, public holidays. Reservations taken on day of performance. **Credit** AmEx, MC, V. **Map D2.**
The only one of the screens in the large Alexandra cinema to show VO films, housed in a grand *Modernista* building. *Air-conditioning. Bar/café.*

Arkadin

Travessera de Gràcia 103 (93 405 22 22) Metro Diagonal/FGC Gràcia/bus 22, 24, 28, N4, N6. **Open** *box office* 15 min before first performance. **Tickets** 725ptas Mon, Tue, Thur, Fri; 600ptas Wed; 750ptas Sat, Sun, public holidays. **No credit cards.**
A small two-screen that occasionally shows VO films. It's a little shabby and cramped, but has reasonable sightlines. *Air-conditioning.*

Capsa

C/Pau Claris 134 (93 215 73 93). Metro Passeig de Gràcia/ bus 39, 45, N4, N6. **Open** *box office* 15 min before performances. **Tickets** 575ptas Mon; 725ptas Tue-Fri; 750ptas Sat, Sun, public holidays. **No credit cards. Map D3.**
A very comfortable cinema, with a pleasant (separate) bar alongside. The seats are tilted back to give a clear view of the screen, and the technical quality of the equipment is high. *Air-conditioning.*

Casablanca

Passeig de Gràcia 115 (93 218 43 45). Metro Diagonal/ bus 6, 7, 15, 22, 24, 28, 33, 34, N4, N6. **Open** *box office* 15 min before first performance. **Late shows** 12.30am or 1am Fri, Sat and eves before public holidays. **Tickets** 575 ptas Mon; 725ptas Tue-Fri; 750ptas Sat, Sun, public holidays. **No credit cards. Map D3.**
Two-screen art cinema mostly showing non-mainstream US and European films. The bar has decent food and late shows, with a programme of revivals, are extremely popular. *Air-conditioning. Bar/café.*

Icària

C/Salvador Espriu 61 (information 93 221 75 85/ bookings 93 221 79 12). Metro Ciutadella-Vila Olímpica/bus 36, 41. **Open** *box office* 11am-11pm Mon-Thur, Sun; 11am-1am

Fri, Sat. **Late shows** 1am Fri, Sat. **Tickets** 550ptas before 2.30pm, 725ptas after 2.30pm, Mon-Sat; 725ptas all day Sun, public holidays. **No credit cards. Map F6.**
This well-equipped 15-screen mega-cinema opened in 1996 in the Olympic Village shopping centre across from the beach. At least half of the films shown at any given time are in English, with a good mix of mainstream and independent work. Their weekend late shows are often interesting.
Air-conditioning. Disabled: toilet, wheelchair access.

Maldà

C/del Pi 5 (93 317 85 29). Metro Liceu/bus 14, 38, 59, N4, N5. **Open** *box office* 15 min before first performance.
Tickets 500ptas Mon; 625ptas Tue-Fri; 675ptas Sat, Sun, public holidays. **No credit cards. Map D5.**
A double-bill repertory programme in VO that changes every week, with classics and recent movies you may have missed. Also the only cinema housed in an eighteenth-century palace, with an imposing staircase for its entrance, just inside the Galeries Maldà shopping arcade near Plaça del Pi.
Air-conditioning.

Méliès Cinemes

Villaroel 102 (93 451 00 51). Metro Urgell/bus 14, 20, 54, 58, 59, 64, 66, N3. **Open** box office 15 min before first performance. *Cine Club tickets* 4pm. **Tickets** 400ptas Mon; 600ptas Tue-Sun; *Cine Club* 550ptas, 10.30pm Thur. **No credit cards. Map C4.**
This two-screen repertory cinema opened in 1997, and quickly developed a faithful audience. They show Hollywood classics, leaning toward film noir, with a frequently-changing programme. Comfortable and run both for film buffs and those who just like a movie that stands the test of time.
Air-conditioning. Disabled: toilet, wheelchair access.

Renoir Les Corts

C/Eugeni d'Ors 12 (93 490 43 05). Metro Les Corts/bus 15, 43, 59, 70, 72. **Open** *box office* 3.45-11pm Mon-Thur, Sun; 3.45-11pm, midnight-1am, Fri, Sat. **Late shows** from 12.30am Fri, Sat and eves before public holidays. **Tickets** 575ptas Mon; 700ptas Tue-Fri; 725ptas Sat, Sun, public holidays. **No credit cards.**
In a nondescript corner a short walk from Les Corts Metro, this six-screen complex opened in 1995 and shows exclusively VO films, usually with at least two in English, and a separate programme for late shows. The auditoriums are well-sized and comfortable, the sound system is excellent, and they have unusually good facilities for disabled people.
Air-conditioning. Café. Disabled: toilet, wheelchair access.

Rex

Gran Via de les Corts Catalanes 463 (93 423 10 60). Metro Rocafort/bus 9, 27, 41, 50, 56, N1, N2. **Open** *box office* 30 min before first performance. **Tickets** 725ptas Mon, Tue, Thur, Fri; 600ptas Wed; 750ptas Sat, Sun, public holidays. **No credit cards. Map B4.**
A one-screen cinema that is the largest venue for VO films. In a plain 1960s building, it's comfortable and has a big screen.
Air-conditioning. Bar/café.

Verdi

C/Verdi 32 (93 237 05 16). Metro Fontana/bus 39.
Open *box office* 15 min before first performance. **Late shows** 12.45am Fri, Sat. **Tickets** 550ptas Mon; 725ptas Tue-Fri; 750ptas Sat, Sun, public holidays. **No credit cards. Map E2.**
The Verdi cinemas in Gràcia are the great success story of Barcelona's VO film houses. In 1992, the Verdi had three screens; in 1993, it added two more, and then in 1995 they opened the four-screen **Verdi Park** around the block. They're popular as meeting-places as well as movie-houses, and on weekend nights all nine *salas* can be packed. Classic revivals are shown alongside contemporary international releases, and there's a separate programme for late shows. The Verdi has

become internationally known for its willingness to screen new independent films. It also has one screen showing children's films, also usually in VO (*see chapter* **Children**).
Air-conditioning. Bar. Disabled: toilet, wheelchair access (Sala 1 & Verdi Park only).
Branch: Verdi Park C/Torrijos 49 (93 217 88 23).

The Filmoteca

Filmoteca de la Generalitat de Catalunya

Cinema Aquitania, Avda Sarrià 31-33 (93 410 75 90). Metro Hospital Clínic/bus 15, 27, 41, 54, N3. **Open** *box office* 1 hour before first performance. **Performances** 5pm, 7.30pm, 10pm; *mid-June-mid-Sept only* 5.30pm, 7.30pm, 10pm, daily. Closed public holidays & Aug.
Tickets 400ptas; 300ptas students and over-65s; 5,000ptas block ticket for 20 films; 10,000ptas for 100 films. **Credit** *for block tickets only* MC, V. **Map C2.**
The official Filmoteca shows a continually-changing slate of three films each day, nearly always in VO, usually in short seasons on themes, countries or directors. The eclectic mix is often fascinating, and the cinema is also exceedingly comfortable. In the past the *Filmo* has been a virtual school for aspiring directors and producers, at one time providing the only opportunity in the city to see classics from other countries. A children's programme is shown at 5pm on Sundays.

Events

Mostra Internacional de Films de Dones de Barcelona (Women's Film Festival)

Venue *Filmoteca de la Generalitat de Catalunya.* **Dates** first half of June.
Held since 1993, this event has been highly successful. It's organised by *Dracmàgic* (93 216 00 04), specialists in socio-cultural events, and aims to be an exhibition – not a competition – of women's cinema, past and present. Directors are invited to speak about their work, with lively debates.

Festival Internacional de Cinema de Catalunya, Sitges (Catalonia International Film Festival, Sitges)

Information *C/Rosselló 257, 3er-E, 08008 Barcelona (93 415 39 38/93 415 30 23/fax 93 237 65 21).*
Dates first half of October.
The new title of the long-running and very popular Sitges Festival of Fantastic Cinema, which began as a small-scale event specialising in all kinds of cinema roughly classed as 'fantastic', from sci-fi to pure fantasy or horror movies. This definition had become ever-looser over the years (to the irritation of real schlock buffs), and in 1997 was dropped from the title. Fantasy and horror still feature strongly in the programme, though, alongside other sections such as retrospectives of classic and lesser-known directors and the *Gran Angular* for new, previously-unseen international independent productions, whether by famous names such as Jean-Luc Godard (with *For Ever Mozart*, his film on Bosnia) or complete unknowns. This section also has its own prize which, as an original touch, is voted by the viewing public. In 1997 it went to *Knocking on Heaven's Door* by German director Thomas Jahn, while the main critics' prize was for Andrew Niccol's *Gattaca*. The festival is aimed both at the film/TV industry and the public, and this is a key to its success. Films are shown in several venues around Sitges, and the drama doesn't end with the show, as many restaurants and bars join in the spirit and stay open through the night. Tickets can also be bought in Barcelona through the Tel-Entrades system of the **Caixa de Catalunya** (*see p183*). *See chapter* **Trips Out of Town: Beaches** for details of how to get to Sitges, and where to stay and eat once you're there.

Gay & Lesbian Barcelona

Gay is in vogue in Barcelona, with clubs and cafés opening across town, and Sitges beach just down the road.

Barcelona boasts a flourishing gay scene throughout the year, with the summer and the February Carnival as highlights. It also has a big added attraction thank to its proximity to the beach town of Sitges, long a gay mecca of the Mediterranean.

As in any big city there's a tried-and-tested nightlife circuit. Also, Barcelona has many mixed venues, popular with a gay crowd rather than catering entirely for one; cafés or bars that are just gay-owned and/or have a welcoming atmosphere and sympathetic clientele can be as important as exclusively-gay locales as gay meeting points. The gay scene is referred to in Spanish as the *ambiente*, which can be deliberately ambiguous as the same word is used just to mean atmosphere, and a bar can be *un poco de ambiente* (a bit gay), or more.

There are many more venues for men than women, but places welcoming both sexes abound. There's a distinct lack of segregation in the scene, and dress codes are virtually non-existent.

As yet, there is no really comprehensive regular listings guide to Barcelona (for those that are available, *see chapter* **Media**), and information about what's on can be hard to find. A good bet is to pop into **Sextienda** or **Zeus** (*see below* **Gay services**), where they have a free map of gay Barcelona and will answer any questions you may have. Also, look for fliers in bars, and check the local gay press (*see below* **Gay & lesbian groups/info**).

Cafés & bars

As well as bars listed here, another drinking hole that is not gay per se but an essential gay-favourites is the wonderful **Cafè de l'Opera** on the Rambla (*see chapter* **Cafés & Bars**). Except where stated none of these bars take credit cards.

La Bata de Boatine

C/Robador 23 (93 318 48 11). Metro Liceu/bus 14, 18, 38, 59, N4, N6. **Open** 10.30pm-3am Tue-Sun. Closed Aug. **Map C5**
A long, narrow bar in the sleazy heart of the Barrio Chino, La Bata (meaning 'quilted dressing gown') was formerly an 'American bar', a prostitutes' watering hole. Now, it's an

intimate, friendly place that throws occasional one-off parties hosted by '*el niño de los zancos*' ('the boy on stilts'), who, in fact, tends to stay on his own two feet.

Café de la Calle

C/de Vic 11 (93 218 38 63). Metro Diagonal/bus 16, 17, 22, 24, 28, N6, N9. **Open** 6pm-2.30am Mon-Thur, Sun; 6pm-3am Fri, Sat. **Map D2**
A small, intimate affair, a bit like a combination of a café and someone's front room, with reasonably-priced drinks, good sandwiches and pleasant music that doesn't thump excessively. A good place to meet up and start the evening, popular with gay men and lesbians.

Café Dietrich

C/Consell de Cent 255 (no phone). Metro Universitat/bus 14, 54, 58, 59, 64, 66, N3. **Open** 7pm-2.30am daily. **Map C3**
Fast becoming the most popular gay bar in Barcelona, this bar/cabaret has quickly stolen clientele from **Este Bar** next door. A long, elegant bar greets you as you pass through a plush velvet curtain entrance. Go early to avoid the crush. Cutting-edge dance music complements the buzz of a place where everyone goes to see and be seen.

Este Bar

C/Consell de Cent 257 (no phone). Metro Universitat/bus 14, 54, 58, 59, 64, 66, N3. **Open** 7pm-2am daily. **Map C3**
A staple of gay Barcelona, Este maintains a small yet loyal clientele (although most cruise over to **Cafe Dietrich** and later return for a more quiet drink). It has bright, colourful décor, with temporary art shows around the walls, and well-chosen house music helps a pleasant atmosphere.

New Chaps

Avda Diagonal 365 (93 215 53 65). Metro Diagonal or Verdaguer/bus 6, 15, 33, 34, N4, N6. **Open** 8pm-2.30am Mon-Thur, Sun; 8pm-3am Fri, Sat. **Admission** 300ptas cover charge. **Map E3**
Once a cowboy hangout, complete with saloon-style swing doors, New Chaps now has chi-chi designer décor with plenty of neon lights, which are atmospherically dimmed when it starts getting full. Very cruisy and popular with an older, cloney crowd. There's a backroom, various dark corners and, for some reason, a swing (answers on a postcard, please).

Punto BCN

C/Muntaner 63-65 (93 453 61 23/93 451 91 52). Metro Universitat/bus 14, 54, 58, 59, 64, 66, N3. **Open** 6pm-2am daily. Closed Carnival Tue. **Map C4**
Prime attraction of Punto is that it opens at 6pm, and so is one of the few gay places where you can meet for a coffee before the rush starts. A huge, bright and friendly place, visited by a cross-section of the gay community, young and not-so-young alike. Also near many of the most popular bars.

*The friendly folk at nouveau-trendy **Schilling**.*

Schilling

C/Ferràn 23. Metro Liceu/bus 14, 18, 38, 59, N6, N9.
Open 10am-2.30am Mon-Sat; noon-2.30am Sun. **Map D5**
Cafe culture in the Barri Gòtic exploded with the opening of
this elegantly trendy bar/café. Although not gay by definition, it has become noticeably gay and cruisy. Enjoy morning coffee or lunch on foccacia sandwiches; it's also very alive
and bustling in the evening. *See also chapter* **Cafés & Bars**.

Tèxtil Cafè

*C/Montcada 12-14 (93 268 25 98). Metro Jaume I/bus
17, 19, 40, 45.* **Open** 10am-midnight Tue-Sun; July, Aug
10am-1am Tue-Sun. **Credit** AmEx, MC, V. **Map D5**
In the gorgeous courtyard of the **Museu Tèxtil** (*see chapter*
Museums) on C/Montcada, this café/restaurant is gay-run,
and provides good food and drink in what must be one of
the most delightful spots in the city. The perfect place for
that pre-lunch Martini. *See also chapter* **Cafés & Bars**.

Clubs

See chapter **Nightlife** for more venues that also
draw a sizeable gay clientele. Unless otherwise
stated, clubs don't take credit cards.

Arena

*C/Balmes 32 (no phone) Metro Passeig de Gràcia,
Universitat/bus 7, 16, 17, N1, N2.* **Open** midnight-5am
daily. **Admission** 1,000ptas (incl one drink). **Map D4**
Barcelona's newest gay disco in the tradition of Martins and
Metro has fast become a staple of gay nightlife. A large, spacious dancefloor and pounding house music attracts men of
all ages. Complete with information centre and dark room.

Arena VIP

*C/Diputació 233 (93 487 83 42).
Metro Universitat/bus all routes to Plaça Universitat.*
Open midnight-5am Fri, Sat; 7-10.30pm Sun.
Admission 500ptas (incl beer or soft drink). **Map C4**
The latest incarnation of a gay venue that has had several
different names, an extremely popular club with a healthy
mix of gays, lesbians and a few straight people. Opened by

the owners of Arena and Punto Barcelona, its sudden success is due to a fun weekend mix of clientele. The music is
an exciting mixture of past and present sounds.

Martins

*Passeig de Gràcia 130 (93 218 71 67). Metro Diagonal/
bus 22, 24, 28, N4, N6.* **Open** midnight-5am daily.
Admission 1,000ptas (incl one drink). **Map D2/D3**
Comprising three floors, Martins is a quieter version of
Metro, playing similar music. Although it has lost a lot of
clientele to Arena and Picasso on the weekends, special
events and theme parties are still popular.

Metro

*C/Sepúlveda 185 (93 323 52 27). Metro Universitat/bus
24, 41, 55, 64, 91, 141, N6.* **Open** midnight-5am daily.
Admission 1,000ptas (incl one drink). **Map C4**
Probably the busiest of Barcelona's gay clubs. Full most
nights, it's packed – sometimes uncomfortably so – at weekends, when every section of the gay male community is in
evidence. Women are welcome but infrequent visitors. Extra
entertainments include speciality nights (foam parties,
S&M), a café, TV and backrooms.

Picasso

*Avda Paral.lel 106 (no phone). Metro Paral.lel/bus 20, 36,
57, 64, N6.* **Open** 2am-6am Sat-Sun. **Admission**
1,500ptas. **Map C5**
Run by the owners of **Octopussy** (*see chapter* **Nightlife**),
this is the favourite weekend haunt of Barcelona's trendier
gay, lesbian and trans-gendered clubbers. Its main dance
area pumps out house and techno, while upstairs you can
check out the other bar and dancefloor with more classic
dance vibrations. The theme parties are not to be missed.

Taller

*C/Mèxic 7-9 (no phone). Metro Espanya/bus 9, 38, 65,
91, 109, N1.* **Open** 2-7am daily. **Admission** 1,000ptas
(incl one drink). **Map A4**
A dark, cavernous venue which has taken over where the
notorious Distrito Distinto was forced to leave off. Empty
until around 4am, it fills up with those who like to party hard.
Extremely cruisy and crushed, with a large backroom
upstairs. Music: house and techno.

Aire

C/Enric Granados 48 (93 451 8462). Metro Passeig de Gràcia, FGC Provença/bus 7, 16, 17, 54, 58, 64, 66, N3. **Lunch served** 1-4pm, **dinner served** 9-12pm, Mon-Sat. **Average** 3,000ptas. **Set dinner** 1,750-3,000ptas. **Credit** MC, V. **Map C3**

Tucked away in one of the prettiest streets in the Eixample, Aire is for serious dining. Its elegant yet laid back atmosphere and friendly staff are very welcoming, and a sophisticated menu offers a nice selection of meat and fish dishes.

Miranda

C/Casanova 30 (93 453 5249). Metro Universitat/bus all routes to Plaça Universitat. **Dinner served** 9-12am daily.

The sights of Sitges

Sitges is popular with gay men from all over the world, thanks to a combination of good beaches, a great climate, a pretty setting and an all-singing, all-dancing nightlife. It was once a sleepy fishing port, and the old town at its core has kept its charm, with its church standing above the sea and the beachfront *passeig* as its backbone.

A major date in Sitges is **Carnaval**, a week usually in mid-February, the main feature of which is the drag parade extravaganza when local queens emerge in all their best finery. Carnival sees the town come alive after the winter, with many bars opening up for the week before nodding off again until summer, when the Sitges gay scene really takes off. Most venues open on weekends in May; then, from the first week in June everything opens nightly until 1 October, when Trailer closes its doors for the end of the season. August is the busiest month. The rest of the year is quiet, but it's still a great place for a quiet day out, to stroll along the beach or eat a paella. For more on Sitges and how to get there, *see pages 226-7.*

Accommodation

It's easy to visit Sitges and get back to Barcelona in a day, but if you want to sample the late-night scene you'll need to stay over. The town naturally has any number of hotels and *hostals*, and many welcome gays: some of the most gay-friendly are **Hotel Romàntic** *C/Sant Isidre 33 (93 894 83 75/fax 93 894 81 67)*, a charming little hotel in a delightful nineteenth-century villa, with friendly staff, 24-hour key access and prices (*single* 7,600ptas; *double* 10,500-11,600ptas) that include breakfast; the same people also run **La Renaixenca** *C/Illa de Cuba 7 (93 894 83 75/fax 93 894 81 67)*, not quite as distinctive but also a historic building. Both have attractive gardens. The **Hotel Liberty** *C/Illa de Cuba 35 (93 811 08 72)*, is a less attractive but still popular place with modern facilities (air-conditioning, satellite TV, minibar, phone) and reasonable rates (*singles* 8,500ptas; *doubles* 9,500ptas). All three are very popular, so book.

Bars

There are bars for every taste and style in Sitges. Some change owners and names from one season to the next, while the traditionally popular ones continue to draw in their regular summer crowds. None except **Trailer** have admission charges, and only a few accept credit cards.

One place that's open year-round is **Bar 7** *C/Nou 7 (no phone)* a fun, 'pub-style' bar with bright décor and drag queen photos (open 10pm-3am). The recently opened **Casablanca** *C/Pau Barrabeitg 5 (93 894 70 82*; open 6pm-3am), is an elegant, cosmopolitan bar/café with beautiful mosaic tilework and candlelit tables. Then there are the classic **Bourbons** *C/Sant Bonaventura 9 (no phone)*, and **El Horno** *C/Juan Tarrida 6 (93 894 09 09)*, popular with an older crowd but a definite stop on a night out during the summer season.

Summer nightlife centres on **Mediterraneo** *C/Sant Bonaventura 6 (no phone)*, Sitges' biggest and most happening bar. It's a two-floor venue with its own terrace and great music from a parade of international DJs, packed nightly from 1am and the place to be seen before heading off to Trailer. **Parrots Pub** *Plaça de l'Industria (93 894 81 78)* with its outside terrace bar, is still popular for that first cold drink after a long day on the beach. Sitges' only all-gay disco, **Trailer** *C/Angel Vidal 36 (no phone)* has a big international crowd: young and trendy on the dancefloor, older around the edges, with DJs from all over playing the latest sounds. The 1,000ptas admission charge includes a drink. It closes around 5am, leaving its customers to do as they will – usually on the beach, which can be as busy by night as by day.

Restaurants

Sitges has many good places where you can eat in style. Gay visitors have always enjoyed the beautiful garden setting at **Flamboyant**, *C/Pau Barrabeitg 58 11)*, featuring a lovely set dinner menu (1,900ptas) as well as à la carte choices. In a quite different setting is **Castell** *C/Carreta 21 (93 894 33 49)*, a cosy and intimate environment where you can enjoy tasty fish, chicken and lamb dishes contrasted with American and British classics.

Average 3,000ptas. **Set dinner** 2,500ptas. **No credit cards. Map C4**

Fast becoming Barcelona's most popular 'gay cabaret' restaurant, with a guilded interior and leopard print seating that are a jungle fantasy come to life. Near many of the popular gay bars, it's a good choice for visitors to the city. Dinner includes a floor show of professional drag acts and other surprises, and the menu is modern and creative.
Booking essential.

La Morera

Plaça Sant Agustí 1 (93 318 75 55). Metro Liceu/bus 14, 18, 38, 59, N4, N6. **Lunch served** 1-3.30pm, **dinner served** 8.30-11.45pm, Mon-Sat. **Average** 1,850ptas. **Set lunch** 925ptas. **No credit cards. Map C5**

A small restaurant in a square just off C/Hospital, close to the Rambla. Owner and staff are all gay, as is a large percentage of the clientele. The food consists of better-than-average Catalan dishes and a good range of salads.
Air-conditioning. Booking essential (Fri, Sat).

La Mossegada

C/Diputació 214 (93 454 7275). Metro Universitat/bus 14, 54, 58, 64, 66, N3, N8. **Dinner served** 9-11pm Mon-Sat. **Average** 2,000ptas. **Set menus** 1,250ptas Mon-Thur; 1,500ptas Fri, Sat. **No credit cards. Map C4**

Latest of a recent string of 'gay' restaurants to open, this spacious place offers grilled and open sandwiches and salads in an informal café atmosphere. Near most of the popular bars, it's a great place to go for a light snack or for the full menu.
Booking essential (Fri, Sat).

Theseo

C/Comte de Borrell 119 (no phone). Metro Urgell/bus 9, 14, 50, 56, N1, N2. **Open** *bar* 1.30pm-1.30am Mon-Thur; 1.30pm-3am Fri, Sat. *lunch served* 1.30-4pm Mon-Sat. **Set lunch** 1,100ptas. **No credit cards. Map C3**

In a bustling area near Mercat de Sant Antoni, this café/restaurant/art gallery has interesting décor of exposed rustic brickwork combined with artistic, funky lighting design. It offers a fantastic creative-cuisine lunch menu mixing classic Spanish recipes with a special twist. Impressive art installations add to the experience.

Gay services

Accommodation

Hotel California

C/Rauric 14 (93 317 77 66/fax 93 317 54 74). Metro Liceu/bus 14, 18, 38, 59, N6, N9. **Rates** *single* 4,500-5,000ptas; *double* 7,000-8,000ptas. **Credit** AmEx, EC, MC, V. **Map D5**

The only hotel in Barcelona to cater for a gay (male) clientele. It's comfortable if not luxurious, and very central. It has 31 rooms (all with bathrooms), and although there's no bar, they can provide breakfast and drinks.
Hotel services *Air-conditioning. English & French spoken. Laundry. Safe.* **Room services** *Minibar (some). Radio. Room service (24hrs). Telephone. TV.*

Bookshops

Antinous

C/Josep Anselm Clavé 6 (93 301 90 70). Metro Drassanes/bus 14, 18, 36, 38, 57, 59, 64. **Open** 10am-9pm Mon-Fri; 11.30am-9pm Sat. **Credit** AmEx, DC, MC, V. **Map D5**

A bright and spacious bookshop with an extensive range of gay literature and magazines, local press and cultural information, and a nice little café in the back to enjoy a coffee.

Complices

C/Cervantes 2 (93 412 72 83). Metro Jaume I/bus 17, 40, 45. **Open** 10.30am-8.30pm Mon-Fri; noon-8.30pm Sat. **Credit MC, V. Map D5**

Barcelona's first gay bookshop. Run collectively by friendly, mainly female staff, it has a wide selection of books and magazines in Catalan and Spanish, as well as foreign titles.

Other shops

B Free

Plaça Vila de Madrid 5 (93 412 27 59). Metro Plaça Catalunya/bus 14, 38, 59, N6, N9. **Open** 10.30am-8pm Mon-Fri; noon-8.30pm Sat. **Credit** MC, V. **Map D4-5**

A 'fashion and gay culture' shop with a wide range of disco and work-out fashions, jewellery, cards and information.

Sextienda

C/Rauric 11 (93 318 86 76). Metro Liceu/bus 14, 18, 38, 59, N6, N9. **Open** 10am-8.30pm Mon-Sat. **Credit** MC, V. **Map D5**

A sex shop that hands out free gay maps of Barcelona and Sitges as well as selling mags, sex aids, condoms, poppers and videos. Friendly, helpful staff.

Zeus

C/Riera Alta 20 (93 442 97 95). Metro Sant Antoni/bus 24, 64. **Open** 10am-9pm Mon-Sat. **Credit** V. **Map C4**

Similar to Sextienda, also very friendly and also offering a free gay Barcelona/Sitges guide and information.

Zona Intima

C/Muntaner 61 (93 453 71 45). Metro Universitat/bus 54, 58, 64, 66, N3. **Open** 10am-2pm, 5-8.30pm, Mon-Sat. **Credit** JCB, MC, V. **Map C3**

Pricey designer clothing and underwear/accessories: a place to go to if you can't go on without a new pair of Calvin Kleins.

Saunas

Each centre has showers, porno lounges and cubicles. On arrival you are given a locker key, a pair of very un-chic plastic sandals and a towel. Drinks are charged to you when you leave. BYO condoms, as they can be difficult to come by inside. Most popular are the Casanova and Thermas, both when the clubs empty out and on weekend afternoons.
Sauna Casanova *C/Casanova 57 (93 323 78 60/93 318 06 38). Metro Urgell/bus 9, 50, 54, 56, 58, 64, 66, N1, N2, N3.* **Open** 11am-5.30am Mon-Thur; 11am-5.30am Mon. **Admission** 1,200ptas Tue, Thur; 1,600ptas Mon, Wed, Fri-Sun. **Credit** MC, V. **Map C4**
Sauna Condal *C/Espolsa-Sacs 1 (93 301 96 80). Metro Urquinaona/bus 16, 17, 18, 19, 24, 40, 45 and all nightbuses to Plaça Catalunya.* **Open** 11am-5.30am Mon-Thur; 11am Fri-5.30am Mon. **Admission** 1,200ptas Mon, Wed; 1,600ptas Tue, Thur-Sun. **Credit** MC, V. **Map D4**
Sauna Thermas *C/Diputació 46 (93 325 93 46). Metro Rocafort/bus 9, 27, 50, 56, 109, 127, N1, N2.* **Open** noon-2am Mon-Thur; noon Fri-2am Sun. **Admission** 1,500ptas. **Credit** V. **Map B4**

Gay & lesbian groups/info

Groups/centres

Actua *C/Gomis 38, baixos (93 418 50 00/fax 93 418 89 74). Bus 22, 73, 85.* **Open** 9am-2pm, 4pm-7pm, Mon-Fri. Modelled on Act-Up groups in the US and Britain, a thriving organisation of people living with HIV, giving counselling and information.
Ca la Dona *C/Casp 38, pral (tel/fax 93 412 71 61). Metro Urquinaona/bus all routes to Plaça Catalunya.* **Open** *office* 10am-2pm, 4-8pm, Mon-Fri. **Closed** Aug. **Map D4**

Barcelona's main women's centre houses several groups including a lesbian feminist outfit and Grup d'ajuda mútua Tamaia, a women's self-help group. See also page 268.
Casal Lambda C/Ample 5 (93 412 72 72/fax 93 412 74 76). Metro Drassanes/bus 14, 18, 36, 38, 57, 59, 64. **Open** 5-9pm Mon-Thur; 5pm-midnight Fri; noon-10pm Sat, Sun. **Map D5**
A gay cultural organisation that runs weekly outings and parties (open to non-members), hosts a range of different men's and women's groups, publishes gay monthly Lambda and also has an attractive patio inside. Used more by men than women, but always welcoming and relaxed.
Coordinadora Gai-Lesbiana C/Buenaventura Muñoz 4 (93 900 601 601/fax 93 218 11 91). Metro Arc del Triomf/bus 39, 41, 51. **Open** 5-9pm Mon-Fri. **Map E5**
Well-established umbrella organisation recognised by the Ajuntament (city council) and working with them on issues such as AIDS. Includes a Body Positive-like self-help group, a lesbian group, Gay Christians, a youth group and the Teléfon Rosa phoneline (see below).
FESLU C/Vidre 10, 2º 3ª (93 412 15 09). Metro Drassanes/bus 14, 18, 38, 59, N6, N9. **Map D5**
The name stands for festes lúdiques, a fancy way of saying 'Free time, party time!', meaning a group of dykes who organise 'entertainments' connected with **La Illa** (see **Lesbian Barcelona**) and the monthly women's disco at Picasso.
Front d'Alliberament Gai de Catalunya (FAG) C/Villarroel 62, 3º 1ª (93 454 63 98). Metro Urgell/bus 9, 14, 20, 50, 56, 59, N1. **Map C3**
An active group that includes various collectives and groups, and produces the Barcelona Gai information bulletin.
Laberint Apt de Correus 5394, 08080 (93 215 63 36). Magazine produced (sporadically) by a radical lesbian group, Red de Amazonas. In Spanish, despite the Catalan title.

Phonelines

AIDS Information Line (93 339 87 56). **Open** 9am-5.30pm Mon-Fri. An official Ajuntament health information service. English speakers are available.
Teléfon Rosa (93 900 601 601). **Open** 6-10pm daily. Very helpful service with advice on AIDS and gay rights, and information on clubs and events. English spoken.

Lesbian Barcelona

Lesbian culture and identity are not particularly marked here, but the Barcelona dyke scene has been growing stronger and more visible. Some of the longest-established bars are within walking distance of each other in Gràcia, but there are many new mixed bars and clubs scattered around the Eixample and Barri Gòtic. There are also regular fun weekend special events and women-only dances, weekly and monthly.

It's useful to recognise a few Castilian phrases: to flirt is tirar los tejos (literally, to throw the tiles at someone); tener pluma (to have feathers) is to look obviously gay; to pick up someone is ligar (to tie or bind); entender (to understand) is to be gay (you understand?) and the scene is the ambiente. Gay Pride day is celebrated with a small parade and celebrations in late June, and has been becoming more and more popular. Barcelona's lesbian and gay bookshop, **Complices** is doing booming business, lesbian films are shown to enthusiastic audiences in the Women's Film Festival each June

(see chapter **Film**), and there's very little hassle on the streets. With growing Gay/lesbian exposure in film and the media, the scene is very much alive.

Cafés, bars, restaurants, clubs

See **Gay** (above) for mixed venues where women are welcome. **Café de la Calle** is a lesbian favourite, and there is a great monthly dyke night at **Picasso**. Unless stated otherwise admission is free and credit cards are not accepted.

Bahia

C/Seneca 12 (no phone). Metro Diagonal/bus 6, 7, 15, 22, 24, 27, 28, 33, 34, N4, N6. **Open** 10pm-3am daily; Christmas Eve 10am-midnight. **Map D2**
Trendy Gothic bar with good music and friendly atmosphere. After-hours session is growing in popularity.

Bar Fortuny

C/Pintor Fortuny 31 (93 317 98 92). Metro Liceu/bus 14, 38, 59, N6, N9. **Open** 10am-midnight Tue-Sun. **Map D4**
Just off La Rambla, this bright, kitsch bar/café is an ideal rest stop when exploring the Raval. The women behind the bar serve a tasty variety of healthy international dishes in the evening, or you can enjoy a pre-dinner drink before moving on. Another place that's not exclusively lesbian, but feminist-orientated and definitely popular with gay women. See also chapter **Cafés & Bars**.

Cheek To Cheek

C/Muntaner 325 (no phone). FGC Muntaner/bus 58, 64, N8. **Open** 10pm-2am daily. **Map D2**
Outside, it looks a bit like an English pub; inside you'll find a pleasant atmosphere and friendly Catalan dykes.

Free Girls

C/Marià Cubi 4 (no phone). FGC Gràcia/bus 16, 17, 27. **Open** 11pm-3am Fri, Sat. **Admission** free. **Map D2**
Formerly known as Imagine, this disco/pub attracts a younger lesbian crowd.

La Illa

C/Reig i Bonet 3 (93 210 00 62). Bus 21, 39, N4. **Open** 7.30pm-1am Mon-Thur, Sun; 8pm-3am Fri, Sat. **Map E2**
Women-only cultural association which is also the best lesbian sandwich bar in town and hosts a range of activities, from bossa nova nights (live music on Thursdays) and dark-room discos (reggae, soul) to lesbian choir sessions (Mondays) and great monthly theme nights.

Members

C/Seneca 3 (93 237 12 04). Metro Diagonal/bus 6, 7, 15, 22, 24, 27, 28, 33, 34, N4, N6. **Open** 9pm-2.30am Tue-Thur, Sun; 9pm-3am Fri, Sat. **Map D2**
A tiny dancefloor, but this is a standard lesbian hangout, mirrored pillars and all. Also now increasingly mixed.

La Rosa

C/Brusi 39, passatge (93 414 61 66). FGC Sant Gervasi/bus 16, 17, 27, 58, 64, 127, N8. **Open** 10pm-3am Thur-Sun, eves of public holidays. **Admission** 350ptas. **Map C2**
This is the centre of the hardcore dyke scene: tacky but still very popular.

La Singular

C/Francisco Giner 50 (93 237 50 98). Metro Diagonal/bus 22, 24, 28, N4, N6. **Meals served** 6pm-2am Tue-Fri; 1pm-2.30am Sat, Sun. **Map D2**
Very friendly dyke-run tapas bar with local home-cooked dishes (around 600ptas) and tasty desserts (450ptas).

Media

*Sport sheets, scandal sheets, neighbourhood radio and
ever more TV: what makes Barcelona tick.*

Barcelona's media world has been characterised by
continual change, and continues to be so. All the
main print and broadcast media have been created
or totally transformed since the 1970s. In the press,
the major newspapers – *El País, El Periódico, La
Vanguardia* – have their places in local life, but
other projects are noticeably volatile, as this year's
success turns into next year's closure.

The pace of change has been greatest in television. Spaniards watch more television than anyone else in Europe – after Britain. In the 1980s the
monopoly of state broadcaster TVE was broken
by the arrival of separate channels for autonomous
regions, first of them the Catalan TV3 in 1983.
Private channels arrived in 1989, transforming
viewing habits, and around the same time satellite
dishes began to spring up on Barcelona's balconies. In the last few years, people willing to pay
for the pleasure have had a steadily increasing
number of channels to zap into. Cable television is
still in its infancy, but licences have been adjudi-
cated and the industry is gaining momentum.

Volatility of a kind also characterises the politics of the media, with a disquieting overlap
between the worlds of politics and journalism.
This became especially marked after the right-
wing *Partido Popular* (PP) of José María Aznar
came to power in Madrid in 1996, since when the
relationship between media and government has
often resembled that of a Latin American country
more than a European democracy. Matters have
come to a head precisely over the expansion of
TV, as moves to change the regulatory framework
in broadcasting have precipitated tremendous
struggles for control of digital, satellite and pay
television (*see* **Partly political broadcasts**).

A feature of the media specific to Catalonia in the
past few years has been the expansion of Catalan-
language broadcasting. Bidding head-to-head for
mass audiences with Spanish media, Catalan TV and
radio have won healthy ratings. In fact, in 1997 TV3
had the highest viewing numbers in Catalonia of any
network. This success, however, contrasts with the
continuing weakness of print media in Catalan.

Malalts de Tele, on **TV3**. *See page 203.*

Malalts de Tele, on **TV3**. *See page 203.*

limited range of papers, the giant news-stands on
the Rambla offer a vast range of magazines –
design magazines, porn, sports, and the inimitable
gossip mags, which, unlike dailies, are the same
from one end of the Spanish state to the other.

Newspapers & magazines

Avui
The *Avui* was launched in 1976 as the first Catalan-language
newspaper published openly for 40 years, and its appearance was heralded as a great national event. However, it soon
established a reputation for stuffiness and failed to win more
than a limited readership. A 1990s redesign has made it more
lively, but its position remains shaky, and some say its days
are numbered, particularly since the aggressive launch in
1997 of a Catalan edition of *El Periódico*.

El Mundo de Catalunya
In Madrid, *El Mundo* is the main rival of *El País*, and won
its reputation through its exposure of the scandals of the previous Socialist government of Felipe González. However,
with its PP allies in power the paper's appetite for inves-
tigative reporting on government seems very diminished. In
1995 it launched a separate Catalan edition, which so far has

Press

All the main dailies are locally-produced – there is
no real Spanish 'national' press – and there are no
true mass-appeal popular papers. In contrast to the

Partly political broadcasts

In Spain, when one party is voted out of power, as the Socialists were in 1996, and another voted in, as was the *Partido Popular*, it means everyone at the huge national public station TVE, from the director general to the anchor person on the 9pm news, has to consider whether they should clear their desk. The fact that the staff are not fixed but depend on a political party for their jobs must lead to a certain anxiety. It certainly leads to a noticeable absence of commitment to quality, and as unabashed a use of the station to stay in power as the ruling party can get away with.

Programme content on TVE 1 has taken a noticeable turn to the right since Aznar came to power. There has also been a blurring of the lines between government, media and the courts that has been extremely distressing to anyone concerned to see truly independent media. Day after day there have been new revelations of media collusion with the politicians. In early 1998, for instance, the editor of the conservative Madrid daily *ABC* confessed that during the

Socialist years he had been part of a group centered around a talk-show on COPE, a radio network owned by the Catholic Church. They were dedicated to conspiring against the then-governing party and their leader, Felipe González. Among them was also Pedro Rodríguez, chief of *El Mundo*. And 1997's media news was dominated by the government's attempt to provide the Teléfonica phone company's Via Digital with the lion's share of the satellite TV market by hook, crook or blatantly illegal methods, going to such extremes as introducing legislation to prohibit the type of decoder used by competitor Canal Satellite (a ban ruled unacceptable by the EU) and bringing criminal charges (later dismissed) against Canal Satellite investors.

In Catalonia, some 'balance' is provided by the fact that TV3 and Canal 33 are dependent not on the Aznar government but on the Generalitat. What this means, though, is that in turn any negative news about Jordi Pujol and *his* team is harder to find on TV3 than the famous needle in a haystack.

survived in a difficult market. In addition, editor Pedro Rodríguez has been involved in ongoing scandals of his own, both political – around his willingness to act as a mouthpiece for the PP – and personal, including a videotape in which he is allegedly seen being whipped by a Dominican prostitute.

El País

Spain's premier daily, and the only one that could claim to be a national newspaper, although to succeed in Barcelona it has a substantially different local edition. Also founded in 1976, *El País* has been a great success story of modern Spain. With Friday's edition comes the *Tentaciones* supplement, with arts features and listings, and Saturday's includes the *Babelia* literature and arts section. Politically it has been sympathetic to the Socialists, and critical of the Pujol administration in Catalonia. Its chairman Jesús Polanco was the subject of criminal charges trumped up by the Aznar government in 1997, trying to force him out of the satellite TV business, and the paper is at loggerheads with *El Mundo*.

El Periódico de Catalunya

The closest local papers to a tabloid, with big headlines, colour, lots of photos and a healthy readership, but still more wordy than a true popular tabloid would be. In politics, more or less left-wing and sympathetic to the Socialists. Since 1997 it has had an edition in Catalan (the one with a blue masthead), with completely the same editorial content as its Spanish one. With breezier style and design, it should provide stiff competition for *Avui*. From July to September it runs a double-page spread in English, French and Italian.

Sport & El Mundo Deportivo

Two papers in direct competition with one another, both entirely devoted to sports. This is where to catch up with the ongoing melodrama of Barcelona FC, which usually takes up over half their pages. Highlights are the vox-pops, when fans-in-the-street have their say on last weekend's game plan.

La Vanguardia

Top-selling paper in Catalonia in living memory, and the only one to rival *El País* in resources and coverage. Founded in 1881, it is the only Barcelona paper to have survived since the Franco years (and beyond). It has done so by revamping itself with a 1980s redesign that has made it a lively, imaginative paper; its international correspondents, particularly in Latin America and the Middle East, are excellent. Politically, *La Vanguardia* has always been conservative and is now generally sympathetic to the Pujol government (dull Pujol stories are frequently on the front page), but one reason why it has survived so well is that it never commits itself too strongly to any position. Very good for listings (*Cartelera*), especially for Catalonia outside Barcelona. Again, some Catalan-language features.

¡Hola!, Semana, Lecturas, Diez Minutos...

Checking up on what's going on in the *prensa del corazón* ('heart press') is an essential part of being in Spain, for after all, as its nationalities move apart, knowing who these celebs are who are marrying, splitting up, recovering from surgery or just showing off their new furniture to the readers could be one of few things that gives the place a common culture. Regulars include international paparazzi-material like Naomi Campbell, David Copperfield and royalty, but there's also a stream of home-grown Spanish attention-grabbers, some of whom seem to do very little *except* appear in the magazines.

Classified ads

The best paper for general classifieds is *La Vanguardia*, especially on Sundays. There are three specialised small-ad magazines: *Primeramà*, published Tuesdays and Thursdays (93 321 40 40), carries general ads, as does *Los Clasificados* (906 30 61 60), every Wednesday, which has a large job ad section. *Mercat Laboral*, out Friday (93 321 65 56), is dedicated to job ads. Placing ads in all three magazines is free.

English-language press

Best places to find international papers are the kiosks on the Rambla and Passeig de Gràcia. For more specialised press try **Crisol** or **Laie Llibreria-Café** (*see chapters* **Shopping** *and* **Cafés & Bars**).

Barcelona Business

A monthly free sheet launched in 1998 with a wide range of news, business and general articles on Catalonia. There's also a 'directory' of useful addresses and numbers. It can be obtained by subscription (fax 93 443 04 40), from stands at the airport, and various venues around town.

Barcelona Metropolitan

A free monthly magazine launched in 1996 aimed mainly at English-speaking Barcelona residents, with classifieds, useful advice and extensive listings of what's on each month in film, music, the arts, and nightlife, plus feature articles on many aspects of local life. Available in cinemas, bars, consulates and a variety of locations around the city.

Listings magazines

The weekly *Tentaciones* supplement of *El País* is an extra source of information, and there are several free magazines that add to the sometimes limited scope of *Guia del Ocio*. For titles, *see chapter* **Music: Rock, Roots & Jazz**.

Guía del Ocio

Published weekly, on Thursdays, with basic what's-on information. Good for cinema and theatre, less so for music.

TV & radio

TV

Today it's possible to receive seven conventional channels in Barcelona, and the subscription channel Canal Plus (usually written Canal+). The coming of private TV in 1989 led to a scramble for audiences, with channels going straight for the mass market with game shows, chat, soaps and true-life drama 'reality shows'. Since the mid-1990s, another audience-grabber has been live football, to the extent of overkill.

All channels, private or not, carry advertising. Films make up a high proportion of programmes and some are shown in the original language with subtitles, particularly on TVE 2 and Canal+. With the right type of set it's also possible to see otherwise-dubbed films in the original language on TV3.

TVE 1 (La Primera)

The state television's flagship network has lost a quarter of its audience to private channels, and in Catalonia to TV3. TVE 1 in Catalonia, is mostly in Spanish, with a few programmes in Catalan. As far as news goes, since the PP victory the entire top echelon of the station has changed; news programmes have become heavily pro-government, and the network's credibility suffers as a result.

TVE 2 (La 2)

TVE's second channel shows slightly more intellectual programming than TVE 1, and more sports, particularly at weekends. In Barcelona, nearly half its programmes are in Catalan. Late-night movies, often in English, are a highlight.

TV3

Set up by the Generalitat in 1983, this all-Catalan-language channel has won healthy audiences with programmes such as the wacky satire show *Malalts de Tele*, amid more routinely conventional material. Original Catalan-language soap operas – a new departure for the channel in the 1990s – have also proven extremely popular, but TV3 also produces the occasional quality documentary, particularly in its Sunday-night prime-time slot *30 Minuts*. One of the main channels

for live football on Saturday nights, and European Barça games on Wednesdays. Programmes shown dubbed on TV3 can be seen in English on sets with a NICAM stereo system.

Canal 33

Opened in 1989 as a second Catalan-language complement to TV3, showing slightly more 'quality' programming, movies and sports. Its Friday night programme *60 Minuts* airs excellent documentaries from around the world.

Antena 3

The first and now most successful of the private channels, its programmes (the same throughout Spain, and thus all in Spanish) are a fairly bland mix of game shows, football, endless chat, and some good-quality films.

Tele 5

Tele 5 started off as pace-setter in the ratings war, grabbing itself an audience with a non-stop stream of prizes, soaps and entertainment extravaganzas, but in the mid-1990s the formula seemed to pale, and the channel became more sober. Recently it's picked up with some lively chat shows.

Canal+

Associated with the similar French channel, Canal+ is only available to subscribers, but many hotels, cafés and bars receive it. It's primarily a movie and sports channel, showing recent films (often undubbed), and has paid out huge sums to win exclusive rights to show most live league football games. It also has the best football show on TV, *El Dia Después* on Monday nights, with former Liverpool man Michael Robinson. Also strong news slots, documentaries, music, and comedy. Canal+ shows US ABC News at 8.05am, daily. This is not codified, and so accessible to non-subscribers.

BTV (Channel 39)

Launched in 1994, the Ajuntament's local public-access channel. It's on-air daily, and material runs from concerts and theatre to talk, sports, general information and occasional film classics. It relies heavily on student broadcasters, but even so its 9pm newscast has won considerable respect. Revamped and reorganised in 1997 as BTV, it's sometimes the best viewing in town, although the signal is weak in some *barris*. At night, when its off the air, there's a single camera trained on the fish at the Aquàrium, with music.

Satellite & cable

Cable is only just beginning here, and only a tiny part of the city is wired to receive CTC (Cable Televisió de Catalunya). Digital satellite TV, though, is going strong. There are two providers: Via Digital, owned by the previously state-owned phone company Telefónica, and Canal Satellite, owned by Canal+ and the company that owns *El País*, PRYSA, among others. The struggle between them is a major political controversy. Both offer a basic programme package for around 3,000 pesetas a month; whether there will be enough subscribers to support them both, or they will merge into one super satellite-provider, remains to be seen.

Radio

There is a healthy underground radio scene; these stations have irregular hours and may be hard to pick up in some parts of town. Ones to try for include **Ràdio Contrabanda** (91.3 FM), which has an English-language slot at 6pm on Saturdays; **Ciutat Vella** (106.8 FM), for multi-varied music; and **Ràdio Pica** (91.8 FM) for a bit of everything. On the above-ground dial, good music stations are **Catalunya Música** (101.5 FM), mainly for classical music, with some jazz, while **Ràdio Associació de Catalunya** (105 FM) has a mix that includes rock, jazz, world music and R&B.

The **BBC World Service** can be picked up on 15070, 12095, 9410 and 6195 KHz Short Wave, depending on the time of the day.

Music: Classical & Opera

Casals, Caballé, Carreras – Barcelona has a rich musical tradition, and soon may actually have the venues to satisfy its concert-goers' demands.

A catastrophe, or just a disaster with a silver lining? It looks as though it's going to be the latter. Barcelona is coming out of the state of shock it went into in January 1994, when a chance spark from a welder's torch sent the **Liceu** opera house up in smoke in just a few hours. Having presided over the Rambla since the 1840s, the Liceu was one of the most venerable cultural institutions in a city that is always creating new ones. It was also a musty old theatre with completely antiquated backstage facilities, the inadequacies of which had been discussed for years.

Work began remarkably quickly on building a new Liceu, retaining the old façade – which had survived the fire – but with entirely new, expanded design and rehearsal spaces. The result, five years and many million pesetas later, is that Barcelona is to acquire a world-class, state-of-the-art opera house behind the old shell. The current line is that the Liceu will reopen in summer or autumn 1999; the date is still open to question, but the intention is to inaugurate the new Liceu with a gala performance of *Turandot*, the opera due to be staged before the fire.

Despite a very old-school elitist image that put off wider audiences – many of Barcelona's grander families held private boxes, which are not going to be replaced in the new opera house – the Liceu had a central position in the musical world because of the particularly strong choral and operatic tradition in Catalonia. Catalans love song, and have produced many great singers, from Francesc Viñas at the turn of the century to Victoria de los Ángeles and today's stars Jaume Aragall, Montserrat Caballé and José (known here as Josep) Carreras. Choral societies have been a Catalan institution since the last century, and the most established – such as the **Orfeó Català** and **Coral Sant Jordi** – are of international standing. Indeed, such is the strength of the Catalan tradition in singing that not only the Liceu but also Barcelona's other great musical venue, the **Palau de la Música Catalana**, was built as a choral and operatic, rather than orchestral, concert hall.

ORCHESTRAL OVERTURES

The Catalan musical tradition is by no means limited to singing, for the country has also been home to many distinguished musicians in other fields: the immense figure of cellist Pablo (known here as Pau) Casals, pianist Alicia de Larrocha, and composers Robert Gerhard, Eduard Toldrà and Xavier Montsalvatge. Barcelona's orchestras, however, have never enjoyed the same prestige as its singers.

Today, Barcelona has two official orchestras, the Liceu orchestra and the cumbersomely named **Orquestra Simfònica de Barcelona i Nacional de Catalunya**, more easily referred to as the **OBC**. Both are considered competent, but neither has received critical acclaim away from home. The city's lack of a world-class orchestra has long been a sensitive point, but things are improving. American conductor Lawrence Foster took over as resident director of the OBC in 1996, with a brief to produce a Barcelona-based symphony orchestra with an international reputation. The absence of adequate musical infrastructure is an area perhaps of more concern to the city's musicians. They are irked by the authorities' willingness to spend vast amounts on grand events while paying much less attention to musical education, or the provision of rehearsal and performance spaces. As far as venues are concerned, the shortage is slowly being corrected, and the success of new private initiatives such as the **Auditori Winterthur** (in the strange setting of a shopping mall on the Diagonal) is demonstrating the appetite for more accessible classical music locales.

Since the Liceu fire a near-impossible burden of activity has been born by Barcelona's most unique concert hall, the *Modernista* **Palau de la Música**. Already altered and extended in the 1980s, this extraordinary building is about to go under the knife in another, desperately needed expansion project conceived by the same architect, Oscar Tusquets. The intention is to tear down an adjacent church and add another 600-seat concert hall by the year 2000. Don't worry, however – the promise is that this renovation will not close the Palau. With any luck, to take the strain off the old place it is hoped the city authorities will complete a project they have had in hand for years, the **Auditori** by Plaça de les Glòries. This box-like building should contain two modern concert halls, abundant rehearsal and ancillary space and a new permanent home for the OBC, the Barcelona Conservatory and even the **Museu de la Música** (*see chapter* **Museums**). However, it has been dogged by delays and has fallen a very long way behind its neighbour the **Teatre Nacional**, now up and running (*see chapter* **Theatre**), and is unlikely to see performances before the millenium.

Whatever its problems in institutions and hardware, Barcelona has a large and enthusiastic audience for classical music, and concert-going is very popular. The city is also the base for a dynamic contemporary music scene. There are several ensembles active in the field, and interesting composers include Joan Guinjoan, Albert Guinovart and the eccentric Carles Santos. The most regular venues for contemporary concerts are the **Fundació Miró**, **Teatre Lliure** and the **Centre de Cultura Contemporània de Barcelona** (**CCCB**, *see chapter* **Art Galleries**), but there are performances fairly frequently at the **Casa Elizalde** and **L'Espai** (*see chapter* **Dance**).

Programmes & tickets

The *Guia del Ocio* has thin coverage of classical music, and the best sources of information, apart from the programme leaflets of individual venues, are the leaflet *Informatiu Musical* and monthly magazine *Barcelona en Música*, both free from tourist offices and many record shops. Procedures for buying tickets in advance vary. At smaller venues, tickets are often available only from the box office, but, as with theatres, tickets for several venues are sold through savings banks (*see p183*). Tickets handled by La Caixa can be bought with a credit card from the Servi-Caixa machines at the bank's branches, or booked by phone with a card on freephone 902 33 22 11; tickets handled by the Caixa de Catalunya can be bought in Plaça Catalunya, over the counter at its branches or by phone with a credit card on freephone 902 10 12 12.

The procedure for obtaining tickets for performances at the **Palau de la Música** also varies. Tickets for the OBC season are obtainable only from the Palau box office (or by post from the Orchestra's office); many are sold in the form of *abonaments* or season tickets for the whole year, and season-ticket holders have priority when booking, so the number of seats on open sale can be quite low. Note, though, that many concert series are organised by independent agencies, especially **Ibercàmera** and **Euroconcert**, who are responsible for bringing big international names to the city. Tickets for these series, and for the Liceu season are available through Servi-Caixa or the Caixa de Catalunya. For all concerts at the Palau, though, demand is very high, and it's advisable to obtain tickets as promptly as possible.

Concert promoters

Euroconcert *Rambla Catalunya 10, 2n 4a (93 318 51 58). Metro Catalunya/bus all routes to Plaça Catalunya.* **Open** 9.30am-1.30pm, 4-7pm Mon-Thur; 9.30am-1.30pm Fri.
Ibercàmera *Gran Via de les Corts Catalanes 636, 1er 2na (93 317 90 50/reservations 93 301 69 43). Metro Passeig de Gràcia/bus 7, 16, 17, 22, 24, 28, 50, 54, 56.* **Open** 10am-2pm, 3-6pm Mon-Fri.

Orchestras & ensembles

La Capella Reial de Catalunya & Grup Hespèrion

Catalan early music specialist Jordi Savall won international acclaim when he played the beautiful baroque score for the French film *Tous les Matins du Monde*. One of the finest performers of renaissance-to-seventeenth-century music in the world, he returns home frequently with his different ensembles to present concerts on original instruments, often in wonderful Gothic settings. Savall concerts are a regular highlight of the **Festival de Música Antiga** (*see below*).

Orfeó Català

Information *Palau de la Música, C/Sant Francesc de Paula 2 (93 268 10 00).* **Map D4**
The Orfeó is a national institution as well as a choir, and such were its status and wealth at the turn of the century that it was able to commission the building of the Palau de la Música. It has undergone radical change since 1985, when, its average age was over 60. Today, the quality of the choir, with 87 singers of all ages, has greatly improved, and new director Josep Vila is considered one of the leading figures in choral music in Europe. The Orfeó's repertoire consists of the great choral classics. It spends most of its time in Catalonia and Spain, but occasionally performs abroad.

Orquestra de Cadaqués

Information *C/dels Arcs 8 (93 302 27 22).* **Map D5**
Created in 1988, this is the brainchild of conductor Edmon Colomer and the **Festival de Cadaqués**. It is Catalan in name only, however, as its young musicians are international. Every other year they sponsor an international competition for orchestra conductor, and the winner receives a contract for 20 concerts. Its emphasis is split between contemporary composers and the recuperation of early Spanish composers, such as Durán, Carnicer and Terradellas. The orchestra isn't a full-time occupation for its members, but it tours several times each year as well as playing in Barcelona, at the festival in Cadaqués itself, where regular conductors include Sir Neville Marriner and Gennady Rozhdestvensky, and at **Perelada** (*see below* **Festivals**).

Orquestra de Cambra Teatre Lliure

Information: **Teatre Lliure** (*see chapter* **Theatre**).
The innovative Teatre Lliure is also a focus for contemporary music, with its own well-regarded chamber orchestra. Programmes are entirely twentieth century, and concerts are usually on Mondays, Thursdays and Sundays. Directed by Josep Pons, the orchestra has a commission to make two recordings a year for Harmonia Mundi, which have included works by Josep Soler, Luis de Pablo and Joan Albert Amargós. They also perform at the Auditori de la Caixa.

Orquestra Simfònica de Barcelona i Nacional de Catalunya (OBC)

Information & postal bookings *OBC, Via Laietana 41 pral, 08003 (93 317 10 96).* **Map D5**
This orchestra was founded as the *Orquestra Municipal de Barcelona* in 1944, and later became the *Orquestra Ciutat de Barcelona*. Its present laborious official title is a give-away that it is now supported, in a rare moment of collaboration, by both the Barcelona Ajuntament and the Generalitat, who have come together with a clear commitment to establish it as a front-rank international orchestra. As part of this, despite its standing engagements at the Palau, the orchestra now tours more frequently. Its musical director is American, Lawrence Foster, with German Franz-Paul Decker as principal visiting conductor. As the old *Ciutat de Barcelona* orchestra it was often accused of complacency and of relying too much on the loyalty of Palau season-ticket holders, and Decker himself had a confrontation with the orchestra's members during a spell as its director in the 1980s, when he

suggested that one quick way to improve it would be to introduce some foreign players. Its membership has since changed considerably, and chic Catalan designer Antonio Miró has recently outfitted them in smart new performing attire. As well as its principal conductors the OBC also performs under leading guest conductors such as Eliahu Inbal or Christopher Hogwood (due to conduct a new Mozart series), and with an international range of soloists who in the 1998 season will include Radu Lupu and Franz Peter Zimmermann. In its musical choices the orchestra has two main areas of emphasis: to present a full and enterprising international repertoire, and also to perform and record the range of Catalan music. Its main concert season at the Palau runs from September to May; there are concerts most Fridays (9pm) and Saturdays (7pm), and hugely popular, lower-price Sunday morning concerts at 11am. Orchestra members also perform in free chamber music concerts in the **Saló de Cent** (*see below*), and many soloists play in chamber groups such as the **Quartet de Corda Gaudí** and the **Quintet de Corda de Barcelona**.

Orquestra Simfònica del Gran Teatre del Liceu

Information *see* **Gran Teatre del Liceu**.
The other full-scale orchestra resident in Barcelona is the permanent resident orchestra of the Liceu, formed in the early 1980s in an attempt to give the opera house more solidity as a musical venue, creating in-house productions rather than relying on visiting companies, and with less of an air of an upper-class social club. Since the Liceu fire the orchestra has performed at various Barcelona venues and at major one-off events such as the **Perelada** festival (*see* **Festivals**).

Orquestra Simfònica del Vallès

Information *C/Narcís Giralt 40, Sabadell (93 727 03 00)*. Founded 1987, this orchestra has become one of the leading ensembles in Catalonia and now offers three different concert cycles, symphonic, traditional and popular, which it performs on weekends from October to June at the magnificent *Modernista* **Teatre Municipal La Faràndula** *C/Alfons XIII, Sabadell (93 725 83 16)*. Some one-off events such as 'Film Classic' concerts are held at the Palau in Barcelona.

Venues

Barcelona has long had a shortage of music venues, but since the Liceu fire the pressure on space has been immense. The **Mercat de les Flors** and **Teatre Victòria** (*see chapter* **Theatre**) have also taken up some of the strain.

Auditori del Centre Cultural de la Fundació La Caixa

Passeig de Sant Joan 108 (93 458 89 07). Metro *Verdaguer/bus 15, 20, 21, 45, 47, 55*. **Open** *box office* 11am-8pm Tue-Sat; *advance sales* box office & Servi-Caixa. **Tickets** *main concert series* 500-2,000ptas; *family concerts* 500ptas; 250ptas under-14s. **Credit** V. **Map E3**
The arts foundation of La Caixa is the city's principal patron of musical activity outside of official funding, and has a concert programme throughout the year in its main cultural centre and art gallery. Its philosophy is both to support young local musicians and to provide Catalan audiences with opportunities to hear well-known performers from abroad. Concerts generally form short series, and the recent **Festival de Músiques del Món** (festival of music from around the world), has enjoyed great success. As well as the main programme there are family concerts on Saturday mornings at 12.30pm, of music selected to engage and appeal to kids, but performed by entirely professional and often well-known musicians. For the main centre, *see chapter* **Art Galleries**; for the **Mediateca** music library, *see page 264*.

Auditori Winterthur

Auditori de l'Illa, Avda Diagonal 547 (93 218 48 00). Metro *Maria Cristina/bus 6, 7, 33, 34, 63, 66, 67, 68*. **Open** information *& box office* 10am-2pm, 4-8pm, daily; *advance sales* box office, from central office at C/Balmes 186 (open 9am-1pm Mon-Fri) & Servi-Caixa. **Tickets** 3,000-6,000ptas. **No credit cards** (box office). Inaugurated in 1996, this modern 650-seater concert hall is oddly located in L'Illa shopping mall. The *Lírica de Barcelona* organisation promotes five concerts a season of popular operatic works and Spanish *zarzuela*, with young singers and established names. OBC chamber ensembles and international chamber orchestras such as the Leopoldinum also play here, and it regularly hosts concerts during festivals (*see below*).

Casa Elizalde

C/València 302 (93 488 05 90). Metro *Passeig de Gràcia/bus 39, 43, 44, 45, 47, N7*. **Open** *information & box office* 10am-2pm, 5-9pm, Mon-Fri. **Tickets** 425ptas. **No credit cards. Map D3**
A multi-purpose city-owned cultural centre in a strikingly ornate Eixample building, with a beautiful courtyard that's sometimes used for performances in summer. It hosts classical concerts, usually on Fridays (8pm), and choral performances every second Wednesday (also 8pm). They feature music soloists, duets or quartets, and some contemporary music.

Fundació Joan Miró

Parc de Montjuïc (93 329 19 08). Metro *Paral.lel, then Funicular de Montjuïc/bus 61*. **Open** *box office* from 7.30pm Thur; *phone reservations* 10am-2pm, 3-6pm Mon-Fri. **Tickets** 700ptas; 1,800ptas for three concerts; 4,000ptas for eight concerts. **No credit cards. Map B5**
The Fundació Miró contains the main centre for contemporary music development in Spain. Its major summer concert series, **Nits de Música**, runs from June to September, with eight concerts spread over that time on Thursdays at 8.30pm. There are also series at other times of year featuring Catalan and international musicians. *See also chapter* **Museums**.

Gran Teatre del Liceu

La Rambla 61. Metro *Liceu/bus 14, 18, 38, 59, N6, N9*. **Information** *C/Ausiàs March 56 (93 485 99 00/93 412 37 90)*. Metro *Arc de Triomf/bus 19, 51, 55*. **Open** 9am-2pm, 3-6pm, Mon-Fri. **Ticket sales** Centre de la Virreina (*see p251*) 4-7pm Mon-Fri, & Servi-Caixa. **Tickets** prices vary according to venue. **Credit** MC, V. **Map D5**
The Liceu itself may be a building site, but the Liceu as an institution seems to have been given a new lease of life, as, freed from its cosy old edifice, it struggles to keep itself alive in public memory and satisfy the passionate audience of local opera-lovers. The phantom Liceu has presented full-floating seasons, with performances in the Palau and the Teatre Victòria. Opera productions are generally at the Victòria and often feature visiting European companies (unfortunately, including rather too many over-tired eastern European touring companies), or collaborative productions; concert performances are staged at the Palau. As well as locally through Servi-Caixa tickets for the Liceu season can be booked from abroad on a special 24-hour phoneline, on 34-93 417 00 60.

Palau de la Música Catalana

C/Sant Francesc de Paula 2 (93 268 10 00). Metro *Urquinaona/bus 17, 19, 40, 45*. **Open** *box office* 10am-9pm Mon-Fri; 3-9pm Sat; 10am-11pm Sun (concert days only); *advance sales* box office, phone & Servi-Caixa or Caixa de Catalunya. **Tickets** *main concert series* 1,600-6,700ptas Fri, Sat; 1,000-4,000ptas Sun. **Credit** MC, V. **Map D5**
The Palau remains Barcelona's main (and only substantial) concert hall. The building, one of the must-sees of the city in itself, is a delightful *Modernista* extravaganza (*see chapter* **Sightseeing**), but it's also an ideally sized auditorium. Its acoustics are up for debate (due to the large amount of metal used in the construction), but musicians love playing here.

*The **Palau de la Música**'s mosaic towers.*

After its earlier major renovation, which included an extension of the concert pit, the decision has been taken to add a new 600-seat auditorium for chamber music and *lied*. The Palau's never-ending agenda includes concerts by international orchestras, singers and soloists, in the Ibercàmera and Euroconcert seasons, as well as its weekly OBC concerts. The only concern might be that this wonderful old building could collapse under the strain now being put upon it, but if it survives the renovation it will give Barcelona an additional important venue, as well as newly open spaces outside to further appreciate the many features of the building.

Sala Cultural Caja Madrid

Plaça Catalunya 9 (93 301 44 94). Metro Catalunya/bus all routes to Plaça Catalunya. **Open** *information* 11am-1pm, 6-9pm Tue-Sat; 11am-1pm Sun. **Tickets** free. **Map D4**
This small concert hall in Plaça Catalunya is run by a Madrid savings bank. Concerts are normally held every Tuesday at 7.30pm, and occasionally on other days of the week, between October and June: its programmes are varied, including piano solos, chamber music and a few orchestral works.

Saló de Cent, Ajuntament de Barcelona

Ajuntament de Barcelona, Plaça Sant Jaume (93 402 70 00). Metro Liceu or Jaume I/bus 17, 40, 45. **Open** *information* 8am-2.30pm, 4-5.30pm, Mon-Fri. **Performances** *Oct-May* 8pm Thur. **Tickets** free. **Map D5**
Every Thursday during the main music season (except public holidays), the magnificent Gothic council chamber in the Ajuntament, the Saló de Cent, is thrown open to free concerts by a chamber ensemble (the **Solistes de l'OBC**) made up of musicians from the OBC. Programmes – once unadventurous – now feature a wide range of chamber pieces including contemporary work, and the concerts offer a matchless opportunity to admire the architecture.

Festivals

The main arts festivals, the **Grec** and the **Mercè** (*see chapter* **Barcelona by Season**), both feature a wide range of music, and the **Festival de la Guitarra** in March-April (*see chapter* **Music: Rock, Roots & Jazz**) brings to the city fine classical guitarists. In summer, there are several festivals around the Costa Brava that give great opportunities to escape the Barcelona heat and listen to music in very enjoyable settings. For travel information, *see chapter* **Trips Out of Town: Beaches**. As well as during festivals, several Barcelona churches host concert series from time to time: tourist offices (*see page 251*) have details.

Festival de Música Antiga

Information *Centre Cultural de la Fundació la Caixa, Passeig de Sant Joan 108 (93 458 89 07).* **Dates** Apr-May. **Tickets** 500-1,500ptas; some concerts free. **Map E3**
Organised by the Fundació la Caixa, this well-established and very successful festival brings together fine performers and ensembles from across Europe in early, renaissance and baroque music. Its fringe cycle, for younger musicians, has become extremely popular, and there are also afternoon family concerts and master classes. A great attractions is its venues: superb Barri Gòtic buildings such as the Saló de Tinell, the chapel of Santa Agata, or the ornately baroque church of Sant Felip Neri.

Festival de Cadaqués

Information *Orquestra de Cadaqués, C/Arcs 8 (93 302 27 22),* or during festival *Oficina de Turisme, Cadaqués (972 25 83 15).* **Dates** mid-July-mid-Aug. **Tickets** 1,000-3,500ptas.
The programme here, in perhaps the most chic town on the Catalan coast, usually consists of the great classics, but also featured are contemporary works and music competitions.

Festival Internacional de Mùsica Castell de Perelada

Castell de Peralada, Peralada, Girona (972 53 82 92). **Information** *Inverama (93 280 58 68).* **Dates** mid-July-late Aug. **Box office** *from 10 June* noon-8pm Mon-Fri *July, Aug* noon-8pm daily; *advance sales* box office & Servi-Caixa. **Tickets** 3,000-10,000ptas. **Credit** MC, V.
Held in the gardens of the castle (now a casino) of Perelada, close to Figueres, this is a notably upmarket festival, and for many the social outing is as important as the (excellent) music. It attracts major international names, and the programme is usually heavily opera-oriented.

Festival Internacional de Mùsica Torroella de Montgrí

Information *Festival Internacional de Música, Apartat 70, Codina 28, 17257 Torroella de Montgrí (972/76 06 05).* **Dates** mid-Jul-late Aug. **Advance booking** from early June, & Caixa de Catalunya. **Tickets** 500-8,000ptas.
In Torroella, a small town north of Begur, summer concerts take place in a beautiful Gothic church or in the main square. Recent highlights have included appearances by tenor Jaume Aragall and the Vienna Chamber Orchestra.

Festival Piano i Bel Canto

Information *(93 245 22 53).* **Dates** Nov-Dec.
Tickets prices vary according to venue; *advance sales* Caixa de Catalunya.
A new festival, launched in 1997, with a crowd-pleasing programme mostly of nineteenth-century classics performed in the Teatre Tivoli, the Palau de la Música, the Saló del Tinell and the Auditori Winterthur.

Music: Rock, Roots & Jazz

The international music scene continues to invade, but live music never loses its Latin flavour.

Barcelona's live music scene has arguably suffered in the last few years through the techno invasion, which has led many music venues to convert to clubs touting big-name DJs. However, there's still plenty on offer in the city from other musical spheres – most, surprisingly, also imported.

Salsa, son, merengue and other Caribbean rhythms continue to be major forces on the local music scene, helped along by the city's ample Caribbean population. Greats such as the queen of salsa Celia Cruz and Los Van Van play regularly to packed houses, while Barcelona-based talent such as the enigmatic Lucrecia and Los Angelitos de Salsa play the local clubs on a regular basis. Ignorance is no excuse for not participating in a sweaty salsa dance session: nearly all of Barcelona's venues hold free dance classes, quite often before the band comes on. Reggae, roots and world music also have their niches carved out. Watch out for any gig that bears the name Club Mestizo, dedicated promoters of reggae and other

world music, as well as the **Grec** and **Mercè** festivals, which always feature top roots artists.

Barcelona also has a vibrant jazz tradition. The city may have lost its living jazz legend, internationally renowned pianist Tete Montoliu, in 1997, but his death has done nothing to dampen the city's love of the music. The scene is sustained by an important festival each October, and two schools – the **Taller de Músics** and **Aula de la Musica**. Performers based in Barcelona include accomplished soulstress Monica Green and singer/piano man Lucky Guri, who does everything from ragtime to be-bop in his own inimitable style. On an international level, watch out for jazz pianist Chano Domínguez, whose recent album *Hecho a mano*, with its fusion of jazz, flamenco and *coplas* (traditional Spanish song) has been getting rave reviews at home and in the States, as has the latest work of saxophonist Jorgé Pardo, who also experiments with fusing jazz with other genres.

'Catalan Flamenco' – as featured at culture-fests such as the **Grec**.

RUMBA RHYTHMS

A few years ago, a big noise began to be made about 'Catalan Flamenco', the sudden boom in flamenco talent from the Andaluz suburbs around Barcelona. Since then the south and Madrid have proved to be more fruitful in terms of new talent, but what the fuss did achieve was the creation of a solid ground in terms of venues willing to host regular *cante jondo* gigs, and it ensured that Barcelona's main culture-fests, such as the **Grec**, include flamenco. This is when the fab five of Catalan flamenco, Maite Martín, Miguel Poveda, Ginesa Ortega and Duquende, take a break from touring internationally to display their extraordinary talents. But there are plenty of good lesser-known names as well, and more often than not you can stumble upon by chance in a spontaneous local bar gig or neighbourhood fiesta.

Rumba, on the other hand, has always boasted a league of die-hard fans within Catalonia's frontiers. The rest of the world may have cottoned on to it via the France-based Gypsy Kings, but gypsy rumba – the flamenco-ish, foot-tapping, hand-clapping music that simply refuses to die – was born in Barcelona. The pattern set by Peret, the gypsy from the Raval who is the king of rumba, is now carried on by Sabor de Gràcia, Ai Ai Ai, and a very active collective of gypsies from the neighbourhood of Gràcia, who have managed to wangle a permanent stage for themselves at the annual **Festa Major de Gràcia** in August *(see chapter* **Barcelona by Season***)*.

Another home-grown strand in the Catalan musical garden is *cançó*, the country's traditional style of protest-folk song that has its roots in the radicalism of the 1960s and 1970s. Joan Manuel Serrat, who, unlike most of his contemporaries, often sings in Spanish as well as Catalan, had huge success on a national and international scale in 1997 with his album *Banda Sonora d'un Temps, d'un País*, the first ever crossover hit for a Catalan language album. Other names that haven't faired as well outside Catalonia but have a strong following here are Maria del Mar Bonet, Lídia Pujol, who mixes her music with poetry, and the eccentric Albert Pla, whose style of *cançó* borders on the theatrical.

Rock Català, the heavy-ish pop-rock that has been well supported by the local industry over the years, is still waiting for its Serrat-type figure to take the music to the rest of Spain. Despite success on the part of its pioneers Sau, Els Pets and more recently Els Goses, it fails to impress further afield. However, with yet more official shove coming in the form of Catalan-language music quotas on the air-waves, it will be interesting to see how the situation develops. More accessible and fun are lighter bands such as the *pop-naïf* of Los Fresones Rebeldes, the rapsters 7 Notas, 7 Colores, techno-punk duo Jellyhead, and the wedding-type band Azucarillo Kings, who do tongue-firmly-in-cheek versions of anything from Bowie to Blur.

VENUES/PROGRAMMES

Barcelona is also a fixture on the European pop/rock tour circuit. While more modest bands are usually lucky enough to play in **Zeleste**, big international acts nearly always appear in one of the Olympic sports venues *(see chapter* **Sports & Fitness***)*; the **Palau Sant Jordi** (which has hosted the Spice Girls and Phil Collins), the **Palau d'Esports** (most frequently used, but with the worst acoustics) and, over the summer, the **Velòdrom** in Horta. The **Estadi Olímpic** goes virtually unused, except for the likes of Michael Jackson and Tina Turner. Tickets for these concerts can be bought at the Plaça Universitat ticket booth *(see page 184)*.

Of the smaller venues, some specialise in a specific type of music, but more often than not they host a mixed bag of musical styles, theatre and even poetry readings. Finding out what's on in Barcelona has been made easier by a boom in free magazines that can be picked up in bars, shops and cafés. Watch out for *AB*, the dance scene's Bible, *Mondo Sonoro* for live rock and pop, *Barcelona Metropolitan* (in English) for a bit of everything and *Ruta Latina* for salsa and Latin. The *Guia de Ocio* is also useful, as is *Tentaciones* supplement in Friday's *El País* *(see chapter* **Media***)*.

Rock/Jazz & Musics Various

Bikini

C/Déu i Mata 105 (93 322 08 00). Metro Les Corts/bus 15, 43, 59. **Open** (three rooms) *Cockteleria/Dry* midnight-4.30am Tue-Wed, Sun; midnight-5am Thur; midnight-6am Fri, Sat; *Rock* 11.30pm-5am Tue-Wed, Sun; 11.30pm-5am Thur; 11.30pm,-6am Fri, Sat; *Salsa* same hours as Rock room, Tue-Sat; 11.30pm-4.30am Sun. **Admission** (incl one drink) 1,000ptas (Tue-Thur, Sat); 1,400ptas (Fri, Sun). **Credit** AmEx, V.
Torn down to make way for L'Illa shopping mall, the original Bikini was the stuff club legends are made of. Membership was like a passport to Barcelona chicdom. Re-built on the same site by the same management, it has changed in décor from tacky to well-tailored (it has been likened to a cinema foyer), but its eclectic musical policy survives. With one-off gigs and concert series featuring specific styles and countries, from world music, salsa and reggae to britpop and dance, Bikini reigns supreme in inner-city music venues. *See also chapter* **Nightlife***.*

La Boîte

Avda Diagonal 477 (93 419 59 50). Bus 6, 7, 15, 27, 33, 34, 63, 67, 68, N8. **Open** 11pm-5.30am Mon-Thur, Sun; 11pm-6am Fri-Sat. **Admission** (includes one drink) 1,500-3,000ptas, depending on the band. **No credit cards.**
Map C2
The dynamic brothers Mas i Mas, who began with the café named after them *(see chapter* **Cafés & Bars***)*, have built up something of a musical empire in Barcelona, taking over long-neglected venues such as the **Jamboree** and **Los Tarantos**. Nobody's complaining, as they have renovated them with taste, improved the acoustics and given a whole new energy to their concert programmes. La Boîte, a small basement club, was their first music venue. It features a menu of jazz, soul, blues and occasionally month-long cycles

of international casino-type performers: recent examples include The Supremes and Boney M. Drink prices are hefty, but all Mas venues offer discounts for advance booking, and cards for each venue offering five or six concerts for 5,000ptas. *See also chapter* **Nightlife**.

Club Apolo/Nitsaclub

C/Nou de la Rambla 113 (93 441 40 01). Metro Paral.lel/bus 36, 57, 64, 91, N6, N9.
Open *disco* midnight-6am Thur-Sat; *gigs* times vary. **Admission** *disco* (incl one drink) 1,200ptas; *gigs* prices vary. **No credit cards. Map C5**
As well as being one of the best clubs in town, this ex music-hall brings in top live acts of the world music/reggae, pop/rock and salsa varieties, and even the odd theatrical-dance performance, both locally based, (under the banner of Apolo's alter-ego Nitsaclub) and from further afield. There are plenty of tables, plus a balcony that ensures a good view even for big-name acts. You can stay on to club after the gig, when the crowds pour in. *See also chapter* **Nightlife**.

Garatge Club

C/Pallars 195 (93 309 14 38). Metro Llacuna/bus 40, 42, 141. **Open** midnight-5.30am Fri, Sat; 6pm-10.30am Sun; *mid-May-mid-Oct* outdoor terrace open from 8pm. **Admission** depends on the band. **No credit cards.**
Offering from rock to punk and anything in between, Garatge Club in Poble Nou is for hard-nosed rock/indie/punk fans who like their music on the noisy side.

Jamboree

Plaça Reial 17 (93 301 75 64). Metro Liceu/bus 14, 18, 38, 59, N4, N6, N9. **Open** 8.30pm-4.30am Mon-Thur, Sun; 8.30pm-5am Fri, Sat. **Admission** *gigs* (incl one drink) 1,200ptas; *disco* free. **Map D5**
Inaugurated in 1959, this Plaça Reial cellar was the first jazz 'cave' in Spain. It closed in 1968, but was re-opened by the Mas i Mas brothers (*see* **La Boîte**) in 1993. Barcelona-based and visiting names in jazz, blues, Latin jazz, funk, gospel and occasionally hip-hop all play at this enormously popular venue, and the Sunday night blues sessions are an institution. A club session continues after the gigs. *See also chapter* **Nightlife**.

Jazzmatazz

Passatge Domingo 3 (93 211 88 97). Metro Passeig de Gràcia, FGC Provença/bus 20, 21, 22, 24, 28, 43, 44, N4, N6. **Open** 9pm-4am Tue-Thur; 9pm-5am Fri, Sat; 8pm-midnight Sun; *gigs* midnight Tue-Sat; 8.30pm Sun. **Admission** free. **Map D3**
Sophisticated club run by three partners from Ireland, Catalonia and Senegal. The diversity of their backgrounds is reflected in the musical menu: funk, soul, Latin, rock and Celtic music from local bands, both native and foreign residents, in concerts from Wednesday through to Sunday, the latter night being a very popular unplugged session. A reasonably priced bar and a soul/funk DJ spinning discs after each performance make Jazzmatazz one of the better places to see out the night in this neck of the woods.

Jazz Sí Club/Café

C/Requesens 2 (93 329 00 20). Metro Sant Antoni/bus 20, 24, 41, 55, 64, 141. **Open** 9am-11pm daily. **Music** from 6pm; 8.30pm Thur-Sat; 7pm Sun. **Admission** depends on the band (and incl one drink); or free (but you must have a drink). **No credit cards. Map C4**
Quirky club/café in a tiny street in the Raval near Ronda Sant Antoni, run by Barcelona's contemporary music school the Taller de Músics (at C/Requesens 5), whose programming is a mixed bag: Wednesdays are jazz; Thursdays salsa; Fridays flamenco; Saturdays rock, and Sundays offers a rock/blues jam session. It's also a meeting point for musicians, and good, reasonably priced snack food is available.

KGB

Alegre de Dalt 55 (93 210 59 06). Metro Joanic/bus 21, 39, 55, N4. **Open** *gigs* 9pm-midnight; *disco* midnight-5am Thur-Sat. **Admission** *gigs* depends on the band; *disco* (incl one drink) 1,000ptas. **No credit cards. Map E2**
Once a famous after-hours joint, from Wednesday to Saturday this long-standing club/music venue now puts on live gigs of the grunge-indie-rock variety from the local and national scene, with a DJ operating after the show. Young, noisy crowd.

London Bar

C/Nou de la Rambla 34 (93 318 52 61). Metro Liceu/bus 14, 18, 38, 59, N6, N9. **Open** 7pm-4am Tue-Sun. **Admission** free. **Credit** MC, V. **Map C5**
A Barcelona institution and a relic from the days when the *Barrio Chino* was at its peak, the bohemian-ish London is usually packed at weekends, mainly with young foreigners. Music tends to the blues/boogie/be-bop side, played by local and resident-foreign bands – fun if you don't mind a noisy, smoky atmosphere. And although it's been thoughtlessly renovated at times, it's managed to save a touch of its original 1910 *Modernista* décor. *See also chapter* **Nightlife**.

Luz de Gas

C/Muntaner 246 (93 209 77 11/93 209 73 85). Bus 6, 7, 15, 33, 34, 58, 64, N8. **Open** 11pm-4.30/5.30am daily. **Admission** (incl one drink) approx 1,800ptas. **Credit** AmEx, DC, MC, V. **Map C2**
This beautiful, *belle époque* former music hall has a fixed programme of soul/jazz, salsa, pop and a touch of country – and even the occasional opera performance – every night of the week. Monica Green has a regular Thursday spot with soul/funk and MOR standards and the pop rock of local outfit, Traditional Tourist. Unfortunately, the club tends to suffer from a sometimes snooty uptown clientele and stroppy management. *See also chapter* **Nightlife**.

Magic

Passeig Picasso 40 (93 310 72 67). Metro Barceloneta/bus 14, 39, 51. **Open** 11pm-6am Thur-Sat and eves of public holidays. Closed Aug. **Admission** *gigs* 500-1,200ptas; *disco* (incl one drink) 1,000ptas. **No credit cards. Map E5**
The revival of Magic, first opened as a hippy hang-out in the 1970s, must be proof that punk and noise-rock still live (in Barcelona at least). If the sound of bands such as The Perverts and Los Negativos grabs you, then this is the place to be. Opposite the Ciutadella, this is the only central venue that programmes indie rock on the hard side; they even get the odd name group as well.

Savannah

C/Muntanya 16 (93 231 38 77). Metro Clot/bus 18, 33, 34, 35, 43, 44, 54, N7, N9. **Open** 11pm-5am Thur-Sat. **Admission** (incl one drink) 1,000ptas; *gigs* depends on the band. **No credit cards.**
Popular rock and blues venue out in Clot, pulling in some lesser-known international (mainly American) players and bigger names from the national scene. Sometimes, it also puts on fringe theatre.

Sidecar Factory Club

C/Heures 4-6 (93 302 15 86). Metro Liceu/bus 14, 18, 38, 59, N6, N9. **Open** 10pm-3am daily; *gigs* normally 10/11pm. Closed Aug. **Admission** depends on the band. **Map D5**
A well-known basement club tucked away in a corner of the Plaça Reial, Sidecar offers all genres of pop-rock from mainly local independent bands most nights of the week. On Tuesdays, the G's Club takes over, offering 'alternative' performances from a local arts collective that can

The festival menu

Barcelona's musical range is enriched every year with a varied spicing of festivals. In summer the city's streets and squares provide perfect outdoor venues, and the sounds of rock, jazz, rumba and other music last well into the night.

The first gathering of the year is actually outside the city in Terrassa, **Jazz-Terrassa** in March, which has featured names such as Milt Jackson and Ray Barretto (information 93 786 27 09; for information on getting to Terrassa, *see page 225*). March through to April sees the **Festival de Guitarra** (information 93 232 67 54), in the Palau de la Música (*see chapter* **Music: Classical & Opera**) and other smaller venues, which brings together guitar music of all kinds (except heavy rock) – from the best flamenco performers to jazz, blues and classical.

An event that has consolidated itself nicely into the upper echelons of groovedom is **Sonar** (information 93 442 29 72) in mid-June, an 'advanced music meeting' that's Europe's only official electronic music and multimedia arts festival. It showcases DJs, techno/dance and experimental groups in gigs, debates and workshops at the **CCCB** (*see chapter* **Art Galleries**) and a nightly club **Pavelló de Mar Bella** on the beach, with all kinds of related attractions alongside.

The city Ajuntament's two major festivals either side of summer both feature musicians from flamenco and African music to Van Morrison or Ray Charles. At the **Grec**, during the balmy nights of July, concerts take place in the Plaça del Rei, Port Vell, the Cathedral steps and Velòdrom at Horta. **La Mercé**, as well as bringing Spanish, Latin, reggae and world music to the city squares in September, has incorporated a modern music festival, **BAM** (information 93 401 97 16). After a shaky start, in the last couple of years it's pulled in big

Paco de Lucia at the Palau de la Musica.

names such as Primal Scream and Nicolette (*see chapter* **Barcelona by Season**).

Not in Barcelona but neatly between these two is a new festival on the circuit, **Dr Music** (information 93 268 28 28), Catalonia's answer to Glastonbury. Set in majestic rolling hills in the pre-Pyrenees near **Escalarre**, the three-day event held over a weekend in July offers top names in rock, pop and dance as well as as bungee jumping, theatre performances, alternative markets and other festival paraphernalia.

Then of course, there's the long-running **Festival Internacional de Jazz** (information 93 232 67 54) in October. Acts like Jazz Crusaders and Georgie Fame play in the Palau de la Música, and in jam sessions at the Harlem Jazz and Jazz Sí. Finally, for experimental, electronic and new-age music fans, **Gràcia Territori Sonar** (information 93 238 40 38) is a new contemporary music collective which offers a running, year-long programme of two gigs each month (usually in the second half) in or around bars and cafes in Gràcia. Artists come from all over, and in some months – dedicated to specific countries – their performances are accompanied by dance or video.

include anything from poetry readings and theatre to video art and experimental music. The 'underground' crowd are friendly.

La Tierra/Costa Breve

C/Aribau 230 (93 414 27 78). FGCProvença/bus 6, 7, 15, 33, 34, 58, 64, N8. **Open** midnight-6am Thur-Sat. **Admission** 1,000ptas (includes one drink). **Credit** V. **Map C2**

A venue with an unclassifiable music programme. Gigs, on Thursday, Friday and Saturday nights, run the range from rumba to funk, jazz and country. Hugely popular with the wannabe set at weekends, when the Costa Breve funk-soul club kicks off after the concerts. *See also chapter* **Nightlife**.

Zeleste

C/Almogàvers 122/Pamplona 88 (93 309 12 04). Metro Marina/bus 6, 40, 42, 141, N6. **Open** *gigs* normally from 9pm; *club* 1-5am Sat, Sun. **Admission** *gigs* 1,500-3,500ptas depending on the band; *club* 700-900ptas (incl one drink). **No credit cards.** **Map F5**

The best medium-sized music venue in Barcelona. If they're not big enough (or don't want) to fill a stadium, all first-rank national and international acts perform here: recent headliners include Portishead, Green Day, and the awful Kelly Family. On the city-side of Poble Nou, it has three halls and also hosts club nights each weekend, when the late-night bar is open to all with no admission fee.

Flamenco

Las Lolas Local

C/Pinzón 3-5 (93 315 89 88). Metro Barceloneta/bus 45, 59, **Open** *approx 8pm-2am daily.* **Admission** *free (but you must have a drink).* **Map E6**

Run by a group of flamenco lovers in the depths of Barceloneta, Las Lolas organises live flamenco jam sessions on the last Friday of every month featuring local musicians, which draw in a fun, ready-to-party crowd. If you are into learning a few steps while you are here, every Tuesday and Thursday they also organise flamenco and *sevilliana* (the famous flamenco-ish folk dance from Seville) dance classes, plus sporadic intensive courses.

La Macarena

C/Nou de Sant Francesc 5 (93 317 54 36). Metro Drassanes/bus 14, 18, 38, 59, 91, N4, N6, N9. **Open** *10.30pm-4.30am daily.* **Admission** *free (but you must have a drink).* **Credit** MC, V. **Map D5**

With an interior like an Almodóvar film set and an owner who could be one of the extras, La Macarena is a once-in-a-lifetime experience. It's totally unpredictable: you could be treated to anything from a thrilling, spontaneous session from visiting flamenco artists or a cursory 10-minute spot from the regulars who hang around the bar. Whatever, you'll be expected to pay. There's no cover charge, but be warned: if they ask you after the show if you would 'like to buy a drink for the artists', it could empty your wallet. An acceptable way out is to leave a tip as you go; the amount should depend on the length and quality of the 'show'. Go late (2am on) and, if possible, with somebody who lives in the city.

El Tablao de Carmen

C/Arcs 9, Poble Espanyol (93 325 68 95). Metro Plaça d'Espanya/bus 13, 61. **Open** *approx 8pm-2am Tue-Sun; flamenco shows 9.30pm, 11.30pm, Tue-Thur, Sun; 9.30pm, midnight, Fri, Sat.* **Admission** *Poble Espanyol* 950ptas; 525ptas students, over-65s, groups; *El Tablao de Carmen copa-espectacle* 4,200ptas (incl one drink & Poble Espanyol); *sopar-espectacle* 7,800ptas (incl dinner & Poble Espanyol). **Credit** AmEx, DC, JCB, MC, TC, V. **Map D5**

High-quality supper/flamenco show venue in the Poble Espanyol (*see chapter* **Sightseeing**), with a full *tablao* show of guitarists, singers and dancers. Great fun, it's frequented by locals and tourists alike. If you book in advance you don't have to pay the Poble admission fee.

Los Tarantos

Plaça Reial 17 (93 318 30 67). Metro Liceu/bus 14, 18, 38, 59, 91, N4, N6, N9. **Open** *10.15pm-4.30am daily; flamenco show (tablao)* 10.15pm-midnight Mon-Sat. **Admission** *tablao* 3,800ptas (includes two drinks); *other performances* varies depending on the artist. **Credit** MC, V. **Map D5**

Since its makeover by the Mas brothers (*see* **La Boîte**), Los Tarantos, long-established as a flamenco show or *tablao* for tourist parties, has become the most important club on the new Catalan flamenco circuit. As well as flamenco, they also feature tangos, Latin and salsa. After the live gigs it becomes the world music part of the Jamboree next door, and the audience is welcome to stay on.

Folk

L'Espai (*see chapter* **Dance**) also acts as a showcase for mostly Catalan artists in different fields of music. There is no specific criteria, and performances can be anything from flamenco to folk and experimental, but their aim is to give talented unknowns a space to display their talent.

Centre Artesà Tradicionarius (C.A.T.)

Travessera de Sant Antoni 6-8 (93 218 44 85). Metro Fontana/bus 22, 24, 28, 39, N4, N6. **Open** *bar* 5pm-midnight Mon-Fri; *gigs* about 10pm Mon, Fri. **No credit cards. Map D2**

A centre is dedicated to the teaching, studying and exposure of different types of indigenous music from Catalonia, other parts of Spain and occasionally the rest of Europe. Concerts are held every Thursday and Friday nights, and during the week classes and workshops are held. They also organise a folk music festival in early March which brings in musicians from every part of the world and fills the pubs and bars of Gràcia with a wonderful diversity of styles and rhythms.

Jazz specialists

La Cova del Drac

C/Vallmajor 33 (93 200 70 32). Metro Muntaner/bus 14, 58, 64, N8. **Open** *6pm-4am Tue, Wed; 9pm-4am Fri, Sat.* **Admission** *(incl one drink); 500-1,500ptas (midnight show).* **Credit** V. **Map C1**

Swish uptown jazz club that now has few echoes of the days when, while located on C/Tuset, it was a bohemian/intellectual hang-out during the final years of Francoism. The current club has live acts (with bigger, 'international' names at weekends) at 11.30pm Thursday to Saturday, after 'new talent' gigs at 9.30pm, which are not necessarily jazz, but rather folk, pop or jazz fusion; at 1.30am, live music gives way to the 'Classic Plastics Disco'. Tuesday nights there's poetry readings at 6pm, followed by a jam session. Drinks are on the pricey side, but La Cova has a reputation for excellence.

Harlem Jazz Club

C/Comtessa de Sobradiel 8 (93 310 07 55). Metro Jaume I/bus 17, 40, 45. **Open** *8pm-4am Tue-Thur, Sun; 8pm-5am Fri, Sat.* **Admission** *free (but you must have a drink).* **No credit cards. Map D5**

A great favourite with Barcelona jazz aficionados, an intimate Barri Gòtic club with a great atmosphere. It presents both local talent and jam sessions by international musicians visiting for jazz festivals and workshops, and lately their programming has branched into the spheres of pop and Latin music as well. Gigs begin about 10.30-11.30pm.

Pipa Club

Plaça Reial 3 (93 302 47 32). Metro Liceu/bus 14, 18, 38, 59, N6, N9. **Open** *10pm-3am daily; gigs* midnight Thur-Sat; *jam session* 11pm Sun. **Admission** 1,000ptas (Thur-Sat); free (Sun). **No credit cards. Map D5**

Pipa means pipe, and during the day 'Pipa Club' is exactly what it says it is – a meeting-place for pipe-smokers. At night it turns into a venue for local and some foreign (mainly contemporary) jazz talent, and you might find boleros, tangos and even African rhythms on some nights.

Latin

Antilla Cosmopolita

C/Muntaner 244 (93 200 77 14). Bus 6, 7, 15, 33, 34, 58, 64, N8. **Open** *9pm-4.30am Mon-Thur; 11pm-6am Fri, Sat; 11pm-4.30am Sun.* **Admission** 1,500ptas (incl one drink); members free. **No credit cards. Map C2**

Great live bands set the crowd moving from Sunday to Thursday in the most popular salsa/Latin venue in Barcelona, and on Fridays and Saturdays there's a 'salsoteca'. There are free dance classes from Monday to Thursday: just turn up at the door, then hang around till the concerts start to strut your stuff. Dance fiends heading for a weekend in the Montseny can also shake a hip at the **Antilla-La Garriga**, Avda Pau Casals 1 (93 871 46 62), in the attractive small town of La Garriga. *See also chapter* **Nightlife**.

Sport & Fitness

In a post-Olympic city like this one, there's no excuse for not finding a sport to help you work up a sweat – and there are even some that don't involve FC Barcelona.

When televised soccer is blamed for restaurants' downturn in trade, you know you're in a city with an appetite for sport. Barcelona's dailies *El Mundo Deportivo* and – wait for it – *Sport!* offer nothing else but match analysis and conjecture, targeted near-exclusively at fans of FC Barcelona. But as omnipresent as *Barça* may appear – in many other sports as well as football – it's not the only sporting flame in town. The 1992 Olympics encouraged a whole new generation of home-grown sports names. Catalan yachtsmen near-monopolised the medals podium, a feat repeated in Atlanta, and the country is also home to world-class tennis players Arantxa Sánchez Vicario and Sergi Bruguera, rally-master Carles Saínz and motorcyclist Alex Crivillé.

Post-Olympic Barcelona is also replete with state-of-the-art installations for sporting participation. Despite early teething problems, most facilities in the city are now running to full capacity, and Ajuntament subsidies keep prices surprisingly low. It's particularly worth noting that water-based sports such as windsurfing and sailing have picked up a lot in the last few years, with clubs based near the heart of the city.

Spectator sport

Many tickets can be bought by credit card through the Servi-Caixa or Tel-entrades systems of savings banks (*see page 183*).

Major sports venues

Estadi Olímpic de Montjuïc *Avda de l'Estadi (Catalan 93 481 00 92/Spanish 481 10 92).*
Palau St Jordi *Avda de l'Estadi (Catalan 93 481 01 92/Spanish 93 481 11 92).*
Both *Metro Espanya, then escalators, or Paral.lel then Funicular de Montjuïc/ bus 13, 61.* **Map A5**
Palau dels Esports *C/Lleida (Catalan 93 481 00 93/Spanish 93 481 10 93). Metro Espanya, Poble Sec/bus 55.* **Map B5**
Velòdrom d'Horta *Passeig Vall d'Hebron (Catalan 93 481 00 93/Spanish 93 481 10 93). Metro Montbau/bus 27, 73.*

This glut of large-scale multi-purpose sports venues left to Barcelona by the 1992 Games is pretty under-used much of the time, although the Estadi Olímpic has taken on more consistent life since it became home to **Espanyol** football games (*see below*). As well as for sports all the venues are used for concerts and other events (*see chapter* **Music: Rock, Roots & Jazz**). The beautiful velodrome, in Vall d'Hebron, tends to be the least used: the **Palau d'Esports** at the foot of

Montjuïc is older than 1992, but was rebuilt for Olympic year. There is a booth in Plaça Universitat which sells tickets and has information on events at all four venues (*see p184*).

American football

Barcelona Dragons

Estadi Olímpic de Montjuïc, Avda de l'Estadi (93 425 49 49). Metro Espanya, then escalators, or Paral.lel then Funicular de Montjuïc/bus 61. **Ticket office** match days only from three hours before match time. **Tickets** 1,300-2,100ptas. **Credit** V. **Map A5**

Part of the 'World League' of American football, the Dragons have been surprisingly successful in gaining support in a city with very little experience of the game. They play in the Estadi Olímpic, usually on Sundays at 7pm from April to June. The promoters try to make it a full day out, with cheerleaders and all the razzle-dazzle Americana attached to the sport. Most players are American, but in accordance with a league rule there are a few locals in the squad (including Johan Cruyff's son-in-law). Tickets can be bought at the stadium on the day or in advance from the ticket booth at Plaça Universitat (*see p184*) or Servi-Caixa machines.

Basketball

Second only to football in popularity. The season runs from September to May, and league games are usually on Sunday evenings; European and Spanish Cup matches mid-week.

FC Barcelona

Palau Blaugrana, Avda Arístides Maillol (93 496 36 00). Metro Maria Cristina, Collblanc/bus 15, 52, 53, 54, 56, 57, 75. **Ticket office** from two hours before match times, or Servi-Caixa. **Tickets** 500-2,700ptas. **No credit cards**.

The basketball arm of *Barça* is fanatically well-supported, and it's advisable to book in advance. League games are mainly on Sundays at 6/6.30pm; Cup and European games 8/8.30pm in the week. In recent seasons the team has lacked the consistency of the early 1990s.

Joventut

Avda Alfons XIII-C/Ponent 143-161, Badalona (93 460 20 40). Metro Gorg/bus 44. **Ticket office** from one hour before match times. **Tickets** 1,000-3,000ptas. **No credit cards**.

Badalona's standard-bearers stand head-to-head with their wealthier neighbours, and unlike them have actually won the European Basketball Cup. Sunday games are at 7.30pm, and the fans are still more passionate than at Barcelona.

Football

The city's two first-division clubs are **FC Barcelona** and **RCD Espanyol**. Such is the all-absorbing power of *Barça* that lower-division teams tend to be reduced to semi-pro status through lack of support, but football completists might check out **Sant Andreu** and **Hospitalet**, forever trying to reach somewhere near the big league.

*Smiling faces at Nou Camp stadium, where **Barcelona FC** are returning to form.*

The season traditionally runs from the first weekend in September to May, and league games are at 5pm on Sundays, although some are now played (and shown live on TV) at 8.30pm on Saturdays or 9.30pm on Mondays. Mid-week cup games are usually at 8.30pm, while European matches take place as late as 10pm at the behest of TV companies. In late August both clubs have pre-season tournaments which involve major European and Latin American sides, with games at 7pm. *See also* **A nation gets its kicks**.

FC Barcelona

Nou Camp, Avda Aristides Maillol (93 496 36 00). Metro Maria Cristina, Collblanc/bus 15, 52, 53, 54, 56, 57, 75. **Ticket office** 10am-1pm, 4-8pm, Mon-Fri; *match days* 10am-1pm, 4pm-match time Mon-Fri; 10am-match time Sun. **Tickets** 2,500-12,500ptas. **No credit cards**.

Although Nou Camp stadium has a capacity of nearly 120,000, tickets to see *Barça* are often hard to come by, as most are reserved for the club's 100,000-plus *socis* (season-ticket holders). The best bet is to phone the club about two weeks in advance and ask exactly when tickets will go on sale; then get to the ground two hours beforehand and queue. Alternatively, you can always try your luck with the ticket touts (scalpers). There's a range of ticket prices, and, since the *entrades generals* areas (for non-members) are often not well placed, it's worth spending at least 3,500ptas for a decent view. Barcelona also has teams in the Spanish second and third divisions and at amateur level. The second-division team, *Barça-B*, plays in the *Mini-estadi*, a 16,000-seater ground connected to the main stadium. Tickets cost about 1,000-2,000ptas, and games are at about 5pm on Saturdays; on days when A and B teams are both at home, a joint ticket allows you to see both games.

RCD Espanyol

Estadi Olímpic (93 424 88 00). Metro Espanya or Paral.lel, then Funicular de Montjuïc/bus 61 (special buses on match days). **Ticket office** 10-1.30pm, 5-8pm, Thur, Fri before weekend games, or daily before important games; match days 10am-match time. **Tickets** 2,000-7,000ptas. **No credit cards**. **Map A5**

It's much easier to see Espanyol games, especially since the club's move to the 80,000-seater **Estadi Olímpic** (*see above*). A problem may be getting up Montjuïc, but on match days there are free buses from a special stop at Plaça Espanya every three minutes from an hour and a half before kick-off.

Greyhound racing

Canódromo Pabellón

C/Llançà 2-12 (93 325 46 08). Metro Espanya/bus 9, 13, 51, 53, 65, 91, 127. **Open** 11am-2pm, 5-9pm, Mon, Fri-Sun, public holidays; 5-9pm Tue-Thur. **Admission** free. **Map B4**

A small track overlooked by apartment balconies just off the Plaça d'Espanya. A relaxed atmosphere and small bets (winners and second place only) with odds to match are the order of the day. A great place to pop in, have a beer and a sandwich, and watch the races, which are every 15 minutes.

Ice hockey

FC Barcelona

FC Barcelona Pista de Gel, Avda Aristides Maillol (93 496 36 00). Metro Maria Cristina, Collblanc/bus 15, 52, 53, 54, 56, 57, 75. **Admission** free.

Once again, it's *Barça* that sponsors the only professional ice hockey team in town. The rink, open to the public on non-match days (*see below* **Ice skating**), is part of the club's vast sports complex. Games are not played all year, and timings vary a lot: a schedule is available from the arena or by phone.

Roller hockey

FC Barcelona

Palau Blaugrana, Avda Aristides Maillol (93 496 36 00). Metro Maria Cristina, Collblanc/bus 15, 52, 53, 54, 56, 57, 75. **Ticket office** two hours before match times. **Tickets** 1,000ptas. **No credit cards**.

A sport almost exclusive to Spain, especially Catalonia. It's played on regular roller skates with a hard ball and field hockey sticks; rules follow ice hockey regulations, with one notable exception: body-checking and most other forms of contact are prohibited, making it more like field hockey. Matches are played in the same hall as basketball, the *Palau Blaugrana* indoor arena. For match times, see the local press, or phone.

Other events

Barcelona Marathon (Marató de Catalunya-Barcelona)

Information & entry forms *C/Jonqueres 16, 9-C, 08003 (93 268 01 14/fax 93 268 43 34).* **Date** mid-March.

The Barcelona Marathon celebrated its twentieth anniversary in 1997. From 1992-6 it ended in the Estadi Olimpic, which required a crippling final climb up Montjuïc. This led to poor times and an absence of international runners, and in 1997 the organisers recognised defeat and decided that in future the race would end on the flat in Plaça d'Espanya. It starts north of the city in Mataró, and thousands take part. The city also holds two half-marathons, and the **Cursa de la Mercè** fun run during La Mercè in September (*see chapter* **Barcelona by Season**). The sports information centre (*see below* **Active sport**) has details of all events.

Motor sports

Circuit de Catalunya *Carretera de Parets del Vallès a Granollers, Montmeló (93 571 97 00). By car A7 or N152 to Parets del Vallès exit (20km/13 miles).* **Times & tickets** vary according to competition.

In Montmeló, near the A7 north of Barcelona towards Granollers, this racetrack was inaugurated in 1991. It hosts the Spanish Grand Prix (usually early May), and many other competitions in different classes, including motorcycle meets. For details of events call the circuit, or check with the **RACC** in Barcelona (*see page 259*).

Tennis

Reial Club de Tennis Barcelona-1899 *C/Bosch i Gimpera 5-13 (203 78 52). Bus 63, 114.* **Open** *club* (members only except during competitions) 8am-10pm daily. **Ticket office** 9am-6pm daily during competitions.

The city's most prestigious tennis club hosts one major international tournament, the ten-day **Trofeig Comte de Godó**, part of the men's ATP tour, generally in mid-April. Agassi, Sampras, Muster and the best Spanish players have all competed in this big-money tournament. Tickets cost 4,500-8,500ptas; they are available through Servi-Caixa, and *bono* tickets are available for admission on several days. A smaller tournament is the **Open de Catalunya**, a women's invitation event usually held in late June at the **Club de Tenis Hispano-Francès** (93 428 12 36) in Vall d'Hebron.

Active sport

The Ajuntament runs an extensive network of *Poliesportius* or sports centres. Activities available at each vary: some have basic gyms and indoor halls suitable for basketball and five-a-side; others a lavish range of facilities including pools and running tracks. Charges are low, and you don't have to be a resident to use them. Information on city facilities (and sports events) can be obtained from the office below. For cycle hire shops, *see page 260*.

Servei d'Informació Esportiva

Avda de l'Estadi 30-40 (information phoneline 93 402 30 00). Metro Espanya, then escalators, or Paral.lel then Funicular de Montjuïc/bus 61. **Open** 8am-2.30pm, 3.45-6.15pm, Mon-Thur; 8am-2.30pm Fri. **Map A5**

The Ajuntament's official sports information service, in an office alongside the **Piscina Bernat Picornell** (*see below* **Swimming pools**). They have leaflets listing district sports centres, or you can phone to ask which is your nearest. Staff are helpful but don't always speak English. You can also find out about the growing number of *festa* days when specific sports are promoted via city-organised events such as *el dia dels patins* (roller-skating) and *el dia de la bicicleta*. The sports authorities have also launched a campaign to encourage use of the beach facilities, so if you fancy taking part in aerobics classes with sand between your toes, this is the place to come.

Billiards, snooker, pool

Many bars have tables for Spanish billiards (*carambolas*, blue, and without pockets) or American pool, and a few full-size snooker tables. If you're unfamiliar with local rules watching a few games should make everything clear. A favourite bar for *billar* is the **Velòdrom** (*see chapter* **Cafés & Bars**), and **Snooker Club Barcelona** (*see chapter* **Nightlife**) has full-size English snooker tables.

Club Billars Monforte

La Rambla 27 (93 318 10 19). Metro Drassanes/bus 14, 18, 38, 59, 64, 91. **Open** 10am-10pm daily. **Membership** 1,000ptas per month; tables 200ptas per hour (one person); 360ptas per hour (two people). **No credit cards. Map D5**

An old-fashioned club in a room of faded glory, with men of a certain age playing cards, dominoes and billiards. Officially it's members only, but non-members are usually made welcome. You need to knock after 10pm, and it doesn't hurt to phone ahead and let them know you're dropping in.

Bowling

Bowling Barcelona

C/Sabino Arana 6 (93 330 50 48). Metro Maria Cristina/bus 7, 59, 67, 68, 70, 72, 74, 75, 114. **Open** 11am-1.30am Mon-Thur; 11am-2.30am Fri; 11am-3.30am Sat; 11am 11.30pm Sun. **Rates** *per game* 200ptas 11am-5pm Mon-Fri; 425ptas from 5pm Mon-Thur, 11am-5pm Sat, Sun; 525ptas from 5pm Fri; 600pts from 5pm Sat, Sun, public holidays. *Shoe hire* 150ptas. **Credit** V.

This centre has recently added additional facilities in a bid to keep up with the nearby Pedralbes bowl. Lunchtime is a good time to go and take advantage of the cheaper day rates.

Bowling Pedralbes

Avda Dr Marañón 11 (93 333 03 52). Metro Collblanc/bus 7, 54, 67, 68, 74, 75. **Open** 10am-2am Mon-Thur; 10am-4am Fri, Sat; 10am-midnight Sun. *Aug* open from 5pm only. **Rates** *per game* 220ptas 10am-5pm Mon-Fri; 380ptas from 5pm Mon-Fri, 10am-5pm Sat, Sun; 500ptas from 5pm Sat, Sun. *Shoe hire* 100ptas. **Credit** MC, V.

A well-equipped operation: you can hire gloves and shoes, and play snooker, pool or darts. There are 14 lanes, a bar and dining area. Best time is early afternoon, as it gets crowded later in the day. If it's full, leave your name at reception and they will page you at the bar when a lane becomes free.

Cricket

Barcelona Cricket Club

Information *(93 488 28 52).*

Yes, the crack of ball on willow can be heard here. The club is part of a 16-team Spanish league, and plays 50-over one-day matches on Saturdays and friendlies on Sundays. They are open to games from visiting teams, so any village or pub side planning a trip to Barcelona can get in touch.

Football

British International Football League

Information *(93 218 67 31/93 665 28 84).*

How do expats bond? By starting a football league, that's how. The BIFL has some 12 permanent men's teams and a regular season of games, and a women's league as well.

A nation gets its kicks

FC Barcelona is the world's richest football club and Spain's fifth largest company. Much of this economic success can be put down to astute marketing, but it was, ironically, Franco who provided his subjects with the key to so many ringing tills. The dictator's censoring of all things Catalan helped consecrate the club and the team's colours as surrogate patriotic symbols. *Barça* became 'more than a club' and football more than a game. It hardly needed King Midas to turn this into gold, but current chairman Josep Lluís Núñez and his directors have kept Camp Nou's coffers brimming not just with average attendances of 90,000 but also a gamut of *Barça*-stamped memorabilia. **Botiga del Barça** in Maremàgnum (*see chapter* **Shopping**) offers the full range.

When the Swiss founder of FC Barcelona Joan (formerly Hans) Gamper gave his team the colours of his native canton's flag, he couldn't have imagined that a century later the same grenadine and blue would embellish not only the football squad's heroics but also those of 19 other sports teams. This diversification means that his successor presides over a budget of 12,000 million pesetas and the support of 100,000-plus *socis* (members). All have a right to vote for the club president, in elections that are as high-profile as any vote on mere politics.

WHAT'S THE SCORE?

Johan Cruyff's managerial reign from 1988 saw in a period of title-winning glory. Four league

wins and a European Cup down the line, though, the Dutchman's legendary luck began to run out. Notions that continental domination might be beckoning were dashed by AC Milan's 4-0 thrashing of *Barça* in the 1994 European Cup final. With Núñez tiring of Cruyff's maverick tongue, few were surprised by his sacking in 1996.

Boardroom sighs of relief at the appointment of Bobby Robson as replacement were met with nail-biting from fans, who suspected the Englishman's signing meant a return to underachievement. To

---

Though it was started by wandering Brits the membership is completely international, and includes many locals. The president, Nick Simons, can provide further information.

Gyms/fitness centres

Califòrnia Look
Plaça de Ramon Berenguer el Gran 2 (93 319 87 25). Metro Jaume I/bus 17, 40, 45. **Open** *Sept-July* 7.30am-10pm Mon-Fri; 11am-3pm Sat; *Aug* 8am-10pm Mon-Fri. **Rates** *short-term* 1,200ptas per day; 4,000ptas one week; 5,500ptas two weeks; 8,500ptas per month; *membership* 7,944ptas per month. **No credit cards. Map D5**
One of few fitness centres in Barcelona that caters to the short-term visitor, with day, one-, two-, three-week and monthly rates. For each period there are two charge rates: basic, which gives the visitor access to all the sports facilities, and a higher rate which includes UV and beauty treatments.

L'Estudi
C/Casp 12 (tel/fax 93 317 28 41). Metro Catalunya/bus all routes to Plaça Catalunya. **Open** 9am-9pm Mon-Fri (may vary in summer). **No credit cards. Map D4**
A wide range of facilities including sauna and whirlpool.

Short-term visitors are catered for: 6,000ptas a week gives unlimited access to all equipment. Some staff speak some English.

Golf

Club de Golf El Prat
El Prat de Llobregat (93 379 02 78). By car Carretera de l'Aeroport (21km/13 miles). **Open** 24 hours daily. **Rates** *non-members* (approx) 12,000ptas per day Mon-Fri; 24,000ptas per day Sat, Sun, public holidays. **Credit** AmEx, MC, V.
Placed in a lavish location on the coast near the airport, this is a premiere 36-hole course that has hosted the Spanish Open six times. Equipment is available for hire, but you must be a member of a federated club to play. From October to May it is members only at weekends; at all times your best chance for a game is to go very early in the day during the week.

Club de Golf Sant Cugat
C/de la Vila, Sant Cugat del Vallès (93 674 39 58). By car Túnel de Vallvidrera (E9) to Valldoreix/by train FGC from Plaça Catalunya to Valldoreix. **Open** 8am-7pm Mon; 7.30am-8.30pm Tue-Fri, public holidays; 7am-9pm Sat-

hold off comparisons with Cruyff's dream team, Núñez embarked on a massive spending spree, enticing Brazilian ace Ronaldo, whose breathtaking season at Barcelona (1996-7) couldn't quite mask a certain lack of order on the pitch. Despite winning three of four titles in play, Robson's *Barça* never quite convinced, and President Núñez again decided it was time for fresh blood.

Bringing in Dutchman Louis van Gaal was as much a bid for his own continuity as a ploy to recall the club's glory days. Long-brewing anti-Núñez feeling was galvanised in May 1997 when Ronaldo slipped through his fingers and signed for Milan. After that he had some skilful manœuvring to do. Announcing presidential elections for July, he gave potential challengers little chance to organise, and won a victory on a low turnout. A curiously-named anti-Núñez group, *l'elefant blau* (the blue elephant), emerged as a force to be reckoned with.

With his dismissal of dissident fans and devotion to note-taking, coach Van Gaal aroused little sympathy in his first months in Barcelona. An initial run of lucky victories was followed by an embarrassing exit from Europe, and his days seemed numbered. More defeats in the new year didn't augur well for 1998. Then, Van Gaal drafted home-grown talents Celades and Oscar into the team and reinstated stalwarts Nadal and Ferrer, and Barcelona gained a welcome consistency. The skills of Rivaldo, Figo and Giovanni were able to flourish, and even the most sceptical fans were left rubbing their eyes. Having won the Spanish league at the first try in 1998, Van Gaal might just earn that famous last laugh… watch this space.

UPSTAIRS DOWNSTAIRS

Aficionados of football glamour may be unaware that Barcelona plays host to another top-flight club, **Espanyol**. Traditionally drawing its support from non-Catalans, *los pericos* (the budgies!) have never had major success. In recent years, though, things have been looking up, due in no small measure to the hard-nosed coaching of Jose Antonio Camacho.

An interesting counterpoint to *Barça*'s school of football, Camacho's Espanyol are a team for lovers of footballing grit. In 1997 the debt-ridden blue-and-whites cashed in on their old Sarrià ground and took up rented accommodation in Montjuïc's giant Olympic stadium. With gates of around 20,000, it's rarely a powder-keg of passion, but Espanyol fans seem to be taking to their new home, and with the purse-straining signings of Argentinian Esnaider and French internationals Oudec and Cobos the squad's workman-like ethic has been complemented by an injection of flare.

The Olympic Stadium and other Montjuïc venues are regularly open to visitors (*see* **Major sports venues** *and chapter* **Sightseeing**). At the Nou Camp, you can combine a tour of their hallowed installations with a stroll around the **Museu del FC Barcelona** (*see chapters* **Sightseeing** *and* **Museums**). An extra treat due in 1999 is a special exhibition to mark the club's centenary, with poster by long-term fan Antoni Tàpies (*left*).

Sun. **Rates** *non-members* 7,00ptas per day Mon; 9,000ptas per day Tue-Fri; 20,000ptas per day Sat, Sun, public holidays. **No credit cards**.

This attractive and very well-equipped course was built in 1919, and saw the professional debut of a young Seve Ballesteros. A major drawback for visitors is that you cannot hire clubs or trolleys, so you will have to bring your own. Green fees allow you access to club facilities such as the bar, restaurant and swimming pool; rates are lower if you go as a member's guest.

Horse riding

Hípica Severino de Sant Cugat

Passeig Calado 12, Sant Cugat del Vallès (93 674 11 40). By car Carretera de l'Arrabassada (exit 5 from Ronda de Dalt). **Open** 10am-1pm, 4-7/8pm, daily. **Rates** from 1,600ptas per one-hour lesson. **No credit cards**.

This school takes groups on rides through the pretty Vallès countryside around the town of Sant Cugat and along the north side of Collserola. All-day rides include a lunch stop along the way. Weekend rides need to be booked at least two days in advance.

Ice Skating

FC Barcelona Pista de Gel

Avda Arístides Maillol (93 496 36 00). Metro Maria Cristina, Collblanc/bus 15, 52, 53, 54, 56, 57, 75. **Open** *Sept-June* 10am-1.45pm, 4-7.30pm, Mon-Thur; 4.30-8.45pm Fri, Sun, holidays; 4.30pm-12,45am Sat. *1-20 July* 10am-1.30pm, 4-7pm, Mon-Thur; 10am-1.30pm, 4-8pm, Fri; 5-9pm Sat, Sun. Closed 21 July-Aug. **Rates** (incl skates) *Mon-Fri* 1,000ptas; 850ptas under-12s. *Sat, Sun, public holidays* 1,200ptas; 975ptas under-12s. **No credit cards.**

Part of the FC Barcelona complex, this is a basic, functional skating rink with skate hire, a bar and a restaurant. Saturdays in season, it's used for ice hockey.

Skating Roger de Flor

C/Roger de Flor 168 (93 245 28 00). Metro Tetuan/bus 6, 19, 50, 51, 54, 55, N1, N3, N4, N5. **Open** *Sept-June* 10.30am-1.30pm Tue; 10.30am-1.30pm, 5-10pm, Wed; 10.30am-1.30pm, 5-10pm, Thur; 10.30am-1.30pm, 5pm-1am, Fri; 10.30am-2pm, 4.30pm-1am, Sat; 10.30am-2pm, 4.30-10pm Sun, public holidays. *July-Aug* 5-10pm Mon; 10.30am-1.30pm, 5-10pm, Tue-Thur; 10.30am-1.30pm, 5pm-1am, Fri; 10.30am-2pm, 5pm-1am Sat; 10.30am-2pm,

5-10pm Sun, public holidays. **Rates** 850ptas; *Skate hire* 450ptas; *glove hire* 100ptas. **No credit cards. Map E3**
A modern rink with bar and restaurant facilities. It offers group discounts if you arrange your visit at least a day in advance.

Jogging & Running

The best place for jogging is along the **seafront**, from Barceloneta past the Vila Olímpica and beyond. Away from the water, the next best spot is **Montjuïc**. You can run up from Plaça d'Espanya at the bottom, or start at the top: either way you'll have to do some climbing. **Tibidabo** and **Collserola** are other good places to run; from Plaça Dr Andreu at the top of the tramline, fairly level, quiet roads lead along the hillside, and have great views. Within the city, street running is not usually pleasant due to the traffic.

Sailing

Until recently watersports were confined to towns up or down the coast, but with the building of the Port Olímpic the city offers completely new sailing opportunities.

Base Nàutica de la Mar Bella

Espigó del Ferrocarril, Platja de Bogatell, Av Litoral (93 221 04 32). Bus 36, 41, 92. **Open** 9am-9pm daily. **Rates** *membership* 20,600ptas per year; *boat hire & courses* rates vary. **No credit cards.**
Experienced sailors can hire many classes of boat at this club (on the third beach along from the Port Olímpic), and courses are run for beginners. There are windsurfing and snorkelling facilities, and well-trained staff.

Centre Municipal de Vela

Moll del Gregal, Port Olímpic (93 221 14 99). Metro Ciutadella-Vila Olímpica/bus 10, 36, 45, 59. **Open** 10am-1pm, 4-7pm, daily. **Rates** introduction 3,000ptas; 20 hour course 26,000ptas. **No credit cards. Map F6**
An unpretentious city sailing club offering courses at reasonable prices. The five-day, 20-hour programme is the same price whatever the class of boat, and for the complete novice, the centre offers a sea-christening session.

Club de Regates Port Olímpic

Moll del Gregal, Port Olímpic (93 221 14 99). Metro Ciutadella-Vila Olímpica/bus 10, 36, 45, 59. **Open** 10am-2pm Mon, Wed-Fri; 10am-10pm Sat, Sun. **Boat hire** from 3,000ptas per hour. Courses from 23,500ptas. **No credit cards. Map F6**
This club deals mainly with competitions, but it also rents out most types of small boat on a one-off basis. Office staff are friendly, and some speak English.

Sport climbing

Catalans are among the world's best climbers, and those who live in the city won't let a lack of mountains get in their way. The city boasts a number of indoor climbing-walls or *rocodroms*, often within municipal *Poliesportius*. Inquire at the **Servei d'Informació Esportiva** (*see above*) for details of centres that have them. Given the nature of this sport, potential climbers should bring proof of their national federation membership or climbing credentials.

Unió Excursionista de Barcelona

C/Jocs Florals 51 (93 332 54 94). Metro Mercat Nou/bus 70. **Open** 7-10pm Mon, Tue, Thur, Fri. **Rates** 125ptas per hour. **No credit cards.**
The premises of this association are open to anyone who can prove membership of their national climbing federation, and foreign visitors are welcomed with a rugged handshake. Once inside you can borrow the club's ropes, but you should bring your own appropriate clothing.

Squash

Squash 2000

C/Sant Antoni Maria Claret 84 (93 458 22 02). Metro Joanic/bus 15, 20, 45, 47. **Open** 7.30am-11.30pm Mon-Fri; 8am-10pm Sat; 8am-3pm Sun. **Rates** from 1,010ptas per half-hour. **Credit** MC, V. **Map E2**
Twelve squash courts, plus a sauna and well-appointed bar and restaurant areas. Courts must be booked in advance.

Swimming pools

There are 27 municipal pools in Barcelona, but before the city reclaimed its beachfront it could be hard to see water in the crush. Now they're not quite so hectic, but still busy. For a full list of pools, contact the **Servei d'Informació Esportiva** (*see above*). The most spectacular of the 1992 pools, the **Piscina Municipal de Montjuïc** used for the diving events, continues to be closed for long periods for repairs.

Club de Natació Atlètic Barceloneta

Plaça del Mar (93 221 00 10). Bus 17, 45, 57, 59, 64. **Open** 6.30am-11pm Mon-Fri; 7am-11pm Sat; *end-Sept-mid-June* 8am-5pm, *mid-June-mid-Sept* 8am-8pm, Sun, public holidays. **Admission** *non-members* 1,000ptas per day; *Baños de San Sebastián* 1,400ptas per day. **No credit cards. Map E6**
Three indoor pools, plus the usual bar and restaurant. It also includes the **Baños Municipales de San Sebastián** (Passeig Joan de Borbó 93, at the very tip of Barceloneta where the Passeig meets the beach), which contains two pools to choose from in summer, indoor and outdoor, as well as a separate massage/sauna area and well equipped gym.

Piscina Bernat Picornell

Avda de l'Estadi 30-40 (93 423 40 41). Metro Espanya, then escalators, or Paral.lel then Funicular de Montjuïc/bus 61. **Open** 7am-midnight Mon-Fri; 7am-9pm Sat; *Oct-May* 7.30am-2.30pm, *June-Sept* 7.30am-8pm, Sun, public holidays. **Admission** *Oct-April* 1,200ptas; 650ptas under-15s; free under-6s. *May-Sept* 650ptas; 450ptas under-15s; free under-6s. **Credit** MC, V. **Map A5**
Built in 1969, this pool was lavishly renovated to be the main swimming venue for the 1992 games. Entry fees are low and it is now heated in spring and autumn.

Piscina Municipal Folch i Torres

C/Reina Amalia 31 (93 441 01 22). Metro Paral.lel/bus 20, 36, 57, 64, 91, N6. **Open** 7am-9.30pm Mon-Fri; 8am-7.30pm Sat; 8.30am-1.30pm Sun, holidays. **Admission** 900ptas. **No credit cards. Map C5**
This city complex on the edge of the Raval has three covered pools, and other facilities such as a sauna and a weights room.

Tennis

Club Vall Parc

Carretera de l'Arrabassada 97 (93 212 67 89). Bus A6/ By car Ctra de l'Arrabassada. **Open** 8am-midnight daily. **Rates** courts 2,200ptas per hour. **No credit cards.**
On Tibidabo, near the Vall d'Hebron, this private club offers 14 open-air courts and two open-air pools. You can hire racquets, but must bring your own tennis balls.

Centre Municipal de Tennis Vall d'Hebron

Passeig de la Vall d'Hebron 178-196 (427 65 00). Metro Montbau/bus 27, 60, 73, 76, 85, 173. **Open** 8am-11pm Mon-Fri; 8am-9pm Sat; *Oct-April* 8am-7pm; *May-Sept* 8am-9pm, Sun, public holidays. **Admission** 1,650-2,150ptas. **No credit cards.**
The city tennis centre purpose-built for the Olympics, some way from the centre of town. It has 17 clay courts, and a full-size court for *pelota*. You need your own racquet and balls.

Theatre

Barcelona's theatre scene may be riven by controversies, but this hasn't stopped dynamic productions from drawing in bigger and bigger audiences.

Catalan has been a literary language since the middle ages, but no dramatic texts of any note appeared until the modern era. Public venues bent on promoting a national theatre have to fall back on a few so-called classics from the last century, such as Frederic Soler's romantic visions of city life and the social-realist dramas of Angel Guimerà. Contemporary textual theatre is generally light, the stuff of writers Josep Maria Benet i Jornet and Sergi Belbel, both of whom also create soap operas for Catalan TV. An important local playwright who writes in Spanish is José Sanchis Sinisterra, founder of the **Sala Beckett**.

Great texts may be lacking, but nevertheless theatre is booming here. Its vitality is not dependent on literary dialogues but on an extraordinary capacity to blend music, choreography, multimedia resources and spectacular production values into a distinctive Catalan style – in shows that are striking and accessible even to those unable to follow the language. This Catalan approach to theatre has drawn ecstatic reactions from critics and audiences around the world for groups like Els Comediants and La Cubana. Only minimal (or no) Catalan is required to enjoy groups like the post-punk La Fura dels Baus, mime humorists El Tricicle or the slew of cabaret-inspired companies in Barcelona like Chicos Mambo Boys, who take drag queen shows to hilarious avant-garde heights.

The vibrancy of this kind of theatre, added to Barcelona people's love for music hall and vaudeville – revived as literary cabaret and home-grown musicals – has helped a spectacular growth in theatre attendances in recent years. One consequence of this is that private promoters and producers now surpass public ones in prestige and power.

Not even the opening of the Generalitat-sponsored **Teatre Nacional de Catalunya** (TNC) in 1997 has altered the balance much. At the first clash between public and private sectors the complaints of local theatre bosses were enough to ensure the firing of TNC head and founder Josep Maria Flotats, in the very month his beloved project opened. A counterpoint to the Teatre Nacional is a city-sponsored project to create a **Ciutat del Teatre** ('City of Theatre') on the side of Montjuïc, around the already-in-operation **Mercat de les Flors**. This converted flower-market, and the summer festival pro-

An eye on the future: **La Cubana**. *See p220.*

grammes, are where the odd English-language production is likely to appear in Barcelona, such as Cheek by Jowl's readings of Shakespeare or other touring shows.

Seasons & festivals

The main theatre season runs from September to June, and local tradition has always been to close theatres down in summer. However, the success of the **Festival del Grec** and the affluence of tourists has now convinced some promoters to present programmes in July and August. The Grec is the best time to catch visiting theatre and dance companies, both international and from other parts of Spain. There is no fringe festival per se in Barcelona (Catalonia's best experimental showcase is in the town of **Tàrrega**, in Lleida, in October), but it's worth watching out for the **Opera de Butxaca** (Pocket Opera) series at alternative theatres like **Artenbrut** and the **Màlic**, or the **Marató del Espectacle** at the Mercat de les Flors around the end of May. For this and all festivals, *see chapter* **Barcelona By Season**.

Tickets & times

Main shows at most theatres start late, around 9-10pm. Many theatres also have earlier (cheaper) matinee performances at around 6-7pm, often on one day midweek and Saturday or Sunday; weekend nights there are also late shows. Most theatres are closed on Mondays. Advance bookings are best made through the ticket sales operations of savings banks (*see p183*). Tickets for many theatres can be bought at branches of the **Caixa de Catalunya**, or by phone with a credit card on the same Caixa's *Tel-entrades* line (**902 10 12 12**); tickets for several others can be bought with a credit card through the *Servi-Caixa* machines of **La Caixa**, or by phone on **902 33 22 11**. There is no additional commission. Which Caixa handles the tickets of a particular theatre is indicated below. Theatre box offices often take cash sales only. The best places to find details of current programmes are the *Guia del Ocio*, newspapers and, for *Tel-entrades* theatres, the *Guia del Teatre* available at Caixa de Catalunya branches.

Major companies

Els Comediants

Over 25 years, around the figure of director/guiding light Joan Font, Els Comediants have developed a unique style of performance based on street theatre, mime, circus, music and Mediterranean traditions of folklore, *festa* and celebration. A Comediants show, often presented in open-air venues such as parks or squares, is as much an event as a piece of 'theatre', with structure but no real script, which makes them particularly appealing to international audiences. Comediants have been accused of being adolescent, and indeed they quite frequently hire themselves out for town festivals and so on without much visible concern for artistic integrity. Like several other companies (Els Joglars, Dagoll Dagom), they arose out of the alternative/street theatre scene of the 1970s, but now tour the world. In Barcelona they have appeared recently at the TNC with *T.E.M.P.U.S*, based around the theme of time.

La Cubana

Perhaps the Catalan company with the widest appeal, La Cubana thrives on a dazzling mix of satire, gaudy showbiz effects, camp music, energy and audience participation. Its productions *¡Cómeme el Coco, Negro!* and *Cegada de Amor* were huge successes, the latter brilliantly exploiting and inter-mixing film and theatre conventions to enthrall audiences. After a year in Barcelona *Cegada de Amor* (Blinded by Love) spent a further year in Madrid, and then blew audiences away in its adaptation for the 1997 Edinburgh Festival. A new production is eagerly awaited for late 1998, and meanwhile La Cubana keeps busy doing TV work.

Dagoll Dagom

Under the direction of Joan Lluís Bozzo this company has honed a Catalan musical genre almost of its own, with striking use of colour and comedy. Their productions *Mar i Cel* and *Flor de Nit* – inspired by the anarchist 1920s – were both box-office hits, as was the more recent *T'Odio, Amor Meu*, with Dorothy Parker texts and Cole Porter music. DD have wowed audiences around Europe. Recent shows include adaptations of *Pygmalion* and *The Pirates of Penzance*.

La Fura dels Baus

With their primitivist rituals, industrial music and latent threat of danger, La Fura burst onto the international scene in the 1980s with provocative productions like *Suz-O-Suz* ('85) and *Tier Mon* ('88), in which water, fire, and raw meat formed part of the messy recipe, treating audience members like shipwreck victims in a sea of noise, power-tools, naked men, shopping trolleys, mayhem and constant motion. Later productions like *Noun* (1991), *MTM* (1994) and *Manes* (1996) have featured more text and narrative content. For 1998 they have produced a version of *Faust* for the TNC, which will then tour. La Fura also generates satellites like the *Mediterranean Sea* piece for the opening of the 1992 Olympics, and CDs, videos and interactive CD-Roms.

Els Joglars

A company that essentially revolves around Albert Boadella, its strong-willed founder, ideologist and leader, who was imprisoned for his political stances in the Franco years. With sardonic humour and text as well as the customary Catalan mime and dance skills, Boadella has kept to a line of caustic satire, with creations such as *Yo tengo un tío en América* ('I've got an uncle in America), detonating the Columbus commemorations of 1992, and *Ubu President*, a reworking of *Ubu Roi* with Ubu unmistakeably based on Catalan President Jordi Pujol. A bit reiterative in their spoofs of Church, state and nationalist clichés, Joglars lately produced a Jekyll-and-Hyde take-off about the eccentric Catalan writer Josep Pla.

Teatre Lliure

Probably Barcelona's most reputable theatre company, since 1976 the Lliure has kept to a line of presenting classic and contemporary drama by Catalan and international authors, in Catalan. Its productions are often sparse, in tune with the small Gràcia space they occupy, but quality is high. In 1998 they revived an earlier production of Heinrich Müller's *Quartet*. The company is an active participant in the Ciutat del Teatre project, which should result in more ambitious productions. The Lliure also has a fine chamber orchestra (*see also* chapter **Music: Classical & Opera**).

El Tricicle

As its name suggests, El Tricicle consists of three actors, a comedy team as much as a theatre group, but whose shows are interlinked pieces, not just sketches. Like Dagoll Dagom and La Cubana they have successfully transferred their live output to TV. Since their work is almost always mime with music, they're well able to cross borders, and their most global audience must have been for their skit in the Olympic closing ceremony of 1992. An ambitious try at a mimed film, *Palace*, and a 1997 stab at pleasing New York audiences both failed, and lately they have been producing dramatic comedies for other performers.

Mainstream theatres

Club Capitol-Sala 1

La Rambla 138 (93 412 20 38). Metro Catalunya/bus all routes to Plaça Catalunya. **Box office** 4-9pm daily; *advance sales* box office & Servi-Caixa. **Tickets** 2,200-2,800ptas; group discounts. **No credit cards. Map D4**
Who would have thought that the theatre boom in Barcelona would lead to cinemas closing to make way for stage spaces? This cinema now has one large hall dedicated exclusively to comedy and musicals. The first show was the very successful routine of Spanish-language comedian Pepe Rubianes.

Mercat de le Flors

Plaça Margarida Xirgu, C/Lleida 59 (93 426 18 75). Metro Espanya, Poble Sec/bus 55. **Box office** one hour before performance; *advance sales* Caixa de Catalunya & Centre d'Informació de la Virreina. **Tickets** prices vary according to performance. **No credit cards. Map B5**
A huge converted flower market with three halls of different sizes, the Mercat is due eventually to become part of the Ciutat del Teatre project. It is already the usual venue for multidisciplinary performances such as those by La Fura dels Baus, and major visiting productions like those of Peter Brook, Quebecois dancers La La La Human Steps and Britain's Cheek by Jowl. Run by the Ajuntament, the Mercat twins with the open-air Teatre Grec for the **Grec** festival, with a multi-varied range of performances (*see chapter* **Barcelona By Season**). Tickets can be bought at La Virreina centre on the Rambla (*see p251*) as well as through a caixa.

Teatre Arnau

Avda Paral.lel (93 441 48 81). Metro Paral.lel/bus 36, 57, 64, N4, N6. **Box office** from two hours before performance times; *advance sales* box office & Caixa de Catalunya. **Tickets** 1,500-3,000ptas. **No credit cards. Map C5**
One of the historic music halls of the Paral.lel, the charming old Arnau now functions more as a theatre, offering comedy and musicals often adapted from English.

Teatre Condal

Avda Paral.lel 91 (93 442 31 32/85 84). Metro Paral.lel/bus 20, 36, 57, 64, N4, N6. **Box office** from 4.30pm Tue-Sun; *advance sales* box office & Caixa de Catalunya. **Tickets** 2,500-3,000ptas; group discounts. **No credit cards. Map C5**
On the Paral.lel, historic heartland of commercial theatre, the Condal is owned by Focus, Spain's largest private theatre

producers. Recently it staged a very funny Catalan play co-authored by Sergi Belbel, *Sóc Lletja* (I'm Ugly), and a Spanish version of Ray Cooney's *Politically Correct* directed by Tricicle member Paco Mir.

Teatre Goya

C/Joaquim Costa 68 (93 318 19 84). Metro Universitat/bus all routes to Plaça Universitat. **Box office** from 3.30pm Tue-Sun; *advance sales* box office & Caixa de Catalunya. **Tickets** from 2,500ptas. **No credit cards. Map C4**
Founded in 1917 and dedicated to modern Spanish theatre, the Goya saw the premières of many works by Garcia Lorca, often starring his favourite leading lady, Barcelona actress Margarida Xirgú. Nowadays anything from cabaret or Noël Coward to an adaptation of the *Iliad* can be seen here. In addition there are productions of great Spanish dramatists such as Valle-Inclán and Lorca, and occasional flamenco concerts.

Teatre Lliure

C/Montseny 47 (93 218 92 51). Metro Fontana/bus 22, 24, 28, 39, N4, N6. **Box office** from 5pm Tue-Sun; *advance sales* box office (5-8pm Tue-Sat) & Caixa de Catalunya. **Tickets** 1,800-2,200ptas; 1,350ptas Thur. **No credit cards. Map D2**
For over 20 years the Teatre Lliure has been the the most prestigious venue in Catalan theatre, a breeding ground for fine actors and directors such as Lluis Pascual, who went on to run major companies in Madrid and Paris before taking on the Ciutat del Teatre project on Montjuïc. With its own rep company (*see above*) and workshops, it is soon to set up in the Ciutat as well. The charming old building in Gràcia was taken over for its present role in 1976: it's small but versatile, continues to inspire great affection, and has an excellent bar-restaurant. Almost all of the productions are in Catalan. *See also chapter* **Music: Classical & Opera**.

The quest for a national theatre

The most impressive theatre building in Barcelona, by a long way, is the Parthenon-like **Teatre Nacional de Catalunya (TNC)**, opened in 1997. A monumental structure by architect Ricard Bofill, the TNC was to be the fulfilment of an enormously ambitious Generalitat effort to showcase quality Catalan theatre. However, as the first season closed with a run of *Guys & Dolls* – hardly the stuff to make a serious dramatic reputation – it became clear that somewhere the noble project had lost its way.

The whole idea of a national theatre has inspired intense infighting in the Catalan theatre world ever since Josep Maria Flotats, a fine, French-trained classical actor who had been a resident member of the Comédie Française, was asked to return home to devise such a thing in the 1980s. Flotats' aim was to create a permanent public theatre with a resident company like the National in Britain or the major theatres he had worked in in France. However, scepticism and jealousy soon arose among other theatre professionals. The Teatre Lliure could justifiably claim that for years their poorly funded, finely tuned troupe had already functioned as a *de facto* national theatre; other companies like Els Joglars and Dagoll Dagom contrasted their untraditional styles to that of Flotats, pointing out that a language without important dramatic texts could better express itself via innovative approaches than through textual theatre. Commercial production agencies, meanwhile, complained that the TNC would provide unfair competition and demanded that they be allowed to use the new facility, which Flotats held to be contrary to his entire conception of a public theatre.

The city Ajuntament came up with its own proposal for a **Ciutat de Teatre** or 'City of Theatre' in former exhibition buildings on Montjuïc, around the city-owned **Mercat de les Flors**. The Teatre Lliure joined this project, and former Lliure director Lluís Pascual returned from his post at the Théatre de l'Europe in Paris to head the scheme. It seemed clear that the Ciutat – due to open in 1999 – was meant to frustrate Flotats' ambition to establish the TNC as sole player in the spotlight.

Needless to say, as the TNC approached completion the local stage scene resembled a loudly ticking bomb. Few imagined the explosion would coincide with the opening night. Before an audience of Catalonia's cultural and political elites, Flotats used his speech to attack the '*quatre gats baladrers*' (four whining cats) who had made his life miserable over the previous decade. This was taken as a grave insult above all by the heads of private-sector companies present. Within the month, not only had they forced Flotats' firing, but the Generalitat had acquiesced in giving over 40 per cent of the TNC's programme space to commercial initiatives. So, rather than becoming the prestigious stage that Catalan theatre had been yearning for, Bofill's Grecian temple now serves as just another building – however grand – where theatre can be seen in Barcelona.

Teatre Nacional de Catalunya

Plaça de les Arts 1 (900 12 11 33). Metro Glòries/bus 7, 18, 56, 62, N3, N9. **Box office** from two hours before performance times Tue-Sun; *advance sales* box office & Servi-Caixa. **Tickets** 2,800ptas; discounts students, over-65s, groups; 50% discount on standby tickets from 50min before performance. **Credit** MC, V. **Map D4**

Teatre Poliorama

La Rambla 115 (93 317 75 99). Metro Catalunya/bus all routes to Plaça Catalunya. **Box office** 5pm to performance Tue-Sun; *advance sales* box office & Servi-Caixa. **Tickets** 1,850-2,850ptas; discounts for students, over-65s, groups. **Credit** V. **Map D4**

This theatre was acquired by the Catalan government in 1984 to house the Josep Maria Flotats company and *Centre Dramàtic de la Generalitat* (CDGC), genesis of the future National Theatre. Since the opening of the TNC it has been given over to commercial producers for shows such as Dagoll Dagom's *Pigmalió*. George Orwell was holed up on the roof of the building for three days during the Civil War street-fighting between anarchists and Communists in 1937.

Teatre Principal

La Rambla 27 (93 301 47 50). Metro Drassanes/bus 14, 18, 38, 59, N6, N9. **Box office** from 4.30pm Tue-Sun; *advance sales* box office & Servi-Caixa. **Tickets** plays 2,000-3,000ptas; *opera* 1,000-4,000ptas; *recitals* 2,000ptas; discounts under-14s, groups. **No credit cards. Map D5**

The Principal stands on the site of Barcelona's first theatre, the Teatre de la Santa Creu, opened in 1597. Destroyed by fire in the eighteenth century, it was rebuilt and renamed in the 1850s, when it entered into competition with the new Liceu for Barcelona's opera crowd. Needless to say it lost. The theatre has just been refurbished, and for the 1998-9 season will return to opera with productions of Gluck, Mozart and Verdi, along with major dramatic classics in Catalan and Spanish.

Teatre Romea

C/Hospital 51 (93 317 71 89/93 301 55 04). Metro Liceu/bus 14, 18, 38, 59, 91, N4, N6. **Box office** noon-1.30pm, 4-8pm Tue-Fri; 4-8pm Sat; 4-6pm Sun; *advance sales* box office & Servi-Caixa. **Tickets** 1,500-2,500ptas; 25% discount students, over-65s, groups. **Credit** V. **Map C5**

Now another theatre of the Generalitat's CDGC, the Romea has been a centres of the Barcelona theatre world for over a century. It offers classical and contemporary theatre, almost always in Catalan, and continues as a public theatre in spite of the tendency of the Teatre Nacional to usurp its role.

Teatre Tívoli

C/Casp 10-12 (93 412 20 63). Metro Catalunya/bus all routes to Plaça Catalunya. **Box office** 11.30am-2pm, 4.30-8pm, Tue-Sun; *advance sales* box office & Caixa de Catalunya or Servi-Caixa (depending on performance). **Tickets** 2,000-4,000ptas; group discounts. **No credit cards. Map D4**

Barcelona's biggest theatre offers a mixed bag of drama, spectacular shows and music, including a long run of La Cubana's *Cegada de Amor*. It has also offered Els Joglars' spoof of Jordi Pujol, and has been a venue for events related to the 1998 centenary of the birth of Federico García Lorca.

Teatre Victòria

Avda Paral.lel 67 (93 443 29 29). Metro Paral.lel/bus 36, 57, 64, N4, N6. **Box office** from 5pm Tue-Sun; *advance sales* box office & Servi-Caixa. **Tickets** approx 1,900-3,500ptas; discounts Wed, Thur. **Credit** V. **Map C5**

Opened 1905, the Victòria is one of Barcelona's largest venues, and notable for its acoustic excellence. Productions vary from concert editions of opera produced by the Liceu, to adaptations of musicals or visiting dance and music groups.

Villarroel Teatre

C/Villarroel 87 (93 451 12 34). Metro Urgell/bus 9, 14, 20, 50, 56, N1. **Box office** from 7.30pm Tue-Sat; 6-7pm Sun; *advance sales* box office (7.30-9.30pm Tue-Sat), phone (9am-2pm, 7.30pm-performance) & Caixa de Catalunya. **Tickets** 2,000-2,500ptas; discounts under-14s, over-65s, groups. **No credit cards. Map C4**

The Villarroel stages mainly non-mainstream theatre, such

as *Dakota* and *Surf* by playwright Jordi Galceran. Its financial situation is often shaky, despite the popularity of its productions, and it always seems to survive by sheer will.

Alternative & fringe theatres

Artenbrut

C/Perill 9-11 (93 457 97 05). Metro Verdaguer/bus 20, 21, 45, 47. **Box office** 8pm till performance Tue-Sun; *advance sales* box office & Caixa de Catalunya. **Tickets** 1,600-2,000ptas. **No credit cards. Map D2/E2**

This small venue has great intentions, with a double bill on weekends usually divided between text-based works and the *Opera de Butxaca* (pocket opera), series, which runs from real mini-operas from classical scores to drag-queen cabaret.

La Cuina & Teatre Adrià Gual

C/Sant Pere Més Baix 7 (93 268 20 78). Metro Jaume I/bus 17, 19, 40, 45. **Box office** two hours before performance Mon-Sat; one hour before performance Sun; *advance sales* box office & Caixa de Catalunya. **Tickets** 1,700-1,900ptas; 25% discount students, over-65s; free Mar, May-June (student productions). **No credit cards. Map D5**

Two stages that serve as outlets for the work of Barcelona's Theatre Institute school, in interesting (and cheap) productions. Both student and professional productions are presented, often directed by prestigious visiting directors. The school should move to the Theatre City on Montjuïc in 1999.

Espai Escènic Joan Brossa

C/Tantarantana 16 (93 310 13 64). Metro Jaume I/bus 39, 51. **Open** *box office* two hours before performance. **Advance sales** Caixa de Catalunya. **Tickets** 1,500-2,000ptas. **No credit cards. Map E5**

One of Barcelona's most curious theatre projects is dedicated to poet and artist Joan Brossa, who wrote wonderful theatrical pieces in the 1960s close to performance art. The space reflects his obsessions: magic and sleight of hand, the commedia dell'arte, the circus and literary cabaret. Shows are often accessible to non-Catalan speakers.

Sala Beckett

C/Alegre de Dalt 55 bis (93 284 53 12). Metro Joanic/bus 21, 25, 39, 55, N4. **Box office** one hour before performance; *advance sales* box office (10.30am-2pm, 4-6pm Mon-Fri) & Caixa de Catalunya. **Tickets** 1,500-2,000ptas. **No credit cards. Map E2**

Founded by the Samuel Beckett-inspired Teatro Fronterizo group, whose founder José Sanchis Sinistierra is one of Spain's best modern playwrights. This small Gràcia space offers varied new theatre, and also contemporary dance.

Teatre Malic

C/Fusina (93 310 70 35). Metro Jaume I/bus 39, 51. **Box office** two hours before performance; *advance sales* box office, phone (10am-2pm, 4-6pm, Mon-Fri) & Caixa de Catalunya. **Tickets** 1,500-2,000ptas. **No credit cards. Map E5**

A tiny (60-seat) theatre in a Born basement, the Màlic has jumped on the mini-musical bandwagon. Other productions include minimalist recitals from modern classics like Albee's *Zoo Story*, and there are kids' shows on weekend mornings.

Versus Teatre

C/Castillejos 179 (93 232 31 84). Metro Monumental/bus 7, 56, N2. **Box office** one hour before performance; *advance sales* box office & Caixa de Catalunya. **Tickets** 1,500-2,000ptas; performances for children 800ptas. **Credit** MC, V. **Map F4**

One of the newer alternative theatres, with its own company as well as strong productions from outside companies. Drama includes twentieth-century works, and Versus joins in the 'Pocket Opera' cycle with inventive offerings.

Trips Out of Town

Getting Started

Escaping from the city roar, by road or rail.

Considering how small Catalonia actually is – all its borders are within a day's reach of Barcelona by car – its scenery and climate are remarkably varied. To the north and east are the Pyrenees and the Mediterranean coastal mountains, while to the west it slopes into a broad plain. In theory at least, it's feasible to wake up to the cold, fresh air of the mountains, and later the same day spend your siesta on the coast with temperatures over 35°C.

The Catalan '*costes*' – Brava, Maresme, Garraf and Daurada – all have their tourist-heavy towns, but there are plenty of lesser-known places, and inland the countryside is a goldmine of beautiful towns, villages and scenery, much of it yet to be discovered by non-Catalan visitors. The Generalitat tourist office in the **Palau Robert** (*see page 251*) and local offices stock a wealth of brochures on areas and districts (*comarques*), national parks, and specific themes (*Modernisme*, or Roman sites). The Generalitat also publishes two comprehensive annual guides, *Hotels Catalunya* and *Catalunya Campings*, available at most bookshops. For travel agents, *see chapter* **Services**.

By bus

Coach services around Catalonia are operated by different private companies, which are now mostly (but not entirely) concentrated at the **Estació d'Autobusos Barcelona-Nord**, C/Ali Bei 80 (Metro Arc de Triomf). General information is on **93 265 65 08**, but each company also has its own phone lines. Two areas better served by buses than trains are the high Pyrenees (with the Alsina-Graëlls company) and the central Costa Brava (with Sarfa).

By road

For many car-mad locals, the greatest of the 1992 additions to Barcelona was the **Rondes**, the obstacle-free ring-road built to ease traffic into, around and out of the city. The **Ronda de Dalt** runs along the edge of Tibidabo, and the **Ronda Litoral** along the coast, meeting north and south of the city. They intersect with several motorways (*autopistes*): from the north, the A17 for Girona, and the A18 for Terrassa, Sabadell and Manresa, which run into Avda Meridiana; the A2 for Lleida and Tarragona, a continuation of Avda Diagonal;

and the A16 for Sitges, reached from the Gran Via. These roads carry tolls, and it's often best to get off them once out of town. Where possible, toll-free alternatives are indicated in the pages that follow. The **Túnel de Vallvidrera**, the continuation of Via Augusta that leads out of Barcelona under Collserola to Sant Cugat and Terrassa, also has a high toll. North of Barcelona, a recent addition to Catalan infrastructure is the **Eix Transversal** motorway between Girona and Lleida via Vic, which significantly reduces journey time between these cities and is intended to reduce the need for so much of the region's traffic to pass through the Barcelona hub.

Thanks to the *Rondes*, traffic on main roads runs fairly freely most days, but return journeys into Barcelona on Sunday evenings are always to be avoided. For more information on driving and car hire, *see page 259*.

By train

Spanish Railways (**RENFE**) operates an extensive network within Catalonia – particularly useful for the coast, Girona, the Montseny and the Penedès. All trains stop at **Barcelona-Sants** station (Metro Sants-Estació), where tickets for regional destinations are sold at the windows labelled *Rodalies/Cercanías*. In the city centre some routes (the coast to the north, the Montseny, the Penedès) pass through **Plaça Catalunya**; others (the coast south, Girona) through **Passeig de Gràcia**.

Trains can be *Regulars*, which stop at every station, *Deltas*, stopping at nearly all of them, and *Catalunya Exprés*, which stop less frequently and cost a little more. Long-distance (*Largo Recorrido*) services also stop at main stations, with supplements for high-speed services. RENFE fare structures are complicated, but there are special tickets giving unlimited travel on regional trains for three or five days, and off-peak days each month (*días azules*, blue days, and usually midweek) when long-distance services are cheaper. For **RENFE information**, call **93 490 02 02** (English spoken).

Some destinations (Montserrat, Igualada, Manresa) are served by Catalan Government Railways (**FGC**). It has two stations: **Plaça d'Espanya**, for Montserrat and Manresa, and **Plaça Catalunya** for the line within Barcelona and trains to Sant Cugat, Sabadell and Terrassa. **FGC information** is on **93 205 15 15**.

The City Fringes

A breath of fresh air is within easy reach of Barcelona's centre.

You don't need to travel far to discover a different side to Barcelona: pine forests and small hill villages are within half-an-hour's journey time. As well as being pretty, these areas also contain some of the most striking examples of Catalan *Modernista* architecture.

The Vallès

The other side of the great ridge of Collserola from Barcelona extends the hilly plain of the Vallès. Just beyond the road and rail tunnels, **Les Planes** is a picnic area on the edge of Collserola, with cheap restaurants and an area called a *merendero*, with tables and charcoal grills that are used by Sunday visitors who bring their own food to barbecue. There's an attractive walk or cycle ride from Les Planes towards **El Papiol**, a town with a medieval castle and the remains of an Iberian settlement.

A little further to the north is **La Floresta**, a leafy suburb of houses scattered between pines up and down steep hillsides. It was once called 'La Floresta Pearson', after the Canadian engineer who brought mains electricity to Barcelona in 1911, and planned the village. In the 1970s it was Barcelona's hippy colony – legendary 'Fat Freddy's Cat' cartoonist Gilbert Shelton even lived here for a while – and the influence survives in the friendly Bar Dada, near the station. La Floresta is a great place for an easy, short walk, with beautiful views.

Below Collserola stands **Sant Cugat**, a fast-growing but pleasant town with a Romanesque **monastery** and, on the Arrabassada road back towards Barcelona, the **Casa Lluch**, a striking 1906 Modernist creation with superb tiling. The main centres of the Vallès are two of Catalonia's major industrial towns, Terrassa and Sabadell. **Terrassa** is rarely seen as a tourist attraction, but has at its centre three beautiful, very ancient Visigothic-Romanesque churches, **Santa Maria, Sant Miquel** and **Sant Pere**, with sections that date from the sixth century. The town also has a host of Modernist buildings connected with the textile industry, such as the extraordinary **Masia Freixa**, a combination of mosque and Disneyland palace, and the Aymerich i Amat factory, which now houses Catalonia's science museum, the **Museu de la Ciència i de la Tècnica.**

The eternal rival of neighbouring Terrassa, **Sabadell** also has plenty of interesting Modernist buildings, including the unmissable covered market, the **Torre de les Aigües** (water-tower), and **Caixa d'Estalvis de Sabadell** savings bank.

Information

Getting there: Les Planes, La Floresta, Sant Cugat *By car* A7 via Túnel de Vallvidrera (exit 8 off Ronda de Dalt, toll), or the winding but scenic Carretera de l'Arrabassada (exit 5 off Ronda de Dalt) for free. *By train* FGC from Plaça Catalunya, Terrassa or Sabadell trains. Journey time 15-25 min. **El Papiol** *By car* A7, then B30 from Molins de Rei. *By train* RENFE from Plaça Catalunya. **Terrassa, Sabadell** *By car* A18 or N150 (exit 1 off Ronda de Dalt). *By train* RENFE or FGC from Plaça Catalunya. **Where to eat:** Les Planes is a traditional picnicking place, La Floresta has the Bar Dada. Sant Cugat has a very good grilled-meat restaurant, the reasonably priced **Braseria La Bolera**, C/Baixada de l'Alba 20 (93 674 16 75). In Terrassa **Casa Toni**, Carretera de Castellar 124 (93 786 47 08; average 3,000ptas), has an impressive range of wines. In Sabadell **Forrellat**, C/Horta Novella 27 (93 725 71 51), is pricey (5,000ptas) but top quality. **Museu de la Ciència i de la Tècnica de Catalunya** *Rambla d'Egara 270, Terrassa (93 736 89 66).* **Open** 10am-7pm Tue-Fri; 10am-2.30pm Sat, Sun, public holidays. **Closed** Mon. **Admission** 400ptas, 275ptas students, over-65s; free under-7s and first Sun of the month. **No credit cards.**

Colònia Güell

The Colònia Güell in the small town of **Santa Coloma de Cervelló**, on the western edge of Barcelona's sprawl, was one of the most ambitious projects on which Gaudí worked for his patron Eusebi Güell. It was intended to be a model industrial village around a textile factory, with a complete range of services for the workers. Like their park in Barcelona, it was never finished.

Nevertheless, the Colònia's crypt – begun in 1898, and the only part of the church to be completed before Güell died in 1918 – is one of Gaudí's most extraordinary and architecturally experimental works. The interior combines great sobriety with a look irresistibly like a giant fairy grotto, with parabolic vaults and tree-like inclined columns that pre-date their use by modern architects by at least half a century. All the fittings, stained glass and pews are the originals, by Gaudí. The other buildings of the 'colony', most by Francesc Berenguer, are also interesting.

Colònia Güell

Santa Coloma de Cervelló (93 640 29 36). By car A2 to Sant Boi exit, then right turn to Sant Vicenç dels Horts (8km). *By train* FGC from Plaça d'Espanya to Molí Nou; the Colònia is a 10-min walk from the station. **Open** 10am-1pm, 4-6pm, Mon-Wed, Fri, Sat; 10am-1.15pm Thur, Sun, public holidays. **Admission** 100ptas. **No credit cards.**

Beaches

There's a lot more to Catalonia's coastal resorts than pure sun, sea and sand, but not everyone seems to have realised this yet.

Since Barcelona managed to clean up its act and make its beaches appealing and user-friendly, the need to catch a train to some sandy haven further along the coastline hasn't been quite as strong as it once was. The coastal towns of Catalonia have other attractions, however, and despite a highly developed tourist industry many are surprisingly unspoilt, managing to retain much of their original charm and beauty.

South

To Sitges & Vilanova

Traditionally Barcelona's own favourite, and nearest, beach has been **Castelldefels**, just 20km (12 miles) to the south – a bit of a dull town, but with kilometres of windswept, uncrowded beaches and fine seafood restaurants. It's used more by locals than foreigners, and has an attractive marina development, **Port Ginesta**, on the west side. If you're travelling by train, it's a much shorter walk to the beach if you get off at Castelldefels Platja, the stop immediately after Castelldefels proper. Only a few minutes' train ride further along is **Garraf**, a tiny village with a clean, small beach served by a couple of beach bars or *xiringuitos*, and the **Celler de Garraf**, another *Modernista* classic designed by Gaudí for the Güells, in 1895.

The Garraf mountains come down to the sea, and just the other side is **Sitges**, one of Catalonia's most famous resorts. Discovered and promoted at the turn of the century by writer/artist Santiago Rusiñol – whose circle included Manuel de Falla, Ramon Casas, Nonell, Utrillo and Picasso – it was also one of the first real resorts, and has a character many others lack. Sitges attracts thousands of visitors from across Europe. Since the 1960s, the town has also become a favourite destination for gays, first from Barcelona and then from around the world (for more on Sitges' gay scene, *see chapter* **Gay & Lesbian Barcelona**). There are nine beaches along the seafront, and quieter beaches at the adjoining (artificial) port of Aiguadolç – to get there, turn left out of the station. For nudist beaches in Sitges, get to the beach, turn right, and keep going until you find them (quite a walk on a hot day). For walks into the Garraf hills behind Sitges, *see page 245*.

Even when crowded, the town still has great charm, with its long promenade, the Passeig Marítim, curving along the beaches. Dominating the view is an especially beautiful cluster of buildings around Sitges' most visible monument, the seventeenth-century church of **Sant Bartomeu i Santa Tecla**. Almost adjacent to it are the old market, the Ajuntament and the **Museu Cau Ferrat** on C/Fonollar (93 894 03 64), Santiago Rusiñol's old home, which he bequeathed to the town as a ready-made museum, chock-full of his collections of paintings, archaeological finds, *Modernista* ironwork, medieval keys, model ships, traditional ceramics and indoor fountains. Opposite is the **Palau Mar i Cel**, another delightful old residence with a finely crafted door, an unusual interior and an eclectic collection of medieval and baroque artwork. A third museum, the **Museu Romàntic** in Casa Llopis, C/Sant Gaudenci 1 (93 894 29 69), has an assortment of household objects from the last century, with a valuable collection of antique dolls. A combined ticket admits you to all three museums.

Vilanova i la Geltrú, the largest port between Barcelona and Tarragona, isn't exactly a holiday resort – although it does have some good beaches – but has several museums, including the important **Biblioteca-Museu Balaguer** on Avda Victor Balaguer (93 815 42 02), with paintings by El Greco, Catalan turn-of-the-century art, oriental artefacts and old weapons and coins. The town also has a distinguished central square, the **Plaça de la Vila**, and is known for its Carnaval each

*Swinging on the beach in **Sitges**.*

'Is that a saddle on your bicycle or are you just pleased to see me?'

February, and its seafood, especially served with a spicy local variant of *romesco* sauce called *xató*.

Information

Getting there: *By car* A16 to Castelldefels, Garraf, Sitges (41km/25 miles) and Vilanova, with an extra tunnel toll between Garraf and Sitges. C246 covers the same distance, but involves a slow, winding drive around the Garraf mountains. *By train* RENFE from Sants or Passeig de Gràcia to Sitges (average 30min) and Vilanova (40min). Trains approx. every 20 minutes; not all stop at Castelldefels and Garraf.
Tourist offices: **Castelldefels** *Plaça Rosa dels Vents (93 664 23 01)*; **Sitges** *Passeig de Vilafranca (93 894 12 30)*; **Vilanova i la Geltrú** *C/Torre de Ribaroges/Platja. (93 815 45 17)*.
Where to eat:
Castelldefels: There are plenty of cheap paella places near the seafront. A good, more upmarket restaurant is the **Nàutic** *Passeig Marítim 374 (93 665 01 74)*.
Sitges: Good value for money are **Sitges** *C/Parellades 61 (93 894 34 93)* and **La Salseta** *C/Sant Pau 35 (93 811 04 19)*. Slightly more expensive, but worth it is **Chez Jeanette** *C/Sant Pau 23 (93 894 00 48)*, with seasonal Catalano-French cuisine. If you want to blow some money on good seafood, avoid the seafront and go straight to **La Nansa** *C/Carreta 24 (93 894 19 27)*.
Vilanova i la Geltrú: **Avi Pep** *C/Llibertat 128 (93 815 17 36)* is cheap and cheerful, while the **Peixerot** *Passeig Marítim 56 (93 815 06 25)* gets the pick of the fish arriving daily at the town harbour. When the seafood gets too much, excellent grilled meat can be had at **Can Pagès** *C/Sant Pere 24-26 (93 894 11 95)* and **El Celler Vell** *C/Sant Bonaventura 21 (93 894 82 99)*.
Where to stay:
Sitges: **Celimar** *Passeig de la Ribera 18 (93 811 01 70)* is a comfortable seafront hotel (about 12,000ptas a double room). **Hostal Maricel** *C/ D'en Tacó 11 (93 894 36 27)* weighs in at 6,000ptas/double, while the **Parellades** *C/Parellades 11 (93 894 08 01)* is one of the best cheaper options. *See also chapter* **Gay & Lesbian Barcelona**.

Tarragona & the Costa Daurada

About two thirds of the way from Vilanova to Tarragona lies **Altafulla**, a small town often bypassed by the tourist trade, despite having one of the best-preserved medieval centres on the coast. The modern section is close to the seafront, where there are beaches of fine, white sand, between rocky outcrops that give shade, and a picturesque seaside castle at nearby **Tamarit**. The old, walled town – crowned by the imposing **Castell d'Altafulla** and floodlit at night – is a ten-minute stroll inland. At **Els Munts**, about half-way between the old and new towns, there is one of Catalonia's best-preserved Roman villas.

Tarragona, a busy provincial capital of over 100,000 people, has been mysteriously overlooked by most foreign visitors, despite the fact that as Roman *Tarraco* it was the capital of an area which covered half the Iberian peninsula, and as a result contains the largest ensemble of Roman buildings and ruins in Spain – an extraordinary architectural legacy that includes the original town walls, an amphitheatre, circus, aqueduct and forum. Much later, the Catalan colonisers who seized the area from the Moors in the twelfth century spent 61 years constructing the **Catedral de Santa Maria**, the Romanesque-Gothic building that dominates the town, in the midst of the *ciutat antiga* or old city, comparable in beauty to the Barri Gòtic of Barcelona. Tarragona also has a breathtaking view of the sea and the city's flat hinterland, the *Camp de Tarragona*, from the long walkway

A grand day out

Opened in 1995, the **Port Aventura** theme park near Salou – the themes being the Mediterranean, Polynesia, China, Mexico and the Wild West – has drawn in the crowds from the first day. Attractions include a waterfall ride, a 'typhoon' corkscrew, canoeing, a steam train, Chinese carousels, log-riding, virtual-reality games, and last but certainly not least, the stomach-crunching Dragon Khan, largest roller-coaster in Europe, with eight 360° loops. There are also (of course) special rides for little kids, and floor shows from Mariachis to Chinese acrobats.

For those who don't usually enjoy this kind of thing, it should be noted that Port Aventura is a more authentic theme park than most: the designs of the buildings were thoroughly researched, and products on sale in the shops actually originate in the countries they're supposed to be from. Those who do like this kind of thing think it's great, and rate it very highly in the international theme-park league. Admission entitles you to an unlimited number of rides, and on-site facilities include video and buggy hire, a purchase collecting service, wheelchair hire and special facilities for disabled visitors. Food and drink cannot be taken into the park, but food outlets (some serving alcohol) make an inevitable appearance on every corner.

Port Aventura
(977 77 90 90). Open Mar-late June, mid-Sept-late-Oct 10am-8pm, *late June-mid-Sept* 10am-midnight, daily. **Admission** *One day* 4,100ptas; 3,100ptas 5-12s, over-65s; free under-5s. *Two consecutive days* 6,250ptas; 4,850ptas 5-12s, over-65s; free under-5s. *Three consecutive days* 8,200ptas; 6,400ptas 5-12s, over-65s; free under-5s. *Night ticket (7pm-midnight, late June-mid-Sept only)* 2,500ptas; 1,900ptas 5-12s, over-65s. **Credit** AmEx, DC, JCB, MC, V.
Getting there: *By car* A2, then A7 to exit 35, or N340 (108km/67 miles). *By train* RENFE from Sants or Passeig de Gràcia (1hr 15min). Port Aventura has its own station, on the Barcelona-Tarragona-Tortosa line; in season seven southbound and ten northbound trains a day stop there.

around the Roman walls called the **Passeig Arqueològic**. Below it there is a busy modern boulevard, the Rambla Nova, a host of other monuments and an attractive fishermen's district with good seafood restaurants, most offering dishes with Tarragona's characteristic *romesco* sauce. The beach, the **Platja del Miracle** ('Beach of the Miracle') lies just beyond the amphitheatre.

A few more kilometres southwest is **Salou**, largest resort of the Costa Daurada, with sand, sea, hotels, discos, bars, calamares'n'chips and sun cream all on tap. It also has some Modernist buildings, and a major new attraction just nearby, **Port Aventura** theme park (*see opposite*).

Information

Getting there: *By car* A2, then A7 via Vilafranca (Tarragona 98km/60 miles). The toll-free N340 (Molins de Rei exit from A2) follows a similar route. *By train* RENFE from Sants or Passeig de Gràcia to Altafulla (Catalunya Exprés 55min), Tarragona (1hr 6min) and Salou (1hr 18min). Trains hourly approx 6am-9.30pm.
Tourist offices: Altafulla *Plaça dels Vents (977 65 07 52)*; **Tarragona** *C/Fortuny 4 (977 23 34 15)*; **Salou** *Passeig Jaume I 4 (977 35 01 02)*.
Where to eat:
Altafulla: Faristol *C/Sant Martí 5 (977 65 00 77)*, an eighteenth-century house converted into a bar-restaurant, is well-priced and has a pleasant outdoor terrace.
Tarragona: Bufet el Tiberi *C/Martí d'Ardenya 5 (977 23 54 03)*, is enjoyable and cheap. The best-known restaurant is **Sol-Ric** *Via Augusta 227 (977 23 20 32)*, famous for its fish-and-shellfish *romesco*, veal with Cinzano and the 400 wines on its list (average 5,000ptas).
Salou: Restaurants are pricey. **Goleta** *C/Gavina-Platja Capellans (977 38 35 66)* does good salt-baked fish.
Where to stay:
Altafulla: Yola *Via Augusta 50 (977 65 02 83)*, is a clean and modern place(around 6,000ptas). To rent rooms in the old town, ask at the English-owned bar **El Corral** *(977 65 04 86)*, near the Faristol (*see above*).
Tarragona: Imperial Tarraco *Rambla Vella 2 (977 23 30 40)*, is luxurious; the attractive **Forum** *Plaça de l'Ajuntament (977 23 17 18)* is a likeable cheap *hostal*.
Salou: El Racó *Platja del Racó (977 37 02 16)* has doubles for 5,500 ptas. If it's full, there are 53 other places to stay in this town of about 8,000 permanent inhabitants.

The Ebro Delta

About an hour further down the coast from Tarragona you'll find the wonderful natural park of the **Delta de l'Ebre**, an ecologically remarkable 320 square km (125 square mile) area that's home to almost 300 species of birds – 60 per cent of all the species in Europe can be found here. There are flamingoes, great crested grebes, purple herons, night herons, marsh harriers, an enormous variety of ducks, and many others. The towns of the delta are nothing special in themselves – and have their share of white box-shaped tourist developments – but the sheer natural beauty of the place, the immense, flat, green expanse of wetlands, rice fields, channels and dunes, makes it fascinating and atmospheric all year round.

The absolute flatness is ideal for walking or cycle tours (bicycles can be rented easily, check at

the information office in Deltebre). Boat tours along the river are also possible. Because it's a good two-hour train ride from Barcelona, plan on spending at least a weekend in the Delta. A good place to base yourself is the central town of **Deltebre**, the base for most park services. From there it is easy to make day trips to the bird sanctuaries, most of which are located on the other, south, side of the river, the primary point of interest being **Punta de la Banya**.

Information

Getting there: *By car* A2, then A7 via Vilafranca, or the toll-free N340 (Molins de Rei exit from A2). Barcelona-Amposta 172km/107 miles. *By train and bus* RENFE from Sants or Passeig de Gràcia to L'Aldea-Amposta (2 hrs), then by bus (HIFE 977 44 03 00) to Deltebre.
Tourist office: Deltebre *Park Information Centre, C/Ulldecona 22 (977 48 96 79)*. There is also a small museum on the different Delta habitats alongside.
Where to stay & eat:
Deltebre: El Buitre *Carretera de Riumar (977 48 05 28)* is a white, box-style hotel outside of town with undertones of low-budget James Bond (about 4,000ptas a double). It also has, though, an above-average restaurant with inexpensive, very good Delta rice dishes (try the *rossejat*, well-browned rice with fish broth). There are two campsites in Deltebre, **L'Aube** *Urbanització Riumar (977 44 51 06)*, and **Riomar** *Urbanització Riumar (977 48 00 06)*, and a youth hostel, **Alberg Mossèn Batlle** *Avda de les Goles de l'Ebre (977 48 01 36)*.

North

The Costa del Maresme

The Maresme coast, immediately north-east of Barcelona, is close enough to the city for easy day-tripping. Two of the best places for a day out are **Caldes d'Estrac**, also known as **Caldetes**, and **Sant Pol de Mar**. Both are small towns with good beaches (some nudist), and plenty of tourists, local and foreign. Sant Pol has the advantage that, unlike in many places along this coast, where railway tracks run close to the beach, some of its beaches are separated from both roads and the rail line by rocky cliffs. Both villages are also worth strolling around. Caldetes has some interesting *Modernista* houses, a spa, and a recently restored park with good views of the coast, and Sant Pol – which has a striking Modernist school, from 1907 – is a mostly unspoilt, if yuppified, fishing village.

Information

Getting there: *By car* N11 from Barcelona to Caldes d'Estrac (36km/22 miles) and Sant Pol (48km/30 miles). *By train* RENFE from Sants or Plaça Catalunya. Trains every half-hour, journey time approx 35min.
Where to stay and eat:
Caldetes: Emma *Baixada de l'Estació 5 (93 791 13 05)* is one of the town's best middle-priced restaurants. If you want to stay over, the **Pinzón** *C/El Callao 4 (93 791 00 51)*, has rooms for about 4,500ptas a night.
Sant Pol: Hostalet I *C/Manzanillo 9 (93 760 06 05)* and **Hostalet II** *C/Santa Clara (93 760 07 43)* are pleasant hotels with doubles for around 5,000ptas. There are some good paella restaurants on the main street.

The Costa Brava

The Costa Brava proper lies within the *comarca* of the **Baix Empordà**. This rocky peninsula was the original 'rugged coast' for which journalist Ferran Agulló dreamt up the name 'Costa Brava' earlier this century. It is still the Costa's most unspoilt section. There are no big sandy beaches, and access by public transport is limited, and so the area has largely escaped the mass tourist boom. Consequently, accommodation facilities are still limited (it is essential to book in high season), as are nightlife and organised activities for children and families. This does not mean the area is undiscovered, though: it's a favourite holiday destination for prosperous Catalans, and in summer it's best to visit midweek to avoid the crowds.

Winding roads connect the main inlets on the peninsula. The northern ones – **Sa Riera, Sa Tuna** and **Aiguablava** – are most accessible from Begur, those further south – **Tamariu**, **Llafranc** and **Calella** – are best reached from Palafrugell.

Begur is an attractive old town dominated by the remains of a fourteenth-century castle. It is set just inland – and so was more protected in its day from piracy – on a rocky hillside commanding magnificent views to north and south. From there it's a steep 3km (2 mile) walk down to the coast. If you're not prepared to hoof it, you'll need your own transport. A little further inland is the very carefully preserved medieval village of **Pals**, now seemingly converted almost entirely into second

Sea sports

Sailing, windsurfing, kayaking

Nearly every town on the coast worth its salt has a *club nàutic* (boat club), where it's often possible to rent a small sailing boat (*estell* – star class –, swordfish or catamaran) or windsurf by the hour. Sea kayaks are also increasingly popular, and are a great way to explore the *calas* of the Costa Brava. If the local club has nothing to offer, there will probably be other rental places in the vicinity that specialise in one type of boat, catamarans being the most common. Some coastal camp sites also have boats for rent. Prices range from 1,500ptas to 3,500ptas per hour. There are also boat hire facilities in Barcelona (*see* chapter **Sports & Fitness**).

Boat hire: south of Barcelona

Castelldefels: Catamaran Center *Port Ginesta, Local 324 (93 665 22 11)*. **Open** All year. All sizes

and classes of catamarans for hire, including a 53-foot catamaran yacht. Sea kayaks also available.
Sitges: Club Nàutic Sitges *L'Espigó s/n (93 894 09 05)*. **Open** All year. Catamarans for hire.
Calafell (near El Vendrell): **Windcat House** *Mas Mel, Passeig Maritim 51 (977 69 30 72)*. **Open** All year. Catamarans and kayaks for rent. Courses also available.

Boast hire: north of Barcelona

Calella de la Costa: Club Nàutic Calella *Passeig de la Platja (93 766 18 52)*. **Open** All year. Catamarans, *estells*, kayaks and windsurfing equipment for hire.
L'Escala: Kayaking Costa Brava *Passeig Lluis Albert 11 (972 77 38 06)*. **Open** All year. Kayak rentals, group excursions (full- or half-day) from Tamariu to Aiguablava. Courses available.

homes with video-intercoms installed next to ancient stone doorways. Pals is nonetheless a remarkable survivor, with several fine twelfth- to fifteenth-century monuments and buildings, and beautiful views over the surrounding countryside.

Sa Riera, at the end of the little road from Pals to the coast, is the northernmost cove of the peninsula and has one of its largest sandy beaches – although there's still only space for 300 bodies – and good views of the Medes islands to the north. There's a popular nudist beach, the *Illa Roja*, in a secluded spot between Sa Riera and La Platja del Racó. From Sa Riera a road leads across a headland to **Sa Tuna**, a picturesque fishing village. Its one *hostal*-restaurant is in an excellent position on the seafront, but the beach is small and stony.

Sant Pere Pescador: La Bellena Alegre
C/Despoblat Sector Sud (972 52 03 02). A Costa Brava campsite that has windsurfing equipment for hire.

Scuba diving

Scuba diving is a very popular sport in Catalonia. The experience may not be quite the same as in the Caribbean or the Red Sea, but there are some very decent dives to be had, particularly on the Costa Brava, with its rocky coves and caves. In just about every town along this coast there's a diving club where you can rent equipment – wetsuit, air tanks– and find a guide to take you down. Mask, fins, and snorkel can also be rented, but it's more common to bring your own. Prices vary: about 5,000-8,000ptas per dive, equipment and guide included. Diver's certificates are required. If you've never dived before, it's possible to try a simple baptismal dive with a guide (about 7,000ptas), or sign up for a course. Courses usually last a few days to a week and cost around 50,000ptas. Many scuba clubs in Barcelona also arrange day trips up the coast, but logically charge a bit more.

The **Illes Medes**, a small group of islands near Estartit, are an official underwater natural park, and one of the last places along this coast where it's still possible to find the Mediterranean's famous red coral. Unfortunately, precisely because of this, the diving scene at the Medes can be intensely crowded, with boatloads of 50 divers at a time being shipped out and dumped into the sea every half hour or so.

Diving Clubs

Barcelona: Aquamarina *C/Castillejos 270 (93 455 29 62).* Metro Sagrada Familia/bus all routes to Sagrada Familia. **Open** All year. Guided tours in Catalonia. Equipment for sale and rent.
Begur: Aqualògik *Cala d'Aiguafreda (972 62 42 47).* **Open** All year. Ten dive routes.
Cadaqués: Sotamar *Avda Caritat Serinyana 17 (972 25 88 76).* **Open** All year. Ten dive routes.
L'Estartit (Illes Medes): **Diving Center La Sirena** *Camping La Sirena (972 75 09 54).* **Open** All year. **Unisub** *Ctra Torroella de Montgrí 15 (972 75 17 68).* **Open** Mar-Nov. **Quim's Diving Center** *Ctra Torrella de Montgri, km 4.5 (972 75 01 63).* **Open** All year.
Roses: Poseidon *C/Bernd i Barbara Mörker (972 25 57 72/972 25 44 07).* **Open** All year. Nine dive routes.

From there a lovely walk (about 40 minutes) along a coastal path takes you northwards through **Aiguafreda**, a small wooded cove, to a spectacular building, once a hotel, cut into the cliff on the promontory beyond. Steps lead down to swimming pools cut into the precipitous cliff-face.

Heading south from Sa Tuna, you'll reach **Fornells** and **Aiguablava**, both in a larger bay with villas dotted around the wooded hillsides. Aiguablava has a small beach with beautiful white sand, a small harbour for yachts, and the old and luxurious Hotel Aiguablava. **Tamariu** is a slightly larger village in a small, intimate bay, with hotels and bars which are known for their excellent seafood. There are several places nearby where you can swim from the rocks. You can also hire boats for exploring the coast or fishing (call Paco Heredia on 972 30 13 10 or 907 29 25 78).

Llafranc is more developed as a resort, thanks to its being connected by a main road with Palafrugell. From here you can walk to **Calella de Palafrugell**, a prettier fishing village just to the south, with another good beach. Tamariu and Llafranc are the only places on this stretch easily accessible by public transport, with regular buses from **Palafrugell**, the main transport centre of the peninsula. It has a lively Sunday market, several seventeenth-century buildings, and a museum dedicated to Josep Pla, one of Catalonia's best twentieth-century writers, who was born here.

Further up the coast to the north is the small town of **Estartit**, a water-sports centre conveniently situated opposite the **Illes Medes**, a clutch of small rocky islets that are Catalonia's only underwater nature park. Glass-bottomed boats leave every hour from Estartit (June-Sept; Apr, May, Oct, according to demand) to tour the rare coral deposits for which the islands are renowned. The more adventurous can go scuba-diving (*see opposite*). A pleasant walk up the road from Estartit is the **Castell de Montgri**, an unfinished but imposing twelfth-century castle with a fine view of coast and hinterland.

Information

Getting there: *By bus* Sarfa (93 265 11 58), nine buses daily from Estació del Nord to Palafrugell (2hrs), some of which continue to Begur. Change in Palafrugell or Torroella for Estartit. *By car* A7 north to exit 6 onto C255; or exit 9 for C250, C253, C255 via Palafrugell (123km/76 miles). Alternatively, take the slower coastal A11, then C250, C253, C255.
Tourist offices:
Begur *Plaça de l'Església 8 (972 62 40 20)*; **Pals** *C/Aniceta Figueras 6 (972 68 78 57)*; **Palafrugell** *C/Carrilet 2 (972 30 02 28)*; **L'Estartit** *Passeig Marítim (972 75 89 10).*
Where to eat:
Begur: Can Torrades *(972 622 28 82)*, in an old house, has good but pricey Catalan home cooking; **Fonda Platja** *(972 62 21 97)* is also quite expensive but has excellent Catalan food. More moderately-priced pizzas can be found at **La Pizzeta** *(972 622 38 83).* On the

outskirts of Begur on the road toward Palafrugell is **Mas Comangau** *(972 62 32 10)*, a traditional restaurant popular for Sunday lunch. In Pals, **Alfred** *C/La Font 7 (972 63 62 74)* has home-cooking for around 3,000ptas. **Aiguablava: Hotel Aiguablava** *(see below)* has a top-class restaurant, and the **Parador** *(972 62 21 62)* offers panoramic views. The restaurant of **Hostal Sa Tuna** *(see below)* is simple but also has a great view. **Tamariu:** There's not much to choose between the restaurants on the sea-front. The family-run **Snack Bar Es Dofí** *(972 61 02 92)*, is the only one open all year. **Llafranc:** One of the area's best restaurants is the **Hotel Llafranc** *Passeig de Cipsela 16 (972 30 02 08)*.

Where to Stay:
Begur: Hotel Begur *C/De Coma i Ros 8 (972 62 22 07)* is centrally placed and open all year (7,500ptas, double); **Hotel Rosa** *C/Forgas i Puig 6 (972 62 30 13)* is less expensive (5,200ptas). **Pals** has the **Barris** *C/Enginyer Algarra 51 (972 63 67 02)*, for 4,700ptas. There are two campsites near Begur: at Sa Riera, **El Maset Platja de Sa Riera**, *(972 62 30 23)*; and on the road to Palafrugell, **Begur** *Carretera de Begur a Palafrugell (972 62 32 01)*.

Sa Tuna: Hostal Sa Tuna *Platja Sa Tuna (972 262 21 98)* is perfectly located but has only eight rooms. **Aiguablava:** In the bay of Aiguablava and Fornells, the four-star **Hotel Aiguablava** *Platja de Fornells (972 62 20 58)*, is still family-run and has a swimming pool, tennis courts and other comforts (12,000ptas, double). **Tamariu: Hotel Hostalillo** *C/Bellavista 28 (972 30 01 58)* is the largest hotel in town (13,900ptas double; open June-Sept only); the **Hostal Vora de Mar** *Passeig del Mar 6 (972 30 05 53)* is open all year (5,000ptas double). **Llafranc: Hotel Llafranc** *(see above)* has double rooms for around 11,000ptas. Or try the two-star **Hotel Casamar** *C/Carrer de Nero 3-11 (972 30 01 04)* for 8,500ptas per double. There are two campsites near Calella: **La Siesta** *C/Chipitea 110-120 (972 61 51 16)*; and **Moby Dick** *C/Costa Verda 16-28 (972 61 43 07)*. **L'Estartit: Santa Clara** *Passeig Maritim 18 (972 75 17 67)* is pleasant, and costs 4,700 ptas per double.

Figueres to France

The indisputable centre of the northern Costa Brava, the *comarca* of **Alt Empordà**, is the town

The Dalí Triangle

Figueres had an on-off relationship with its most famous son during his life, but since Salvador Dalí's death the town has become an obligatory visit for anyone interested in (or just curious about) the great masturbator's special universe. The **Teatre-Museu Dalí**, in Figueres' former theatre, was designed by the man himself as a kind of static spectacle complete with music, optical illusions, cars with rain inside and many other installations. It also contains his tomb. From July to September, the museum stay opens later, with Dalí's own choice of lighting and music as well as a free glass of *cava*. The **Torre Galatea**, Dalí's egg-topped Figueres residence, is next door.

In addition, 1998 is the first year in which the two other Empordà properties associated with the great man have been opened to the public on a regular basis by the Dalí estate, forming what has been labelled a *triangle dalinià* for aspiring surrealists to disappear into. Dominating **Port Lligat** just outside **Cadaqués** is his own favourite house, a Dalí image in itself with its two giant cracked heads on the top wall seen against the rocky hillside and azure sea of the bay. Built for Dalí with many strange features, the house was all but abandoned for over ten years and is in poor condition, and only eight people are allowed in at a time (so reservations are essential). In **Púbol**, about 35km (22 miles) south of Roses near La Bisbal in the Baix Empordà, is the twelfth-century castle that Dalí bought for his wife and 'muse' Gala. There she entertained a string of young men, while Dalí

himself was famously not allowed to visit without an appointment. Today, reservations are not obligatory except for groups of over 30 people.

Daliesque sites
Casa-Museu de Port Lligat *(reservations 972 25 80 63)*. **Open** *14 Mar-14 June, 16 Sept-1 Nov* 10.30am-6pm, *15 Jun-15 Sept* 10.30-9pm, daily. Closed Nov-Mar. **Admission** 1,200ptas. **No credit cards.**
Castell de Púbol *(inquiries to Teatre-Museu Dalí, 972 51 18 00)*. **Open** *14 Mar-14 June, 16 Sept-1 Nov* 10.30am-6pm, *15 Jun-15 Sept* 10.30-9pm, daily. Closed Nov-Mar. **Admission** 600ptas. **No credit cards.**
Púbol is best reached via Girona, not Figueres: by train to Girona or Flaçà, and then Sarfa bus from either to La Bisbal, which stops at Púbol village. With a car, take the N11 north from Girona, and then the C255 towards La Bisbal.
Teatre-Museu Dalí *Plaça Gala-Salvador Dalí 5, Figueres (972 51 18 00)*. **Open** *Oct-June* 10.30am-5.15pm Tue-Sun; *July-Sept* 9am-7.15pm daily. **Admission** *Oct-June* 700ptas; 400ptas students, over-65s; *July-Sept* 1,000ptas; 700ptas students, over-65s. **Credit** AmEx, MC, V.

of **Figueres**, from where it's possible to travel by car, bus or train to every other place of interest in the area. The *tramontana* wind sweeps this area at regular intervals and, according to the rest of Catalonia, leaves its inhabitants slightly touched (read, crazy), a fact apparently borne out by two of Figueres' most famous sons: Narcís Monturiol, the utopian socialist and penniless inventor of (some say) the first submarine, and Salvador Dalí. Another thing the Empordà is known for is its fine food, especially *mar i montanya* dishes of meat and seafood.

Figueres is an attractive town in itself, with a lively central Rambla, and not just the site of one of Catalonia's most visited attractions, the **Teatre-Museu Dalí** (*see opposite*). Also worth visiting is the **Museu de l'Empordà** (972 50 23 05), on the Rambla, for a comprehensive, well-presented overview of the district's art and history.

A straight road leads east from Figueres to **Roses**, once a major trading port and now the area's largest tourist town. It has a glut of hotels, discos and overpriced restaurants, but also attractive beaches and a sixteenth-century citadel, the **Ciutadella**. To the south are the **Aiguamolls de l'Empordà**, a nature reserve in the marshlands at the mouth of the Fluvià river that's great for walking and birdwatching (*see below*).

From Roses the road starts to climb in order to take you through precipitous switch-backs with wonderful views into **Cadaqués**, at the end of the Cap de Creus peninsula. This is the town where high-rise hotel-building was barred during the boom years of Costa hotel speculation, so that it kept its little, narrow streets and whitewashed houses. Barcelona's cultural élite made Cadaqués their favourite summer resort in the 1960s, and it's since been popular with well-heeled bohemians from all over Europe. Its cultural season includes its very own music festival each August (*see chapter* **Music: Classical & Opera**).

Consequently, Cadaqués is relatively expensive, but it's still strikingly beautiful, and all around the Cape there are tiny, rocky coves offering the chance of complete relaxation. The town's native population, whose ancestors lived for centuries in total isolation from anywhere inland, are well-known for their lack of interest in outsiders.

A short walk to the next bay and you're in **Port Lligat**, the tiny bay where Dalí built his favourite Catalan residence (*see opposite*). Beyond there a road continues on to another place of Dalinian associations, **Cap de Creus** ('Cape of Crosses'), with a lighthouse, a nature reserve and unique, pock-marked rock formations that have led it to be used as a location in several science-fiction movies.

Port de la Selva, on the north side of the Cape, has never received the accolades showered on Cadaqués, yet is similarly unspoilt, quieter in summer, and closer to the magnificent monastery of

Sant Pere de Rodes, sometimes lost in clouds on the mountain above the town. One of the oldest and most beautiful Romanesque buildings in Catalonia, it was founded in 1022, but large sections are still intact. A little further north again is **Llançà**. The modern part of this fishing village gives onto several bays and beaches, and is just a short walk from the beautiful old centre. Llançà also has good connections to the French border, for those headed in that direction.

Alternatively, if you head south from Figueres to the opposite end of the Alt Empordà you will come to the well-preserved remains of the ancient city of **Empúries**, founded in 600 BC by the Phoenicians, re-colonised by the Greeks and finally taken over by the Romans, in the year AD 2. Ruins of buildings from all three periods, and the line of the original Greek harbour, are clearly visible, and it's a very attractive and atmospheric ancient site, right next to a beach. The nearest modern town is **L'Escala**, an attractive port noted for its anchovies, and birthplace of Caterina Albert, author of the classic Catalan novel *Solitud*.

Aiguamolls de L'Empordà

The wetlands (*aiguamolls*) of the Empordà south of Roses are a bird-watcher's paradise. Some 300 species winter, nest or rest on their migratory routes here. The garganey is the natural park's symbol. Amphibians, fish and mosquitos (take insect repellent) are also common here. Some areas of the park are shut to the public in the spring nesting season.

There is a great long walk through the reserve from Castelló d'Empúries to Sant Pere Pescador (it takes about 7½hrs, if you do the full route). From Castelló, take the G IV-6216 road, signposted to **Sant Pere Pescador**. At the fork with the road to Empúria-brava, follow the GR-92 to the Natural Park Information Centre at **Mas Cortalet** (972 45 22 22; if you're doing this the easy way, with a car, drive straight there). Continue on the path towards La Muga Vella. The track parallel to the sea leads to small birdwatching shelters overlooking **La Massona** lagoon. From there go on past Mas Matà to rejoin the road, and head left to Sant Pere Pescador. **Caramany** island has undisturbed woods.

Getting there: *By bus* Sarfa buses to Roses from Estació del Nord stop at Castelló d'Empúries, and there are more frequent services from Figueres. From Sant Pere Pescador there are buses to Figueres. *By car* A-7 and N-II to Figueres, C260 to Castelló d'Empúries. *By train* RENFE to Figueres, then bus.

Sant Pere de Rodes

Open *Oct-May* 10am-1.30pm, 3-5pm, *June-Sept* 10am-7pm, Tue-Sun. **Admission** 300ptas; 150ptas students. **No credit cards.**

Information

Getting there: *By bus* Barcelona Bus (93 232 04 59), several buses daily to Figueres from Estació del Nord (2hrs 30min). Sarfa (93 265 11 98) runs a direct service to Roses and Cadaqués (two buses daily; 2hrs 15min). The easiest way to get to anywhere on the coast is to take a train to Figueres, and then a Sarfa bus from the depot next to the station. Sarfa has services to Llança, Roses, Port de la Selva, Cadaqués and L'Escala. *By car* A7 or N11 to Figueres (120km/74 miles). From Figueres, C260 to Roses. *By train* RENFE from Sants or Passeig de Gràcia to Figueres (1hr 45min, Catalunya Exprés) or Llançà.

Tourist Offices:
Figueres *Plaça del Sol (972 50 31 55)*; **Roses** *Plaça de les Botxes (972 25 73 31)*; **Cadaqués** *C/Cotxe 2-A (972 25 83 15)*; **Llançà** *Avda d'Europa 37 (972 38 08 55)*; **L'Escala** *Plaça de les Escoles 1 (972 77 06 03)*.

Where to eat:
Figueres: Bars on the Rambla are fine for a drink, but most restaurants are in the old town. Those in C/de la Jonquera are cheapish and have tables outside in summer. **Presidente** *Ronda Firal 33 (972 50 17 00)* provides quality Catalan food for about 3,000ptas.
Cadaqués: Best-known restaurant is **La Galiota** *C/Narc's Monturiol 9 (972 25 81 87*; average 5,000ptas).
Casa Anita *C/Miguel Roset (972 25 84 71)* has excellent seafood and is very popular; cheaper but also good is **Pizzeria Plaza** *Passeig Maritim 10 (no phone)*.

Where to Stay:
Figueres: Hotel Duran *C/Lasauca 5 (972 50 12 50)* has doubles for 8,800ptas; **Hostal Bon Repòs** *C/Villalonga 43 (972 50 92 02*) is a good budget option.
Roses: There are dozens of places in the town. **Marian** *Platja Salatar (972 25 61 12)* gives onto the beach and costs 5,700ptas per double. **Hostal Can Salvador** *C/Puig Rom 43 (972 25 78 11)* is one of the cheaper *hostals* at 4,500ptas for a double room.
Cadaqués: Book ahead: the town has few hotels for the summer demand, while out of season smaller *hostals* may be closed. The tourist office has a list, and one of families who rent rooms. Try **Hostal Marina** *C/Frederic Rahola 2 (972 25 81 99)* at 7,000ptas a double, and the **Pension Vehí** *C/de l'Esglèsia 6 (972 25 84 70)* at 5,000ptas a double.
Port de la Selva: German *C/Poeta Sagarra 11 (972 38 70 92)* is a reasonably-priced small hotel (6,000ptas, double). **Porto Cristo** *C/Major 48 (972 38 70 62)* is the luxury option (17,000ptas, double).
Llança: Try the **Florida** *C/Floridablanca 16-18 (972 12 01 61)* for 5,000ptas a double, or for greater comforts the **Berna** *Passeig Maritim 13 (972 38 01 50)* at 9,250ptas.
Empúries: If you have a car, the best place to stay in the area is the village of Sant Marti d'Empúries, which has the comfortable, beautifully situated **Riomar** *Platja del Riuet (972 77 03 62*; 7,500ptas a double), or the cheaper **Can Roura** *Plaça de l'Esglèsia 12 (972 77 03 05)* for a mere 4,800ptas per double. The **Youth Hostel** *(972 77 12 00)* is on the beach by the ruins, but often full. An IYHF card is required, and beds cost 1,500ptas per night.

The Balearics

Since **Mallorca, Menorca, Eivissa** (aka **Ibiza,** in Spanish) and **Formentera** form Europe's number-one holiday patch, it's actually nearly always cheaper and easier to reach any of them by direct flight from northern Europe than in a two-stage journey via Barcelona. Even so, it's worth remembering that they're only a short hop from Catalonia.

Familiar to millions, the islands still have many unspoilt areas, and each has a very individual character. Ibiza, hub of international club culture, is a desert island that burns yellow each summer, while small Formentera alongside it is more desert-like still. Go in February and you can even have large bits of it to yourself. Mallorca, taken from the Moslems by Jaume I of Aragon in 1229, has remote, mountainous areas inland, and an attractive capital in Palma with another Catalan Gothic cathedral.

Menorca, greenest of the islands, with beautiful coves around its shores, was held by Britain for 70 years in the eighteenth century, an occupation that left strange traces – door latches, sash windows, and some of the world's best gin, result of a happy encounter between Navy grog and a Mediterranean skill with herbs. Unknown to most visitors, the modern inhabitants of the Balearics have also produced a rich literature in Catalan, the main language of the islands.

Information

Getting there by air: Over 10 flights daily, Barcelona-Mallorca, and three daily to Ibiza and Menorca. Since the removal of the state monopoly on domestic flights three companies – Air Europa, Spanair and Iberia/Aviaco – have been engaged in a price war: return flights to Mallorca cost about 12,500ptas for a weekend or 10,000ptas if you stay a bit longer, but this may vary.

Getting there by sea: Transmediterrània, *Estació Maritima de Balears, Moll de Barcelona (93 443 25 32)*, is the sole ferry operator to the islands. All ferries leave from the Estació Maritima, opposite the Drassanes at the foot of the Rambla (Metro Drassanes). There are ferries daily to Mallorca at 11pm (journey time 8hrs), plus a 1pm sailing on Sundays; ferries to Menorca or Ibiza also leave at 11-11.30pm (both 9hrs), but only on certain days of the week. Unless you sit up all night, ferries cost more than flying. One-way fares to Palma are around 6,000ptas seat-only, or 14,300ptas per person for a cabin shared by two, with a 15 per cent discount for return tickets. Advantages are that you can take a car or bike, there are great views on arrival, and tickets are more readily available.

Tourist offices: Ibiza & Formentera: *Paseo Vara del Rey 13, Ibiza (971 30 19 00)*; **Mallorca:** *Avda Jaime III, Palma (971 71 22 16)*; **Menorca:** *Plaça Esplanada 40, Mahón (971 36 37 90)*.

Inland

Mountains, ancient monasteries, green valleys and cava cellars: the Catalan countryside has a wonderful combination of lushness and ruggedness.

Over the last half-century several million people have visited the Catalan coasts, but only a fraction have ventured more than a short distance away from the shore. Rural Catalonia, though, is exceptionally beautiful. Mediterranean colours and rugged hills are mixed with a lush verdure, merging into truly alpine landscapes in the Pyrenees. The valleys that ascend into the Pyrenees are one of the birthplaces of Romanesque architecture, with exquisite early-medieval buildings in every second town and village.

Montserrat

Perched half-way up this dramatic ridge (the literal translation, 'saw-tooth mountain', describes it accurately) stand the monastery and hermitages of **Montserrat**. The fortress-like atmosphere is emphasised by difficult access – the road meanders hair-raisingly and there are frequent delays. The only other way up, more spectacular still, is by cable-car.

Hermits were attracted to this isolated place as early as the fifth century, and a Benedictine monastery was founded here in 1025. The so-called 'Black Virgin', a small wooden figure of the Madonna and child, was installed here in the twelfth century, although it's claimed the statue is much older. All kinds of legends and traditions have grown up around it over the centuries. It is the patron virgin of Catalonia, and Montserrat is still the most common name for Catalan women.

In the Middle Ages, the monastery became an important place of pilgrimage. It grew rich and powerful, its remote position helping to ensure its independence. During the Franco era, the monastery was a bastion of Catalan nationalism.

The **shrine of the Black Virgin** is in the sixteenth-century basilica, where it can be visited – and touched – by joining the queue to the right of the main door and climbing up behind the altar. Two museums display gifts given to the virgin, which include some Old Master paintings and three works by Picasso. First-time visitors be warned, however, that the monastery itself is not particularly interesting. The cafeterias and souvenir shops also tend to take the edge off the place's spirituality, although connoisseurs of religious kitsch might feel they justify the whole trip.

The walks and views around the site are truly spectacular. The whole of the mountain, 10km (6 miles) long, is now a nature park, and the monastery occupies only a very small part of it. As well as the cave where the virgin was discovered – 20 minutes' walk from the monastery – there are 13 hermitages dotted around the mountain, the most accessible of which is **Sant Joan**, at the top of a funicular that runs from beside the monastery. If you walk it instead, the 20-minute path to the hermitage has superb views. There are also much longer walking routes around Montserrat (*see page 245*), including a circuit of all the hermitages and the (relatively easy) trek to the **peak of Sant Jeroni**, at 1,235m (4,053ft). Rock climbing is popular amid the unique geology of Montserrat, and enthusiasts can find several thrilling climbs on well-marked routes (inquire at the tourist office).

At the foot of the mountain, on the south side, is the village of **Collbató**. It's in a beautiful location, and has several illuminated caves – *les coves de Salitre* – that are open to visitors (93 777 03 09).

Information

Getting there: *By bus* Julià-Via from Sants bus station, at 8am (June-Sept); 9am (Oct-May). The journey takes about 80min. Julià also run guided tours to Montserrat (*see chapter* **Sightseeing**). *By car* N11 to exit at km 59; or A2 to Martorell exit, then through Abrera and Monistrol (60km/37 miles). The road to the monastery is often crowded and very slow. *By train* FGC from Plaça d'Espanya, every 2hrs from 7.10am daily, to Aeri de Montserrat (journey time approx 1hr); then by cable car to the monastery, every 15min. Return fare (including cable car) is 1,770ptas.
Tourist office: **Montserrat** (*93 835 02 51*).
Where to eat: Restaurants on Montserrat are expensive and unimpressive. The café at the top of the Funicular de St Joan is better and usually less crowded, but only open in summer.
Where to stay: The two hotels run by the monks – the **Hotel Abat Cisneros** (8,360ptas double; reductions mid-Nov to mid-Mar), and **Hotel Residéncia Monestir** (5,100ptas per double; no singles; closed mid Mar to mid-Nov) – are both reasonable. To book a room at either, phone *93 835 02 01*. There is a **camp site** (*93 835 02 51*) beyond St Joan funicular; look for the sign.

The Royal Monasteries

Montblanc, 112km due west of Barcelona, is one of the most beautiful towns in western Catalonia, yet all but unknown to foreign visitors. It also has

Staying in a *Masia*

Masies are perhaps the most characteristic sight of the Catalan countryside. The prototypes of these giant manor-farmhouses, with massive stone walls and sloping roofs, date from the centuries following the collapse of the Roman Empire, and there are still plenty that have been in continual use since the fourteenth century or earlier. Part home, part shelter for animals and part fortress, these solid dwellings were first built for very practical reasons, and any embellishments were added later.

Nowadays many *Masies* are still working farms, while others have been made into second homes by affluent urbanites. Somewhere between these two extremes are about 800 *masies* across Catalonia which offer a very reasonably-priced bed-and-breakfast service. Often owned by families who still work the land, they provide a great way to experience the Catalan countryside close-to.

Prices for double rooms are usually about 4,000ptas, with a maximum of 15 people to a house, although usually there are far fewer than that. Some *masies* can be rented complete, as fully equipped independent, self-catering accommodation.

The Generalitat publishes a guide to the houses, *Guia de Residències – Cases de Pagès*, with details of prices, services, capacity, and location. It costs 500ptas and can be found in bookshops or at the **Palau Robert** information office (*see page 251*), where you can also consult it for free.

---

around it, roughly forming a triangle, three exceptional Cistercian monasteries: **Poblet** – almost as much a national symbol as Montserrat, and a more attractive building to boot – **Santes Creus** and **Vallbona de les Monges**.

In the Middle Ages Montblanc was a prosperous town with an important Jewish community, a past reflected in the *Carrer dels Jueus* ('Jews' street'), the magnificent thirteenth-century town walls – two-thirds of which remain intact – the churches of **Santa Maria la Major**, **Sant Miquel** and **Sant Francesc**, the **Palau Reial** (Royal Palace) and the **Palau del Castlà** or castle-keeper's palace.

The great monasteries of this region were unusually grand because they enjoyed a uniquely close relationship with the Catalan-Aragonese monarchs, and were all built partly with the intention that they should house royal tombs. **Poblet**, a few kilometres west of Montblanc, was founded in 1151 by Ramon Berenguer IV, the Count-King who created the joint Catalan-Aragonese monarchy. He also seized this area from the Moslems and undertook its re-population, and to assist the process gave generous grants of land to the Cistercian order. Poblet was a royal residence as well as a monastery, and has within it a fourteenth-century Gothic royal palace. Especially impressive are the fifteenth-century chapel of Sant Jordi and the main church with the tombs of most of the Count-Kings of Barcelona, but the entire complex is remarkable. The monastery can be seen by guided tour only, conducted by a monk.

Santes Creus, founded in 1158 and possibly still more beautiful than Poblet, grew into a small village when a group of families moved into abandoned monks' residences in 1843. Within its strongly fortified walls there are the **Palau de l'Abat** (abbot's palace), a monumental fountain, a twelfth-century church with some more royal tombs, and a superb Gothic cloister and chapterhouse. Visits to Santes Creus now include an audio-visual presentation, hence the relatively high price.

Vallbona de les Monges, third of these Cistercian houses, was unlike the others a convent of nuns, and was particularly favoured by Catalan-Aragonese Queens, especially Violant of Hungary, wife of Jaume I. She is buried here, while her husband lies at Poblet. It has a fine, part-Romanesque cloister, but is less grand than the other two. A small village was built around it in the sixteenth century when it was ordained that nuns should not live in isolated and unprotected buildings. All three monasteries still house religious communities.

Monestir de Poblet

(977 87 02 54). **Open** *Mar-Sept* 10am-12.30pm, 3-6pm, Mon-Fri, 10am-12.30pm, 3-5.30pm, Sat, Sun; *Oct-Feb* 10am-12.30pm, 3-5.30pm,daily. **Admission** 500ptas; 300ptas students, over-65s.

Monestir de Santes Creus

(977 63 83 29). **Open** *Oct-May* 10am-1.30pm, 3-6pm; *June-Sept* 10am-1.30pm, 3-7pm, Tue-Sun. **Admission** 600ptas; 500ptas under-21s, over-65s.

Monestir de Santa Maria de Vallbona

(973 33 02 66). **Open** 10.30am-2pm, 4.30-6.30pm, Tue-Sat; noon-2pm, 4.30-6.30pm, Sun. **Admission** 250ptas; 200ptas over-65s.
Hours may vary according to times of religious services.

Information

Getting there: *By bus* Hispano Igualadina (93 430 43 44) runs daily services to Montblanc from C/Europa (behind the Corte Inglés on Avda Diagonal; Metro Maria Cristina).

There are more services from Valls and Tarragona. *By car* A2, then A7, then again A2 direct, or N340 to El Vendrell then C246 for Valls and Montblanc (112km/69 miles). For **Poblet**, take N240 west from Montblanc and turn left in L'Espluga de Francolí. **Santes Creus** is connected by a slip road to the C246. For **Vallbona de les Monges**, take the C240 out of Montblanc towards Tàrrega and turn left at the relevant side road, which is clearly signposted. *By train* RENFE from Sants or Passeig de Gràcia to Montblanc, five trains a day (journey time approx 2hrs).
Tourist office: Montblanc & Poblet *(977 86 00 09)*.
Where to eat: Montblanc has an inn, **Fonda Colom** *C/Civaderia 3 (977 86 01 53)*, just behind the Plaça Major, with a five-course set meal for around 3,000ptas. You can also eat well at **Els Àngels** *(see below)*.
Where to stay: Highly recommended in Montblanc is **Els Àngels** *Plaça dels Àngels 1 (977 86 01 73)*, which also has a restaurant. Failing that, the **Colom** *(see above)* has a few rooms. Poblet's neighbouring village of Vimbodí has the **Fonoll**, *C/Ramon Berenguer IV 2 (977 87 03 33)*. Santes Creus has the equally cheap **Hostal Grau** *C/Pere III 3 (977 63 83 11)*, and Vallbona de les Monges has no place to stay at all.

The Montseny to the Pyrenees

Vic & Rupit

Vic is an easy town to visit from Barcelona, surrounded by nature reserves: the wonderful mountains of Montseny, Les Guilleries and Collsacabra, ideal for a weekend's walking. A town of 30,000 people which began life as the capital of an Iberian tribe known as the Ausetians, Vic was made a city by the Romans, and later fell briefly into the hands of the Moors. They lost it to Wilfred the Hairy *(see page 13)* in the ninth century, since when it has remained an important religious, administrative and artistic centre. In the nineteenth century it produced one of Catalonia's greatest poets, Jacint Verdaguer, and philosopher Jaume Balmes.

Vic has many late-medieval houses – now mainly used as administrative and university buildings – and its **Plaça Major** is one of the finest and liveliest town squares in the whole of Catalonia. Monuments worth seeing are the **Temple Romà** (Roman temple), now an art gallery, and the neoclassical **Catedral de Sant Pere**, which contains a set of sombre twentieth-century murals painted by Josep Lluís Sert, and has a perfectly-preserved eleventh-century belltower. The **Casa de la Ciutat**, in one corner of the Plaça Major, dates from the fourteenth century. The square is most animated on Saturdays – market day – and during the traditional livestock market, the *Mercat del Ram*, held during the week before Easter. Vic is famous for its high-quality *embotits* or charcuterie, and shops selling *botifarres*, *llonganisses* and other sausages can be found in almost every street.

The district of Osona, of which Vic is the capital, is unusually full of interesting villages, such as **Centelles**, **Manlleu**, and **Montesquiu**. The most rewarding route is up the main C153 road towards Olot into the region known as Les Guilleries, turning off to the right along local roads for **Tavertet** – a perfectly preserved seventeenth-century village with panoramic views over the Ter valley – and **Rupit**, a remarkable village built against the side of a medieval castle, with an old town from the sixteenth century and an eleventh-century church, **Sant Joan de Fàbregues**. From Rupit, several impressive traditional farmhouses, such as **El Bac de Collsacabra** and **El Corriol** (which has a collection of traditional ceramics and historical artefacts), are within walking distance.

Information

Getting there: *By bus* Empresa Sagalès (93 231 27 56) from the corner of Passeig Sant Joan and C/Diputació (Metro Tetuan) to Vic. There is no direct bus to Tavertet and Rupit from Barcelona, but the best way to get there is to get a train or bus to Vic and then get one of the Pous company (93 850 60 63) local buses. *By car* N152 from Barcelona, direction Puigcerdà, to Vic (65km/40 miles). For Tavertet and Rupit, take C153 out of Vic (signposted to Olot). *By train* RENFE from Sants or Plaça Catalunya to Vic, approx two trains per hour (journey time 1hr).
Tourist office: Vic *Plaça Major 1 (93 886 20 91)*.
Where to eat: Vic has several good medium-priced restaurants. The **Basset** *C/Sant Sadurní 4 (93 889 02 12)*, has great seafood dishes (2,500-5,500ptas). **Ca l'U** *Plaça Santa Teresa 4/5 (93 889 03 45)*, is a more traditional (and cheaper) inn-style place with plenty of pork specialities. For something special, take the N152 toward Ripoll, and just before Sant Quirze de Besora turn onto a 2km, signposted road to the **Rectoria d'Oris** *C/Rectoria (93 859 02 30)*. It's one of the best restaurants in the area, and has a terrific view.

The thirteenth-century cloister of **Poblet**.

Gentrified for good reason, the old mountain slate village of **Queralbs**.

Where to stay: Vic's luxury hotel is the three-star
Ciutat de Vic *C/Jaume el Conqueridor (93 889 25 51)*,
at 11,000ptas a double; whereas the **Ausa** *Plaça Major 4
(93 885 53 11)*, is slightly cheaper, still comfortable and
gives onto the main square. Rupit has a good inexpensive
hostal, the **Estrella** *Plaça Bisbe Font 1 (93 852 20 05)*.

Ripoll to the Vall de Núria

Ripoll, the next medium-sized town on the road
north of Vic, grew up around the unique church
and monastery of **Santa Maria de Ripoll**.
Known as the 'cradle of Catalonia', it has a superb
twelfth-century portal that is one of the finest
examples of early Romanesque stonework in
Europe. This valley was the original fiefdom of
Hairy Wilfred, Guifré *el Pilós*, before he became
Count of Barcelona (*see page 13*). He is buried in
Santa Maria, which he founded in 879.

Wilfred the Hairy also founded the monastery
and town of **Sant Joan de les Abadesses**,
10km (6 miles) up the C151 road east, and worth
a visit for its restored Gothic bridge as well as the
twelfth-century monastery itself. The monastery
museum (972 72 00 13) covers a thousand years
of local life.

The road from Sant Joan leads on to
Camprodon, on the fast-flowing river Ter,
which is known for a kind of crunchy biscuit
called a *carquinyoli*, and has a fine Romanesque
church. Veering to the left from Camprodon, a
local road leads up the valley to the tiny mountain village of **Setcases**, a famous beauty spot

now heavily taken over by second homes. By
now you are well into the Pyrenees, and the Ter
valley road comes to an end at **Vallter 2000**
(972 13 60 75), the easternmost ski station in the
mountains. As with all ski resorts in the area, the
best way to spend more than a day there is by
booking a package, available at any travel agent
in Barcelona.

Ribes de Freser, the next town up on the
other main road from Ripoll, the N152 north, is an
attractive place and a good base from which to
travel to the picturesque if gentrified villages in
the surrounding area, **Campelles** and especially
Queralbs. Ribes is also the starting point for the
cremallera, the FGC's narrow-gauge 'zipper train',
which runs via Queralbs all the way up to the sanctuary of **Núria**, through the valley of the same
name along the Freser river.

Núria itself, nestling by a lake in the middle of
a plateau at over 2,000m (6,500 feet), is the home
of the second most famous of Catalonia's patron
virgins, a wooden statue of the Madonna carved
in the twelfth century, and was already a refuge of
hermits and place of pilgrimage long before then.
The massively solid monastery around the shrine,
most of it nineteenth-century, is not especially
attractive, but its location is spectacular, and the
zipper-train makes it an easily accessible place to
try some relatively light high-mountain walking
(the tourist office has maps of nearby paths). It's
also a winter-sports centre (972 73 07 13), suited to
novice skiers.

Information

Getting there: *By bus* TEISA (972 20 48 68) from the corner of C/Pau Claris and C/Consell de Cent to Ripoll, Sant Joan de les Abadesses and Camprodon. *By car* N152 direct to Ripoll (104km/64 miles), from Avda Meridiana. For Sant Joan de les Abadesses and Camprodon, take the C151 out of Ripoll. *By train* RENFE from Sants or Plaça Catalunya, approx two trains each hour (journey time to Ripoll approx 1hr 30min). For **Queralbs** and **Núria** change to the *cremallera* train in Ribes de Freser.
Tourist offices: Sant Joan de les Abadesses (*972 72 01 00*); **Ribes de Freser** (*972 72 71 84*); **Núria** (*972 73 07 13*).
Where to eat:
Ripoll: **El Racó del Francés** ('The Frenchman's Corner'), *Plà d'Ordina 11 (972 70 18 94)*, as its name suggests, serves French dishes (average 4,500ptas).
Sant Joan de les Abadesses: Sant Pere *C/Mestre Andreu 3 (972 72 00 77)*. Local food at reasonable prices.
Queralbs: The one good place to eat is **De la Plaça** *Plaça de la Vila 5 (972 72 70 37)*.
Where to stay:
Ripoll: Decent rooms are available at **Ca la Paula** *C/Berenguer 8 (972 70 00 11)*, for 4,500ptas a double (no private bathrooms); **La Trobada** *Passeig Honorat Vilamanya 4 (972 70 23 53)*, is more comfortable (7,500ptas).
Sant Joan de les Abadesses: Janpere *C/Mestre Andreu 3 (972 72 00 77)*, is the best, at 6,000ptas per double. There is very little accommodation at Vallter; most people stay in towns further down the valley.
Ribes de Freser: Catalunya Park Hotel *Passeig Salvador Mauri 9 (972 72 71 98)*, is very comfortable (7,000ptas per double); cheaper rooms are available at **Traces** *C/Nostra Senyora de Gràcia 1 (972 72 71 37)*.
Queralbs: L'Avet *C/Major (972 72 73 77)*, is tiny; slightly larger is **Sierco** *C/Major 5 (972 72 73 77)*. In **Núria**, there's a three-star hotel, the **Vall de Núria** *C/Santuari Mare de Dèu de Núria (972 73 20 00)*, for 9,100ptas a double, and a youth hostel, the **Alberg Pic de l'Aliga** *(972 73 00 48)*.

Berga & Puigcerdà

Some 50km (31 miles) west of Ripoll on the C149 (or on the C150, from Vic) is **Berga**, capital of the *comarca* of the Berguedà. The **Serra del Cadí**, one of the ranges of the 'Pre-Pyrenees' or Pyrenees foothills, looms impressively above the town to the north in spectacular giant cliffs. Berga also has an imposing medieval castle, **Sant Ferràn**, sitting above the town to provide a suitably storybook air. Mainly visited by other Catalans, Berga has a charming old centre, with a Jewish quarter from the thirteenth century. It's also a town with character, famous for the frenzied festival of devils, drink and drums called **La Patum** in May (*see page 241*), but also for its mushroom-hunting competition, held the first Sunday of October in the Pla de Puigventós. Enormous basketloads of different *bolets* (wild mushrooms) with names like *rovellons*, *camagrocs* and *senderuelas* are weighed in before an enthusiastic public. Prospective participants should contact the tourist office, which can also provide basic information as to where to hunt.

Heading north from Berga along the C1411, uphill into the Cadí, you'll come to the small town of **Bagà**, with partially preserved medieval walls and a central square with Romanesque porticoes. It marks the beginning of the **Parc Natural del Cadí-Moixeró**, a gigantic mountain park covering 41,300 hectares (150 square miles). Established by the Generalitat in 1983, the Cadí park contains some 20 or so ancient villages, as well as wildlife and forest reserves. All retain some medieval architecture, and many offer stunning views of the surrounding mountains.

Picasso stayed and painted in one village, **Gósol**, for several weeks in 1906, when it was utterly remote. Rugged and austerely beautiful, the Cadí is rich in wildlife and can feel more like the American West than the Mediterranean. Chamois roam the mountain slopes, as do re-introduced roe and red deer. There are also golden eagles, capercaillies, and black woodpeckers. Detailed information on the park is available in English at the tourist office in Berga or the **Palau Robert** in Barcelona (*see page 251*).

Above Bagà the C1411 road enters the Tunel del Cadí, a major infrastructure project of the 1980s. It emerges into the wide, fertile mountain plateau of the **Cerdanya**. Described by writer Josep Pla as a 'huge casserole', the Cerdanya is as much of a natural unity as any geographical feature could be; however, since a treaty of 1659 the frontier between France and Spain has run right across its middle. To make things even stranger, there's one Spanish village, **Llívia**, that was left as an 'island' within French territory. The Cerdanya is also crossed by the Segre, a famous trout-fishing river.

The snow-capped peaks that ring the valley are laced with ski resorts, including **La Molina** (972 89 21 75), and **Masella** (972 89 21 75). The capital of the area (on the Spanish side), **Puigcerdà**, is a sizeable town heavily touristed by Catalans and the French. Accordingly, there's an array of discos and après-ski bars mixed in with the remnants of things medieval. Other places of interest in the area are **Lles**, site of a Romanesque church and a cross-country ski resort, and **Bellver de Cerdanya**, a beautiful hilltop village that was the unlikely scene of a battle between anarchists and Communists during the Civil War. It sits on the northern edge of the Cadí-Moixeró park, and has an information centre.

Information

Getting there: *By bus* ATSA (93 873 80 08) runs five buses daily to Berga from corner of C/Balmes and C/Pelai (journey time approx 2hrs). Alsina Graells (93 265 68 66) has a daily service to Puigcerdà from Estació del Nord (3 hrs). *By car* C1411 via Manresa to Berga (118km/73 miles) and Bagà. For Gósol turn off before Bagà on to B400. From Bagà continue on C1411 through Túnel de Cadí (toll) for Puigcerdà; an alternative is the longer, more scenic N152 through Vic and Ripoll to Puigcerdà. Lles and Bellver are both off the N260 west from Puigcerdà. *By train* RENFE from Sants or Plaça Catalunya to Puigcerdà, about two trains each hour (journey time approx 3hrs).

Tourist Offices: Berga (*93 822 1500*). **Puigcerdà**
C/Querol, Baixos (*972 88 05 42*). **Bellver de Cerdanya**
(*973 51 02 29*).
Where to eat:
Berga: La Sala *Passeig de la Pau 27* (*93 821 11 85*),
serves very good, if pricey, local dishes such as *patates
enmascarades*, a rustic blend of mashed potato and black
sausage. And, of course, excellent mushroom dishes.
Puigcerdà: Good regional food, moderately priced, is
served at **El Galet** *Plaça Santa Maria 8* (*972 88 22 66*).
A pizzeria that also offers good regional dishes is **La
Tieta** *C/Dels Ferrers 20* (*972 88 01 56*). In **Bolvir**,
5km/3 miles outside Puigcerdà, there is the five-star hotel
Torre del Remei *C/Camí Reial s/n* (*972 14 01 82*),
which has the best and most expensive restaurant in the
area (and perhaps one of the best in Spain).
Where to stay:
Berga: **Estel Hotel** *C/Sant Fruitos 39* (*93 821 34 63*),
is modern and well-run (5,000ptas for a double). In the
medieval centre of town is **Queralt Hotel** *Plaça de la
Creu 4* (*93 821 06 11*), with doubles for 4,700ptas.
Bagà: **La Pineda** *C/Raval 50* (*93 824 45 15*), is
inexpensive (5,200ptas/double) and has a restaurant.
Gósol: **Triuet** *Plaça Major 4* (*973 37 00 72*), is in the
central square of the village, and cheap (2,600ptas a
double; 5,000ptas, meals included).
Puigcerdà: There are plenty of hotels and *hostals* in the
town centre; the **Avet Blau** *Plaça Santa Maria 14* (*972
88 25 52*), has rooms at 12,000ptas a double, **Hotel
Alfonso** *C/Espanya 5* (*972 88 02 50*), is more moderate
at 5,000ptas/double. A little further out is the **Torre del
Remei** (*see above*), first class but a hefty 26,000ptas.
Lles has an inexpensive *pension*, the **Domingo**
C/Travessera 8 (*973 51 50 87*), at 3,500ptas, and a
private farmhouse, **Casa Barber** *C/Major s/n* (*973 51
52 36*), which charges 3,400ptas for a double room.
Bellver has the **Pendis** *Avda Cerdanya 4* (*973 51 04
79*), at 3,800ptas a double, or the larger **Mesón Matias**
Ctra Puigcerdà s/n (*973 51 00 39*), at 3,600ptas.

Girona, Besalú & Olot

The most interesting and vibrant Catalan city after
Barcelona, **Girona**'s origins go way back: it was
one of the first Paleolithic farming communities in
the region, a major trading town under the
Romans, and a flourishing centre throughout the
Middle Ages. Its legacy from that era is one of the
most impressive collections of medieval buildings
in Catalonia. The magnificent **Cathedral**, built
from the eleventh to the fifteenth centuries, has a
Romanesque cloister, a soaring Gothic nave and a
five-storey tower. From the main façade, 90 steep
steps lead down to the main street and the river
Onyar, where the buildings packed along the river
have been attractively renovated in varied colours.

Back at the top, just off the Cathedral square is
the Carrer de la Força, leading to the uniquely
atmospheric **Call**, the medieval Jewish quarter,
which has a centre for Jewish studies run by the
last surviving native Jewish community in the
peninsula. Add to this the **Passeig Arqueològic**,
a walk around the city's old wall; the **Banys
Àrabs** – a thirteenth-century Moslem/Jewish
bathhouse; seven other churches dating from the
eleventh to the sixteenth centuries; an iron bridge
designed by Eiffel; and the **Palau Episcopal**,

with a fine art museum, and you'll have a rough
idea of the overall beauty of Girona. The city today
is also a highly active artistic and literary centre.

Banyoles, 16km (10 miles) north of Girona, is
an attractive town divided into the **Vila Vella**
(Old Town) and **Vila Nova** (New Town), both of
which contain medieval buildings. Its main attraction, though, is the **Estany de Banyoles**, a natural lake in an ancient volcanic crater occupying
over a million square metres, surrounded by several smaller lakes and containing rare species of
fish. It is a very delicate environment, and only eco-
friendly watersports are permitted, but it hosted
the rowing events in the 1992 Olympics.

Besalú, another 14km (8 miles) north, is one of
the gems of Catalonia, a small, wonderfully peaceful medieval town founded in the tenth century.
With hardly any modern buildings, it seems suspended in time, and the whole town centre has
been declared a monument. Of special interest are
the streets of the old Jewish **Call** and the *mikveh*
(Jewish baths), the two main squares and the
church of **Santa Júlia**, but most eye-catching of
all is the spectacular and entirely intact twelfth-
century **fortified bridge** over the Fluvià river.

The N260 road continues west, past extraordinary villages such as **Castellfullit de la Roca**,
perched atop a precipitous crag, to **Olot**. The
medieval town was destroyed in an earthquake in
1427, but it has eighteenth-century and *Modernista*
buildings that are unusually imposing for a town
of this size. In the last century it was home to a
school of landscape painters, and the local **Museu
de la Garrotxa** (*972 27 91 30*) has works by them
and Casas, Rusiñol and other Modernist artists.
Olot's most unusual feature, though, is that it is
surrounded by some 30 extinct volcanoes and
lava-slips, sometimes no more than green humps
in the ground, which give the **Parc natural de
la zona volcànica de la Garrotxa** a unique
landscape. Just south of the town on the Vic road
there is a museum and information centre, the
Casal dels Volcans (*972 26 67 62*) dedicated to
them. On the beautiful back road south-east from
Olot to Banyoles there is a small but delightful
beech forest, **La Fageda d'en Jordà**, made
famous by poet Joan Maragall, grandfather of
Barcelona's former mayor (for walks in the park,
see page 246).

Information

Getting there: *By bus* Barcelona Bus (*93 232 04 59*) to
Girona from Estació del Nord; TEISA (*972 20 48 68*) runs
to Banyoles, Besalú, Olot from the corner of C/Pau Claris
and C/Consell de Cent. *By car* A7 or toll-free N11 to
Girona. For Banyoles, Besalú, Olot, take the C150 from
Girona (direction Besalú). *By train* RENFE from Sants or
Passeig de Gràcia to Girona, trains hourly approx 6am-
9.15pm (1hr 15min, Catalunya Exprés).
Tourist offices: Girona *Rambla Llibertat 1* (*972 20 26
79*). **Banyoles** (*972 57 55 73*). **Olot** *C/Bisbe Lorenzana
15* (*972 26 01 41*). These offices also have information
on places to stay in the area, such as farmhouse lodgings.

Festa!

Every village and town in Catalonia has at least one major *festa* (*fiesta*, in Spanish), usually in the summer. Most include features common to just about all Catalan celebrations, such as *sardanes* and *castells* (*see chapter* **Barcelona by Season**), alongside others that are much more specific. The only festivity shared throughout the country is Sant Joan, the celebration of the summer solstice with bonfires and fireworks on the night of 23 June.

Easter, though in general a much less important event than in other parts of Spain, sees several, fairly sober traditional festivals. Passion plays are performed in the streets of **Cervera** (Lleida) and **Olesa de Montserrat** (Barcelona). In **Vergés** in the Empordà, northeast of Girona, the mysterious 500-year-old *Dansa de la Mort* ('Dance of Death') is renacted every year on the night before Good Friday. A procession of people dressed as skeletons moves through the village in an eerie, meandering dance, to a mesmeric drum beat.

Festivals later in the year are more exuberant. Catalonia's wildest and most berserk *festa* is **La Patum** in **Berga**. It has been held on Corpus Christi, 60 days after Easter Sunday (and so usually in May), since 1394; it was moved to this date by the Church in an effort to christianise it, but the unique beasts that make up the *Patum* folklore are very pagan in origin. Celebrations go on for several days, reaching a peak on Corpus Thursday. The streets are filled with fantastic figures – dwarfs, the Angelknight, the dragon-like *guites*, the magic eagle – which career through the crowds amid deafening noise, throwing out sparks and fireworks all the while. Be warned that the *Patum* is a very loud and rowdy festival. Revellers get very drunk, but this rarely leads to trouble; problems are more likely to be caused by the sheer size of the crowds, which grow by the year.

A much more gentle, smaller-scale event can be seen around the same time in **Ripoll**. A nineteenth-century Catalan country wedding is re-enacted evry year on the first Sunday following 12 May; bride and bridegroom arrive at the church on horseback dressed in local costume, and invite all those attending to wine, snacks and canapés. More information on the full range of local festivals is available at the **Palau Robert** (*see page 251*).

Information

For Berga, *see p239*; for Ripoll, *see p238*.
Getting there: **Cervera** *By bus* Alsina Graells (93 265 68 66) from Estació del Nord, four buses daily. *By car* A2 to Martorell, then N-II (106km/66 miles). *By train* RENFE from Sants, two trains daily. **Olesa de Montserrat** *By car* A2 to Martorell, then N-II (40km/25 miles). *By train* FGC from Plaça d'Espanya, at least two trains each hour. **Vergés** *By car* A7 or N11 to Girona, C255 east, then left to Torroella de Montgri and Vergés (120km/74 miles). *By train and bus* RENFE to Girona, then Sarfa bus.

Where to eat:
Girona: **Albareda** *C/Albareda 7 (972 22 60 02)*, is in a historic building and has high-quality fare for around 4,000ptas. Cheaper (3,000 ptas) and simpler is **Casa Marieta**, *Plaça Independència 5 (972 20 10 16)*.
Banyoles: **La Rectoria** *C/Espinavesa (972 55 35 51)*, a famous gourmet restaurant (around 5,000ptas).
Besalú: Best restaurant is **Fonda Siqués** *Avda Lluis Companys 6-8 (972 59 01 10)*; cheaper and attractive is the **Cúria Reial** *Plaça de la Llibertat 15 (972 59 02 63)*.
Olot: **Ramón** *Plaça Clarà 10 (972 26 10 01)*, is the best value. With transport, **La Deu** *(972 26 10 04)*, on the Vic road, is well worth a visit – not least for its view.
Where to stay:
Girona: **Reyma** *C/Pujada del Rei Marti 15 (972 20 02 28)*, is a comfortable *hostal* near the Jewish Quarter, for about 6,000ptas a double. More upmarket (15,000ptas) is the **Carlemany** *Plaça Miquel Santaló (972 21 12 12)*.
Banyoles: **Can Xabernet** *C/Carme 27 (972 57 02 52)*, has double rooms for 7,000ptas; **L'Ast** *Passeig Dalmau (972 54 61 54)*, has a swimming pool and garden.
Besalú: **Venència** *C/Major 8 (972 59 12 57)*, is cheap at 4,000ptas a double, or try the riverside **Siqués** above the Fonda Siqués restaurant (*see above*).
Olot: The **Borrell** *C/Nònit Escubós 8 (972 26 92 75)*, has wheelchair access (8,000ptas); **Garrotxa** *Plaça de Móra 3 (972 26 16 12)*, is a bargain (3,500ptas a double).

The High Pyrenees

The *comarques* of the high Pyrenees, west of Andorra, reach altitudes of over 3,000m (9,800 feet), and contain some of the most spectacular scenery in the whole mountain range. They are Catalonia's main districts for real mountain walking, adventure sports and skiing. Too far from Barcelona to be comfortably visitable in only a couple of days, they are great places to explore over a week or a long weekend.

The Pallars Sobirà

The Pallars Sobirà runs up to the French frontier alongside Andorra, a region of steep-sided valleys and flashing rivers, snow-covered in winter and idyllic in summer, with centuries-old villages of stone and slate that seem encrusted into the mountain sides. The capital of the *comarca* is **Sort**, the centre for organised sports in the area. Companies in Sort organise rafting and kayaking trips, caving and other adventure sports, and hire out equipment. The tourist office has details of all of them.

For winter, the area has two ski stations: **Super Espot** (973 62 40 15), near the village of **Espot**, 24km (15 miles) north of Sort on a turn to the left after **Llavorsí**, a large, fully equipped resort, and the smaller **Port Ainé** (973 62 03 25), near the town of **Rialb**, just to the north of Sort. As at Vallter (*see page 238*) they are best booked direct from Barcelona.

From spring to autumn there are different attractions. The same road that leads to Espot continues to the nature reserve of **Aigüestortes**, with a network of paths through alpine wilderness. At its centre is the **Estany de Sant Maurici**, a fabulously beautiful, crystal-clear mountain lake, but there are smaller lakes dotted all through the mountains. In the park there are mountain shelters with full-time wardens, and given the remoteness of most areas you are advised to contact the park information centre in Espot (973 62 40 36) before embarking on any long hikes.

Rafting Llavorsí

Carretera Vall d'Aran, Sort (973 62 21 58).
This company's mainstay is white-water rafting down the fast and perky Noguera Pallaresa river, through spectacular gorges. Rides of about 15km (9 miles) last a few hours and cost 400ptas per person. They also run kayak and canoe tours in more tranquil waters, bungee jumping from bridges, a sort of do-it-all river tour called 'barranking', and **treks on horseback** into the mountains (2,000ptas an hour).

Information

Getting there: *By bus* Alsina Graells (93 265 68 66), one bus daily to Sort from Estació del Nord, leaves 7.30am and arrives 12.20pm. *By car* For Sort (approx 250km), take A18 to Manresa, C1410/C1412 to Tremp and then N260 north-east via Pobla de Segur.
Tourist office: Sort (*973 62 11 30*).
Where to eat:
Sort: There are plenty of traditional *fondes* in the old town, but **Hotel Pessets** *C/Diputació 3 (973 62 63 55)*, specialises in high-quality local cuisine, with a rich wild boar stew (*civet de porc senglar*).
Espot: Casa Palmira *C/Unic (973 62 40 72)*.
Where to stay:
Sort: The **Ramón** *C/Major 3 (973 62 01 33)*, is central and reasonably priced (3,700ptas a double); **Pessets II** *C/Diputació 3 (973 62 00 00)*, gives you a bar, pool, tennis courts, garden and restaurant for 8,000ptas.
Espot: The luxury hotel is **Saurat** *C/Sant Martí (973 62 41 62)*, costing 7,800ptas for a double room. **Sant Maurici** *C/Afores (973 62 40 61)*, is a cheaper two-star.

The Val d'Aran

North of Sort, if you are travelling on the old C142 route, the road begins to wind ever more tightly up to one of the most spectacular mountain passes in Europe, the **Port de la Bonaigua** at 2,072m (6,800ft), which makes it very clear that the valley you are entering, the **Val d'Aran**, is actually on the north side of the Pyrenees, the source of the river Garonne, which meets the sea at Bordeaux. The valley is a district with an architectural style, administration and even language (Aranese, a

dialect of Provençal) of its own, and that it is Spanish territory is purely an accident of history.

Vielha e Mijaran (usually just called Vielha), capital of the Val d'Aran, is a town worth visiting in its own right, for medieval houses such as **Çò de Rodés** and churches such as **Sant Pèir d'Escunhau** and **Sant Miquèu**. The valley is another great walking area, but is best known for winter sports, at its two big ski stations: **Tuca-Malh Blanc** (973 64 10 50), south of Vielha near the village of Betren, and the giant **Baqueira-Beret** (973 64 44 55), patronised by the Spanish royal family.

Information

Getting there: *By bus* Alsina Graells (93 265 68 66), two buses daily from Estació del Nord, at 6.30am and (via Sort) 7.30am (journey time 5hrs 45min, more if via Sort). *By car* From Sort (*see above*), C147 and C142 continue to Port de la Bonaigua (55km/34 miles, but journey takes well over one hour). Most direct route from Barcelona is A18 to Manresa, C1410/C1412 to Tremp and N260 north-east from Pobla de Segur, to enter Val d'Aran by the Vielha tunnel at western end of the valley. Distance to Vielha 320km/199 miles.
Tourist office: Vielha *C/Sarriulera 6 (973 64 01 10)*.
Where to eat:
Vielha: Good and cheap is **Nicolàs** *C/Castèth 10 (973 64 18 20)*, while **Era Mola** *C/Marrec 8 (973 64 24 19)*, is the city's most typically Aranese restaurant.
Betren: La Borda de Betren *C/Major (973 64 00 32)*, is a rustically decorated restaurant near Tuca-Malh Blanc
Where to stay:
Vielha: The town is quite expensive, but **Aran** *Avda Castiero 5 (973 64 00 50)*, is reasonably priced at 9,500ptas a double in high season. Cheaper (3,500ptas double) is the **Busquets** *C/Major 9 (973 64 02 38)*.
Baqueira: The ski resort has **Val de Ruda** *Carretera de la Bonaigua (973 64 58 11)*, a two-star hotel dwarfed by two nearby, very expensive luxury hotels.
Betren: There is only one hotel, the **Tuca** *Carretera Salardú s/n (973 64 07 00)*, complete with disco, pool and everything else for 7,100-15,500ptas per double.

Fruits of the earth: *cava* & wines

Catalonia's most famous wines and all of its *cava*, or sparkling wine, come from the **Alt Penedès** west of Barcelona, one of the most respected wine-producing areas in Spain. **Vilafranca del Penedès**, capital of the *comarca*, has a **Museu del Vi** (wine museum), with a fascinating display of wine-making equipment from across the centuries.

The region's largest winemaker, **Bodegues Torres**, also offers guided tours from Monday to Saturday (93 890 32 26; booking essential).

On the riverfront in **Girona**.

Some of the hundreds of rolling wine-acres of the Penedès.

Sixty per cent of the Alt Penedès is given over to vineyards. If Vilafranca is the main centre for table wine and brandies, neighbouring **Sant Sadurní d'Anoia** is the capital of the *cava* industry. **Codorniu** was the first company to begin *cava* production here, after Manuel Raventós, heir to the estate, spent time working in the Champagne region in the 1870s and reproduced the *méthode champenoise* in his native land.

The vast cellars of the Can Codorniu building, from 1896-1906, are a beautiful *Modernista* work by Josep Puig i Cadafalch. All visits include a short film, a mini-train ride through the cellars and a *cava* tasting session, and at weekends, visitors receive a free champagne glass as well. The free weekday visits have the extra plus that you see the cellar at work.

Caves Freixenet, established in the 1920s, conducts cellar tours on weekdays only. Tours are free, and give a full run-down on their cellars and *cava* manufacturing process, as well as a tasting session. As well as these two, there are many more *caves* in Sant Sadurní that offer free tours; the tourist office has a full list. All the tours are given in English as well as several other languages.

Catalonia has several other *denominació d'origen* wine-producing regions, such as the small **Alella**, around the town of the same name just east of Barcelona and best known for its whites, and more importantly **Priorat** and **Terra Alta**, on either side of the River Ebro, west of Tarragona. Falset and Gandesa, respectively, are the district capitals. The wines of both areas are heavier,

stronger and less consistent than their Penedès equivalents, but can be of high quality: try the Priorat Scala Dei reds and Gandesa rosés. Local tourist offices have information on vineyard visits and tastings; in Gandesa, look out too for the **Cooperativa Agrícola**, another great Modernist contribution to the wine industry.

Caves Codorniu
Avda Codorniu, Sant Sadurní d'Anoia (93 818 32 32). **Open** 8am-12.30pm, 3pm-4.30 pm, Mon-Fri; 10am-1.30pm Sat, Sun. **Admission** Mon-Fri free; Sat, Sun 200ptas.

Caves Freixenet
C/Joan Sala 2, Sant Sadurní d'Anoia (93 891 70 00). **Tours** 9am, 10am, 11,30am, 3.30pm, 5pm, Mon-Thu; 9am, 10am, 11.30am, Fri. **Admission** free.

Museu del Vi
Plaça Jaume I 1, Vilafranca del Penedès (93 890 05 82). **Open** 10am-2pm, 4-7pm, Tue-Sat; 10am-2pm Sun. *June-Sept* 9am-9pm Tue-Sat; 10am-2pm Sun. **Admission** 400ptas.

Wine Festivals
Most of the main wine-towns of Catalonia have festivals in autumn to celebrate the grape harvest (*verema*). In **Alella** it takes place very early, around the first weekend in September, when the year's first crushed grapes are blessed. Much larger are the events in **Vilafranca**, the first Sunday in October, and **Sant Sadurní**, usually a week later. At each there are concerts, dances, exhibitions, tastings and other things going on, and in Sant Sadurní there's the crowning of the *Reina del Cava*, the Cava Queen, while most of the crowd get several free glasses of the product as well. Smaller towns have their own events; tourist offices have details.

Information
Getting there:

Alt Penedès: *By car* A2 then A7 direct to Sant Sadurní (44km/27 miles) and Vilafranca del Penedès (55km/34 miles), or A2 then turn on to toll-free N340 at Molins de Rei, which is much slower. *By train* RENFE from Sants or Plaça Catalunya, trains hourly 6am-10pm (45min).
Alella: *By bus* Autocars Casas (93 798 11 00) from corner of Gran Via and C/Roger de Flor. *By car* N11 north to Montgat, left turn to Alella (15km/9 miles).
Falset & Gandesa: *By car* A2, then A7 via Vilafranca, to Reus, turn right on to N420 for Falset (143km/89 miles) and Gandesa (181km/112 miles). *By train* RENFE from Sants or Passeig de Gràcia to Marçà-Falset. Six trains a day; journey time approx 2hrs. For Gandesa, continue to Mora d'Ebre (another 20min) and catch local bus.
Tourist offices: **Vilafranca del Penedès** *C/Cort 14 (93 892 03 58);* **Sant Sadurní d'Anoia** *Plaça de l'Ajuntament 1, baixos (93 891 12 12);* **Gandesa** *Avda Catalunya (977 42 06 14).*

Walking the hills

Hiking and hill-walking have long been hugely popular in Catalonia. It's not surprising, for Barcelona is surrounded by easily-accessible mountain regions with spectacular landscapes. Many are now national parks. The mountains in these areas are mostly low to medium height, and walking is made easier in some places by GR (*gran recorregut*) long-distance footpaths, marked by red and white route signs.

If you venture out walking you should take local walking maps and, naturally, be suitably clothed and shod (with light walking boots) and have with you water and food supplies.The best shop in Barcelona for walking maps is **Llibreria Quera**, and **Altair** also has a good selection (for both, *see chapter* **Shopping**). As usual, the **Palau Robert** (*see page 251*) is also a good source of information.

Below we give a selection of possible walks, ordered in a rough arc from west to east around Barcelona and to the north of the city. But there are many more.

Organised walks

Several clubs and companies take guided walks around the Catalan countryside, and further afield. They include:
Centre Excursionista de Catalunya (CEC), C/Paradís 10 (93 319 01 00).
Unió Excursionista de Catalunya (UEC), Gran Via de les Corts Catalanes 580 (93 453 11 65).
These clubs plan walks for members only, usually at weekends and lasting one or two days.
Spain Step by Step C/Casp 55, 3° 11ª (93 245 82 53).
Tailor-made accompanied or unaccompanied group walking tours all over Spain, by arrangement only.

Garraf

This arid, almost desert-like nature park in the hills above Sitges is fascinating to geologists. Karst outcrops abound, cliffs fall sharply to the sea, and the margallo palm – the only native European palm – and numerous African plant species are common.

Olesa de Bonesvalls to Sitges

(4hrs 30Min) Leave the village of Olesa along the road past the medieval Hospital d'Olesa. Take the GR-5 towards Sitges, traverse the deep Avenc de l'Esquerrà, past an ancient *masia*, Can Grau, on through Jafre and past the Maset de Dalt. Cross the cols at Pota de Cavall and La Fita and drop down the old connecting paths of La Fita and Del Capellans to Sitges.

Begues to Sitges (5hr)

(5hrs). This walk begins at Begues, on the western edge of the Barcelona urban area. From the village, follow the GR-92 southwards, and pass the *masias* at Can Baró and Can Roure. Climb **La Morella** (595m/1,900ft) and enjoy the view before continuing to Vallgrasa col and on to Plana Novella. Walk along the banks of the Jafre until you get to the Maset de Dalt. Pick up the GR-5 here for Sitges.

Getting there

By bus Mohn bus from Plaça d'Espanya to Begues and Olesa de Bonesvalls. *By car* A-16 or C-246 to Gavà and Sitges, BV-2411 from Gavà to Begues and Olesa de Bonesvalls. *By train* RENFE (Sants) to Sitges.

Sant Llorenç del Munt i l'Obac

This park has a wild craggy landscape cut with narrow ravines hosting a range of interesting flora. Its highest point is **La Mola** (1,104m/3,620ft) crowned by the eleventh-century monastery of **Sant Llorenç del Munt**.

Circular route from Matadepera via Sant Llorenç del Munt

(4hrs) From Matedepera village, follow the Les Arenes stream, then leave it to bear right towards Can Prat. Pick up a signposted track that runs left off a sharp bend to connect with the *Camí dels Monjos* (C-31). Walk along this marked track and climb, zig-zagging at times, to the peak of **La Mola** (where there is a Nature Park Information Centre). Continue north to a rocky outcrop, the Morral del Drac (Dragon's Snout), and drop down into the ravine of Canal de Santa Agnès, until a path on the right marked with an X, the *Camí de la Font Soleia*. Follow it until it meets the *Camí dels Monjos*, to return to Matadepera by the same route.

Getting there

By car A-18 and N-150 to Terrassa, then BV-1221 to Matadepera. *By train and bus* RENFE or FGC from Plaça Catalunya to Terrassa, then Thireo bus to Matadepera.

Montserrat

The most emblematic and most visited massif in Catalunya, shaped into pinnacles and near-vertical ravines by erosion. For the monastery and information on how to get there, *see page 235.*

Circular route from the monastery via Sant Jeroni

(4hrs 30min) Walk up the steps from the **Font el Portal** by the monastery to the Via Crucis, and cross the stream, the **Torrent de Santa Maria**. Follow this up to its source, through the passes of Pas dels Francescos, the Pla dels Ocells and the Basses de Sant Antoni. Continue up to the hermitage of **Sant Jeroni** on the col at **Pou de Calaç**; this is about 15 minutes below the peak of Sant Jeroni. Return to the monastery down the steep ravine of Sant Jeroni, turning right on to the GR-72 (also called the *Camí de l'Arrel*), which skirts the north-east face of the main massif, before you reach the road. Continue to the monastery via the Pla de la Trinitat.

The 'Hermitage Route'

(3hrs) Leave the main monastery the same way as the previous route and follow the path to the **Plaça de Santa Anna**. Turn right here towards the hermitage of **Sant Benet** (now a refuge) and the cave-hermitage of **Sant Salvador**. Continue on over a less steep stretch and turn left when you reach the Pla dels Ocells. Traverse the small peak of Trencabarrals to pick up the *Camí Nou de Sant Jeroni*. From this path you can take in the circuit of panoramic views and hermitages, including **Sant Jaume**, **Sant Onofre**, **Sant Joan**, **Santa Caterina** and **Santa Magdalena**. Return to the Monastery via the *Camí de Les Ermites* and *Camí de Sant Miquel*, along the top of the main ridge.

Montseny

The massif of the Montseny, due north of Barcelona, is sacred to Catalan ramblers, and has been a Reserve since 1978. Several of its peaks top 1,700m (5,500ft), and woodland covers about 60 per cent of its area.

Circular route from El Figueró via Tagamanent

(5hrs) From the station in Figueró walk along the track towards Vallcárquera until you get to the **Font del Molí** and the church of **Sant Pere**. Continue, leaving the Vallcárquera stream on your right, and pick up another track signposted Tagamanent via the col at Sant Martí. Climb up to the rocky promontory from here to the hermitage of **Santa María de Tagamanent**. From the peak, drop down again to the col and go on to Can Bellever and L'Agustí. Turn right here along a path through woods to La Roca Centella, which you leave on your left. Drop down, bearing to the right towards the Romanesque hermitage at **San Cristòfol** and a col at La Creu de Can Plans. Follow the power line to the Vallcárquera *riera* (stream) to return to El Figueró.

Circular route from Aiguafreda via Serra de l'Arca

(4hrs) From Aiguafreda village take the track along a stream called the *Riera de l'Avencó*. After crossing bridges at Pere Curt and La Bisbal (by a *masia* at Casa Nova de Sant Miquel), reach the third bridge at Picamena, but don't cross it. Continue along the track to the left through holm oaks to **Pla de la Creu**, a beautiful mountain pasture above the Serra de l'Arca. There is a neolithic dolmen nearby, at Pla del Boix. Go on south-west along the GR-92 path, and take it to the left until you reach another dolmen. At a fork soon after that, go right past two dolmens to the dolmen at **Cruïlles**. Pass the abandoned *masia* at Can Serra and return to Aiguafreda.

Getting there

By bus Sagalès from corner of Passeig de Sant Joan-C/Diputació to El Figueró and Aiguafreda. *By car* N-152 (El Figueró 40km/25 miles). Also A-7 or C-251 to Sant Celoni and BV-5301 to Montseny. *By train* RENFE from Sants or Plaça Catalunya to El Figueró and Aiguafreda, Vic line (approx two trains hourly).

Montnegre & El Corredor

The Montnegre and El Corredor *massifs* run northeast of Barcelona between the Tordera valley (with the main A7 motorway) and the sea. Dominant vegetation is Mediterranean woodland; fields, farmhouses, medieval churches, Iberian remains and neolithic dolmens are scattered about the area.

Sant Celoni to Canet de Mar

(6hrs) From Sant Celoni, on the south side of the Montseny, walk via Pertegas towards Vilardell, and continue until you

see signs for the GR-5 path. Cross the Boscos de Montnegre woods following the signs and walk on to **Sant Martí de Montnegre**. Follow the path to the right, now the GR-92, and skirt Turó d'en Vives mountain. Drop down to the hermitage of **Sant Iscle de Vallalta**, and walk on to Safigueras col. The route finishes by the sea in the beautiful village of **Canet de Mar**, by the castle of Santa Florentina.

Llinars del Vallès to Sant Celoni

(5hrs) From Llinars village follow the B-510 towards **Dosrius**, until you get to Can Bordoi and the church of **Sant Cristòfol**. Take the GR-92 path from here; this runs close to an Iberian settlement site at Turó del Vent. Continue on to El Far and the **Santuari del Corredor**, with a Nature Park Information Centre and fine views of the woods of Montnegre. Proceed along the path to Can Pradell de la Serra, which connects with an itinerary signposted with green and blue; follow these signs to the left to the dolmen at **Pedra Gentil**, supposedly a witch's coven. Walk on to the B-511, which runs down to Sant Celoni.

Getting there

By bus Sagalès from Passeig Sant Joan-C/Diputació to Llinars del Vallés, and Autobuses Barbà from Pla del Palau to Sant Celoni. *By car* A7 to Granollers, C-251 to Llinars del Vallés (36km/22 miles) and Sant Celoni (49km/30 miles). A-19/N-II to Canet de Mar. *By train* RENFE from Sants or Passeig de Gràcia to Llinars and Sant Celoni (Girona line) or Canet (Blanes line).

Olot & La Garrotxa

There are over 20 old larva flows and about 30 volcanic cones around Olot, many well preserved with visible craters. **El Croscat** was the last to erupt, about 11,500 years ago. The forms, textures and colours of the lava contrast strongly with the leafy, damp forests. For the town of Olot, *see page 240*.

Circular route from Olot via Fageda d'en Jordà & the volcanoes of Santa Margarida & El Croscat

(7hrs) Leave the Nature Park Information Centre (Casal dels Volcans) and follow itinerary three (green) through the beech forest of Fageda d'en Jordà, sited on an old lava flow from El Croscat. At the junction with itinerary two (red), follow it to the right. Pass the eleventh-century Romanesque church of **Sant Miquel de Sacot** and walk up the southern slope of **Santa Margarida**. There is a hermitage in the centre of the crater here. Drop down the northern slope until you get to the car park at Santa Margarida, cross the GI-524, and continue round El Croscat to the information centre at Can Serra. Pick up itinerary three here back to Olot.

Circular route from Olot via Volcà del Racó & Puig Redón

(5hrs 30min) Take itinerary three (green) from the Casal dels Volcans as far as the **Font Moixina** spring, and pick up itinerary nine (dark blue), which runs through the Bosc de Tosca and past Pocafarina to the **Racó** volcano. Get on to itinerary 12 (grey) and walk up the northern slope of the Sierra del Corb to the car park at Xenacs. Go on to **Puig Redón** (909m/2,980ft), which has fabulous views. Return to Xenacs and follow itinerary 10 or the shorter number 11 to **Les Presses**. Walk back to **Olot** along a disused railway, now a cycle route.

Getting there

By bus TEISA from the corner of C/Pau Claris and C/Consell de Cent. More frequent services from Girona. *By car* A-7, N-II and C-150 to Banyoles and Olot (130km/80 miles). Or N-152 to Ripoll, C-150 to Olot. *By train* RENFE to Girona, then TEISA bus.

Directory

Directory

Essential Information

Before arriving

Visas & immigration

Visas are not needed by European Union nationals, or by US, Canadian and New Zealand citizens for stays of up to three months. British and all non-EU citizens must have full passports. Citizens of Australia, South Africa and some other countries need visas to enter Spain; they can be obtained from Spanish consulates in other European countries as well as in the home country. Spain is also one of the EU countries within the Schengen agreement, under which a visa issued by another member state should also be accepted as valid for Spain.

EU citizens intending to work, study or live permanently in Spain should register with the police within 15 days of arrival to obtain a Residence Card

(*carta de residencia*). Non-EU nationals who wish to work or study in Spain for more than three months officially should have the relevant visa before entering the country. For more on living in Spain, *see pp262-3*.

Customs

EU residents do not have to declare goods imported into Spain for their personal use if tax has been paid on them in the country of origin. Customs can still question whether large amounts of any item really are for your own use, and random checks are also made for drugs. Quantities accepted as being for personal use are:
• up to 800 cigarettes, 400 small cigars, 200 cigars and 1kg of loose tobacco
• 10 litres of spirits (over 22% alcohol), 90 litres of wine (under 22% alcohol) and 110 litres of beer.

Limits for non-EU residents:
• 200 cigarettes **or** 100 small cigars **or** 50 cigars **or** 250 grams (8.82 ounces) of tobacco
• 1 litre of spirits (over 22% alcohol) and 2 litres of wine or beer (under 22% alcohol)
• 50 grams (1.76 ounces) of perfume

There are no restrictions on cameras, watches or electrical goods, within reasonable limits, and visitors can carry up to 1 million ptas in cash. Non-EU residents can also reclaim Value Added Tax (IVA) paid on some large purchases when they leave Spain. For details, *see p165* **Shopping**.

Insurance

EU nationals are entitled to make use of the Spanish state health service, provided they have an E111 form, which in Britain is available from

Language cocktails

As far as foreigners are concerned, Barcelona's status as a bilingual society seems to confuse (or even irritate) some, and engage, attract or entrance others. Catalan is the preferred tongue of around 60 per cent of the population, and ever more the principal language of public life. All streets are now signposted (and maps printed) exclusively in the language. Other fields are less straightforward, for there are still plenty of Spanish-speakers around, and Catalan and Castilian Spanish are regularly intermixed, with a spectrum of usage between the two. Linguistic toing and froing is second nature to locals: stay here a while and you can pick up a new hobby in cataloguing the more bizarre incidences of verbal seasoning.

Elsewhere in Spain you may easily hear the paranoid wail that the Catalans have now become impossible, and expect even innocents straight off the train to understand their obscure tongue. There are Catalans who will speak to you from the outset in their own language, but you are far, far more likely to meet people who still expect to deal with visitors in Spanish. Any recognition on your

part of the Catalan language, however, if only in a few phrases, will always be appreciated, and is an effective ice-breaker. You will also find it easier to find your way if you can at least recognise Catalan place names (soft *g*s and *j*s instead of the guttural Spanish *ge*). If you are thinking of staying here for any length of time, it is strongly advisable to learn Catalan, as otherwise you will only be ghettoising yourself. Catalan is a Latin language with no special difficulties (and, thanks to shared vowels, it's actually easier for English-speakers to get a good Catalan accent than a Spanish one). The Catalan government and universities provide a range of inexpensive courses in the language, and there are also private schools (*see page 267*).

We have followed current Catalan and local usage in addresses in this Guide, but be prepared to meet Castilian-Spanish equivalents that can be substantially different. With other terms, where both forms are equally useful we have given both, always with the Catalan first. For useful phrases in both languages, *see pages 254–5*.

Emergencies

All services are on call 24 hours daily.
For information on police forces, *see page 252*.
Ambulance/*Ambulància* *061/93 300 20 20.*
Fire Service/*Bombers/Bomberos* *080.*
Municipal Police/*Policia Municipal* *092.*
National Police/*Policia Nacional* *091.*
Catalan Government Police/*Mossos d'Esquadra* *93 300 22 96.*
Guardia Civil *062.*

Emergency repairs

All lines are open 24 hours daily; *900* numbers are freephone
lines. Which electricity company you need to call will be
indicated on your electricity meter.
Electricity Enher *900 77 00 77;* Fecsa *900 74 74 74;*
Hidroelèctrica de Catalunya *900 78 78 78.*
Gas/*Gas Natural* *900 75 07 50.*
Water/*Aigües de Barcelona* *93 231 90 00.*

post offices, health centres and Social
Security offices. This will cover you
for emergencies, but using an E111
involves dealing at least a little with
Spanish health bureaucracy, and for
short-term visitors it's usually simpler
to take out private travel insurance
before departure, which will also
normally cover you for stolen or lost
cash or valuables as well as medical
costs. Some non-EU countries have
reciprocal health-care agreements
with Spain, but, again, for most
travellers it will be more convenient
to have private travel insurance. For
more on health services, *see p261.*

Communications
Mail

If all you need are normal-rate
stamps for cards or letters, you
can buy them in any *estanc* or
tobacco shop (*see page 253*).

Correu Central
*Plaça Antoni López (93 318 35 07/902
197 197). Metro Jaume I/bus 14, 17,
36, 40, 45, 57, 59, 64.* **Open** 8am-
10pm Mon-Fri; 8am-8pm Sat; *some services only* 9am-1pm Sun. **Map D5**
In the imposing main post office all
the different postal services are
available at separate windows
around the main hall: parcel post,
telegrams, telex and so on. All post
offices also offer a fax sending and
receiving service, but they are more
expensive than private fax bureaux.
At the Correu Central there is an
information desk by the main
entrance. Note that within the
general opening times not all

services are available at all times;
also, some post offices close during
August. Letters sent Poste Restante
(General Delivery) to Barcelona
should be addressed to *Lista de
Correos, 08070 Barcelona, Spain.*
To collect them go to window 36,
with your passport. To send
something by express post, say you
want to send your letter *urgente.*
Other city centre post offices
*(open 8.30am-2.30pm Mon-Fri;
9.30am-1pm Sat):*
Plaça Bonsuccès.
Metro Catalunya/bus all routes to
Plaça Catalunya.
C/Aragó 272. Metro Passeig de
Gràcia/bus 7, 16, 17, 22, 24, 28, 39, 45.
C/València 231. Metro Passeig de
Gràcia/bus 7, 16, 17, 20, 21, 43, 44.

Postal rates & post boxes
Letters and postcards weighing up to
20gm cost 35ptas within Spain;
70ptas to the rest of Europe; 115ptas
to the US, Canada, Africa and Middle
East; 155ptas to Australasia and the
Far East. Mail to other European
countries generally arrives in three to
four days, to North America in about
a week. Aerogrammes (*Aerogramas*)
cost 85ptas for all destinations.
Normal post boxes are yellow, with
two horizontal red stripes. There are
also a few special red post boxes for
urgent mail, with collections about
every two hours.

Postal Exprés
Available at all post offices, this is an
efficient express post system with
guaranteed next-day delivery to
Spanish provincial capitals, and 48-
hour delivery elsewhere in Spain. The
most convenient and reliable way of
sending small packages within Spain.

Telephones

Telefónica, the Spanish phone
company, is a much-disliked
institution. Charges are high,
especially for international
calls. Calls are cheaper after
10pm and before 8am, Monday
to Saturday, and all day on
Sundays. For mobile phone and
fax rentals, *see page 183.*

Phone numbers
In April 1998 Telefónica made it
necessary to dial provincial area
codes with individual numbers for all
calls, even in the same street. Hence
all Barcelona numbers have to begin
with *93* whether for local or long
distance calls. This change was
announced very abruptly, and the *93*
will not be shown on the stationery of
many companies, hotels and so on for
some time. Numbers beginning *900*
are freephone lines.

Public phones
The most common model of phone
now in use accepts coins, phonecards
and credit cards, and also has a
digital display with instructions in
four languages including English.
The minimum charge for a local call
is currently 13ptas, for which you will
need to insert at least three *duros*
(5ptas coins). This type of phone will
also give you credit to make further
calls without having to reinsert your
money. If you are likely to make more
than a couple of calls it's best to get a
phonecard, available for 500, 1,000,
2,000 or 5,000ptas and bought in post
offices or *estancs*. There are also still
some of the older model, coin-only
phones, in which you insert coins into
an aperture at the top of the phone
before dialling. The coins begin to
drop when the call is answered, and
change is not given if you put in a 25
or 50ptas coin for a local call. In
addition, most bars and cafés have a
telephone for public use. They usually
accept 5 and 25ptas coins, but in some
bars they are set to take only 25ptas,
an illegal but not-uncommon practice.

International & long-
distance calls
To make an international call, dial 07,
wait for a loud continuous tone and
then dial the country code: **Australia**
61; **Canada** 1; **Irish Republic** 353;
New Zealand 64; **United Kingdom**
44; **USA** 1, followed by the area code
(omitting the first zero in UK
numbers) and number. To call
Barcelona from abroad, dial the
international code (00 in the UK), then
34 for Spain. If you are calling
Barcelona from anywhere else in
Spain, the number is now the same as
the local number, beginning with 93.

Directory

Phone centres

At phone centres (*Locutorios*) you are allotted a booth and pay at the counter when you've finished your calls, so avoiding the need for pocketloads of change.

Centres: *La Rambla 88. Metro Liceu/bus 14, 18, 38, 59.* **Open** 10am-11pm daily. **Map D5**

Main vestibule, Estació de Sants. Metro Sants-Estació/bus 44, 109. **Open** 8am-10pm Mon-Sat; 9am-10pm Sun, public holidays. **Map A3**

Vestíbulo, Estació d'Autobusos del Nord, C/Ali Bei 80. Metro Arc de Triomf/bus all routes to Arc de Triomf. **Open** 9am-9.30pm Mon-Fri. **Map E4**

Operator services

Normally in Catalan and Spanish only.
National directory enquiries 1003
International directory enquiries 025
National operator 1009
International operator *Europe & North Africa* 1008; *Rest of World* 1005
Telephone breakdowns 1002
Telegrams 93 322 20 00
Time 093
Weather information 094
Alarm calls 096
Once the message has finished (when it starts repeating itself), key in the number you are calling from, followed by the time at which you wish to be woken, in four figures, ie 0830 if you want to be called at 8.30am.
General information 098
A local information service provided by Telefónica, with information particularly on duty pharmacies in Barcelona. Otherwise, it is generally less reliable than the 010 line (*see p251*).

Disabled travellers

Barcelona is a city where disabled people, especially wheelchair users, have mixed experiences. Accessible buses are in use on a growing number of routes, and there is a limited special taxi service. The main railway stations, Sants, França, Passeig de Gràcia and Plaça Catalunya, are also fully accessible to wheelchairs. An official guide to transport access in Barcelona and area is available from the transport information office at Metro Universitat (93 318 70 74). Wheelchair access points are also indicated on most public transport maps.

This and the existence of a special transport information phoneline for the disabled (93 412 44 44, English speakers sometimes available) are evidence of an official desire to improve facilities. The resources given to this in practice, though, are limited. A programme is in hand to provide access at all Metro stations, but when it will be completed is another question; so, some stations, such as Universitat, have lavish facilities, while others have none.

Through the 1990s, however, spurred on by the experience of the 1992 Paralympic Games, there has been a noticeably greater awareness of the need to take disabled requirements into account. The city's newest museums, such as **MACBA**, and some that have been recently remodelled, such as the **MNAC**, incorporate model facilities for full access. Older museums can be more of a problem. Thanks to ONCE (Spain's lottery-funded organisation for the blind) more has been done on behalf of blind and partially sighted people. Most street crossings in the city centre are identifiable by knobbled paving and low kerbs.
Institut Municipal de Disminüits *C/Comte d'Urgell 240 (93 439 66 00). Metro Hospital Clinic/bus all routes to Hospital Clinic.* **Open** 9am-2pm Mon-Fri. **Map C3.** The official city organisation for the disabled collates information on changes in access and facilities, and produces a range of leaflets on access in different fields (museums, theatres and so on).

Buses

All buses on the **Aerobús** service from the airport and most on the **Bus Turístic** route are fully accessible to wheelchair users, with low-entry doors, wheelchair points and so on. In addition, similar fully adapted buses alternate with standard buses on some regular city routes, including the **14, 20, 24, 33, 44, 47, 59, 64, 72** and the night buses **N1, N2** and **N3**.

Metro & FGC

Banks of steps and a lack of lifts close off most Metro and FGC stations to wheelchair users, but all stations on line 2 (Paral.lel-La Pau) and the Montjuïc Funicular (*see chapter* **Sightseeing**) have lifts and ramps to provide full access. It is planned to extend these facilities, but so far only some stations on line 1, and Provença on the FGC, are fully accessible.

Taxis

All taxi drivers are officially required to transport wheelchairs (and guide dogs) for no extra charge, but their cars can be inconveniently small, and in practice the willingness of drivers to co-operate varies widely. Special minibus taxis adapted for wheelchairs can be ordered through **Barnataxi** on 93 357 77 55; say that you want a *Taxi Amic* when ordering. Fares are the same as for standard cabs, but the numbers of such taxis in Barcelona are limited, so call well in advance to get a cab for a specific time.

Holidays

On public holidays (*festes/fiestas*) virtually all shops, banks and offices, and many bars and restaurants, are closed. Public transport runs a Sunday service, or a very limited service on Christmas Day and New Year's Day, and some museums are also open, if for shorter-than-usual hours. Efforts have been made to reduce the impact of public holidays, but when one falls on a Tuesday or Thursday some people still take the intervening day before or after the weekend off as well, in a long weekend called a *pont/puente* (bridge). Few offices now close for the whole of Easter Week, but activity diminishes greatly from midday on the Wednesday. For a calendar of city festivals, *see pages 5-11* **Barcelona by Season**. The usual official holidays, with some variations each year, include:
New Year's Day (Cap d'Any) 1 January; **Three Kings (Dia de Reis)** 6 January; **Good Friday (Divendres Sant)**; **Easter Monday (Dilluns de Pasqua Florida)**; **May Day (Festa del Treball)** 1 May; **Whit Monday (Dilluns de Pasqua Granada)**; **Saint John/ Midsummer's Day (Sant Joan)** 24 June; **The Assumption (L'Assumpció)** 15 August; **Catalan National Day (Diada Nacional de Catalunya)** 11 September; **Our Lady of Mercy (La Mercè)** 24 September; **Discovery of America (Dia de la Hispanitat)** 12 October; **All Saints' Day (Tots Sants)** 1 November; **Constitution Day (Dia de la Constitució)** 6 December; **Immaculate Conception (La Immaculada)** 8 December; **Christmas (Nadal)** 25 December; **Boxing Day (Sant Esteve)** 26 December.

Information

Both the city council (the *Ajuntament*) and the Catalan regional government (the *Generalitat*) provide tourist information offices, and the city runs an efficient information service for local citizens that's also useful to visitors. The best information on what's on in music, theatre and so on will be in local papers and listings magazines (*see chapter* **Media**).

City tourist offices sell multi-journey transport tickets, tourist bus tickets and the *Barcelona Card* discount card. For details of these schemes, *see page 47* and *page 257*. The city of Barcelona has a website at *www.bcn.es* and the Catalan government site is at *www.gencat.es*.

Centre d'Informació Plaça Catalunya

Plaça Catalunya (general information 93 304 31 35/hotel information 93 304 32 32). Metro Catalunya/bus all routes to Plaça Catalunya. **Open** 9am-9pm daily. **Map D4**
The main office of the City tourist board *Turisme de Barcelona* is right in the city centre and has a full information service (with good maps), a money exchange desk and a souvenir and book shop. There is also a hotel booking service, which is not available at the smaller offices.
Branch offices: Ajuntament *Plaça Sant Jaume. Metro Jaume I/bus 17, 40, 45.* **Open** 10am-8pm Mon-Sat; 10am-2pm Sun, public holidays. Closed 25 Dec, 1 Jan. **Map D5**.
Barcelona-Sants station *Metro Sants-Estació/bus 27, 43, 44, 109.* **Open** *Oct-May* 8am-8pm Mon-Fri; 8am-2pm Sat, Sun, public holidays; *June-Sept* 8am-8pm daily. Closed 25 Dec, 1 Jan. **Map A3**.
Palau de Congressos (Trade Fair office) *Avda Reina Maria Cristina. Metro Espanya/bus all routes to Plaça d'Espanya.* **Open** *during trade fairs only* 10am-8pm daily. **Map A4**

Temporary offices & 'Red Jackets'

Information Booth located at *Sagrada Família.* **Open** *24 June-25 Sept* 10am-8pm daily. **Map F3**
In summer Turisme de Barcelona opens up this temporary booth (no accommodation service). In the same period information officers called 'Red Jackets' in red uniforms also roam the Barri Gòtic, La Rambla and Passeig de Gràcia, ready to field questions in a heroic variety of languages, 10am-8pm daily.

Palau Robert/Oficines d'Informació Turística

Palau Robert, Passeig de Gràcia 107 (93 238 40 00). Metro Diagonal/bus 7, 16, 17, 22, 24, 28. **Open** 10am-7pm Mon-Sat; 10am-2.30pm Sun. Closed public holidays. **Map D3**
The Catalan government's lavishly equipped new information centre occupies the Palau Robert, a turn-of-the-century mansion at the junction of Passeig de Gràcia and the Diagonal, with a beautiful garden. It does not have quite as much on Barcelona itself as the City offices – although it still has city maps and other essentials – but it does have a huge range of information on other parts of the country and different activities.
Branches: Airport Terminal A *(93 478 47 04).* **Open** 9.30am-3pm Mon-Sat; **Terminal B** *(93 478 05 65).* **Open** 9.30am-8pm Mon-Sat *(mid-June-mid-Sept* 9.30am-8.30pm), 9.30am-3pm Sun, public holidays.

Centre d'Informació de la Virreina

Palau de la Virreina, La Rambla 99 (93 301 77 75). Metro Liceu/bus 14, 38, 59. **Open** 10am-2pm, 4-8pm, Mon-Fri. Ticket sales 11am-2pm, 4-7pm Tue-Sat; 11am-2pm Sun. **Map D5**
Not a tourist office as such, but the information office of the City cultural department, with information on exhibitions, concerts, theatres and so on, and a free monthly listings leaflet, *Fet a Barcelona*. Also the best place to buy tickets for events in the **Grec** summer festival (*see p9*), and productions at the **Mercat de les Flors** (*see chapter* **Theatre**) during the rest of the year. In the same building is the **Llibreria de la Virreina** bookshop, with a comprehensive choice of books on Barcelona, some in English editions.

010 Phoneline

Open 8am-10pm Mon-Sat.
A City-run information line that's again primarily directed at local citizens, but will answer queries of any and every kind. Calls are taken in French and English as well as Catalan and Spanish, but you may have to wait for an English-speaking operator. To call from outside Barcelona, phone 93 402 70 00.

Maps

Metro and central area street maps are included at the back of this guide. Tourist offices provide a reasonably detailed free street map, and the City tourist offices also have a better map for 200ptas. Metro maps are available free at all Metro stations (ask for '*una Guia del*

Metro') and city transport information offices (*see page 258*), which also have free bus maps. Metro and bus maps indicate access points for the disabled on to public transport.

Money

The Spanish currency is the *peseta*, the usual abbreviation of which is *ptas* (*pesseta, ptes,* in Catalan). There are coins for 1, 5, 10, 25, 50, 100, 200 and 500 pesetas. Confusingly, there are several different kinds of 5, 25, 50 and 200ptas coin, including a range of commemorative editions. A 5ptas coin is called a *duro*. Notes begin with the green 1,000ptas, and continue through 2,000 (red), 5,000 (brown) and 10,000ptas (blue).

Banks & bureaux de change

Banks and savings banks readily accept travellers' cheques (you must show your passport), but are less keen to take personal cheques with a Eurocheque guarantee card. Commission rates vary a good deal, and it's worth shopping around before changing money. Given the rates charged by Spanish banks, the cheapest way to obtain money is often through a cash machine with a credit card rather than with travellers' cheques, despite the fees charged for cash withdrawals. It is always quicker and more trouble-free to change money at larger bank offices rather than at local branches.

Bank hours

Banks are normally open 8am-3pm, Mon-Fri, and from 1 October to 30 April most branches also open 8am-1.30pm Sat. Hours vary a little between different banks: some open slightly earlier or later, while several branches stay open until 4-4.30pm one day a week, usually Thursday. Savings banks (*Caixes d'Estalvis/Cajas de Ahorros*), which offer the same exchange facilities as banks, open 8am-2.30pm, Mon-Fri, and from Oct-May also 4.30-7.45pm Thur. They never open on Saturday. Banks and *caixes* are closed on public holidays.

Out-of-hours services

Outside normal hours there are bank exchange offices open at the **airport** (Terminals A and B, open 7am-11pm daily), **Barcelona-Sants** station (open 8am-10pm daily) and the **Estació de França** (open 8-10am, 7-9pm, daily). There are also several private bureau de change (*cambio*) offices, mostly in the Rambla, the city centre and Sants station. Some in the Rambla are open until midnight, or till 3am in the July-Sept summer season. *Cambios* do not charge commission, but their exchange rates are usually less favourable than bank rates. At the airport, Sants and outside several banks around Plaça Catalunya there are automatic cash exchange machines that accept notes in major currencies, so long as they are in good condition.

American Express

C/Rosselló 261 (93 217 00 70). Metro Diagonal/bus all routes to Passeig de Gràcia. **Open** 9.30am-6pm Mon-Fri; 10am-noon Sat. **Map D3**
Bureau de change, poste restante, card replacement, travellers' cheque refunds and an ATM for AmEx cards. Money transfers from AmEx offices anywhere in the world within 24 hours (charges paid by the sender).

Western Union Money Transfer

Loterías Manuel Martín
La Rambla 41 (93 412 70 41). Metro Drassanes/bus 14, 18, 38, 59, N4, N5. **Open** 9.30am-midnight Mon-Sat; 10am-midnight Sun. **Map C5**
The quickest, if not the cheapest, way of having money sent from abroad.
Branches: Mail Boxes *C/València 214 (93 454 69 83).* **Open** 9am-2pm, 4.30-8pm Mon-Fri; closes earlier in August; also at Avda Meridiana 316.

Credit cards

Major credit and charge cards are widely accepted in hotels, shops, restaurants and many other services (including Metro ticket machines, and pay-and-display parking machines in the street). With major cards you can also withdraw cash from most bank cash machines, which provide instructions in different languages at the push of a button. Exchange rates and handling fees are often more favourable than with cash or travellers' cheque transactions. Banks also advance cash against a credit card, but prefer you to withdraw the money directly from a cashpoint.

Card Emergencies

All lines have English-speaking staff and are open 24 hours daily.
American Express *(card emergencies 91 572 03 03/travellers' cheques freephone 900 99 44 26).*
Diner's Club *(93 302 14 28/24-hour helpline 91 547 40 00).*
MasterCard/Access/Eurocard/Visa *(93 315 25 12).*

Opening times

Most shops open from 9-10am to 1-1.30pm, and 4.30 to 8-9pm, Mon-Sat, although many do not reopen on Saturday afternoons. Markets open earlier, at 7-8am, and except for the central Boqueria market generally close by 3pm. Major stores, malls and a growing number of shops in the city centre are open all day 10am-9pm, Mon-Sat. These larger stores are also allowed to open on a few Sundays and holidays during the year, and every Sunday in the month up to Christmas. The only shops always open on Sundays are *pastisseries/ pastelerías* (cake shops), which to compensate usually close on Monday. For other shops open outside normal hours, *see page 166*.

In business, more and more offices now follow an 'intensive' schedule of 9am-6pm, Mon-Fri. The tendency is also growing towards staggered holidays, but many restaurants and shops still close up completely for all or part of August. Most (but not all) museums are open at weekends, but close for one day each week, usually Monday. They do not close in summer. For restaurant hours, *see page 118*.

Police & crime

In the 1980s Barcelona won a certain ill-fame as a black spot for petty theft and street crime. Nowadays, following a string of police and social measures, the incidence of street crime is very much less, but it's still advisable to be cautious in some areas. Violent muggings are now rare, but bag-snatching and pickpocketing still happen, above all in and around the lower Rambla and Plaça Reial.

Most street robberies, though, are aimed very much at the unwary, and could be avoided with a few simple precautions. Stated bluntly, the suggestions below may suggest a degree of paranoia, but they are really just a question of common sense and need not interfere with your enjoyment of your stay once taken on board:
• When sitting in a café, especially outside, **never** leave your bag on the floor, on the back of a chair, or on a chair where you cannot see it clearly. If in doubt, keep it on your lap.
• Wear shoulder bags pulled to the front, not at your back. Keep the bag closed and keep a hand on top of it.
• Avoid pulling out large-denomination notes to pay for things, especially in the street late at night; try not to get stuck with large notes when changing money.
• Be aware that street thieves often work in pairs or groups: one may ask you the time, start a conversation about football or whatever to distract you while his friend hovers behind you and then grabs your bag. This is often done very crudely so it's not hard to recognise. Ignore any sudden requests to shake your hand, as they will try and pull you toward them. Another variant is the 'chocolate' trick: someone stops you, says you have something on your back and offers to help clean it off. While you are rearranging your things, someone else makes off with your bag. Sometimes they actually will spray chocolate sauce, ketchup or similar gunk on your back. Either way it's best to ignore them, keep walking and if necessary clean it up later.

Police forces

Like most European countries Spain has several police forces. In Barcelona the most important are the local *Guàrdia Urbana*, in navy and pale blue, and the *Policía Nacional*, in black and white uniforms. Each force has its own set of responsibilities, although at times they overlap. The *Urbanos* are principally concerned with traffic and parking problems and various local regulations. The force with primary responsibility for dealing with crime are the *Nacionales*. The *Guardia Civil*, in military green, are responsible for policing inter-city highways, customs posts, and for guarding some government buildings, but are not often seen within Barcelona. The Catalan government police, the *Mossos d'Esquadra*, are gradually taking over several of the Guardia Civil's responsibilities.

Reporting a crime

If you are robbed or attacked you should report the incident as soon as possible to the special *Turisme-Atenció* station on the Rambla, a service set up by the *Guàrdia Urbana* in association with the *Policía Nacional* to provide information and assistance for foreign visitors in any kind of difficulty. Officers on duty can speak French, German, Italian and English. If you report a crime you will be asked to make an official statement (*denuncia*). It is of course unlikely that anything you have lost will be recovered, but you will need the *denuncia* to make an insurance claim. At other times or in other areas report the incident to the nearest *Policía Nacional* station (*Comisaría*), which are listed in the local phone book. For emergency phone numbers, *see p249*.

Turisme-Atenció
La Rambla 43 (93 301 90 60). Metro Liceu/bus 14, 18, 38, 59, N4, N5. **Open** 7am-10pm daily. **Map D5**

Lost passports

The loss or theft of a passport must be reported immediately to the police and your national consulate (*see p261*). If you lose a passport over a weekend and have to travel immediately, the consulate will charge for having to open the office specially and issue you with an emergency passport. Spanish authorities and most airlines are often prepared to let you out of the country even without one if you do not look suspicious and have other documents with you, including the police *denuncia* confirming the loss of your passport, but in such cases it's advisable to be at the airport in plenty of time. You will also have to explain the lack of documents at the other end.

Seasons

Barcelona is a coastal city and its weather, while rarely extreme, can often produce surprises, with cold snaps in mid-spring and occasional heavy rains at the height of summer. In general, though, the seasonal pattern is pretty clearly marked.

Spring *Average temperature 15°C (59°F)*. March is unpredictable, with bright sunny days still interspersed with rain or chilly winds, but clear skies become more consistent from early April. Easter Week is when locals finally cast off winter coats: café tables appear around the streets, and May is one of the most enjoyable of all times to be in Barcelona, warm enough to sit out through the night but never oppressive.
Summer *Average temperature 24°C (75°F)*. In early summer the weather is delicious, and Barcelona's streetlife is

at its most vibrant. The real heat hits from late July to mid-August; more of a problem than the actual temperature is the humidity, which can be very heavy and muggy. In August many locals still escape the city altogether: for the visitor this has the compen-sation that there is much less traffic, and the part-empty city has an atmosphere all of its own. Many businesses are closed, but recently fewer people have abandoned Barcelona for the whole month, and for those who are around there are events such as the *Festa Major* in **Gràcia**. Amid the heat, there may be brief, intense but refreshing thunderstorms.
Autumn *Average temperature 16°C (61°F)*. In September the weather is again beautiful, warm and fresh, and ideal for the beginning of the football season and a range of arts events leading up to Barcelona's biggest festival, **La Mercè**. In October the summer visibly 'breaks', sometimes with torrential rain. Pavement tables are mostly taken in by November, although some remain all year.
Winter *Average temperature 11°C (53°F)*. It can snow in Barcelona, but winter weather is more likely to be damp, with snatches of crisp sunshine. One of the busiest times of the year for business and the arts, but also with the **Christmas** and **Carnaval** festivities.

Tipping

There are no fixed rules, nor any expectation of a set ten per cent or more, and many locals tip very little. It is common to leave around five per cent for a waiter in a restaurant, up to and rarely ever over 500ptas, and people may also leave something in a bar, maybe part or all of the small change, according to how much they have had and the level of service. It's also usual to tip hotel porters, toilet attendants, and the ushers in the more traditional cinemas. In taxis, the usual tip is around five per cent, but more is given for longer journeys, or if the driver has helped with luggage.

Useful points

Electricity

The standard current in Spain is today 220v. A few old buildings still have 125v circuits, though, and it's advisable to check before using electrical equipment in hotels, parti-cularly in older, cheaper places.

Plugs are all of the two-round-pin type. The 220v current works fine with British-bought 240v products, with a plug adaptor. They are available locally at **El Corte Inglés** (*see chapter* **Shopping**). With US 110v appliances you will also need a current transformer.

Estancs/Estancos (tobacco shops)

The tobacco shop, usually known as an *estanc/estanco* and identified by a brown-and-yellow sign with the words *tabac* or *tabacos*, is a very important Spanish institution. First and foremost, as the name suggests, they supply cigarettes and every other kind of tobacco to the majority of the local population still devoted to the weed, but they are also the main places to buy postage stamps, and the only shops where you can obtain the official money vouchers (*papel de estado*) demanded by Spanish state bureau-cracy in all kinds of minor procedures. They also have sweets, postcards and a range of other less usual items.

Queuing

Catalans, like other Spaniards, have a highly developed queuing culture. In small shops and at market stalls people may not stand in line, but they are generally well aware of when it is their turn. Common practice is to ask when you arrive, to no one in particular, '*Qui es l'últim/la última?*' ('Who's last?'); see who nods back at you, and follow after them. Say '*jo*' ('me') to the next person who asks the same question.

Smoking

It's unusual to find non-smoking areas in restaurants or bars – especially cheaper ones – although smoking bans in cinemas, theatres and on trains are generally respected. Smoking is also banned throughout the Metro and FGC, but many people take this to mean on the trains only, and not the station platforms. For places to buy tobacco, *see chapter* **Shopping**.

Time

Local time is one hour ahead of British time, except at the beginning and end of summer. Clocks are changed earlier than in the UK, so that for a while the two usually coincide. For most of the year, though, when it's 6pm in Barcelona, it's 5pm in London, and midday in New York.

Water

Barcelona tap water is perfectly safe and drinkable, but has a rather minerally taste. By preference, most people drink bottled water, and if you ask for water in a restaurant you will automatically be served this unless you specifically request otherwise.

Vocabularies: Spanish...

Note that in Catalonia, still more than in the rest of Spain, this language is generally referred to as *castellano* (Castilian), rather than *español*. Like other Latin languages, it has different familiar and polite forms of the second person (you). Many young people now use the familiar *tú* form most of the time. For foreigners, though, it's always advisable to use the more polite *usted* with people you do not know, and certainly with anyone over 40. In the phrases listed here all verbs are given in the *usted* form. For help in making your way through menus, *see also pages 122-3*.

Spanish pronunciation

c, before an i or an e, and z are like th in thin
c in all other cases is as in cat
g, before an i or an e, and j are pronounced with a guttural h-sound that doesn't exist in English – like ch in Scottish loch, but much harder
g in all other cases is as in get
h at the beginning of a word is normally silent
ll is pronounced almost like a y
ñ is like ny in canyon
A single r at the beginning of a word and rr elsewhere are heavily rolled

Useful expressions

hello *hola*
hello (when answering the phone) *hola, diga*
good morning, good day *buenos días;* **good afternoon, good evening** *buenas tardes;* **good evening** (after dark), **good night** *buenas noches*
goodbye/see you later *adios/hasta luego*
please *por favor;* **thank you (very much)** *(muchas) gracias*
you're welcome *de nada*
do you speak English? *¿habla inglés?;* **I don't speak Spanish** *no hablo castellano*
I don't understand *no entiendo*
can you say that to me in Catalan, please? *¿me lo puede decir en Catalán, por favor?*
what's your name? *¿cómo se llama?*
speak more slowly, please *hable más despacio, por favor*

wait a moment *espere un momento*
Sir/Mr *señor (sr.);* **Madam/Mrs** *señora (sra.);* **Miss** *señorita (srta.)*
excuse me/sorry *perdón*
excuse me, please *oiga* (the standard way to attract someone's attention, politely; literally 'hear me')
OK/fine/(or to a waiter) **that's enough** *vale*
where is...? *¿dónde está...?*
why? *¿porqué?;* **when?** *¿cuándo?;* **who?** *¿quién?;* **what?** *¿qué?;* **where?** *¿dónde?;* **how?** *¿cómo?*
who is it? *¿quién es?*
is/are there any...? *¿hay...?*
very *muy;* **and** *y;* **or** *o*
with *con;* **without** *sin*
open *abierto;* **closed** *cerrado*
what time does it open/close? *¿a qué hora abre/cierra?*
pull (on signs) *tirar;* **push** *empujar*
I would like... *quiero...*(literally, 'I want'); **how many would you like?** *¿cuántos quiere?*
how much is it *¿cuánto es?*
I like me *gusta*
I don't like *no me gusta*
good *bueno/a;* **bad** *malo/a;* **well/badly** *bien/mal;* **small** *pequeño/a;* **big** *gran, grande;* **expensive** *caro/a;* **cheap** *barato/a;* **hot** (food, drink) *caliente;* **cold** *frío/a*
something *algo;* **nothing** *nada;* **more/less** *más/menos;* **more or less** *más o menos*
do you have any change? *¿tiene cambio?*
price *precio;* **free** *gratis;* **discount** *descuento;* **bank** *banco;* **alquilar to rent; (en) alquiler** (for) **rent,** *rental;* **post office** *correos;* **stamp** *sello;* **postcard** *postal;* **toilet** *los servicios*

Getting around

airport *aeropuerto;*
railway station *estación de ferrocarril/estación de RENFE* (Spanish railways)
Metro station *estación de Metro* **entrance** *entrada;* **exit** *salida*
car coche; bus *autobus;* **train** *tren*
a ticket *un billete;* **return** *de ida y vuelta;* **bus stop** *parada de autobus;* **the next stop** *la próxima parada*
excuse me, do you know the way to...? *¿oiga, señor/señora/etc, sabe cómo llegar a...?*
left *izquierda;* **right** *derecha;* **here** *aquí;* **there** *allí;* **straight on** *recto;* **to the end of the street** *al final de la calle;* **as far as** *hasta;* **towards** *hacia* **near** *cerca;* **far** *lejos*

Accommodation

do you have a double/single room for tonight/one week? *¿tiene una habitación doble/para una persona para esta noche/una semana?*
we have a reservation *tenemos reserva*
an inside/outside room *una habitación interior/exterior*
with/without bathroom *con/sin baño;* **shower** *ducha;*
double bed *cama de matrimonio;*
with twin beds *con dos camas*
breakfast included *desayuno incluido*
air-conditioning *aire acondicionado;* **lift** *ascensor;* **swimming pool** *piscina*

Time

morning *la mañana;* **midday** *mediodía;* **afternoon/evening** *la tarde;* **night** *la noche;* **late night** (roughly 1-6am) *la madrugada*
now *ahora;* **later** *más tarde*
yesterday *ayer;* **today** *hoy;* **tomorrow** *mañana;* **tomorrow morning** *mañana por la mañana*
at what time...? *¿a qué hora...?*
in an hour *en una hora;* **the bus will take 2 hours (to get there)** *el autobus tardará dos horas (en llegar)* **at 2** *a las dos;* **at 8pm** *a las ocho de la tarde;* **at 1.30** *a la una y media;* **at 5.15** *a las cinco y cuarto;* **at 22.30** *a veintidos treinta*

Numbers

0 *zero;* 1 *un, uno,una;* 2 *dos;* 3 *tres;* 4 *cuatro;* 5 *cinco;* 6 *seis;* 7 *siete;* 8 *ocho;* 9 *nueve;* 10 *diez;* 11 *once;* 12 *doce;* 13 *trece;* 14 *catorce;* 15 *quince;* 16 *dieciséis;* 17 *diecisiete;* 18 *dieciocho;* 19 *diecinueve;* 20 *veinte;* 21 *veintiuno;* 22 *veintidos;* 30 *treinta;* 40 *cuarenta;* 50 *cincuenta;* 60 *sesenta;* 70 *setenta;* 80 *ochenta;* 90 *noventa;* 100 *cien;* 200 *doscientos;* 1,000 *mil;* 1,000,000 *un millón*

Days, months & seasons

Monday *lunes;* **Tuesday** *martes;* **Wednesday** *miércoles;* **Thursday** *jueves;* **Friday** *viernes;* **Saturday** *sábado;* **Sunday** *domingo*
January *enero;* **February** *febrero;* **March** *marzo;* **April** *abril;* **May** *mayo;* **June** *junio;* **July** *julio;* **August** *agosto;* **September** *septiembre;* **October** *octubre;* **November** *noviembre;* **December** *diciembre*
spring *primavera;* **summer** *verano;* **autumn/fall** *otoño;* **winter** *invierno*

...and Catalan

Catalan is a Latin language that is readily comprehensible with a little knowledge of French or Spanish grammar. The extent to which Catalans expect visitors to speak it varies greatly (*see page 248*), but it is certainly useful to have some recognition of the language to be able to read signs, understand what's said to you and pronounce place names correctly. Catalan phonetics are significantly different from those of Spanish, with a wider range of vowels and soft consonants. Catalans use the familiar (*tu*) rather than the polite (*vosté*) forms of the second person very freely, but, again, for convenience verbs are given here in the polite form. For food and menu terms, *see pages 122-3*.

Catalan pronunciation: some basics

In Catalan, as in French but unlike in Spanish, words are run together, so *si us plau* (please) is more like *sees-plow*.
à at the end of a word (as in Francesc Macià) is an open **a** rather like when you say **ah**, but very clipped
ç, and **c** before an i or an e, are like a soft **s**, as in sit
c in all other cases is as in cat
unstressed **e**, in a plural such as cerveses (beers), or Jaume I, is a weak sound like centre or comfortable
g, before an i or an e, and **j** are pronounced like the **s** in pleasure; **tg** and **tj** are similar to the **dg** in badge
g after an i at the end of a word (Puig) is a hard **ch** sound, as in watch
g in all other cases is as in get
h beginning a word is normally silent
ll is like the **lli** in million
l.l the 'split double-l', most unusual feature of Catalan spelling, refers to a barely audible difference, a slightly stronger stress on a single **l** sound
o at the end of a word is like the **u** sound in flu; **ó** at the end of a word is similar to the **o** in tomato;
ò is like the **o** in hot
A single **r** beginning a word and **rr** are heavily rolled; **r** at the end of a word strengthens the previous vowel but is almost silent, so *carrer* (street) sounds like *carr-ay*
s at the beginning and end of words and **ss** between vowels are soft, as in sit

A single **s** between two vowels is a **z** sound, as in lazy
x is like the **sh** in shoe, except in the combination **tx**, which is like the **tch** in watch
y after an **n** at the end of a word or in **nys** is not a vowel but adds a nasal stress and a y-sound to the n

Things everyone here knows

please *si us plau;* **very good/great/OK** *molt bé*
hello *hola;* **goodbye** *adéu*
nothing at all/zilch *res de res* (said with both s silent)
price *preu;* **free** *gratuït/de franc;* **change, exchange** *canvi;* **llogar** *to rent;* **(de) lloguer** (for) *rent, rental*
entrance *entrada;* **exit** *sortida*
open *obert;* **closed** *tancat*
up with Barcelona FC *Visca el Barça* (corny as hell, but every foreign footballer who comes here has to say it, and it often gets a cheap laugh)

More expressions

hello (when answering the phone) *hola, digui'm*
good morning, good day *bon dia;* **good afternoon, good evening** *bona tarda;* **good night** *bona nit*
see you later *fins després*
thank you (very much) *(moltes) gràcies;* **you're welcome** *de res*
do you speak English? *parla anglès?;* **I'm sorry, I don't speak Catalan** *ho sento, no parlo català;* **I don't understand** *no entenc*
can you say it to me in Spanish, please? *m'ho pot dir en castellà, si us plau?;* **how do you say that in Catalan?** *com se diu això en Català?*
what's your name? *com se diu?*
Sir/Mr *senyor (sr.);* **Madam/Mrs** *senyora (sra.);* **Miss** *senyoreta (srta.);*
excuse me/sorry *perdoni/disculpi*
excuse me, please *escolti* (literally 'listen to me')
OK/fine *val/d'acord;* **enough** *prou*
how much is it *quant és?*
why? *perquè?;* **when?** *quan?;* **who?** *qui?;* **what?** *què?;* **where?** *on?;* **how?** *com?;* **where is...?** *on és...?;* **who is it?** *qui és?;* **is/are there any...?** *hi ha...?/n'hi ha de...?*
very *molt;* **and** *i;* **or** *o;*
with *amb;* **without** *sense*
I would like... *vull...* (literally, 'I want'); **how many would you like?** *quants en vol?;* **I don't want** *no vull*
I like *m'agrada;*
I don't like *no m'agrada*
good *bo/bona;* **bad** *dolent/a;*
well/badly *bé/malament;*

small *petit/a;* **big** *gran;* **expensive** *car/a;* **cheap** *barat/a;* **hot** (food, drink) *calent/a;* **cold** *fred/a*
something *alguna cosa;* **nothing** *res;* **more** *més;* **less** *menys;* **more or less** *més o menys*
toilet *el bany/els serveis/el lavabo*

Getting around

a ticket *un bitllet;* **return** *d'anada i tornada;* **card expired** (on Metro cards) *títol esgotat*
left *esquerra;* **right** *dreta;* **here** *aquí;* **there** *allí;* **straight on** *recte;* **at the** (street) **corner** *a la cantonada;* **as far as** *fins a;* **towards** *cap a;* **near** *a prop;* **far** *lluny;* **is it far?** *és lluny?*

Time

In Catalan quarter- and half-hours can be referred to as quarters of the next hour (so, 1.30 is two quarters of 2)
morning *el matí;* **midday** *migdia;* **afternoon** *la tarda;* **evening** *el vespre;* **night** *la nit;* **late night** (roughly 1-6am) *la matinada*
now *ara;* **later** *més tard;* **yesterday** *ahir;* **today** *avui;* **tomorrow** *demà;* **tomorrow morning** *demà pel matí*
at what time...? *a quina hora...?*
in an hour *en una hora;* **the bus will take two hours (to get there)** *l'autobús trigarà dues hores (en arribar)*
at 2 *a les dues;* **at 8pm** *a les vuit del vespre;* **at 1.30** *a dos quarts de dues/a la una i mitja;* **at 5.15** *a un quart de sis/a las cinc i quart;* **at 22.30** *a vint-i-dos-trenta*

Numbers

0 *zero;* 1 *u, un,una;* 2 *dos, dues;* 3 *tres;* 4 *quatre;* 5 *cinc;* 6 *sis;* 7 *set;* 8 *vuit;* 9 *nou;* 10 *deu;* 11 *onze;* 12 *dotze;* 13 *tretze;* 14 *catorze;* 15 *quinze;* 16 *setze;* 17 *disset;* 18 *divuit;* 19 *dinou;* 20 *vint;* 21 *vint-i-u;* 22 *vint-i-dos, vint-i-dues;* 30 *trenta;* 40 *quaranta;* 50 *cinquanta;* 60 *seixanta;* 70 *setanta;* 80 *vuitanta;* 90 *noranta;* 100 *cent;* 200 *dos-cents, dos-centes,* 1,000 *mil;* 1,000,000 *un milló*

Days, months & seasons

Monday *dilluns;* **Tuesday** *dimarts;* **Wednesday** *dimecres;* **Thursday** *dijous;* **Friday** *divendres;* **Saturday** *dissabte;* **Sunday** *diumenge*
January *gener;* **February** *febrer;* **March** *març;* **April** *abril;* **May** *maig;* **June** *juny;* **July** *juliol;* **August** *agost;* **September** *setembre;* **October** *octobre;* **November** *novembre;* **December** *desembre*
spring *primavera;* **summer** *estiu;* **autumn/fall** *tardor;* **winter** *hivern*

Getting Around

Barcelona's distinctive geometry, visible at a glance on any map, makes it easy for newcomers to get their bearings. At its core, running back from the port between Avda Paral.lel and the Ciutadella park, is a tight, lozenge-shaped mass of narrow streets that is old Barcelona, until the last century the entire city, divided through the middle by the great avenue of La Rambla (*Ramblas* in Castilian Spanish).

At the top of the Rambla is Plaça Catalunya, the city's centre and main hub of the Metro and bus networks. It also marks the beginning of the regular grid of the *Eixample*, the nineteenth-century 'extension' to the city. Beyond that, there are districts that were once separate villages, such as Sants or Gràcia, the new beach and port areas, and the two mountains of Montjuïc and Tibidabo. Equally evident are the great arterial avenues that run through the Eixample, the Gran Via de les Corts Catalanes (better known just as *Gran Via*), Avinguda Diagonal and Passeig de Gràcia. One oddity of the city is that, because it fits so neatly between Tibidabo and the sea, it is virtually never drawn on maps with north at the top. Due north is actually on the line of Avda Meridiana, as the name suggests.

Barcelona is a compact city that's easy to explore on foot. For longer journeys, a fast, safe Metro (underground/subway) system and buses enable you to get to most places in half an hour or less, during daytime.

A car, on the other hand, is often the slowest means of travelling within Barcelona. More handy in the traffic is a bike or moped, although a car is a great advantage for trips outside the city. For transport outside Barcelona, including Balearics ferries, *see page 224*. **Note: all local transport and taxi fares are subject to revision each January.**

Arriving & leaving

By air

Barcelona's **Aeroport del Prat**, rebuilt for 1992, is 12km (7½ miles) south of the city in Prat de Llobregat. Foreign airlines use Terminal A; Iberia international flights usually come in at Terminal B. In both there are tourist information desks, cash machines that take credit cards, and exchange offices (open 7.30am-10.45pm daily). From the airport there are three ways of getting into town: bus, train or taxi. For airport information, call **93 298 38 38**.

Aerobús

This special bus service is usually the most convenient means of getting to central Barcelona, if also the most expensive after taxis. Buses pick up outside all the terminals, and run to Plaça Catalunya with stops at Plaça d'Espanya and on the Gran Via. Buses to the airport also pick up at Sants railway station. Buses leave the airport every 15 minutes, 6.05am-midnight Mon-Fri (6.35am-midnight Sat, Sun); and in the opposite direction from Plaça Catalunya, 5.30am-11.15pm Mon-Fri (6am-11.20pm Sat, Sun). The trip takes about 30 minutes; a single ticket costs 475ptas. Two local buses also run between the airport and Plaça d'Espanya, the **EA** and **EN** (6.20am-2.40am daily from the airport; 7am-3.15am daily from Plaça d'Espanya). The fare is 140ptas, but the journey, with many stops, can take over an hour.

Airport trains

Getting to the airport station involves a walk that can be laborious with luggage in tow. To find it, walk out of the terminal buildings to the long bridge (with moving walkway) between Terminals A and B. All trains stop at four stations in Barcelona: Sants, Plaça Catalunya, Arc de Triomf and Clot-Aragó, all of which are also stops on the Metro system. Trains leave Prat at 13 and 43 minutes past each hour, 6.13am-10.43pm, and from Plaça Catalunya at 8 and 38 minutes past the hour, 6.08am-10.08pm, Mon-Fri. At weekends and on public holidays, timings vary slightly but there are still trains every half-hour. The journey takes 30 minutes (20 minutes to/from Sants), and the current fare is 305ptas (350ptas Sat, Sun, public holidays).

Taxis from the airport

The taxi fare to central Barcelona should be about 2,500-3,000ptas, including a 300ptas airport supplement, although fares are slightly higher after 10pm and at weekends (*see p258*). There is a minimum charge for trips to/from the airport of 1,500ptas, and also a supplement for larger items of luggage placed in the car boot. It's advisable to ignore any cab drivers who approach you inside the airport; take only the next cab in line at the ranks outside each terminal.

Airlines

British Airways *Passeig de Gràcia 85 (93 215 69 00/information & reservations 902 111 333). Metro Diagonal/bus 7, 16, 17, 22, 24, 28.* **Open** 9am-5pm Mon-Fri. **Credit** AmEx, DC, JCB, MC, V. **Map D3** This address may change at the end of 1998, but the information number will remain the same. *Airport office (93 379 44 68/baggage enquiries 902 131 024).* **Open** 7am-7pm daily.
Delta Airlines *Passeig de Gràcia 16, 5B (93 412 43 33). Metro Catalunya/bus to Plaça Catalunya.* **Open** 9am-2pm, 3-5.30pm Mon-Fri. **Credit** AmEx, DC, MC, V. **Map D4**
Iberia *C/Diputació 258 (information/ reservations 902 400 500). Metro Passeig de Gràcia/bus 7, 16, 17, 22, 24, 28.* **Open** 9am-6pm Mon-Fri. **Credit** AmEx, DC, MC, V. **Map D4**
TWA *C/Consell de Cent 360, 5° (93 215 81 88). Metro Girona/bus 7, 47, 50, 54, 56.* **Open** 9am-5pm Mon-Fri. **Credit** AmEx, DC, JCB, MC, $TC, V. **Map E3** *Airport office (93 298 33 21).* **Open** 8am-2pm daily.

By bus

Eurolines international coach services (information 93 490 40 00) from Britain and other parts of Europe stop or terminate at the **Estació d'Autobusos Barcelona-Sants**, by Sants railway station and Sants-Estació Metro. **Linebus** international services and most long-distance coaches from rural Catalonia and other parts of Spain operate from the **Estació d'Autobusos Barcelona-Nord** at C/Ali Bei 80, next to Arc de Triomf station on Metro line 1 (**Map E4**; general information 93 265 65 08; individual companies have their own phone lines). Some coaches stop at both. *See also page 224*.

By train

Most Spanish state railways (RENFE) long-distance trains terminate at or pass through the giant **Barcelona-Sants** station (**Map A3**). It's a little way from the centre, but has a Metro (Sants-Estació), at the junction of two lines, line 3 (green) and line 5 (blue). The green line is the most direct route to the centre. At Sants there are exchange facilities, a tourist information office, a hotel booking office and other services. Some international rail services from France do not stop in Sants but terminate at the lavishly restored 1920s **Estació de França**, near Ciutadella park and Barceloneta Metro. On many trains you can choose either station, and many also stop between the two at the central **Passeig de Gràcia** station, which can be the handiest place to get off. *See also page 224.*

RENFE information

General information 93 490 02 02. **Open** 7am-10pm daily. *International information & reservations (93 490 11 22).* **Open** 8am-8pm Mon-Fri.

Left luggage

All have automatic, coin-operated luggage lockers.

Luggage lockers

Aeroport del Prat *Terminal B.* **Open** 24 hours daily. **Rates** 635ptas per day.
Estació d'Autobusos Barcelona-Nord
C/Ali Bei 80. Metro Arc de Triomf/bus all routes to Arc de Triomf. **Open** 24 hours daily. **Rates** 300, 400, 600ptas per day.
Estació Marítima (Balearics Ferry Terminal) *Moll de Barcelona. Metro Drassanes/bus 18, 36, 38, 57, 64, N4, N6.* **Open** 8am-midnight daily. **Rates** 300, 500ptas per day.
Train Stations:
Open 4.30am-midnight daily. **Rates** 400, 600ptas per day. There are lockers at Sants, Passeig de Gràcia and França (6am-11pm only), but not at the smaller Barcelona stations.

Public transport

The Metro is generally the quickest, cheapest and most convenient way of getting around the city, although there are some 'holes' in the network – places without a well-located Metro station – notably around Plaça Francesc Macià, for which buses are more useful. Metro and local buses are run by the city transport authority (TMB), but one of the underground lines (from Plaça Catalunya to Reina Elisenda or Les Planes, with a branch to Avda Tibidabo) and the line from Plaça d'Espanya to Cornellà are not part of the Metro but run by Catalan government railways, the *Ferrocarrils de la Generalitat de Catalunya* or FGC, which also has services out into the surrounding countryside. However, the systems connect.

Fares & tickets: get your *targeta*

The basic fare for a single ticket on the Metro, FGC and buses is the same, currently 140ptas, and each trip costs the same no matter how far you travel. Unless you plan to make only a few journeys, however, buying single tickets is a waste of money: it's much better to buy one of the different kinds of multi-journey tickets or *targetes*. Some can be shared by two or more people, so long as one unit is cancelled on the card for each person travelling.

Most types of *targeta* are valid for Metro and FGC. There are no barriers between Metro lines; if you change between Metro and FGC (at Catalunya, Diagonal/Provença or Espanya) with a T2 or T50/30 *targeta* you must insert the card into the ticket machines again, but a unit will not be deducted (with single tickets, you must pay

twice). The outlets at which *targetes* can be bought vary, and they cannot be bought on buses. T2 and T50/30 cards can be bought by credit card from *Servi-Caixa* machines in savings banks (*see page 183*).

Targeta varieties

T1 Valid for ten trips on buses and Metro (but **not** the FGC). It costs 775ptas and is sold at Metro stations, transport offices, some news-stands and over the counter at most savings bank (*Caixa d'Estalvis*) offices.
T2 Valid for ten trips on Metro and FGC. Available from transport information offices, *Servi-Caixa* and ticket desks and automatic machines at Metro/FGC stations, for 760ptas.
T50/30 Gives 50 trips within any 30-day period on Metro and FGC.

From transport offices, *Servi-Caixa* and ticket desks and machines at Metro/FGC stations, for 3,175ptas.
T-Mes Unlimited travel on all three systems for one month, for 5,250ptas. Note, though, that this means a calendar month, not 30 days from date of purchase. With your first month's card you must obtain an identity card (which costs 200ptas and requires a photograph), available only at the TMB and FGC offices. In succeeding months you can renew your card at any Metro/FGC station.
T-Dia Unlimited travel for one person on Metro, FGC and buses for one day (575ptas). Sold at transport offices and Metro/FGC stations.
3 Dies Unlimited travel for one person on Metro and buses (but **not** the FGC) for three days, for 1,350ptas. Available from the same outlets as the T-Dia, plus the Plaça Catalunya and Sants tourist offices.
5 Dies The same, but valid for five days' travel, for 2,000ptas.
Aerobús+Bus+Metro The same as the previous two cards, but also including a return bus trip from and to the airport. Valid for three days (1,800ptas) or five (2,300ptas) and available at the airport.

For transport information call the city information line (010, *see page 251*). Barcelona also offers a choice of special sightseeing services and rides, from the 'Tourist Bus' to the Tibidabo tram; for these, and organised tours, *see chapter* **Sightseeing**.

TMB information office

Vestibule, Metro Universitat (93 318 70 74). **Open** 8am-8pm Mon-Fri. **Map C4**. **Branch offices**: Ronda Sant Pau 43; Vestibule, Metro Sagrada Família; Vestibule, Metro Sants-Estació.

FGC information

Vestibule, Catalunya FGC station (93 205 15 15). **Open** *Sept-July* 7am-9pm, *Aug* 8am-8pm, Mon-Fri. **Map D4**

Metro & FGC

The five Metro lines are identified by a number and a colour on maps and station signs. At interchanges, lines in a particular direction are indicated by the names of the stations at the end of the line, so you should know which they are when changing between lines. On FGC lines, note that some suburban trains do not stop at every station.

Metro hours

Mon-Thur 5am-11pm **Fri, Sat & days preceding public holidays** 5am-1am **Sun** 6am-midnight; **Public holidays midweek** 6am-11pm The FGC runs later, with a last train from Plaça Catalunya to Sant Cugat via Sarrià at 1.30am daily.

Boarding the train

At Metro and FGC stations, with a single ticket or a *targeta* from one of the automatic machines, you insert the ticket into the machine at the platform gate, which cancels one unit for each trip, and will reject expired tickets. Tickets are not checked or collected at station exits. Trains run about every 5 minutes on weekdays, and every 7-9 minutes after 9pm and at weekends. The Metro gets very crowded during peak hours (7.30-9.30am, 6-8.30pm), but trains are rarely excessively full at other times.

Buses

City bus stops are easy to find: a great many routes originate in or pass through Plaça Catalunya, Plaça Universitat and/or Plaça Urquinaona. Because of the many one-way streets buses often do not follow exactly the same route in both directions, but run along parallel streets.

Taking the bus

Most routes run from about 4.30am-11pm, Mon-Sat, with buses about every 10-15 minutes on each route. On Sundays and public holidays times vary a great deal, with no service at all on some routes. You board buses at the front, and get off through the doors at the middle or rear of the bus. Only single tickets can be bought on board. If you have a T1 *targeta*, insert it into the machine to the left of the doors as you board, which automatically clips off one unit. If you change buses you must pay again. With a travel card for one or more days, just show it to the driver. On suburban services fares increase on a zone system outside the city limits, and tickets must be bought on board.

Useful routes

22 Plaça Catalunya to Pedralbes via Passeig de Gràcia, C/Gran de Gràcia or Via Augusta, the *Tramvia Blau* tram, Sarrià and Pedralbes monastery.
24 C/Parlament to Carmel via Plaça Universitat, Plaça Catalunya, Passeig de Gràcia, C/Gran de Gràcia or Via Augusta and the Parc Güell (the best way to get from the centre to the park).
41 Vila Olímpica to Plaça Francesc Macià via the Ciutadella, Plaça Urquinaona, Plaça Catalunya and C/Calàbria or C/Viladomat.
45 Passeig Marítim, by the beach, to Horta via the Barceloneta, Via Laietana, Plaça Urquinaona, Passeig de Sant Joan and Hospital de Sant Pau.
64 Barceloneta to Pedralbes via Pla del Palau, Colom, Avda Paral.lel, Ronda Sant Antoni, Plaça Universitat, C/Aribau or C/Muntaner, Sarrià and the Pedralbes monastery.
66 Plaça Catalunya to Sarrià via Plaça Universitat, C/Aribau or C/Muntaner and Plaça Francesc Macià.

Night buses

There are 13 *Nitbus* (night bus) routes (N1-N6, N8-N14), which mostly operate from 10.30pm-4.30am nightly, with buses about every 30 minutes. All N routes originate in or pass through Plaça Catalunya, and some run out into surrounding towns such as Badalona or Castelldefels. Standard *targetes* are **not** valid on night buses; instead, you must buy single tickets (155ptas) or the special ten-trip night bus *targeta* (990ptas), both available only on board.

TombBus

A special shoppers' bus service (the name means 'round trip', nothing to do with graveyards) that runs between Plaça Catalunya and Plaça Pius XII on the Diagonal, 8am-9.30pm Mon-Fri, 9am-9.30pm Sat. Again, *targetes* cannot be used; single tickets cost 170ptas.

Local trains

For trips into the suburbs and surrounding towns there are, as well as buses, regional rail lines run by the FGC and RENFE. The two main FGC stations in Barcelona are in **Plaça Catalunya** (the same as for the FGC line within the city), for trains to Sabadell, Terrassa and the small towns immediately beyond Tibidabo, and **Plaça d'Espanya**, for services towards Hospitalet and Montserrat. The centre of the RENFE local network (signposted *Rodalies/ Cercanías* at mainline stations) is **Plaça Catalunya**. This is the main station for lines along the coast and toward the Pyrenees, although for some destinations, especially to the south-west, there may be more frequent services from the **Estació de Sants** or **Passeig de Gràcia**. Some towns are served by both systems. Fares vary according to zones. For more on rail services, *see page 224.*

Taxis

Barcelona's 11,000 black-and-yellow taxis are among its most distinctive symbols, and at most times easy to find. Fares are reasonable. Taxis can be hailed on the street when they show a green light on the roof, and a sign saying *Lliure/Libre* (Free) behind the windscreen. There are also taxi ranks at railway and bus stations, the main squares and at several other locations throughout the city. When giving instructions to the driver, it's a good idea to know the name of the district you are heading for and maybe a local landmark, as well as just the address. *See also page 256.*

Fares

Current official rates and supplements are shown inside each cab. The minimum fare at time of writing is 295ptas, which is what the meter should register when you first set off. The basic tariff applies 6am-10pm, Mon-Fri; after the first 1.75km fares increase at a rate per kilometre, or on a time rate at slow speeds. At all other times (including midweek public holidays) the additional rate is higher, although the initial charge remains the same. There are also supplements for each item of luggage larger than 55cm x 35cm x 35cm (100ptas), and for animals (125ptas). If you require a taxi to wait, you will be charged 2,200ptas per hour. Note also that taxi drivers are not officially required to carry more than 2,000ptas in change, and that very few accept credit cards.

Receipts & complaints

To obtain a receipt, ask for *'un rebut, si us plau/un recibo, por favor'*. If you have a complaint of any kind about a cab you must insist that the receipt is made out in full, with the time, beginning and end of the journey, details of the fare and driver's signature. Make a note, too, of the licence plate and taxi number, shown inside and on the rear doors of the cab. Call transport information on *010* to explain your complaint to them, and follow their instructions.

Phone cabs

The companies listed below take phone bookings 24 hours daily. Only some operators will speak English, but if you are not at a specific address give the name of a street corner (ie *Provença/Muntaner*), or a street and a bar or restaurant, where you want to wait. You'll be asked your name. Phone cabs start the meter from the moment the call is answered.
Barnataxi *(93 357 77 55)*; **Fono-Taxi** *(93 300 11 00)*; **Ràdio Taxi** *(93 225 00 00)*; **Servi-Taxi** *(93 330 03 00)*; **Taxi Groc** *(93 490 22 22)*; **Taxi Miramar** *(93 433 10 20)*; **Taxi Mòbil** *(93 358 11 11)*; **Tele-Taxi** *(93 212 22 22)*.

Driving

Driving in Barcelona can be wearing. Jams are frequent, parking space is at a premium, and tempers run short. Locals' devotion to their vehicles flies in the face of the sheer inefficiency of the private car as a means of getting around the city. It is a great asset, though, for trips further afield (*see chapter* **Trips out of Town**). If you do drive in or around Barcelona, points to bear in mind are listed here.
• You can drive in Spain with a valid licence from most other countries, but it is useful also to have an international driving licence, available in Britain from the AA and RAC.
• Keep your driving licence, vehicle documents and insurance Green Card with you at all times.

• It is obligatory to carry a warning triangle in your car, and to wear seat belts at all times on main highways and, officially at least, in cities.
• Children under 14 may not travel in the front of a car.
• Speeding fines imposed on motorways (*autopistes*) and other main highways, policed by the Guardia Civil and the Mossos d'Esquadra, are payable on the spot.
• Do not leave anything of value, including a car radio, in your car, and do not leave bags or coats in view on the seats. Take all of your luggage into your hotel when you park your car.
• In general drivers go as fast as they can, irrespective of the speed limit. At traffic lights at least two cars will follow through on the amber light as it changes between green and red. Do not therefore stop sharply when you see a light begin to change, as the car behind will not be expecting this and could easily run into you.
• When oncoming drivers flash their lights at you this means they will *not* slow down (contrary to British practice). On main highways, flashing of lights is usually a helpful warning that there is a speed trap ahead.

Spanish residents

If you become resident in Spain you must exchange your foreign licence for a Spanish one. The best way to do so is by becoming a member of the **RACC** (*see below*), who will take care of all the paperwork for you for about 14,000ptas. EU citizens do not need to take another driving test on exchanging their licences, but citizens of other countries may have to.

Car & motorbike hire

Car hire is quite expensive here, but price structures vary widely, and with a little effort you can probably find what you need. You must have a driving licence, and will need a credit card for a deposit or have to leave a large amount in cash. Check whether 16 per cent IVA (VAT) tax is included in the price.

Hertz

C/Tuset 10 (93 217 80 76).
Bus 6, 7, 15, 16, 17, 27, 33, 34.
Open 8am-2pm, 4-7pm, Mon-Fri; 9am-1pm Sat. **Credit** AmEx, DC, JCB, MC, V. **Map C2**
If you are 25 or over, you can hire a car here for 11, 500ptas per day, 43,400ptas per week or 15,500ptas for the weekend (including tax, insurance and unlimited mileage). With the international agencies you will often get a better deal if you book from your home country.
Branch: Airport *(93 298 36 40)*.
Open 7am-midnight daily.

Sprint

C/Melcior de Palau 161 (93 322 90 12). Metro Sants Estació/bus 43, 44, 109. **Open** 9am-2pm, 4-8pm, Mon-Fri. **Credit** AmEx, DC, MC, V. **Map A3**
Small car rental for weekends (pick-up Fri, return Mon am) for 20,000ptas including mileage, insurance, IVA. A week with unlimited mileage costs 6,000ptas a day, all inclusive. You must have had a licence for two years.

Vanguard

C/Londres 31 (93 439 38 80/ 93 322 79 51). Bus 15, 27, 41, 54, 66. **Open** 8am-2pm, 4-8pm, Mon-Fri; 9am-1pm Sat, Sun. **Credit** AmEx, DC, MC, V. **Map C2**
Good weekend deals in all ranges: from 13,800ptas incl IVA, insurance and unlimited mileage. Vanguard is also the best place to rent scooters and motorcycles. All-inclusive weekend rates run from 8,120ptas for a 50cc Honda to 26,680ptas for a Yamaha 600. You must be 18 and have had a licence for a year to hire a moped; 25 with three years' driving experience for larger bikes.

Breakdown services

If you are taking a car to Spain it is advisable to join a motoring organisation such as the AA or RAC in Britain, or the AAA in the US. They have reciprocal arrangements with the local equivalent, the **RACC**. Main dealers for most makes of car are in the local yellow pages under *Automòbils/Automóviles*.

RACC (Reial Automòbil Club de Catalunya)

C/Santaló 8 (200 33 11/24-hour breakdown assistance & medical emergencies 902 106 106). Bus 6, 7, 14, 15, 27, 30, 33, 34, 58, 64. **Open** *Phonelines* 24 hours daily. *Office Sept-May* 9am-2pm, 4.30-7.30pm, Mon-Fri; *Aug-mid-Sept* 9am-2.30pm Mon-Fri; *24, 31 Dec , 5 Jan* 9am-2pm. **Map C2**
The RACC has English-speaking staff and will send immediate assistance if you have a breakdown. Outside Barcelona, call the same emergency number, but you may be referred to a local number. The RACC also provides a range of other services for foreign drivers at low prices, and for free or at a discount for members of affiliated organisations

Midas

Via Augusta 81-83 (93 217 81 61). FGC Gràcia/bus 16, 17, 25, 27. **Open** 8am-8pm Mon-Fri; 9am-2pm Sat. **Credit** AmEx, DC, MC, V. **Map D2**
An exhaust, brakes and filter repairer, with while-you-wait service. There are 14 more branches in Barcelona.

Neumáticos Roger de Flor SA

C/Roger de Flor 133 (93 231 66 16).
Metro Tetuan/bus 6, 7, 18, 51, 54, 55, 56, 62. **Open** 9am-9pm Mon-Fri; 10am-2pm Sat, Sun. **Credit** V. **Map E4**
A quick-service tyre repair workshop.

Vidrauto

C/Mallorca 342 (93 458 36 44/93 459 03 64). Metro Verdaguer/bus 6, 15, 33, 34, 55. **Open** 9am-1.30pm, 3.30-8pm, Mon-Fri; 9am-1.30pm, 4-7.30pm, Sat. **Credit** AmEx, MC, V. **Map E3**
Can replace all kinds of autoglass.

Parking

Parking is never easy in central Barcelona. The Municipal Police readily give out tickets (which many people never pay), or tow cars away, which leaves you with no option. Be careful not to park in front of doorways with the sign *Gual Permanent*, indicating an entry with 24-hour right of access. In some parts of the old city, notably La Ribera and the Barri Gòtic, not just parking but also entering with a car is banned to non-residents for much of the day. Large signs indicate when this is so.

Pay & display areas (*Zones Blaves*)

Many streets in the central area and the Eixample are pay-and-display areas (*Zones Blaves*, Blue Zones), with parking spaces marked in blue on the street. Ticket machines will be nearby. Parking restrictions in these areas apply only 9am-2pm, 4-8pm, Mon-Sat. During these times you are allowed to park for a maximum of two hours; the charges are 60ptas for 15 minutes, 125ptas for 30 minutes, 255ptas for one hour and 510ptas for two hours. If you overstay your time and are given a penalty ticket you can cancel the fine by paying an additional 500ptas. To do so, press the button *Anul.lar denúncia* in the ticket machine, insert 500ptas and take the receipt that then comes out. The machines accept credit cards (AmEx, MC, V), but do not give change.

Car parks

Central car parks *C/Àngels, Plaça dels Àngels, Avda Francesc Cambó, Plaça Gal.la Placídia, Moll de la Fusta, Avda Paral.lel, C/Urgell .*
Open 24 hours daily.
The 23 municipal underground *parkings* are indicated by a white 'P' on a blue sign, with another to indicate if spaces are available: *Lliure/Libre* means there are, *Ple/Lleno* means full. Rates vary slightly, at around 110-120ptas per half-hour and 220-240ptas per hour. You can also buy special payment cards, usable at any city car park, valid for periods from ten hours (2,000ptas) to 100 hours (16,500ptas). You are especially advised to use a car park if you have a car with foreign plates.

Metro-Park

Plaça de les Glòries. **Open** 24 hrs daily. **Credit** AmEx, DC, MC, V. **Map F4**
The Metro-Park is a special car park service on a park-and-ride principle, and can be recommended to anyone coming in to Barcelona with a car from the coast for a day, and so not really needing it while they are here. For 650ptas you can leave your car for a whole day, and receive a card giving unlimited travel for one person for one day on Metro and city buses (but not the FGC). For 2,700ptas you can leave your car every day for a week. The car park is in the middle of Plaça de les Glòries, conveniently at the junction of the Diagonal, Meridiana and the Gran Via, and by Glòries Metro, on line 1.

Towing away & car pounds

(092/93 274 32 44).
Credit AmEx, DC, MC, V.
If your car has been towed away by the Municipal Police they will leave a yellow sticker on the pavement near where you left it. Call either number (open 24 hours) and quote your car number to be told which of the city car pounds your vehicle has gone to. Staff do not normally speak English. It will cost 14,600ptas to recover your vehicle during the first four hours after it was towed away, plus 245ptas for each additional hour after that.

Petrol

Most stations (*gasolineres*) now have unleaded fuel (*sense plom/ sin plomo*) as well as regular (*super*). Diesel fuel is *gas-oil*.

24-hour petrol stations

Several have round-the-clock hours.
Raval/Poble Sec: Campsa Avda Paral.lel 37, corner of C/Palaudaries. **Credit** AmEx, MC, V. **Map C5**
Poble Sec/Plaça d'Espanya: Total Avda Paral.lel 140, corner of C/Parlament. **Credit** MC, V. **Map B5**
Eixample: Cepsa C/Casanova 89, corner C/Aragó. **Credit** MC, V. **Map C3**
Near Plaça Macià: Cepsa C/Comte d'Urgell 230, junction Avda Sarrià. **Credit** AmEx, MC, V. **Map C2**
Arc de Triomf: Cepsa C/Roger de Flor 58, near Estació del Nord. **Credit** AmEx, V. **Map E4**
Clot: BP C/Clot 2, junction with Avda Meridiana heading north. **Credit** MC, V (no shop).
Ronda de Dalt: BP Via Favència 75-121, near Parc de la Guineueta, on north side. **Credit** MC, V.

Riding a bike in Barcelona might seem foolhardy, but several cycle routes (*carrils bici*) have been established, particularly around the Ciutadella, the port, along the Diagonal and from Sants to Montjuïc. They are popular for recreational cycling, if less for everyday transport. The beach-side routes, also, are now used just as much by rollerbladers. More information on these routes is available from tourist offices and the city sports information service (*see page 213*).

Bike & skate hire

Bike rental shops tend to be clustered near the Ciutadella park and the old port, or the Olympic port and the beach, the most popular areas for weekend cycling. At week-ends, some shops by the Ciutadella also rent bikes and *bicicars*, four-wheelers with side-by-side seats, just for use in the park. Many shops near the beach now also hire out **rollerblades** and equipment in answer to a booming demand.

Un Cotxe Menys

C/Esparteria 3 (93 268 21 05). Metro Barceloneta/bus 14, 16, 17, 39, 45, 51. **Open** 10am-2pm, 5-8pm, Mon-Fri; 10am-3pm Sat, Sun, holidays. **No credit cards**. **Map E5**
The name means 'One car less', and this La Ribera shop offers an imaginative range of services. Bike hire is 600ptas per hour; 1,500ptas a half day; 2,000ptas per full day. Also guided cycle tours (*see chapter* **Sightseeing**).

Icària Esports

Avda Icària 180 (93 221 17 78). Bus 41,71. **Open** *Oct-Mar* 4.30-11pm Mon-Sat; 10.30am-1.30pm, 4.30-11pm, Sun, holidays; *Apr-Sept* 10.30am-1.30pm, 4.30-11pm, Mon-Fri; 10.30am-2.30pm, 4.30-11pm, Sat, Sun. **No credit cards**. **Map F5**
Mountain bikes from this Vila Olímpica shop cost 650ptas per hour, 2,000ptas a half-day, 3,000ptas a full day. Also street bikes, tandems and rollerblades with equipment (650ptas per hour). Opening hours may vary in winter.

...al punt de trobada

C/Badajoz 24 (93 225 05 85). Metro Llacuna/bus 36, 92. **Open** 8am-9.30pm daily. **No credit cards**.
Also near the Vila Olímpica and the beach: mountain bikes cost 500ptas per hour, 1,500ptas a half-day and 2,500ptas a whole day. Rollerblades are 500ptas per hour, 1,500ptas for a half-day, with discounts on weekdays.

Resources

Computer services

For quick access to cyberspace, the best places are Internet cafés (*see chapter* **Cafés & Bars**).

Cinet

Passeig Lluis Companys 23 (93 268 26 40/fax 93 268 07 00/e-mail info@cinet.es). Metro Arc de Triomf/ bus 19, 39, 40, 41, 42, 55, 141. **Open** 9am-2pm, 4-7pm, Mon-Fri. **Map E5**
Internet service provider who can connect you directly or via the phone company's *Infovia* system. Also consultancy services and PC and modem hire.

Data Rent

C/Muntaner 492, 5° 4° (93 434 00 26/fax 93 418 78 83). FGC Pàdua/bus 16, 58, 64, 74. **Open** *Oct-May* 9am-2pm, 4-7pm, Mon-Fri; *June-Sept* 8am-3pm Mon-Fri. **Map C1**
PCs and occasionally Macs, printers and presentation equipment for hire.

Consulates

A full list of consulates in Barcelona is in the phone book under *Consulats/Consulados*. Outside office hours all have answerphones that will give you an emergency contact number. There is no Canadian consulate in Barcelona; Canadian citizens in difficulties should contact the embassy in Madrid on 91 431 43 00. For more on what to do if you lose a passport, *see page 253*.

Consulates

American Consulate *Passeig Reina Elisenda 23 (93 280 22 27). FGC Reina Elisenda/bus 22, 64, 75.* **Open** 9am-12.30pm, 3-5pm, Mon-Fri.
Australian Consulate *Gran Via Carles III 98 (93 330 94 96). Metro Maria Cristina/bus 59, 70, 72, 75.* **Open** 10am-noon Mon-Fri. Closed Aug.
British Consulate *Avda Diagonal 477 (93 419 90 44). Bus all routes to Plaça Francesc Macià.* **Open** *end Sept-mid-June* 9.30am-1.30pm, 4-5pm, Mon-Fri; *mid-June-mid-Sept* 9am-2pm Mon-Fri. **Map C2**
Irish Consulate *Gran Via Carles III 94 (93 491 50 21). Metro Maria Cristina/bus 59, 70, 72, 75.* **Open** 10am-1pm Mon-Fri.
New Zealand Consulate *Travessera de Gràcia 64, 4° 2° (93 209 03 99). FGC Gràcia/bus 16, 17, 27, 58, 64, 127.* **Open** *for appointments* 9.30am-1.30pm, 5-6.30pm, Mon-Fri. **Map C2**

Courier services

Estació d'Autobusos Barcelona-Nord

C/Ali Bei 80 (information 93 265 65 08/courier service 93 232 43 29). Metro Arc de Triomf/bus 40, 42, 141. **Open** 7am-7.45pm Mon-Fri; 7am-12.45pm Sat. **No credit cards**. **Map E4**
Inexpensive service at the bus station for sending parcels on scheduled buses to towns within Spain. Pick-up and delivery provided in larger towns.

Eurocity

C/Milanesado 15 (93 203 95 04/fax 93 205 45 71). FGC Tres Torres/bus 16, 70, 72, 74, 94. **Open** 8.30am-7pm Mon-Fri. **No credit cards**.
An efficient local courier company. The basic charge to send a package within Barcelona is 1,150ptas for non-account customers. Also offers national and international services.

UPS

C/Miguel Hernández, corner of C/Indústria, Polígon Industrial Zona Franca, L'Hospitalet de Llobregat (freephone 900 10 24 10/fax 93 263 39 09). **Open** 7am-8pm Mon-Fri. **Credit** AmEx, MC, V.
Reliable international courier company with competitive rates. You must call by 5pm for pick-up at your door by 7pm and next-day delivery. The depot is in the Zona Franca industrial area, and if you need to drop off or collect in person it's hard to get there except by car or cab.

Health

All visitors can obtain emergency health care through the local national health service, the *Seguretat Social/Seguridad Social*. EU citizens are entitled to basic medical attention for free if they have an E111 form (if you can get an E111 sent or faxed within four days, you are still exempt from charges). Many medicines will be charged for. In non-emergency situations short-term visitors will usually find it quicker to use private travel insurance rather than the state system. Similarly, non-EU nationals with private medical insurance can also make use of state health services on a paying basis, but other than in emergencies it will be simpler to use a private clinic.

If you become resident and register formally with the state *Seguretat Social/Seguridad Social* (*see pages 261-2*) you will be allocated a doctor and a local health clinic. Further information on all health services is available from the city health institute, or the 010 information line (*see page 251*).

Institut Municipal de la Salut

Plaça Lesseps 1 (93 415 00 66). Metro Lesseps/bus 22, 24, 25, 27, 28, 31, 32, 74. **Open** 8.30am-8.30pm Mon-Fri. **Map D1**
The city health administration also operates a phoneline (not English-speaking) for information on local health services or related matters.

Emergencies

In a medical emergency the best thing to do is go to the casualty (signed as *urgències*) department of any of the main hospitals. All are open 24 hours daily. In the central area, go to the **Clínic** or the **Perecamps**. If necessary, call an ambulance on **061**.

Hospitals

Centre d'Urgències Perecamps *Avda Drassanes 13-15 (93 441 06 00). Metro Drassanes/bus 14, 18, 38, 59, N4, N5, N6.* **Map C5**
A centrally-located specialised clinic dealing only in emergencies.
Hospital Clínic *C/Casanova 143 (93 227 54 00). Metro Hospital Clínic/bus 14, 54, 58, 59, 63, 64, 66, N3, N8.* **Map C3**
The main city-centre hospital, in the *Esquerra* (left side) of the Eixample.
Hospital de la Creu Roja de Barcelona *C/Dos de Maig 301 (93 433 15 51). Metro Hospital de Sant Pau/bus 15, 19, 20, 25, 45, 47, 50, 51, N5.* **Map F3**
Hospital del Mar *Passeig Marítim (93 221 10 10). Metro Ciutadella/bus 10, 36, 45, 59, 71, 92.* **Map E6**
This hospital has a special clinic for infectious diseases, including AIDS.
Hospital de la Santa Creu i Sant Pau *C/Sant Antoni Maria Claret 167 (93 291 90 00). Metro Hospital de Sant Pau/bus 15, 19, 20, 25, 45, 47, 50, 51, N1, N5.* **Map F2**

Directory

Living & working in Barcelona

During the 1990s people from other European Union countries have been able to work in an increasingly wide range of fields in Barcelona – medicine, the drinks trade, architecture, publishing. However, while the Catalan economy has remained quite healthy, in Spain as a whole unemployment is high, close to 20 per cent, and for foreigners some kinds of jobs are still not easy to come by. If you've just arrived and don't have any specialised skills, your best chances of finding work are still in the old standbys, English teaching and/or translation. Bear in mind, though, that Barcelona is one of the world's most popular destinations for EFL teachers, and the market is increasingly saturated. Alternatives may well be better paid and give you more freedom of action.

If you are looking for teaching work it is advisable to have a relevant qualification, preferably the RSA Diploma. If you get work in a school, it will usually only be on a nine-month contract to begin with. There is always private teaching work, although so many people offer private classes in Barcelona nowadays that rates can be very low; try not to accept anything under 2,000ptas an hour. To get your first classes, try putting up ads on the noticeboards at the **British Institute**, C/Amigó 83 (93 209 63 88), in English-language bookshops (*see chapter* **Shopping**) or at the various Barcelona universities, or ask around among English teachers.

If you stay and work here there are some bureaucratic hurdles to negotiate; you can maybe ignore them for a while, but in the long run this will be counter-productive. If you come to work for a company having been contracted in your country of origin, these procedures should be dealt with by your employer.

Bureaucracy

EU citizens working for a company/*Cuenta ajena*

In the last few years paperwork has become at least a little easier for EU citizens working in Spain. Work permits as such no longer exist, but you must become a resident to work legally (you will also require a *NIE/NIF, see below* **EU citizens working freelance**). To become a resident you will need to have a contract or a firm offer of work (which can be for only three hours a week and with no stipulated duration) and make out an application at the special office for foreigners' affairs at the **Delegación del Gobierno** (*see below*). There are separate sections for *nacionales comunitarios* (EU) and *no-comunitarios*; for *comunitarios* procedures normally go through in a day or so.

The office will also require two photocopies of the information pages of your passport and four photographs, and around 850ptas in *papel de estado*, official money vouchers, which must be purchased in *estancs*, tobacco shops. Keep copies of all documents submitted. You may also be asked for a medical certificate and/or proof of sufficient funds. You will normally be given a Type A residency permit, valid for 12 months and not automatically renewable. This ties you to the company and business sector for which you have registered, and in theory you should leave the country on its expiry. If you reapply successfully at that time, you will be issued a Type C permit, which lasts for five years and is renewable.

EU citizens working freelance/*Cuenta própia*

To work freelance, as a *trabajador autónomo/a* or *trabajador por cuenta própia*, an essential first step is to obtain a *Número de Identificación Fiscal* (*NIF*, tax code), which as a foreigner will be the same as your *Número de Identificación de Extranjero* (*NIE*). You will find it very difficult to do any consistent business without one. You will also find it virtually indispensable to contract the services of a *gestor* (*see pxxx*) to advise you on legal procedures and tax; without one, you will waste both time and money. A *NIF/NIE* can be obtained from the Delegación del Gobierno (*see below*), your local Tax Office (*Delegación de Hacienda*), the address of which is in the phone book, or through your *gestor*, which is the easiest way to do it. Once you have this number you can open a bank account, request a telephone line, be paid by other businesses (the most essential reason for having one) and so on.

Local clinics (*Centres d'Assistència Primària*)

A *CAP* is a lower-level local health centre where you will receive first aid and, if necessary, be sent on to a hospital. All are open 24 hours daily.
Central area:
Casc Antic *C/Comtal 24 (93 310 14 21/93 310 50 98).* **Map D4**
Drassanes *Avda Drassanes 17-21 (93 329 44 95/93 329 39 12).* **Map C5**
Esquerra de l'Eixample *C/Manso 19 (93 325 28 00).* **Map B4**

Raval/Plaça Universitat *C/Torres i Amat 8 (93 301 24 82/93 301 24 24).* **Map C4**

Private health care

Centre Mèdic Assistencial Catalonia (Dr Frances Lynd)

C/Provença 281, baixos (93 215 37 93). Metro Diagonal, FGC Provença/bus 20, 21, 43, 44. **Open** 8am-8pm Mon-Fri. **Credit** V. **Map D3**

Dr Lynd is a British doctor who has practised in Barcelona for many years. She is at this surgery 3.30-6.30pm Wed; at other times, call to make an appointment and she will ring you back.

AIDS/HIV

There are facilities for AIDS/HIV treatment at all the main hospitals, and a special clinic at the **Hospital del Mar**.

Next stop is also in the Tax Office: at the *Actividades Económicas* desk fill in form 845, specifying which sector (*Enseñanza*, for teaching) you wish to work in, and form 036, the *Declaración Censal*, and keep copies of both. Next, officially, is a visit to a local Social Security office (*Delegación de Seguridad Social*) to say you want the *alta como autónomo*; this is one point where the advice of a *gestor* is particularly important, as the contributions you are theoretically obliged to pay can be very high (30,000ptas per month), and he/she can suggest alternatives. As an *autónomo* you will have a Social Security number, and will have to make annual tax declarations. With this initial documentation you can apply for a *Cuenta própia* residency permit at the Delegación del Gobierno, with the same information (passport, proof of earnings) as for the *Cuenta ajena* permit (*see above*). If you are looking for work in areas other than teaching, with a *NIF* you can also use the Generalitat employment service (*Servei Català de Col.locació*, 902 221 111/ 902 221 044/93 228 57 57).

Non-EU citizens

In parallel with the relaxation of access to Spain for other EU nationals there has come a more restrictive situation for people from other parts of the world. Americans and Antipodeans will never feel the presence of the police in the same way that Algerians do, but the state still likes to remind people that its immigration laws are not to be taken lightly with, for example, occasional nationality checks on buskers on the Rambla, and deportations of those who are held to have overstayed their tourist status.

Officially, first-time residency applicants need a special visa, for which you must apply at the nearest Spanish consulate in your home country, although you can start the ball rolling in Spain if you don't mind making at least one trip back

home. Basic documents needed are a contract or firm offer of work from a registered Spanish company, a medical certificate and a certificate of good conduct from your local police force. You must present these with several passport-style photos and translated copies of relevant qualifications to the consulate, who pass them on to the Labour Ministry in Madrid. If they approve them, the consulate will then issue your special visa (this can all take six months). If you apply to work freelance or start your own business, procedures are slightly different and you will also be asked for proof of income. Once back in Spain the procedures for applying for residency are similar to those for Europeans, but you also need a work permit, obtained from the **Dirección General del Trabajo**. One way some long-stayers get round paperwork is by acquiring an EU passport: Ireland and Italy are the most generous in granting them to those who show grandparental links with the mother country.

Students

Students who stay in Spain over three months, including EU nationals, also officially require a residence permit, and those enrolled on full-time courses might find it creates difficulties if they do not get one. To do so, you will need to show the Delegación del Gobierno a confirmation of enrolment on a recognised course; confirmation of income for the duration of the course (estimated at around 800,000ptas for a year); and confirmation of health insurance status, private or public.

Delegación del Gobierno

Avda Marqués de l'Argentera 2 (93 482 03 00/93 482 03 11). Metro Barceloneta/bus 14, 16, 17, 36, 39, 45, 57, 59, 64. **Open** 9am-2pm Mon-Fri. Still known to most people by its old name of *Gobierno Civil*, the foreigners' section has a separate entrance. To avoid the biggest queues, go on a Friday.

Dirección General del Trabajo

Travessera de Gràcia 303-311 (93 401 30 00). Metro Joanic/bus 21, 39, 55. **Open** 9am-2pm Mon-Fri. Shorter queues at 9am.

Renting a flat

Since the 1992 boom passed by it has been easier to find vacant flats in Barcelona on reasonable terms. For property ads, look in *La Vanguardia* (under *alquileres*), or small-ad magazines (*see chapter* **Media**); otherwise, just look for signs headed *es lloga* (Catalan) or *se alquila* in apartment-block doorways. The fundamental element in determining rights and obligations as a tenant is the individual rental contract (*contracte de lloguer/contrato de alquiler*) signed by you and the landlord. They vary a great deal, and before signing it's important to be clear on the exact conditions in the contract, particularly regarding responsibility for repairs; if in doubt, have it checked by a *gestor*.

Contracts of over 12 months' duration are subject to an annual rent increase of not more than the official inflation rate, the *IPC* (*Índice de Precios al Consumo*, retail price index, published in the press). Landlords, though, may be keen to keep good tenants, and might be willing to waive the first year's increase, or make other concessions. For residents rent paid is tax deductible, provided you have all the necessary receipts.

Alternative medicine

Centre de Medicina Integral

Plaça Urquinaona 2, 3er 2na (93 318 30 50). Metro Urquinaona/bus all routes to Plaça Urquinaona. **Open** *information* 10am-1pm, 4-8pm, Mon-Fri. Closed August. **Map D4**
Acupuncture, homeopathy, chiropractics and other forms of complementary medicine. There are some English-speaking practitioners on the staff.

Contraception & women's health

Condoms (*condons/ condones*) and other forms of contraception are available in most pharmacies, although there is a very small number of pharmacists in the city that still refuse to stock them on religious grounds.

Specialised clinics

Ambulatori les Drassanes/Centre de Planificació Familiar
Avda Drassanes 17-21 (93 329 44 95). Metro Drassanes/bus 36, 57, 64, 91. **Open** 9am-2pm Mon-Fri. **Map C5**
A specialised family planning clinic that's within the large Drassanes CAP, but run separately. The all-women staff are friendly and helpful, if frequently overworked.

Centre Jove d'Anticoncepció i Sexualitat *C/La Granja 19-21 (93 415 10 00). Metro Lesseps/bus 24, 31, 32, 74.* **Open** *approx Oct-May* 10am-7pm Mon; noon-7pm Tue-Thur; 10am-2pm Fri; *June-Sept* 10am-5pm Mon-Thur; 10am-2pm Fri. Closed Easter & Aug. **Map E1**
A family planning centre aimed at young women, with very friendly staff and a tolerant attitude towards questions of social security status and residency papers.

Dentists

Dental treatment is not covered by EU reciprocal agreements, so private rates, which can be costly, apply.

Centre Odontològic de Barcelona

C/Calàbria 251, baixos (93 439 45 00). Metro Entença/bus 41. **Open** 9am-9pm Mon-Fri; 9am-2pm Sat. **Credit** DC, MC, V. **Map B3**
Well-equipped clinics providing a complete range of dental services. Several of the staff speak English.
Branch: Institut Odontològic de la Sagrada Família *C/Sardenya 319, baixos (93 457 04 53). Metro Sagrada Família/bus 19, 50.* **Open** 9am-1pm, 3-8pm, Mon-Fri.

Pharmacies

Pharmacies (*farmàcies*) are signalled by large green, usually flashing, crosses, and are plentiful throughout the city. They are normally open 9am-1.30pm, 4.30-8pm, Monday to Friday, and 9am-1.30pm on Saturdays. At other times a duty rota operates: every pharmacy has a list of *farmàcies de guàrdia* (duty pharmacies) for that day posted outside the door. Those marked in blue are open all day 9am-10pm, and 9am-1.30pm on Sundays.

Those marked in red are on permanent emergency duty (*servei d'urgència*) for the full 24 hours. This list is also published in local newspapers, and information is available on the 010 and 098 phonelines (recorded message, in Spanish only, 24 hours daily). Note that at night duty pharmacies often appear to be closed, and it's necessary to knock on the shutters to be served.

Helplines

AIDS Helpline

(93 339 87 56). **Open** 9am-5.30pm, *June-mid-Sept* 8am-3pm, Mon-Fri. Has some English-speaking staff.

Alcoholics Anonymous

(93 317 77 77). **Open** 11am-1pm, 5-9pm, Mon-Fri, Sat, Sun; answerphone at other times. There are several English-speakers among the local AA groups.

Telèfon de l'Esperança

(93 414 48 48). **Open** 24 hours daily. A privately funded local helpline that caters for a wide range of needs, from psychiatric to legal. English sometimes spoken, but it's not guaranteed.

Libraries

Barcelona has a good network of public libraries: the *Guia del Ciutadà*, consultable at city information offices, has a list.

Ateneu Barcelonès

C/Canuda 6 (93 318 86 34). Metro Catalunya/bus all routes to Plaça Catalunya. **Open** 9am-10.45pm daily. **Map D5**
Anyone spending time in Barcelona might consider joining this venerable cultural and philosophical society founded in 1836, which has the best private library in the city, open every day of the year, including Christmas. Initial membership costs 20,000ptas (payable in instalments), and the subsequent fee is 2,000ptas per month; there are special rates for anyone living more than 45km (28 miles) from the city. As a member you gain access to its Mediterranean-gentlemen's club atmosphere and the deliciously peaceful interior garden patio and bar.

Biblioteca de Catalunya

C/Hospital 56 (93 317 07 78). Metro Liceu/bus 14, 18, 38, 59. **Open** 9am-8pm Mon-Fri; 9am-2pm Sat. **Map C5**
The largest of the city's libraries, the Catalan national collection, housed in the Medieval **Hospital de la Santa Creu** and with a wonderful stock reaching back centuries. Readers' cards are required, but one-day visitors are normally allowed in on presentation of a passport, and full cards are not hard to obtain. It's not open-access, and book delivery is slow. Further information and an on-line catalogue are on the Internet at *www.gencat/es/bc*.

Institut Municipal d'Història/Ca de l'Ardiaca

C/Santa Llúcia 1 (93 318 11 95). Metro Liceu, Jaume I/bus 17, 40, 45. **Open** 9am-8.45pm Mon-Fri; 9am-1pm Sat; *Aug* 9am-2pm Mon-Fri. **Map D5**

The city newspaper archive, with an exhaustive stock of Barcelona's press, many papers from other parts of Spain, and extensive book, map, graphics and document collections. It occupies the **Ca de l'Ardiaca** in front of the Cathedral, with one of the prettiest patios in the Barri Gòtic. A reader's card is required, for which you will need two photos.

Mediateca

Centre Cultural de la Fundació la Caixa, Passeig Sant Joan 108 (93 458 89 07). Metro Verdaguer/bus 6, 15, 33, 34, 55. **Open** 11am-8pmTue-Fri; 11am-3pm Sat. Closed Aug. **Map E3**
An extraordinarily useful facility run by the arts foundation of 'la Caixa' savings bank, in the **Fundació la Caixa's** main centre on Passeig de Sant Joan (*see also chapter* **Art Galleries**). It's a high-tech art, music and media library that allows you to explore latest technologies (CD-Rom, Internet), watch satellite TV or videos, read magazines from all over the world, listen to (and borrow) records, tapes or CDs, check out a huge art slide collection, attend talks and workshops, and browse in a whole array of references on contemporary culture. Most materials are open-access, but a card is needed to use some a-v materials or borrow materials (to get one, take your passport). A *User Guide* in English is available. On Internet at *www.fundacio.lacaixa.es*.

Lost property

Airport & rail stations

If you lose something land-side of check-in at **Prat Airport**, report the loss immediately to the *Aviación Civil* office in the relevant terminal, or call central airport information on 93 298 38 38. There is no central lost property depot for the RENFE rail network: if you think you have mislaid anything on a train, look for the *Atención al Viajero* desk or *Jefe de Estación* office at the nearest main station to where your property has gone astray, or call ahead to the destination station of the train. To get information by phone on lost property at main rail stations call their general information numbers and ask for *Objetos Perdidos*.

Municipal lost property office

Servei de Troballes *Ajuntament, C/Ciutat 9 (93 402 31 61). Metro Jaume I/ bus 17, 40, 45.* **Open** 9am-2pm Mon-Fri. **Map D5**
All items found on public transport and taxis in the city, or picked up by the police in the street, should eventually find their way to this office, with an entrance on the C/Ciutat side of the city hall. Within 24 hours of the loss you can also try ringing the city transport authority (93 318 70 74). For taxis, call the city hall office.

Public toilets

Public toilets are not common in Barcelona. There are clean toilets with an attendant at main rail stations and in the RENFE vestibule in Plaça Catalunya, and also a toilet at the back of the Boqueria market. Around the centre there are several new-style pay-on-entry cubicles that cost 25ptas. Apart from that, you are best advised to pop into a bar or café if in need. Major stores and fast food restaurants are, of course, the staple standbys.

Religious services

Anglican & Protestant

St George's Church *C/Sant Horaci 41 (93 418 60 78). FGC Sarrià/bus 14, 22, 64, 58, 75.* **Services** 12.30pm Wed; 11am Sun.

Catholic Mass in English

Parròquia Maria Reina *Carretera d'Esplugues 103 (93 203 41 15). Bus 63, 75, 114.* **English Mass** 10am Sun.

Jewish

Sinagoga de Barcelona *C/Avenir 24 (93 200 61 48). FGC Gràcia/bus 58, 64.*

Moslem

Centre Islàmic *Avda Meridiana 326 (93 351 49 01). Metro Sagrera/bus 62.* **Prayers** 2.45pm Fri.

Removals

AGS

C/Provença 288, pral (93 487 23 42). Metro Diagonal/bus 22, 24, 28. **Open** 8.30am-8.30pm Mon-Fri. **No credit cards. Map D3** International household goods movers with door-to-door service to anywhere in the world, and also a storage service.

F Gil Stauffer

C/Pau Claris 176 (93 215 55 55). Metro Diagonal/bus 7, 16, 17, 18, 20, 21, 22, 24, 28, 39, 43, 44, 45. **Open** 9am-7pm Mon-Fri. **No credit cards. Map D3** Reliable national and international movers with associated link companies throughout the world.

Business

Historically, Barcelona has been Spain's most important city for international trade, a Mediterranean crossroads ever since Roman times. Today Madrid, as Spain's capital, is the number one business centre in the country, but Barcelona runs it a very close second.

It's a cliché, but nevertheless true, to say that Catalans show a greater openness to new ideas and projects than other peoples of the Iberian peninsula. Spain's bureaucracy is intricate and cumbersome, however, and since its re-establishment Catalonia's autonomous government, the Generalitat, has fallen into many of the habits of its older counterpart. There are also EU rules to be taken into account.

It's a waste of time trying to handle this system single-handed. A visit to the **Cambra de Comerç** is a must to sort out what you need to do and who to consult for advice and permits. Locals often use intermediaries such as a *gestoria* (*see below*) rather than deal with formalities themselves.

Institutions & info

Anyone working in Barcelona for more than just a passing visit will need to know about the different official bodies and their

respective areas of competence. A good first stop is your own consulate, which will have lists of English-speaking professionals. For consulates, and more on residency, *see pages 261 and 262-3*.

Government

EU office: Patronat Català Pro-Europa *C/Bruch 50, 2° (93 318 26 26). Metro Urquinaona/bus 7, 18, 47, 50, 54, 56, 62.* **Open** 9am-2pm Mon, Fri; 9am-2pm, 4-6pm, Tue-Thur. *June-Sept* 9am-2pm Mon-Fri. **Map E4** Information on EU regulations and their effect on Spain, and EU grants. **Central government: Delegación de Hacienda** Your business will need a tax number (*Número de Identificación Fiscal* or *NIF/NIE*), issued by the local tax office. There are several district offices (*see p262* **EU citizens working freelance**). It is advisable to obtain this via a *gestoria*. **Catalan government: Generalitat de Catalunya** *Plaça Antoni Lopez 5 (information 902 416 000). Metro Jaume I/bus 14, 17, 36, 40, 45, 57, 59, 64.* **Open** *15 Sept-30 Apr* 9am-2pm, 3-5.30pm, Mon-Fri. *1 May-14 Sept* 8am-3pm Mon-Fri. **Map D5** The Generalitat provides a range of services for foreign investors. English-speaking operators can direct you to the department you need. **City council: Ajuntament de Barcelona** *Plaça Sant Miquel 4-5 (93 402 70 00). Metro Jaume I/bus 17, 40, 45.* **Open** 8.30am-6pm Mon-Fri; *July, Aug* 8.15am-2.15pm Mon-Fri. **Map D5** Permits for new businesses are issued by the ten municipal districts; for details, ask for the *Ajuntament de Districte* (district town hall) of the neighbourhood where you will be establishing your business.

Other institutions

Borsa de Valors de Barcelona (Stock Exchange) *Passeig de Gràcia 19 (93 401 35 55). Metro Passeig de Gràcia/bus 7, 16, 17, 22, 24, 28.* **Open** *visits* 9am-6pm, *library* 9am-noon, *departments* 9am-2pm, 4-6.30pm, Mon-Fri. **Map D4** **British Society of Catalunya** *Via Augusta 213 (tel & fax 93 209 06 39). FGC Bonanova/bus 14.* **Open** no fixed opening hours. Keep in touch with fellow expats in monthly events. Membership 1,500ptas a year. **Cambra de Comerç, Indústria i Navegació de Barcelona (Chamber of Commerce)** *Avda Diagonal 452-454 (93 416 93 00). Metro Diagonal/bus 6, 7, 15, 27, 33, 34, 127.* **Open** *Oct-May* 9am-5pm Mon-Thur; 9am-2pm Fri; *June-Sept* 8am-3pm Mon-Fri. **Map D3** The most important institution for business people, with a wealth of information: advice on business viability, fiscal, commercial and legal consultancy services, market studies, databases by sectors, and a guide to all the steps to take when setting up a business.

Business services

Conference services

Barcelona Convention Bureau *C/Tarragona 149 (93 423 18 00). Metro Tarragona/bus 27, 109, 127.* **Open** 9am-2.30pm, 4-7pm, Mon-Thur; 9am-3pm Fri. **Map A3** A specialised arm of the city tourist authority that assists organisations or individuals wishing to hold conferences or similar events in the city, with full information, lists of venues and/or service companies and so on.

Centre de Relacions Empresarials

Aeroport del Prat (93 478 67 99).
Open 8.30am-8.30pm Mon-Fri. *July, Aug* 8.30am-2.30pm Mon-Fri.
The **Cambra de Comerç** provides this 'meeting point' within the airport terminals, with eight meeting rooms and access via network to most of the information available at their main office. Information services are open to all; use of meeting rooms must be arranged through a member company of the Chamber. The Chamber can also provide conference halls, seating from 15 to 500, in the historic medieval Stock Exchange, the **Casa Llotja** (*see chapter* **Sightseeing**). For information and bookings, call 93 416 93 30.

Fira de Barcelona

Avda Reina Maria Cristina (93 233 20 00). Metro Plaça Espanya/bus 9, 13, 51, 53, 65. **Open** 9am-2pm, 4-6pm, Mon-Fri; *June-Aug* 9am-2pm Mon-Fri. **Map A4**
The Barcelona trade fair is one of the largest permanent exhibition complexes in Europe, hosting over 60 major events each year. In addition to the main area at Plaça d'Espanya it includes a state-of-the-art new site, **Montjuïc-2**, in the Zona Franca towards the airport, with over 100,000 sq m of exhibition and convention space in halls of various sizes. The Fira also administers the **Palau de Congressos** conference hall within the Plaça d'Espanya site. It can be let separately (direct lines 93 233 23 71/93 233 23 41).

Gestorías – administrative services

The *gestoría* is a very Spanish institution, the main function of which is to lighten the weight of local bureaucracy by dealing with it for you. A combination of bookkeeper, lawyer, notary and business adviser, they can be very helpful in getting you through paperwork and pointing out shortcuts that foreigners are unaware of. Unfortunately, employees at local *gestorías* rarely speak English.

Gestoría Tutzo

C/Aribau 226 (93 209 67 88). Metro Diagonal/bus 6, 7, 15, 27, 33, 34, 58, 64. **Open** 8.30am-2pm, 4-7pm, Mon-Fri; *July, Aug* closed pm Fri. **Map C2**
Very professional and with years of experience, Tutzo offers all the administrative services you may need – legal, international, fiscal, accounting, social security, contracts and so on – and the staff speak English.

Law & accountancy

Gabinete Echevarría

C/Roger de Llúria 36, àtic (93 412 18 99). Metro Urquinaona/bus 7, 18, 50, 54, 56. **Open** 9am-1.30pm, 4-7pm, Mon-Fri. Closed Aug. **Map D4**
Law practice associated with US firm Saffery Champness.

Santacana Grup

Passatge Forasté 7 (93 417 30 30). FGC Av Tibidabo/bus 17, 22, 73. **Open** 9am-1.30pm, 3.30-7pm, Mon-Thur; 9am-1.30pm Fri. Closed Aug. Affiliated with London accountants Moore Stephens, this firm provides not only standard accountancy and consultancy services but also those usually offered by *gestorías.*

Office services

Office space

Centro de Negocios *C/Pau Claris 97, 4º 1ª (93 301 69 96). Metro Passeig de Gràcia/bus 7, 18, 50, 54, 56, 62.* **Open** 8am-9pm, *Aug* 9am-3pm, Mon-Fri. **Map D4** Very near the city centre, with office space, desk space in a shared office, mail box addresses, meeting rooms, secretarial services and a wide range of administrative services for hire.
Ofitten *C/Galileu 303-305, 4º (93 321 08 12). Metro Les Corts/bus 15, 43, 59.* **Open** 8.30am-8pm, *Aug* 8.30am-2.30pm, Mon-Fri. Furnished and unfurnished offices, with secretarial services available.

Temp agencies

Adia *C/ Mallorca 221-3, 3º 2ª (93 454 38 08). FGC Provença/bus 7, 16, 17, 20, 21, 43, 54, 64, 66.* **Open** 9am-7pm Mon-Fri. **Map D3**
Manpower *C/Aragó 277 (93 487 68 68). Metro Passeig de Gràcia/bus 7, 16, 17, 22, 24, 28.* **Open** 8am-7pm, *Aug* 8am-6pm, Mon-Fri. **Map D3**

Translation agencies

BCN Consultores Lingüísticos *C/Balmes 69, 3º 2ª (93 454 51 12). Metro Passeig de Gràcia/bus 7, 16, 17, 20, 21, 43, 44.* **Open** 9am-7pm, *Aug* 9am-3pm, Mon-Fri. **Map D3** Professional translators and interpreters; prices are quite high.
DUUAL *C/Ciutat 7, 2º 4ª (93 302 29 85). Metro Jaume I/bus 17, 40, 45.* **Open** 9am-2pm, 4-7pm, Mon-Thur; 9am-2pm Fri. **Map D5** A sophisticated agency with competitive rates and state-of-the-art DTP equipment. It can handle eastern European languages, and also Chinese, Japanese, Greek and Arabic.

Traductores Jurados (Official Translators)

In Spain official bodies often demand that foreign documents be translated by legally certified translators. Rates are higher than for conventional translators.
Teodora Gambetta *C/Escorial 29-31, escala C, àtic, 2ª (tel/fax 93 219 22 25). Metro Joanic/bus 21, 39.* **Open** by appointment. **Map E2**
Luís Pérez Pardo *C/Dr August Pi Sunyer 11, 6º 1ª (tel/fax 93 204 43 27). Metro Maria Cristina/bus 7, 63, 68, 74, 75, 114.* **Open** by appointment.

Students

There are eight universities in Catalonia, of which five – four public, one private – are in or near Barcelona. Choice at university level is limited in Spain: the British or US system whereby you can select a university on its reputation is envied by Spanish students, who are required to attend a local university unless they are studying a course that it does not offer. Since the Barcelona universities are some of the most comprehensive in the country, few Catalan students study in other parts of Spain.

Barcelona universities have been particularly adept in seeking and forging links with other universities and colleges in the European Union. Catalonia is ardently Europhile and its universities enthusiastically support the various European inter-university exchange programmes. Catalan universities have attracted more than 90 per cent of the 3,000 students studying in Spain under the EU's Erasmus scheme.

Most Spanish degree courses now last for four years, leading to a *Llicenciatura*, although some run for three, for a *Diplomatura*. The main teaching language in Barcelona universities is now Catalan, except in certain subjects such as Spanish language and literature. Foreign students who stay for over three months, including those from EU countries, are required to have a residence permit: for details, *see page 263*.

Punt d'Informació Juvenil, Secretaria General de Joventut

C/Calabria 147-C/Rocafort 116 (93 483 83 83/punt d'informació juvenil 93 483 83 84). Metro Rocafort/bus 9, 41, 50, 56. **Open** *Punt d'informació juvenil* 9am-2pm, 3-8pm, Mon-Fri; *Aug* 9am-2pm Mon-Fri. *Travel agency* 10am-8pm Mon-Fri; 10am-1.30pm Sat. *Aug* 10am-8pm Mon-Fri; 10am-2pm Sat. **Map B4** A 'youth information point' run by the Generalitat, with information on accommodation, youth travel and other fields. Foreign students enrolled at Barcelona universities can use the accommodation service.

Universities

EU Programmes: Socrates, Erasmus & Lingua

The **Erasmus** student exchange scheme and **Lingua** project (specifically concerned with language learning) are the most important parts of the EU's **Socrates** programme to help students move between member states. Barcelona's universities have exchange arrangements with many British and Irish colleges and universities, covering a wide range of subjects. Erasmus is open to students from their second year onwards; anyone interested should approach the Erasmus co-ordinator at their home college. General information is available in Britain from the *UK Socrates & Erasmus Council, R & D Building, The University, Canterbury, Kent CT2 7PD (01227 762 712)*.

Universitat Autònoma de Barcelona

Campus de Bellaterra, 08193, Bellaterra (93 581 10 00/student information 93 581 11 11). By train FGC from Plaça Catalunya to Universitat Autònoma (Sabadell line). **Open** *information Sept-June* 9am-2pm, 3-5pm, Mon-Fri; *July, Aug* 8am-2pm Mon-Fri.
The Autonomous University occupies an unlovely 1960s campus outside the city at Bellaterra, near Sabadell, but with frequent FGC train connections. On the Internet at *www.uab.es/*.

Universitat de Barcelona

Gran Via de les Corts Catalanes 585 (93 403 54 17). Metro Universitat/ bus all routes to Plaça Universitat. **Open** *information (Pati de Lletres entrance)* 9am-2pm, 4-8pm, *July, Aug* 9am-2pm, Mon-Fri. **Map C4** Barcelona's oldest university has faculties in the main building on Plaça Universitat, in the giant Zona Universitària on the Diagonal and scattered through other parts of the city. Information is also available by Internet on *www.ub.es/*.

Universitat Politècnica de Catalunya

Avda Dr. Marañon 42 **Student Information Office** *C/Jordi Girona 1-3 (93 401 62 00/student information 93 401 73 96). Metro Zona Universitària/bus 7, 67, 68, 74, 75.* **Open** *student information office* 9am-6pm Mon-Thur; 9am-3pm Fri. Closed Easter and August. Specialises in technical subjects such as engineering and architecture. Most of it is in the Zona Universitària, but it also has faculties in Terrassa and other towns. On the Internet on *www.upc.es/*.

Universitat Pompeu Fabra

Pla de la Mercè 10-12 (information 93 542 22 28/93 542 17 00). Metro Drassanes/bus 14, 36, 38, 59, 64. **Open** *information Sept-mid-June* 10.30am-1.30pm, 4.30-6.30pm, *mid-June-Aug* 8am-2pm, Mon-Fri. **Map D5** An economics and social sciences-based university with faculties in central Barcelona, many in the old city. Founded only in 1991, it is on the web at *www.upf.es/*.

Universitat Ramon Llull

Central office *C/Sant Joan de la Salle 8 (93 253 04 50). FGC Tibidabo/bus 22, 64, 75.* **Open** *information* 9am-2pm, 4-7pm, Mon-Fri. Closed Easter and Aug 1-18. A private university founded to bring together a number of previously separate institutions owned and/or run by the Jesuits, although this does not mean there is a strong religious presence in teaching. Fees are high. On the net at *www.url.es/*.

Language learning

Centres de Normalització Lingüística

Central office *Consorci de Normalització Lingüística, C/Pau Claris 162 (93 482 02 00). Metro Passeig de Gràcia/bus 20, 21, 22, 24, 28, 39, 43, 44, 45.* **Open** *Sept-June* 9am-2pm, 3-5.30pm, *15 Jun-15 Sept* 8am-3pm, Mon-Fri. **Map D4**

The official Generalitat organisation for the support of the Catalan language has several centres around the city that provide inexpensive Catalan courses from beginners' level upwards, with intensive courses in summer.

Escola Oficial d'Idiomes

Avda Drassanes (93 329 24 58). Metro Drassanes/bus 14, 18, 38, 57, 59, 64, 91. **Open** 10.30am-12.30pm, 4.30-5.30pm, Mon-Fri. **Map C5** The 'official school' has courses at all levels in Spanish and Catalan, and in several other languages for local students. They're cheap, and hence are often overcrowded; demand is such that in enrolment periods (usually, June and September) they have a ticket-and-queue system which means that you have to wait around to see if you can sit the entry test that day. Arrive early to be in with a chance.

International House

C/Trafalgar 14, entresol (93 268 45 11). Metro Urquinaona/bus 19, 39, 40, 41, 42, 55, 141. **Open** 8am-9pm Mon-Fri; 9.30am-1.30pm Sat. **Map E4** Intensive Spanish courses all year round, beginning every two weeks. Courses consist of four hours' class time every weekday (9.30am-1.30pm).

Instituto Mangold de Idiomas

Rambla Catalunya 16 (93 301 25 39). Metro Catalunya/bus all routes to Plaça Catalunya. **Open** *offices* 9am-9pm Mon-Thur; 9am-7pm Fri. *Activities for children Oct-June* 10am-1pm Sat. **Map D4** A well-regarded, centrally located school that gives intensive Spanish courses throughout the year. Courses last about three/four weeks, with 20 hours of classes each week. Non-intensive Catalan courses are also offered.

Universitat de Barcelona

Gran Via de les Corts Catalanes 585 (93 318 42 66). Metro Universitat/bus all routes to Plaça Universitat. **Open** *language course information* 9am-1pm Mon-Fri. The university runs reasonably priced courses for foreigners in both Catalan and Spanish, some also including higher-level studies in literature, culture and so on. Ask for the *Servei de Llengua Catalana (93 403 54 77/e-mail slc@slc.ub.es)* for information on Catalan courses; *Estudios Hispánicos (93 403 55 19/e-mail est-hispa@d1.ub.es)* for Spanish. Courses are held throughout the year, and there are intensive language courses in July and September.

Other courses

Business schools

ESADE *Avda de Pedralbes 60-62 (93 280 61 62/93 204 81 05). FGC Reina Elisenda/bus 22, 63, 64, 75, 114.* **Open** *information* 10am-2pm, 4-7pm, Mon-Fri. Mornings only at Easter. Closed three weeks Aug. A prestigious private business school in Pedralbes, set up under Jesuit auspices in 1958 and now associated with the **Universitat Ramon Llull**. Its highly-regarded bilingual MBA programme has full- and part-time options: included are comprehensive language studies. The first year of the course can be studied in English or Spanish.

IESE *Avda Pearson 21 (93 253 42 00). Bus 63, 75, 114.* **Open** *information* 9am-1.45pm, 3-4.45pm, *July, Aug* 9am-2pm, Mon-Fri. An offshoot of the University of Navarra, another private Catholic university, which offers a two-year bilingual MBA programme.

European summer school

Information: Estudis de Formació Continuada de la Universitat de Barcelona *Palau de les Heures, recinte Llars Mundet, Passeig de la Vall d'Hebron, 08035 (93 428 45 85). Metro Montbau/bus 27, 60, 73, 76, 85, 173.* The University of Barcelona runs an annual European summer school in its faculty in the Vall d'Hebron, with courses in management, human resources, information technology and other areas, aimed at graduates or professionals. Most are in English, and teachers are drawn from the whole of Europe.

Music

Àrea de Música, Departament de Cultura
Departament de Cultura, Portal de Santa Madrona 6-8 (93 316 27 80). Metro Drassanes/bus 14, 18, 38, 57, 59, 64, 91. **Open** *information Sept-mid-June* 9am-2pm, 3-5.30pm, *June-15 Sept* 8am-3pm, Mon-Fri. **Map C5**
The Generalitat Culture Department runs a course on early music in Catalonia, usually in August, with provision for English speakers.

Women

The women of Barcelona consider themselves to be significantly more liberated than those in the rest of Spain, and the Catalan capital is in many respects a very female-friendly city. A woman drinking alone in a bar usually needs to watch her bag more than her behind, and is unlikely to invite leery comments – more than can be said for many comparable cities elsewhere.

The change in the position of women is often cited as the most far-reaching of all the transformations that have swept over Spain in the last 25 years. One index is the birth rate: from having the second-highest in Europe (after Ireland) in 1975, Spain (and Catalonia especially) now has the lowest in the world. Feminism, on the other hand, is a different matter. When asked the question, 'What is a feminist?', Barcelona women gave hundreds of different answers – including, 'A feminist is someone who believes profoundly that biology played a dirty trick on us, and hopes it won't last forever', and 'A feminist is a bad person, isn't she?'

One reflection of the limited interest in feminism *per se* is that women-only spaces are almost non-existent in Barcelona, although there are women's organisations in every neighbourhood or *barri*. A few are actively feminist in outlook, but the majority reflect the still-prevailing sense of community that exists in Catalonia, and range from immigrant pressure groups to support groups for widows and educational workshops. Barcelona has one feminist bookshop, **Pròleg** (*see chapter* **Shopping**).

Useful publications

Guia d'Entitats i Grups de Dones de Barcelona This free volume lists all women's organisations operating in Barcelona, and can be obtained from the Ajuntament in Plaça Sant Jaume, the Consells de Districte or the Centre Municipal d'Informacio i Recursos per a les Dones (93 318 78 79).
Guia de Dones/Guía de Mujeres Also from the Ajuntament, this interesting 'alternative' guide to Barcelona by Isabel Segura is in the form of a series of itineraries around areas of the city connected with female historical figures from Roman times to the present day. In Catalan and Spanish editions, it's available from the **Llibreria de la Virreina** and other bookshops (1,800ptas).

Organisations

Associació Catalana de la Dona

C/Providència 42, 2° 2ª (93 213 34 40). Metro Fontana/bus 39. **Open** by appointment. **Map E2**
An independent association for the promotion and defence of women's rights. It organises cultural events and has spaces available for discussion groups and workshops.

Ca la Dona

C/Casp 38, pral (93 412 71 61). Metro Catalunya/bus all routes to Plaça Catalunya. **Open** *office* 10am-2pm, 4-8pm, Tue-Thur. Closed Aug, Christmas and Easter. **Map D4**
Ca la Dona women's centre acts as an umbrella for a variety of groups, houses the *Coordinadora Feminista de Catalunya*, the most important local feminist organisation, and hosts a range of activities that include video groups and a lesbian group. A good place to get general information. It also publishes a quarterly magazine of the same name (in Catalan, 300ptas), with information on women's events.

FESLU

C/Vidre 10, 2° 3ª (93 318 08 02/93 412 15 09). Metro Liceu/bus 14, 18, 38, 59, N4, N5. **Map D5**
Formally described as 'a women's cultural activity group', FESLU roughly translated means 'Free Time, Party Time'. Women of various nationalities put together parties wherever they can, and run **La Illa** women's café (*see also chapter* **Gay & Lesbian Barcelona**).

Institut Català de la Dona

Head office *C/Viladomat 319, entresol (93 495 16 00).* **Map B3**
Information centre *C/Portaferrissa 1-3 (93 317 92 91). Metro Liceu/bus 14, 18, 38, 59, 91.* **Open** *16 Sept-31 May* 9am-2pm, 4-7pm, *1 Jun-15 Sept* 8am-3pm, Mon-Fri. **Map D5**
The women's affairs department of the Catalan government. It has an extensive resource service (the *Centre de Documentació*), organises conferences, exhibitions and courses and administers grants available for women's projects. Main services are in C/Viladomat, while the information office is in C/Portaferrisa. Some departments close in August.

Further Reading

Several useful books on Barcelona are produced locally in English-language or bilingual editions, both by the city council (Ajuntament de Barcelona) and independent publishers, especially the Editorial Gustavo Gili. Places to find them are the **Llibreria de la Virreina** city bookshop and the main tourist office (*see chapter* **Shopping** *and page 251*) or the **Fundació La Caixa** (*see chapter* **Art Galleries**).

(*see chapter* **Shopping** *and page 251*)

Guides & walks

Amelang, J, Gil, X & McDonogh, GW: *Twelve Walks through Barcelona's Past* (Aj. de Barcelona).
Well thought-out walks by historical themes ('Barcelona of the Merchants', 'Bohemian Barcelona'). Original, and much better-informed than many walking guides.
García Espuche, Albert:
The Quadrat d'Or (Aj. de Barcelona).
Building-by-building guide to the central Eixample, the 'Golden Square' of *Modernista* architecture.
González, A & Lacuesta, R: *Barcelona Architecture Guide 1929-1994* (Ed. Gustavo Gili)
Thorough paperback guide to all of Barcelona's contemporary architecture.
Güell, Xavier: *Gaudí Guide* (Ed. Gustavo Gili)
Handy, with good background on all his work.
Pomés Leiz, Juliet, & Feriche, Ricardo:
Barcelona Design Guide (Ed. Gustavo Gili)
An eccentrically wide-ranging but engaging listing of everything ever considered 'designer' in BCN.

History, art, architecture, culture

Elliott, JH: *The Revolt of the Catalans*
Fascinating, highly detailed account of the Guerra dels Segadors and the Catalan revolt of the 1640s.
Fernández Armesto, Felipe:
Barcelona: A Thousand Years of the City's Past
A solid, straightforward history.
Figueras, Lourdes: *Domènech i Montaner*
Beautifully produced, bilingual-edition study of the classic *Modernista* architect.
Fraser, Ronald: *Blood of Spain*
An oral history of the Spanish Civil War and the tensions that preceded it, the most vivid account of this great conflagration; especially good on July 1936 in Barcelona.
Hughes, Robert: *Barcelona*
The most comprehensive single book on Barcelona in any language: tendentious at times, erratic, but wonderfully broad in scope and beautifully written, and covering every aspect of the city's history, legends, life and culture up to the 1900s.
Kaplan, Temma: *Red City, Blue Period – Social Movements in Picasso's Barcelona*
An interesting tracing of the interplay of avant-garde art and avant-garde politics in 1900s Barcelona.
Orwell, George: *Homage to Catalonia*
The classic account of Barcelona in revolution, by an often bewildered, but always perceptive observer.
Paz, Abel: *Durruti, The People Armed*
Closer to its theme, a biography of the most legendary of Barcelona's anarchist revolutionaries.

Richardson, John: *A Life of Picasso, Vol. I, 1881-1906*
The definitive biography: volume I covers the whole of Picasso's Barcelona years among the Modernistes, and his later important visits to Catalonia.
Solà-Morales, Ignasi:
Fin de Siècle Architecture in Barcelona (Ed. Gustavo Gili)
Large-scale and wide-ranging description and evaluation of the city's *Modernista* heritage.
Tóibín, Colm: *Homage to Barcelona*
Evocative and perceptive journey around the city: good on the booming Barcelona of the 1980s, but also excellent on Catalan Gothic, Gaudi and Miró.
Vázquez Montalbán, Manuel: *Barcelonas*
Idiosyncratic but insightful reflections on the city and its history by one of its most prominent modern writers.
Zerbst, Rainer: *Antoni Gaudi*
Lavishly illustrated and comprehensive survey.

Literature

Calders, Pere:
The Virgin of the Railway and Other Stories
Ironic, engaging, quirkily humorous stories by a Catalan writer who spent many years in exile in Mexico.
Català, Victor: *Solitude*
The pseudonym of a woman novelist, Caterina Albert; this is her masterpiece, an intense story from 1905 that shocked readers with its open, modern treatment of female sexuality.
Martorell, Joanot, & Joan Martí de Gualba:
Tirant lo Blanc
The first European prose novel, from 1490, a rambling, bawdy shaggy-dog story of travels, romances and chivalric adventures.
Mendoza, Eduardo:
City of Marvels and *Year of the Flood*
Mendoza's sweeping, very entertaining saga of Barcelona between its great Exhibitions, 1888 and 1929, and a more recent novel of passions in the city of the 1950s.
Moncada, Jesús: *The Towpath*
A powerful, contemporary novel of rural Catalonia.
Oliver, Maria Antònia: *Antipodes* and *Study in Lilac*
Two adventures of Barcelona's first feminist detective.
Rodoreda, Mercè: *The Time of the Doves* and
My Cristina and Other Stories
A translation of *La Plaça del Diamant*, most widely-read of all Catalan novels, the poignant, finely-worked story of a great survivor, Colometa, from a Gràcia shop in the 1930s to the aftermath of the Civil War. Plus a collection of similarly bitter-sweet short tales by the same author.
Vázquez Montalbán, Manuel:
The Angst-Ridden Executive and *An Olympic Death*
Two thrillers starring Vázquez Montalbán's detective and gourmet extraordinaire, Pepe Carvalho.

Food & drink

Andrews, Colman: *Catalan Cuisine*
A mine of information on food and much else besides (but also with usable recipes). Unfortunately no longer in print in the UK, but worth looking for.
Casas, Penelope: *Food and Wines of Spain*
A useful general handbook.

Index

Advertisers' Index

Maps

Pedestrians

Possibilities

Time Out | London's Living Guide.

http://www.timeout.co.uk

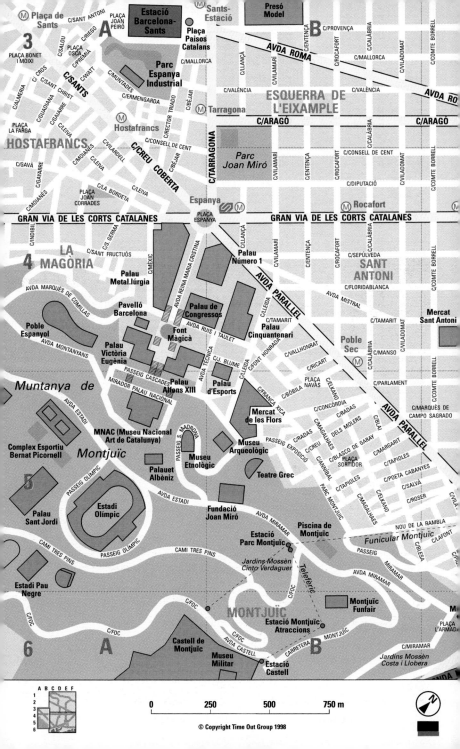

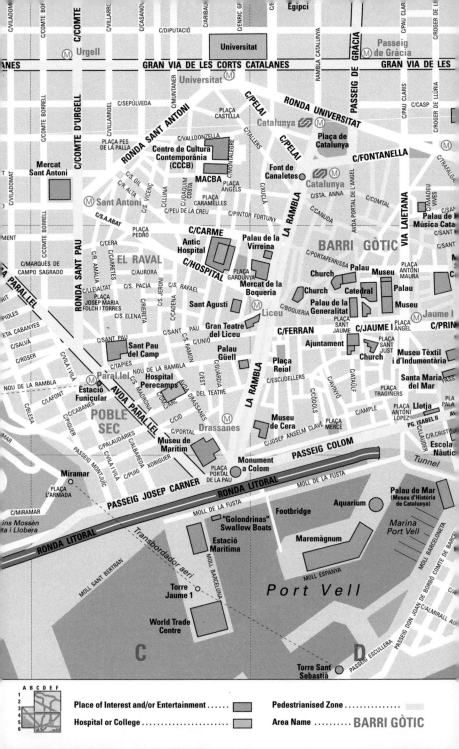

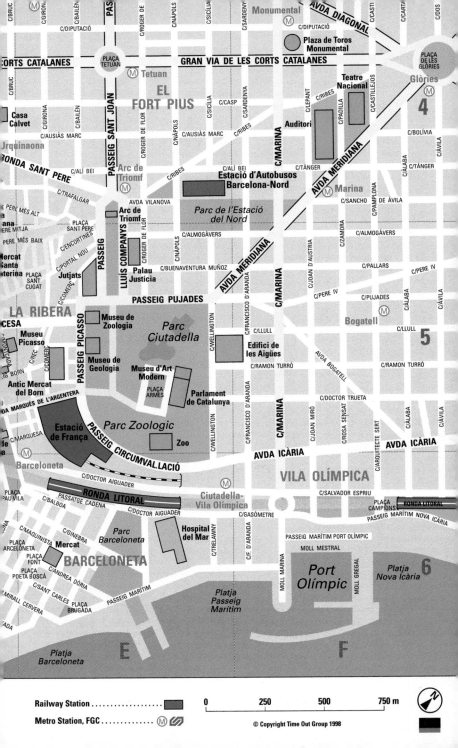

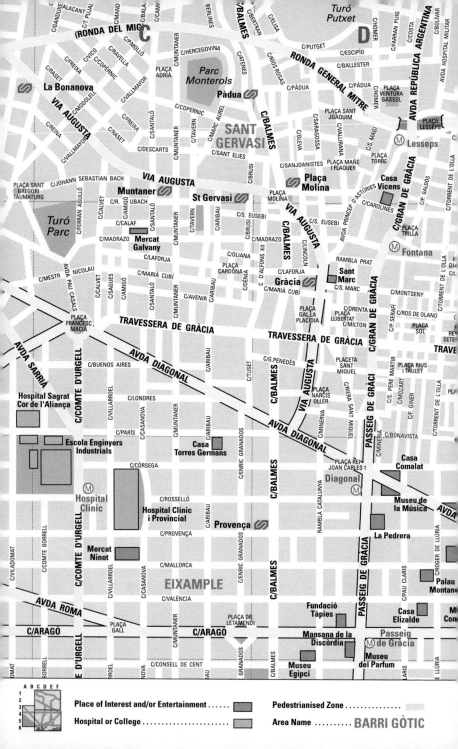

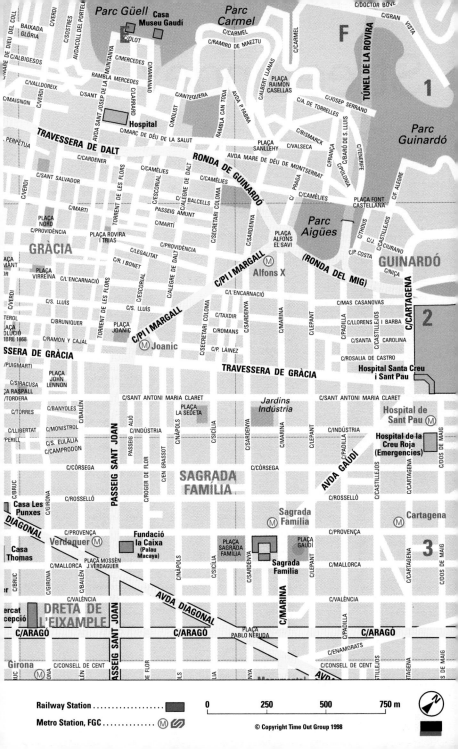

Street Index

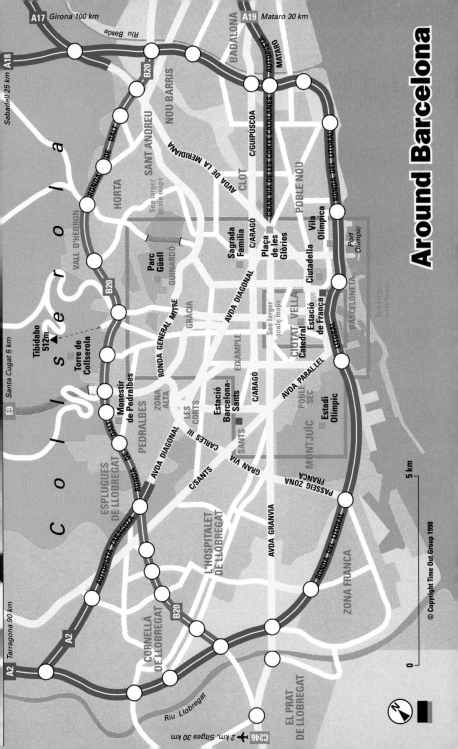

Around Barcelona

© Copyright Time Out Group 1998

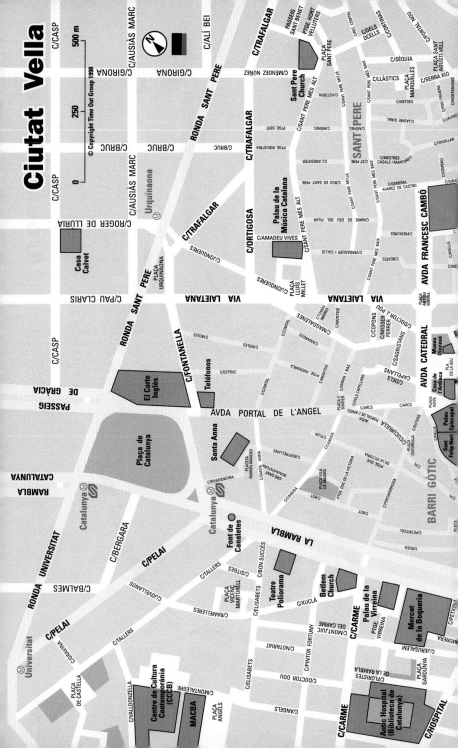

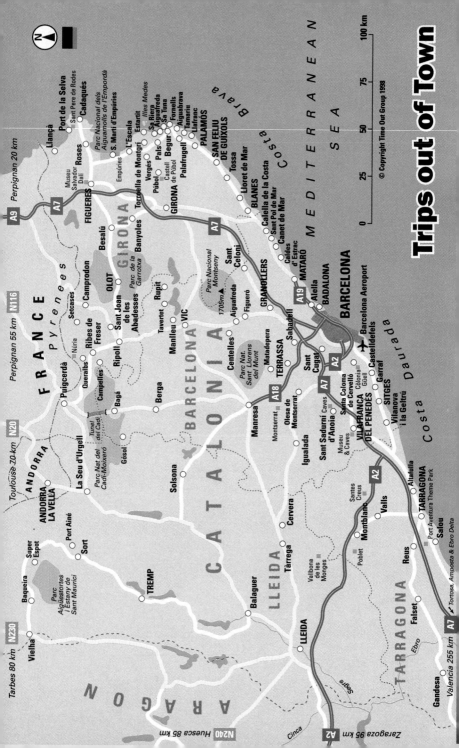
Trips out of Town

Night bus routes

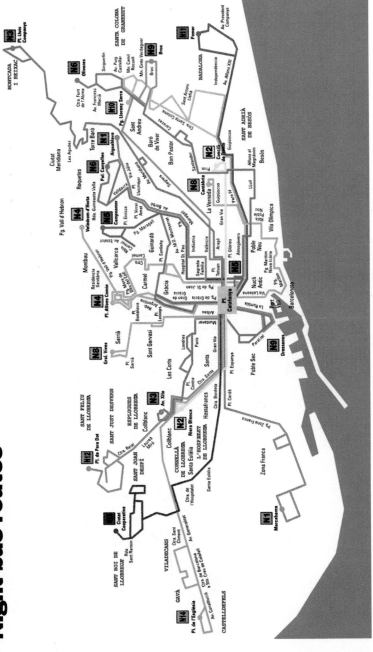

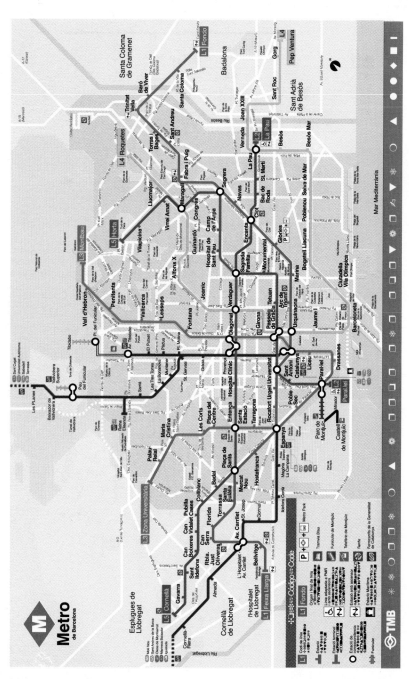